Late Marxism

Late Marxism

Adorno, or,
The Persistence
of the Dialectic

◆

FREDRIC JAMESON

VERSO

London · New York

First published by Verso 1990
© Fredric Jameson 1990
All rights reserved
Reprinted 1992

Verso
UK: 6 Meard Street, London W1V 3HR
USA: 29 West 35th Street, New York, NY 10001-2291

Verso is the imprint of New Left Books

British Library Cataloguing in Publication Data
Jameson, Fredric
Late Marxism: Adorno, or, the persistence of the dialectic.
1. German philosophy. Adorno, Theodor W. (Theodor
Wiesengrund), 1903-1969
I. Title
193

ISBN 0-86091-270-1
ISBN 0-86091-981-1 pbk

US Library of Congress Cataloging-in-Publication Data
Jameson, Fredric.
Late Marxism: Adorno, or, the persistence of the dialectic/
Fredric Jameson.
p. cm.
Includes bibliographical references.
Includes index.
ISBN 0-86091-270-1. — ISBN 0-86091-981-1 pbk.)
1. Adorno, Theodor W., 1903-1969   I. Title.
BV4526.2.J35 1990
193-dc20

Typeset in Garamond by BP Integraphics, Bath, Avon

Printed in the U.S.A. by Courier Companies, Inc.

For
Perry Anderson

Contents

A Note on Editions

and Translations

I have here often retranslated quotes from Adorno's works afresh (without specific indication). The available translations are uneven, to say the least; E.F.N. Jephcotts's *Minima Moralia*, and more recently, Rodney Livingstone's *In Search of Wagner*, are elegant Anglo-English; John Cumming's *Dialectic of Enlightenment* has a stronger German accent, which I for one must welcome since I believe, with Pannwitz, that the translator should allow 'his language to be powerfully affected by the foreign tongue ... [and should] expand and deepen his language by means of the foreign language'.[1] In particular, Adorno's sentences try to recover the intricately bound spatial freedom of Latinate declension, objects that grandly precede subjects, and a play of gendered nouns that the mind scans by means of the appropriately modified relative. Chiasmus here becomes the structural echo by one part of the sentence of another, distant in time and space; and the result of these internal operations is the closure of the aphorism itself; definitive, yet a forthright act that passes on, not into silence, but into other acts and gestures. Adorno should then be the occasion of forging a powerful new Germanic sentence structure in English; and this is why I must find altogether misguided the strategy of Christian Lenhardt, the English translator of *Aesthetic Theory* who breaks up sentences and paragraphs and produces a literate and respectable British text which I can no longer even recognize (but see on this his exchange with Bob Hulot-Kentor[2]).

Thus, unfortunately, this whole monumental undertaking will have to be done again, something that must also be said for E.B. Ashton's even more unfortunate version of *Negative Dialectics*, where the most basic terms are misrendered, making whole passages (which are already difficult enough at the best of times) altogether incomprehensible. Readers obliged to go on using this version should make a note of the most urgent howlers: *Tauschverhältnis* is in particular not 'barter' but simply 'exchange system' (very much as in 'exchange value'): *Vermittlung* is scarcely 'transmission' but will be again recognizable as the well-known 'mediation' (and note that *mittelbar* and *unmittelbar* – normally 'mediated' and 'immediate' – are here frequently 'indirect' and 'direct' for some reason); *Anschauung* is, finally, not 'visuality' but is conventionally rendered, since the very first Kant translations, as 'intuition'. The first group of these errors (along with the significant but incomprehensible excision of the name of Karl Korsch at one point) might lead a paranoid to believe that this translation aimed precisely at producing a post- and non-Marxist Adorno 'for our time'; the third, however, could only imply a complete innocence of the philosophical tradition. Still, all the translations strike occasional sparks, and I am fortunate in having had them all to rely on.

Page references to the most frequently quoted works are given within the text, first to the German, and then to the English, versions (even where the latter has not been used), and designated by the following abbreviations:

AT *Aesthetic Theorie*, Gesammelte Schriften, vol. 7 (Frankfurt: Suhr-kamp, 1970)
    Aesthetic Theory, transl. Christian Lenhardt (London: RKP, 1984)

DA *Dialektik der Aufklärung* (Frankfurt: Fischer, 1986, original 1944)
    Dialectic of Enlightenment, transl. John Cumming (New York: Herder & Herder, 1972)

MM *Minima Moralia* (Frankfurt: Suhrkamp, 1986, original 1951)
    Minima Moralia, transl. E.F.N. Jephcott (London: Verso, 1974)

ND *Negative Dialektik* (Frankfurt: Suhrkamp, 1975, original 1966)
    Negative Dialectics, transl. E.B. Ashton (New York: Continuum, 1973)

NL *Noten zur Literatur* (Frankfurt: Suhrkamp, 1981)

PNM *Philosophie der neuen Musik* (Frankfurt: Europäische Verlagsan-stalt, 1958)
    Philosophy of Modern Music, transl. Anne G. Mitchell and Wesley V. Blomster (New York: Seabury, 1973)

W   *Versuch über Wagner* (Frankfurt: Suhrkamp, 1952)
    In Search of Wagner, transl. Rodney Livingstone (London: Verso, 1981)

INTRODUCTION

Adorno in the Stream

of Time

This book offers detailed readings of three major works written wholly or in part by Adorno at various stages in his career: *Dialectic of Enlightenment*, published in 1947, the *Negative Dialectic* of 1966 and the posthumously published *Aesthetic Theory*. I have, however, drawn extensively on other books – the essays called *Noten zur Literatur*, the *Minima Moralia*, and the Wagner book, as well as other relevant materials. I have considered these writings synchronously, as parts of a single unfolding system, as though the various Adornos, in the various stages of their youth and decay (as in *2001*), were all 'sitting around a table in the British Museum' together.

In historiography – whether it is that of a form, a national population, or a single productive psyche – the decision about continuity or discontinuity is not an empirical one; as I've said elsewhere, it is taken in advance, as a kind of absolute presupposition, which then determines your subsequent reading and interpretation of the materials (sometimes called 'the facts'). We are very well placed to see that today, we who have witnessed the unfurling of a great wave of counter-revolutionary historiography designed to 'prove', for example, that the French or Russian revolutions accomplished very little save to interrupt, with their mindless bloodshed, a peaceful economic progress already on course and well under way. Such 'history' offers a true Brechtian estrangement-effect, which runs in the face of common sense (that is to say, our received ideas) and gives us something new to argue about: the argument will be most productive if it also includes some rethinking of periodization itself, which has come to be one of the central theoretical issues for an age that is at one and the same time profoundly ahistorical and avid for historical narratives and narrative reinterpretations of all kinds – an appetite, as it were, for

poststructural gossip (including the newer histories) that is something
like a compensation for the weightlessness of a fall out of history unlikely
to last for long.

The alternative – an account of Adorno's career in various stages,[1]
including as its obligatory backdrop the exciting wartime flights across
Europe and North America, and the postwar return to a Germany in
rubble (with the subsequent emergence of a student movement in the
sixties), done in the various appropriate Hollywood and Tv-docudrama
styles – has generally ignored the philosophical or aesthetic components,
whose lifelong persistence it is not difficult to show,[2] and fastened on
the easier matter of political opinion: in other words, when did he stop
believing in Marxism? (or rather, since Horkheimer and the 'School'
are the inescapable intellectual and financial context here, when did
'they' stop believing in Marxism?). I will argue against this rather shallow
view of the nature of political commitment, ideological choice, and
philosophical and literary production. Apostasies are real enough, and
excellent dramatic material; but this is not at all what happened to
Adorno during the Cold War and after the return to Restoration Germany
in the Adenauer period. He went on, indeed, to write his two major
works, examined in the present study: projects that establish him as one
of the greatest of twentieth-century Marxist philosophers; and as my
title suggests, it is to document the contributions of Adorno to contemporary Marxism that the present book was written.

It is not, indeed, people who change, but rather situations. This can
also account for the alterations in my own views of Adorno, whose
work has itself varied in significance for me according to the historical
decade: Adorno was for me a crucial methodological discovery in the
declining years of the Eisenhower era, when it seemed urgent to invent
some conception of the dialectic itself in the North American context.
This was then the period in which I used Adorno's musical analyses
(to which I will revert very little in the present volume) as practical
demonstrations of the ways in which what we used to call the 'social
and historical background' – indeed, the class and ideological background
– was not *extrinsic* but very precisely *intrinsic* to the business of formal
analysis.

Readers of *Marxism and Form*, however, will have sensed my increasing
distance, by 1971, when the book was finally published, from what I
took to be Adorno's hostility towards the Soviet Union, the Third World,
and (reading it overhastily from his essays on jazz, like everyone else)
the Black movement in this country. But the new decade, known in
retrospect as the sixties, meant (for me at least) sympathy with all those
things. In the age of wars of national liberation, Adorno's sense of Apoca-

lypse seemed very retrogressive indeed, focused as it was on the moment of Auschwitz, and obsessed with the doom and baleful enchantment of a 'total system' that few enough – in a 'pre-revolutionary' moment defined notoriously by the sense that *'tout est possible!'* – sensed impending in our own future in the middle distance.

The seventies – the age, in this country at least, of Theory and theoretical discourse, of *jouissances* that ranged from structuralism to poststructuralism, from Maoism to narrative analysis, and from libidinal investments to Ideological State Apparatuses – were essentially French; Adorno (along with Lukács and so many other Central European thinkers, with the signal exceptions of Benjamin and Brecht) seemed an encumbrance, not to say an embarrassment, during the struggles of that time, and prompting those still committed to him into elaborate translation schemes to 're-concile' Adorno with Derridean orthodoxy. While all this was going on over here, the French intelligentsia was in the meantime in the process of full de-Marxification; so that the next decade drew the curtain open on a wealthy and complacent, depoliticized Europe, whose great theoreticians were dead and whose indigenous philosophical traditions were buried. (I will say more about the fortunes of Adorno and the dialectic in the Bundesrepublik today in the conclusions to this volume.) To that Europe, learning analytic philosophy and pioneering its own forms of business management and international trade, the America of the postmodern made echo: losing its industries like fleas but leading a whole new world economic system, into which even the former Eastern bloc seemed eager to leap.

Here at length, in this decade which has just ended but is still ours, Adorno's prophecies of the 'total system' finally came true, in wholly unexpected forms. Adorno was surely not the philosopher of the thirties (who has to be identified in retrospect, I'm afraid, as Heidegger); nor the philosopher of the forties and fifties; nor even the thinker of the sixties – those are called Sartre and Marcuse, respectively; and I have said that, philosophically and theoretically, his old-fashioned dialectical discourse was incompatible with the seventies. But there is some chance that he may turn out to have been the analyst of our own period, which he did not live to see, and in which late capitalism has all but succeeded in eliminating the final loopholes of nature and the Unconscious, of subversion and the aesthetic, of individual and collective praxis alike, and, with a final fillip, in eliminating any memory trace of what thereby no longer existed in the henceforth postmodern landscape. It now seems to me possible, then, that Adorno's Marxism, which was no great help in the previous periods, may turn out to be just what we need today. I will return to the relations between Adorno and the postmodern in my conclusions.

As for Marxism, however, it would be too easy to add that anyone
surprised by the characterization of Adorno as a Marxist has not read
much of his admittedly difficult writing, and also that most available
secondary discussions tend to leave the Marxism out, as though it were
some curious set of period mannerisms which a postcontemporary discussion no longer needs to take into consideration. But to those – non-
Marxists and anti-Marxists as well as the Marxists themselves – who think
it is interesting to argue about the degree and authenticity of Adorno's
Marxism (was he not really, after all, just as Hegelian, if not indeed
rather a post-Marxist?), I will suggest that it might be productive, for
one brief moment, to revive the old distinction between science and
ideology which has fallen, like so much else, into disrepute today.
'To be a Marxist' necessarily includes the belief that Marxism is
somehow a science: that is to say, an axiomatic, an organon, a body
of distinctive knowledges and procedures (about which, were we to develop the argument, one would also want to. say that it has a distinctive
status as a discourse, which is not that of philosophy or of other kinds
of writing).

All science, however, projects not just ideology but a host of possible
ideologies, and this is to be understood in a positive sense: ideology as
the working theory of a specific practice, the latter's 'philosophy' as
it were, and the ensemble of values and visions that mobilize it and
lend it an ethic and a politics (and an aesthetic as well). The various
Marxisms – for there are many of them, and famously incompatible
with one another – are just that: the local ideologies of Marxian science
in history and in concrete historical situations, which set not merely
their priorities but also their limits. To say, then, that the Marxism of
Lenin, or of Che, or of Althusser, or of Brecht (or indeed of Perry
Anderson or of Eagleton, not to speak of myself), is *ideological* now
simply means, in the critical sense of the term, that each one is situation-
specific to the point of encompassing the class determinations and cultural
and national horizons of its proponents (horizons which include, among
other things, the development of a working class politics in the period
in question).

As for Adorno's Marxism, it is obviously also determined (that is to
say, limited) by all those things, which used to be called 'factors'. What
is odd is only that a standpoint such as that of historical materialism
– for which the primacy of the historical situation is central – should
show as much perplexity in the face of this plurality of Marxist 'ideologies'
as any 'bourgeois philosophy'. To acknowledge Adorno's Marxism in
this spirit certainly does not mean to endorse his positions as a program

(indeed, much of Adorno's philosophical work turns precisely on this question of how we are to engage a living thought that is no longer historically current). In particular, his views on political art have been a stumbling block for some, who forget that these opinions were the price he paid for keeping alive a now unseasonable conception of the deeper political vocation of modernism itself. His attitudes towards 'actually existing socialism' were clearly class-conditioned (as was his lack of sympathy or understanding for Third World revolutions); but at a time in which the socialist countries themselves are engaged in a momentous process of transformation, they need no longer detain us, except as historical testimony to the dilemmas of left intellectuals during the Cold War. But he seems to have had more sympathy for the student movement of the sixties than he was willing to express publicly[3] (a sympathy not a little tarnished by the deathless shame of having called the police into the University).

But any assessment of Adorno's political positions must not omit his academic praxis as such – his systematic intervention into the intellectual life that survived the war in what became the Federal Republic (involving any number of influential academic survivors of Hitler's universities) and in particular the responsibility he actively took for the reconstruction of sociology – a turn of destiny all the more unusual for a one-time aesthete and expert on musical questions. Adorno's vigorous and voluminous polemics and *mises au point* on the nature and function of sociology (which constitute a missing third term alongside *Negative Dialectics* and *Aesthetic Theory* and which I will discuss in the course of the first part) seem to have involved two stages or concurrent propositions. The so-called Frankfurt School returned to Germany surrounded – legitimately or illegitimately[4] – by the prestige of American empirical research: Adorno was capable of using this to pound his more metaphysical enemies in German social philosophy, while also turning on empiricism itself (and positivism) and subjecting that in turn to the critique of the dialectic (a word he used a great deal more in his sociological writings than in his philosophical ones). We have today come to a far keener sense of the significance and the objective dynamics of those 'ideological state apparatuses' which are the professions and the disciplines, something which ought to put us in a better position to appreciate what can now be called a genuine form of praxis in this area on Adorno's part.

Nor are these lessons outmoded either, even though the brief triumph of the dialectic on the West German scene seems to have given way to new and undialectical currents – that of Habermas, which of course critically descends from Adorno and Horkheimer, while modifying them beyond recognition[5] – and that of the various Anglo-American

influences, which are all decidedly hostile to dialectical thought. But –
except in anthropology, where the worldwide impact of Lévi-Strauss's
structuralism had a distantly comparable role in transforming the discipline – the other social sciences, unless I am mistaken, do not seem to
have known any comparable internal 'revolution' (save, belatedly, for
the extraordinary one-man effort of Pierre Bourdieu in sociology, whose
general impact cannot yet be assessed). The dialectic remains for
them a methodological timebomb; it can also be expected to play a significant role in the very different traditions of the social sciences in
the socialist countries, where it may spark new thoughts and new possibilities for intellectuals not primarily committed to whoring after Western
gods.

In any case, it is worth noting that the emphasis on sociology now
completes the traditional philosophical triad of the good, the true and
the beautiful as that is uniquely inflected in Adorno's work: the modulation of ethics into sociology (of a historical cast) is clearly the crucial
strategic move here, and thereby the least immediately recognizable
formal intervention. So it is that in Adorno the academic disciplines,
having missed their chance at reunification in Marxism itself, live on
in outwardly respectable but inwardly problematized forms.

But as to how Marxist this all may be, I would like, on a theoretical
level, to continue to insist on the relevance of the distinctions proposed
in *The Political Unconscious* to judgements of this kind: Adorno was
indeed not far from my mind when I suggested that the levels of the
political (immediate historical events), of the social (class and class consciousness), and of the economic (the mode of production), remain for
us in some paradoxical interdependent independence from each other
(or are relatively autonomous, if you prefer that language). This recognition was meant, if not to solve, then at least to neutralize what seemed
to me false problems and meaningless polemics in such areas as those
of the 'transition to capitalism', where proponents of an active shaping
role of working people seemed to confront those for whom the disem-
bodied forces and logic of capital were somehow at work. These however
seemed to me to offer two utterly different ways of construing or con-
structing the object of study, along with 'explanations' of utterly distinct
levels of abstraction: so that at length it becomes problematic even to
affirm that disagreement or contradictory, incompatible 'interpretations'
are involved here.

Something of the sort is also what I would wish to affirm about the
spirit of Adorno's Marxism, and in particular the notorious absence from
it of class judgement (actually, at all the crucial polemic moments, Adorno
is quite capable of making local class-ideological judgements of a particu-

larly decisive and devastating kind).[6] Adorno's contribution to the Marxist tradition is not, however, to be sought in the area of social class, on the second level of my tripartite scheme: for that one goes elsewhere (to E.P. Thompson, for example).

Where he does have an indispensable contribution to make, which we will not find elsewhere, is on my third 'level', that of analysis in terms of the economic system or mode of production. The originality, indeed, of his philosophical work (discussed here by way of a commentary on *Negative Dialectics*, in Part I) as well as in his aesthetics (Part III is a commentary on *Aesthetic Theory*, while Part II attempts to characterize Adorno's social view of art itself, partly on the basis of *Dialectic of Enlightenment*), lies in his unique emphasis on the presence of late capitalism as a totality within the very forms of our concepts or of the works of art themselves. No other Marxist theoretician has ever staged this relationship between the universal and the particular, the system and the detail, with this kind of single-minded yet wide-ranging attention (few contemporary thinkers have in any case combined this philosophical sophistication with a properly aesthetic sensibility; only Croce and Sartre come to mind, while Lukács, still in many ways a far greater historical figure, looks in this respect like something of a caricature). To be sure, in a period, the poststructuralist, in which we no longer have 'concepts' – in a period, the postmodern, in which we no longer have 'works of art' either – Adorno's offering may seem like a useless gift. At the least, it may serve to instruct the enemies of the concept of 'totality' in the meaning and function of this kind of thinking and interpretation, to which I will pay close attention in the following pages; in any case, Adorno's life work stands or falls with the concept of 'totality'.

As for the current ratings of Adorno's stock, I have been surprised by the increasing frequency of comparisons with his arch-enemy Heidegger[7] (whose philosophy, he once observed, 'is fascist to its innermost cells'[8]): the basis of these *rapprochements*, besides a kind of general neutralization of everything threatening for consumer society in both these philosophies, evidently has to do with the tendential mystique in Adorno of the so-called 'non-identical', or Nature. Meanwhile, the stress of the Frankfurt School on motifs of domination has seemed to awaken fleeting similarities with Foucault (who in any case, in a moment of abandon, suggested his own 'affinities' with these Germans he had not read until the end of his life[9]). The tortuous and hypersubtle 'undoings' of *Negative Dialectics* in its way with the Concept have also seemed to many to offer the proverbial family likeness with Derrida and deconstruction. (In my opinion, no very solid foundation for a 'dialogue' between this last and Marxism will be laid by wishing away the basic differences;

I have myself in another place suggested that Adorno's fundamental problematic is in some ways closer to de Man than to Derrida.[10])

Against all these comparisons I want to argue the following: what looks
like an approach to a more Heideggerian idea of Nature – Being here
replaced by Non-identity – is set in an altogether different perspective
if we grasp the fundamental role of natural history in Adorno. But this,
meanwhile, will also modify our stereotypes about the Frankfurt School
attitude towards science (they are normally thought to be against it)
and also in turn dispel the impression of some deeper similarity with
Foucault, since their very conception of natural history itself removes
everything that is anthropological and ideological about the latter's theme
of 'power'. As for deconstruction, I think that the impression of a family
likeness here rests on the ambiguity of the so-called 'history of Western
metaphysics', borrowed from Heidegger, and in its grandly mythical and
unhistorical lines seeming not unlike 'dialectic of enlightenment' itself.
But Error, what is called metaphysics or identity, is in Adorno the effect
of an increasingly powerful social system, while in Heidegger it is that
of an increasing distance from some original truth: even though, for
him, power, in the form of Latin and the Roman Empire, plays a part
in the distortion, sapping, and repression of that truth. Of course power
for Heidegger returns in modern technology; but it cannot be said that
he stresses the omnipresence of the social within the forms of error or
the inner constraints of metaphysical thought, as Adorno tries to do.
Meanwhile any stress on subjective error as a force of agency in its own
right is bound to slip into idealism.

I should, in the light of these attitudes towards philosophical comparison, now probably say something about my own approach to Adorno's
philosophical texts, which it may not be sufficiently clarifying to characterize in terms of narrative analysis. Indeed, if a narrative can be detected
at work in a philosophical essay – and one can easily imagine its exoteric
forms, the 'adventures' of a concept, the struggle between the protagonist-
concept and its enemies or opposite numbers, the Propp-style passage
through a series of tests and trials, philosophical synthesis as marriage,
and so forth – it seems more interesting to stage this narrative structure
in more modernist or 'reflexive' terms – that is to say, in terms of the
crisis of representation. At that point, what becomes interesting in a
philosophical text is not merely how its 'concept' manages to win
through, but how it managed to get said in the first place, and at what
price. 'Modernism' is in this sense that deeper skepticism about the possibility of representing anything – which is to say, finally, about saying
anything at all – that in the face of the palpable fact that sometimes
things do get said or represented gives way to a curious exploration of

the structures and the preconditions, the electoral fraud, cheating, rigging in advance, and tropological footwork that enabled such representation in the first place; not excluding a cool analytic assessment of what had to be abandoned *en route*, left unsaid, lied about, or misrepresented.

In modernism, however, the referent itself still survives, albeit problematically; so that the possibilities of the speaking subject (or its structural impossibilities) can also be staged in function of the structure of the object – in the present case, that turns out to be a kind of 'preestablished harmony' between Adorno's own modernism and the approach I am proposing. It is, in other words, because Adorno is himself so keenly aware of the nature of philosophical writing as a linguistic experiment, as *Darstellung* and the invention of form, that it becomes interesting and appropriate to look at his own work in the same way. But then I need to correct this formulation of the matter in turn, and to insist that although Adorno certainly does have a 'style' (like the rest of the 'modern masters', for whom this category is an objective and a historical one), and although I sometimes talk about it as such, I doubt if the reading I propose can be thought of as a literary one in the restricted or trivialized sense.

Adorno's modernism precludes assimilation to the aleatory free play of postmodern textuality, which is to say that a certain notion of truth is still at stake in these verbal or formal matters. As with aesthetic modernism itself, indeed, what you are able to construct in language has a certain truth by virtue of that very wresting of language, not merely from silence as such, but from the baleful properties of the proposition form, the perils of thematization and reification, and the inevitable (and metaphysical) illusions and distortions of the requirement to begin and end at certain points, and to appeal to this or that conventional standard of argument and of evidence. So the deeper message of my book, at the level at which Adorno himself in his particularity becomes indistinguishable from the dialectic, has to do with celebration of the dialectic as such. This may at least today have the benefit of a certain novelty.

So may my title, which simply introduces a German expression of long standing (*der Spätmarxismus*) to the English-speaking public. I find it helpful above all for a sharpening of the implication I developed above: namely, that Marxism, like other cultural phenomena, varies according to its socioeconomic context. There should be nothing scandalous about the proposition that the Marxism required by Third World countries will have different emphases from the one that speaks to already receding socialism, let alone to the 'advanced' countries of multinational capitalism. Even this last is of course profoundly 'uneven' and 'non-synchronous' and other kinds of Marxism are still vitally relevant to it. But this book argues the special relevance of Adorno's Marxism, and of its unique capacities within our own equally unique 'late' or third stage of capitalism. The word means nothing more dramatic than that: still, better late than never!

Killingworth, Connecticut
August, 1989

PART I

Baleful Enchantments

of the Concept

One

Of the two most influential misreadings of Adorno – as a post-Marxist and as a postmodernist – the second will be dealt with in our conclusions. The notion of his post-Marxism, however, rests on a misunderstanding of one of Adorno's basic leitmotivs, namely 'non-identity', from which, thematized and reified and turned into a philosophical program of some sort, all kinds of unwarranted consequences are drawn, as will be shown below.

Adorno is, however, the philosopher of Identity in a very special sense: it is with identity as such that both *Dialectic of Enlightenment* and *Negative Dialectics* begin: for this word can subsume the 'concept' and the 'system' fully as much as 'enlightenment' or 'science'. To write a philosophy of identity, however, does not mean to celebrate it or to pose as its ideologue: what has often been described as the Frankfurt School's 'critique of Reason' is in fact a systematic exploration of a standardization of the world imposed fully as much by the economic system as by 'Western science'. *Negative Dialectics* must be approached by way of this fundamental conceptual premiss, which constitutes the absolute and contradictory situation of philosophy itself, as well as of the various local polemics and skirmishes staged in the book's separate chapters. Before that, however, *Dialectic of Enlightenment* had sealed the fortunes of this concept by making it available in the form of a mediation, and above all one which included the 'existential' materials of daily life (along with those, famously, in which the identity-form is printed on mass culture). As befits a deliberately discontinuous work, we will deal with *Dialectic of Enlightenment* episodically throughout this book, returning at later moments to its conception of culture, its diagnosis of anti-Semitism, and its vision of natural history.

Here, however, at the threshold of a philosophical analysis of identity, it seems appropriate to insist on the face it wears and turns on daily life – namely repetition as such, the return of sameness over and over again, in all its psychological desolation and tedium: that is to say, neurosis. In that limited appropriation which Adorno makes of Freudian conceptuality (and which in some contexts looks crude and old-fashioned, when it does not, as in others, open up new layers and levels of the analysis), neurosis is simply this boring imprisonment of the self in itself, crippled by its terror of the new and unexpected, carrying its sameness with it wherever it goes, so that it has the protection of feeling, whatever it might stretch out its hand to touch, that it never meets anything but what it knows already. To put it that way, however, is to begin to wonder – not merely 'psychologically' – what it would take to have the strength to stand the new, to be 'open' to it; but even more: what that new might be, what it might be like, how one would go about conceptualizing and imagining what you can by definition not yet imagine or foresee; what has no equivalent in your current experience.

At that point, there slowly emerges the counter-image or -mirage of the neurotic self locked utterly into its own 'identity' – namely, the unrepresentable vision of the ceaseless flow of the absolutely new, the unrepetitive, the great stream which never comes twice and which Deleuze calls the 'flux' of perpetual change, in which neither subject nor object can yet be imagined, but only the terror and exhaustion of radical difference without markers or signposts, without moments of rest or even those spatial folds into which, like the bull into its *querencia*, we withdraw to lick our wounds and to know a few instants' peace. To shed our defenses and give ourselves over absolutely to this terrifying rush of the non-identical is of course one of the great ethical fantasy-images of the postmodern and the very delineation of the 'schizophrenic hero': why postmodern social space – the most standardized of all 'administered societies', from which the Other and otherness has been the most successfully exorcized – should be thus fantasized as the primal flux of schizophrenic difference is another and a puzzling question, which can only be answered sociologically (a word I use here for shorthand, until we can replace it with the much more complicated conception of the dialectic Adorno will spell out for us).

These two absolutizing and frightening glimpses of a closed self and a primal flux are, however, useful in grasping the *function* of the compromise formations that variously come into being throughout human history with their more familiar everyday shapes: garden-variety 'psychic identity', for example, which filters away enough of the radically new to allow what is left to be tolerable to experience, while it tirelessly reassures us that we really still do have a persistent identity over time, that my personal consciousness is still somehow 'the same' throughout all the unexpected peripeties of the biographical adventure, and that all the new dawns still reveal a world and an expanse of objects which, however they have changed their places, retain their older names and remain somehow, and however distantly, familiar. Ego is thus, in that larger sense of personal identity, a defense mechanism but also a weapon, an instrument of praxis and survival.

But Adorno only marginally includes an anthropology and a social psychology, and will open these levels, and that of the psychic subject itself, up to other forms of conceptuality, as we shall see in a moment. It is, however, worth pausing here in order to characterize the situation with which thought itself is confronted by the terms of the preceding discussions, a situation or a dilemma which then not only accounts for a certain philosophical ideal in Adorno's practice but also for the significance for him of certain peculiar aesthetic strictures as well.

If the concept is grasped as 'the same', as what makes things the same as well as inscribing a sameness – a return of recognizable entities – on the psyche, then the struggle of thought (at least at a certain moment of its history) has to undermine that logic of recurrence and of sameness in order to break through to everything sameness excludes: I put it this way in order to be able to describe this last – the 'non-identical' – both in terms of otherness and of novelty (rather than in the conventional terms of either the real or the referent, which would reconvert all this into a dualism: the concept being for Adorno just as real as anything else). But we must reach this experience of the new and of the other through conceptuality: that operation in Adorno which most closely approximates Habermas's critique of irrational philosophies turns rather on various intuitionisms (Bergson, Husserl, even Heidegger in a certain sense) which are stigmatized for their tendency to abandon conceptuality as such and to try for a more direct, immediate contact with the 'real'. Is it possible to do something to the concept, which otherwise tendentially locks us into sameness, in order to use it as a mode of access to difference and the new?

> Thought need not rest content in its logical regularity; it is capable of thinking against itself, without abolishing itself altogether; indeed, were definitions of the dialectic possible, that one might be worth proposing. (ND 144/141).

It is therefore not a matter of jettisoning the inherited categories of philosophy, which in any case continue to inform daily life in the guise of common-sense realism; no more than intuitive immediacy, the invention of new utopian concepts and neologisms offers no escape from the 'iron cage' of the concept and its identities. But how the concept can be used against itself is a complicated matter which we will try to characterize later on.

For the moment, that other feature of what the concept represses – the New – reminds us that this situation, this dilemma, is in some sense also an aesthetic one and, particularly in the area of so-called modernism, knows specifically aesthetic and artistic equivalents, which we will discuss at some length in a later context. It seems more worthwhile at this point to underscore the significance of Adorno's interest in a somewhat more traditional aesthetic and linguistic structure, namely the epic, about which it has not sufficiently been observed that he also has a theory, to be derived from several points in his work; implicitly, in the 'Odyssey' commentary in Dialectic of Enlightenment, which stages the emergence of epic language and narrative from the ever-sameness of myth; and explicitly in two crucial essays in the Noten zur Literatur, 'On Epic Naïveté' and the enormous 'Parataxis', on Hölderlin (and not exclusively given over to the obligatory onslaught on the famous Heideggerian exegesis of the poet).

Adorno does not seem to have known Erich Auerbach's influential analysis of epic in terms of this same category of parataxis (but as part of an unstable dualism between the additive time of epic – 'and ... and ... and ...' – and the more syntactical and periodic linear and causal temporality of what he calls 'hypotaxis', using the Old Testament as a strong form and Ur-counterpart to Homer).[1] Both commentators share, of course, the traditional view of the stasis of epic time – its 'serenity' as a series of isolated moments and 'centered' sentences which themselves have something of the mesmerized stillness of the tableau. But where Auerbach assumes that these epic sentences simply follow one upon another in all the regularity of the paratactic stream, it will come as no surprise to find Adorno posing the problem in terms of our preceding description: namely, as that of generating the new moment, temporal change, out of mythic repetition and sameness. The focus is on the syncategorematic and the particle, connectives that link these seemingly stable and monadic sentences, which turn on themselves like the solar system, together in a larger sequence or passage of textual time; and on the anaphoric echoes and reprises that weave the separate sentences desperately into some larger temporality.

What Adorno reads, however, is not the serene logic of such connectives – the 'and' – but rather the violence of the yoking of the sentences and the epic illogicality of the sense of these otherwise functional words:

'but', 'however', 'meanwhile', Hölderlin's *nämlich* – a sense which, by denying the continuity at the same moment that it establishes it, foregrounds the peculiarity of the epic operation itself and stages 'parataxis' as a wilful inscription of the new and the break within the stable reproduction of a sameness and a repetition often associated with epic, but in reality far more deeply characteristic of the mythic world which epic seeks to cancel and transcend. There is a way in which this peculiar classical syntax can stand as an emblem for Adorno's philosophical practice fully as much as the more obvious formal inventions and solutions of the modern. In particular, the remarkable way in which death finds itself inscribed in the tranquil imperturbability of Homeric language – the grisly execution of the maids, whose commentary concludes the '*Odyssey*' chapter in *Dialectic of Enlightenment* – suggests interesting parallels with some of the ultimate aims of *Negative Dialectics* itself.

We must now, 'however', return to the matter of the concept, and in particular to the multiple and rotating significance of the term 'identity' as Adorno deploys it. This functional polysemousness has earlier historical and philosophical parallels:

> In the history of modern philosophy, the word 'identity' has had several meanings. It designated, for example, the unity of personal consciousness: that an 'I' remains the same throughout all its experiences. This is what was meant by the Kantian 'I think, which should be able to accompany all my representations [*Vorstellungen*]'. Then again identity meant what was supposed to be regularly or nomothetically [*gesetzlich*] present in all rational beings, or in other words thought as logical universality; including the equivalence with itself of every object of thought, the simple A = A. Finally, the epistemological meaning: that subject and object, however mediated, coincide. The first two levels of meaning are by no means strictly differentiated, even in Kant. Nor is this the result of a careless use of language. Identity rather shows up as the zone of indifference between psychology and logic within idealism itself. (ND 145, note/142, note)

The sea-changes in meaning of the concept are therefore here already designated as levels – that is, as the epistemological space of emergent disciplines and specialized codes (so that it is perhaps not irresponsible to grasp the term *gesetzlich* – literally, 'lawful', and here standing for the conceptual regularities and uniformities of Reason itself – as a hint and foreshadowing of the emergence of some properly juridical or legal level as well – the identity of the *legal* subject – something rarely developed in Adorno himself but in which many of us today are keenly interested). Nor is the ultimate level – the economic – here evoked, but it will emerge at its proper time and place.

We have at any rate here moved from the psychic level of identity, the unity of the subject, to the properly logical one, at which for the first time the central space of Adorno's deployment of identity and non-identity comes into view: namely, that of the *concept* (*Begriff*, rather than *Idee*, 'idea', which has a very different meaning in Hegel, and also in the great 'Epistemo-Critical Prologue' to Walter Benjamin's *Origin of German Tragic Drama*, a text of supreme importance for Adorno, both in his first philosophical years and then again in *Negative Dialectics* itself, and one to which we will return).

In the philosophical framework, therefore, the *concept* is the strong form of identity, subsuming a great variety of different, really existing objects under the same term or thought (the objects being different by definition, since they all exist separately). The primacy of the concept therefore implies a historical moment in which universals come into being, in which abstractions are wrested from the primal flux of sheer names that would seem to characterize preconceptual thinking: when we think, however, of Lévi-Strauss's analysis of this last as perceptual or qualitative science [*pensée sauvage*], and also of Adorno's account of the dynamics of enlightenment, a process which for him has no beginning, then it would begin to seem that functionally the primacy of the concept (in Western philosophy) is not so different after all from the elaboration of magical names, since both are forms of 'enlightenment' in the sense in which they secure domination over nature, and organize the 'blooming, buzzing confusion' of the natural state into so many abstract grids.

Meanwhile, the concept – any concept – asserts and enforces the conviction that it corresponds to the thing, to its object: how that relationship is conceived surely plays across a broad variety of epistemological fantasies, from notions that it represents some inner truth of the thing all the way to the feeling that it is somehow 'like' the thing. Rare indeed are those who, like the Dickens character, celebrate the capacity of the philosopher to produce concepts utterly unlike the thing itself: 'If you was to take and show that man the buoy at the Nore ... and ask him his opinion of it, Wal'r, he'd give you an opinion that was no more like that buoy than your uncle's buttons are.' It is true that Althusser, whose epistemology is in this sense radically non-identitarian, liked tirelessly to remind us that 'the concept of sugar does not taste sweet'; but the therapeutic shock of this reminder cannot last long, and my hunch is that anyone trying to conceptualize the property of sweetness will ultimately end up persuading himself that the mind triumphant manages to incorporate sweetness within itself as part of its thought.

The failure is not simply the result of the mind's weakness, or its attachment to an outmoded philosophical ideology or epistemology: it

is, on the contrary, inscribed in the concept itself, whose whole dynamic
seeks to secure and perpetuate the feeling that it reunites subject and
object, and reenacts their unity. Adorno, who still uses the language
of ideology and false consciousness, will sometimes go so far as to suggest
that this primal illusion of the identity of the concept with the thing
is the strong form of ideology itself and provides its very definition:

> Ideology by no means always takes the form of explicitly idealistic philosophy.
> It does its secret work within the very foundational construction [*Substruktion*]
> of something affirmed as first or primary (no matter what the latter's content),
> within the implicit identity of concept and thing, which justifies the world
> as it is, even when a doctrine summarily teaches the dependence of conscious-
> ness on being. (ND 50/40)

We will return to the matter of firstness later on in the framework of
Adorno's view of philosophical *Darstellung* or writing-form; what might
be added to the remarks just quoted is only the supplementary turn
of the screw that the identification of the concept with the thing also
implicitly (but also often explicitly) has the result of our believing that
the concept is a thing, of our living among our concepts as though they
were the things of the real world. The term demanding to be pronounced
at this point is clearly the word 'reification'; and that Adorno's leitmotiv
of identity can be seen as his variant on the now traditional apparatus
of the critiques of reification (from Marx on) seems to me demonstrable,
but also paradoxical in the light of his not infrequent denunciations of
vulgar or schematic Marxism in general and of reification theory in particular. Such passages seem, however, to involve two kinds of anxiety,
one of form and one of content, so to speak. Adorno's materialism,
which specifically makes a place for a life among objects and things,
senses a kind of moralizing spiritualism in the use of the slogan of reifica- *(Protestant)*
tion as a reproach – as though it were desirable to divest oneself altogether
of material furnishings! In particular, the reifying impulse in modern
art is affirmed as a necessity and evaluated positively. But this amounts
to something a little more complicated than a reversal of Marx's reproach
that Hegel confounded alienation with objectification; since Adorno's
perspective historicizes the problem and includes reification as such (as
an intensified effect of commodity production) within even non-alienated
objectification today.

Formally, however, the problem posed by the term 'reification' is of
another kind and turns, as we shall see later in more detail, on the
unwanted 'thematization' of the single-shot motif or explanation, no
matter how locally valid. This then becomes a substantive ideological

or even anthropological 'theory' in its own right, at which point its form contradicts its content by virtue of conveying an autonomous message in the first place. In short, Adorno's objection would frequently seem to be the (pertinent) one that most often the concept of reification is itself reified, or at least easily reifiable. Characteristically, then, Adorno criticizes 'reification' in the name of the moment of truth of reification theory.

As for identity itself, however, in so far as it has been characterized functionally in terms of domination and repression, an alternate or complementary description emerges negatively, in the direction of what identity excludes. Even the classical dialectic (still organized around identity) 'must unquestionably pay the price of a bitter sacrifice in the qualitative multiplicity of experience' (ND 18/6). Hegel himself is still at one with the older identitarian philosophical tradition in his indifference 'to non-conceptuality, individuality, and particularity; to what has been since Plato written off as transitory and incapable of promotion to genuine philosophical significance [unerheblich], and on which Hegel himself plastered the label of "lazy existence"' (ND 20/8). The suggestion here of a certain asceticism in conceptuality, of renunciation coupled with ressentiment at that very renunciation, is certainly present and very consistent with Adorno's attitudes (not only towards the repressive functions of identity); elsewhere he derides the aversion to rhetoric of traditional philosophers, 'who consider the body of language as sinful' (ND 66/56).

Yet clearly enough, as such overtones of a language of desire and repression indicate, this moment – in which we approach the nature of identity by way of a characterization of 'non-identity' – discloses that zone of Adorno's thinking in closest proximity to many of the now familiar thematics of poststructuralism. We have already tactically evoked the Deleuzian flux: here the word 'heterogeneity' seems inescapably to impose itself, and to draw along behind it a whole ideological baggage tending to reassociate Adorno with postmodernism and post-Marxism, an association against which we argued in the introduction to the present volume. A rather different perspective on Adorno's conception of otherness and the non-identical will emerge later in the discussion of *Aesthetic Theory*, where a thematic of nature and natural beauty equally unexpectedly seems to turn Adorno back into a much more traditional kind of aesthetic philosopher, but one no less incompatible with dialectics and Marxism than the poststructural kind. It is certain that his emphasis on the way in which reason and the concept tendentially filter out the qualitative (the perceptual and even the bodily) is a congenial theme at the present time, while the repression of the particular by the general and of the individual by the universal seems to return us decisively to precisely those anti-'totalitarian' and anti-utopian positions from which Adorno's anti-identity theory must be sharply distinguished (that it involves a historical critique of the nominalist tendency in modern art fully as much as an acknowledgement and a foregrounding of it will be clear only later on, in our discussion of *Aesthetic Theory*).

A passing remark, early in *Negative Dialectics*, makes it clear, however, that all of these themes are first and foremost to be grasped within another tradition, namely the Marxist one. This crucial phrase identifies 'what cannot be subsumed under identity' – that is to say, everything that has been evoked above variously under the notions of difference and heterogeneity, otherness, the qualitative, the radically new, the corporeal – as 'what is called in Marxian terminology *use value*' (emphasis added; ND 22/11). This is the decisive clue, not merely to the basic philosophical argument that subtends Adorno's conception of identity and non-identity – *Capital*, volume I, Book I, Part I – but also to the ultimate identity of 'identity' itself, which we have observed to take on the forms of psychic identity and of logic and epistemology before coming to rest (at least provisionally) in the economic realm of exchange and the commodity. The weak form of the argument merely supposes a *homology* between these processes (economic abstraction is structured *like* psychic abstraction, which in its turn is structured *like* philosophical abstraction or unity); while its stronger form asserts a priority of the 'economic', in the sense that stamping goods as uniform and producing uniform goods is a more complex functional activity than the production of uniform thoughts.

Marx's classic chapter is in effect a meditation on the mysteries of identity (which we take for granted): how is it, when the consumption (or 'use') of any specific object is unique, and constitutes a unique and incomparable temporal event in our own lives as well, that we are able to think of such things as 'the same'? Sameness here is not merely the concept of the category of this particular object (several different things being steaks, cars, linen, or books) but also, and above all, the equivalence of their *value*, the possibility we have historically constructed of comparing them (one car for so many pounds of steak), when in terms of experience or consumption – in other words, of use value – they remain incomparable and speculation is incapable of weighing the experience of eating this particular steak against that of a drive in the country. Exchange value, then, the emergence of some third, abstract term between two incomparable objects (an abstraction which, by way of the historical dialectic narrated by Marx in this chapter, ultimately takes the form of money), constitutes the primordial form by which identity emerges in human history.

The 'exchange relationship' [*Tauschverhältnis*] is the other great leitmotiv that sounds throughout Adorno's work, and it is strictly 'identical'
with that more philosophical leitmotiv named 'identity' which we have
been tracing here. Now the philosophical and anthropological evocation
of the will to domination inherent in the identical concept gives way
to a more vivid sense of the constraints of the economic system (commodity production, money, labor-power) secretly inherent in all manifestations of identity itself; meanwhile, this infrastructure of the concept
then also makes it clear why its effects (sometimes also called 'ideology'
as we have seen above) cannot simply be thought away by the thinking
of a better thought, by new forms of philosophizing and more adequate
(or even more Utopian) concepts. History already thinks the thinking
subject and is inscribed in the forms through which it must necessarily
think.

'Society precedes the subject' (ND 132/126); thought's categories are
collective and social; identity is not an option but a doom; reason and
its categories are at one with the rise of civilization or capitalism, and
can scarcely be transformed until the latter is transformed. But Habermas
is wrong to conclude that Adorno's implacable critique of reason (*Verstand* rather than *Vernunft*) paints him into the corner of irrationalism
and leaves him no implicit recourse but the now familiar poststructural
one of *l'acéphale*, cutting off the intolerable, hyperintellectual head of
the formerly rational being. He thinks so only because he cannot himself
allow for the possibility or the reality of some new, genuinely dialectical
thinking that would offer a different kind of solution in a situation in
which the limits and failures – indeed the destructive effects – of non-
dialectical 'Western' reason are well known.

Two

Everything therefore turns on whether we can imagine such a radically different, alternative way of thinking or philosophizing, let alone ourselves practice it. Dialectical thinking has often been described as reflexivity, self-consciousness, 'thought to the second power', the distancing of ordinary thought 'procedures [so] as to widen its own attention to include them in its awareness as well'.[2] That is a way of putting it, but its effectiveness depends very much on the freshness of this rhetoric of self-consciousness, which, at a time when 'consciousness' itself has been called back into question as a concept or a category, has apparently ceased to convey very much. Reflexivity (if you prefer) is part of the baggage of a modernist thinking no longer very authoritative in the postmodernist era.

Negative Dialectics gives us another way of characterizing the dialectical process (now purged of Hegelian idealism, at least so far as Adorno is concerned). We are now asked (but the figures are mine) to think another side, an outside, an external face of the concept which, like that of the moon, can never be directly visible or accessible to us: but we must vigilantly remember and reckon that other face into our sense of the concept while remaining within it in the old way and continuing to use and think it. If the notion of the 'Unconscious' seems occasionally to impose itself, we should resist it as some ultimate philosophical solution and see that notion also as a kind of shorthand, one figure among many others which equally sought to endow the thinking mind with a dimension of radical otherness that, at least on Lacan's and Lévi-Strauss's reading of Freud, must always structurally elude us, and remain forever out of reach. Like the astronomer (Lévi-Strauss's comparison[3]) we can reckon the presence out there of some massive invisible body or gravitational source which can never be part of our experience, even though we can use its hypothesis to rebuke and therapeutically to discredit unmediated conscious thinking.

But this way of putting it offers a misleading way of characterizing Adorno: the Frankfurt School's pioneering use of Freud applied the latter's categories as a kind cf supplementary social psychology (repression and the damaged subject as indices and results of the exchange process and the dynamics of capitalism) but never as any centrally organizing concept.[4]

In order to see how thought could be imagined to 'think against itself', we must return to the starting point of the first chapter, which set out to rewrite stereotypical (post-Marxist) versions of two fundamental concepts in Adorno, identity and totality. Of identity we have seen that it is in fact Adorno's word for the Marxian concept of exchange relationship (a term he also frequently uses): his achievement was then to have powerfully generalized, in richer detail than any other thinker of the Marxist or dialectical tradition, the resonance and implications of the doctrine of exchange value for the higher reaches of philosophy. Of totality we will now assert that Adorno is not merely not an enemy and a critic of this copiously stigmatized idea, but that it comes very precisely as the solution to the problem of thinking with and against the concept that has been posed above. The fundamental operation whereby the concept can be retained and dereified all at once (to use a different kind of shorthand) involves its reinsertion into totality or system (a term whose slippage between notions of a philosophical system and of a socioeconomic system will be significant and even crucial, as we shall see shortly). As for totality, it plays a strategic role in freeing us from the 'spell' of the concept, as the following preliminary characterization (an argument against Croce) already suggests:

> What is differentiated will appear divergent, dissonant, negative just as long as consciousness is driven by its own formation towards unity; just as long as it measures what is not identical with itself against its own claim for totality. It is this which dialectics exhibits to consciousness as a contradiction. (ND 17/5-6)

Yet there is a suggestion in this passage that the drive towards totality (Lukács's *Totalitätsintention*) may have something illicit about it, expressing the idealism and the imperialism of the concept, which seeks voraciously to draw everything into its own field of domination and security. Something of this is certainly present in Adorno, nor is it alien to other thinkers who have been stigmatized as 'totalitarian' in their insistence on the urgency and centrality of the notion of totality; the misunderstanding lies in drawing the conclusion that philosophical emphasis on the indispensability of this category amounts either to celebration of it or, in a stronger form of the anti-utopian argument, to its implicit perpetuation as a reality or a referent outside the philosophical realm. In that case no critique, satire or representational denunciation would ever be possible, since it would simply reconfirm what it claimed to be stigmatizing.

The moment of truth in this misunderstanding becomes more visible when we turn to that more purely philosophical modulation of the notion of totality which is the notion of a philosophical system, or of the ideal of systematic thinking. *Negative Dialectics* is certainly on the face of it a repudiation of the ideal and the practice of philosophical systems (even that of Hegel); as has already been observed, it seems to urge a practice of thought which at its outer limit would authorize the writing of just those provisional, fragmentary, self-consuming conceptual performances celebrated by properly postmodern philosophy.[5]

What must now be affirmed, however, is the opposite of all this: namely, that no matter how desirable this postmodern philosophical free play may be, it cannot now be practiced; however conceivable and imaginable it may have become as a philosophical aesthetic (but it would be important to ask what the historical preconditions for the very conception of this ideal and the possibility of imagining it are), anti-systematic writing today is condemned to remain within the 'system'. We may make a beginning on this paradox by returning to certain anti-utopian arguments associated with so-called post-Marxism: for it is certain that in denouncing philosophical system, in proposing some radically unsystematic dialectics, in arguing against 'system' itself, Adorno retains the concept of the system and even makes it, as target and object of critique, the very center of his own anti-systematic thinking. This is the sense in which it can – and must – be affirmed that he perpetuates the primacy of system as such: his most powerful philosophical and aesthetic interventions are all implacable monitory reminders – sometimes in well-nigh Weberian or Foucauldian tones – of our imprisonment within system, the forgetfulness or repression of which binds us all the more strongly to it, in ways reminiscent of the illusions of identity, with which it is of course in one sense virtually synonymous.

Identity is, however, something like occluded system, totality forgotten or repressed, at the same time that it continues the more effectively to perform system's work. This is the sense in which the conscious reintroduction of system or totality comes as a solution to the closure of identity; it cannot free us from the latter's illusions and mirages, since no mere thinking can do that, but it suddenly makes these last visible and affords a glimpse of the great magic 'spell' [*der Bann*] in which modern life is seized and immobilized. (This essentially romance figure has a paradoxical dynamic in contemporary thought, since it is precisely enlightenment and the *desacralization* of the world – Weber's *Entzauberung* – which can be characterized as the realm of a whole new fetishization: a term Marx explicitly borrowed from eighteenth-century anthropology).[6]

System is very precisely that outer face of the concept, that outside forever inaccessible to us, evoked above; yet to see how this might be so, we need experimentally to record the inner transformations or dialectical polysemousness of this twin notion of system/totality in much the same spirit as our account of the levels of reference in the concept of identity. What looks like the ideal of philosophical system is, then, in a second moment deconcealed as the claims of reason and the universal – indeed, of abstraction as such: whose systematizing operations within the concept it may be convenient to register by way of the dialectic of form and content. The in-forming presence of system within even the most isolated and free-standing 'concept' can be detected in its form, which remains abstract and universal, whatever its local content may happen to be. But this clarifies the figure we have proposed of another 'face' or an 'outside' of the concept, since we cannot think the form and the content of a given concept simultaneously or in the same way: attention to the form of a thought seems at once, in a kind of Gestalt perception, to discredit the thought's content – that is to say, its official meaning or reference: to bracket it, so that it falls to the level of an optional example and its inherent 'belief' evaporates or becomes fictional.

Thinking the concept in the usual fashion, however, means 'believing' it and attending to its content, in such a way that the perception of its form becomes a trivial annoyance and a distracting interruption. What needs to be invented, therefore – and what in my opinion Adorno's dialectics proposes – is a new kind of stereoscopic thinking in which the concept continues to be thought philosophically and cashed at face value, while in some other part of the mind a very different kind of intellectual climate reigns, a cruder and more sociological set of terms and categories, in which the form of that concept is noted and registered in shorthand and in which the existence of the financial and banking system thereby presupposed is somehow reckoned in.

For as we have seen in our discussion of identity, abstraction itself – very much including its most sophisticated philosophical equivalent in logic and in the form of universals – is revealed at another level to be at one with the logic of equivalence and exchange; that is to say, with the logic of capital. The exchange relationship, the abstract value form in which identity is primordially conceived, cannot exist as a punctual event, as an occasional matter or an isolated, optional or random act; it is at one with the exchange system itself, so that it is at this point that the philosophical term 'system' modulates into the essentially social or socioeconomic concept of totality (something Adorno often invokes in the sociological and even Weberian terminology of bureaucratic or 'administered' society [*die verwaltete Welt*], but more often and less euphemistically simply as 'late capitalism'). This ultimate deconcealment of the nature of the systematic makes it clear why we cannot simply renounce 'system' and let it go at that; even more why 'totality' remains an indispensable name for the infrastructural dimension of reason and abstract thought today – its other or family name, as it were:

> The dialectical mediation of the universal and the particular does not allow a theory that opts for the particular to treat the universal overzealously as a soap bubble. If it did that, theory would be incapable of registering the pernicious supremacy of the universal in the current state of things, nor could it project the idea of another state of things in which the universal would find itself stripped of its bad particularity insofar as individuals were restored to what rightly belonged to them [namely, *Besonderheit*, which is to say precisely specificity, particularity, individuality]. Nor are on the other hand conceptions of a transcendental subject acceptable, a subject without society and without those individuals whom for good or ill it integrates. (ND 199-200/199-200)

Adorno's language here will, however, be misleading to the degree to which the philosophical concepts he manipulates (universality, particularity) seem in this passage to be on the same level with each other, as though one could simply think them together in a 'synthetic judgement', with whatever inversion of the philosophical and logical hierarchy of subject and predicate seems desirable. But the burden of his critique of Hegel lay precisely in the accusation that Hegel thought the relationship between the two poles from the point of view of universality: 'the difference between the universal and the particular developed by the dialectic is the one dictated by the universal itself' (ND 18/6). This distortion is the effect of the very form of universalizing philosophical language, which, in trying desperately to designate what is other than the universal, continues to use an abstract terminology and the very form of logical opposition or dualism to convey its protest against the operations of that language and that logical form. To say 'particular' is to reinforce the 'universal', no matter what you go on to do with these words.[7] I stress the effect at this point, not merely to illustrate the preceding discussion of the lateral distortion by the philosophical and universalizing

systemic form of its content, but also because Adorno's warning, in spite
of itself, tends to obscure the radicality of the double standard he himself
practices, which we have begun to describe here.

This is to say that purity in philosophical thinking or writing (Adorno
already approaching the poststructural position that these are in fact the
same), the unmixed or 'intrinsic', is as impossible as it is undesirable:
something that holds for the individual concept as well and also – paradoxically for those who think of Adorno as in this area the very quintessence
of the aesthete – for the work of art. What the concept cannot say must
somehow, by its imperfection, be registered within it (just as the monadic
work of art must somehow 'include' its outside, its referent, under pain
of lapsing into decorative frivolity): otherwise the powerful force of identity will reign through it unchecked. Those for whom dialectical thought
in general, and Adorno's writing in particular, are uncongenial have seen
this impurity at work more vividly than the sympathizers: they evoke
long, heady, supersubtle 'dialectical' disputation, followed by the inevitable lapse into vulgar-Marxist interpretation of a summary type, the
'explanation' in terms of late capitalism that solves everything.

Nor is it wrong to observe that the 'interpretant' – late capitalism,
'administered society', the fragmentation of psychic subjects in the monopoly period, etc., etc. – is never the object of the same kind of prodigious
intelligence deployed in the great philosophical periods that precede it
and to which it gives a kind of closure. But the double standard does
not mean the establishment of a boundary between topics that are fair
game for the dialectic and truths that are supposed to be left untouched
(since they constitute the foundational or Archimedean point in terms
of which the other kinds of operations are conducted). It means rather,
within the same thought, designating the outside of that thought which
can never be mastered by it on its own terms.

The summary deictic indication in passing of late capitalism, system,
exchange, totality, is not a reference to other sets of thoughts or concepts
(such as Grossman's or Pollock's theory of late capitalism,[8] or Weber's
of bureaucracy) which can be criticized in their own terms for their
coherence and validity and their ideological quotient. It rather gestures
towards an outside of thinking – whether system itself in the form of
rationalization, or totality as a socioeconomic mechanism of domination
and exploitation – which escapes representation by the individual thinker
or the individual thought. The function of the impure, extrinsic reference
is less to interpret, then, than to rebuke interpretation as such and to
include within the thought the reminder that it is itself inevitably the
result of a system that escapes it and which it perpetuates: even there
where it seeks radically to grasp and confront the element in which

it bathes and which infiltrates and determines its subjective processes fully as much as the objects for which it seeks to account.

We therefore find ourselves obliged to take form into account if we want to deal seriously with content; for Adorno's 'theories' of late capitalism are inseparable from what we may call the 'totality-effect' in his writing and *Darstellung*. It is an effect that might be evoked in terms of Deleuze's great (Leibnizian) theory of the filmic modern,[9] as a continuous loop between the present of the image or shot, the world-totality behind it of which it is only an aspect, but which expresses itself only through that aspect, and the mobile sequence by which the shots succeed one another (and also convey the modifications in the totality beyond them). Adorno's sentences are, then, just such individual 'shots', edited into a larger formal movement (the constellation or model, as we shall see shortly), small- and large-scale dimensions through both of which the absent totality perpetually feeds. (Indeed, by way of Eisenstein, Deleuze characterizes one form of this modernist and 'totalizing' system as the dialectic itself.)

The philosophical objection that can be made to this form of thinking or writing is therefore essentially no different from the problem which on the level of language produced the notion of the 'hermeneutic circle': if we must pass through the individual sentences, or even through their larger locally staged argument and architectonic, where would that conception of totality, which is supposed to open up the other face of their particular meanings ever come from in the first place? How could we ever acquire a conception of the universal or the total system – if we are condemned to pass through particulars? The obvious response – that we evidently acquired the notion of the universal somewhere, since we now have it – is vitiated by a postmodern situation in which it seems possible to read particulars one by one without any transcendent universal or totality from which they derive their meaning; and in which we also harbor the deep suspicion that such universals as may still survive are in reality stereotypes that include no new information content.

A more satisfactory (although not at all satisfying) response may be afforded by turning the problem into its own solution: this very contradiction between the universal and the particular constitutes Adorno's diagnosis of the modern world, and cannot in that sense be solved but only thematized and foregrounded, taken as a symptom in its own right. In his post-Hegelian philosophical language, reconciliation [*Versöhnung*] – whether this is understood philosophically, existentially, socially, or aesthetically – is very precisely to be taken as a lifting of the tensions and contradictions between the universal and the particular: the common understanding that it involves a reconciliation of subject and object is

thus erroneous, except to the degree to which object here designates
the larger social order and subject the individual or particular. From
this perspective, then, interpretation as such – the reading of the particular
in the light of the absent universal – is dialectically transformed and
'sublated': producing a new mode of interpretation in which the particular
is read, not in the light of the universal, but rather in the light of the
very contradiction between universal and particular in the first place.
Interpretation now means turning the text inside out and making it into
a symptom of the very problem of interpretation itself.

But this philosophical solution – if it is one – scarcely removes the
local discomfort of garden-variety interpretive acts and operations; nor
does it effectively address the malaise readers have sometimes felt with
Adorno's own interpretations. That he was keenly aware of the issue
may be judged by the following remark on interpretation in a more
specifically literary or aesthetic context:

> What is self-defeating [*das Fatale*] about all forms of interpretation of art,
> even the most philosophically responsible kinds, is the way in which they
> find themselves obliged to express what is shocking and unaccustomed by
> way of what is already familiar, in so far as they must necessarily express
> it by way of the Concept; they thus explain away what alone demands explana-
> tion: as passionately as works of art long for interpretation, they all equally
> passionately betray conformism, even against their own will.[10] (NL 101)

The consequence is that 'conformism' – in this case, conformism to the
preexisting idea or stereotype – returns in the form of interpretation
to defuse and domesticate what in the work – as sheer unassimilable
particularity and uniqueness – struggled to resist it. This is the spirit
in which, in one of the grimmer caricatures of Adorno's own 'method',
a hostile critic enumerates the 'findings' of Adorno's principal essay on
Proust (including page references to the complete edition of the *Noten
zur Literatur*):

> The whole is the untrue (p. 203), bourgeois society as a closed system of
> preestablished disharmony (p. 206), non-identity of the ego (p. 206 ff.), the
> breakdown of experience in alienation, beauty's continuing existence as mere
> appearance (p. 207 ff.), impossibility of love in the function-dominated totality
> (p. 209 ff.), etc.[11]

This seemingly definitive etcetera does not take into account the remarkable evocations of Proust in the concluding chapter of *Negative Dialectics*:
references that surely constitute a luminous 'interpretation' of a wholly

novel stamp (although it may be agreed that the critical faculty flags somewhat in the essay in question, without conceding any of the implied critique of Adorno's method itself).

This operated, at its moments of greatest intensity, as a kind of Gestalt modification of the hermeneutic circle. The logical relationship of the particular to the universal is in any case never that of the traditional Aristotelian subsumption of species under genus. Still, in so far as the reader habitually sorts judgements out into the canonical major and minor premisses, Adorno's propositions may be said deliberately to invert these, by way of a perceptual play on the blurred zones of our lateral perception. The attention systematically directed to the particular, to the text or phenomenon to be interpreted – and for which the interpretandum is the presupposed totality summoned to the outlying field of vision – finds that what has been said, unexpectedly, addresses that totality itself and modifies it, not the particular that was its pretext. Meanwhile, a thematization of the totality (monopoly capitalism, for instance) that drew in this or that isolated historical particular as a mere example or illustration proves itself to have been a subterfuge for the striking modification, the interpretation by way of shock and novelty, of the putative example itself. Adorno himself describes this process – which can clearly not lend itself to a 'linear' argument about anything – in connection with the elective affinity of the essay as a form with cultural matters:

> [The essay] sinks itself into cultural phenomena as into a second nature, a second immediacy, not in order to 'reduce' those, but rather to lift their illusions by its persistent immanence. It is as little deluded as 'philosophies of origin' about the difference between culture and what underlies it. But for the essay culture is not some epiphenomenon above being that must be eradicated, but rather its object of criticism, what it posits [*thesei*], is the underlying itself, the false society. This is why origins mean no more to the essay than superstructures. It owes its freedom in the choice of objects, its sovereignty over all priorities of subject-matter or theory, to the fact that for it in some sense all objects lie equally near the center: that is to say, to the principle that everything is bewitched. (NL 28)

Rhetorically, then, we may say that Adorno's way with interpretation, and the dimension of an outside and an absent system that he seeks to reconfer on particulars of experience, turn on the possibility of shifting the positions perpetually between particular and universal, transforming the putative universal without warning into a particular, unmasking the alleged particular as a universal in true sheep's or grandmother's clothing.

This play of positions may indeed be traced down into the very syntax of the sentences themselves, about which we have already noted an excessive fondness for the transformation of nouns in subject positions without warning into objects.

Three

It may now be useful in passing to specify at least two kinds of thinking which are not to be confused or identified with the dialectical stereoscopy or 'double standard' we have observed at work in Adorno. It may now seem, for example, increasingly urgent to return to our hesitations about the rhetoric of self-consciousness and reflexivity, and to specify more explicitly (as we shall also do when we come to Adorno's aesthetics) the ways in which 'a thoroughgoing critique of identity gropes its way towards the preponderance of the object' (ND 184/183).

It would be a great mistake to suppose that the kind of awareness of the outside of thought we have been describing here can be achieved by heightened and more alert introspection of the phenomenological type (it should be recalled that Adorno began his philosophical career with a radical critique of Husserl). The only way in which the subjective processes of the mind can be prevented from sealing us back into idealism is to seize on those fitful moments in which, they unexpectedly betray their objective nature: something the logicians have always sought to show about the forms and syntax without, however (even in Hegel's *Logic*), taking the next step towards specifying the *derivation* of those objective 'mental structures' and their relationship to that larger realm of objectivity (or reality),[12] which is of course for Adorno the social rather than the natural (even though, following the example of Marx's relationship to Darwin – human history as a part of natural history – he also develops an interesting conception of natural history, which will be examined later).

The difficulties of achieving a new dialectical objectivity are evidently asymmetrical, since owing to the inequality in the concept of mediation, the subject falls into the object in an utterly different way than the latter into the former. Object can only be thought by way of subject, yet ever perseveres as an other to this last; subject on the other hand is in its very structure and from the outset also object. The object cannot be thought away from the subject as an idea; but the subject can certainly be removed from the object in thought. (ND 184/183)

This final asymmetry reminds us, if we needed the reminder, that Adorno's celebration of the preponderance of the objective, here and throughout, has nothing to do with the positivistic (or even empiricist) excision of subject positions altogether.

Nor is the slogan of objectivity in Adorno the symptom of that rather different kind of anti-subjectivity which seeks to humiliate the subjective dimension in a spirit of ascesis, self-hatred, or *ressentiment*: on the contrary, it is meant to generate a new space for the emancipation of the subject itself; while at the same time its own realization depends on precisely that emancipation:

> In what are, at the present historical stage, most often called oversubjective judgments, what really happens is that the subject has merely automatically echoed the consensus omnium. It could restore the object to its own rights, instead of being satisfied with a bad copy, only where it resisted the least common denominator of such objectivity and freed itself qua subject. Objectivity today depends on that emancipation, rather than on the tireless repression of the subject. The oppressive power of the objectified within subjects, a power that blocks them from becoming subjects, also blocks knowledge of the objective; such is what happened to what used to be called the 'subjective factor'. Subjectivity toc v is rather mediated as objectivity, and such mediation demands analysis more urgently than the traditional kind. That objectivity to which every kind of subject, including the transcendental one, is yoked, finds its own mediatory mechanisms prolonged by the subjective ones. (ND 172–3/170–71)

But it is very precisely the emergence in Adorno of the analysis of just such hidden forms of objectification within the subjective that we have been outlining here: the concealment of identity within the very form of the concept, the perpetuation of external system by the very nature of abstraction or universalizing thought; and it seems quite correct for Adorno to see this as the most original feature of his own dialectical practice. To reveal the social dimensions of abstract thought: to put it that way is to ignore the dialectic of the explanandum and the intricacies at work within any reified conception of the social and within sociology itself. Discussing Weber, Adorno remarks that in fact, philosophical conceptuality is the most adequate area for dealing with the thing itself [*Grund der Sache*], in so far as social research at least becomes false when it limits itself to those interdependencies within its own domain that ground the object, and ignores the latter's determination by the totality itself. Without the overarching [philosophical] concept such internal interdependencies mask the realest dependency of all, namely that on society, and society cannot be adequately ranged under the individual *res* that has its concept 'under' itself. Society, however, appears only through the particular, thereby enabling the [properly philosophical] concept to be transformed on the occasion of determinate knowledge. (ND 166-7/164-5)

It is hoped that the reader will by now not be tempted by this rather tortured passage to conclude that Adorno is merely advising the sociologists to add a philosopher to their team and to let him provide the ultimate theoretical framework. On the contrary, we have tried to show that no 'philosophical concept' is adequate either: each one must be analyzed symptomatically for what it excludes or cannot say. What Adorno reproaches the sociologists with generally is that they do not get on with that work, but rather assume that the larger or more abstract 'concepts' – such as society itself, freedom, bureaucracy, domination – are the end-point of thinking and the ultimate framework for interpretation. On the contrary, those concepts demand dialectical analysis the most urgently, and it is by way of their formal pseudo-universality and 'scientific' abstraction that the ultimate shackles which the social imposes on our thinking about the social become revealed although not removed.

This is clearly the moment to say something more about Adorno's role and work as a sociologist, which can easily be misunderstood if the only work that springs to mind is the famous volume on anti-Semitism called *The Authoritarian Personality* and published in the United States virtually at the moment of the postwar return to Germany. Indeed, to put it this way is also to compound the misunderstanding and to assume that Adorno was interested in 'authoritarianism' for what it had to say about 'prejudice', rather than the other way round. Even in the chapter of *Dialectic of Enlightenment* officially consecrated to anti-Semitism, this phenomenon (not, to be sure, a matter of mere disinterested curiosity for its authors, just as one must not imagine that the funding of the *Studies in Prejudice* project was unmotivated) is not, as for liberalism, a mere aberrant empirical matter, which may be studied in isolation from 'late capitalism' generally, but is in its function, and in its significance as a psychic symptom, at one with the fabric of this last, the social totality itself, that remains the principal object of study and the dialectical framework in which alone such local inquiries can take on their meaning.

Anti-Semitism, then, which betrays the regression of the psyche under industrialization and rationalization, along with its violent mesmerization by the archaic modes of appropriation and relationships to nature its victims seem to represent, is grasped as a form of cultural envy that reveals the relationship of the subject to the social totality under modernization in a peculiarly privileged way (as we will see later on, in a different context). What is characteristic of Adorno's sociological perspective is then this attempt to cross the particular with the general and hold them together in their contradictory tension, which is lost at once when the empirical lapses back into the status of yet another mere research project.

Viewed from the other perspective, however, from that of the 'general' rather than the 'particular', Adorno's sociological propositions tend towards a lapidary concision that transforms brief essays, such as the fundamental statement simply entitled 'Society',[13] into verbal objects of great density, like shrunken dwarfs: this is to be explained by the fundamental asymmetry between subject and object, and by the consequent fact that 'society', the universal, the system itself, is as 'fictive' and non-empirical as it is real. The social totality 'cannot be grasped in any immediate fashion, nor is it susceptible of drastic verification'.[14] In practice, this means that Adorno's sociological theorization will always be metacritical, separating the necessarily imperfect use of the sociological concept out from the materials it seems in the process of interpreting, and finding the conceptual coinage of the sociologists fully as historically and socially revealing as the data they thought they were collecting. But it is not a matter of the sociology of sociologists exactly, although the emergence and function of the discipline are present to Adorno's mind, particularly in those moments when it becomes uncritical and apologetic, lapsing into an ideational reproduction of the status quo; rather, even at their most intellectually energetic, the concepts of sociology cannot but be flawed and fractured, since their very object is contradictory, faithfulness to it thereby requiring a certain transfer of the social contradiction into thought.

So it is that just this subject–object tension – the real 'individual' caught in an 'imaginary' social order, the existential fact itself produced by the universal system of identity that obliterates it, the psyche whose very solitude, anomie, and irrational spasms are somehow social and collective to their very core – reproduces or externalizes itself in the very history of the emergent sociological discipline by way of the twin antithetical figures of Weber and Durkheim, both of whom are right and wrong, true and false, simultaneously. To Weber's forms of 'comprehension' – the elaborate typologies of the ratio of means to ends – corresponds Durkheim's insistence on the alienating objectivity of the social 'fact': very precisely because 'society is both known and not known from the

inside'.[15] To Weber's grasp of a certain subjectivity at the moment of
its eclipse by rationalization, then, asymmetrically corresponds Durkheim's great dictum that the explanation of social phenomena in psychological terms must always be false, as well as his insistence on the primacy
of the collective (which has in modern times become invisible). But the
truth cannot be said to lie somewhere in between them, any more than
the tension can be resolved by means of some conceptual synthesis or
the invention of a 'third way', since it corresponds very precisely to
social objectivity: Adorno's sociology thus poses the embarrassing question whether the comprehension or intuition of a contradiction can itself
be other than contradictory, unless it involves the production of the
concept of contradiction.

All of this is reproduced and acted out in more contemporary forms
in the relations between sociology and psychology (or psychoanalysis),
which cannot be 'synthesized' any more than they may be allowed to
'succumb to the temptation to project the intellectual division of labor
onto the object of their study'.[16] The rift between public and private,
social and psychological, is a dramatic externalization (although not the
only one or even the only type) of the epistemological contradictions
of 'a society whose unity resides in its not being unified'.[17] It seems clear
that Adorno sometimes felt his sociological mission better served by
forcing his readers to confront such paralogisms than by the other intellectual practice available: to work one's way through them in dialectical
steps, which involves the construction of mediations. That these exist
is virtually given in advance by the dilemma and the contradiction, which
causes the seemingly psychological to convert without warning into a
social datum, while social 'facts' dissolve ceaselessly back into ideolo-
gemes.

So it is that Weber squares this circle by way of the intuition of a
'rationality of self-preservation',[18] which links the existential to the social
order and keeps them at arm's length from each other at one and the
same time: Adorno's formulation, indeed, suggests a greater relevance
of Weber for the construction of *Dialectic of Enlightenment* than might
have been deduced from its Freudo-Marxian-Nietzschean trappings. Psychology meanwhile becomes 'sociological' not merely in the origins of
its drives ('scars inflicted by society',[19] 'the dimension of split-off irrationality that complements the prevailing rationality'[20]), but also in their social
possibilities of expression and gratification

> which have today become wholly a function of profit interests.... Even the
> man whose calculating rationality yields all the advantages it promises cannot
> attain to real happiness through them but must, like all the other

customers, knuckle under once again and take what those who control production offer.[21]

But it could be argued that even these 'mediations' are little more
than reenactments of the fundamental contradiction, which essentially
allows for no more satisfactory methodological resolution than the sheer
alteration of the two perspectives:

> The separation of sociology and psychology is both correct and false. False
> because it encourages the specialists to relinquish the attempt to know the
> totality which even the separation of the two demands; and correct in so
> far as it registers more intransigently the split that has actually taken place
> in reality than does the premature unification at the level of theory. Sociology
> in the strict sense, despite constant tendencies to subjectivize it (also on the
> part of Max Weber), never loses sight of the objective moment of the social
> process. But the more rigidly it disregards the subject and his spontaneous
> impulses, the more exclusively it comes to be dealing with a reified, quasi-
> scientific *caput mortuum*. Hence the tendency to imitate scientific ideals and
> approaches, which are, however, forever incapable of accounting for specifi-
> cally social phenomena. While priding themselves on their strict objectivity,
> they have to settle for the already mediated end-products of the scientific
> procedure, with sectors and factors, as if they were the real, unmediated object.
> The upshot is sociology minus society, the replica of a situation in which
> people have lost contact with themselves.[22]

The objection can now be entertained that Adorno's is essentially a philosopher's sociology – that is to say, a critique of the sociological tradition
from a somewhat different conceptual and disciplinary level: that he calls
for such a thing, indeed, we have already seen, just as he will call for
an analogous primacy of philosophy over art criticism at the end of
Aesthetic Theory. But surely the very force of the arguments just summarized goes a long way towards discrediting the distinction, implicit in
this kind of reproach, between sociological practice and theory, production and mere criticism, between doing sociological field-work and sitting
at home to rethink the basic categories and concepts. For the premiss
is not merely the obvious one: that our conceptualization of society
has real and practical consequences for its objective existence; but above
all, the inverse of this proposition – that repression of the concept of
society and the social system has a vital part to play in perpetuating
its domination. This is the sense of the warning, even more timely today
than when it was issued in the sixties: 'Not only theory, but also its
absence, becomes a material force when it seizes the masses.'[23]

The critique of sociology thereby becomes a form of praxis in its own right, as exemplified by Adorno's polemic struggles within a postwar but not altogether reformed German sociology: these struggles, as has already been observed and according to the structure of the social contradiction itself, were necessarily battles on two fronts at once, and aimed as much at promoting a certain kind of empirical research within an otherwise relatively metaphysical and speculative tradition as at criticizing the unreflexive and merely operational use of contradictory categories as though they were classificatory concepts. It has often been pointed out, however (most notoriously by Althusser), that metaphysics and empiricism are two dialectical sides of the same ideological coin: so that the so-called positivism debate,[24] the implacable war on positivism that became the way in which Adorno conceived of his sociological vocation, ended up resuming both strands of the critique. I will return at the end of this book to the relevance of such a mission in the contemporary intellectual situation.

Of no less practical relevance than this 'critique of the subject', however, is the 'critique of the object' that is at one with it, and can be formulated in terms of a denunciation of the market of no less unexpected actuality:

> The first objective abstraction takes place, not so much in scientific thought, as in the universal development of the exchange system itself; which happens independently of the qualitative attitudes of producer and consumer, of the mode of production, even of need, which the social mechanism tends to satisfy as a kind of secondary by-product. Profit comes first. A humanity fashioned into a vast network of consumers, the human beings who actually have the needs, have been socially pre-formed beyond anything one might naively imagine, and this not only by the level of industrial development but also by the economic relationships themselves into which they enter, even though this is far more difficult to observe empirically. Above and beyond all specific forms of social differentiation, the abstraction implicit in the market system represents the domination of the general over the particular, of society over its captive membership.[25]

This passage, then, reconfirms the primacy of exchange in Adorno's philosophical diagnoses of identity and abstraction, which can now be summarized by way of the following themes.

Abstraction is first of all collective and not individual; objectivity is present within the subject in the form of collective linguistic or conceptual forms which are themselves produced by society, and thereby presuppose it. This has very much to do with the division of labor, and in particular with the primal separation of manual from intellectual labor which is the precondition of abstract thought itself. But we shall also see – particu-

larly when we come to deal with some of the extraordinary formulations
of *Aesthetic Theory* – that it also has very much to do with that classical
Marxian notion which is the development of productive forces: these
too, as a social and historical phenomenon, are inscribed in the 'concept'
and lend it their force, capitalism in that sense being the achievement
of ultimate abstraction by way of machinery. Finally, this social language
should not displace the in-forming presence of history itself within the
concept and its form: not merely the history of philosophy as this lies
concealed and encapsulated within the most apparently free-standing and
unattributable neologism, but also the history at one with the raw material
– language – on which philosophical abstraction essentially works,[26] and
which continues to mark it at the very moment in which such raw
material is transformed, beyond recognition, into the Idea:

> Whenever philosophy became equal to itself, it seized on the non-conceptual
> as its object along with the historically existent: and this, not merely beginning
> with Schelling and Hegel but already *à contrecœur* in Plato, who baptized
> the existent as the non-existent and yet wrote a doctrine of the state in which
> the eternal Ideas have a family likeness and an intimate relationship with
> empirical determinations such as exchange value and the division of labor.
> (ND 141/137)

Four

This insistence on the social, the collective, exchange, the division of labor, the dynamics of history, however – in other words on the 'preponderance of the objective' within abstract thinking – now demands a complementary warning and caution on the other side of the matter; and to do justice to the complexity of Adorno's position obliges us to differentiate it sharply from another methodological alternative with which it may sometimes seem to have no little in common – namely, the sociology of knowledge. For Adorno equally tirelessly insists that his dialectic is not to be confused with that, which he denounces equally implacably, and whose master thinkers – Mannheim, but also Veblen and Spengler – are the object of some of the most brilliant critiques in that volume of Adorno's most centrally consecrated to sociology – above all to the sociology of ideas and of culture – namely, *Prisms*.

The external classification schemes of the 'sociology of knowledge' were an abomination to him, but symptomatic of something else. Mannheim is dispatched in this way: 'the sociology of knowledge sets up indoctrination camps for the homeless intelligentsia where it can learn to forget itself',[27] a vision that already has something in it of that 'end of ideology' which Cacciari and Tafuri learned specifically from the Frankfurt School: namely, the interest technocracy has in 'Enlightenment'-type critiques and 'demystification' of belief and committed ideology, in order to clear the ground for unobstructed planning and 'development'.[28] What stands in the way, like the unique accidents of a terrain that must be levelled, is the content of the past – organic and inherited forms, superstition, collective habits, the resistance of a specific cultural history or social psychology: rooted beliefs that for Enlightenment are an impediment

to Reason in its universalizing and identitarian vocation, and which block
the perfect fungibility of subject and object alike, in a postmodernism
which from this perspective stands revealed as the triumph of bureaucratic
technocracy over the remnants and survivals, the lags and residual content,
against which it struggled for so long during the modern period.

To put it this way, however, is to grasp a deep affiliation between
the sociology of knowledge and the 'sociology of culture' which is homologous with it and in which the deeper aporia of both is, if anything,
even more dramatically revealed. For Adorno's critique of the sociology
of culture begins with what endows this last at its most powerful with
the very motive power of its perception: very precisely the loathing
for culture as such, *ressentiment* for the aesthetic 'supplement' in all its
forms, a jaundiced eye alert to all those moments in which the pretense
of culture to its own autonomy and rightful function shows its shabby
edge: the first of such moments being the very use of the reified word
'culture' itself, which separates and trivializes its objects in advance so
that lengthy demonstrations of its distance from 'life' or 'reality' become
unnecessary (a dialectic worked out on the philosophical level by Marcuse's great essay 'On the Affirmative Character of Culture'). Thus, not
only Spengler and Huxley, in their fashion, but above all Veblen are
driven by an anti-cultural, anti-aesthetic impulse which constitutes their
object of study (by separating it out) in such a way that its very sham
and impotent autonomy serves to condemn itself.[29] Yet this power of
the great *Kulturkritik* is not the result of personal idiosyncrasy, but has
its own historical specificity:

> With respect to aesthetics, the conclusions Veblen derives from his critique
> of consumption as mere ostentation are very close to those of functionalism
> [*die neue Sachlichkeit*], which Adolf Loos formulated at about the same time.
> Where the practical is concerned they resemble those of technocracy.[30]

The violence with which Loos repudiates 'ornament' and the 'ornamental', identified by him on the one hand with crime as such and on the
other with 'perversion', is a strategic move in the high modernist purge
of academic and 'fine-arts' canons of 'beauty' at the same time that it
prepares the hygienicist ethos of Le Corbusier: but to condemn it solely
for its puritanism is to preempt the most interesting part of the analysis
in the name of psychological diagnosis. What must be noted is, first,
that Adorno marks the philosophical prolongation of this attitude in
pragmatism, contemporary with Veblen, whose dislike of 'transcendent'
ideas and abstractions (today sometimes stigmatized as 'theory' itself)
is thus assimilated to this revulsion against ornament, against what supple-

ments sheer immanence and stands as a form of philosophical luxury or indulgence (abstract or 'continental' philosophy and system here coming to play the role of decorative 'culture' on the other level).

Yet these contemporary identifications and family likenesses (*Kulturkritik*, pragmatism, functionalism) also make it plain that we encounter in them a historical impulse which cannot simply be rebuked by choosing a different philosophical option. But the deeper reason why this anti-aesthetic impulse cannot simply be 'disproved' lies in the fact that it is at work within the works of art themselves and at the very heart of the production of modernism, whose motif of the guilt of art (Thomas Mann's *Doktor Faustus*) and nominalistic impatience with the 'lie' of art and the complacencies of old-fashioned aesthetic appearance [*Schein*] are among the most crucial features for any understanding of the modern, as we shall see in the next chapter. We cannot, therefore, simply refuse the critique of culture and go on celebrating this last under the guise of some disengaged aestheticism: we must somehow go all the way through it and come out the other side (Adorno's 'solution' here will therefore be the very paradigm of that 'impure' mode of thought we have been trying to characterize on the philosophical level).

The dilemma of the cultural has in fact very significant consequences – as Adorno demonstrates in one of the most brilliant 'fragments' of *Minima Moralia*, entitled 'Baby with the Bath Water' (47–50/43–5) – for what has often been thought of as one of the essential working principles of the Marxist tradition: the distinction between base and superstructure: it being understood that very serious qualms and reservations about this, ranging all the way to the most drastic proposals for its total removal, are also a recurrent part of the Marxist tradition, virtually from Engels himself onward. Raymond Williams's extensive and influential critique of the doctrine is thus only one of the most recent of many suggestions that we give it, as Perry Anderson once put it about another staple of the Marxist tradition, a decent burial; the post-Marxists did not bother to wait for the family's permission. It is one thing, however, to drop the matter altogether; but quite another to find a better and more satisfactory *substitute* for it, as Williams tries to do by proposing the Gramscian notion of hegemony. What happens is that in so far as the new idea proves to be an adequate substitute, and performs the functions of the old one in a suitable way, all of the arguments against the old concept return in force against the new one; whereas if it turns out to be relatively unassailable, what gradually dawns on us is that it is not a substitute at all, but a wholly new and different idea. (Much the same can be observed about proposals to substitute for the old and shopworn concept of ideology any number of new terms and ideas, such as discourse, practice,

episteme, and the like.) My own position has always been that everything
changes when you grasp base-and-superstructure not as a full-fledged
theory in its own right, but rather as the name for a problem, whose
solution is always a unique, ad hoc invention.

But we must initially separate the figuration of the terms base and
superstructure – only the initial shape of the problem – from the type
of efficacity or causal law it is supposed to imply. *Überbau* and *Basis*,
for example, which so often suggest to people a house and its foundations,
seem in fact to have been railroad terminology and to have designated
the rolling stock and the rails respectively, something which suddenly
jolts us into a rather different picture of ideology and its effects. Engels's
notion of 'reciprocal interaction', meanwhile, sounds like the positivistic
science textbooks of his day; while Gramsci's military and strategic conceptions of 'hegemony' seem far enough removed from the placid landscape of those older Second International dwellings and foundations.
Benjamin suggested, in the *Passagenwerk*, that the superstructure might
be thought to *express* the base – thus giving us a kind of linguistic model
(albeit a prestructuralist one). It would not be doing violence to Sartre's
thought, meanwhile, to suggest that for him the *situation* (in the multi-
dimensional class and psychoanalytic senses he gave to that term) stood
as the infrastructure to which the act of 'free'choice brought a superstructural response and solution. But if we stress the limiting force of the
situation and minimize the creative features of the freedom inventing
itself within it, we then have something closer to Marx's own remarks
on the relationship between ideologues and class-fractions in *The Eighteenth Brumaire*, from which the elaborate Lukácsean system of ideological epistemology in *History and Class Consciousness* subsequently derives.

Meanwhile, we have here essentially been concerned to argue that
Adorno's stereoscopic conception of the coexistence of the universal and
the particular constitutes his particular version of the base/superstructure
opposition, since the universal (concept, system, totality, exchange system
itself) is the immediately unknowable infrastructure, while the particular
stands as the act or event of consciousness or culture that seems to be
our only individual reality, at the same time that equivalence controls
it like a force field.

But none of these figures (and others are surely conceivable) fatally
suggests the operation of any inevitable causal or deterministic law. What
is distinctive about the Marxist problematic lies in the centrality of this
problem and this question, conceived to be the most urgent and fundamental one – namely, the relationship to be established between 'culture'
(or consciousness, or 'existence') and its socioeconomic context, or 'base'.
Once the problem is acknowledged, the local solutions may range from

the most lawful of all – the most vulgar and demystifying registration of ideological reflex and collective bad faith – to the local hypothesis of a mysterious autonomy of the cultural under certain circumstances, not excluding situations where culture runs on ahead and seems itself for a brief time 'determinant'. It is when one has decided in advance that the relationship to be thus established is no longer an interesting or an important question that we may speak, using Adorno's formula, of throwing the baby out with the bath water.

To be sure, Adorno also means it the other way round, in the spirit of his analysis of Veblen: to see culture as a 'superstructure' is also already to have thrown the baby out with the bath water, for it implies that culture must always be grasped as something like a functional lie, creating 'the illusion of a society worthy of man which does not exist', so that it would be preferable, on such a view, to do away with those illusions and to 'demand that relationships be entirely reduced to their material origin, ruthlessly and openly formed according to the interests of the participants'. Thus a (perfectly proper) denunciation of illusion turns into a new kind of illusion in its own right: 'this notion, like all expostulation about lies, has a suspicious tendency to become itself ideology'. A Marxian materialism, then, tends under its own momentum towards an anti-aesthetic anti-culturalism in which it oddly meets the *ressentiment* of its fascist opponents:

> Emphasis on the material element, as against the spirit as a lie, gives rise to a kind of dubious affinity with that political economy which is subjected to an immanent criticism, comparable with the complicity between police and underworld. (MM 49/44)

As can be imagined, this is very precisely the kind of paradigmatic situation and contradictory dilemma for which 'negative dialectics' has been devised in the first place:

> If material reality is called the world of exchange value, and any culture whatever refuses to accept the domination of that world, then it is true that such refusal is illusory as long as the existent exists ... [yet] in the face of the lie of the commodity world, even the lie that denounces it becomes a corrective. That culture so far has failed is no justification for furthering its failure. (MM 49/44)

The methodological conclusion, then – a conclusion which holds not merely for *Kulturkritik* but for thinking on all its other levels – is that we must denounce culture (as an idea but also as a phenomenon) all the time we continue to perpetuate it, and perpetuate it while continuing tirelessly to denounce it. It is with culture as with philosophy, which famously 'lived on because the moment to realize it was missed' (ND 15/3); there is, as we shall see, a utopian power in keeping alive the impossible idea of philosophizing (as of producing culture) even while ruthlessly exposing the necessary failure to go on doing it today. (In the same way, according to my own proposal, the stigmatizing term of superstructure needs to be retained in order to remind us of a gap that has to be overcome in some more adequate way than forgetting about it.) For like philosophy, culture is itself marked by the original sin of the division between manual and mental labor:

> Cultural criticism is, however, only able to reproach culture so penetratingly for prostituting itself, for violating in its decline the pure autonomy of the mind, because culture originates in the radical separation of mental and physical work. It is from this separation, the original sin as it were, that culture draws its strength. When culture simply denies the separation and feigns harmonious union, it falls back behind its own notion.[31]

The point of this digression on cultural theory in Adorno has been to emphasize the presence at work within its dilemmas of the same contradictions we have underscored in philosophical thought, in the analysis of the 'concept', which can neither be taken at face value as an autonomous instrument for grasping some Real distinct from it, nor debunked in the fashion of the sociology of knowledge or vulgar *Ideologiekritik* for that dimension of the lie and the illusion which is, in our society, inherent in it. What is not yet clear is what it might mean, in concrete situations, to think by means of a concept which is itself somehow 'false' in its very form. As for the peculiar contradictions in which the sociology of knowledge and sociological critique of culture thereby find themselves imprisoned, these are rather to be grounded in some deeper philosophical notion of the *heteronomy* of critique itself – the paradox of the possible distance of a part, the mind, from the whole of which it is a part – which will be examined later.

Five

'It is an innate peculiarity of philosophical writing', Walter Benjamin once said, in a statement which will be of the greatest significance for us in the present context, 'to confront anew, with every radical turn in thought, the question of *Darstellung*.'[32] This question – that of philo- sophical *presentation* or *representation*, of the very form of the laying out of philosophical conceptuality in the time of the text, as well as of the traditional genres of that form (Benjamin mentions the Spinozan pseudo-Euclidean 'demonstration', the great nineteenth-century system, the esoteric essay by which mystical doctrine is transmitted, and the scholastic tractatus) – will now return again in Adorno as the clue and the key to the ways by which the philosophical concept, with all its truths and untruths, can be 'set in motion' (to quote Marx's own oblique reference to his *Darstellung*).

The matter of *Darstellung* will also afford some final insight into the status of 'totality', of which we have said both that the concept, in some sense its body serf, reproduces its untruth and its form of domination, and that it is itself somehow unthinkable and unrepresentable, very speci- fically in our present sense of the word. Yet the isolated thought about anything (what has here and throughout pompously been termed the 'concept') – however accurate and pertinent it may otherwise be – carries its untruth invisibly, within its very form (identity and exchange): talking about it means talking about its content, and adjustments in that remain within a Newtonian world from which the other one lies hidden virtually by definition. It is therefore tempting to suppose that the formal untruth of every individual concept might be driven into visibility by the process of revealing their links and interrelationships with one another. Yet the

49

system that might thereby emerge – something like Hegel's 'objective spirit': the great absolute web of all the error and delusion and passionate conviction held together and believed and spoken at any moment in human history – would that not also (if we begin by denying it validity as an after-image of objective totality) be something like a representation, at best the object of a structural sociology of the epistemes of our period?

Either project – the system of our concepts or the system of the things to which these concepts try to correspond – fatally reintroduces the mirage of system itself, not to speak of the old antithesis between subjective and objective of which we now know at least that, although it cannot be eluded, it cannot be dealt with head on in that immediate form, but must be only provisionally outsmarted by some ruse (to which Adorno's dialectics seemed to provide us with a handbook and an operating manual).

It is as though, in *Negative Dialectics*, these totalizing dilemmas of a systematizing philosophy (it being understood that, owing to its object, genuine philosophy is always somehow driven by that impulse) were to be disarmed by the acting out (or the mimesis) of a kind of pseudo-totality (the shamanistic overtones of this formulation are authorized by the Frazerian tribal speculations included in *Dialectic of Enlightenment*). Pseudo-totality: the illusion of the total system is aroused and encouraged by the systematic links and cross-references established between a range of concepts, while the baleful spell of system itself is then abruptly exorcized by the realization that the order of presentation is non-binding, that it might have been arranged in an utterly different fashion, so that, as in a divinatory cast, all the elements are present but the form of their juxtapositions, the shape of their falling out, is merely occasional. This kind of *Darstellung*, which seeks specifically to undermine its own provisional architectonic, Benjamin called configuration or constellation, terms to which Adorno added the apparently more awkward 'model', offering three formal demonstrations of it in the second half of *Negative Dialectics*.

An initial qualification needs to be set in place, however, before we try to characterize this peculiar structure, and that has to do with the notion of the fragment, so often loosely evoked in connection with Benjamin as much as with Adorno, and sometimes vaguely assimilated to the Nietzschean aphorism when not to Schlegel's aesthetics itself.[33] That this impressionistic notion does not take us very far is indeed already apparent from these comparisons, since there does not on the face of it seem to be much that is fragmentary about a 'simple form' like the aphorism, so powerfully dominated by an aesthetic of closure. That modern thought or experience is somehow 'fragmentary' might be an instructive feature of yet another *Kulturkritik* of modern times, but only if fragmentation is seen as the situation and the dilemma to which modern thought responds, not as one of its general qualities or properties: where in any case the very universality of the phenomenon makes it less than useful as a way of specifying what is distinctive about Adorno or Benjamin. Nor is a short piece like 'Baby with the Bath Water', referred to above, in any meaningful sense fragmentary: it is a complete statement, whose closure is not the least stunning thing about it; while many of the alleged fragments from Benjamin are just that: notes and jottings recovered post-humously, which this writer was accustomed to transform into essays that, however idiosyncratically, obeyed the formal logic of the discursive genre.

Some clarification is surely to be gained by differentiating between the fragmentary and the discontinuous: for this last is a basic fact of life in both Adorno and Benjamin, sometimes foregrounded by the blanks and gaps between the paragraphs, sometimes exacerbated by their very absence and by the wilful elimination (particularly in Adorno) of virtually any paragraph breaks at all, in the towering wall of water of a text that carries us forward across bewildering shifts and changes in its topics and raw material. The distinction imposes itself not least because the notion of the fragmentary seems to designate the object, while that of disconti-nuity stresses the distance between those objects: the stars that make up a constellation are not normally thought to be 'fragmentary' without a good deal of preliminary metaphorical footwork. That the notion of the configuration, the constellation, or the model demands a correspond-ingly micro-category seems clear: a way of dealing with the elements or building-blocks fully as dramatically as a snapshot of those heavens from over a great distance does for their relationships. We will return shortly to the way in which the individual 'concept' is positioned in this momentary and provisional 'total system'. Later on, however, the account of the overall formal *Darstellung* of such constellations will be augmented by attention to the 'mimetic' sentences that make it up.

As is well known, Benjamin staged two major demonstrations of this form – one of which, owing to his untimely death, remained 'fragmentary' in the literal sense of that word. These are *The Origin of German Tragic Drama* and the legendary Arcades project or *Passagenwerk* ('Paris – Capital of the Nineteenth Century'), some nine hundred pages of which were finally assembled in book form a few years ago. It is customary to dis-tinguish these two efforts in terms of their philosophical outlook: thus the book on tragic drama, particularly on the strength of that obscure and enigmatic 'Prologue' from which we have already quoted above, is generally described as idealistic, when not somehow mystical in some more thoroughgoing sense; while the Arcades project, on the basis of its raw materials as well as of our biographical knowledge about the

author during this period, is said to be Marxist and materialist and
accounted a 'contribution' to the development of historical materialism,
particularly in the area of cultural historiography. This is all surely right
on some level of generality, although it seems to me to presuppose propositions about belief, intellectual development, and ideological commitment
which are very crude indeed and probably demand rethinking.

Another such proposition – closely related to those and comparable
for the persistence in it of a very traditional conception of the individual
subject – has to do with 'influence'. That Benjamin had a decisive influence
on Adorno the path-breaking work of Susan Buck-Morss has established
beyond any doubt.[34] But is influence to be understood simply as the
transfer of some new thought from one person's head to another's? In
that case, it might be preferable to talk about the awakening of new
interests (not to say a whole new problematic) in the mind of the individual on the receiving end of the 'influence' in question. Perhaps, however,
Adorno's omnipresent theme of 'mimesis' offers a new way to use this
notion of influence, which designates something that really happens just
as surely as it misinterprets it. 'Influence' in this new sense would then
describe the ways in which the pedagogical figure, by his own praxis,
shows the disciple what else you can think and how much further you
can go with the thoughts you already have; or – to put it another way,
which for us is the same – what else you can *write* and the possibility
of forms of writing and *Darstellung* that unexpectedly free you from
the taboos and constraints of forms learnt by rote and assumed to be
inscribed in the nature of things. This, at any rate, is the way in which
I want to grasp Benjamin's 'influence' on Adorno, as just such a liberation
by mimesis and as the practical demonstration of the possibility of another
kind of writing – which is eventually to say: another kind of thinking.
At that point, then, the putative idealistic content of the book on tragic
drama, as that is contrasted with the 'materialist' content of the Arcades
project, becomes less significant than the conception of philosophical
form they both share, which Benjamin seems to have been able to awaken
in Adorno's mind as a philosophical aesthetic and ambition.

We must therefore begin again with the notorious 'Epistemo-Critical
Prologue' [*Erkenntniskritische Vorrede*] to *The Origin of German Tragic
Drama*, in order to capture the terms in which, at that time, Benjamin
thought his own writing praxis. The 'Prologue' begins with a fundamental
distinction between truth and knowledge which, although something
like it is everywhere at work in modern thought, has not yet found
its philosophical historian (it is, for example, an inaugural distinction
in many existentialisms, but also at work in oppositions between science
and ideology in the Marxist tradition, and finally finds its echo in Adorno's

differentiation of 'truth-content' from that ideological false consciousness which can be present simultaneously with it, in certain kinds of works; see the example of Wagner below).

This opposition will then gradually be rearticulated along the lines of a form–content distinction between Idea [*Idee*] and Concept [*Begriff*], a distinction which does not return in Adorno although its effects can be strongly felt in him, as I will show. His avoidance of the word *Idea* – we have seen that the notion of the *Concept* is everywhere in his work – easily translates into our own contemporary discomfort with the conceptuality of the transcendent or the metaphysical: something I now propose to express by way of the suggestion that (although Plato is explicitly evoked here) we postpone the facile solution of describing Benjamin's position as 'Platonic', a characterization which at once consigns it to a realm of past thinking virtually by definition inaccessible to us, as does the related category of 'mysticism'. The distinction between Idea and Concept is of course crucial to Kant, and also very much present in Hegel, however dialectically transformed, but it cannot be said to be the most vital and usable part of their heritage. It seems best, therefore, to leave all such traditional connotations aside from the outset, and try to deduce a fresh meaning from Benjamin's own argument.

Concepts stand on the side of things and knowledge of things, Ideas on the side of 'truth'. Concepts are therefore instruments of analysis of phenomena, and also mediations, whereby the empirical realities – otherwise mired in immediate experience and in the here-and-now – somehow gain transmission and access to the realm of truth: so far Kant! Concepts are therefore by their nature somehow always multiple:

> Phenomena do not ... enter into the realm of ideas whole, in their crude empirical state, adulterated by appearances, but only in their basic elements, redeemed. They are divested of their false unity, so that, thus divided, they might partake of the genuine entity of truth. In this their division, phenomena are subordinate to concepts, for it is the latter which effect the resolution of objects into their constitutive elements. (OGT 213–14/33)

It is therefore as though the fundamental mission of the concept were to destroy the apparent unity of ordinary realities, analyzing and disjoining these last into a swarm of concepts which can then be reassembled in some new and unaccustomed way. The individual concepts remain fixed and trained on the multiple aspects of the reality in question; but it seems to be the very fact of their multiplicity (no single one 'equals' the object or can claim 'identity' with it) that lends them their mediatory function, which Benjamin oddly describes in a dual fashion:

> Through their mediating role concepts enable phenomena to participate in
> the existence of ideas. It is this same mediating role which fits them for the
> other equally basic task of philosophy, the representation [*Darstellung*] of
> ideas. (OGT 214/34)

If mysticism there be here, it would surely lie in this suggestion that
the 'contemplation' of the ideas ('truth') can somehow be disjoined from
their presentation or representation in the philosophical text: even if
one insisted on distinguishing between thinking on the one hand and
writing or language on the other, it would not take much ingenuity
or effort to imagine 'thinking' as pre-sketch and trial run (the Heideggerian *Vor-wurf*) of writing, *Darstellung* or expression. In any case Benjamin
will shortly take pains to exclude all overtones and suggestions of the
contemplative and of that static, intuitive-perceptive *Anschauung* systematically repudiated by Adorno as well in a variety of contexts: meanwhile
the tireless emphasis on representation or *Darstellung* which marks the
stunning originality of this text would also seem, in advance, to undermine
the possibility of some experience of truth that might be separated from
its laying out in time and in language:

> Knowledge is possession. . . . For the thing possessed, representation is second-
> ary; it does not have prior existence as something representing itself. But
> the opposite holds good of truth. For knowledge, method is a way of acquiring
> its object – even by creating it in consciousness, for truth method is self-
> representation and is therefore immanent in it as a form. (OGT 209/29–30)

With these qualifications, then, we reach the heart of the matter, which
is the relationship between *Darstellung* or representation and the Idea.
Now suddenly, in a flash of light, the grand formulations are possible
and stand revealed:

> Ideas are to objects as constellations to stars. This means, in the first place,
> that they are neither their concepts nor their laws. (OGT 214/34)

The Idea is therefore simply the 'system' of concepts, the relationship
between a group of concepts: as such it has no content in its own right,
is not a quasi-object (as the concept is) nor the representation of one:
'ideas are not present in the world of phenomena' (OGT 215/35), any
more than constellations 'really exist' in the sky. Meanwhile, it becomes
clear that philosophical writing or *Darstellung* will consist in tracing the
constellation, in somehow drawing the lines between the empirical concepts thus 'configured' together. But the concepts represent *aspects* of
empirical reality, while the Idea (and its philosophical notation) represents

the *relationships* between them. We must also stress the way in which Benjamin's characteristic language here seems to ward off and to evade the temptation of the subjective, to forestall in advance (without in any way resolving them satisfactorily) rhetorical questions that might reposition such an 'Idea' within the human mind (does not the constellation exist only as a projection of the human viewer? And is not the relationship between phenomena or between the concepts of phenomena, essentially an achievement, or at least an operation, of the mind itself?). The pseudo-Platonic language, then, might be seen as a way of going around behind the great Kantian 'solution' and somehow preempting it.

But now a doubt still remains and we need to get some handle on the content of these mysterious Ideas, whose form now seems clear enough. Despite the warning – and in the absence of any examples or illustrations – the slippage back into Plato still seems fatally to impose itself, and we continue to wonder whether such Ideas are not finally to be grasped 'merely' as the old Platonic abstractions: of the Good or the Beautiful, or of Justice (or Kant's freedom, God and immortality of the soul). But this is not at all the kind of philosophizing Benjamin has in mind, although he takes a peculiar detour to outflank it. For the next topic in the 'Prologue' then again raises the mirage of Benjaminian mysticism with a vengeance, as it restages the archetypal motif of magical language: the act of naming, in which, not unexpectedly, Adam reappears to displace Plato:

> The structure of truth ... demands a mode of being which in its lack of intentionality resembles the simple existence of things, but which is superior in its permanence. Truth is not an intent which takes its determinations and characteristics from empirical reality; rather truth consists in the power that stamps its essence on that empirical reality in the first place. The state of being, beyond all phenomenality, to which alone this power belongs, is that of the name. This determines the manner in which ideas are given [or are revealed as data, *Gegebenheit*]. But they are not so much given in a primordial language as in a primordial form of perception, in which words possess the nobility of their naming function, unimpaired by the operations of knowledge as such. (OGT 216/36)

> Ideas are displayed, without intention, in the act of naming, and they have to be renewed in philosophical contemplation. (OGT 217/37)

Now we can move more quickly; as the context of the 'Prologue' suggests, and as Benjamin will tell us in another page or so, 'tragedy' is just such a 'name' and an 'Idea', and will here become the object of a properly philosophical *Darstellung*, the tracing of an enormous constellation out of 'empirical' concepts. In hindsight, we also know that a similar name, a similar idea, is somehow inherent in the notion of the 'arcade' in the later project. Suddenly, the traditional Platonic repertoire of abstractions – whatever their social and historical content may have been in Plato's day – is radically transformed into a flood of modern 'ideas' of a far more concrete and historical type, such as *capital* itself, or bureaucracy, or dictatorship, or even Nature or History, in their modern senses, or finally 'Paris – Capital of the Nineteenth Century'!

These new 'ideas' are not to be seen as some 'fall' of the Platonic problematic into the secular dynamics of modern times. Rather, these new abstractions – like Adorno's system or totality, they are at one and the same time utterly non-empirical (not given as knowledge or immediately) and the realest matters to us in the world, the matters which constrain us the most absolutely – pose new 'epistemological' problems to which Benjamin's deliberately archaic solution provides a fresh answer that is retained in *Negative Dialectics*. The discursive context of the Benjamin 'Prologue', therefore, would be more adequately grasped by juxtaposing it with efforts like Weber's cumbersome attempt to theorize the sociological 'ideal types' than with the Platonic or even Hegelian predecessors in the older philosophical tradition.

Before documenting Adorno's own faithfulness to this notion of the constellation or configuration, a few final features of Benjamin's conception need to be set in place. First, owing very precisely to his sense of the originality and the non-traditional nature of his proposal, Benjamin will seek sharply to differentiate it from traditional conceptions of abstraction – such as the general and the particular, or the typical – which would draw his whole argument about the Idea and the concepts back into familiar logical categories. The individual concepts, for example, which register various aspects of the empirical reality and whose configuration makes up its Idea, far from being somehow representative, characteristic, typical or average, must register its extremes; only in its ultimate, convulsive manifestations can the real be grasped, not in its least common denominators (OGT 215/35). This perverse emphasis on the atypical and on the dissonance between 'species' and 'genus' would be enough to distance Benjamin decisively from both Plato and Weber; its spirit can be most immediately grasped in the literary problematic of the book on tragic drama, where it makes more sense to approach a genre from its most uncharacteristic and extreme productions than in its low-level routine reproductions. But it will also be appropriate to translate this methodological insistence of Benjamin into Adorno's very different language, thereby stressing the way in which conceptuality in our time necessarily approaches the nominalistic, and fastens under its own momentum on the unique cases and events – rather than, as before, to their pallid abstractions, which have for us become empty words.

Words indeed pose the second question on which we must dwell for a moment; for it does not seem to me overingenious but indispensable, and still very much in Benjamin's own spirit, to augment his account with a further remark on the way in which the language of the Idea necessarily overlaps that of the concepts. What is absolutely undesirable is to be misled by the terms of the discussion back into the effort of isolating a group of Idea-words which are distinct from those used in conceptuality: such a sacred list would return us, in all kinds of ways, to the Platonic system. For it is obvious, when we begin to think about it concretely, that the same words will have to change places frequently. The study of a certain kind of existential metaphysic, for example, may well involve the posing, as Idea, of the objective existence of the 'tragic' (as in Unamuno's *Tragic Sense of Life* or Raymond Williams's *Modern Tragedy*). But 'tragic' here in Benjamin simply designates a feature of the reality of the form, perhaps an extreme one, which is reformulated into one of the group of concepts that will at length be organized into the 'name' of the overall phenomenon – that is to say, the Idea. Thus, although the book on tragic drama itself certifies the existence of an Idea of 'tragedy', the concept of the 'tragic' in our contrasting example has nothing to do with that 'Idea' and operates on a different level altogether.

In the same way, it might be found useful to come at some general idea of the market by way of a concept of the 'free' (as in free trade, freedom of contract, and the like): such a concept would take its place in a whole constellation, but would have little enough to do with that very different thing, the Idea of freedom (as we will in fact shortly observe Adorno to map it out). We can in fact appeal to Benjamin's own text for authority to add this new methodological complication to his account: for in a passage already quoted above, he has specified the word for an Idea to be very precisely a *name*, and now we can better understand why the matter of naming is a crucial step in his argument and in his differentiation between ideas and concepts. In the Idea, as we recall, 'words possess the nobility of their naming function, unimpaired by the operations of knowledge as such'. This is to say that 'freedom' is a word now used as the name of an Idea; whereas the attribute 'free' does not involve such naming, but stands as a non-naming word that has a function in the process of knowledge and of knowing the object.

Finally, it will be necessary to complete this account with Benjamin's idiosyncratic description of the relationships between Ideas as such. This remains an astronomical figure, very precisely to distinguish it from the relationship between concepts to each other which was described as a constellation. Here, however, among the Ideas, autonomy reigns along with harmony:

> These latter can stand up on their own in perfect isolation, as mere words never can. And so ideas subscribe to the law which states: all essences exist in complete and immaculate independence, not only from phenomena, but especially from each other. Just as the harmony of the spheres depends on the orbits of stars which do not come into contact with each other, so the existence of the *mundus intelligibilis* depends on the unbridgeable distance between pure essences. Every idea is a sun and is related to other ideas just as suns are related to each other. (OGT 217–18/37)

They are related to each other in so far as each one is also a star; yet a star that hangs like a sun in any particular heaven becomes thereby incomparable, the horizon of a whole world and the only true reality or referent, as Derrida once put it. Within that hegemony, only the one unique sun is conceivable and cannot be thought together in the same breath as the glittering swarm knowledge vainly identifies as other suns. Concepts are those distant stars whose juxtaposition can be grasped in the figure of the constellation; Ideas, meanwhile, although multiple and equally discontinuous, offer no analogous standpoint beyond them from which to grasp their star-like coexistence: which is to say, returning to the question from which we began, that they cannot be yoked together in the form of philosophical system, and that the philosophical exposure to any single Idea blots the others out with its light. The discontinuities of *Negative Dialectics* are therefore already implicit in this Benjaminian figure – which, however, returns in a somewhat more explicit form in the realm of Adorno's aesthetics, as we shall see later on.

Six

Adorno has other, alternate figures for the constellation as the form of philosophical *Darstellung* – even though this last is centrally positioned in *Negative Dialectics* (163–8/161–6), where it is more loosely celebrated as a method that unpacks the historical content of the *concept* (as has been observed, Adorno abandons the vocabulary of Idea and returns to a more general Hegelian usage):

> Cognition of the object in its constellation is cognition of the process stored in the object. As a constellation theoretical thought circles the concept it would like to unseal, hoping that it will fly open like the lock of a well-guarded safe-deposit box: in response, not to a single key or a single number, but to a combination of numbers. (ND 166/163)

That the contents of this box will not look like the findings of a 'history of ideas' any more than those of a 'sociology of knowledge' we have already assured ourselves. Meanwhile, since Benjamin's modern readers have always been perplexed by his insistence on the 'timelessness' – about the Ideas, of which we have tried to argue that they are in fact social and historical in nature – it is worth observing the way in which Adorno here uses the spatiality of the figure of the constellation to argue explicitly against 'linear causality', but in the name of history itself (he is evoking Weber as an unconscious practitioner of the constellation method):

> But the capitalist system's increasingly integrative trend, the fact that its elements entwine into a more total context of functions, makes the old question about *cause* – as opposed to *constellation* – more and more precarious. (ND 168/166)

Meanwhile, the sciences themselves 'probably operate not so much with causal chains as with causal networks' (ND 263/266). This however, is a rather different kind of timelessness than the eternal Platonic one; and it seems perfectly proper to associate it with the name it has received in another compartment of contemporary thought – to wit, that of the *synchronic*, which does not imply any stasis of time or history, but rather a thinking which does not involve the temporal as such: timeless in its suspension of the category of time and temporality, rather than in its otherworldly invariance. Having gone that far, we might as well identify this account of causal networks and constellations with Althusserian structural causality: an intersection whose significance is reinforced by Althusser's interest in the problem of *Darstellung* in Marx; without, however, having the same kind of formal results for his own philosophical practice as those we shall observe in Adorno.

There are, however, other, non-astronomical figures for that practice which are no less instructive. They need to be prefaced by a proposal: I think it would be helpful for those of us who write on Adorno to eschew with all rigor and self-discipline, and for an indefinite period, those inevitable musical analogies that have become virtually a convention of Adorno criticism, save in instances where they are absolutely unavoidable. Such is unexpectedly the case right now: *Negative Dialectics* in fact offers three full-dress demonstrations of what we have been calling the constellation method; these are the three concluding monograph-length studies of freedom, history, and 'metaphysics'. These chapters are however explicitly designated as 'models', a term that has always seemed to me aesthetically and philosophically inappropriate in this otherwise linguistically very self-conscious writer, whose relationship to the reified inertia of sheer terminology is normally subtle and alert, gun-shy and ever on the point of dialectically stampeding. 'Model', however, strikes one as just such an inert term, and one borrowed from the most reified forms of scientific and social-scientific discourse at that: the discipline of sociology is of course always present in Adorno's mind, even during his most formal philosophizing, but what is present of it is more often its constitutive limits and the mark left on it by history in the form of specialization, rather than its right to supersede philosophy, particularly in matters of terms and names.

At best, it might seem as though the awkwardness of this word reflected a malaise in Adorno's practice which he himself generally displaced onto other people (most notably Kant and Sartre, in the 'Freedom' chapter, ND 222-5/223-6) – namely, the dilemma of the philosophical *example*, whose optionality immediately disqualifies the authority of the concept it was supposed to illustrate. But it is difficult to read these three 'model' chapters as anything but 'examples' of the new method, thereby at once transforming it into that 'methodology' which it sought above all to avoid becoming. A star can no doubt serve as the example of 'starness' generally; but the sun cannot be an example of anything. The term 'model' might then, unconsciously, acknowledge that kind of failure, by the very way in which it draws attention to itself.

Everything changes, however, when we discover that the word 'model' has in fact for Adorno a specifically *musical* provenance, and was appropriated by Schoenberg from a loose and common-sense acceptation as 'exercises' (one of his books is called *Models for Beginners*) for an increasingly specialized and articulated meaning, which will be instructive for us here. Model, in later Schoenberg, designates the raw material of a specific composition or its thematic point of departure: which is to say, for twelve-tone music, the specific row itself, the particular order and configuration of the twelve notes of the scale which, chosen and arranged in advance, *becomes* the composition, in so far as this last is 'nothing more' than an elaborate series of variations and permutations – both vertical and horizontal – of that starting point. What in classical music was separated – the initial 'themes' and their later 'development' – is here reunited. Speaking of the moment of Beethoven in *Philosophy of Modern Music*, Adorno has the following to say:

> Now, in association with development, variation serves in the establishment of universal, concretely unschematic relationships. Variation becomes dynamic. It is true that it still strongly maintains the identity of its initial thematic material – what Schoenberg calls its 'model'. Everything remains 'the same'. But the meaning of this identity reveals itself as non-identity. The initial thematic material is so arranged that preserving it is tantamount to transforming it. There is in fact a way in which it no longer exists 'in itself', but only with a view towards the possibility of the whole composition. (PNM 57/55–6)

If the philosophical analogy we have attributed to Adorno on the strength of this new meaning of the word 'model' is accurate, then a certain earlier or classical philosophy might also be described in much the same way, as the ostensible separation of an 'initial thematic material' – the philosophical idea or problem – and its ulterior development – philosophical argumentation and judgement. This separation means that the concept in question precedes the philosophical text, which then 'thinks' about it, criticizes and modifies it, solves or refutes the problem: such a text presumably has a narrative time not unlike that of sonata form, where something climactic and decisive finally happens – the climax in the philosophical argument is reached – after which a coda shuts down the process by drawing the conclusions. (In the passage just quoted, of course, Adorno characteristically raises the valences of this account, since he also wants to argue that something like Schoenberg's solution is already secretly at work in Beethoven as well: just as one might also want to argue that certain crucial texts of classical philosophy are already 'negative dialectics' without being aware of it.)

What we must retain, however, is the implication that 'twelve-tone' philosophy will do its work differently from the classical text: the concept or problem will not be independent of the *Darstellung* but already at one with it; there will be no conceptual events, no 'arguments' of the traditional kind that lead to truth climaxes; the text will become one infinite variation in which everything is recapitulated at every moment; closure, finally, will be achieved only when all the possible variations have been exhausted. It does not seem superfluous to add, in the light of the numerological obsessions of artists Adorno admired, like Thomas Mann or Schoenberg himself, that – most uncharacteristically for this author – the third and final 'model' of *Negative Dialectics*, on metaphysics, is divided into 'chapters' and printed in the form of twelve numbered sections.

Seven

All of this, however, still defines the larger movement of Adorno's way with concepts, the way in which a twelve-tone philosophy plays out the configurations and the constellations it finds in its path and invents all at once. The texture of this philosophy is, however, not yet reached by such description, which might also, as we have said, obtain in some measure for the Benjaminian projects that preceded it. Yet what strikes one as radically original in Adorno, and as a practice and a philosophical micro-politics that has finally very little in common with Benjamin any longer, is his deployment of the dialectical sentence itself, to which even the energy of Marx's great chiasmatic syntactical acts offers but a distant family likeness. The truest precursor here would seem to be not Benjamin, and certainly not Nietzsche, but the extraordinary Austrian rhetorician Karl Kraus, not so much untranslatable as shamelessly ignored in English, perhaps because the greatest of his self-producing utterances – which rise from the journalistic immediacy of the week-by-week Vienna of his day and of his private journal, *Die Fackel* – tend to rend their contexts and to blast apart the essay framework that offered the pretext for their production, so that Kraus's writings cannot really be read, but only his isolated rhetorical periods:

> In these great times which I knew when they were this small; which will become small again, provided they have time left for it; and which, because in the realm of organic growth no such transformation is possible, we had better call fat times and, truly, hard times as well; in these times in which things are happening that could not be imagined and in which what can no longer be imagined must happen, for if one could imagine it, it would not happen; in these serious times which have died laughing at the thought

that they might become serious; which, surprised by their own tragedy, are reaching for diversion and, catching themselves redhanded, are groping for words; in these loud times which boom with the horrible symphony of actions which produce reports and of reports which cause actions; in these times you should not expect any words of my own from me – none but these words which barely manage to prevent silence from being misinterpreted.[35]

What Adorno found here, I want to suggest, is the very paradigm of an expressive syntax, in which the actual machinery of sentence structure is itself pressed into service, in all its endless variety, and mobilized to convey meaning far beyond its immediate content as mere communication and denotation. To Kraus, far more than to Adorno himself, might well apply Benjamin's idea that 'speech communicates itself',[36] and perhaps also his idiosyncratic notion of language as 'non-representational mimesis'.

It is not clear to what degree Adorno discovered the possibilities of the notion of mimesis in Benjamin's infrequent use of it: what is certain is that he went on to make it mean much more than Benjamin did – perhaps too much more (involving at length a whole anthropology in *Dialectic of Enlightenment*) and at the same time something just slightly distinct, just slightly different. If anything, comparability is afforded by a different Benjaminian word and notion: for nothing in the older writer offers quite so many purely formal analogies to the peculiar status of *mimesis* in Adorno – a foundational concept never defined nor argued but always alluded to, by name, as though it had preexisted all the texts – as Benjamin's notion of *aura*, which otherwise has nothing to do with it.[37] It is as though, in both these writers, a kind of repressed foundational longing found its way back into their writing by way of these magical terms, which are evoked to explain everything without ever themselves being explained, until at length we become persuaded that they could never themselves be explained or grounded, and mark the root of some archaic private obsession, as in the Ur-sounds and names of the great modern poets. 'Aura' and 'mimesis' are therefore the hostages given to the unique and the particular which free an extraordinary universalizing thought and language to go about its business.

Yet there is one sense of the otherwise protean term 'mimesis' which *Negative Dialectics* allows us to specify and to use: the price for this new applicability lying, to be sure, in a reduction and a specialization that radically cut it off from Adorno's other deployments of the charged word. At the local climax of his discussion of causality, in a remarkable passage that would merit the closest commentary, Adorno complexly rehearses the dialectic of subject and object at work in that very 'dialectic of enlightenment' that produced the concept of causality in the first place, as a handle on the objective relations, hierarchies, interactions, dominations and subordinations at work in the world of things. Projection (a later and degraded psychic phenomenon, developed at the greatest length in the 'Anti-Semitism' chapter of *Dialectic of Enlightenment*) is not at all what Adorno has in mind when he evokes a certain necessary 'affinity' between the subject and things that is presupposed by any form of knowledge: enlightenment builds on this just as surely as it wishes to exterminate it:

> Consciousness knows only so much about its other as the latter resembles it, but not by extirpating itself along with that resemblance. ... The less it tolerates any affinity to things, to that degree its drive towards identity increases ruthlessly. (ND 267/270)

All these considerations would be at work in a genuine critique of the concept of causality, about which he also says that it is a privileged place to observe the operation of identity on the non-identical. And then he says this about the concept itself:

> In it thinking fulfills its mimicry of the spell it had itself cast on things; it does so on the very threshold of a sympathy before which that spell would vanish altogether. Between the subjective component of the concept of causality and its objects there exists an 'elective affinity' that is in fact a premonition of what happened to those objects at the hands of that subject. (ND 267/270)

This notion of a mimicry – a strong form of mimesis – at work within the very technical concepts of science and philosophy themselves, a mimetic impulse that embarrasses them and which they seek to deny (in the strong Freudian sense), if not to repress altogether, seems to me to offer useful clues to Adorno's own philosophical practice, which would then in this sense constitute a virtually psychoanalytic acting out or talking cure, *abreaction*, of precisely that repressed mimetic impulse, allowing us once again to grasp some older relationship of the mimicking subject to its other or nature: a relationship we cannot reinstate or reinvent as such in 'modern times', any more than the Freudian therapy invites us really to become children again, yet whose recovery by way of memory – indeed, whose anamnesis – is therapeutic in its own right.

Whether philosophy can actually do that, whether the most powerful or formally ingenious or evocative philosophical sentence structure can intervene with effects of this kind in the reader's mind, is open to some doubt; nor is that doubt reduced or even usefully articulated by the

way in which Adorno, following Benjamin's strong lead, systematically
excludes issues of reception from his aesthetics and therefore, implicitly,
from his account of the power of the texts of 'critical theory' as well.
Or rather, he disposes of a powerful account of the refusal to receive
– that is to say, of resistance – in the Nietzschean doctrine of *ressentiment*
(see Part II, below); as for reception, however, or the possibility in our
time for a subject to take a critical stance in the first place, this is inscribed
as a description of the uncharacteristic trajectory of the individual subject,
and generally evoked as the anachronistic survival of an older individualism and an older set of class attitudes into the new world of the total
system and the 'administered' or bureaucratic society (ND 50–51/40–41)
– that is to say that the possibility of reception is generally explained
as the accident of class privileges that isolate the critical subject from
the tendential movement of social and systemic *Gleichschaltung*.

   None the less, and leaving its possible effects aside, it would seem plausible to examine Adorno's sentences in terms of their mimetic component:
something often meant anyway when philosophical practice is loosely
described in terms of aesthetics:

> To represent the mimesis it supplanted, the concept has no other way than
> to adopt something mimetic in its own conduct, without abandoning itself
> to it utterly. (ND 26/14)

The force of this will not adequately be felt, however, unless we underscore the qualifier and remind ourselves of Adorno's absolute hostility
to the assimilation of philosophy to aesthetic writing, to play, to art,
to *belles-lettres* generally; this absolute differentiation of philosophical
thought from artistic production – most unseasonable in the present
intellectual climate – is the price to be paid for the detection of those
features of the philosophical argument which do have something in common with artistic practice:

> The freedom in a thought can be found there where it transcends that object
> of its thinking to which it has bound itself in resistance. It is a freedom
> that follows the expressive drive of the subject. The need to lend suffering
> a voice is the precondition of all truth. For suffering is the objectivity that
> weighs the subject down; what it experiences as its most subjective capacity,
> expression, is objectively mediated. (ND 29/17–18)

It will be seen that here already, in the philosophic defense of a mimetic
moment in philosophy, the mimetic has begun to act itself out in Adorno's
language. This is something that can be clarified by substituting a more
recent terminology for that of mimesis, a terminology which was not

available in its contemporary forms to Adorno and which, like all trans-coding, imposes a certain interpretive violence on his thought: namely, the language of *narrative*. For on the face of it, and beyond the Cratylism of this or that isolated word or name (as, for example, in poetic diction), it is not obvious how sentences could be said to be mimetic in the first place, without making a laborious detour through the language system by which they are produced, a detour that ultimately involves a compara-tive view of the various possible structures of human language. Such a detour, which causes the work of a Humboldt or a Whorf to rise up like an immense monument or mountain range, then permits the analyst to grasp the unique syntactical spirit of a given language or system of languages as one form of the mimesis of the relationship of those speakers to being and to the world in general (the tense system, presence or absence of subjects and objects, nomination, etc.). Without that global perspective (which might be implicit in some attempt to grasp the relation-ship of the dialectic to the structure of the German language, say) the mimetic possibilities of the individual sentence can be grasped only as the way in which they tend to form themselves into micro-narratives, and as it were to act out the content of what is in them abstractly grasped as philosophical thinking or argument.

This tendency is, however, surely very strong in Adorno himself, who supplements the content of his philosophical conceptions with a well-nigh gestural picture of the interaction of their components. The conception of enlightenment – that is to say, Reason generally and the inner drive of all abstract thinking in particular – as a form of domination obviously yields in advance a rich narrative schema, with *actants* and motives and violent and dramatic events: something that will be closest to the surface when we evoke the inaugural moments of Western reason itself, as in the following remark:

> Whenever something that is to be conceived flees from identity with the concept, this last will be forced to take extreme steps to prevent any doubts as to the seamlessness, closure and accuracy of the thought-product from arising. (ND 33/22)

As if this were not already ominous enough, the micro-narrative now takes on even more precise detail, and the mists of the homology lift to disclose the jungle itself:

> This system [rationalism], in which the sovereign mind imagined itself to have been transfigured and transformed, has its Ur-history in the pre-mental, in the animal life of the species. Predators are voracious; the tiger-leap on their prey is difficult and often dangerous. Additional impulses may be necess-

ary for the beast to dare it. These fuse with hunger's unpleasure into a rage at the victim, expression of which then usefully terrifies and cripples this last. In the progress towards humanity this process is rationalized by way of projection. (ND 33/22)

This is a picture whose philosophical argument may be thought to presuppose a certain anthropology (we have already expressed a certain discomfort with these features of Adorno's thought) or on the other hand, those anthropological components might well be seen, in Russian Formalist fashion, as the content Adorno had to talk himself into in order to write vivid sentences of this kind. In that case, the more interesting prolongation of this dimension of this work – not 'anthropology' as a preconception about human nature, but the entire, truly philosophical meditation on the relationship between human history and natural history – would be something like what the Formalists called a 'motivation of the device', a belief that justifies your own aesthetic after the fact. It is at any rate in the 'model' on natural history that we find the final twist in the micro-narrative outlined above, a reappropriation of the narrative for conceptual and philosophical uses, above all in the sentence that caps the discussion of the relationship of the 'instinct' of self-preservation (for Adorno the primal curse of our own fallen world) to the structures of consciousness and, indeed, to 'false consciousness' itself: 'if the lion had a consciousness, his rage at the antelope he wants to eat would be ideology' (348/342).

It is therefore the mimetic component of the individual philosophical sentence – its tendency to narrativize the conceptual – that finally springs the isolated abstract concept out of its bad identity and allows it, as it were, to be thought from the inside and from the outside all at once: an ideational content transformed mimetically into a quasi-narrative representation. This micro-work of the sentence on the isolated concept is, then, what undermines its apparent rational autonomy and pre-forms it (to hark back to the musical analogy) for its multiple positions in the larger movement of the constellation or the 'model'. The mimetic or the narrative may be thought to be a kind of homeopathic strategy in which, by revealing the primal movement of domination hidden away within abstract thought, the venom of abstraction is neutralized, allowing some potential or utopian truth-content to come into its own.

Is it necessary to add that this significance in Adorno of a mimetic mode of philosophizing by no means marks him as a mere 'littérateur'; it in no way implies the substitution of aesthetics for philosophy, since the mimetic impulse is common to both, but takes distinct forms in each. In any case, in *Negative Dialectics* Adorno argued at some length against the supersession of philosophy by literature ('no matter how hard we try for a linguistic articulation of the historicity of our topics, the words we have to use remain concepts' (ND 62/52–3).

Yet the form of the sentences must now also be seen as a form of philosophizing in its own right:[38] we shall see later, for example, the unexpected significance of that animal imagery which expressed the imperialism of the concept in the illustration just given (it sounds, indeed, the theme of the whole dimension of natural history as that is part and parcel of Adorno's philosophical 'system'). The same must now be said about the economic images and figures that lend such closure to sentences thereby transformed into veritable aphorisms. The comparison, which stages the particular with metaphoric vividness, also includes a whole economics, and this turns largely, throughout Adorno, on the relationship between individual subjects and the tendential laws of late or monopoly capital. We have already noted one proto-economic area of philosophical significance in the notion of the concept and identity, which correspond to Marx's account of value in simple commodity exchange. A whole second dimension of economic logic, however, turns on the more complex and dialectical relationship between universal and particular, which it may be convenient to separate into two general groups, the first having to do with the division of labor within the individual subject, while the second dramatizes the precarious position of individuation itself under monopoly conditions.

Thus, to take this second group first, the traditional image of the rebel is not merely objectively precarious but perhaps even subjectively illusory. Of the Hollywood rebel, for example – they seem to have had Orson Welles in mind – Adorno and Horkheimer observe that even his dissidence can be accommodated as a style or an eccentricity: 'Once his particular brand of deviation from the norm has been registered and classified by the culture industry, he belongs to it as the land reformer belongs to capitalism' (DA, 118/132). Outflanked, 'coopted', the most revolutionary peasant demands now reintegrated into a larger market strategy that seeks very precisely to break up the great estates in order to create private property and to foster a henceforth landless proletariat – the heroic simile includes this whole epic process, which constitutes a capsule textbook on agrarian reform as seen by Marxist analysis; but it also includes a preview of a whole newer film history for which stylistic innovation of the Welles type is considered a form of marketing try-out that allows Hollywood to modify and modernize its technique, while drawing innovation itself back inside the stereotypical product.[39] On the other hand, all of this can be rewritten in terms of the first mode of analysis mentioned above, the internal division of labor: 'No wrestling match is without a referee: the whole brawl has been staged by society internalized in the individual, which both supervises the struggle and takes part in it' (MM 175/134).

The more standard case, however, is that of the individual subject as anachronism: the comparison is with small business in the age of the great trusts and monopolies, and just as 'the possibility of becoming a subject in the economy, an entrepreneur or a proprietor, has been completely liquidated' (DA 137/153), so also the psychic subject, the producer of autonomous art or independent action or thought, is also eliminated; or becomes, where it survives, a precarious holdover, a sport of nature:

> When the big industrial interests incessantly eliminate the economic basis for moral decision, partly by eliminating the independent economic subject, partly by taking over the self-employed tradesmen, partly by transforming workers into cogs in the labor unions, the possibility of reflection must also die out. (DA 177-8/198)

But this economic homology – now a full-dress theory of the psyche under monopoly capitalism (see esp. DA 181-2/202-3) – opens up a number of directions. It can, for example, be pressed into service for an account of the nature and quality of the residual individual potentiality under monopoly:

> The Utopia of the qualitative – the things which through their difference and uniqueness cannot be absorbed into the prevalent exchange relationships – takes refuge under capitalism in the traits of fetishism. (MM 155/120)

In the same way, but more succinctly, the more familiar theme of reification is thus laid down: 'The more reification there is, all the more subjectivism will there be' (W92/74). (The maxim, Adorno adds, 'holds good for orchestration just as much as for epistemology'.)

But the homology can also be interrogated for its own conditions of possibility, at which point the relationship between the individual psyche, private property and time itself slowly comes into view: 'historically, the notion of time is itself formed on the basis of the order of ownership' (MM 98/79; see also ND 362/369). In this form, however, the sentence remains a kind of abstract affirmation, a mere philosophical proposition of a relatively static kind. It does not become a mimetic figure until the 'subject' enters the force field of late capitalism where the association between personal identity and private property threatens to come apart: at that point a tendency becomes visible, whose story can be told:

The individual has been, as it were, merely invested with property by the class, and those in control are ready to take it back as soon as universalization of property seems likely to endanger its principle, which is precisely that of withholding. (MM 77/64)

The figure can finally produce its own global theory out of itself, and as a figure for its own existence: this is what happens when, in one of the most stunning of the *Minima Moralia*, the figures of the tendential restriction of the individual subject, and its increasing penetration by the social division of labor, rejoin the language of *Capital* itself, and Adorno can speak of an 'organic composition of capital' within the psychic subject: that is to say, an increasingly higher percentage of mental machinery and instrumental operations as opposed to living human labor, to the free subjectivity whose role is ever more diminished. Now human creativity shrinks to machine-minding and reason to a fitful organic impulse: 'the will to live finds itself dependent on the denial of the will to live: self-preservation annuls all life in subjectivity' (MM 308/229).

But this particular figure explicitly corrects its own misreading: this is not, Adorno specifies, the thesis about 'the 'mechanization' of man', which 'thinks of him as something static which, through an "influence" from outside, an adaptation to conditions of production external to him, suffers certain deformations'. Rather, the figure is itself dialectical and includes Marx's analysis of the organic composition of capital as such.

These 'dialectical tropes', then, mobilize on the level of the individual sentence the relations between the universal, or the totality, and the particular, that have been described in an earlier chapter. They confirm what was argued there: that the term corresponding to the totality or social system is not merely presupposed in the form of inert knowledge or preexistent belief: rather it is itself specified by what happens to its opposite number, the individual subject. These figures therefore yield information about a specific moment of the operation of the social totality in its monopoly period: the adherence, indeed, to the 'state capitalist' model of the economy,[40] a model overtaken by the development of multinational capitalism today and no longer current, permits a kind of measurement of the 'damaged subject' we no longer dispose of, a measurement whose 'registering apparatus' includes images of the constriction of space, of tendential exclusion, of the obliteration of possibility and creative novelty by intensified repetition and sameness. This process could be registered in narrative or mimetic form by Adorno (and Horkheimer) because they lived through the transitional period in which smaller business and entrepreneurship were once visible, so that their absence at a later stage remains a dramatic symptom, still perceptible to the observer.

This is of course an advantage over our own period, in which social homogenization is far more complete, the past has been more definitively disposed of, and this kind of temporal or modernist dialectic seems inoperative.

Eight

In fact, far from being an 'open' or aleatory composition, *Negative Dialectics* imitates – as over a great distance, with radically different building materials, and in that 'prodigious erosion of contours' of which Gide, following Nietzsche, liked to speak – the plan of Kant's *Critique of Pure Reason*. (I am tempted to say that it *wraps* it as a postmodern reconstruction – glass shell, arches – wraps an older monument; except that Adorno is not postmodern and the more fitting analogy would be what Thomas Mann does to Goethe's *Faust*.) The uses and abuses of what we call dialectic, what one can and cannot properly think with it, and in particular the relationship to the logical forms of identity and non-identity – all this stands in for Kant's central concern with Reason itself and its legitimate and illegitimate functions.

The illegitimacy of transcendental speculation, then; the dogmatic or theological wandering among entities we cannot know (in Kant's for us now antiquated usage, the transcendental *dialectic*) – in the secular world of the mid twentieth century this place of error, temptation and confusion is clearly that of Heidegger, to whom once again a substantial section will be devoted (which we will not particularly examine here, even though a hostile critic has suggested that Adorno's principled antagonism to Heidegger, from the earliest years onward, was 'the one fixed point' in his philosophizing[41]). Kant's other asymmetrically positioned adversary, empiricism – whose overcoming was famously so important and so full of content for him – can in Adorno's period only be that far more dehumanized thing he calls positivism, something that plays a significant role in his arguments rather as a historical situation (sometimes also called nominalism) than as a significant set of philosophical positions (like Hume's) with which he has to come to terms.

Meanwhile, the structure of the 'dialectic of enlightenment' itself, as a deduction both derived and derivational, and the enigmatic concept of 'mimesis', constitute allusions at least as omnipresent, and often as inexplicable, as Kant's categories and schemata; while finally the three great transcendental ideas, whose essential unthinkability is as exhaustively demonstrated as their indispensability is affirmed – Immortality, Freedom and God – can be shown to have their counterpart in the three 'models' with which *Negative Dialectics* concludes its work. Immortality, of course, returns as such in the final section on the possibility or the impossibility of metaphysics, a most unKantian reinvention of Kant's central problematic for our own time: in Kant, this particular 'idea', or necessary but indefensible transcendental value, returns to dawn over the failure of the paralogisms of pure reason, which were unable to ground the substantial existence of the soul (which stands in for the subject's unity, the famous 'transcendental unity of apperception').

Freedom, however, corresponds to the problem of the antinomies of pure reason – that is to say, the impossibility of establishing the causalities of the universe, and whether it has a beginning or an end, is infinite or bounded, and so forth: the relevance of what we might today think of as a subjective or a psychological matter (freedom) is clarified with the antinomies of causality itself, and whether the same string of events could be read in two distinct and incommensurable ways, as a causal series (determined, as we might say today, by the social as well as the psychoanalytic) and as a concatenation of free choices and responses. The point is that for Kant this problem is not a subjective but an objective one, and here Adorno's bias towards the objective, his systematic defamiliarization of the subjective in terms of the 'preponderance of the object', is very consonant and indeed overshoots the Kantian mark by encompassing at this point ethics and those ethical paradoxes that Kant reserved for another panel of his triptych (whence the absence of a properly Adornian 'critique of practical reason', since that is already implicit here).

The idea of God, finally – that 'ideal of pure reason' that completes the contingency of the empirical world by its necessity, just as it grounds the nature and existence of the particulars of that world – becomes, in Adorno's post-Kantian and post-Hegelian intellectual context, the problematic of the Hegelian world spirit, a question about the nature of universals and the universal as such (the traditional function of the older idea of God), but also one which deploys the concept of History itself, in Adorno, as we shall see, dialectically reproblematized in terms of the 'identity' and 'non-identity' between human and natural histories. And there are other points of contact between the two texts: 'a complete enumeration of which would be a useful and not unpleasant, but in this place a perfectly dispensable, occupation'.[42]

This ambitious operation does not, then, elaborate the conditions of possibility for the validity of Marxism itself, as Kant's *Critique* did for the natural science of his own period; it is not in that sense exactly a philosophy of Marxism or a working out of its philosophical scaffolding and underpinnings (something which Lukács's *History and Class Consciousness* can be said to have done in a far more idiosyncratic and less traditional way). Its philosophical conclusions – which can be formulated as the threefold emergence of new conceptions (if not transcendental *ideas*) of mortality and materialism, of the essential impurity or heteronomy of ethics and action, and of the deep substratum of natural history at work in human history – are if anything philosophical complements to a Marxian view of history itself; as vast as is the purview of this last, which expands to include virtually all human activity and to rivalize with the philosophical bases of the various disciplines in its claim to ground them all, these three zones then fall beyond or outside even that enlarged one. Adorno's 'critical' or 'negative-dialectical' philosophy – taken now no longer as a method of some kind, but as a set of substantial philosophical results and concepts – can in that sense be said to correspond to what Sartre (not altogether happily) called an 'ideology', that is a corrective to Marxism as the 'only untranscendable philosophy of our time',[43] an unfreezing of what had dogmatically hardened in this last, and a reminder of those issues – so often called the 'subjective factor', consciousness or culture – that lie beyond its official boundaries.

On the other hand, the Kant parallel also suggests that Adorno's later preoccupation with 'non-identity', and in particular the role that nature and natural beauty come to take on in *Aesthetic Theory*, can itself be seen as a (very Kantian) slippage beyond the bounds assigned to such 'transcendental ideas', and a lapse encouraged by the very block itself (which in Adorno is what separates identity from non-identity): the atheistic and skeptical Kant, indeed, would have renounced ideas of this kind, which the deistic Kant welcomes back.

Finally, if the formative subterranean – I would prefer to say subtextual rather than intertextual – role of the *Critique* described here is plausible, then it becomes equally clear why we can rarely take the Adorno of the essay manifesto (and the open work, the fragmentary probe) at his word. These 'models' now scarcely seem chosen at random, but to have a deeper and more systematic logical relationship and to 'participate' at least in the internal coherence of Kant's own text as a fundamental historical symptom and geological upthrust of thought in the early bourgeois period.

Indeed, if the wonderful formula of the essay is to be taken at face value, that to conceptualize 'essayistically'

> is comparable only to the conduct of someone obliged in a foreign country to use the foreign language practically, rather than to cobble its elements together in schoolroom fashion (NL 21)

then it must be observed about these 'essays' of *Negative Dialectics* that what they try to speak is at least an Indo-European language related to the writer's native one.

Nine

But freedom – in the sense of free will, determinism, responsibility and choice, all things we last glimpsed in Sartre's existentialism, now so long ago – is today a rather old-fashioned problem, or rather, better still, springs as a term and a local problem from a whole seemingly antiquated problematic, redolent of a time before psychoanalysis and behaviorism, when not also smacking lightly of the dustiest academic philosophy contained in long-unopened tomes on ethics somewhere. It is therefore appropriate for Adorno to invite us to reflect on the significance of the old-fashioned and the no longer actual, in philosophy and in culture as well, if only by way of grasping more vividly the way in which this 'problem' also was implicit in the great opening move of the work, in the spectacle of philosophy somehow 'living on' and surviving itself. Elsewhere, in a remarkable meditation on Ibsen and feminism in *Minima Moralia* (No. 57), in which what looks old-fashioned about *A Doll's House* is not the 'social issue' it raises, which is no longer current, but rather the fact that it *is* precisely old-fashioned – in other words, that it has not been solved, is still with us, but in ways we no longer wish to be conscious of. Outdatedness would then be the mark of repression – 'the shame that overcomes the descendant in face of an earlier possibility that he has neglected to bring to fruition'(MM 116/93). So also with ethical philosophy, and in particular with Kant: it stands as a token and a reminder of a moment in the past in which it seemed more plausible and more 'realistic' to speculate about the freedom of the subject and of its acts than it does today.

The historicality of the concept was, however, already previewed in an earlier chapter of *Negative Dialectics*:

77

Emphatically conceived, the judgement that a man is free refers to the concept
of freedom; yet the concept itself turns out to be more than what is predicated
of the man, just as the man turns out in his other determinations to be
more than the concept of his freedom. Its concept not only asserts that it
is applicable to all individual men defined as free. It is nourished by the
idea of a condition in which individuals would have qualities attributable
to no one under current circumstances. To praise someone as free has its
specificity in the *sous-entendu* that something impossible has been ascribed
to him, simply because it has manifested itself in him; it is this secret thing
that strikes the eye which animates every judgement of identification that
is worth making. The concept of freedom lags behind itself as soon as it
is empirically applied. (ND 153-4/150-51)

The temporality of the concept lies not merely in its past history, therefore, but also in its future, as a 'broken promise' and a utopian thought
that overshoots the mark, mistakenly imagining itself to have become
universal.

The formal question raised most insistently by this 'model' (as by the
others) then involves the *Darstellung* of such a peculiar entity in time,
let alone the problem of its own antinomies and inner contradictions.
Kant had already argued that freedom was what is today called a 'pseudo-
problem'; but was far from wanting us to forget about the matter altogether, as positivism seems to have done, despite the fact that the word
continues to be used in the juridical and penal processes as well as in
what few 'ethical' dilemmas still come up from time to time. *Negative
Dialectics* will not want to 'solve' this old problem exactly, nor to produce
some new and more non-contradictory 'philosophy' of freedom than
is to be found in the earlier efforts of the tradition:

> the topics to be discussed must be reflected on, not in the sense in which
> one makes a judgement as to the existence or non-existence [of the problems
> to which they correspond], but rather by reckoning into their determination
> the impossibility of nailing them down as well as the necessity of continuing
> to think them. (ND 211-12/212)

In the case of Kant's version of freedom – in which that account of
action is inconsistent, or at least incommensurable, with the causality
of the phenomenal world (where I may well freely will to do something,
but it gets done by my body, under the laws of gravity, etc.); so that
the Prussian philosopher will consign the language and conceptuality
of freedom to the realm of things-in-themselves, while retaining it in
this other one as a 'regulative idea' – Adorno can still benefit from Horkheimer's old lessons in ideological analysis:

Since the seventeenth century great philosophy had marked out freedom as
its own specific property interest; under a tacit mandate from the bourgeoisie
to ground it apodictically. Yet that interest is structurally contradictory. It
opposes the old oppression of feudalism and promotes a new one, that dwells
within the rational principle itself. What is required is a common formula
for freedom and oppression: the former is ceded to rationality, which then
limits it, and is thereby distanced from an empirical world in which one
does not wish to see it realized at all. (ND 214/214)

Yet the matter is not thereby disposed of once and for all: for, as the
aesthetic writings codify the distinction more clearly and more crudely,
ideological function must here still be differentiated from 'truth-content'
(*Wahrheitsgehalt*); while even in the realm of ideology, Kant's ingenious
satisfaction of the twin contradictory ideological requirements proves
to be little more than a provisional resting place on a road that could
only go downhill after his own time, where in particular psychology
– as an empirical science of cause and effect – was only at the beginnings
of its colonization of subjectivity, in our time so thoroughgoing as to
make one wonder where 'freedom' might be lodged somehow, let alone
what it was in the first place. Ironically, however, even reflections on
'determinism sound archaic, as though dating from the early period of
the revolutionary bourgeoisie' (ND 215/215): 'Indifference to freedom,
to the concept as well as to the thing itself, is actualized by the integration
into society, that happens to subjects like an irresistible force' (ND 215/
216). Yet this must also be described as an ideology and a choice, fully
as much as a historical process; Adorno therefore significantly adds this
second sentence: 'Their interest in being provided for has paralyzed the
interest in a freedom they fear would leave them unprotected.'

The rest of this first section seeks, however, to show how within a
range of conceptions of unfreedom, some concept of freedom none the
less remains presupposed. The argument, here and throughout, that the
two opposites dialectically entail each other, will later on become the
practical recommendation for a deliberate heteronomy in ethical thinking. Here, however, the unity of opposites is expressed genealogically:

The identity of the self and its alienation accompany each other from the
very beginning; whence the bad romanticism of the concept of alienation
in the first place. A precondition of freedom, identity is at one and the same
time also and immediately the principle of determinism itself. (ND 216/216-17)

But society, the principle of identity and integration and of the repressive
disarticulation of the psyche, also requires and posits freedom as its own
precondition; while the psychic ego is also nourished by and grounded

on that anamnesis of the archaic infantile instincts which it is its function
to control and domesticate. Even Kant's *Darstellung* – his reluctant mar-
shalling of 'examples' in the form of primary ethical 'texts' and cruxes
– dramatizes the unstable yet inevitable mediation between some pure
notion of freedom and its contingent circumstances, which in the long
run forbid generalization or universalization.

Yet the opposite of this is also true: so at the end of this section Adorno
comes to the astonishing proposition that even the seemingly inadequate
Kantian conception of the 'will' (conceived as 'a faculty to make oneself
act according to the idea of certain laws' [Kant, quoted in ND 226–7/227])
displays, when it is visible, a kind of bizarre supplement or additional
charge (Adorno's expression is *das Hinzutretende*) in which freedom does
seem to be vividly added on to normal acts and conscious or chosen
behavior. But what this is might just as easily be described, in modern
terms, as coming from below fully as easily as coming from above:

> The impulse, intramental and somatic all at once, transcends the sphere of
> consciousness to which in another sense it still belongs. With such an impulse
> freedom now reaches into the world of experience; this animates its concept
> as that of a state that could as little be blind nature as it could nature's
> repression. The fantasy picture of such a state, which reason will not let
> any proof of causal interdependency talk itself out of, is that of a reconciliation
> of nature and spirit. Nor is it as alien to reason as it appears in Kant's own
> identification of reason with will; it doesn't fall from heaven. It only strikes
> philosophical reason as something radically other, because will assigned to
> pure practical reason is a mere abstraction. The supplementary charge [*das
> Hinzutretende*] is precisely the name for everything that has been burnt out
> of that abstraction; free will could not possibly achieve reality without it.
> It is a flash of light between the poles of something long past and grown
> almost unrecognizable and what might someday come to be. (ND 228/228–9)

This rectification and recuperation of the old doctrine of will – definitively
dissolved, one would have thought, by Sartre, who demonstrates that
what we take to be the exercise of 'conscious' will-power is only a game
we play with ourselves within a more general non-reflexive free choice
deployed in order to allow us to reap the prestige of its exercise (and
also, most often, to fail) – seems to stress something closer to an ontological leap of being, rather than the application of redoubled effort.

However that may be, the next section of the model swings around
into the reversal of this argument and seeks rather to renumerate the
ways in which all concepts of freedom also include their own unfreedom.
Kant himself, on the personal and social level, seems to dramatize this
in a particularly regrettable (if perhaps now comic) fashion: 'Like the

idealists who followed him, Kant cannot bear freedom without compulsion' (ND 231/232). On the other hand, even if the pure formalism of duty and universal law can often (particularly in its German manifestations) look ruthless and oppressive in Kant himself and in the Enlightenment, 'there still survives in it, despite and even because of its very abstractness, real content, namely the egalitarian idea' (ND 235/236). Yet this same abstract universality requires contingent material in order to exist at all: freedom is in this Kantian sense still dialectically the same as chance:

> Freedom needs what Kant calls the heteronomous. Without what according to the criteria of reason itself is called the accidental or the contingent, freedom could as little exist as could reason's own logical judgements. The absolute separation between freedom and chance is as arbitrary as the equally absolute one between freedom and rationality. For an undialectical standard of legality something about freedom will always seem contingent: the case demands reflection, which then lifts itself above the categories of both law and chance alike. (ND 236/237)

It is, incidentally, clear from Adorno's infrequent yet mesmerized returns to the question of chance throughout his work as a whole that such reflections are very much stimulated and inspired by the speculative developments on chance and contingency in Lukács's *History and Class Consciousness*.[44]

But in order to ground his own dialectical and heteronomous conception of freedom, Adorno must first undo Kant's Third Antinomy, which purports to demonstrate the impossibility of both the concept of phenomenal freedom and of its opposite (causality without freedom) alike, and therefore sets a gap between the two too great to be bridged by any dialectic. In doing this in the next section, however, Adorno takes the opportunity to repudiate what he takes to be Marx's equally intolerable solution, the collapsing of theory and practice together in such a way that the former disappears: as can be expected, this is the occasion for a characteristically Frankfurt School plea for the contemplative in and for itself.

The sequel, however, is of the greatest interest in so far as Adorno now focuses in turn on the other column of the antinomy, in order now to rescue, not freedom, but causality. Kant's (and the Germans') ideological and class biases are again foregrounded in his identification of causality with the law: whatever 'follows in line with a rule' (quoted, ND 245/247). Substantively, what can be said about this rather compulsive notion of causality is that it is in this respect identical with Kant's definition of freedom ('following the rules') and ought then rather to apply

to 'what is distinguished from compulsion' (ND 247/249). Yet the failure
of Kant's operation and the palpable derivation of the transcendental
description of freedom from the phenomenal rather than from the noume-
nal realm (ND 252/255) now open the basic structures of Kant's ethics,
and above all that of the Categorical Imperative itself, to a more properly
social derivation: in particular the logical argumentation by way of distinction between means and ends clearly draws on a historically original
social experience:

> the distinction between subjects as the commodity of labor power, from which
> value is to be extracted, and those people who, while still themselves commodi-
> fied, are also those subjects for whom the whole apparatus is set in motion, an
> apparatus that forgets and only incidentally also satisfies them. (ND 254/257).

The utopian moment in the great Kantian imperative seems to have
been tarnished for Adorno, not merely because its chance to be realized
(in the political universalism of the bourgeois revolution) was missed,
but also because of the stubbornly repressive character of the doctrine,
which wants to have nothing whatsoever to do with happiness, let alone
pleasure, in its pursuit of a universal moral law as abstract as the law
of non-contradiction itself. Finally, however, this seems to be attributable,
fully as much as to Kant himself, the Enlightenment and the eighteenth-
century German bourgeoisie or Prussian state, to the deeper operation
of the principle of identity; and this will of course be Adorno's ultimate
refutation of the Third Antinomy:

> The subject need only pose the inescapable alternative between free will and
> its lack of freedom to be lost in advance. Each drastic thesis is false. At their
> core the theses of freedom and determinism coincide. Both proclaim identity.
> (ND 261/264)

Yet at the same time both theses are also true:

> The antinomy between the determination of the individual and the social
> responsibility that contradicts such determination is not due to a misuse of
> concepts, but is real, and the moral form taken by the non-reconciliation
> between the universal and the particular. (ND 261/264)

Yet this new antinomy – Adorno's rather than Kant's – now drives
his thought forward into its ultimate formulation, and the most elaborated
statement of his conception of heteronomy:

> Freedom is, however, so entangled with unfreedom that unfreedom is not
> merely its impediment but also a premise of freedom's concept. No more

than any other one can this one be separated off as an absolute. Without
the unity and the domination of reason, nothing like freedom would ever
have been thought of in the first place, let alone brought into being: to
that the history of philosophy itself can testify. There is no available
model of freedom but this one: that just as consciousness intervenes in
the total constitution of society, so also it intervenes, through that
very intervention, in the complexion of the individual. The reason this
notion is not itself chimerical is that consciousness as a form of diverted
libidinal energy is itself a drive, and therefore a moment of what it
actively intervenes in. Without that affinity that Kant so violently
denies [between the universal and the empirical, between freedom and
the phenomenal world], that very idea of freedom, in whose name he
refuses the expression of such affinities, would not exist in the first place.
(ND 262/265)

It is a doctrine of the mixed or the impure – or, in another language,
of the identity between identity and non-identity – which we will find
returning in the aesthetics, whose artistic works or monads are both
closed intrinsic forms and objects saturated by the social to which they
ceaselessly refer in the strong semantic sense. Yet it also draws its force,
as we shall see shortly, from Adorno's philosophically original deployment of the notion of natural history (into which, in the above passage,
'consciousness' is reinserted in so far as it is also 'a form of diverted
libidinal energy').

With this climax, then, as in a local coda, Adorno's reflection then
proceeds down the other slope of the heteronomous concept, as though
'what happened to the idea of freedom also seems to be happening to
its counterpart, the concept of causality' (ND 262/265): he has in mind
essentially the sea-change from the linear causality still central for Kant
to an essentially synchronic conception, 'operating not so much with
causal chains as with causal networks' (ND 263/266).

Causality has similarly withdrawn into totality ... each state of things is
horizontally and vertically connected to all the others, illuminates all of them
[tingiert] just as it is illuminated by all in turn. The last doctrine in which
Enlightenment used causality as a decisive political weapon, the Marxist doctrine of infrastructure and superstructure, now lags innocently behind a condition in which not only the machineries of production, distribution and
domination, but also economic and social relationships along with ideologies
are inextricably interwoven, and in which living people have themselves
become bits of ideology. Where ideology is no longer added on to things
as their justification or their mystification or glamorization, but has been
transformed into the appearance of the inevitability and therefore the legitimacy of the status quo, a critique that operates with the unequivocal causal

relationships of base and superstructure misses the mark. In the total society all things are equidistant from the center; such a society is fully as transparent, and its apologia as threadbare, as those people grow extinct who once saw through it. (ND 264-5/267-8)

It is then with such a causality – the 'magic spell' of late capitalism, as we shall see later on – that the subject and freedom have – pace Kant – a certain affinity; with such an objective dimension that the truth of the subject can alone be revealed. 'Affinity' is in this sense 'determinate negation' – that is to say, 'critical theory', 'negative dialectics'; it is also, in some hitherto undisplayed sense, mimesis:

> In it [affinity as critique] thought completes its mimicry of that spell on things which it has itself laid around them, on the threshold of a sympathy before which the spell itself would disappear. The subjective principle within causality has its elective affinity with objects in the form of a dim, unformulated realization of what happened to them at the subject's hand. (ND 267/270)

Mimesis can thus now be seen to offer a peculiar reversal or corrective of the Viconian principle of verum factum, in so far as it does not merely yield insight into the deeper nature of what human beings and their social order have done to the world but also grants some distant, simultaneous sense of how that might be repaired. The thought thus oddly echoes the great Brechtian principle of estrangement, which sought, by demonstrating that what we took to be natural was in reality social and the result of human praxis, to reawaken the awareness that human praxis was equally capable of turning it into something else.

Two final sections, as it were alternative endings, review the contemporary alternatives (psychoanalysis, personalism, existentialism) to Kantian ethics, or to ethics altogether; and also the doctrine of the intelligible world and the intelligible character, which Kant consigns to the world of the noumena or things-in-themselves. In the first of these concluding discussions, the heteronomy of ethics is again decisively staged in the debate on the execution of the Nazi war criminals:

> acquittal would be a barefaced injustice, but a just atonement would be infected by that very principle of brute force, in the resisting of which alone humanity consists. Benjamin anticipated this dialectic by his remark that the carrying out of the death penalty might be moral, but never its legitimation . (ND 282/286)

In the second, along with a systematic repudiation of the 'heroism' of moral or ethical beings as such, the Utopian motif is once again sounded:

If we dared to confer its true content on the Kantian X of the intelligible character (as that asserts itself against the total indeterminacy of the aporetic concept), that content would probably turn out to be the most historically advanced, ephemerally flaring and just as quickly extinguished consciousness in which the impulse to do right dwells. This is the concrete yet intermittent anticipation of sheer possibility, neither alien to human beings nor identical with them. (ND 292/297)

In the absence of this itself no more than intermittent anticipation of the future, Adorno notes, no ethics are really feasible in and of themselves: we either try to change the system altogether or 'try to live in such a way that we can believe ourselves to have been good animals' (294/299).

This conclusion to the freedom model, however, in fact brings us back to the *Minima Moralia* of the immediate postwar years, one of whose central programs consisted in the (well-nigh Kantian) disproof of the feasibility of ethics by way of their antinomies. A series of very small-scale 'models' rehearse, with remarkable economy and equally remarkable dialectical tact, the internal 'impossibility', in our time, of marriage (No. 10), convention (No. 16), a proper life with things (No. 18), and love (No. 110). Marriage, for example, is corrupted by its institutional association with interest, but in such a way that even if interest is absent, owing to the accident of the parties' personal worth, the institution ensures its own logic; even for those without interest, the rich and privileged, who 'are precisely those in whom the pursuit of interests has become second nature – they would not otherwise uphold privilege' (MM 29/31).

As for convention – that is, a certain prearranged artificial distance between social actors – it is in all domains (from art to ethics) a transitional phenomenon, since it must be freely chosen and thus distinct from traditional, externally imposed constraints and norms, while the impulse to liberate ourselves from those constraints necessarily ends up destroying convention itself. As for our relationship to possessions and the object world, it has been problematized by new monopoly forms of property and by an excess of consumer goods, and offers no conceivable mean:

> a loveless disregard for things ... necessarily turns against people too; and the antithesis, no sooner uttered, is an ideology for those wishing with a bad conscience to keep what they have. (MM 42/39)

Love, meanwhile, tries to negotiate its way between the requirement of asocial spontaneity and the fact that it is bourgeois society that itself defines it as what is not social:

'the love ... which, in the guise of unreflecting spontaneity and proud of its
alleged integrity, relies exclusively on what it takes to be the voice of the
heart, and runs away as soon as it no longer thinks it can hear that voice,
is in this supreme independence precisely the tool of society. (MM 227/172)

What each of these fables gives us to contemplate is not merely the contradictory nature of the phenomenon, nor only the impossibility of establishing a non-contradictory ethics to govern such an area, but above all the
explanatory link to a historical stage of the social order, whose peculiarities alone account for these impasses, just as, more proximately, that
history also illuminates the origin of the value we seek but no longer
find realizable within them. They are thus all designed to show that
one cannot 'get out' of ethics by means of ethics; that ethical dilemmas
are socially and politically, as a series of lapidary conclusions suggest:
'wrong life cannot be lived rightly' (MM 42/39); 'no emancipation without
that of society' (MM 228/173).

Yet the articulation between the ethical dilemma and the social contradiction is in all these cases expressed in terms of what we have called
the crisis of nominalism, that is to say, the tension in modern society
between the realm of the general and the realities of the particular. 'The
universal is revealed in divorce as the particular's mark of shame, because
the particular, marriage, is in this society unable to realize the true universal' (MM 31/32). Meanwhile, liberated convention, 'emancipated tact ...
meets with the difficulties that confront nominalism in all contexts' (MM
37/36).

A remarkable and extended paragraph, then (No. 16, 'Just hear, how
bad he was'), draws the larger conclusion by mediating on the ever more
gaping distance between events in the abstract, and in particular large-scale
collective catastrophes, and the micro-logical happenings of importance
to ourselves, in which alone forms of sympathy are capable of making
a spontaneous appearance. 'Wherever immediateness posits and
entrenches itself, the bad mediacy of society is insidiously inserted' (MM
240/182) – something, Adorno adds, which is 'not without relevance to
the doctrine of reason of state, the severance of morality from politics'
(MM 237/180). But as he goes on to show, it is also not without relevance
to questions of aesthetic representation (and indeed is further developed
in the central sections on cultural representation and in particular on
the problem of historical and political representation in our time: No.
94, 'All the world's not a stage'). Yet this diagnosis – which has its most
immediate affinities with Benjamin's analyses of the breakdown of traditional forms of experience – is here prolonged beyond aesthetic contradictions and the crisis of representation on into the more social and

philosophical issue of the various zones of autonomy and semi-autonomy in modern life.

What the paragraphs already cited demonstrate with respect to ethics – that even though to all appearances it is autonomous and demands its own specific thinking and intellectual solutions, the antinomies at work in those disprove the initial premiss of the autonomy of the ethical itself – now proves to be a lesson one can learn over a wider variety of areas, from culture (No. 22, 'Baby with the Bath Water') to folk art (No. 131, 'Wolf as Grandmother') and from politics to philosophy. Modernity, as we have since been taught by Luhmann,[45] consists in increasing differentiation, in the relative autonomization of a whole range of social levels and activities from one another: the 'liberation' of culture from the sacred, for example, or the 'liberation' of politics from ethics. Yet from another perspective it is precisely all these things together, in a coexistence and an internal overlap or identification, which make up secular society as such, that does not, however, exist empirically as an autonomous object and is not available for independent inspection. The semi-autonomy of its spheres and levels is therefore as false as it is true; the vocation of the dialectic lies in the attempt to coordinate and to respect this validity along with this sham ideological appearance. This it does, as these small-scale 'models' in *Minima Moralia* testify, by acknowledging the autonomy of a secular sphere such as ethics whose practical dependence on the social totality it then infers by way of the contradictions that result from the attempt to endow it with an autonomous theory. The heteronomy of the concept of freedom is thus merely a special case of this more general critique of the autonomy of social spheres and zones (and of philosophical subdisciplines).

Ten

It is in the Hegel 'model' of *Negative Dialectics* that Adorno's most sustained 'defense' of the Marxian view of history as such will now be staged. The characterization must, however, immediately be qualified in two ways, for as we have already made clear Adorno does not in that sense ever argue in any systematic or 'sustained' fashion. This chapter will therefore not yield his basic positions 'about' history; it will not in particular shed much light on his conception of late capitalism as an economic system; rather, essentially, it comments on the *concept* of history and on the *concept* of late capitalism (as these already exist in Hegel and in Marx and elsewhere), rotating these ideas into a variety of cross-lights, measuring their variable ideological implications, demonstrating the local paradoxes of their use (which involves both paralogisms and antinomies), and finally formulating a proposition as to the mode in which the impossible yet indispensable concept is to be handled.

This seemingly aleatory yet comprehensive treatment – it might be called something like a constellative critique – involves a systematic positioning of Hegel (his bias against the individual and the particular is tracked implacably, yet freshly, without any of the hoary remarks about the Prussian state which are normally obligatory), as of Marx, whose bias for necessity is rebuked, not least in the light of our own situation ('what corresponds to the impending catastrophe today would rather seem to be the hypothesis of some irrational catastrophe at the very beginnings of time' ND 317/323). Yet the chapter has an underlying momentum and, as it were, a thematic *telos* quite different from that of the other two models (had we not forbidden musical analogies, it would be tempting to evoke the formal differences between the various movements of a

sonata): what is argued in effect is the ultimate objectivity of that absent
and invisible totality which is history; this means in effect that we steer
a variable but steady course for the conception of natural history that
has already been promised.

The second feature of the chapter which will disorient those seeking
outright statements on Adorno's 'theory' of history has to do with its
terminology or, if you prefer, the philosophical thematics of the discussion, in which the obvious problems of those two contemporary *bêtes
noires*, the concept of totality and so-called 'linear history' (both associated
with Hegel in the popular mind), form by no means its central focus;
nor are these themes or terms exactly enlisted in the argument, which
turns centrally on that other great issue of the universal and the particular.
It will, then, be in the light of this very different problem that totality
and historical and narrative causality will be thought and rewritten.

Meanwhile, it will come as no surprise to find that, within such a
theoretical framework, virtually the central issue raised by the relationship between the universal and the particular – namely, the mechanisms
that block their coordination and turn their opposition into a generalized
crisis (existential, social, aesthetic, philosophical, all at once) – is what
Adorno will call positivism (along with its accompanying value, 'nominalism'). It seems to me desirable to understand this term in as generalized
a cultural and intellectual fashion as possible: in particular it scarcely
any longer, even in Adorno's period, designates positivistic philosophers
as such, but rather the more general positivistic tradition in the social
sciences. Meanwhile, our own situation, with respect both to philosophy
and to sociology, has been significantly modified in the twenty-some
years since the publication of *Negative Dialectics*, in at least its personnel
and its fashions, if not its deeper tendencies: we will miss the usefulness
of Adorno's diagnosis of positivism for us if we do not recognize that
the tendencies he designated under that name have if anything intensified
since his own death and are now, in the virtual eclipse of his own philosophy as well as of dialectical thinking generally, virtually hegemonic
and unchallenged – which means that they look somewhat different.

'Positivism' is, then, in general to be taken to mean a commitment
to empirical facts and worldly phenomena in which the abstract – interpretation fully as much as general ideas, larger synchronic collective units
fully as much as diachronic narratives or genealogies – is increasingly
constricted, when not systematically pursued and extirpated as a relic
and a survival of older traditional, 'metaphysical', or simply old-fashioned
and antiquated thoughts and categories. But this diagnosis – which can
be extended over a wide variety of contemporary social phenomena,
as has already been suggested – must be sharply distinguished from the

(undoubtedly affiliated) conservative or reactionary laments about the disappearance of values, moral and otherwise, the obsolescence of the Platonic (or even the Kantian) Ideas, the breakdown of collective identities (for them, the Nation, or 'Western civilization', are the relevant entities) or the decay of conventional forms, whether in culture or in manners.[46]

These complaints about modern times and its degenerescence are as closely related to those of Adorno – who can sometimes sound like this, to be sure, in some of the more querulous notations of *Minima Moralia* – as the first aristocratic and reactionary critiques of capitalism to the left and radical analyses of the new social order that appeared a few decades later. The basic structural difference lies in the status of the 'universal' in each: for the conservatives, that term exists already and has content (of the traditional type) – the crisis of what Adorno calls positivism can then simply be resolved by reinvigorating the older collective institutions and, as part of the same process, by tracking down the forces that weakened those values in the first place, by weeding out the agents and propagators of a bad 'nominalism' and antinomianism.

Adorno's conception of the relationship between universals and particulars is, however, not of this hierarchical or Aristotelian type, where the ones become subsumed beneath the others in the classical form of Order. For one thing, the universals are as affected as the particulars by the crisis; these are now 'bad' or baleful universals, and were perhaps always that: the point of the vocation of philosophy to reidentify their operations and to make them once again visible is not in order to celebrate them, but rather to do away with them altogether. Nor is the figure of subsumption – a sign and trace of violence and domination – the way in which to imagine even an ideal *Versöhnung* or 'reconciliation' between the universal and the particular. But the argument aims at anything but producing a concept of such subsumption or logical 'reconciliation'; rather, in the name of intensifying the tensions between universal and particular, of bringing everything that is incommensurable between them to consciousness as a historical contradiction and a form of suffering for the mind, it seeks to stigmatize the repression of that fundamental tension – as in the positivistic dismissal of universals as sheer metaphysical survivals, or Heidegger's mystique of the universal as such – as a form of violence, the domination of the universal over the particular, which, however, takes the placid form of the unproblematical appearance of everyday reality.

The 'excursus' thus begins very properly with the dissatisfaction of the particular – that is to say, in this initial context, the individual, the personal subject – with whatever too insistently wants to remind him or her of the invisible shaping power of history, which everywhere exceeds the existent or the isolated fact, just as it betrays its omnipresence in all the contents of my consciousness, from the social to my very language, none of which belongs to me. The birth of history is just that acknowledgement of the totality that it has become inescapable to notice within the inexplicable swerve of the individual objects and subjects towards some unknown end. This, which Hegel called the *Weltgeist* (notoriously, he glimpsed it once incarnated on horseback during the extraordinary opening of the brief Napoleonic era), is, however, endowed with this strange invisible power

> because society's law of motion has for thousands of years been abstracting from its individual subjects, degrading them to mere executors, mere partners in social wealth and social struggle, even though it is no less true, and equally real, that none of this would exist without them and their individual spontaneities. (ND 299/304)

This 'stored labor' of abstraction is the capital that endows History or Society with its real power, like Feuerbach's God or Durkheim's collectivity: the god of this world which, however, unlike Hegel, we must not worship. The individual waxes and wanes according to the vicissitudes of World Spirit: 'one is tempted to associate periods of ontological participation in world spirit, and some more substantial luck and happiness than the merely individual, with the unleashing of productive forces' (ND 301/306), while on the other hand Adorno is intent on inscribing the unruly stupidities of the human collective, as in committee meetings ('a reminder, in its invariance, of how little the power of the universal changes throughout history, of how much of it still remains prehistoric' [ND 303/308]). All this now suddenly hardens into the Law and the antinomies of the juridical and its institutions: universals, about which it is amusing to find Hegel assure us that 'conscience will consider [them] with good reason most hostile to itself' (ND 304/310) – something Kant seems to have felt to be an advantage. But law is only the obvious and visible of all the abstractions in which individuality is straitjacketed, a lesson which nevertheless, as was pointed out at the beginning of this chapter, no one wants to hear: 'to look the supreme power of the universal in the eye does all but unbearable psychological damage to the narcissism of all individuals and of a democratically organized society' (ND 306/312).

The next section briefly recalls the fundamental principle of Adorno's thought (as of Hegel and also Durkheim) – 'the positing of an equivalence between logical categories and those of society and history' (ND 311/317); while the one that follows returns to the historiographic question itself (is a universal history possible?), which it rightly associates with the prob-

lem of necessity. Yet the category of Necessity in our time awakens
the incompatible historiographic commitment to discontinuity, as the
form nominalism takes in the realm of individual and collective storytelling: death, or the generations, along with demography, break up what
would otherwise have the logic of a seamless web of acts and consequences.
To this all but universal contemporary visceral objection to so-called
Hegelian 'master narratives' (if they are not called 'linear history' instead),
Adorno assents, while characteristically also dissenting in his fashion,
since the worst is always certain: 'No universal history leads from the
wild animal to the genuinely human being, but one indubitably leads
from the slingshot to the megaton bomb' (ND 314/320). The question
he wishes to raise with Marx, however, is whether it would not be better
(politically better? more efficacious?) to think of history in terms of con-
tingence rather than necessity; to attribute the fall into violence, state
power, and capital to a catastrophe that need never have taken place
(this was Lévi-Strauss's position on the emergence of 'civilization') rather
than to see even this first invention of antagonism as 'inevitable'.

A number of painful quotations from Hegel follow, which abundantly
document the latter's enthusiastic commitment to the party of the universal but are also used to argue the peculiar detemporalization which this
partisanship brings to his conception of time, and finally the premature
suspension of his own dialectic to which it forces him. A new section,
however, shows us that of one offense, at least, Hegel is innocent: there
are no Hegelian master narratives! The story of *Geist* – impressive enough
as a superstructural dialectic – was unable to take on genuine historiographic content without a significant mediation, which doesn't work,
although it has its own dynamic and semi-autonomy – namely the *Volks-
geist*, or what we might now call the *national* principle fully as much
as that of this or that *people*. But acknowledgement of this contingent
fact which is the multiplicity of nations and peoples, and still seems
to be equal to itself two centuries later under late capitalism, introduces
a structural ambiguity into the plan for universal history: for if nations
are universals as far as those existential individuals who are their subjects
are concerned, they are themselves individuals with respect to some putative overall historical *telos*. They have too much individuality to be
reduced to stages or moments of anything; and not the least feature of
Adorno's analysis is the way he links, to this breakdown, the dysfunc-
tionality of the great Hegelian concept of the 'ruse of reason' (also known
as the 'ruse of history'):

Hegel saw through the fiction of individuality's historic being-for-itself as
through that of every other unmediated immediacy, and by means of the

theory of the ruse of reason (which dated back to Kant's philosophy of history), he classified the individual as an agent of the universal, a role in which it had served so well over the centuries. In doing so, and in keeping with a habitual thought structure that both schematizes and repeals his conception of the dialectic simultaneously, he conceived of the relationship between the world spirit and the individual, including their mediation, as an invariant: thereby even he, Hegel, lies in thrall to his own class, that has to eternalize its most dynamic categories in order to prevent itself from becoming conscious of the ultimate limits of its continuing existence as a class. Guiding Hegel is the picture of the individual in individualist society. This is an adequate one, since the principle of exchange society can realize itself only by way of the individuation of the contracting parties; and also because the *principium individuationis* is literally its very principle, that is to say its universal. It is inadequate because in the totality of functional relationships that requires the form of individuation as such, individuals have been relegated [by Hegel's theory] to mere executive organs of the universal. (ND 336/342)

In such a passage, the shadow of Marx falls across Hegel's nation states and a new principle of world history emerges, distinct from that of language or national culture, which is that universal 'spell' cast by exchange value over all individuality and across the frozen landscape of isolated particulars. As can be imagined, the vision of this magical spell inspires Adorno, in the scant pages to come, to his most eloquent formulations.

A short penultimate section returns to the subjectivity of the historical individual, tendentially reduced by modern psychology and psychoanalysis, which reflect the structural diminution of the contemporary psychic subject as so many symptoms but do not name the essential, or in other words happiness itself, about which we can only think negatively. This massive tendential movement, in which universal and particular alike have in the preceding pages both been equally, albeit asymmetrically, revealed as somehow objective in their truth and their reality, now at length flows into the long-awaited conclusion: on natural history itself.

Eleven

For the various background narratives in Adorno must all be completed by a more 'fundamental' but also a more enigmatic one. It has often been noticed[47] that the writer's early academic lecture on 'The Actuality of Philosophy' (1931) could in many ways be seen as a sketch for the whole program written up over thirty years later in *Negative Dialectics*; the other significant text from that same period – called 'The Idea of Natural History' – has received less attention and remains something of an enigma. One cannot say of it that it is finally worked out and given embodiment in the mature works; the last few pages of the 'Hegel' chapter in *Negative Dialectics*, to be sure, return explicitly to the theme of natural history, but merely repeat the motif, reawakening the suspicion, so often muttered by Adorno's critics and enemies, that he was constitutionally unable to transform the local flash and the local insight into the sustained duration of full-blown philosophical argument. But perhaps he was able to do something else with it.

Indeed, 'The Idea of Natural History' seems to me to offer a methodological proposal, rather than a set of theses on the matter. We are better placed today, after the extraordinary reinvigoration of evolutionary thought and the powerful rereading of Darwin himself by Stephen Jay Gould and others, to grasp what might be at stake in the strategic but unclearly motivated act of repositioning this problem at the heart of the Frankfurt School project of that period. Marx's own relationship to Darwin is well known; the abortive dedication of *Capital* Volume I (1867) to the author of *The Origin of Species* (1857) was a little more than a salute from one initiator of a Copernican revolution to another. It was meant to affirm the subsumption of human history – for the first time scientifically disengaged by historical materialism – under natural history – something henceforth indissociable from Darwin's own work and theorization. Marx's own position, he tells us in the Preface to *Capital*, 'grasps the development of the economic formation of society as a process of natural history'. Yet it was an ambiguous project; and the very concept of class struggle itself, in the somber atmosphere of Social Darwinism and the ideological leitmotiv of the survival of the fittest, is later on susceptible to all the lurid half-lights and tones of protofascism.

As for us today, looking back from the prosperous shelter of some postmodern far future, disquisitions on the prehistory of the planet and its flora and fauna surely have a strange and irrelevant unreality about them: only the old distinction between science and truth can perhaps account for a situation in which we bring assent and belief to the correctness of the facts of the matter – what our handbooks tell us about the Pleistocene, along with George Washington – without any real conviction. We remember the archeological as a sequence in Disney's *Fantasia*; and if the ancients 'believed' firmly in a host of legends and superstitions they must have also known to be preposterous, we 'disbelieve' equally in these facts and hypotheses, embodied in whole scientific disciplines which we know, *grosso modo* to be correct.[48] This is because our historical metabolism has undergone a serious mutation; the organs with which we register time can handle only smaller and smaller, and more and more immediate, empirical segments; the schematism of our transcendental historical imagination encompasses less and less material, and can process only stories short enough to be verifiable via television. The larger, more abstract thoughts – what is more totalizing than natural history, after all? – fall outside the apparatus; they may be true but are no longer representable – it is worse than old-fashioned to evoke them, rather a kind of social blunder is involved. Nor is this astonishing triumph of some ultimate positivism – which has in a few years conquered the whole earth, like Islam or Christianity – itself necessarily altogether positive for the ideological interests of the power structure; it would have been desirable to tap a few myths still, and Daniel Bell and others find themselves wishing that a little religion were still available. But it doesn't work any more; and even the new diseases cannot be made illicitly vivid to the imagination by the evocation of epic medieval or classical plagues. Still, the plague is, if anywhere, the place where human history and natural history most dramatically intersect, before the naked eye.

For there is a nightmare of natural history that is even grislier than that of the human one; and it is this that the postmodern mind has been able to repress fairly successfully (save for biological death itself) for reasons that are scarcely mysterious: what better way to avoid being reminded of the nightmare of nature than to abolish nature altogether? Yet a glimpse into the interstices that not merely open to view the pecking order of all living species, a hideous eternity of domination and hierarchy designed at least to leave its subjects alive, but also and finally the violence of nature itself, organisms obliged to eat their whole waking life long, and to eat each other (in Adorno's most frequent characterization of it) – this dizzying perspective brings with it a nausea more fundamental than the sight of the malice with which humans attempt to culturalize their own internecine slaughter. Animals, which still live here and there among us, sometimes give us some of this to see; and it has not often been noticed that, if virtually alone among the Western Marxists the Frankfurt School had a meditation on the domination of Nature and can be counted among the philosophical ancestors of the ecology movement, it also made its contribution to animal rights. The long note on 'Man and Animal' appended to *Dialectic of Enlightenment*, and perhaps attributable to Horkheimer, is surely one of central 'constellations' of that work (although Adorno included other noteworthy reflections on animals in *Minima Moralia*:

> every animal suggests some crushing misfortune that took place in primeval times ...: The masses, having been forced to toe the same line, are becoming so oblivious of the transformation they are undergoing ... that they no longer need to have it symbolically displayed. Now and again, if we scan the trivial news-items on the second and third pages of a newspaper – the front page is crammed with men's frightful deeds of glory – we may come across a few lines about a circus fire or poisoned elephants. ... Goethe's aversion to apes also indicated the limits of his humanitarianism. ... Nature herself is neither good, as the ancients believed, nor noble as the latter-day Romantics would have it. As a model and goal it implies the spirit of opposition, deceit, and bestiality. (DA 221/247, 224/251, 225/253, 227/254)

Unsurprisingly, this set piece also modulates through the 'woman question' and is also a rare but characteristic specimen of Frankfurt School proto-feminism, suggesting that gender also and preeminently marks the spot where human and natural histories bewilderingly intersect, and reminding us of the high stakes in their disentanglement.

In this form, however, natural history remains a 'vision' of nature, or in other words a *Weltanschauung* – which is to say an ideology and an anthropology – that ranges itself somewhere in between Hobbes and Robert Ardrey or sociobiology; the competing 'vision' – that of Rousseau, say – is no less aesthetic than its alternative; nor does it matter very much that the Frankfurt School can in some respects be said to combine

BALEFUL ENCHANTMENTS OF THE CONCEPT   97

both, in their call for a return to nature without domination at the
end of what Marx called 'prehistory'. But we have learned to distinguish
the very status and structure of such 'visions of the world' – in whose
representations as it were, the imagining subject is personally involved
– from that rarer and very different thing associated with science, which
seems to give us a discourse without a subject and a way of thinking
phenomena such as historical succession or diachronic change which does
not involve representation as such. This is indeed, I take it, what the
debate staged by the Althusserians around Marx's early writings aimed
to bring out: to stigmatize these last as 'humanist' was in effect to characterize them as ideological and to underscore the way in which the vision
of human nature and its potentialities, as well as of the possibilities of
alienation, remained an anthropological one. This did not mean, I also
take it, that such an ideological vision of human nature was necessarily
wrong (let alone unattractive); merely that as discourse it functioned
on the same level as the competing 'visions' (Stirner's existentialism,
the pessimism of Schopenhauer, with those of Hobbes and Rousseau
still vividly alive in the background). *Capital*, which was not a representation as such and made no place for the subject – the intoxicated spectator,
witness and solipsistic but contemplative victim of the grand metaphysical
spectacle – constituted, then, a kind of discourse as different from this
one of the early Marx as Darwin himself from Social Darwinism.

Yet is not any return to natural history, any attempt to recover the
'natural' basis of and perspective on human history, threatened with
just such a regression into this or that primal 'vision of the world'?
If we wish to eschew such pictures, would it not be preferable, with
Vico, to separate human history from natural history, to confine ourselves
to the human arena, the space of human praxis, and let Nature 'be in
its being'? But this alternative is what the Frankfurt School seems to
have felt to be profoundly idealistic, in its omission of biology and death,
of the brute *fact* of the generations (history has no trouble accounting
for their *content*), and finally of what Sartre called the contingent metaphysical fact of scarcity itself, the struggle for life against Nature (as the
Ur-datum on which that profoundly historical thing which is production
and the modes of production is founded). But would this supplement
of nature and biology do any more for us than add some additional
volumes on the history of protein and calorie intake, on the archaic
susceptibility to microbes, or the comparative erg-power of the male
and female musculatures throughout the ages?

The originality of Adorno's proposal is, then, to have cut across these
alternatives in an unexpected way, implying that we will not succeed
in repressing the metaphysical impulse, but that it would be undesirable

to achieve complete success in doing so anyhow, since that would clearly spell the triumph of positivism and empiricism as such (something to which the last chapter of *Negative Dialectics* returns). The unstable coexistence of metaphysics and its dissolution in Kant is an admirable, but unusable analogy. Meanwhile, we will not stop doing either social or natural history (that is, the 'human sciences' and the natural sciences) but, no matter what our acknowledgement of the call to unify them, will continue to alternate them only. Under these circumstances, commitment to the idea of natural history suggests this provisional solution:

> If the question of the relationship of nature and history is to be seriously posed, it can hold out the prospect of an answer only if we succeed in grasping historical being in its most extreme historical determination, that is to say, there where it is most historical, as a form of natural being, or if we succeed in grasping Nature where it persists most deeply within itself as nature, as on the contrary a form of historical being.[49] (ND 353/359)

The dualism, in other words, cannot be undone by the taking of a thought or by frontal assault – such dualisms are in any case themselves the mark and scar of profound historical developments and contradictions – but its poles may be allowed dialectically to short-circuit one another. Thus the Marxian conception of modes of production acquires the uncanny half-light of a different dimension altogether when we inspect its findings, not merely through the telescope of Lévi-Strauss's astronomer-anthropologist, but above all through the disincarnated eyes of Olaf Stapledon's space traveller in *Star Maker*, moving from galaxy to galaxy and from civilization to civilization of beings increasingly different from us biologically: from hominoids to 'nautiloids', symbiotic partner existences, crab-like beings and sentient vegetal life. But when the view from the epicycle of Mercury begins to strengthen fatalism, as in some increased conviction about the limitations placed on social life and development by biological contingencies, then one must roll this whole mental operation over and turn even this naturalization of history inside out by the defamiliarization of Nature itself as a kind of social being.

At that point Darwinian reality, unmodified, shrinks to the intellectual acts of Darwin himself and the social preconditions of his 'discoveries' in the English capitalism of the early nineteenth century: what is 'historical' about Nature now is then suddenly our own capacity to discover or to represent it as social beings, and to project it out beyond the human social world. (That this kind of transformation of nature [or scientific discovery] into a social fact is not 'relativistic', exactly, that social determinations can somehow be thought together in the mind with scientific 'truth', is one of the crucial paradoxes rehearsed by the contemporary history, sociology and philosophy of science.)

What is involved here is a reciprocal defamiliarization of the two incommensurable poles of the dualism of Nature and History, but clearly enough – and on Adorno's own formulation – this must be a perpetual process in which neither term ever comes to rest, any more than any ultimate synthesis emerges. The scanty references to Lukács's early notion of society as a 'second nature' (in *The Theory of the Novel*) do not, however, tell us very much about what such a process might look like; until it ultimately dawns on us that *Dialectic of Enlightenment* is itself its representation and its working out, an insight that would seem considerably to clarify that peculiar and idiosyncratic text. Indeed, many of us have worried at great length over what now looks like a false problem: namely the question of whether the book is to be thought of as espousing 'essentially' Nietzschean positions, or Marxian ones, or in fact Weberian ideas and principles. Perhaps, we sometimes speculated, it may be a synthesis of all of those (just as Lukács earlier performed, in the concept of reification, the supreme synthesis between a certain Marx and a certain Weber); but such a hypothesis then raised the embarrassing supplementary theoretical question of how you would go about verifying the 'success' of the new chemical combination, or on the contrary its failure to cohere.

For the book begins with fear and vulnerability[50] in the face of what is yet not even nature: but the temporality of this beginning – which ought to be mythic in the grand sense (as in Hobbes or Rousseau) and would then reconfirm the frequent and frequently bewildered characterization of *Dialectic of Enlightenment* as the staging of a kind of myth in its own right – is at once rectified and booby-trapped by a dialectical operation now most commonly associated with poststructural synchronics (especially since Althusser seems to have coined the most apt expression for it – the 'always-already'). Adorno and Horkheimer specify, indeed, that it is rather the process by which fear and vulnerability are mastered that brings temporal succession into being in first place, along with historical *telos*.

In this sense, the present – the most up-to-date form of the dialectic of enlightenment – produces the past, and more specifically that immediate past of its own present which is now stigmatized as archaic, old-fashioned, mythic, superstitious, obsolete or simply 'natural'; but this is true as far back into the past as we can see or imagine, and indeed the temporal dialectic proposed here might better be analogized in terms of optics, where with every shift in visual attention a new lateral field establishes itself, forever out of reach. Whether this is inconsistent with the Marxian vision of modes of production, and in particular with that of tribal society or primitive communism – indeed, whether the Marxian conception itself implies nostalgia for some golden age (on the order of the tradition of Rousseau, as for example in Sahlins's extraordinary 'First Affluent Society'[51]) – remains to be seen.

In any case, it should be noted that the peculiar originality of Adorno's and Horkheimer's conception of a 'dialectic of enlightenment' is that it excludes any beginning or first term, and specifically describes 'enlightenment' as an 'always-already' process whose structure lies very precisely in its generation of the illusion that what preceded it (which was also a form of enlightenment) was that 'original' moment of myth, the archaic union with nature, which it is the vocation of enlightenment 'proper' to annul. If it is a matter of telling a historical story, therefore, we must read Adorno and Horkheimer as positing a narrative without a beginning in which the 'fall', or dissociation, is always there already; if, however, we decide to reread their book as a diagnosis of the peculiarities and the structural limits and pathologies of historical vision or narrative itself, then we may conclude, in a somewhat different fashion, that the strange after-image of 'primal unity' always seems to be projected after the fact onto whatever present the historical eye fixes, as its 'inevitable' past, which vanishes without a trace when frontal vision is in turn displaced onto it.

The most dramatic paradox by way of which this 'dialectic' is rehearsed is, however, appropriately enough the discussion of myth itself, along with the anthropological paraphernalia of ritual and shamanistic techniques (which Adorno and Horkheimer probably found in Frazer). For these are also 'enlightenment': the shaman's aim and function – like that of philosophers and scientists in later history – remains that of controlling nature (encouraging fertility, bringing rain, propitiating the gods), and the techniques of the sacred must also be supposed to have a history that corresponds to the more general dialectic of enlightenment, in so far as the more efficient religions cancel out the more primitive and archaic ones, and the very coming into being of rites and ceremonies – let alone their codification and refinement – is itself enlightenment 'progress'. This serves as a piquant twist on traditional enlightenment narratives (the eighteenth century imagined itself to be the scourge of residual traces of the sacred and of superstition in general); but the rationale for subsuming witchdoctors under Western science and reason is given in the very structure of the rituals themselves, as we shall see shortly.

As for the description of this perpetual present of control and domination – of self-protection and self-preservation – it is of course immediately identified as Reason (but as what Hegel would call *Verstand* rather than *Vernunft*, and what Sartre would call analytic rather than dialectical reason) and can clearly be identified in its later and more contemporary stages as what will more generally and culturally be stigmatized as positivism (among other things, as a program and a set of mental operations, it must radically eschew self-consciousness [DA 8/4]). But in order to surprise and observe the operation of this single, totalizing, tendentially unified process at work in a variety of social materials and historical developments (each of which can then stand, succinctly and narratively formulated, as its allegory) it is the identity of the process throughout all its forms, rather than its identification with any one of them, that Adorno and Horkheimer wish to stress in their basic presentation ('The Concept of Enlightenment'): a number of the more properly philosophical versions of these same themes then recur in *Negative Dialectics*, but the contexts are more varied here, so that the two texts complete each other: the former by its articulation of the argument, the latter by its demonstration of a more existential, social and historical relevance. Both begin, however, with the matter of identity and equivalence (at which point ritual is itself unmasked as a process of mimetic substitution homologous to what will happen at later stages of scientific thought); and this first account of what Adorno will later call the magic spell [*der Bann*] logically enough leads on into its effects in necessity and time, and above all in *repetition* as a tendential structure of human life and thought (and of Benjaminian experience) under achieved Enlightenment and its domination of nature.

That this is to be grasped subjectively as well as objectively the authors stress again and again, not least by way of the image of Odysseus, whose 'resourcefulness' presupposes his equally extraordinary self-control. For the domination of the self is simultaneous with the domination of external nature; even the most modest control over threatening forces in the outside world presupposes all the initial forms of psychic repression (whose inextricable relationship to 'civilization' Freud posited in *Civilization and its Discontents*): these are then also to be numbered among the forms and achievements of Enlightenment, and can be observed, recapitulated, in children's discipline and pedagogy (or in that of the national cultures themselves, as in Norbert Elias's histories). But it will be most appropriate to grasp this repression, this domination of inner nature (which may also, with Lacan, be called the construction of the subject) in a somewhat different way as the transformation of the subject into an instrument and a weapon, a means. What remains of it as an end in itself (it would be better to think of this as the great Utopia of aimless floating and gazing at the sky - as in MM, '*Sur l'eau*', 155 - rather than the already highly repressed and disciplined Kantian imperative) is then little more than its continuing existence, or in other words self-preservation - always,

in Adorno, the mark of violence, whose absence, if it were possible or
even conceivable, would at once constitute Utopia (the world 'almost
unchanged', as he liked to say, following Benjamin on the Talmudic
conception of the world transfigured by Messiah).[52]

Speculation on the consequences of just such a general removal of the
need for a survival instinct leads us well beyond the bounds of Adorno's
social life-world and class style (or our own), and into a Utopia of misfits
and oddballs, in which the constraints for uniformization and conformity
have been removed, and human beings grow wild like plants in a state
of nature: not the beings of Thomas More, in whom sociality has been
implanted by way of the miracle of the utopian text, but rather those
of the opening of Altman's *Popeye*, who, no longer fettered by the constraints of a now oppressive sociality, blossom into the neurotics, compul-
sives, obsessives, paranoids, and schizophrenics whom our society
considers sick but who, in a world of true freedom, may make up the
flora and the fauna of 'human nature' itself.

Now three great dimensions of 'civilization' are rewritten in terms
of the dialectic of Enlightenment, as tendential histories: language, thinking and philosophy, and society and the division of labor. The 'history'
of language (which includes art within itself) runs a paradigmatic course
between the sacred name and nominalism, the ultimate desacralization
of language under positivism, which ends up in the literal and the scientific. The process is registered at an overlapping, but somewhat later
stage when we rewrite it in terms of the the history of abstract thinking,
which finds its ultimate forms in positivism and mathematics. With the
division of labor, however, and the culmination in capitalism of the processes at work in the various modes of production, society becomes itself
that totality and that Fate which was once attributed to its opposite
number, Nature; and at this point the paradoxicality of the authors'
formulations recapitulate the most bewildering chiasmatic pronounce-
ments of Rousseau's Second Discourse: 'the enforced power of the system
over men grows with every step that takes it out of the power of nature'
(DA 38/38).

Even Rousseau, however, proposed not some impossible return to a
state of nature (which Horkheimer and Adorno could posit even less),
but rather the far more imperfect Social Contract: here, the breaking
of the magic spell of enlightenment is still envisioned in the celebration
of the dialectic ('determinate negation'/ DA 23/24); the evocation of that
more profoundly Marcusean retrieval called anamnesis (DA 39/40); and
finally, the forthright call for 'true revolutionary praxis' (DA 40/41),
beyond which some Utopia of the non-repressive and the non-coercive
might lie.

What must also be said about the multiple paths and trends of this dense chapter is that, taking as its theme equivalence, it reduces everything to equivalence; identifying the achievements of enlightenment as so many forms of repetition, it subjects its varied raw materials to a single implacable logic that makes all human history into repetition as such. The dominant form taken here by the descriptions of this repetitive process does not yet deploy the code of identity we have found at work in *Negative Dialectics*; rather, it would seem plausible to identify it as the great Weberian movement of the effacement of ends by means, which he called rationalization and the present authors instrumental reason. To be sure, Weber's selected historiographic exhibits of this process (from the sociology of religion to the history of the legal system)[53] afford nothing quite so grandiose as the '*Odyssey*' commentary here, where Odysseus's adventures become allegories of the stages of 'civilization' as they encounter and repress monsters and marvels that are reminders of so many more archaic modes of production as well as markers for deeper, more instinctive layers of the psyche that Reason must thrust further down as it emerges from it.

That the social consequences of such repression in rage, *ressentiment*, and cultural envy should then be laid in place in the 'Anti-Semitism' chapter is altogether logical; while the Enlightenment reduction of ethics itself to an instrumental and sometimes inhuman remnant (described in the 'Kant/Sade' chapter) is perhaps less inconsistent with Weber's own program, although it would certainly have surprised him (the impossible contradiction in contemporary ethics is then rehearsed in a different way, as we have seen, in *Minima Moralia*). Still, these chapters also confirm the feeling of an essentially Weberian thesis, characterized by the implacably repetitive character of the tendential enlargement of enlightenment itself, as well as by the essentially political terms – of domination, violence, and power – in which the tendency is described. This sense of the Weberian elective affinity can only intensify the question about its compatibility with a Marxian view of history.

Before that question is addressed, however, two features of the 'vision of history' outlined in *Dialectic of Enlightenment* must be addressed, which seem to complicate the picture we have given of a simple essentially Weberian mechanism replicating itself over and over again (at higher levels of sophistication) throughout the historical record. These are the intervention of the concept of 'mimesis', whose relationship to 'enlightenment' is not initially obvious; and the notorious analysis of the so-called Culture Industry, whose function here is not so clear, even though its bleakness and pessimism are consonant with the rest. (As for the addenda, they tend to confirm the repetitive structure of the analysis, which can thus be stopped anywhere, or go on forever; *Minima Moralia* can then in that sense be taken as the sequel, and the sign of the feeling that even so, not everything has been said.)

What is most enigmatic about 'mimesis' is not the content but rather the status of this concept, about which – alluded to everywhere in *Dialectic of Enlightenment* (as though we already knew what it was) – we are then in later works referred back to this volume as to its full-dress official philosophical presentation. The philosophical traditions of antiquity are mainly useful to mark conceptual differences: Platonic or Aristotelian imitation, in particular, is conceived as a handicraft potentially resulting in a product,[54] something quite distinct from the sheer activity of mimesis for Adorno, which is bounded on the one side by sheer mimicry and on the other by Frazer's concept of 'sympathetic magic' (and in particular the imitative variety, based on metaphor, as opposed to the metonymic forms of homeopathic or 'contagious' magic, to which Adorno seems relatively more indifferent). Although the (in this form relatively more recent) concept of narrative plays no formal part in Adorno's thinking, we have already seen that a deep affinity can be established between what we call narrative and what he reserves the word mimesis for. 'Mimesis' thus displaces metaphor as a fundamental category of Adorno's thought, and can be said often to function as a more adequate substitute for the primal relationship of subject and object (so often reified in post-Hegelian usage): 'mimesis' forestalls dualistic thinking by naming the dualism as such and as an operation (just as the notion of 'instrumentalization' seemed to do for the Weberian means/ends dialectic).

What it seems to superimpose, however, by way of an excess of implication, is in general the anthropological – namely, the sense everywhere of mimesis as an archaic activity, and one that at least implicitly risks being attributed to some conception of human nature (implications never present in the concept of metaphor as such, or in the abstract subject-object relationship). This opens up depth and perspective when the concept is deployed, a historical space demanding the proto-narrative of a genesis or a genealogy; but it also strengthens the 'always-already' appearance of this peculiar word, which behaves as though we knew it already, and as though it had come from some other place in which its credentials were already firmly established (it would be ironic if Adorno's lifelong principled hostility to definitions – a cause in which he rightly enlists the authority of Kant and Hegel – were mainly motivated by the will to evade this particular definition in advance).

But the role of mimesis in *Dialectic of Enlightenment* is a structurally peculiar one, since this is above all the point on which the issue of the continuity or discontinuity of the history of so-called Western reason is played out. The notorious account of Odysseus as the 'prototype of the bourgeois individual' (DA 42/43) is a mere impertinence which raises only the vaguest forebodings about some slippage between class and economic materials and interpretations in Frankfurt School thought in general; the postclassical reappropriation of Odysseus as a culture hero would be enough to justify it. But most modern historiographic traditions (from idealist histories of ideas to Marxist ones) have insisted with sufficient determination on the structural specificity of Western science – which is to say, of capitalism – for the larger impertinence of *Dialectic of Enlightenment* – the genealogy of enlightenment in prehistorical times, the assimilation of scientists to shamans and animists – to require some further justification.

Is human history, in other words, to be seen as one enormous continuity – in which case what would seem to hold it together is essentially the omnipresence of power, in the form of violence and domination: that is, essentially, the *political* – or does it know some fundamental break or leap or mutation with the emergence of a purely *economic* and desacralized system in that 'minor promontory of Asia' that is Europe, a break also characterized by the emergence of science as the first henceforth purely secular form of human thought? The second alternative, however, which can scarcely posit an absolute break, demands the invention of a dialectic, in which the same term remains but is modified, as it secures the modulation from the first moment to the second (indeed, in my opinion, the modern dialectic arose from the problem of conceptualizing this social and historical double standard in the eighteenth and early nineteenth centuries).

In this case, it is very precisely the concept of mimesis which will afford this dialectical possibility: the turn of so-called Western science will now be seen as a result of the anti-mimetic taboo and of anti-mimetic regression – that is to say, the passage from a perceptual 'science' based on the senses and on quality to notations and analysis based on geometry and on mathematics. But this description, which then displaces the specificity of 'science' onto its representation and its languages, thereby allows the continuity between science and ritual – as forms of domination – to remain intact. It is in any case probably more owing to psychoanalysis than to Hegel or Marx that we are today so willing to grant dialectical continuity to the same impulse and what represses it, and to see the mimetic impulse and the anti-mimetic taboo as a single phenomenon (with contrary effects); while the psychoanalytic construction can then authorize Adorno to develop the principle further (in the Anti-Semitism chapter) and to evoke a 'return of the repressed' of this same repressed mimetic impulse. Finally, we may observe an unusual 'antithetical sense of primal words' at work in his own ambivalence about the taboo, which in the spirit of any number of post-Weberian critiques of rationality, is clearly hostile, when it designates science, but becomes strangely positive and mystical when it alters just slightly to admit the 'taboo on graven images' that justifies our reluctance to describe Utopia, or even to mention happiness itself.

The second apparent hitch in the continuous history of domination afforded by *Dialectic of Enlightenment* presents itself on the occasion of the 'Culture Industry'; that chapter seems more relevant from the American-notebooks perspective than it does from that of a general critique of Western science (or of positivism). The American perspective is, however, also that of the theory of 'monopoly' of 'state' capitalism (developed by Pollock and Grossman), for it is essentially that which secures their convergence theory of the similarities between the United States of the New Deal and Hollywood, and Nazi Germany. Such comparisons, which are frequent throughout the chapter, will arouse less pious indignation if it is understood that what is meant – besides the similarities between American repressive conformism and the rapid stifling of opposition under Hitler – is what most authorities acknowledge anyhow: namely, the originality of the nascent media technology throughout this period, as it is pioneered above all in the USA and Germany and has significant impact on their respective public spheres.[55]

Minima Moralia is then what this critique of the USA looks like when the 'convergence' hypothesis is removed, and a more conventional European background perspective is restored: it now stages a unique counterpoint, as it were, between Proust and Hollywood, between social and cultural observations nourished by the twenties and by the persistence of an older aristocratic European tradition, and those that complain about the raw and brash materialism of American life (particularly as seen through the eyes of the *émigrés*). That contrast also turns on economics, but of a rather less theoretical type: 'in Europe the pre-bourgeois past survives in the shame felt at being paid for personal services or favours' (MM 259/195). This says it all, from immediate reactions to the Americans and their culture as a 'people without dignity' all the way to the horror of wage labor (particularly for intellectuals) and at length to the well-nigh metaphysical theme of self-preservation itself, as a doom laid upon the human race. In this context the occasional evaluation of the anti-capitalism of Marxists like Adorno as a set of mandarin rather than working-class attitudes takes on some plausibility.

But that is not particularly the perspective of the 'Culture Industry' chapter, which rarely stresses the economic as such, and in which working class people do appear as gullible victims ('the slow-witted, who are the ones who suffer for everything anyhow' [DA 125/139]). This chapter can be clarified, I feel, and some of the more aimless polemics about it dispersed, by the realization that it does not involve a theory of culture at all, in any sense this word has come to have for us at least since Raymond Williams. But even in the anthropologists, and in Benjamin as well, culture is a realm of protection and adaptation in which the infrastructural asperities of nature or of the economic system are mediated, rationalized, palliated and sometimes transfigured in utopian or anticipatory fashion: culture, in Benjamin, wards off the kaleidoscopic shocks of the nineteenth-century urban environment; it is evidently enough a breeding ground for false consciousness, but also for demands in which embellishment and luxury symbolically express the will to achieve some freedom beyond sheer necessity.

It is important to see that 'culture' means none of these things in Adorno; the 'Culture Industry' chapter has to do with individual works or signatures – from Toscanini to Victor Mature and Betty Grable; it also has very much to do with individual subjectivity and its tendential reduction and subsumption; but it does not include a concept of culture as a specific zone or structure of the social. This is why it is a mistake to suppose that Adorno's 'elitist' critiques of the 'Culture Industry' in any way define his attitude or position towards 'mass culture', grasped now not as a group of commercial products but as a realm of social life: irrespective of the enormous changes and mutations undergone by 'mass culture' since wartime Hollywood and on into postmodernism, Adorno does not conceive of culture as a realm of social life in the first place; and it is rather this, indeed, which needs to be objected to in his theory (unless – the other way round – the contemporary concept of culture is itself to be grasped as a reflex of the tremendous expansion of the cultural sphere and the acculturation of daily life since the 1960s).

But if the false problem of Adorno's 'theory' of culture is removed, then it becomes clear how the chapter fits into the plan of *Dialectic of Enlightenment* as a whole: it pursues the implacable expansion and penetration of 'enlightenment' (or of 'positivism', if you prefer another version) into the mind itself, into individual subjectivity, in modern times. The irony and impertinence of the Kant reference (the Culture Industry has developed a streamlined form of Kantian schematism for its products [DA 112/124]) draws its density from the privileged position of aesthetics in the period of classical German idealism, and at the beginnings of capitalism: a position based not on some canon of masterpieces but rather on the space it still offered for the exercise of a non-alienated subjectivity that was neither business nor science, neither morality nor pure reason. This enclave is what the Culture Industry now begins to colonize, a kind of last frontier and final unexplored territory for the dialectic of Enlightenment. Degraded individual works of 'art' are therefore not here evaluated for purely aesthetic reasons, from some rigid 'standard' of high art (we will see in our examination of *Aesthetic Theory* that that 'standard' excludes the products of the Culture Industry altogether); rather, they have become so many symptoms of the degradation of subjectivity.

Apart from that, the Culture Industry, as Adorno and Horkheimer see it, is not art or culture but rather business as such, and indeed a place in which the tendential convergence between monopoly and instrumentalization can be observed more clearly than in other kinds of commodity exchange. Theoretically, indeed, this chapter has the additional significance and interest of an experimental combination of two kinds of analysis often confused with each other but less compatible than is ordinarily supposed: commodification and instrumentalization. The final pages, dealing with radio, raise the paradoxical problem of what to do with a commodity which is free: are these offerings (but by extension television images as well) thereby less commodities or more (and are there degrees in commodity structure)? The same pages, however, also stage the climax of the narrative of language and its dissolution, begun in the first, enlightenment chapter: for the first magical name does not come to rest in the reifications of scientific language, but rather here, with Hitler and the American radio industry, in the final form of a language become sheer brand name.

We must now try to close this enormous parenthesis, which enumerated the peculiarities of *Dialectic of Enlightenment* in order to reposition this influential text within Adorno's work as a whole. All the features described above become clarified if we now grasp this book in terms of Adorno's thesis on the alternation of social and natural history, where it clearly becomes the natural-history variant of a more Marxian social history. The two alternatives are now to be thought of as immense rewriting programs, neither of which contradicts each other, but which ceaselessly recode the findings of each in an incompatible language. The requirement for an alternation between these languages arises from an acknowledgement that no synthesis between them is today conceivable, and also that, as has already been observed, either one in isolation is misleading. It is therefore unnecessary to suppose that because *Dialectic of Enlightenment* mobilizes non-Marxist forms of explanation, it thereby constitutes a move beyond Marxism or a renunciation of the Frankfurt School's essentially Marxist programs of the 1930s (an interpretation which makes it difficult to account either for Adorno's later work, particularly in *Negative Dialectics*, or for the uses the radical student movement made of this early text along with its predecessors).[56]

For the perspective of natural history, which seems to be a theoretical alternative based on other kinds of explanations, is in fact rather a kind of *defamiliarization*, a view of the same phenomena (including their explanations) as it were from the epicycle of Mercury.

> Mind arose out of existence, as an organ for keeping alive. In reflecting existence, however, it becomes at the same time something else. The existent negates itself as thought upon itself. Such negation is the mind's element. To attribute to it positive existence, even of a higher order, would be to deliver it up to what it opposes. (MM 328/243)

This essentially anthropological perspective on consciousness clearly feigns a view from the outside, from the Martian observer; and subsumes any concrete historical content of the mind at whatever stage it has been observed in. Within any one of those stages, a certain technological level of consciousness goes on 'reflecting' the division of labor, solving 'such problems as the evolution of the mode of production has posed', generating a certain intellectual class, throwing out a subsidiary web of ideology whose functions are consistent with the class arrangements in question. The anthropological perspective has little to say in the analysis of this concrete moment, little to add to the findings of a more properly socioeconomic theory; it intervenes when we are tempted to eternalize the idealist perspective on the object – mind or consciousness: a perspective required provisionally for its local analysis, but one which must then be redissolved into the larger materialist vision of natural science before it begins to imply the independent or autonomous existence of 'entities' – such as mind or culture, or indeed politics or economics themselves – which are rather to be considered moments in a dialectical totality. Natural history thus intervenes at those moments of methodological contradiction we have already examined, in which the 'critique of culture' or the 'sociology of ideas' (or, in another way, ethics as such) prove impossible to establish as separate non-contradictory disciplines.

But of course the anthropological perspective itself – such as the resonance of the notion of 'mimesis' – implies a different code or vocabulary from the socioeconomic, and tends to stress domination rather than production. These are the resonances of *Dialectic of Enlightenment* that have often been taken by its readers to reflect Nietzschean or Weberian, often even Social Darwinistic, presuppositions. According to our hypothesis here, however, which is essentially that of a rewriting strategy, there is nothing particularly exclusive in the choice to read a particular mode of production as a way of dominating nature, provided this new description serves as a reminder of natural history rather than a new theory in its own right: following Adorno's methodological rule, then, 'domination' must itself next be unmasked as an essentially social and historical concept, and the contents of this whole historiographic line must then be reversed and rewritten again in social terms. But if nature is absolutized as a first or fundamental code, then it decays into ideology even more rapidly than do the more obviously produced and class-bound ideologies of history, and is dismissed rudely in the next chapter, 'even where it takes itself for the bedrock of Being, as the projection of the wretched cultural wish that in all change things must stay the same' (ND 361/368). Thus we rejoin the basic differentiation with which we began, a dialectic of history in which even the laws of its change are modified at each stage, and that other kind of 'dialectic' – called, of enlightenment – in which repetition is a monotonous law of its seeming enlargement over time. But how can we tell if this repetition is a doom or an anxiety that feeds a wish-fulfillment?

Indeed, at a time when the relationship of ecological to socialist politics is very much on the agenda practically, and when also within Marxism the question of nature (and of natural science) has been significantly raised again in a variety of ways (after the relative disinterest of most of so-called Western Marxism in science), this new dialectical double-standard and alternating discursive relationship suggested by Adorno not merely problematizes conventional views of the Frankfurt School as hostile to science (a critique of reason, but also a call to natural history!) but also suggests a new and suggestive strategy and paradigm.

The ultimate terms of any vision of history in the light of nature are, however, those of the ceaseless stream of the generations themselves, the perpetual transformation of the river of organisms into which one never steps twice, the dizzying perspective of Kafka's *Josephine the Mouse-Singer*, and the omnipresence of ephemerality and death – what is signified by the untranslatable German word *Vergängnis*, with which indeed this section on natural history, and the entire chapter on Hegel's World Spirit, significantly concludes. But such a language, which reduces the dust of human events and actions to the swarm of the non-human, would deem to lead us out of history altogether, whether natural or social, into the realm of metaphysics itself. It is indeed to that realm that Adorno now turns in the concluding 'model' of *Negative Dialectics*.

Twelve

Adorno's final movement comes closest to a kind of 'literary' text – in other words, one which has to be read thematically rather than philosophically – with the result that each reading will be just 'slightly distinct' from the rest. What accounts for this imperceptible difference is no doubt the content of the chapter, which stages incompatible positions on 'metaphysics' – positions that are untenable and unavoidable all at once, and inconsistent with one another; the resultant rhythm is thus quite different from the rotation of the concept itself in the 'Freedom' chapter, in which differences were internally generated by the object of study; or the momentum towards natural history we observed in the chapter on world spirit. Yet even Kant's three transcendental ideas turned out to project very different kinds of internal dysfunction: the paralogisms were not at all the same as the antinomies, while the impossibility of the ontological proof ended up a very different matter from either. We must not therefore approach this final model with the expectation of drawing the same kinds of conclusions or walking away with the same kinds of results in hand: those were in any case distinct in the earlier two models – the structural doctrine of the radical impurity or heteronomy of ethics constituting something more fundamentally substantive than the methodological call for an alternation between social and natural history.

The 'Metaphysics' chapter, however, does seem to involve Adorno's own paralogisms: death is everywhere and omnipresent, perhaps above all in this late capitalist society after Auschwitz; but on the other hand we seem to have eliminated the very thought of it from the fabric of everyday life. Kant's supreme value for us lies in the way in which he embodies the last possible demand for metaphysics in modern secular

society; but he is also the first positivist and provides an arsenal of arguments for the elimination of the metaphysical as such. Metaphysics is
not, as Comte thought, a breakdown stage in the secularization of theology; rather, it embodies its own specific value – truth – but then in
that case perhaps theology is better still in so far as its supreme value
– the body – is materialistic and transcendental all at once. As for some
putative 'third stage' in thinking, the dialectic, it is indispensable only
on condition that it ultimately abolish itself: this final, logical stage in
'negative dialectics' seems to me the only moment in which Habermas's
fear – that this profound critique of reason and rationality might end
up in the cul de sac of irrationalism – seems potentially justifiable; even
though what cancels the rational and dialectical thought in Adorno is
not the instinctual, nor even the lure of false immediacies, but rather
materialism and the bodily wish.

What I wish to retain of this short but bewilderingly suggestive chapter
is above all a certain tension between two kinds of temporality in
Adorno's thought and experience: these are the temporality of the
constitutively incomplete, of gratification by way of unfulfillment, and
the temporality of survivorhood, or of uneven devolopment: the temporality of Proust and the temporality of Auschwitz (or of philosophy itself).
Both are thus forms of temporal experience that exclude any mirage
of full presence, of ultimate satisfaction, reconciliation, or historical consonance – the one by way of the future, the other by way of the past;
the first of these odd ec-centric forms finally seems to turn on the experience of the individual subject, or happiness, while the second very much
involves the experience of history and its 'end' – whether in catastrophe
or in achieved revolution and utopian society.

For the philosophical appeal to death and suffering in Adorno is a
paradoxical one that has nothing of the mystique of Heidegger's 'being-
unto-death'; or any particular morbid fascination with the thing itself.
What seems to have happened to Adorno, rather, is not merely the fact
of Auschwitz – which, horrifying as it may be to imagine, includes no
foolproof guarantee of a response any more than any other atrocity in
history, which we can sometimes grasp and sometimes not – but the
peculiar way in which he experienced that fact: in other words, the way
in which his own life-experience mediated the thing itself. This is also
to be understood against a certain distance in his identification with
Judaism; as a 'half-Jew', for example, Adorno seems to have felt perfectly
secure in returning to a now Hitlerian Germany during summer months
throughout the 1930s. The specific form, then, in which he lived the
news about Auschwitz could be called 'unexpected survivorhood': what
seems to have horrified him was not that he himself was in danger after

the fact, or that he also might have been swept into the camps and gassed, however Jewish he did or did not feel himself to be. Rather, it was the idea that by the same kind of accident (and even without knowing it at the time) he himself proved unexpectedly to have outlived those who were herded into the gas chamber. This, then, is an experience of 'death' and 'mortality' which is transmitted not by some vivid imagination of the death anxiety, but rather through life itself, and the guilt of living on, the gift of life as sheer accident, the emptiness of a peacetime existence which is somehow felt to have taken the place that should have been occupied by someone else, now dead. *'Das Leben lebt nicht'*. This famous sentence, which we have earlier read (not incorrectly) as designating the maimed and damaged nature of human living under late capitalism, now can also be seen to express the gratuitous survival of existence, its aimlessness and pointlessness, after genocide; it being understood that, unlike those contemporary ideologues who manipulated the Holocaust in function of their anti-communism, for Adorno as for Horkheimer, 'they have nothing to say about fascism who do not want to mention capitalism' (the 'state of exception' of Nazi Germany remaining very much a part of the logic of monopoly or state capitalism, according to the various economic theories of the Frankfurt School).

What must now be observed, however, is a structural homology between this form of 'unexpected survivorhood' in guilt and retroactive anxiety and that equally notorious survival of philosophy as such, with which one of the most famous sentences Adorno ever wrote confronts us on the very first page of *Negative Dialectics*: 'Philosophy lives on because the moment to realize it was missed' (ND 15/3). This complicated proposition, which inscribes the failed revolution in the advanced capitalist countries at the same time as it endorses Marx's vision of the eventual coincidence of theory and praxis in a socialist society,[57] also serves as the philosophical basis for that systematic refusal of immediate forms of practice and political relevance implicit in the Frankfurt School's defense of the autonomous moment of critical theory as such. What so often seems to be special pleading and the defense of intellectuals and of the contemplative as privilege and class luxury has its source here, in a vision of necessary historical unevenness that greatly transcends and problematizes Bloch's or Trotsky's, ending up abolishing even the concept of the necessary in history. Yet a certain private guilt surely still clings to this distance from life (as it also clings to the exercise of artistic autonomy), as witness the luminous fable of 'Shaw on his way to the theater, showing a beggar his identification with the hurried remark, 'Press'!' (ND 356/363).

I have suggested in the Introduction that this critical and contemplative

distance from praxis[58] became another kind of praxis in its own right
with the emergence of the new academic spaces in the 1960s, and with
Adorno's embrace of an anti-positivist vocation to struggle within the
disciplines of restoration Federal Republic Germany; which is to say
that the social role of the intellectual can be seen to undergo a profound
mutation within his own personal career: from *émigré* to professor. The
rhythms of this historical unevenness – which seems to confirm the tendential vision of triumphant positivism forecast in *Dialectic of Enlightenment* by its very remoteness from the paradigms of any Marxian social
dialectic – in our own time proceed to abolish both of these 'positions',
on the one hand by transforming the memory of Auschwitz into Jewish
neo-ethnicity and nationalism; on the other by suppressing the last imaginable Archimedean space for critical theory or negative thinking in the
submergent flood tide of a now omnipresent 'cynical reason' (Sloterdijk).
('Society seems intent, by a deathly elimination of tension, on making
a noteworthy contribution to entrophy' (MM 160/123).

The other form of temporal non-coincidence – separated from this
one by a *'presque rien'* that transforms it altogether – is what seems to
have borne for Adorno the name of Proust, who first wrote out the
'identity of identity and non-identity' in the realm of the existential and
registered the peculiar property of experience never to be fully lived
for the first time but only in its reexperience: something which both
affirms and denies all at once the possibility of experience to be fully
gratifying. Something like this seems for Adorno to have been the other
dimension of metaphysics as such, at one and the same time the contemplation of death and the mediation on the possibility of happiness:

> What metaphysical experience is like can best be felt perhaps by those who
> are reluctant to derive it from so-called primal religious experience, in such
> Proustian forms as the happiness of the naming of villages such as Otterbach,
> Watterbach, Reuental, or Monbrunn. You have the feeling that if you ever
> go there, you will reach fulfillment, as though that really existed. Once you
> go, however, that promise retreats into the distance like a rainbow. Yet you're
> not really disappointed; rather, you have the feeling that you can't see it
> now because you're standing too close. (ND 366/373)

Yet this embodiment of gratification through its own failure is not fundamentally different, in Adorno's allegory of the existential, from despair
itself, the promise of gratification being still equally maintained within
its denial. Indeed, Adorno nowhere touches the outer limits of metaphysical speculation with so transcendental a formulation (whose genuine affinity with Benjamin and Bloch is a rare event in his work) as in the
affirmation of happiness as a 'waiting in vain', a *promesse de bonheur*

that, unfulfilled, can also be said to be at one with nihilism and the negative: here passages from Berg's *Wozzek* and *Lulu* join the literary expression of Proustian anticipation. As can be imagined, pages in *Minima Moralia* also rise to these occasions, most notably the childhood reminiscences such as 'Heliotrope' (MM 234/177): 'When a guest comes to stay with his parents, a child's heart beats with more fervent expectation ... '[59] The religious and salvational analogies, however, are important above all in the way in which they once again activate the familiar 'ban on graven images', to which we will return in a moment. Politically, however, the obvious ambivalence must be noted of a conception of inevitable non-fulfillment that stills desire (a reproach that this same 'ban on graven images' would nevertheless go a certain distance towards forestalling). Wisely, however, Adorno generally takes pains to sunder this existential and metaphysical dialectic (along with ethics itself) from a political materialism: 'that no one shall go hungry any more' (MM 206/ 156). Only after this is in place can we entertain the Utopia of *'Sur l'eau'*: *'Rien faire comme une bête*, lying on water and looking peacefully at the sky ... ' (MM 208/157).

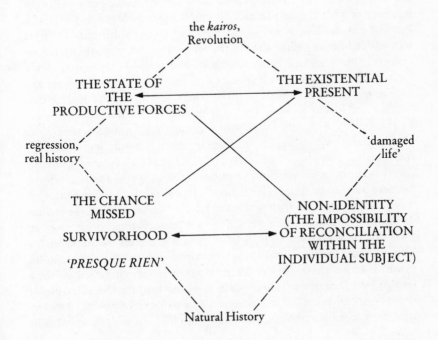

The diagram is premature to the degree to which it anticipates what we will discover in *Aesthetic Theory*: namely, the resolute (and very orthodox) insistence on the significance of productivity and the forces of production. Far more than the possibility of revolution or achieved systemic transformation of the social totality (about which it is a schoolboy philosophical debating point to say that it is presupposed by the conception of the missed opportunity) the conception of productive forces can alone, in Adorno as well as in Marx himself, underwrite a concept of history which, in the full complacency of celebrations of its 'end' in a First World fat with commodities, beats its wings urgently in the debtor nations of the Third World. A reading of loops and regressions in the real historical world is possible only at this price, while the 'existential' realm of the maimed and damaged subject (we are still here in the domain of the anti-hero and of 'anomie') takes its meaning and resonance from situations of under- and over-development, in relative autonomy from the longest *durée*, the mindless biological stratum of natural history itself.

From such a 'world-view', it would seem that transcendence is utterly absent; indeed, of this final chapter of *Negative Dialectics* it might well be said that it deals with the metaphysical only by way of the ban on its image and on its overt expression: at its most routine, then, this can result in a mystical formula of the 'not this ... not that' kind. At its most energetic, however, we seem on the point of touching those ultimate boundaries with the non-thinkable which Kant surveyed and carefully marked out, leading Hegel to observe that if he could think them as barriers and limits he had already thought his way beyond them. Hitler, however, made metaphysics materialist, and included the mortal body irrevocably within any such speculation; but at a time when, 'after the decline – long ratified in secret – of the objective religions that had pledged to rid it of its sting, death itself has now been rendered utterly alien by the socially determined decline of continuous experience as such' (ND 363/370). Meanwhile, 'the idea of absolute death is hardly less scandalous for thought than that of immortality' (ND 364/371): Adorno does not thereby imply secret religious impulses (of the type of the later Horkheimer) but rather simply, with Kant's immortality thesis as well, that we know all about our own death but, unable to imagine it, never include its knowledge in our conscious action: our projects thus presuppose our own immortality, even though this last is not merely unthinkable for secular beings such as ourselves, but perhaps always was. The conclusion towards which the force of this paralogism is then impelled is not a leap of faith, but rather the critique of positivism, the denunciation of the anti-metaphysical 'current situation' in which this impossible and contradictory tension in thought cannot even itself be felt with the scandalous force it merits. The dialectic is then precisely this step above the impossible thought which takes its very impossibility as its own starting point, instead of a desperate attempt to solve it anyway with non-rational means.

So it is that even metaphysics itself and the 'last things' bring us back to a critique of this society and its magical spell: 'Kant's epistemological question, "How is metaphysics possible?", yields to a question from the philosophy of history, "Is it still possible to have metaphysical experience?"' (ND 364–5/372). It can of course also, as has been suggested above, be answered in the language of *natural* history:

> [The indifference of contemporary consciousness to metaphysical questions] conceals a horror that would take men's breath away if they did not repress it. One is tempted to the anthropological speculation whether the evolutionary dialectic that led to consciousness, including that of death, does not contradict an equally evolutionary animal constitution that prevents people from bearing such consciousness in the first place. (ND 388/395)

The perspective of human – that is to say, socioeconomic – history, however, discloses something like a web of actions within which something like a conspiracy, with agents, is embedded (my language, rather than Adorno's). The narrative will now turn on the fate of philosophy, whose index is its metaphysical function – or, in other words, what used to be called *truth*. But this traditional preoccupation does not distance Adorno from poststructuralism as greatly as might be imagined, since his theme also is the impossibility of 'truth' in our own time, the enfeeblement of the category itself, the debility of such mental operations and judgements.

It is a theme whose verbal enactment leads him to some of his most magnificent and contemptuous formulations: 'Even if it were a fact, it could not be the truth that Carnap and Mises are truer than Kant and Hegel' (ND 377/385). It is a paradox that turns on the life of dead cultures and approaches the Gadamerian preoccupation with the 'historical effectivity' of tradition from a non-historicist perspective, even though the perspective of social history necessarily binds thinking to its historical function and context. So Kant's 'block' – the critique of all the metaphysical illusions and pretenses of the more 'transcendental' uses of the mind: 'a system of stop signals' (ND 380/388), as Adorno calls it in passing – is evidently part of a larger social process and 'ruse of history':

> Socially there is good reason to suspect that block, the barrier erected against the absolute, of being at one with the necessity to labor, which in reality holds mankind under the same spell that Kant himself transfigured into a philosophy. The imprisonment in immanence, to which he honestly and brutally condemns the mind, is the imprisonment in self-preservation, as it

is imposed on men by a society that preserves nothing but the taboos that are no longer necessary anyhow. (ND 381–82/389)

Kant is, however, also the place in which the metaphysical impulse is for one last instant preserved and animate, less in the three great transcendental Ideas than in the impossible conception of the things-in-themselves as a *mundus intelligibilis* (to which Adorno here devotes a remarkable subsection).

The paradoxicality of this approach (which, however, began with the by now well-known first sentence of *Negative Dialectics*) lies in the way in which philological or historicist questions about the intellection of the philosophical canon are here transformed into the occasions for a thoroughgoing critique of the social order and late capitalism: as though the old rhetoric of relevance had been dialectically inverted, a palpable contemporary 'irrelevance' thus becoming the most burning and relevant fact of the matter in the current situation. We have already noted that only a commitment to a Marxist view of history can differentiate the stance of these sometimes querulous complaints from that of the (generally right-wing) *laudator temporis acti*; what may now be added is another type of reproach, namely that of a certain philosophical self-referentiality inherent in this perspective, which risks turning all of Adorno's analyses (on whatever topics) back into a purely formal reflection on the limits and possibilities of contemporary philosophy – that is to say, on Adorno's own practice. This optic, more than most others, underscores what is modernist about Adorno's writing (particularly since it at once raises the great central modernist issue of representation). It seems to me to pose the strongest general objection for his philosophy as a coherent position; and can probably not be parried from the outside, but only by way of a certain philosophical solidarity with that position (something that must today, as I will explain in conclusion, take the form of postmodernism theory).

But metaphysics, on this most desperate and negative recuperation, then itself turns into something else – namely theology, about which Adorno's most outrageous propositions assert its twofold relationship to materialism, by way of the emphasis on the body and also by way of the *Bilderverbot* or ban on graven images, to which we now return and which has the additional advantage of emptying 'theology' here of all its theological content. The idea had already been developed in the luminous final pages of the methodological section of *Negative Dialectics*, where even the most unacceptable dualisms of Kantian idealism (the raw 'sensations' organized into intuitions and concepts by the categories), along with Hume's related doctrine of 'impressions', are celebrated as the last epistemological quiver of the somatic element before that element is totally expelled. It lives on in knowledge as the latter's unrest, that it sets in motion and continues to reproduce, unassuaged, in its progress; the 'unhappy consciousness' is no mere delusion of the mind's vanity but rather inherent in it, the one authentic dignity conferred on it by the separation from the body. This dignity is the mind's negative reminder of its physical aspect; its very capacity to feel it is alone the mind's source of hope. (ND 203/203)

And of wishing and desire, of need [Bedürfnis], one would want to add as well, since it is with this that *Negative Dialectics* itself concludes: the affirmation of the deeper affinity between philosophizing and sheer bodily need. At this point, however, what is affirmed is something more paradoxical – namely that genuine materialism must be somehow 'imageless'. To evoke the ban on graven images, even by way of everything that Proust has now come to mean – whose whole expression of landscape, most notably in its climactic pages on Venice, turns on it – is perhaps not as useful as an account of the interference of images themselves that would be more congenial to the subjects of an image-and-spectacle society. Even the phenomenological threatens to convert an internal experience into a mere image of this last; while vulgar materialism, as a philosophy in its own right, is characterized by its external relationship to our deeper materialist experience – that is to say, by a conversion of that into an image, or at least a representation. Adorno's materialism thus wishes above all to elude the representational; in it fulfillment and the somatic realization of the object world must somehow exclude the intermediation of the image:

> Consciousness that interpolates some third thing, the image, between itself and what it thinks, unwittingly reproduces idealism; a corpus of representations is substituted for the object of knowledge, and the subjective arbitrariness of such representations turns out to be that of hierarchy and domination. The materialist longing to grasp the thing wills precisely the opposite of that; the full object can be conceived only in the absence of images. This absence of images converges with the theological ban on graven images. Materialism secularizes that, by excluding the possibility of giving any positive vision of Utopia: such is the content of its negativity. It is at its most materialist outer limit that materialism unexpectedly coincides with theology. It longs for the resurrection of the flesh. (ND 207/207)

As with modernism itself, here representation touches its outer limits, something like an aesthetic Kantian block: *mais il voulait cela dans un autre monde ...*' (*La Condition humaine*) ... 'but not here, not now!' (*A Passage to India*) ... Were these ideas possible as philosophy, then

at this point Adorno would finally be at one with Bloch: but they are
not: and *Negative Dialectics* concludes more modestly with the wish that,
as its ultimate act, the dialectic would cancel itself out altogether. Here,
then, the mystique of nature and the 'non-identical', which we will find
looming larger in *Aesthetic Theory*, seems again to confirm Habermas's
foreboding about the ultimately anti-rational thrust of this philosophy.

But in fact, the ban on graven images ought to exclude the vocation
of all such representational metaphysics from philosophy, which – now
aware of its historicality – can overtly conceive of itself as an instrument
for taking the temperature of History itself: not in the sense in which
it might somehow positivistically 'reflect' its moment of history, but
rather in that this moment remains alive in it, just as in works of art, where
we are asked to grasp 'the poem as a sundial of the philosophy of history'
[*geschichtsphilosophische Sonnenuhr*] (NL 60), a sundial that marks the
stages of collective self-realization and contradiction, but as it were from
within the experience of history and not, by adding up the signs of
material progress, from the outside. 'A message in a bottle' (PNM 126/
133)? Perhaps as well; and such was the way in which Adorno characterized
Schoenberg's music which, unheard, carried in it the secrets of the twentieth century on to some unimaginable future. But it is surely in his
tribute to his teacher Siegfried Kracauer that, in virtually Dantean accents,
we find expressed a lesson we must now ourselves apply to what Adorno
left us:

> From the very beginning I learned, under his direction, to grasp [Kant's]
> work, not as some mere epistemological theory or the analysis of the precondi-
> tions of scientifically valid knowledge, but as a kind of coded text from out
> of which the historical position of Spirit was to be deciphered, with the
> vague expectation that in doing so something of truth itself was to be won.
> (NL 388)

PART II

Parable of the

Oarsmen

One

The central tension in Adorno's aesthetics is that between his formal project of desubjectifying the analysis of aesthetic phenomena and his commitment – inevitable, one would think, in any attempt to prolong the traditional framework of philosophical aesthetics – to the description of aesthetic *experience*: some last remnant of absolutely subjective categories which the desubjectifying impulse cannot wish to dissolve. What happens, of course, is that under these circumstances aesthetic experience retreats into the ineffable and the unsayable: since anything that can be said or formulated or thematized about it at once falls into the force field of the desubjectifying dialectic and is transformed into symptoms and evidence of *objective* processes:

> The spirit of works of art is objective, and that without any recourse to philosophies of objective or subjective spirit as such; the very content of the works is this objective spirit, and it passes judgement over them: spirit of the thing itself, that appears by way of appearance. Its objectivity can be measured by the power with which it infiltrates appearance. (AT 135/129)

The concrete detail of *Aesthetic Theory* is then the unexpected, unforeseeable result of the encounter between these two contradictory impulses, which must first be characterized in some more general ways. The project of desubjectifying our thinking about aesthetics can be seen in a variety of frameworks, of which the largest historical one is surely the turn of contemporary philosophy away from what are now known as 'philosophies of the subject' – that is to say, from the earlier modern attempt to ground truth in consciousness, the transcendental subject, and a variety of other subjective experiences and phenomena. This radical turn away

from and against subjectivity can be genealogized in a number of narratives, which alternately begin with structuralism, with Heidegger, with
Nietzsche, or even with Hegel or with Kant himself. It is objectively
ambiguous, in so far as the case might also be made that this tendency
in contemporary philosophy thereby replicates the tendencies and interests of the modern state and of monopoly capitalism: these last can be
seen as having a stake in the planification of the individual, the reduction
of individual and subjective choice in the era of organized society, the
penetration and colonization of the older autonomous ego, but also of
the Unconscious and desire, by the forces of the market.

The difficulty in affirming this other reading, this counter-interpre-
tation, of modern philosophy's objectivizing project, lies in the fact that
no reaffirmation of the subject or of subjectivity can be offered in opposition to it: since those various regressions and reversions to myth and
to archaic forms of subjectivity are not political responses to the power
and development of late capitalism, on the one hand; and since they
are probably all marked and maimed by its objectifying tendencies, on
the other – being, in other words fully as much symptoms of that process
as they are forms of resistance to it.

Within the world of culture, this anti-subjective project of contemporary thought – which should now be identified as contemporary interpretation in the broadest sense, rather than that of contemporary philosophy
alone – can also be described in a very different language, as an essentially
materialist repudiation of idealism and its ideologies. This description
does not, however, evade the negative and even paranoid scenario I offered
a moment ago, which can always subsume and invert it: materialist intellectuals thus being seen, by a Hegelian 'ruse of reason', as being unwitt-
ingly mobilized in the service of objective social processes. What this
second framework does offer, however, is a displacement of the first
one into the realm of culture and ideology, of texts and 'daily life', of
the superstructure and its dynamic (as opposed to an infrastructure which
more immediately generates thought and its categories in its own likeness).

The materialist kinds of cultural studies which have developed in the
contemporary period can thus be seen, if you like, as a component in
some vaster tendential project of liquidating the older subject and effacing
its archaic ideologies; but if one believes in the priority of the material
dynamics of culture, not only is it difficult to imagine the commitment
of intellectuals to a different project than this one; there is also a perspective in which it is assumed that such demystifying interrogation will
also ultimately reveal and unmask those very social and political forces
of late capitalism which might have found the anti-subjective cultural
project useful in the short term. At any rate, Adorno's various targets

among traditional and modern aesthetic categories – the notion of genius; the conception of the work as subjective or lyric expression; the various psychologies of the aesthetic (from Aristotle to reception theory); traditional psychoanalysis as well as conventional readings of Kant; the 'religion' of art (in art-for-art's-sake as well as in the notion of the compensatory function of the cultural sphere); the centrality of 'intention', even the philosophical (and Hegelian) reappropriation and dissolution of art in the service of meanings of various kinds – these have all intermittently been the targets of contemporary literary and cultural criticism, from the New Criticism on. Even the ultimate turn-of-the-screw of contemporary theory is not absent from Adorno's speculative explorations; namely, the position that Language, in whichever forms, is not subjective, and that language-centered analyses offer the most effective repudiation of older subject-centered categories.[1] In this sense, *Aesthetic Theory* offers a recapitulation, if not a summary, of the concerns and commitments of a varied tendency of contemporary criticism and theory today, probably the dominant one.

On the existential and ideological level, finally, there is surely a sense in which the moderns are all, in one way or another, eager to escape the kinds of interiority bequeathed us by traditional bourgeois culture and its values: the cultivation of subjective refinements and of heightened ethical discriminations enabled by social exclusion and class privilege, the fetishization of Experience as a kind of spiritual private property, the aesthetic individualism which becomes a privatized substitute for the life and culture of groups in business society.[2] It is not clear how much of this T.S. Eliot had in mind in his famous 1919 statement 'Poetry is not a turning loose of emotion, but an escape from personality. But, of course, only those who have personality and emotions know what it means to want to escape from these things.'[3] This concluding pointed sentence, of course, rechannels the significant anti-subjectivizing impulses of high modernism (shared by Adorno) into an equally period-characteristic conservative disdain for the 'anonymous' and 'inauthentic' masses (something that Adorno's analysis of the so-called Culture Industry has often been accused of as well). However, Adorno's dialectic can also show us how the unseating of the subjective can be pursued within the mind:

The notions of subjective and objective have been completely reversed. Objective means the non-controversial aspect of things, their unquestioned impression, the façade made up of classified data, that is, the subjective; and they call subjective anything which breaches that façade, engages the specific experience of a matter, casts off all ready-made judgements and substitutes relatedness to the object for the majority consensus of those who do not even look at it, let alone think about it – in other words, the 'objective' itself. Just

how vacuous the formal objection to subjective relativity is, can be seen in
the latter's most intimate field, aesthetic judgement. Anyone who, drawing
on the strength of his precise reaction to a work of art, has ever subjected
himself in earnest to its discipline, to its immanent formal law, the compulsion
of its structure, will find that objections to the merely subjective quality
of his experience vanish like a pitiful illusion ... (MM 84/69–70)

This is a defense of the objectivity of the subjective which clearly holds
fully as much for artistic production as for its reception. That this hermeneutic impatience, this passion for breaking through to some real, material
world beyond subjectivity and beyond texts, can be explained in terms
of the status of intellectuals and its contradictions does not empty it
of truth-content on other levels: it would not be the first time that the
ideological vested interests of a group also – by some 'preestablished
monadic harmony' or 'ruse of reason' – expressed the objective tendencies
of the social system itself. At any rate, Adorno's 'objectification' of the
aesthetic seems to me to satisfy other contemporary demands raised not
merely by the contradictions of the aesthetic in our time, but also, as
will be argued in greater detail later on, by the dilemmas of contemporary
historical consciousness.

Two

But now we must register the contradiction in Adorno's thought, and the presence in *Aesthetic Theory* of a very different element which may well, in the context of the desubjectifying tendency that has just been described, look like a remnant or survival of just that 'philosophy of the subject' against which the other tendency was directed. This is the conception, and the organizing absent presence, of genuine aesthetic *experience*: full and achieved experience or listening (music being always, in Adorno, the ultimate test case of the aesthetic), the engagement with 'form'; the achievement, on the aesthetic plane, of ideal comprehension or *Verstehen*: and just as this last term introduces some relationship to history into aesthetic experience, so also does another language – the approach to the 'truth content' [*Wahrheitsgehalt*] of the work – lend it a seemingly traditional philosophical dimension.

The differentiation of aesthetic experience was, of course, always one of the central preoccupations of philosophical aesthetics as a discipline and a tradition: Aristotle on the one hand, and Kant and his successors (including the Lukács of the early and late aesthetics) on the other. Hegel, however, marks the onset of a very different approach, which aims at transforming art into philosophy and subsuming it altogether under considerations of 'truth- content' (with the result that something like the historical 'end of art'[4] becomes thinkable). As for Kant, Adorno's dealings with him are brilliantly unprincipled and suggestive: some guerrilla raids into the *Critique of Judgement* turn it inside out and rewrite it as a virtual Copernican revolution of the new anti-subjective aesthetic (where Kant is traditionally supposed to have virtually invented the issue of the differentiation of aesthetic experience as a subjective 'object of study' in the first place); other forays, however, identify and denounce Kantianism as the anticipation in advance of the whole manipulative program of the Culture Industry (the schemata, which persist in Kant's description of Beauty, becoming the prototype of 'degraded' Hollywood stereotypicality, and the source of that bad familiarity which characterizes 'popular music' and its fetishization of hearing).

But *Aesthetic Theory* is not at all a return to such traditional theorizing of aesthetic experience; in many ways, indeed, it challenges the very conception and ideal of a philosophical aesthetics (just as *Negative Dialectics* can also be read as a challenge to the very structure of the traditional philosophical project). The status of Adorno's stubborn commitment to some notion of 'genuine aesthetic experience' therefore demands clarification; along with the very form of this posthumous book, whose discursive or generic status remains unclear, and which often implicitly or explicitly raises the disturbing question whether we really need a 'philosophical aesthetics' any longer in any form, and whether that 'genre' or form of thinking has not somehow, at least in our time, become contradictory and impossible.

Adorno's thinking about these matters takes place on two distinct axes, which often intersect, but cannot be combined or conflated. On the one hand, he systematically distinguishes between 'art' in general and the experience of individual works: this opposition is then clearly the space in which the practices of contemporary literary criticism and theory conflict with the project of a traditional aesthetics, and not only in Adorno's own work. At least in the force field of the modern, literary criticism has tended to conceive its mission as the identification and description of what is unique in specific works, of their incomparability and radical *difference*. But the formal vested interest of traditional aesthetics lies in identifying what is common to all genuine works of art and their experience, and producing some generic concept of the 'artistic' within which the specificity of unique works, from Greek tragedy to Joyce and Picasso, dissolves away. (Contemporary criticism has, however, often been willing to entertain the possibility of a different kind of general or generic concept, in which various distinct works – by the same author, or from the same period, or in the same genre – somehow participate; but this kind of aesthetic thinking – historical rather than eternal – descends from Hegel rather than from Kant, and has also tended to disrupt and problematize the traditional constitution of aesthetic philosophy and its 'object of study' in a different way.)

Contemporary theory has therefore tended to fasten at once on the individual texts, and to elude the larger question of 'art' or the 'aesthetic' altogether, often by assimilating it to psychoanalytic questions of desire in general, or to dynamics of a textuality evident across the board in other, formerly philosophical or disciplinary, realms such as those of politics, anthropology, or sociology. But Adorno has his reasons for wishing to retain a question and a problem that seems otherwise to have become an anachronistic embarrassment: 'Art can never be completely subsumed in the various works of art, in so far as artists always also work on art itself, and not merely on their individual works' (AT 272/261). The distinction between art and the individual work of art remains, in other words, a dilemma, in so far as it marks a relationship as well as an opposition. It will become clear later on, indeed, that the dilemma is also a productive one, since it is by way of this very conflictual coexistence of art and the art-work – of work on an individual object which is also work on the nature of art itself (as in T.S. Eliot's conception of that 'slight' modification or alteration by the new work of the entire preexisting 'ideal order' of 'existing monuments') – that history enters the aesthetic and that Adorno is able to deploy his remarkable conception of the profound historicity of all individual works of art.

But more is at stake, in the difference between art and the individual work, than the *interpretive* access to history: in it is also inscribed the social, and the very experience of class struggle, as it is transmitted through the primal myth of Adorno's aesthetic theory – namely, the 'Sirens' episode from Book XII of the *Odyssey*. Evoking the pain and the contradiction of that repression of the self and of nature which the 'dialectic of enlightenment' holds out as the price of self-preservation, Adorno and Horkheimer describe Odysseus's twofold solution, the twin yet mutually contradictory possibilities of salvation:

> The first he prescribes for his crew. He plugs their ears with wax, and they must row with all their strength. Whoever wants to survive must not give ear to the enticements of what will never come again [*des Unwiederbringlichen*], and he is able to do this only by being able not to hear them. It is an eventuality for which society has always made arrangements. Fresh and intent, the workers must always face forward and ignore the incidental [*was zur Seite liegt*]. They must doggedly sublimate, through redoubled effort, the impulse to diversion. They thereby come to incarnate the practical realm. – Odysseus, the feudal baron for whom others labor, reserves the second possibility for himself. He listens, only bound impotently to the mast; the greater the temptation, the more strongly does he order his bonds tightened, just as later on the bourgeoisie will forbid itself happiness all the more single-mindedly the closer it approaches by virtue of their increasing power. What is heard remains for him without aftermath; he can only move his head to demand release; too late, however; for the crew, who hear nothing, know only the danger of the song, but nothing of its beauty, and leave him at the mast in order

to save him and themselves. They thereby reproduce the very life of the oppressor together with their own, while he himself can no longer step outside his own social role. The bonds with which he has irredeemably shackled himself to praxis at one and the same time sunder the Sirens from it; their temptation, thereby neutralized, becomes a mere object of contemplation, it becomes Art itself. The prisoner is attending a concert, listening motionless just like the audience at concerts later on in history, and his enthusiastic call for freedom already sounds like applause as it dies away. So it is that already in prehistory art appreciation and manual labor become disjoined. (DA 34/34)

This remarkable retelling of Hegel's master/slave dialectic reproduces its ironic twist (the 'truth' of the slave turning out to be the master, while the truth of the master 'only' turns out to be the slave): in effect, Odysseus experiences Art, while his unhearing laborers learn something more profound about the 'individual work of art' to which they themselves are deaf: namely, *das Unwiederbringliche*, what cannot be called back from the past; the work's 'truth-content'.

But Adorno's conception of the individual work will be dealt with later on: for the moment, it is the generic concept of art which concerns us, and about which this passage has revealing things to imply: above all, the sheer guilt of Art itself in a class society, art as luxury and class privilege, a ground bass that resonates throughout all of Adorno's aesthetic reflections without a break, even where its vibration has become a virtual second nature in our sensorium, so that from time to time we no longer hear it consciously. This culpability irreparably associated with all artistic activity is, then, the deeper motive for the radical separation, in Adorno, between Art in general and the individual works: for what these last do, what they 'work on' in the artistic process, is to engage this universal sense of guilt, to address it with lacerating acuity, to bring it to consciousness in the form of an unresolvable contradiction. The individual works of art can never resolve that contradiction; but they can recover a certain authenticity by including it as content and raw material, as what the individual work of art must always confront anew, in all its virulence. In this sense, the guilt with which all works of art are suffused will be one of the mediations by which the otherwise monadic work is profoundly and internally related to the otherwise external social order (but only one possible mediation among others, as we shall see shortly).

It is also the deeper reason why a philosophical aesthetics in our time is not merely impossible, but intolerable. For it is not merely the radical difference of the individual work that general theories of beauty, or of art, or of the aesthetic, both miss and repress; it is also the will to the transaesthetic, to a truth beyond the work and a worldly referentiality in some more general sense, the vocation of Joyce or Aeschylus, of Dante or of Po Chu-yi, to engage the world itself and to be something more than mere 'art', that remains unregistered and invisible in the accounts of a traditional philosophical aesthetic. This is the moment, then, to sound for the first time the major theme and paradox of *Aesthetic Theory* – a principle that will return later in our exposition for fuller development, but whose first provisional formulation speaks to this issue: 'Where art is experienced purely aesthetically, it fails to be fully experienced even aesthetically' (AT 17/9).

As for the guilt of art in general, however, all this needs to be inverted and rearranged: the universal transformation achieved here by a philosophical aesthetics at its most successful and powerful turns all the individual works, in their difference and their various transaesthetic aspirations, back into one long uninterrupted 'aesthetic experience', thereby ejecting us brutally into a social world in which, in the midst of torture and misery, the unjustifiable luxury of art appreciation becomes an irrepressible and unavoidable conviction of every moment. Yet what we have said about contemporary theory also implies that the converse, a framing of the works that goes straight for their 'truth-content', is no less an evasion of this objective guilt, which is a fact of our world; for the metaphysical innocence of that theoretical intercourse with individual works of art, Adorno's formula might well be reversed in order to stress the way in which, when art is experienced only transaesthetically, in the apprehension of its truth content, this last is also missed, and its transaesthetic vocation is itself lost to such experience.

Two final remarks about this as yet provisional motif: first, it will be the form, taken in the aesthetic realm, of what Adorno elsewhere calls the 'determinate negation', the only authentic form of critical thinking in our time – in other words, a consciousness of contradiction which resists the latter's solution, its dissolution either into satiric positivism and cynical empiricism on the one hand, or into utopian positivity on the other. To succeed in thinking art as both aesthetic and anti-aesthetic at one and the same time is to achieve, in this area, the determinate negation. One's second thought, however, must be the awareness that it is very precisely from this dual position that Adorno's unremitting repudiation of political art springs: for it is not only the idle pastimes of the aesthete that are rebuked here, but also the impatience and philistinism of the militant. But we need not yet take a position on this supplementary opinion and consequence, which is also more complicated and paradoxical than it may look in this bald form.

These remarks, however, are all premature: for our first, exploratory concern here has been the status of the concept of Art in general in Adorno, and thereby the relationship of his discourse and form to that of traditional aesthetics: the twist and unexpected reversal in his position can then be characterized as follows – the preoccupation with the nature of art, the very foundation of aesthetics and also the least interesting topic in a situation in which only the individual works of art are interesting and authentic, must none the less be maintained and prolonged, because it is primarily in the area of art in general, as social activity, that the profound culpability of the aesthetic can be registered and identified. *Aesthetic Theory* is thus still an 'aesthetic', as it were, by its negative side, and owing to its commitment to a social perspective in which the inconsequentiality of the aesthetic is an inescapable fact of life.

But we must now turn to the other axis of Adorno's thinking about art, which is in dialectical tension with this first one, in which Art in general finds itself opposed to the individual works. In a second perspective, however, Art in general, now very much including the individual works and indeed precisely consisting of them, will be opposed to everything which is not art; or, more exactly, to everything 'cultural' in the general sense which is not 'really' art. This, the working premiss of *Aesthetic Theory*, must at first be laid out as scandalously and as baldly as possible: all art is 'great art'; there are no degrees in the aesthetic experience or even partial, promising, middling, incomplete aesthetic experience; there is only the thing itself, or else its absence; that is, in this area, the only kind of experience worth talking about, as long as one adds the embarrassing proviso that in case it cannot really be talked about at all in any expository propaedeutic sense; either you know what it is already, or no one can tell you. In this sense, *Aesthetic Theory* presupposes a primitive accumulation of the capital of aesthetic experience; it speaks to you about experiences you have already had, its sentences allude to the already known, the already familiar; and it stands or falls on your agreement with and interest in those descriptions. A brilliant essay in literary criticism might well open up possibilities of reading, or rereading, some hitherto opaque, dull, or exasperatingly perverse text; thereby enabling the emergence in you of some new reading experience (as though, no doubt, for the first time) and even disengaging the formation of some new aesthetic or poetic within your mind. *Aesthetic Theory* does not do that, and does not want to – in that sense also it remains within the confines of the philosophical aesthetic as an a posteriori clarification of what has already been felt.

But we might as well acknowledge our embarrassment with this first peremptory methodological decision: art is by definition 'great art'. What must first be noted is that this position also immediately excludes all the traditional questions about value, which is here presupposed in advance (in a kind of reversal of Northrop Frye's methodological decision to consider all types of narrative, whatever their putative 'value'). Value will come back, however, in another, more historical and social form. Meanwhile one does not so easily exorcize the mocking spirit of the arch-adversary Brecht, the tempter (and the corrupter of Benjamin) whose scenes flash up into the memory, most notably the drunks in *Mahagonny* gazing with wonderment at the player piano and exclaiming, '*Das ist die ewige Kunst!*'

It should be added that Adorno systematically makes a place for something that has tended to be suppressed altogether in the development of contemporary mass and commercial culture – namely, the practice of 'lighter' forms of art (as in the expression 'light opera'): composers like Lehar are as technically expert and admirable in their own way as the 'masters': ' "Light" art as such, distraction, is not a decadent form' (DA, 121/135). But it is a space within a specifically bourgeois culture, which the tendential development of that culture obliterates:

> Light art has been the shadow of autonomous art. It is the social bad conscience of serious art. The truth which the latter necessarily lacked because of its social premises gives the other the semblance of legitimacy. The division itself is the truth: it does at least express the negativity of the culture which the different spheres constitute. Least of all can the antithesis be reconciled by absorbing light into serious art, or vice versa. But that is what the Culture Industry attempts. (DA, 121–2/135)

The famous remark about the 'two halves that don't add up' does not therefore refer to high art and mass culture, but only to high art and light art, whose initial differentiation is itself eliminated by commercialization.[5] Meanwhile, a place is also made for a certain kind of traditional form, as the role played by fairy tales (or archaic late products like the *Struwwelpeter*) suggests. But here too one looks in vain for any politically reassuring traces of populism: indeed, the fundamental mediation on this new opposition – between mass culture and traditional or 'folk' art – is bleak, but also historiographically complex and 'unlinear'. The fundamental social relations in folk art 'are those of masters and servants, gainers and losers, but in an immediate, not wholly objectified form' ('Wolf as Grandmother', MM 272/204). What was ideological about these older forms is revealed in hindsight by the ideological structure of the new mass culture:

> The film has a retroactive effect: its optimistic horror brings to light in the fairy tale what always served injustice, and shows dimly in the reprimanded

miscreants the faces of those whom integral society condemns, and to condemn whom has from the first been the dream of socialization. (MM 272/204).

Brecht himself had recourse to the traditional and the archaic for ends not terribly different from this one.

But as a matter of fact, these positions of Adorno – so easily reducible to 'elitist' opinions, to 'aestheticism', or to a social mandarinism which looks outmoded and culturally alien from within the mass-cultural democracy of the postmodern superstate – are probably better dramatized as moves against a variety of other imaginary or ideal-typical protagonists. In what follows, at any rate, the various positions become characters, and their abstract ballet turns out to be transferable to areas very different from art.

The initial move, which separates some genuine experience of art from everything that is *not* that, seems to be inherent in any philosophy organized around the experiential, which must necessarily reach its constitutive limit in what it is not ('determination is negation'). But in the case of 'experience', a peculiarly paradoxical situation is confronted, since virtually by definition what is not experience cannot be known or formulated, so that such philosophies are unable to include an account of their own boundaries. Interesting non-reflexive strategies therefore emerge: in Merleau-Ponty's phenomenology, for example, the experience of the body finds its Archimedean point outside itself in the peculiar borderline exceptionalities of the so-called 'phantom member' – that is, the continuing sensations 'in' limbs which have been amputated. Only by way of the absent presence of such withdrawn zones is Merleau-Ponty able to organize his descriptions of the full phenomenological body.

In other existentialisms, the problem of the borderline appears in two related but distinct areas: that of meaning and that of death. Only from another, external standpoint can the situational meanings inherent in any life-project be revealed as sheer constructions without natural foundation: but that standpoint – not given within the life-world of the existential philosopher, for example – tends to veer into positivity, so that its absence of meaning now slowly turns into a concept and a philosophy in its own right – namely, the so-called 'absurd'. Meanwhile, in Sartre, death – another constitutive limit of this kind – ceases to be something we can contemplate like an energizing mystery within life (as is still the case in Heidegger's *Sein-zum-Tode*) and becomes the meaningless other side, an event by definition outside life and which to that degree, as it were, ceases to concern us. (Heidegger's 'solution' to the problem of limits, as Habermas is only the latest to have insisted, reverts to a mythic history, by setting the 'outside' of our fallen world of the existent in repressed and forgotten Ur-time, as a genuine experience and presence of the mystery or the question of Being of which we have, in historical time, lost even the memory.)

So it is that, approaching the description of one of the constitutive features of art as play, as riddle and enigma, Adorno finds himself rehearsing the argument from the 'phantom member' and recommending 'the study of unartistic people', of people 'without artistic sensibilities', *amusischer Menschen* (AT 183/177):

> It is quite impossible to explain to them what art is; and if it were possible to do so intellectually, they would still not be able to square this insight with their experience. For them the reality principle is so powerful as to repress aesthetic behavior completely. Urged on by the official cultural approbation of art, such insensitivity to art frequently shades over into aggression, and this plays no little role in the general tendency today towards the 'deaestheticization' of art [*Entkunstung*, literally 'de-arting' – that is to say, the stripping from art of its conventional artistic features and signals, such as *Schein* (aesthetic illusion and fictionality), along with the attempt to rejustify such aesthetic activity by passing it off as something else, as in happenings, advertisements, certain forms of political art, etc. – *FJ*].

The explanatory features introduced here – the 'reality principle', the 'official cultural approbation of art', the relationship to 'aggression' – open up a variety of social and historical forms into which the 'non-artistic' [*Amusie*] can develop into (and which we will examine in a moment). But this first global privative position is determined by the sheer logic of Adorno's inquiry (as we have argued above); what can be observed in this passage is the way in which it now becomes rhetorically staged within the text as one kind of *reader*: very precisely the one to whom we have already made incidental reference – namely, that reader who approaches *Aesthetic Theory* with no previous experience of what the aesthetic is, and is here dramatized as a reader who is unable, for whatever 'natural' or 'constitutive' reason, to 'have' aesthetic experience in the first place.

Anthropologically, of course, such a reader is inconceivable: a being utterly without negativity (in the Hegelian sense), so completely mired in the immediate that its consciousness would eschew even that relative and minimal distance from the world which we attribute to the 'higher' animals. Fantasy, the capacity for fiction or for the mental entertainment of images of what is not (and even what is not yet, or what is past), is thus not some incidental, supplementary adjunct power of human consciousness but virtually its constitutive feature. But once again, as I have suggested above, attempts to 'define' consciousness (one thinks of the way in which Sartre's definition of consciousness as negation and distance necessarily passes through a description of the 'imaginary') find themselves positing this inconceivable privative position to get about their business. In the same way, descriptions of language at some outer limit need the fantastic and internally contradictory representation of non-linguistic beings – such as the Grand Academicians of Lagado in Swift, whose plan to abolish language and substitute the 'things themselves' (carried around for just such communicative purposes) might have served Adorno as a figure for some quintessential positivism.

Adorno's privative term will thus very rapidly take on what the narrative semioticians call the features of 'surface manifestation', becoming a 'lifelike' character (or several) with the appropriate social and historical determinations (something that already begins to happen in the passage cited, as we have observed above). But at the outset the '*amusischer Mensch*', the person bereft of all aesthetic sensibility, is something like the Other in the text: that ultimate non-reader against whom one argues, or, if that fails (as it must by definition), whom one vilifies and ridicules in order to ratify one's solidarity with the 'proper' reader, who is thereby encouraged to assume – against this Other – the perspective constructed by the text itself. It is tempting to imagine that all texts – at least in the earlier stages of genres in formation: that is, in the process of institutionalization – find themselves obliged thus to include the 'bad' or 'undesirable' reader in the form of just such privative positions: these do not, of course, have to be anthropomorphic 'characters' in a narrative but are most dramatically visible as such – as, for example, in those works of science fiction or of occult genres which systematically include the Rationalist, the Skeptic, the Non-believer, *within* the text in order to confute him and thereby to neutralize undesirable readings.

In a sense, of course, Adorno's non-artistic position has already achieved 'actantial manifestation' in a primary narrative: in the form of Odysseus's oarsmen in the 'Sirens' episode, whose ear-stoppers make them over into people who know that art exists but can have no conception of its experience or powers. It is certain that in some larger social sense, as the class allegory of the Sirens makes explicit, these non-artistic people are identified with the laboring masses. They reappear in another astonishing passage of *Dialectic of Enlightenment*, when Adorno and Horkheimer make the (improbable) suggestion that one might suddenly switch the entire Culture Industry off, without anyone caring:

Such closures [e.g., of the movie theaters] would not be reactionary Luddism or machine-breaking. The disappointment would be felt not so much by the enthusiasts as by the slow-witted, who are the ones who suffer for every-

thing anyhow. Despite the films themselves, which are meant to complete
her integration, the housewife finds in the darkness of the movie theater
a place of refuge where she can sit for a few hours with nobody watching,
just as she once used to look out of the window, when there were still private
homes and 'free time' after work. The unemployed of the great cities find
coolness in summer and warmth in winter in these temperature-controlled
locations . . . (DA 125/139)

This populism (which we probably owe to Horkheimer) is clearly rather
different from the conservatism of the same period, with its analyses
of 'mass man' or of the inauthenticity of mass industrial culture (Heidegger's 'das Man', or Ortega's 'revolt of the masses') to which it is nevertheless, ideologically related: here, however, the 'marginals' of contemporary
radical rhetoric already make their appearance – in the persons of women
and the unemployed, and not least in the pathos of those ultimate victims,
the stupid or retarded, to which Döblin's *Alexanderplatz* is the monument.
The comforting darkness of the great movie theaters then becomes the
after-hours resting place of the oarsmen of Odysseus, who pay no more
attention to the mesmerizing images on the screen than they did to the
Sirens' song.

But what if they did? At this point, Adorno's negative or privative
position – non-Art, the quality of people radically unable to have aesthetic
experience in the first place – splits in two, as it begins to enter real
history; and with this bifurcation in his figures, the notorious conception
of the Culture Industry itself begins to appear. For alongside those who
have no conception of artistic experience, a place must now be made
for those who think they do, and a characterization and an analysis
of *ersatz* art must now be devised for all those viewers and listeners
who, believing themselves to be engaged in cultural experience, still turn
out not to know what art is and never to have achieved 'genuine aesthetic
experience', and never even to have known they were deprived of it
in the first place.

The 'Culture Industry' does not play a major role in *Aesthetic Theory*,
but has already been negatively presupposed by it: indeed, the earlier
text poses the most serious philosophical problem for the later project
as a whole – namely, how to deal with the exception or the possible
middle ground, with a kind of 'aesthetic experience' which is neither
'genuine' (an apparent 'art' which is obviously not 'great art', in Adorno's
sense) nor is it non-art altogether. The chapter on the 'Culture Industry'
in *Dialectic of Enlightenment* confronts this structural problem in advance,
by excluding the dilemma of theorizing a kind of art which is not 'really'
art (nor is it 'bad art' exactly, since that is a non-concept) and a real
experience which is not really aesthetic, even though it is not anything

else either (in Kant's terms, it is also neither practical nor epistemological). To say, as Adorno also does here, that this mass-cultural experience is in fact that of the commodity form is also to stress that it is objective (it is not a 'pseudo-experience), but not yet to articulate the relationship of this new code (commodity fetishism) to the traditional aesthetic categories rehearsed here.

Three

But it is difficult today to discuss the notion of the Culture Industry, surely Adorno's single most influential – and also provocative, and even notorious – concept, without including something like the history of the 'fortunes' of this concept in the discussion. Although first outlined, in *Dialectic of Enlightenment*, in a language that wished to combine the sociological and the philosophical, this Ur-text (along with *Minima Moralia*) can also be reread (or rewritten) as work in an older literary genre: namely, that travel literature produced by Europeans as a result of their often horrified contact with the new North American democracy, and in particular with the originality of its political, social and cultural forms, which unlike those of Europe came into being independently of the class struggle with an aristocratic *ancien régime*, whose influence persisted in the Old World, at least until very recent times, in the marks and the survivals of a pre-bourgeois conception of culture (even where, as in Bourdieu's 'distinction', such aristocratic forms and categories were adopted and restructured by the bourgeoisie itself). But the anthropological shock of the contact of these Central European mandarins with the mass-democratic Otherness of the New World was also uniquely conditioned by an unexpected historical conjuncture: the simultaneous rise, in Europe, of Hitlerian fascism.

Today this conjuncture has come to seem less paradoxical and contingent: if indeed it is so, as the historians now seem to suggest, that the Hitlerian moment was in fact Germany's long-postponed bourgeois revolution, and that its violent and petty-bourgeois social, political and cultural *Nivellierung* had as its objective result the destruction of the last remnants of some surviving aristocratic forms, then the two historical phenomena – American mass democracy, the Nazi interregnum in Germany – are closely related. But it was the originality of Adorno and Horkheimer first to have linked these two phenomena culturally, and to have insisted, with an implacability that must surely be counted as a form of political commitment, on the indissociability of the Culture Industry and fascism; and to have mingled their American and their German examples and illustrations throughout their exposition in a provocative fashion that could not fail to scandalize. That the Second World War concluded with the victory of the Culture Industry over its Nazi competitor and rival is then grasped as variation within a single paradigm, rather than the victory of one paradigm over another.

The concept of the Culture Industry thus originally masked and expressed – via some new philosophical stylization and abstraction – one of those Tocqueville-Dickens-Trollope voyages to the United States, whose generic familiarity has always allowed American intellectuals to discount them as so much snobbery and aristocratic prejudice. But for other, left-wing American intellectuals – less wedded to notions of American exceptionalism – the Adorno-Horkheimer critique could also lay the basis for a cultural critique of capitalism itself, by way of that identification of mass culture and the commodity form which has already been mentioned: and in the United States this cultural critique was established independently of the modernist aesthetic values on which it depended philosophically in Adorno and Horkheimer, yet in a situation where, by the 1950s, artistic modernism had become hegemonic and canonical and had conquered the university system. In the ensuing years (shortly to become the 1960s) several of these variables changed and, along with them, the very situation of cultural critique itself. It seems fair to assert that this field of study, with its motivations and values, has remained since then associated with the left in this country (it is only in very recent years that the hitherto episodic forms of right-wing cultural critique have won any legitimacy).

But the American left, as it was reborn socially in the 1960s, also rediscovered its older populist traditions and began to reformulate its cultural positions in an essentially populist idiom. Meanwhile, the essentially European traditions of aesthetic modernism, now canonized in the academy, ossify and are felt to be 'academic' in the bad sense; the repudiation of this kind of modernism by the populist left then merges with an anti-intellectualism which in American business society has paradoxically been a political tradition here on the left as well as on the right; while finally modernism itself, as an artistic movement, for whatever larger systemic and socioeconomic reasons, comes to an end during or shortly before this period (and this means the dissolution of that moment in

PARABLE OF THE OARSMEN

which, as Adorno describes it, 'art [read: modern art, technically advanced art] was by definition politically left' [AT 377/360]).

But now another feature of the new mass culture of the 1960s (prolonged into our own historical period) must be reckoned into the description: so-called popular culture now becomes technically advanced (very much in the spirit of Adorno's description of modernism, as we shall see later on). The formulation is no doubt inaccurate, and undialectical, in so far as it suggests that the 'technologically advanced' was there already, but that finally mass culture made its way to it. What really happened was, on the contrary, a simultaneous leap forward both mass-culturally and technologically, in which for the first time the two developments were also consciously interlinked: resulting in the emergence together of what we now call the media and the new media-oriented culture. This development must be stressed, in order to replace *Dialectic of Enlightenment* in a historical perspective and to read it as something which has *become* historical, whatever other claims its arguments may have on us. The products of Adorno's Culture Industry must now be identified as standard Hollywood Grade-B genre film (before the latter's reorganization by *auteur theory*), as radio comedy and serials of a thirties and forties variety ('Fibber McGee and Molly', for example) and, in music, as Paul Whiteman (the proper referent for what Adorno calls 'jazz', which has little to do with the richness of a Black culture we have only long since then discovered); it has something to do with Toscanini as well (whose contemporary reevaluation was in many ways anticipated by Adorno himself),[6] and arguably also anticipates the first television programs of the late 1940s (such as Milton Berle). Whatever contemporary nostalgia may have recently come to invest such artefacts, the structural break between their forms and those of our own mass culture seems obvious enough to warrant our positing a similar and equally historical break between the analytic thinking (or 'determinate negation') inspired by them and the theory contemporary mass culture has seemed to demand.

This last can be characterized in terms of populism to the degree to which it shows increasing impatience with theories of manipulation, in which a passive public submits to forms of commodification and commercially produced culture whose self-identifications it endorses and interiorizes as 'distraction' or 'entertainment'. New conceptions of reading begin to cast a certain doubt on these conceptions of reception; while paradoxically Foucault's description of the universal web of micro-power in contemporary societies (a description more baleful and totalizing than anything to be found in the Frankfurt School) turns out to authorize counter-conceptions of 'resistance' utterly inconsistent with its French source (where resistance is always an atomized but individual, desperate,

guerrilla effort doomed to failure). The mass-cultural theories of resistance, of rewriting, of the appropriation of the commercial text by groups
for whom it was not destined in that form, would rather seem to reflect
some sense of the deeper utopian impulses at work in cultural production
and consumption alike – where, as Bloch showed us, the mole of collectivity still burrows away through the frivolous individual gratifications
of a privatized and atomized society.

The Utopian origins of such theories are then (via Marcuse) far more
evident in the sociopolitical theories of the New Left, where it is precisely
commodification, and the consumption desires awakened by late capitalism, that are themselves paradoxically identified as the motive power
for some deeper dissatisfaction capable of undermining the system itself.
Philosophically, something of this position persists in Habermas, for
whom the very promises of the bourgeois revolution and of bourgeois
legality and democracy retain potential that can lead to social change
and evolution. In any case, ironically, the utopian component of those
New Left theories of mass culture which replaced Frankfurt School
notions of manipulation by the Culture Industry itself ultimately derives
from the other, utopian face of Frankfurt School thinking.

The belated theorization of the new forms of mass culture as so many
manifestations of 'postmodernism' now seems to complete these new
positions at the same time that it profoundly problematizes them. The
technological perfection of mass culture today (in a postmodern 'image'
in which high technology is also inscribed as content, and which also,
as a commodity form, signifies the technologically new as the very object
of cultural consumption) seems indeed to render more plausible the new
dignity of all these commercial art-objects in which a kind of caricature
of Adorno's conception of art as technical innovation now goes hand
in hand with the acknowledgement of the deeper unconscious Utopian
wisdom of precisely those consuming masses whose 'taste' it validates.
Meanwhile, the virtual disappearance of what Adorno used to oppose
to it as 'high culture' – namely, modernism itself – clears the field, and
leaves the impression of a now universalized culture, whose logic now
describes a continuum from 'art' to 'entertainment' in place of the older
value oppositions of high and low.

The Archimedean point of some 'genuinely aesthetic experience' from
whose standpoint the structures of commercial art are critically unmasked
has thus disappeared; what has not disappeared, however, is still the
ancient philosophical problem of true and false happiness (from Plato
to Marcuse) and whether watching thirty-five hours a week of technically
expert and elegant television can be argued to be more deeply gratifying
than watching thirty-five hours a week of 1950s-type 'Culture Industry'

programming. The deeper utopian content of postmodern television takes
on a somewhat different meaning, one would think, in an age of universal
depoliticization; while even the concept of the Utopian itself – as a political version of the Unconscious – continues to confront the theoretical
problem of what repression might mean in such a context – in particular,
it remains to be determined what political content may be assigned to
works whose unconscious meaning alone is political. Such texts might
well be social symptoms of a deeper political and collective need or longing
without in themselves having any political or politicizing function. Perhaps today, where the triumph of more utopian theories of mass culture
seems complete and virtually hegemonic, we need the corrective of some
new theory of manipulation, and of a properly postmodern commodification (which could not in any case be the same as Adorno and Horkheimer's now historical one).

In fact, however, the 'Culture Industry' chapter does not propose a
theory of culture at all, in the modern sense; and the passionate responses
it has most often aroused have tended equally often to stem from this
misunderstanding and from thinking that it does. It is enough, however,
to reread Raymond Williams's now classic account of 'hegemony' for
it to be clear that there is no equivalent concept anywhere in Adorno's
work (or Horkheimer's either):

> a whole body of practices and expectations, over the whole of living: our
> senses and assignments of energy, our shaping perceptions of ourselves and
> our world. It is a lived system of meanings and values – constitutive and
> constituting – which as they are experienced as practices appear as reciprocally
> confirming. It thus constitutes a sense of reality for most people in the society,
> a sense of absolute because experienced reality beyond which it is very difficult
> for most members of the society to move, in most areas of their lives. It
> is, that is to say, in the strongest sense a 'culture'... [7]

The contrast is all the more striking when Williams reverts to his central
theme here (for it is of hegemony and not initially of culture that all
this is affirmed!), and adds: 'but a culture which has also to be seen as
the lived dominance and subordination of particular classes', something
that would clearly be appropriate to the matter of the Culture Industry
itself, if Adorno and Horkheimer had been able to conceive of it in
this way in the first place. But they do not: at least partly because, as
Minima Moralia is there to testify, the experience of the 'damaged life'
– but also of Weimar and of Nazism, and even of the brash and materialistic United States – leaves no place for the stability of this kind of evocation of social reproduction. It will not be until Negt and Kluge that
accents echoing those in Williams's passage here find their German equiva-

lent.[8] Indeed, it is also possible that the traditional equivalent, *Bildung*, is too tainted a class concept and too redolent of all the complacency of the 'immature' German bourgeoisie, for Adorno and Horkheimer ever to have been tempted by it.

Thus, the 'Culture Industry' is not a theory of culture but the theory of an *industry*, of a branch of the interlocking monopolies of late capitalism that makes money out of what used to be called culture. The topic here is the commercialization of life, and the co-authors are closer to having a theory of 'daily life' than they are to having one of 'culture' itself in any contemporary sense. For Williams's theory is, despite his seeming nostalgia, a very contemporary one indeed, which corresponds to an acculturation of social life far more thoroughgoing and 'total' than could have been conceived in the 1930s (when, with industrial mass production of cultural goods – so-called Fordism – the process was only beginning). Adorno and Horkheimer remain 'modern' in this sense because although they presciently enumerated a whole range of tendencies in what was to become image-society, they could scarcely anticipate the dialectical transformation of quantity into quality that the intensification of the process would entail. Theirs remains therefore, not a *Kulturkritik* but an *Ideologiekritik*: as in classical Marxism, 'ideology' is still here the central concept and has not yet been modified by the demands of a postmodern social order (as, for example, in Althusser's revision).

Four

At any rate, the Adorno-Horkheimer theory of the Culture Industry provides a theoretical description of mass cultural experience which can scarcely be reduced to sheer opinionated or elitist vituperation against 'bad art'. To be sure, the philosophers' argument commits them to differentiate mass-cultural 'experience' from the genuinely aesthetic type: this is achieved by separating 'entertainment', 'amusement', and even 'pleasure' itself off from what happens in art, which cannot be described in those terms. Indeed, the worst fears of those for whom a Germanic dialectic is virtually by definition humorless in its very essence[9] will be confirmed by the obsessive diatribes against laughter that appear and reappear throughout this book; a somewhat different light is shed on this odd prejudice by the realization that laughter is here conceived as essentially Homeric – that is, as a ferocious vaunting, with bared teeth, over the victim, as exemplified, for example, by Wyndham Lewis's Tyros; while we should also read into the record Adorno's frequent exception – from such denunciations of sheer malicious 'fun' – of the genuinely zany, such as the Marx Brothers, and his otherwise astonishing insistence on the deeper mindless silliness or 'simplicity' [*Albernheit*] of all true art.

The analysis of pleasure, however, takes place within a framework of the theory of the alienated labor process and has been prolonged by any number of contemporary discussions of the commodification and colonization of leisure:

> Amusement under late capitalism is the prolongation of work. It is sought after as an escape from mechanized work, and to recruit strength in order to be able to cope with it again. Meanwhile, however, mechanization so

dominates the resting worker's leisure and happiness, and so profoundly determines the manufacture of amusement goods, that his experiences are inevitably
mere after-images of the work process itself. The ostensible content is merely
a faded foreground; what sinks in is the automatic succession of standardized
operations. What happens at work, in the factory or in the office, can be
evaded only by approximation to it in one's leisure time. All amusement
suffers from this incurable malady. Pleasure hardens into boredom because,
in order to remain pleasure, it must demand no effort and thereby moves
rigorously in the worn grooves of association. (DA 123/137)

This concluding word, 'association', needs to be retained, and the historical weight of its philosophical connotation further developed, since, as
we shall see, it functions as the mediation between the labor process
and whatever pleasurable experience may be attributed to mass-cultural
works in the first place. For even the most implacable theory of manipulation in mass culture (and the Adorno-Horkheimer theory is a good deal
subtler than that) must somehow acknowledge the experiential moment
in the mesmerization of the masses before the television set; if only then
to dismiss it as the fix, addiction, false pleasure, or whatever. The great
definition of art which Adorno and Horkheimer borrow from Stendhal
and make their own – art as the *'promesse de bonheur'* – suggests, however,
that for them much will be at stake in coming to terms theoretically
with just such false happiness, just such deceptive pleasure (about which
the utopian positions of a Bloch or a Marcuse will suggest that true
happiness or pleasure is somehow inscribed within this false experience).[10]

In fact, Adorno and Horkheimer make the only really consequent
and rigorous move open to them: they sunder pleasure decisively from
happiness, while at the same time denying the possibility of either as
some full experience or plenitude in its own right. Pleasure thereby
becomes an evanescent natural release, which can never be sustained:

pleasure [*Vergnügen*] always means not thinking about anything, forgetting
suffering even where it is shown. Helplessness is its foundation. It is in fact
flight; but not, as is often said, flight from a wretched reality, but on the
contrary flight from any last thought of resistance left open by this last.
(DA 130/144)

In this form, whatever is left of pleasure in the older sense comes to
invest the position of the ultimate victims, 'the ones who suffer for everything anyhow'. As for the ultimate mystery of sexuality – so often taken
as the very prototype of pleasure in general, and sometimes inconsider-
ately (even by Adorno himself in passing) assimilated to the experience

of art itself – it may be preferable, in true Lacanian fashion, to deny its relationship to pleasure altogether:

> Delight [*Lust*] is austere: *res severa verum gaudium*. The monastic theory that not asceticism but the sexual act denotes the renunciation of attainable bliss receives negative confirmation in the gravity of the lover who apprehensively stakes his life on the fleeting instant. In the Culture Industry, jovial renunciation takes the place of the pain that lies at the heart of ecstasy and asceticism alike. (DA 126–7/141)

Pain as the very truth of pleasure: with this deeply felt paradox we touch the central dialectic of Adorno's conception of experience and his notion of authenticity. The related but distinct notion of happiness also, as we shall see later on, follows this pattern, but as it were on a temporal or historical continuum, very much in the spirit of Bloch's 'not yet': happiness is possible, here and now, only as what does not yet exist, as what is not yet possible or achievable. The Stendhal formula takes on its power when we stress its constitutive incompletion: art is not bliss, but rather the latter's *promise*. The Frankfurt School then rewrite it in their own grimmer idiom: 'The secret of aesthetic sublimation is its representation of fulfillment as a broken promise' (DA 125/140).[11] What is inauthentic in the offerings of the Culture Industry, then, is not the remnants of experience within them, but rather the ideology of happiness they simultaneously embody: the notion that pleasure or happiness ('entertainment' would be their spurious synthesis) already exists, and is available for consumption.

This is, then, one crucial thematic differentiation between 'genuine art' and that offered by the Culture Industry: both raise the issue and the possibility of happiness in their very being, as it were, and neither provides it; but where the one keeps faith with it by negation and suffering, through the enactment of its impossibility, the other assures us it is taking place ('Not Italy is offered, but eye-witness evidence of its existence' [DA 133/148]).

This is then the moment at which we must return to the implication of the word 'association' (already stressed above), but less in the sense of the tradition that emerges from Locke than, rather, in its final twist and solution in Kant himself, and in the theory of the categories and the mental schemata. This is of course the point at which, as has already been mentioned, the stereotypicality of Hollywood and Culture Industry products is, with malicious playfulness, attributed to the *Critique of Pure Reason* as its caricature and ultimate outcome; to be sure,

Kant's formalism still expected a contribution from the individual, who was
thought to relate the varied experiences of the senses to fundamental concepts;
but industry robs the individual of his function. Its prime service to the
customer is to do his schematizing for him. Kant said that there was a secret
mechanism in the soul which prepared direct intuitions in such a way that
they could be fitted into the system of pure reason. But today that secret
has been deciphered. (DA 112/124)

The Kantian problematic is not, to be sure, exhausted by this particular
application and appropriation of its mechanisms: for the question of perceptual schemata (and of their opposite number, something like a perceptual or aesthetic *nominalism*) persists in 'genuine art' and returns
episodically in *Aesthetic Theory* as the problem of the 'universal' and
the 'particular'. Here, however, schematism, in the Kantian sense, provides the crucial mediation between the labor process and 'degraded'
entertainment, which seeks the same – repetition and the familiar – as
its very element: Taylorization, the rationalization of the labor process
and of mass production, is here to be grasped both in production and
reception in well-nigh indistinguishable fashion (but the identification
of reception with production is constant in Adorno, and holds for 'high
art' as well, which will in some sense also constitute another more self-
conscious version of this synthesis, and be characterized as something
like a reception of production – but of advanced production, of 'high'
technology).

Here we seem to pass beyond a straightforward analysis of mass-cultural
artefacts in terms of commodification; or, to be more precise, the emphasis
at this point shifts from the emphasis on the ideological dimension of
the commodity – that is to say, on the 'religious' mysteries of commodity
fetishism – to what may be called its existential or even metaphysical
dimension in Marx – namely, the effects of exchange itself, and in particular of *equivalence* as a new form imposed on reality and on *abstraction*
in the broadest epistemological sense as a historically emergent mode
of organizing the world. This is, of course, the point at which the analysis
of the Culture Industry loops back into the larger framework under
which it was subsumed: the evocation of the 'dialectic of Enlightenment',
of what Weber called rationalization and Lukács reification: the coming
into being of 'identity' as a mental operation which, as we have seen
in the preceding chapter, is at one and the same time a primary instrument
of domination and embodiment of the will to power.

The first chapter of *Capital*, indeed, stages 'equivalence' as anything
but a natural process, and shows it to be at one and the same time a
creative mental act, an extraordinary cultural invention, which is also
a brutal and revolutionary intervention into the objective world: nothing

in the senses endorses the conceptual leap whereby the famous coat becomes equivalent 'in value' to the equally famous twenty yards of linen. Nor can a metaphysics of Number – according to which, eventually, one pound of iron shavings is discovered to be equivalent to one pound of feathers – ground this new value *form*, whose historical evolution culminates in the so-called 'general form of value' or money: it has not been sufficiently appreciated that Marx's four stages of value project a whole history of abstraction as such, of which the commodity form is but a local result (and Weber's rationalization, Simmel's intellectualization, and Lukács's reification constitute its global generalization, at the other end of time). Abstraction in this sense is the precondition of 'civilization' in all its complex development across the whole range of distinct human activities (from production to the law, from culture to political forms, and not excluding the psyche and the more obscure 'equivalents' of unconscious desire), whose very different histories the history of abstraction might therefore be called upon to underwrite.

'Equivalence' retains these senses in *Dialectic of Enlightenment*, where it excludes difference and heterogeneity, and 'excises the incommensurable' (15/12), transforming the unlike into the same, banishing the fear of the new and allowing comparable and measurable quantities to be manipulated. On the other hand, Adorno and Horkheimer also dispose of an alternate characterization of this primal process (which constitutes the very dynamic of 'enlightenment' as such, and of science and 'instrumental reason'): as we have seen, they also call it *mimesis*, and thereby open up a thematic alternative to the Marxian doctrine or problematic of equivalence – a second language or code which, intended to incorporate anthropology (since the grandest dialectical move in the book lies as we have seen in its assimilation of myth to enlightenment), secures mimetic activity as a genuine drive or impulse, and thereby draws this whole new theory into the mythic proper, reprojecting it as an anthropological narrative of the transformation of primal mimetic impulses into Western science. Now a 'scene of origins' will be necessary; so that the Ur-motivation of the mimetic is staged as fear and impotence before Nature, which ritual mimesis and, after it, science, are called upon to master (by domination of the self); while the evident break of 'modernity', the emergence of science – in, for example, the emblematic passage from perceptual 'science', '*pensée sauvage*', alchemy, into mathematical and non-representational thinking – is attributed to a mimetic taboo, or 'ban on graven images', which is itself, however, dialectically as profoundly mimetic (in the anthropological sense) as what it seeks to repress and cancel.

Habermas has shrewdly suggested[12] that this alternate mythic

conceptuality – the code of the mimetic – is ultimately imposed on
Adorno and Horkheimer by the inner logic of their positions: as reason
and rationality are for them implacably identified as 'instrumental reason'
(as *Verstand* rather than *Vernunft*) they no longer have any positive space
for the development of conceptual alternatives to 'enlightenment' and
are thereby forced back into a type of mythic thinking of their own.
He also stresses the unrealized capacity of the notion of mimesis as inter-
personality, and as the space for relations with other people (whom we
understand by mutual imitation): this possibility, which for Habermas
himself is clearly fundamental, is generally, however, in Adorno and
Horkheimer, conceived as something fully as baleful as it might be socially
and intellectually promising, let alone productive.

Meanwhile, it seems clear that the theory of the Culture Industry is
itself unduly limited and restricted by these rather more metaphysical
propositions about the mimetic impulse, which to be sure 'explain' the
deeper power and attraction of a mass culture that has none of the power
and attraction of Art; but explain it too easily and naturalistically (the
schematisms of alienated labor invested by some deeper human 'drive'),
thereby forestalling those more complex lines of speculation and inquiry
that postmodern mass culture seems to demand.[13] In particular, the matter
of repetition in contemporary mass culture has not only become a more
complicated and interesting phenomenon than the one Adorno and Horkheimer had in mind: it would also seem to suggest mediations of a type
they could obviously not elaborate with the originality of daily life in
late capitalism, and in particular with the newer structures of an image
or spectacle society (which are also scarcely even foreshadowed in Benjamin's alternate theory of mass culture, staged under the sign of the mecha-
nically reproducible work of art). As for the 'stereotypical', the current
revival of the term 'formulaic' to designate some of these mass-cultural
structures suddenly opens up analogies with cultural production and
reception in non- or pre-capitalist societies, which are equally excluded
from the historical framework of *Dialectic of Enlightenment*.

Five

Our inquiry into the way in which Adorno conceives of the negative or 'opposite' of art, however, is still not complete. We have in effect identified not one but two such oppositional terms, which do not quite overlap conceptually: there is on the one hand an absence of art altogether [*das Amusische*], a position occupied by Odysseus's crewmen; and alongside that the somewhat stronger negative term of the anti-art or 'bad art' of the Culture Industry, with its betrayed and victimized public:

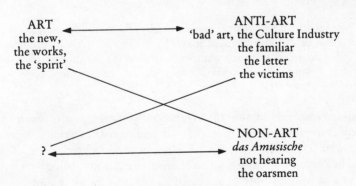

ART
the new,
the works,
the 'spirit'

ANTI-ART
'bad' art, the Culture Industry
the familiar
the letter
the victims

?

NON-ART
das Amusische
not hearing
the oarsmen

The missing fourth term in this system is secured less by a new form of culture (or its absence) than by a generalized negation of the other three terms that, playing across a range of thematic levels, can itself only be identified allegorically as a character in Adorno's deeper ideological and phantasmatic narrative. This 'slot' constitutes the negation of 'anti-art', for example, not by way of the end of the Culture Industry and the emergence of some new and positive 'negation of the negation'; but rather as the opposite number to the latter's drama of victimization, as the agency of that victimization and the place of the production of the Culture Industry itself. Beyond them, of course, the term expands to include the *philistines* in general, who are not, in Adorno's scheme of things, those who passively consume mass culture, nor are they the oarsmen, who are deprived of the very sense organs for any culture, whether authentic or commercial, but rather those who carry in their hearts some deeper hatred of art itself.

The philistines are not first and foremost, therefore, those who do not 'understand' art or, better still, who do not 'understand' modern art; rather, they understand it only too well:

> What our manipulated contemporaries dismiss as unintelligible secretly makes very good sense to them indeed. This recalls Freud's dictum that the uncanny is uncanny only because it is secretly all too familiar, which is why it is repressed. (AT 273/262)

The philistines in this sense are not to be grasped in terms of categories of taste; their project is a more active one, and their refusal is a gesture that has a social meaning which ultimately transcends the matter of art itself and the more limited sphere of the aesthetic:

> The increasing spirituality [or abstraction] of a henceforth secular art spurs the rancor of those excluded from culture, thereby generating a new kind of consumption art over against itself, while at the same time their revulsion against this last drives the artists themselves on to ever more desperate and imprudent forms of spiritualization. (AT 28/20)

This encapsulated mythic history, whose context is a discussion of the peculiar unpleasurability of modern art (and even its vocation to be resolutely unpleasurable), dramatizes the moment of differentiation of what will become the three distinct positions that come into being over against art: those who are initially excluded (Odysseus's crew), those who come to demand consumer pleasure in the place of what they have been excluded from (the public of the Culture Industry), and finally those who, more keenly aware of the whole process (and of what Odysseus is able to hear), conceive a more generalized reaction to it, which must now be identified: it is none other than the great figure of *ressentiment* most dramatically elaborated in Nietzsche.

For what the philistines 'understand only too well' in the (modern) works they hate and characterize as incomprehensible is of course the deepest vocation of art itself – the *'promesse de bonheur'*, in the form of art's 'broken promise', which keeps the idea of happiness alive at the moment of denying its present existence. It is, then, this ultimate relationship to 'happiness' and to utopian fulfillment which is symbolically at play in the passion of the *'homme du ressentiment'*, and can thereby become manifest on a range of other social levels. In fact, the strong form (or narrative manifestation) of Adorno's philistine is to be found not in the 'Culture Industry' chapter of *Dialectic of Enlightenment*, nor anywhere in *Aesthetic Theory*, but rather in the final chapter of the former work, which deals with anti-Semitism. This extraordinary utopian analysis of anti-Semitism in terms of cultural envy now stages the anti-Semitic passion as the very hatred of happiness itself:

> The rights of man were designed to promise happiness even to those without power. Because the cheated masses feel that this promise – as a universal – remains a lie as long as classes exist, it stirs their rage; they feel mocked. Even as a possibility or an idea they repeatedly repress the thought of such happiness, they deny it ever more passionately the more imminent it seems. Wherever happiness seems to have been achieved in the midst of universal renunciation, they must repeat that gesture of suppression which is really the suppression of their own longing. Everything that occasions such repetition and such repression, however miserable it may be in itself – Ahasverus and Mignon, alien things which are reminders of the promised land, or beauty that recalls sexuality, or the proscribed animal reminiscent of promiscuity – draws down upon itself the destructive lust of the 'civilized', who could never wholly fulfill and realize the painful process of civilization itself. To those who spasmodically dominate nature, a tormented nature provocatively reflects back the image of powerless happiness. The thought of happiness without power is unbearable, because only then would it be true happiness.
> (DA 154-5/172)

Elsewhere in this chapter (and alongside various alternate explanatory models of more doubtful interest) Adorno and Horkheimer develop their analysis further in the direction of the relationship of anti-Semitism to the archaic – both social and 'natural' – and to their own theme of mimesis, at least implicitly enlarging this conception of a rage at the idea of happiness to include the envy for what is fantasized as the less alienated state of an older community or collectivity (very much in the spirit of their *'Odyssey'* commentary, in which the Enlightenment spirit of Odysseus is read as a series of cancellations and repressions of pre-capitalist forms). Along with Sartre's theory of anti-Semitism, this 'utopian' analysis surely remains one of the most powerful and convincing

diagnoses of what has otherwise been attributed to sheerly psychological
and irrational impulses (and thereby structurally consigned to what is
by definition incomprehensible). This particular analysis is also independent of the psychologizing perspective of Adorno's *Authoritarian Personality*, where the meaning of *ressentiment* as a social act is recontained
and reified into a theory of character structure.

The emergence of the 'anti-Semite' as a strong manifestation of the
social form of the 'philistine' in general now also makes a little clearer
the cultural 'convergence theory' of *Dialectic of Enlightenment*, in which
a Hollywood and New Deal USA is structurally characterized as bearing
a family likeness to Hitlerian Germany. The deeper continuity is precisely
secured by this figure, who, anti-Semite in the Nazi social order, is in
the United States identified as the seemingly more benign figure of the
philistine of the Culture Industry: both negative embodiments of the
deeper *ressentiment* generated by class society itself. Meanwhile, the valorization of art now finds its deeper function in precisely this diagnosis,
as the guilty and fragile place of a promise of social and personal happiness
persisting within a social order deformed by class and tending towards
an ever more universal bureaucratic control. With this larger framework,
then, the external positioning of the aesthetic is complete, and *Aesthetic
Theory* proceeds to its central topic, which is the exploration of the internal dynamic of art and form.

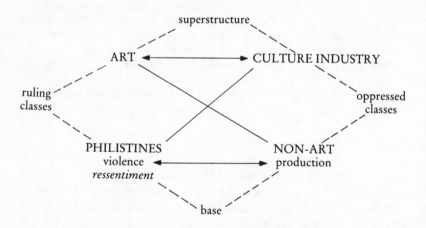

PART III

Productivities

of the Monad

One

The shifting and ambiguous ideological implications of this defense of art against its enemies or its deceptive equivalents are, however, radically changed the moment we complete the move – already anticipated in advance above – from some general notion of art as a process or a value to the individual works of art themselves. This shift in focus – which modifies the whole tenor of the discussion and reveals everything that is still vital and unexploited in what might today be called Adorno's critical method – can be characterized in terms of one of Adorno's great themes, that of *nominalism*, whose multiple significance can even here at the outset be briefly sketched.

Nominalism is for Adorno a philosophical tendency which is at one and the same time a historical event. In aesthetic terms it means the repudiation of the universal: for example, the refusal of the Hegelian objectification of art into genres and styles (a dialectical advance in the form of a strategic withdrawal or limitation: Adorno quite properly mentions Croce as the moment in which this thematic emerges, without yet developing into an exploration of the consequences which then practically ensued in the emergence of what we call 'modern' – that is to say, nominalistic – art [see AT 398/377]). The repudiation of these kinds of historicizing aesthetic universals (Hegel's three great forms of the symbolic, the classical and the romantic, for example) is accompanied by critical mixed feelings about those even more local historical universals or abstractions which are the 'isms' of the avant-garde movements (deployed, much against the spirit of Adorno, in the present book): they still have their truth, but as intellectual signs and symptoms of the *Novum* rather than as stylistic or period terms under which one could subsume the individual works as a particular is subsumed philosophically under a general.

Here Adorno comes the closest to that contemporary (or postmodern) *Bilderverbot* leveled on historiographic narrative itself, on the various stories of art history, on the larger historical paradigms of period and evolution, from which the freshness of the present (including the 'present' of the individual works of art) has always, since Nietzsche, seemed to evaporate. The difference between Adorno and these anti-historical anxieties of poststructuralism lies in the informing presence of an Event (the concept of nominalism implies a causality, identified with the tendencies of history), but also in a migration of history into the work's very form (which now becomes more profoundly social and historical than would have been the case when it merely served as a privileged example of some larger historical or social narrative).

Yet behind the spurious 'universals' of this still historical type, nominalism also tracks the more static universals of the Kantian type, to which reference has already been made above: for us today, such schemata sort themselves out along a wide range of henceforth distinct specializations. They can be grasped as a kind of proto-psychology, in which case the business of aesthetics is reduced to the analysis of various kinds of stimuli, from the machinery of the Culture Industry all the way to Aristotelian catharsis (which Adorno quite consequently denounces – [AT 354/339]). They can, on the other hand, be viewed as the detection of various kinds of conceptual grids and categories within the experience of what we normally call perception: in which case, for Adorno, they are to be denounced as the illicit attempt to transform bodily immediacy into more 'spiritualized' and idealistic forms of abstract thinking, a repression by way of sublimation and a mind-oriented, philosophical dread of what cannot, in aesthetic experience or elsewhere, be philosophized.

Here, then, the work of art is dissolved into sets of abstract patterns, which the universalists are able to draw and exploit in various directions: towards structuralist descriptions, for example, which seek grounding outside the traditional psychological categories; towards metaphysical meanings of the loftier and most traditional high-philosophical type (wherein the individual works – and even, for Adorno, their individual truth-contents – are still replaced by the universals of religious or existential or aestheticizing-religious 'experience'); or finally towards the specific universals of specialized philosophical aesthetics, including such categories as harmony, consonance, proportion, aesthetic appearance [*Schein*], expression, and the like. Such specifically aesthetic or formal categories – which already, as can be seen, span a variety of distinct historical experiences of the aesthetic – are, however, not merely false in the philosophical sense, for they carry within themselves, and within their empty conceptuality, the sedimented experience of specific historical works as such.

Indeed, the project of yet another philosophical aesthetics after the end of aesthetics as a philosophical discipline remains entangled in this dead conceptuality which it cannot jettison but must somehow untangle and provisionally readapt for new purposes, while definitively devaluing and discrediting it. What very different concepts such as proportion or mimesis or expression all illicitly by their very formal nature strive for – and what must be blocked and forestalled in all of them – is the vocation to yield a single-shot 'definition' of the work of art in general (a vocation we already know to be misguided by the very assimilation within it of Art in general and the individual work); something Adorno has taught us to see not as the relationship of the general to the particular, but rather as a deep contradiction and an unresolvable tension within the individual works fully as much as within Art itself.

This means, however, that traditional aesthetic concepts can still be pressed back into service dialectically when the identification of what contradicts and de-universalizes them is systematically secured: thus ugliness must rise up at once against proportion, and the concept of the fragment rebuke the value of harmony; mimesis must be painfully shackled to its irreconcilable opposite, expression, and aesthetic appearance itself – the untranslatable *Schein* – undermined at once at the moment of its triumphant emergence by that omnipresent drive to transcend the aesthetic and to be more than mere aesthetic appearance (an undermining which can also be identified as yet another of the protean forms of what we have here begun to evoke with the name of nominalism). This inducement of a state of war between the traditional aesthetic and formal concepts, then, at once discloses their varied historicity and their deeper situational taproot in specific forms of artistic practice in this or that historical moment.

But in this Adorno must also argue against himself: in so far as his is still an *aesthetic*, in the traditional sense, he also has his single-shot descriptive formal category, which will shortly be identified as that of *construction*, and also has its specifically historical praxis-situation – namely, the nominalist or minimalist moment of aesthetic modernism (from Schoenberg's expressionism to Beckett's theater). Whether his own privileged formal category – which is, to be sure, often released into the local dialectical maelstrom of oppositions with other local formal categories – is as a concept structurally distinct enough from the traditional kinds to sustain this function and this organizational centrality; whether, indeed, it can project its formal claim beyond its own historical aesthetic moment (which is now a thing of the past with enough power

to speak to our own very different one) – these are the ultimate problems
with which *Aesthetic Theory* confronts us.

The matter of nominalism, however, is by no means exhausted by
these conceptual difficulties, which have until now been registered on
the side of the 'notion' or the 'idea', as Hegel might have said; they
have their equivalent on the side of the psychic subject, whose resistance
to universals nominalism also is. Indeed, there is a widespread commitment of contemporary (or poststructural) philosophy to descriptions or
even valorizations of fragmented subjectivity, of the 'decentering of the
subject', of 'schizophrenia', of the repressive function of the ego or the
illusions of personal identity or of biographical continuity, all the way
to the 'waning' of the subject, its eclipses, drops in *'niveau'*, swoons,
breaks, the fitful glimpses of the effects of determination of consciousness
by something that is not itself (whether the unconscious, language, or
an otherness of doxa and ideology). Such contemporary phenomena or
formulations are all, from Adorno's dialectical standpoint, to be seen
as so many symptoms of a nominalism that has penetrated subjectivity
itself and conferred on a variety of punctual subjective 'experiences' an
immediacy that is not to be reduced or defused by their assimilation
to something more general, or more abstract, or more intellectual-generic.
What this means is not merely that the aesthetic tastes of this fitful postcontemporary subjectivity will be very different in kind from those of
the controlled and more comfortable identities of older bourgeois or
aristocratic publics: although that is so also, and spells the end of any
universal aesthetics or doctrine of aesthetic invariables, the tendency even
goes so far as to challenge the very conception of aesthetic unity and
of the closure of the work itself (something which poses a crucial threat
to Adorno's aesthetic project; the notion of Leibniz's *monad* will be
invoked to parry it, as we shall see later on).

Subjective nominalism also means that these fragments of a former
subjectivity have now paradoxically become objective, and can therefore
be seen as constituting themselves materials, building blocks, the stone
and glass and aluminum, of the work's construction (alongside the more
traditional aesthetic raw material and artistic languages out of which
the work was once, traditionally, thought to be made or formed). As
has already been suggested above, this dialectical reversal of the subjective
into the objective is – in what it eliminates of false problems, as well
as in the new and virtually inexplored interpretive possibilities it opens
up – the central heritage of Adorno's aesthetic positions, comparable
in that only to some of the more intuitive speculations of the Russian
Formalists. The predominant exposition throughout in terms of music
is, from this perspective, scarcely a specialized limitation, but rather opens

a door wide for speculative analogies of the most creative kind with the other arts.

Finally, we must note what is in many ways the most central sense of the term nominalism as Adorno uses it throughout *Aesthetic Theory* – namely, as an event, and in particular as something that happened to the history of art itself. The historical paradigm remains that familiar one of the emergence of modernity (as we have learned to understand it in Marx's account of the commodity form, and in Weber's account of rationalization) and of modernism (as it is registered in the forms of the artists, most emblematically, from the European perspective, in Baudelaire). This mythic 'fall' – into capitalism and into modernization – was, as we have seen, already paradoxically inscribed in the very title of *Dialectic of Enlightenment*, where a repressive mimetic and self-sublating process of abstraction and control – projected back into the very origins of human history, and beyond Homer all the way to the first forms of the magical domination of nature – now suddenly, in the eighteenth century, seems to know a dialectical leap in which, brutally canceling its older magical and superstitious, overtly mimetic forms, it pursues the mimetic process on a higher level of abstraction, keeping faith with the deeper impulse of mimesis by systematically expunging all traces of mimesis itself, in what Adorno and Horkheimer will call the *Bilderverbot*, the ban on graven images of a henceforth secular, skeptical, mathematizing thought.

What is to be retained in the aesthetic context of these older descriptions of scientific rationality is the way in which each state produces historicity and the past in the very process of canceling it: scientific 'progress' is thus synchronic rather than diachronic, not merely sweeping away its older mode of production as *pensée sauvage*, but with each new act transforming the very precursor steps of its own, now 'rationalistic', scientific activity into superstition and metaphysical survival. Adorno and Horkheimer are of course, in their earlier work, crucially concerned with the way in which the theoretical component of such enlightened science ruthlessly converts its own official philosophies into unenlightened myths; so that even positivism, which more effectively turned all previous philosophy into theology than any Marxian vision of the former's end and realization, then itself, in its Comtean form, became a peculiarly Hegelian or even occult vestige of superstitious error to be stamped out in its turn.

That discussion, however, seeks to dramatize the inherent vanishing point of theory itself, the ultimate black hole into which, as Reason, Munchausen-like, draws itself up by its own pigtail and kicks its ladder away from under itself, it ultimately repudiates the last vestiges of its own theoretical foundations and finds its extreme abstract vocation in the elimination of thinking altogether, as some earlier, archaic, henceforth dispensable stage. This scientific 'nominalism', then, also seeks the abolition of what used to be called subjectivity; to be sure, its dynamic is henceforth intertwined with the 'economic' (in the larger Marxian sense of the labor process and the commodity form, and in particular, as we have already seen, with the emergence of equivalence and the abstractions of 'identity'); nor is the emergence of the 'aesthetic' at the dawn of modernizing Enlightenment – its radical dissociation from the rational and the scientific; the flight of the sensory and the sensible, the representational and the mimetic, into this newly constituted marginal space of rejection and compensation – in any way a secondary or non-constitutive process, but so essential to the description of Enlightenment that henceforward, as we have seen, only the 'degraded' Culture Industry offers a vivid picture of the prolongation of its colonizing logic.

None the less, the temporality we have attributed to science is significantly analogous (just as a caricature is also an analogy) to the historical dynamic of the aesthetic monad; the paradoxes of the first may illuminate those of its opposite number, and in particular the troublesome problem of the 'New' or the *Novum*. For there is a sense in which the aesthetic *Novum* also cancels its prehistory and converts the very techniques on which its innovations depended into outmoded and obsolete technology: if the word synchronic has been insisted on, however, it was evoked in order – more effectively than the older aestheticizing terminology of 'intrinsic' and 'extrinsic' – to exclude or to dispel the illusion that such innovation could be detected and registered from the outside, from the vantage point of some 'diachronic' narrative from which we calmly observe the emergence of the chromatic (in Wagner), or of 'point of view' (in Henry James), enumerating them furiously on our score card as they pass by, conjoined with notations on the various players and dated volumes.

The historicity in question within the individual work, however, includes that past in the moment of canceling it; so that it might be said of it that however idealistic the Hegelian doctrine of *Aufhebung* may well be elsewhere – in a human history of material breaks and convulsions in which the past of individuals and of collectivities vanishes into death without a trace – here alone, within the aesthetic monad, *Aufhebung* remains true, as a well-nigh materialist descriptive concept (much as Adorno will also say, of Leibniz's concept of the monad itself, that it is the inspired, deformed, mystified anticipation of that very peculiar 'material' object which is the work of art alone). The experience of the 'New' is therefore not something which comes to the experience

of the work of art from the outside, owing to fresh philological or icono-
graphic information, say (although such information has its role to play
in preparing us for that experience): it is at one with aesthetic experience,
it is itself in some deeper way the work's 'truth content' (*Wahrheitsgehalt*).

We must pause here to reemphasize a consequence that has already
been mentioned, namely, that given the traditional valorization of the
'New' and of innovation in all the modernisms, in effect such an aesthetic
assimilates all 'genuine art' to what had hitherto been considered a single
period within artistic history, namely modernism 'proper'. The basic
problem with such an assimilation is not the most obvious one of periodization (or, in other words, what one does with Bach, or Chrétien de
Troyes, or Propertius): emergent money and commercial economies pass
their internal logic and their dynamisms on unevenly to the processes
of cultural production. The very impudence of the time frame of *Dialectic
of Enlightenment* (which describes Odysseus as the first 'bourgeois') suggests that a 'capitalist' cultural dynamic is not to be narrowly construed
within the (still rather short) lifespan of industrial capitalism; and also,
on the other hand, that that 'modernism' preeminently characteristic
of the second or 'imperialist' stage of triumphant European capitalism
in the late nineteenth century may also be seen as something like the
'inner truth' of earlier, slower, seemingly more representational cultures.
What is more scandalous, and yet no doubt logically consistent with
these positions, is their radical exclusion of what may anthropologically
be called non-capitalist art: the cave paintings of Altamira were evoked,
but as an example of magical mimesis – that is, of the proto-Enlightenment
domination of nature – not as some radically different form of art or
culture as such from our own. Nor is the status of non-Western music
imaginable, except as some Hegelian 'end of art' in our Western sense.
The central unspoken proposition – that all great music is bourgeois
music[1] – is thinkable (well beyond the current issues of postmodernism
and its relation to the great tradition) only as a utopian projection of
radically different societies and modes of production in which what we
think of as art – and in particular as the 'work of art', no longer socially
differentiated in our fashion – would have to be called something else.

Were the atomic structure of society to be transformed, then art would no
longer have to sacrifice its Idea – how the particular is possible in the first
place – to some social universal: as long as the particular and the universal
diverge, freedom cannot exist. Freedom would, however, accord the particular
those rights which are today aesthetically in evidence only in the idiosyncratic
constraints artists find themselves obliged to submit to. (AT 69/62)

We will return later to the exceedingly characteristic idea that the contemporary artist's freedom is to be found not in free-floating subjectivity somewhere, whether in choice or caprice, but rather in the objective constraints of the material itself. But it would be a mistake to deduce, from the way in which this passage traditionally stages philosophical 'reconciliation' as the harmony between the universal and the particular, that such a vision plays any normative role in Adorno's aesthetics: there indeed such harmony ('the concrete universal') is not merely normative in all the bad senses, but historically unrealizable in a situation (for which we have been using the word nominalism) in which precisely the most authentic works reveal the incommensurability between the particular and the universal, and are therefore all, in the traditional normative sense, determinate 'failures'.

As for Adorno's conception of the *Novum*, a fuller account cannot be given until we have some better sense of the relationship between the 'productive forces' – or what Marx called the 'level of development attained by social production' – and the work of art itself. What has already been implied, however, is that the 'New' is not a temporal concept in the phenomenological sense; and also that its very conception and theorization (at the dawn of the Modern, with Baudelaire) has a great deal to do with nominalism itself: the universal now being the repetitive and the return of the same, whose only resistance – fragile as that may be – would seem to be the unique here and now, without a name, incomparable, the unrepeatable conjuncture, what can be exchanged with nothing else, and what thereby becomes the 'New' by default, since there are no longer any generic categories to classify it under. Yet nominalism in that sense is not merely a form of resistance to the bad Universal, but also a dilemma and a generalized historical situation, a crisis, whose results for the work of art we must now examine.

Two

The most familiar and widely read version of Adorno's account of the crisis of art (or the emergence of modernism) we owe not to him but to Thomas Mann, who appropriated its earlier formulation (in *Philosophie der neuen Musik*) for his novel *Doktor Faustus*. The heart of the matter is there thematized as the crisis of *Schein*, a convenient term for which English has no easy equivalent and which has frequently been rendered as 'aesthetic appearance' or 'show' or, alternately, as 'aesthetic illusion': expressions which tendentially imply the existence of something else *behind* that appearance or illusion and which, besides the obvious presence of an 'original', may also suggest things as diverse as the 'true meaning' of the work, or on the other hand its primary and quite unaesthetic materials, such as oil paint, or words, or bodies wearing costumes and make-up. What is troublesome about these versions is not so much the implication that in a given situation *Schein* might vanish away and utterly evaporate, abandoning its spectators to the idle activity of staring at pieces of smeared canvas or witnessing, with no little embarrassment, a little group of people striding around a platform waving their arms improbably and opening their mouths (the well-known defamiliarizations of art itself in Flaubert and in Tolstoy).[2] Such moments of the eclipse of illusion (or the sudden wakeful disintoxicated demise of our 'belief' in it) are on the contrary useful as a kind of aesthetic version of the theory of the phantom member – the moment when we step outside the thing and have some more vivid sense of what it really was.

The difficulty is, rather, that such a vaguer sense of 'aesthetic illusion' as mere adornment, as an outer ornamentation superadded to some thing itself, then encourages speculation as to what an art would be like that had the courage to throw off such 'illusions' and to be what it really was in the first place. As a matter of fact, this is exactly what seems to happen in the artistic history of the new or the modern (a process which for Adorno, as we have seen, can be conceived as extending backwards into the *ancien régime*): each successive form or generation then repudiating its immediate past as an affair of romance, lies, the grossest trumpery, in contrast to which its own offerings draw their novelty from a more passionate vocation for truth and a greater commitment to exactitude and detail. Here already, but in restricted form, we see the 'ban on graven images', the anti-mimetic impulse, deployed as a therapeutic instrument against a limited past. Nor is this generational critique of *Schein* or aesthetic appearance always staged in terms of that value called realism: 'truth' – or, more recently, 'authenticity' – will work equally well; neither seems quite so bound to any normative aesthetic. Yet even 'realism' can be used against itself, as when only yesterday Robbe-Grillet attacked the ideological illusions at the heart of Balzacian realism in the name of some more revolutionary commitment of the *nouveau roman* to 'reality'.

The crisis of *Schein* can thus, properly restricted, be pressed into service as the primary motor-power of the modernist aesthetic 'permanent revolution' or the ceaseless fashion changes of artistic innovation in modern times. But for some outside observer – or, at least, for the aesthetic historian whose sense of the ever more rapid dynamics of this process opens a certain bemused distance from it – it is the end or vanishing point of the momentum which becomes a matter for speculation, returning us to the ultimate question of whether an art utterly divorced from aesthetic appearance is conceivable, or on the contrary (the great Hegelian concept of the 'end of art' itself) whether the suspicion that attaches to *Schein* will not finally result in the abolition of art altogether: a *Bilderverbot* that triumphantly annihilates all its graven images without a trace.

The deeper motive for the stigmatization of aesthetic appearance we have already learned: it is the ultimate social guilt of art itself, as that was revealed nakedly and without comment at the very dawn of 'Western' culture in the story of the Sirens' song. But this 'original sin' is evidently intensified in class society by rationalism and secularization (Enlightenment in its narrower historical sense), with the result that the only place where 'aesthetic appearance', 'aesthetic illusion', lives on comfortably, with a clear conscience, is the Culture Industry. Genuine art, which cannot abolish *Schein* altogether without destroying itself and turning to silence, must none the less live its illusory appearance and its unreal luxury status as play in a vivid guilt that permeates its very forms, and is sometimes oddly called reflexivity or self-consciousness. 'Fiction', how-

ever – another powerful proper name for *Schein*, which inflects its meaning in instructive directions – is evidently, in a variety of styles and
forms, the principal commodity the Culture Industry has to sell (the
poststructural variant is called 'representation'): still, endless talk shows,
quiz programs, game shows, lotteries, mock courts, and even the news
itself, suggest not so much that appetite for truth that Dziga Vertov's
documentaries hoped to arouse as well as to satisfy in a socialist society,
as rather some secret worm eating away even at the gratifications of
the fictional and representation in mass culture: the crisis of *Schein* now
extending even into that commodified and degraded precinct in which
it was to have been safely practiced.

The substitute term 'fiction' is, however, more suggestive when we
try it out on areas outside its official domain, where all the conceivable
internal and external permutations of storytelling in novel and film are
only too familiar (from the anti-novel to the documentary). What, however, would a non-fictional architecture be?[3] unless it is simply a matter
of some resolute functionalism for which decoration and embellishment
are very precisely the fictional elements to be expunged. Meanwhile,
a non-fictional painting, far from being unimaginable, is the very foundational concept of a henceforth stereotypical history of this art, in which
storytelling is tracked down, denounced and exterminated to the point
only the painterly materials themselves – and even after them, only their
abstract idea or 'concept' – remain the object of aesthetic contemplation.
(Such was at least, until yesterday, the hegemonic master narrative of
a certain modernist tradition.) But fiction's other identity – *Schein* –
still presumably lives on in these rudimentary materials, at least when
appropriately framed by the museum and the institution of the viewing
experience. Adorno's own account of 'abstraction' is rather different from
this one and may serve as an initial staging of his own idiosyncratic
dialectic, which will be described at greater length shortly; for it focuses,
not on the opposition between the commodity form and 'great art',
but rather on their identity:

> Baudelaire neither struggles against reification nor does he simply offer a
> representation of it; he protests against it by way of the very experience
> of its own archetypes, the medium of such experience becoming poetic form
> itself. This is what lifts him authoritatively above all late Romantic sentimen-
> tality. The historical originality of this work lies in the way in which the
> overwhelming objectivity of the commodity form, which absorbs all remnants
> of the human into itself, is syncopated with that objectivity of the work
> of art which is prior to living subjectivity: the absolute work of art thereby
> coincides with absolute commodification. The residue of abstraction in the
> concept of the modern is the tribute levied on this last by the commodity

itself. If what is consumed in monopoly capitalism is no longer use value, but exchange value, by the same token the abstractness of the modern work – that irritating indeterminacy about its nature and function – becomes the very index of what it is. ... From its very beginnings, aesthetic abstraction, in Baudelaire still rudimentary, and a kind of allegorical reaction to a world itself become abstract, was something like a taboo on graven images. The taboo is specifically directed against what the provincial Germans hoped to salvage under the slogan *Aussage* [message], namely some meaningfulness still left in appearance; after the catastrophe of meaning, appearance itself becomes abstract. (AT 39–40/31–2)

What is sacrificed, on this analysis of abstraction, is less the 'fictive' dimension of the work than, rather, its 'meaningfulness' or, if one prefers, the pretense that the particular and the general – the thing and its meaning – are still in any, even distant, way 'organically' or experientially related. Nominalism here dissociates the remnant of lived immediacy itself from its 'universal', which has now become the universal equivalence and abstraction of the commodity form: the work of art, however, stubbornly holds on to both, in order to preserve the truth of their contradiction. With such an account, we are evidently far enough from those questions of *Schein* with which we began; unless we have to do here precisely with an extraordinary mutation in aesthetic appearance itself, in which the omnipresent power of the commodity form is now paradoxically pressed into the service of that aesthetic impulse it sought to master (and, in what is called the Culture Industry, succeeded in doing so). What is paradoxical here, however, is that in this case the modern – or, for Adorno, the work of art in general – is coterminous with the power of the commodity form, so that to evoke some 'aesthetic impulse' that preceded this situation (the taste for beauty, for example) becomes a logical non sequitur.

Commodification, however, is only one of the alternate codes in which Adorno dramatizes the crisis and the agony of aesthetic appearance. Its related Marxian thematics – the question of the dynamics of production – will be dealt with in a later chapter; here, it is appropriate merely to stress the philosophical relationship between commodification and that language of nominalism which has already been touched on and which – far more than 'non-identity' – constitutes something like the primary 'key' of *Aesthetic Theory* (in so far as one can assign priorities in a text as variable and atonal as the great 'pieces for orchestra' of the second Viennese school that looms so large within it). The commodity form, then, is to the situation of nominalism as the false universal to the bereft particular: the former's empty abstraction determines a heterogeneity of isolated data – whether in the world or the self – that can no longer be made to *mean*, if one understands 'meaning' in the traditional way as the subsumption of a particular under a general.

The ultimate and fundamental aesthetic medium in which this situation is explored – that of music – returns us to the crisis of aesthetic appearance (or *Schein*) in a way which now concretely mobilizes all these analytic categories. To ask the question about the fictionality of music – whether a non-fictive music is conceivable? how a music might be imagined which would resolutely attempt to confront the guilt of the fictional and the original sin of aesthetic appearance and to absolve itself of it? – to raise such questions in the musical realm is now to begin to identify *Schein* and 'fiction' with the *time* of the work itself; it is to pose issues of the whole and the part in a new way, which at once engages the historical 'psychic subject' that can or cannot hear and remember such relationships (the 'fetishization of hearing') and also at once problematizes the very concept of a 'whole' or overall form in terms of which particulars might be perceived; it is finally to make unavoidable the primacy of construction as such, which the dynamics of other artistic media might well inflect in the direction of more partial aesthetic categories: in language, towards that of *expression*, or in painting, towards that of *mimesis*.

Such oppositions, inherited from various moments of traditional aesthetic reflection, reemerge and disappear in various permutations throughout *Aesthetic Theory*: *Schein* versus *Ausdruck* (expression), for example (AT 168/161); or the mimetic versus the constructive (AT 72/65); or montage versus meaning (AT 231-3/221-3). These oppositions are in Adorno to be read as shifting constellations: that is, no definitive terminological solution or philosophical resolution is to be derived from them – the bias or the tendency towards the valorization of something like a concept of construction is evident, but the term itself should as far as possible not be reified or privileged (something that would turn Adorno's book back into a traditional aesthetics). Meanwhile, each oppositional conjuncture is historicized, on two levels: the opposition between montage and meaning, for example, expresses a specific historical moment in the development of modern art; but it also emerges at a specific 'historical' or narrative moment in Adorno's text, so to speak, and is thereby as situational and as provisional in the text as it is in some 'external' history of form.

Finally, all of these oppositions can be mobilized within the discussion of a specific artistic medium: in music, for example, the opposition of *Schein* and expression designates the historically crucial moment of expressionism and of the breakthrough year 1911: the moment in which the nominalist impulse to absolute expression of the subject collides, in the most archetypal of all confrontations, with the ultimate inner formal

commitment of the work of art to some remnant of *Schein*. If it is understood that, in music, this last corresponds to time itself, to the length
of the work, to the sheer duration of musical development; if it is also
understood that for Adorno 'expression' is somehow always the expression of suffering, the cry of pain, sheer dissonance as such – then the
dramatic nature of this confrontation or contradiction will begin to be
clear, as well as the relevance of the 'problem' of a non-fictive music
raised above. Fictionality, in music, is then simply temporal duration,
which is also the *Schein* or aesthetic appearance of the musical work.
How much time do you need for something properly musical to happen?
Are a few notes already 'musical' in that sense? Would the utterance
of a single musical 'sentence' – that is to say, an intelligible phrase or
theme, melody or tune – be enough? The sonata form, however, speaks
against this, implying that the phrase or theme is not really uttered,
even for the first time, until it is somehow (after suitable variation)
repeated and confirmed:

> The reprise is the very crux of the sonata form. It endowed what was decisive
> since Beethoven – the dynamics of thematic development [*Durchführung*] –
> with a retroactive confirmation, like the effect of a film on a viewer who
> stays on after the ending and watches the beginning all over again. Beethoven
> mastered this by way of a *tour de force* which became his trademark: in the
> optimal moment of the final reprise, he presents the result of those dynamics
> and of that process as the ratification and justification of the earlier moment,
> of what had already been there in the first place. This marks his complicity
> with the guilt of the great idealistic systems in philosophy, with the dialectician
> Hegel, in whom finally the very essence of the negations, and thereby of
> becoming itself, flows back into the theodicy of the already existent. By way
> of the reprise, then, music – itself a ritual of bourgeois freedom – remains,
> like the society in which it exists and which exists in it, in thrall to mythic
> unfreedom. It manipulates the cyclical relationship to nature in such a way
> that what returns, by virtue of the simple fact of its return, seems greater
> than itself, and becomes metaphysical meaning proper, or the Idea.[4]

The sonata form, then, works to produce an Idea or a feeling of necessity
which is socially ideological, and confirms and justifies the totality of
what is: at the same time – and in so far as Adorno's thought has a
metaphysical dimension, which will become clear when we discuss the
relationship between art and nature – this ideological function and menda-
city of the sonata form is itself but a distorted historical reflection or
manifestation of the deeper metaphysical dilemma of all art:

> how a making can disclose something which is not made; how what is not
> even true to its own concept can have a truth content. One could grasp

this only if the content were somehow distinct from its appearance and in a form of its own. (AT 164/157)

How there can be something like a 'natural truth' of the *constructed* will then be the central issue of this metaphysical dimension of Adorno's aesthetics, which will be dealt with in a later chapter.

Here, however, in our immediately musical context, the problem becomes rather that of the authenticity of constructed musical time, and the tendential reduction of expressionist music to a few brief instants is only the outward symptom of this ultimate crisis in aesthetic appearance, and but the formal result and end-product of a whole musical nominalism which eschews the intelligibility of the lengthy and elaborated musical phrase. It does so, however, less in the name of some ultimate musical point or note than in the name of the dissonant cluster, whose formal drama lies in the fact that even it needs some minimal time in order to register its expressive pain. Even the most facile philosophical dialectic reminds us that dissonance still needs consonance to be registered as such; but if we think of that consonance as a habit of the ear, and as a traditional musical culture of the first shocked listeners, then we are led to reflect on the 'aging of modern music' and the paradoxes of a *Novum* which, like any other event, has it in itself to become ancient history.

If, on the other hand, we think of the consonance that dissonance still needs as a framework in time, a minimal duration apt to set in place the preconditions for its own violent cancellation, then we register the historical situation of the crisis of *Schein*, which must perpetuate itself as even the briefest of temporal extensions in order for its truth – not *Schein* itself, but its very crisis, its guilt, its inauthenticity and impossibility ('poetry after Auschwitz') – to come to expression. Adorno's disillusionment with the 'solution' to this expressionist crisis – later Schoenberg and the twelve-tone system, from which the very idea of consonance, and along with it the authenticity of dissonance, vanishes altogether – has been discussed elsewhere. What may be observed here is the interesting historical trajectory whereby his commitment to this moment of extreme expressionism is then unexpectedly fulfilled thirty years later by the forms of Samuel Beckett; the secret history of what it would be frivolous to think of as nothing but Adorno's personal tastes then stands revealed as a discontinuous spark that leaps from expressionism to minimalism. On the other hand, if it is a question of disengaging those tastes with some precision, it must be added that the purity of Webern's minimalism is equally repugnant to him; Berg's radical impurity – the true model, rather than either Schoenberg or Stravinsky, for

the orgiastic later compositions of Thomas Mann's Leverkuehn – he
seems much to have preferred. An impure minimalism, then! – which
oddly absorbs bits and pieces of a degraded mass culture all around it.

A rather different philosophical conception of the history of modern
art thereby strangely displaces the more conventional one that runs from
Baudelaire to some exhaustion of the modern (for example, to the impasse
of Schoenberg's twelve-tone system, to use a kind of formal shorthand).
This alternate history – in which modernism is transformed back into
'great art' in general – now finally makes the ultimate function of the
omnipresent motif of nominalism clear; for the latter is required philosophically to ground the former. From the perspective of the dilemmas
of nominalism, indeed the historical position of Beethoven, for example,
'whose music is no less haunted by the nominalistic motif than the philosophy of Hegel' (AT 329/315), is metamorphosed from that of a pre-
modern classic into the very showplace of the most modern dialectic
of *Schein* and construction:

The power of the crisis of aesthetic appearance can be measured by the fact
that it strikes even that music in appearance least inclined to the values of
illusionism. Even in such non- or anti-illusionistic music, the very sublimated
forms of fictive elements die off, not merely expression (as of non-existent
feelings), but also fictions of structure itself, such as that of total or overall
form, which here emerges as being unrealizable. In great music like that of
Beethoven, but probably well beyond the confines of the temporal arts as
such, the so-called primary materials, those ultimate building blocks that analysis reaches in its ultimate stage, turn out to be virtually empty of content
and in themselves vacuous or worthless [*nichtig*]. Only in so far as they asymp-
totically approach nothingness can they fuse together, in their becoming,
as a whole. Yet as distinct formal components, their deeper impulse is always
once again to turn back into *something*: whether a motif or a theme. This
immanent nullity of its most elementary determinants draws all integral art
down towards the amorphous, whose force of gravity increases proportionally
to its degree of organization. Only the amorphous confers the power of integration on a work of art. It is in the very moment of formal completion,
at the greatest distance from the formlessness of nature, that the natural
moment, that of the not yet formed and of the unarticulated, returns in
strength. On the closest inspection of a work of art its most objectivized
forms and images are transformed into a swarm of elements, texts dissolving
into sheer words. When you think you have the basic details of a work
of art firmly in your hands, they suddenly melt away into the indeterminate
and the undifferentiated: such is the nature of artistic mediation. Such is also
the way in which aesthetic appearance takes up its presence in the structure
of works of art. The particular, the very life element of the work, flees the
viewing subject, its concreteness evaporates under the micrological gaze. Pro-

cess, which has in every work of art coagulated into the appearance of an object, now begins to undermine its status as a static thing, and flows away again to where it came from. (AT 154-5/148-9)

What is being proposed is a good deal more scandalous than the simple opinion that Beethoven is not a particularly melodic composer; it is, rather, that his greatest themes or phrases are never anything more than an appearance of something like 'melody' in the first place – this last existing no doubt only in the Culture Industry as a kind of fetish. Rather, the functional power of the great themes is proportionate to the artificiality of their construction, which is motivated by the functional demands of the form (they must be modifiable here, susceptible to variation or the appropriate modulation there, serviceable by way of minimal reconstruction as transitions or as bridge-passages – in short, they come to sound like prefabricated architectural components or Le Corbusier's modular units); and yet, and for those very reasons, they come before us as meaningful aesthetic form, or *Schein*. Beethoven's is thus a minimalism fully as much as Beckett's, but one which *looks* organic and Romantic, and with the promise of late-Romantic lushness already stirring in it like an alien mirage. Adorno's Beethoven is thereby, like Pierre Menard's rewriting of Cervantes, exactly the same as the 'original' and yet a radically different historical text. ('To compose the *Quijote* at the beginning of the seventeenth century was a reasonable undertaking, necessary and perhaps even unavoidable; at the beginning of the twentieth, it is almost impossible,' etc.)

Anachronistic as it may seem, therefore, Beethoven's music is *montage* and as non-fictive as Eisenstein or Juan Gris: montage, the most consequent campaign 'against the art work as a coherent structure of meaning [*Sinnzusammenhang*]' (AT 233/223), is also the moment of triumph of the constructional principle itself:

> The aesthetic constructional principle, the peremptory primacy of the planned whole over detail as such and the latter's relationships within the microstructure, now stands as the correlative [to this seeming surface disorder]; in this sense, and in terms of its micro-structure, all modern art may be considered montage. (AT 233/223)

But the corollary of this doctrine of the worthlessness of the elementary components of the work, and the illusory nature even of their seemingly meaningful or harmonious combinations, turns out to be a modification in the subjective power attributed to the artist (let alone the 'genius'). It is a conclusion we will explore more fully when we deal with the dynamics of productivity; still, some initial consequences need to be drawn here, for paradoxically the constructional materials are meaningless or *nichtig* only in terms of human agency, of the composer or the listener. In reality they have their own meaning within themselves as a historically specific material or technique, which dictates its own formal development:

> How intimately related technique and content really are – conventional wisdom notwithstanding – was demonstrated by Beethoven himself in the remark that many of the effects normally attributed to the genius of the composer are in fact the results of little more than adroit manipulations of the diminished seventh. (AT 320/307)

The relationship of the part to the whole, therefore, redolent not merely of traditional aesthetic theory but also of a form of aesthetic taste and a type of classicizing aesthetic practice which is today utterly alien to us, recovers an astonishing and well-nigh postmodern relevance when, as supremely in *Aesthetic Theory*, it is reformulated as a historical crisis and an unresolvable structural contradiction. It is therefore appropriate to conclude this section on nominalism and construction in Adorno with a lengthier final *mise au point* on Beethoven himself:

> Beethoven confronted the antinomy [between unity and particularity], not by schematically extinguishing the individual component in the spirit of the prevailing practice of the preceding century, but rather – very much in kinship with the developing bourgeois natural sciences of his own time – by deperceptualizing it and stripping it of its qualities. He thereby did more than simply integrate music into the continuum of a new kind of becoming or process, thereby preserving musical form from the intensifying threat of empty abstraction. For the individual moments, as they sink in value, begin to interpenetrate each other and thereby to determine the very form itself through the very process by which they themselves tendentially disappear. The individual components in Beethoven are (but on the other hand are also not) the very impulse towards total form, in so far as they can have their existence only by way of that whole that allows them to be in the first place; whereas in and of themselves they tend towards the relative indeterminacy of the basic tonal relationships and thereby towards amorphousness. If you hear or read his exceedingly articulated music closely enough, it comes to resemble a continuum of nothingness. The *tour de force* of each of his great works lies in the way in which – as though taking Hegel absolutely literally – it determines the transformation of a totality of nothingness into a totality of Being – yet only as appearance [*Schein*], not with any claim to absolute truth. Yet even this last is at least suggested, by way of the immanent rigor which is the work's ultimate content. The latently diffuse and intangible, on the one hand, the supreme power that compels it to form together into something, on the other – these are the two poles of nature itself at work. Over against the daimon, the composing subject, who forges and flings great blocks of

material, there stands the undifferentiation of the tiniest unities into which each of his movements becomes dissociated, ending up no longer even as raw material but rather as the abstract system of tonal relationships themselves. (AT 276/264-5)

In fact, the problem of Adorno's minimalism is at one with the ambiguity of his very enterprise. If *Aesthetic Theory* is ultimately the expression of Adorno's personal aesthetic experience, and thereby projects his own limited biographical 'taste', then its philosophical positions become relativized in a more than historical fashion, and the work shrinks to the status of a document (albeit one of extraordinary intelligence and resourcefulness). If, on the other hand, more universal truths about the work of art are, for whatever reason, to be generalized from minimalism as a unique and privileged moment in the history of art, then we find ourselves unexpectedly back within a more traditional philosophical aesthetic, which still seeks to deduce the general from the particular in a manner peculiarly unacceptable for postcontemporary thought.

Characteristically, to be sure, this minimalism also includes a critique of minimalism (just as its framework denounces 'isms' in the first place). Thus the movement of detail evoked above in the analysis of Beethoven – the becoming 'anti-essential' and non- or anti-foundational of detail as such, its consequent and modern refusal of any internal self-justification, what Hegel would have called the loss or tendential impoverishment of its 'content' – is elsewhere identified as the very 'death wish' of detail itself (AT 450/421); while the triumph of Adorno's central principle of construction – in Constructivism as a historical avant-garde movement – spells the end of art itself: 'in fact, Constructivism has no place left for invention [*Einfall*], for the unplanned and the involuntary' (AT 450/421). The fact that Adorno, like Hegel, goes on to fantasize an art beyond the end of art, or even several, is intriguing enough: the conception of models developed in *Negative Dialectics* returns briefly in the supplementary fragments to suggest that artists may continue to invent and project models of art in a situation in which art-works can no longer concretely be realized (AT 452/423) (hence the stimulation postmodern painters find in theoretical writings about art, which seems today to have replaced the practical stimulation that used to be afforded by the work of other artists). In another place, indeed, Adorno prophetically suggests a return of the tonal after the most implacable forms of atonality, under whose hegemony it once again becomes strangely new: something that seems in fact to be happening in postmodern music (AT 62/54).

Yet the proper use of the doctrines of minimalism and of construction would appear to be those that seek to do without their fatal positivity:

not norms, then, but rhetorical features and parts of the constructed or reconstructed representation of a contradictory situation, pushed to the limit, in which the impossibility of art is not the occasion for pathos, but rather the deconcealment of an articulated structure that is in fact a concrete historical contradiction. What is then achieved, and the effectiveness of praxis, can thereby be measured and evaluated only after the fact. In art also, the slogan 'pessimism of the intellect, optimism of the will' is the only truly energizing ethic.

Three

But with this contextualization of Adorno's judgements, which 'sets them in motion' dialectically and rewrites them into the form of a situation and a contradiction, we again confront the issue of the status of the historical dialectic in the author of *Negative Dialectics*, and in particular the old problem of correspondence or reflection (or even, if you prefer, of base and superstructure): the essentially linguistic question of how the relationship between the cultural or aesthetic act and the social situation is to be expressed. *Aesthetic Theory*'s ingenious philosophical solution to this problem – the concept of the work of art as a windowless monad, which will be examined in the next chapter – in fact, for all practical intents and purposes, leaves it intact. The monad is, in other words, at one and the same time a reflection and not a reflection, just as the work of art itself is social and non-social all at once – or, better still, social through and through by virtue of its very antisociality (see below). This is of course the classical form of the Hegelian dialectic, the identity of identity and non-identity.

What complicates the classical formulation is that there are two forms of non-identity to be confronted, rather than one: Nature, the absolute Other, on the one hand; but also society, a very different kind of other from the first, and certainly nothing like the 'second nature' of the tradition, even though it is often evoked in the language of ontology as the 'totality of what is'. The reflexes of the well-known Great Refusal, then, are, here – where society is in question – peremptory and absolute (and go a long way towards explaining Adorno's hostility to left politics – unless, indeed, it is the other way round): '*denn wahr ist nur, was nicht in diese Welt passt*' [nothing complicitous with this world can have

any truth (AT 93/86)]. But this imposes a very different kind of negativity
from the classical form of non-identity (and introduces the supplementary
terminological difficulty one always has when explicating the Frankfurt
School – namely, that the words 'positive' – associated with positivism
– and 'affirmative' – as in Marcuse's 'affirmative character of culture'
– are always for them negative in connotation).

There fatally reappears, then, that dualistic alternative present in all
radical thought: the differentiation, under whatever form or in whatever
terminology, between the positive and the negative, the progressive and
the reactionary (or regressive), what resists and what submits, between
the radical (or the utopian) and the ideological, between refusal and com-
plicity. Adorno's concrete analyses include these judgments and are
inseparable from them (even the stigmatized political word 'progressive'
reappears, albeit in the rather different context of the development of
productive forces, which we will examine later on). That such judgements
are at one with the old problem of correspondence and reflection (or
of the base-and-superstructure model) seems evident, since only a distance
between the work of art and the social could allow them to come into
play in the first place; that the old correspondence model is complicitous
with the doctrine of the autonomy of the work of art may at first seem
more paradoxical – yet Peter Bürger has shown us persuasively how
it was the very doctrine (and institution) of aesthetic autonomy that
liberated the possibility of such political judgements in the first place.[5]
Here is Adorno's most incisive statement of the matter:

> Art is social, not merely by virtue of its process of production, in which
> at any given moment the dialectic of productive forces and productive relations
> is at work, not even only in the social origins of its contents and raw materials.
> Rather it becomes social by virtue of its oppositional position to society
> itself, a position it can occupy only by defining itself as autonomous. (AT
> 335/321)

What I want to show, however, is that this seemingly clear-cut opposition-
ality is in Adorno a good deal more complicated and dialectically variable.

Take for example the reading (or the rewriting) of Kant's circumscrip-
tion of the aesthetic as 'disinterested interest' or 'purposefulness without
a practical purpose' [zwecklose Zweckhaftigkeit]. This, historically the classical first form of the doctrine of aesthetic autonomy, is reissued by Adorno
with a powerfully dialectical modification:

> The shadow of the most passionate practical interest must be associated with
> the concept of the 'disinterested' if it is to be anything more than mere indiffer-
> ence, and there is reason to think that the dignity of a work of art can be

measured against the very strength of the interest from which it has been wrested (AT 24/16).

(He will elsewhere [AT 396/375] interpret 'disinterest' as a suspension of that drive to self-preservation which was identified as the source of the will to power of the dialectic of enlightenment.) But almost at once this 'positive' reevaluation of disinterestedness becomes dialectically problematized:

> As soon as the art work takes up a position with respect to the negativity of reality, however, the very concept of disinterestedness is modified. Works of art involve in their very nature a relationship between interest and its denial, contrary to both the Kantian and the Freudian interpretations. Even the contemplative relationship to the work of art, wrested away from the objects of action, is lived as a repudiation of immediate praxis and thereby as being itself a form of praxis, a refusal to play the game. Only those works of art which can be felt as modes of action [*Verhaltensweise*] really justify their existence. (AT 25-6/17)

What therefore began as a suspension and a negation of the fallen praxis of a business and commodity society here slowly turns around into a higher form of praxis, which now annuls the earlier concept of 'disinterestedness' or 'purposelessness' and becomes a higher form of interest and a more authentic *telos*.[6]

The other – and antithetical – component of Kant's formula, the nature of that 'purposefulness' or interest-like quality that the art-work does seem to possess, is the object of even more complex dialectical transformations, since it seems most closely affiliated to the dynamic of the social itself, and thereby, as an impulse, the most dubious and contaminated:

> The Kantian notion of 'purposefulness', which secures the link for him between art and the inner essence of nature, is in fact most closely related to *Technik* [a term which in German associates the twin connotations of *technique* and *technology*]. The way in which works of art 'purposefully' organize themselves so as to distinguish themselves from mere being, is called technique; only through technique do they acquire this illusion of 'purposefulness' (AT 321/308).

By thus transferring Kantian teleology from nature to human science, Adorno deliberately introduces into the very heart of the aesthetic the dynamic of 'enlightenment' and the original sin of Western rationality and domination which he was concerned elsewhere to denounce. The later adventures of this perverse resocialization of the Kantian aesthetic will be traced below, in the dialectic of the aesthetic 'forces of production'.

What seems more immediately instructive for Adorno's practice of the dialectic itself will be the prolongation of this theme in the cognate concept of reification [*Verdinglichung*], which plays an equally crucial and equally ambiguous role in his analysis of the work of art.

For reification is, in Adorno's aesthetic, first and foremost a positive, that is to say a valorized, concept – a reversal of its conventional position in the Marxist tradition.[7] There it designated not merely the substitution for human relations of thing-like ones (money, the 'cash nexus') but also – in the form of so-called commodity fetishism – a peculiar pathology of the material in which the former solid things of a world of use values are transmogrified into abstract equivalencies which none the less now project the mirage of a new kind of libidinally invested materiality in the commodity: in this sense 'reification' is virtually at the other extreme from matter itself, which it seems to transform into strangely spiritualized objects which none the less seem more thing-like than the things themselves.

As a materialist Adorno cannot ground his anti-capitalist aesthetic – whose context is that well-nigh universal commodification of the world already diagnosed in *Dialectic of Enlightenment* – in convenient forms of anti-material spirituality, which he plainly loathes and which is included in the denunciation of all forms of 'inwardness' and subjectivization that runs through *Aesthetic Theory* as one of its philosophical programs (to be more closely examined in its proper place). Nor does he have recourse to those conceptions of praxis whereby a Gramsci or a Sartre, in their very different ways, sought to cut the Gordian knot of the dualisms of idealism and materialism and to replace them with something else. What results, therefore, is a restless series of transfers whereby reification – for Adorno absolutely essential to the work of art – changes its valences as it passes from the social to the aesthetic (and vice versa).

'What is called reification gropes, where it is radicalized, towards the language of things. In effect it tries to move back towards the Idea of that nature extirpated by the primacy of human meaning' (AT 96/89). By a kind of ruse, then, the radicalization of the force that destroyed nature is pressed into the service of its at least ideal reestablishment. But this is no mere local strategy: 'reification is essential to works of art, and at the same time contradicts their nature as emergences [*Erscheinendem*]; their thing-like character is no less dialectical than their status as what is to be contemplated and observed [*ihr Anschauliches*]' (AT 153/146). But it is a deadly counter-poison:

> works of art are negative a priori by virtue of the very law that condemns them to objectification: they kill what they objectify by wrenching it from

its living immediacy. Thus their own life feeds on death. This is in fact the qualitative barrier beyond which the modern begins. Works of art mimetically abandon their images to reification, their deathly principle. The hope of successfully escaping this principle is the moment of illusion in art which it, since Baudelaire, seeks to shake off, without thereby resigning itself to becoming again mere thing among things. The heralds of the modern, Baudelaire and Poe, were as artists the first technocrats of the aesthetic. Without the homeopathic ingestion of the poison itself – reification as the virtual negation of the living – the pretense of art to resist subsumption under 'civilization' would have remained a helpless pipe-dream. By absorbing into art, since the beginnings of the modern, objects alien to it that can never fully be transformed by its own internal formal laws, the mimetic pole of art yields to its counter-principle, and this all the way up to the emergence of montage. (AT 201/193)

At this point, then, reification is borrowed back from the social, in order to permit the aesthetic a continuing and ever more precarious existence in a wholly reified world – from which, however, the counter-poison somehow protects it. But in a final moment, reification seems to have been transformed into a more active weapon (against itself); arguing for and against that property of art still called *Geist* or spirituality, Adorno stresses the produced or constructed nature of the work of art, 'which specifically includes the objectivity of its spirit. Aesthetic reflection must sanction that as the expression of the work's objectivity at the same time that it seeks critically to dissolve it' (AT 274/263). Such passages, in which critical and receptive activity seem to become independent of the work itself and to be endowed with a supplementary power and function not implicit in the art-object, are rare enough in Adorno, who rejects the exploration of reception in the general spirit of his anti-subjective program; by the same token, his very project of a belated aesthetics (whose problematic nature and internal contradictions have already been touched on) can also be read as a displacement and a repudiation of the autonomy of literary criticism and interpretation that has come to be affirmed in the present moment of the hegemony of the theoretical. None the less, the sense of the passage is clear: the commodity form must somehow be made available and tangible in order for the activity of its dissolution to have any point: the work must designate itself as a commodity in order to acquire the means of escaping that status. But none of these formulations is quite so peremptory and astonishing as our final one: 'art remains alive only through its essentially social powers of resisting society; *unless it submits to reification, it becomes a mere commodity*' (AT 335/321; emphasis added).

Four

Whatever the orthodoxy of Adorno's Marxism, it can be argued that of all Marxist aestheticians he is the most faithful to Marx's own method, or mode of *Darstellung*. To be sure, the great formal architectonic of *Capital* is no longer historically available to him, like some earlier moment of sonata or symphonic form which, undermined by nominalism, can no longer be reconstructed as such. But *Aesthetic Theory* stubbornly keeps faith with the methodological lessons of the 1857 Preface to the *Grundrisse*: that while one category – production – may have structural primacy over all the others, in the writing it must never be allowed to become the dominant theme or motif; it must never, to switch to the language of poststructuralism, be allowed to organize the terms around itself into a specific code (or 'private language'). So in Marx the category of production rises and sinks, sometimes becomes the terminological partner of lesser categories (distribution, consumption), sometimes disappears from sight altogether, and at other moments, with a thunderclap, is revealed as the very motor of history itself. The concept is here still held at a certain mediate distance from the term which is its name, and which threatens to absorb it altogether into a linguistic identity that approaches the condition and dynamic of poetic language at the same time as it marks the triumph of conceptual reification (we have already observed the intimate relationship between the two).

So it is that this aesthetics can speak a variety of speculative languages, none of which ever finally freezes over into Adorno's 'method', which might then be laid out in the theoretical handbooks with a convenient tag, like Lukács's, Bloom's, Macherey's, Bakhtin's, or Derrida's. We have just seen, for example, that reification plays as fundamental a role in

Adorno's formal analyses as it does in Lukács's thought, and is often more intricately related to his readings than anything in Lukács's own expositions: one does not, for all that, turn to Adorno as the primary source for 'reification theory'. The history of aesthetic situations is here as omnipresent and inescapable as in Sartre; but Adorno does not, as Sartre did at least twice in his life, try to write a 'linear history' of those.[8] The contradiction between parts and wholes is as exhaustively rehearsed as anything in contemporary bourgeois theory, from the aestheticians to the New Criticism; but that dynamic is never codified as a doctrine, about whose formulations endless philosophical argument might be generated: at the last moment before codification the problem is always enlarged, its terminology transformed, and we turn out *also* to have been talking about something else, which needs a different kind of development.

Proving equal to Adorno, therefore, doing right by him, attempting to keep faith with the protean intelligence of his sentences, requires a tireless effort - always on the point of lapsing - to prevent the *thematization* of the concept of production, to use Paul de Man's suggestive phrase. That the notion of production somehow underpins the valorization of construction in Adorno, authorizes it and grounds it, is not wrong but only misleading: rather than a logical process, in which deeper presuppositions are reached and then unfolded in their own name and right, it seems more prudent, for the moment, to think of the one as something like a modulation of the other, which takes us into a different conceptual or sonorous dimension altogether. In that case, the method might be Marx's, but the philosophical form something closer to *Finnegans Wake*.

In so far as *Aesthetic Theory* is also in certain respects an abstract writing up of concrete analyses worked out elsewhere, the more immediate reference for this doctrine of the aesthetic categories will appropriately enough be Adorno's *Versuch über Wagner*, his first full-length musical monograph (written in exile in 1937-8) and a splendor, in which an ideal mimesis of Benjamin's book on tragic drama produces what stands in Adorno's own work as the equivalent of the older critic's virtually contemporaneous 'On Some Motifs in Baudelaire' - a description of the simultaneous emergence of modernism and mass culture.

The dialectic of Wagnerian form - which draws its remarkably 'modern' innovative technology from the relatively untutored simplicities of the composer's essential dilettantism - throws up a virtual textbook opposition between construction and expression, where the driving insistence of the second of these impulses interferes with the architectonics of the first, as it is exemplified in the first Viennese school, with its elaboration of sonata-form temporality. But expression is also not an autonomous category, and knows its own idiosyncratic fate in Wagner, where its 'moment of uncontrolled intensification can scarcely tolerate the mid-space of temporal consciousness and is released in the form of external gestures' (W 35/39), by which Adorno means the Wagnerian leitmotivs, as these seem, sometimes with a virtually cartoon-like larger-than-life crudity, to dramatize the peremptory movements of the Wagnerian characters themselves. But even in terms of this still minimal account of the 'gesture' in Wagner, it is clear that this cannot persist as an auton-omous category either, but must enter into tension and contradiction with the category of 'expression' from which it seemed to derive:

> the problem is compounded by the fact that the moment of expression, which is supposed to lead from one gesture to another in the basic sequence (in the most famous of all, that of the *Tristan* Prelude, the expression is 'yearning' or 'longing'), in fact excludes all repetition of the type of interpolated tonal dance forms and calls out for that very thoroughgoing variation against which the gestural character of the leitmotivs originally struggled but which can be replaced by the Wagnerian principle of 'psychological variation' only in the most rationalistic fashion that does violence to the musical forms them-selves. (W 37/42–3)

What happens, therefore, to the abstract aesthetic categories is that they become transformed into the instruments by which a concrete musical (or productive) situation is measured and characterized. They do not finally themselves (even historically) become harmonized into this or that more comprehensive or dialectical theory or aesthetics as such; rather, it is their very immediate incompatibility and contradiction that describes the technical and historical problems whose solution will constitute the *Novum* of the new work. This, then, is a rather different relationship between the general and the particular than is conveyed either by the traditional philosophical subsumption of species under genres, or by the nominalistic transformation of a particular into the generality of a 'unique style': here the notion of the historical situation, problem, or contra-diction itself mediates between the general and the particular, between the eternal aesthetic categories and the unique and incomparable text.

There are evidently deeper reasons why this richest of all explorations of the modern should finally come to us from music, rather than from the verbal, visual or architectural areas in which prophets and ideologues of the modern have been most vocal and strident. For music seems to be the art in which the distance between producer and ideal consumer is the minimal imaginable, and tendentially abolished: as a composer, Adorno seems to have been able to hear musical works as though he were composing them – from a specialist or expert's standpoint, which has always alternately intimidated or irritated the critics of the other arts, for whom other equally authentic positions of reception seemed available and worth defending against it.[9] Here, however, it is as though there is no outside: a paradoxical outcome indeed for an art that, more than all the others, seems to have its *esse* in its *percipi* and to enjoy little existence of its own beyond the moment of hearing it.

On the other hand, it is precisely this tenuousness of musical object-hood, this more thoroughgoing passage of the artistic object into the sense organ itself – from which for a time it seems indistinguishable – that suddenly seems to put a different face on the old subject–object problem, without 'solving' it by violence, abandoning it as false or meta-physical crux, or projecting a mirage of reconciliation or spurious atone-ment between the poles. Yet this new projection of the work of art also issues from that field in which sheer technical knowledge – and an evolutionary development of that knowledge seemingly as rigorous as what happens in the natural sciences – is massively preponderant and inescapable throughout the entire history of music (as distinct from the local role some more exact knowledge of the metric potentialities of a given language or the psychophysiological dynamics of color or optics may have played in key but discontinuous moments of the history of poetry or painting).

The musical experience thus permits the coordination of a very special account of the subject–object relationship with an emphasis on objective technical dynamics: from this unusual conjuncture will miraculously emerge, reborn long after its tiresome ideological exhaustion in the various ideologies of the modernisms, the concept of the New.

The first of these issues – which will take the form of a reinvention of Leibniz's notion of the 'windowless monad' – constitutes an outcome to the subject–object dialectic which will also 'solve' the traditional Marxian dilemma of base and superstructure, or of the 'correspondence' of the aesthetic work to social reality (or its 'reflection' thereof). The aesthetic translation of Hegel's great formula – the identity of identity and non-identity – is peremptory: 'if the work of art is experienced in a purely aesthetic fashion, it is not even aesthetically properly appre-hended in the first place' (AT 17/9). The doctrine of the aesthetic auton-omy of the work of art is the correct one; but it is true only if grasped as the very opposite of an aestheticizing doctrine, or a kind of philosophi-cal 'art for art's sake'. The work is social and historical through and through: only thus can it become autonomous. The religion of art, the glorification of the cultural and the aesthetic, is a social conduct and an ideology that has nothing to do with the work of art itself.

To put the problem in a somewhat different way: it is clear that every

work of art is 'of the world' and that everything about it is social –
its materials, its creator, its reception, art itself (or culture) as a leisure
class activity, and so forth; as a thing in the world it is social, yet the
most important thing about it is not 'in' the world at all, in that sense.
As a thing-in-the-world it is either a luxury item, which can be set in
opposition to real human need and suffering (or some deeper infrastructural reality of human experience and social life) or else, as some small
fragment of the world, it can try to 'reflect' other larger segments of
that reality, doing so in either a frivolous or a socially responsible way.

From these standpoints, then, the work of art might be, so to speak,
'more' or 'less' social; 'more' or 'less' historical. But it is precisely that
kind of measurement that Adorno thinks nonsensical, when one has
to do with 'genuine' works of art. The bad ones: kitsch, decoration,
the applied arts and handicraft, Culture Industry products – all these,
being already things and commodities in the social world, are fair game
for such evaluative exercises; nor is the deeper guilt of art and culture
itself denied, rejustified or rationalized away at any moment, as we have
seen in Part II. But what we saw there also was that the true work
of art is something radically different from both these sets of things
(art objects, or the institution of art).

It is to solve this peculiar problem – how we are to think about something every part of which is social but which itself is somehow not social
– that the doctrine of the monad is invoked:

> The work of art is what rationalistic metaphysics at its very height proclaimed
> to be the principle of the world, namely the Monad: a force field and a
> thing all at once. Works of art are closed off against each other and blind,
> yet in their very hermetic closure they represent what lies outside themselves.
> Thus have they traditionally offered themselves, as that autarchic principle
> of life that Goethe was wont, in synonymity with the concept of the monad,
> to call entelechy. It seems conceivable that the more problematical teleological
> concepts became in the world of organic nature, they grow even more intens-
> ively appropriate for the work of art. As the moment of an overarching
> system of relationships in the spirit of a given age, intertwined with history
> and society, works strain beyond their monadic condition without ever being
> endowed with windows. (AT 268/257)

Entelechy, the mind–body problem, the doctrine of the soul as the inner
form of its external parts: such idealistic references raise the deepest suspicions about the tendencies of Adorno's monadology only if we fail to
grasp the crucial historical distinction that for him, those older problems
– consciousness, the soul, creation and cosmology – are precisely idealistic
and false, but that their pseudo-solution in an older metaphysics – most

specifically now this one of Leibniz – can be reread as the distorted and mystified solution to the very different materialist problem of the work of art, where it alone has validity:

> That society 'appears' in works of art, with polemic truth and also ideologically, is a fact that can easily lead to the mystifications of the philosophies of history. Speculation can all too easily fall prey to some doctrine of a preestablished harmony between society and the work of art that has been conveniently arranged in advance by the world-spirit. But theory cannot capitulate before this problem of the relationship between art and the social. The process which is completed and brought to fulfillment in works of art is to be thought of as having the same meaning as the social process in which they are embedded: they represent it, following Leibniz's formula, in windowless fashion. The configuration of elements in an artistic whole obeys immanent laws which are related to those that prevail in the society outside. Social forces of production and social relations of production return in the very form of the work, divested of their facticity, because artistic labor is also social labor; works of art are also the products of social labor. Nor are the productive forces within the work of art distinct in and of themselves from those in society, but only by virtue of their constitutive absence from the concrete social order. One can scarcely imagine anything performed or invented within the work of art that does not have its equivalent – in however latent a form – within social production itself. (AT 350/335)

So it is that the doctrine of the monad – and above all the windowless closure that constitutes it as an idea (and has nothing philosophically to do with current discussions of 'open' and 'closed' works) – at once permits the most sweeping affirmations of the sociality and the historicity of art:

> It is the historical moment that is in the work of art constitutive: the most authentic works are those that give themselves over to their historical raw material without reservation and without any pretense to floating above it somewhere. Works of art are in this sense unconsciously the historiography of their own epoch; history is not the least form of knowledge they mediate. That is precisely why they are incommensurable with historicism, which seeks to reduce them to a history external to them, rather than to pursue their genuine historical content. (AT 272/261)

But at this point a caution must be inserted: a price must be paid for that separation from the world that endows the monad with its capacity to be as profoundly historical and social as history and society itself. It cannot be *political*, something which will come as no surprise to readers familiar with Adorno's views on socialist realism (or on Sartrean *engage-*

ment) as well as with his deep antagonism to Brecht. 'Praxis' is thereby dispatched in what will by now have become a familiar thought-figure: 'Praxis does not lie in the effect of the work of art, but rather encapsulated in its truth-content' (AT 367/350). Adorno is in any case very clear about the separation of the three levels of the historical, the social and the political (in a way which paradoxically reconfirms the tripartite scheme of *The Political Unconscious*):

> Social struggles and class relationships are expressed and articulated through the very structure of the works of art; such political positions as these may take, however, are in contrast *mere* epiphenomena, which generally hinder the formal elaboration of the work and finally even impair its social truth content. (AT 344/329)

The political vehemence such statements and positions of Adorno frequently arouse on the left (this one is an obvious provocation) should not lead anyone to forget that there has never been any kind of left consensus on the possibility, or even the desirability, of a properly political aesthetics; nor even on the immediate political effectivity of the most 'committed' works of art. Meanwhile, the futility of the discussion becomes clear when you realize how easy it is to move allegedly 'political' works over into another, more respectable category, as Adorno often does with the parts of Brecht he likes.

But the spirit of these remarks, and the methodology they inspire, is clear enough. The informing presence of society within art and language is all the greater when it is indirect and invisible, 'all the more complete, the less any representation of the ego and of society is made thematic, and the more involuntarily it crystallizes such a representation out of itself' (NL, 55).

Almost the basic question about this cultural politics, then, would be why these views do not simply settle back into a stereotypical Romantic opposition between the individual and society: they cannot do so precisely because society is already within the 'individual', sapping and undermining an individuation and an individuality for which it is itself responsible. And this will oddly, paradoxically, for good or ill, be the reason given for the repudiation of overtly political art:

> For the theory of committed art, as it is current today, presupposes a superiority and an invulnerability to the basic reigning fact of life of exchange society – namely, alienation between human beings and also between objective spirit and the society that it expresses and judges all at once. The theory of commitment demands that art speak directly to people, as though the immediate could realize itself immediately in a world of universal mediation. (NL 120)

Five

Adorno has, however, another, equally provocative way of turning the tables in this situation: 'the social thinking on aesthetics', he observes with feigned astonishment, 'has customarily neglected the concept of productive forces' (AT 69/62). And it is certain that very few Marxist aesthetics have taken the concept of economic production – rather than the conventional ones of class affiliation and struggle, ideology, or political position – very seriously, despite the extensive use of a rhetoric of production in the 1960s and 1970s. Certainly no one – least of all the cultural Stalinists themselves – has had the audacity to suggest a relevance for aesthetics of the even more vulgar-materialist notion of sheer economic productivity (that is to say, the primacy of productive *forces* – machinery and technology – over production *relations* – class positions and consciousness, collective versus authoritarian organization of the shop floor, and so on). Yet it is precisely this conception of production that for Adorno will subsume both the historical and the social dimensions of the work of art, whose relationship to history is marked and dated, as it were, by the advanced character of its production process, while its essential sociality is given in advance by the collective social nature of production itself.

I want to overemphasize this matter of productive forces for a moment, not merely because it is the least familiar or traditional feature of Adorno's aesthetics, but also because it at once reopens the possibility of conceptualizing the 'New' or the *Novum*, so central in all modernism, discussion of which we have found ourselves obliged to suspend heretofore on the merely negative injunction that, whatever else it was, it was not a temporal or a phenomenological concept. This now clearly has something to do

with modernization, in the sense in which, from the very onset of capitalism, new and more productive machinery has driven out its predecessors
and made them obsolete: a historical paradigm which is surely very much
akin to Adorno's own vision of the history of artistic 'progress', where
the new ruthlessly annihilates older forms and conventions, and where
– particularly in the history of music – something like scientific and
technological invention is at one with artistic construction.

The paradigm is a familiar one and constitutes the fundamental master
narrative of all the ideologies of the modern, from the Russian Formalists
to Pound and passing through the most varied manifestos of the most
artistically dissimilar avant-garde movements: what is unique in its rehearsal by Adorno is the philosophical appeal to the only economic theory
capable of providing an adequate grounding to what otherwise becomes
an ever more frantic story of styling changes and the dynamics of fashion
– namely, Marxism itself:

In many authentic manifestations of the modern, the level of industrial content
was strictly avoided thematically, owing to the mistrust against the pseudo-
metamorphoses of machine art, but none the less in them – and perhaps
above all in them! (in Klee, for example) – made its irresistible dynamics
felt, negatively, by way of the reduction in the permissible or the tolerable
and in the intensification of construction proper. This feature of the modern
has changed as little as the very fact of industrialization itself as a force in
people's daily lives: hence the extraordinary appearance of an invariable that
the aesthetic idea of the modern has taken on. To be sure, the aesthetic realm
affords no less developmental space for this historical dynamic than does
industrial production itself, which has in a century been transformed from
classical nineteenth century factories to automation, passing through the
period of mass production proper. The formal process of artistic modernism
draws the power of this its historical content from the fact that the most
advanced types of material production and organization at a given historical
moment are not limited to the immediate area from which they derive. In
a fashion still inadequately analyzed by sociology, their influence is felt even
in those areas of life most distant from them, and penetrates deeply into
the zone of a purely subjective experience which is unaware of such influence,
against which it thinks itself sheltered. That art alone is modern which, according to its own specific modes of experience and by way of the very crisis
of experience itself, absorbs what the most advanced state of industrialization
under the then dominant relations of production has made current. Yet this
involves something like a negative canon, the taboo on what such modernisms
repudiate in their procedures and their technique: a specific set of negations
which in fact turns out to form something like a canon of what remains
to be accomplished. (AT 58/50)

These final remarks deserve special emphasis, for they supply some unexpected clues to the enigmatic nature of the 'New' in art – that 'blind spot' of the modern, 'as empty as the immediate here and now of the thing before us' (AT 38/30) – about which Adorno's technological rhetoric risks suggesting that it is somehow in the mint shininess of streamlined or futuristic machinery that the perpetual *Novum* of great art is to be sought: an impression instantly tarnished by the memory that nothing becomes quite so quickly antiquated as such once 'advanced' equipment.

The problem is meanwhile compounded by the fact that aesthetic phenomena – being cultural; that is to say, formations of a superstructure that is only a functional part of the whole it claims to be the equivalent and the substitute for – are also ideological. The 'New', therefore, is also an ideological compensation, as well as an aesthetic value and a historically original category of capitalist production. Thus, in a slashing paragraph of *Minima Moralia*, Adorno suddenly outdoes Benjamin in his identification of the 'cult of the new, and thus the idea of modernity' as a 'rebellion against the fact that there is no longer anything new' (MM 316/235). The whole of the modern now becomes (very much in the spirit of Benjamin's own essay 'On Some Motifs in Baudelaire') 'the first consciousness of the decay of experience'. The New here becomes sensation, in its most garish media senses ('in a statement at the time of the first pogroms, Goebbels boasted that at least the National Socialists were not boring' [MM 319/237]); and the lurid light shed back by modern politics on modern art now virtually causes the 'truth-content' of the latter to pale away into little more than a repetition which, like artificial stimulus in general, wishes it were a new experience: 'not for nothing were Poe, Baudelaire, Wagner addictive types' (MM 320/238). This drug, however, no longer looks much like the art demanded by the avant-garde, 'a music that astonishes the composer like a new substance that appears in the chemist's retort'.[10]

How one is then to 'remember' the 'New' none the less remains the nagging doubt at the heart of this aesthetic value. Detemporalizing what seems an irrevocably temporal concept demands that we restructure the problem to which it responds in some less immediately phenomenological or experiential way, if that is possible. The worry clearly turns on the status of formerly 'new' works of the past, thereby reawakening that complex of issues that swarm around the term 'historicism', whatever immediate meaning one decides by fiat to limit that to. But as so often it is a mistake to confront the mystery of our understanding [*Verstehen*] of the past in the Cartesian manner, reconstructing its a priori possibility as it were deductively from zero – that is, from an imagined starting point in which the past does not yet exist and we are, as it were, as

yet without memory altogether. We must rather begin from the fact
and the premiss that we do occasionally 'understand' the past in some
stronger sense: that, from time to time, we have been able to have the
conviction that we 'know' what Lenin was thinking on the occasion
of this or that intervention; that we sense what the Paris of the 1830s
felt like as a life-world; that we know how Lu Xun's first writings must
have struck his contemporaries; that we can feel the excitement of the
outbreak of World War I in the various European capitals or the intellectual animation of the devisers of the first vernacular *canzoni*.

Such moments of conviction about the past, unverifiable, ephemeral,
and subject to endless sober revision and fresh doubts, may be metaphysi-
cally illusory; but can be examined in their own right for what they
contain and what goes on in them. I have tried to show elsewhere, following Collingwood, that they involve the reconstruction of a situation and
a problem or a question, whose 'answer' then takes on the value and
the freshness of an act in which we seem to reparticipate.[11] Adorno's
aesthetics does not pose such issues of historicism or *Verstehen* as such:
but his conception of art as production is usefully consistent with this
view, and affords it additional possibilities of development.

What the present passage suggests, for example, is that our most intense
approach to what is 'new' about the old involves a sudden intuition
of taboos and constraints, negatives, restrictions, prohibitions, reluctances
and aversions. But these are not inherited dogma or aesthetic moralism,
and have nothing to do with the respectable tastes and unexamined
aesthetic good conduct of the conventional public sphere. They are *new*
taboos; indeed, what is new about the *Novum* is less the work itself
(whose most spankingly new innovations, in all their self-conscious Sunday pride, may well come to seem the most pitiably antiquated thing
about it) than these new prohibitions, about which it would therefore
be better to say, not that they tell you what not to do, but rather that
they spell out what is *no longer* to be done; what you cannot do any
more; what it would be corny to do again; or about which something
(Socrates' Daimon) warns you that it is somehow not quite right and
ought to be avoided, for reasons you yourself do not quite understand
and may never fully grasp.

Such taboos can bear on the widest range of aesthetic materials: a certain
kind of sentence, for example, which one had better no longer indulge
in, a feeling or an emotion which may be real enough and very widespread
but which had best from now on be left out (so that it becomes interesting
to see whether you can think of characters who have never had such
feelings and could not imagine them); a boring sound combination, a
narrative whose structure makes you impatient, a philosophical argument

which one would be embarrassed to repeat, no matter how true it may be. The New, then, is what happens when one excludes those things, providing what results is something other than silence. This is, of course, a reasoning that leads to minimalism by its very internal momentum, and in which minimalist values are somehow structurally inscribed: but more often in the history of modern art the devaluation of the older aesthetic technology, the obsolescence of a whole range of now prohibited contents and forms, has felt like a liberation to which invention responds with a flush of new forms that seems very rich indeed.

There is therefore no insurmountable problem about sensing what it was Beethoven could no longer allow his instruments to do; the problem is now the other way round – how we are to prevent ourselves from attributing what he did find to make them do to the sheerest subjectivity or 'genius'. 'The subjective component of the work is itself a piece of objectivity' (AT 69/61). How to demonstrate this, how to undermine our tendencies to subjectivism in some persuasive and definitive way – without thereby capitulating to positivism – is, as we suggested at the very outset, one of the most fundamental vocations of *Aesthetic Theory*.

That the raw material of the work of art is historical through and through is a useful lesson that we cannot learn often enough, which may not, however, fully complete that particular task. Those of us who learned our modernist historicity from Proust, for example, will appreciate Adorno's corrective rewriting of the doctrine:

Proust (and after him Kahnweiler) took the position that painting transforms our very mode of seeing and thereby the objects themselves along with it. As authentic as may be the experience to which this doctrine corresponds, the formulation may well be too idealistic. Precisely the reverse of this formulation may not be altogether unconvincing either: that it is the objects themselves which have historically changed, so that the human sensorium adapts to those changes and painting ultimately invents the appropriate indices for them. Cubism could in that sense be interpreted as a reaction to a new level of rationalization within the social world itself, which geometrizes that world's nature by way of new forms of planification; it may be seen as the attempt to make available this new situation, which is in itself hostile to the experiential, to and for experience itself, just as Impressionism had done in the preceding, not yet wholly planified stage of industrialization. This would then mark what is qualitatively new about Cubism with respect to its predecessor: that whereas Impressionism sought to reawaken and to rescue the vitality paralyzed within the commodity world by means of its own internal dynamic, Cubism despairs of doing so and embraces the heteronomous geometrization of the world as its new law and its new order, in order to secure some new guarantee of objectivity for aesthetic experience. (AT 447/418)

But even the example of the visual arts still leaves the door too far ajar
for some differentiation between the objects out there and the 'techniques'
that are invented to register their modification. Yet it was that very
distinction Proust's aesthetics sought with such paradoxical novelty and
force to obliterate, inventing, *avant la lettre*, 'defamiliarization' as a concept whose first effect is very precisely intellectual defamiliarization. In
Adorno, where the tendential distinction between subject and object is
somehow not yet even available, music will, as always, perform this
function more adequately. Here is Adorno's lesson on the fugue, for
example:

> The fugue is bound to tonal relationships; its very invention is somehow
> called forth by the *telos* of the transformation in which modality is set aside
> and tonality comes to reign supreme over an imitative musical praxis. Specific
> procedures such as the real or tonal answer constituted by a fugal theme
> make musical sense only in a situation in which an outmoded polyphony
> sees itself confronted with the new task of transforming the older homophonic
> center of gravity of tonality, of integrating tonality into polyphonic space,
> of making room for contrapuntal and harmonic progressions in musical
> thought together. All the peculiarities of this new form – the fugue – can
> be deduced from this objective necessity of which the composer seems by
> no means to be conscious. The fugue is the specific organizational form of
> a polyphony become tonal and thoroughly rationalized; this is the general
> meaning of the form, beyond any of its individual realizations, without which
> it would not, of course, exist in the first place. The tendential loosening
> of the fugal schema, and even the eventual liberation from it, is therefore
> inscribed in advance within it. Once tonality is no longer binding, the funda-
> mental categories of the fugue – such as the distinction between *dux* and
> *comes*, the stereotypical structure of the fugal response, and above all the
> reprise-like motif that facilitates the return to the dominant key – lose their
> function and become technically false. But the moment the articulated and
> dynamized expressive needs of the individual composers no longer long for
> the fugue (itself far more complexly differentiated than later ideologies of
> musical freedom were willing to suppose), this form has, *qua* form, become
> objectively impossible. (AT 297–8/286)

The composing subject need not, therefore, be conscious of the historical
situation of productivity as such, any more than the great inventor-entre-
preneur (Edison) of a certain stage of capitalism need worry particularly
about the system itself as a whole. Yet in that the composer-inventor,
by composing, registers the objective needs of the system – Adorno uses
the word desire [*begehren*], but it is the composer's whole sensibility,
his 'expressive needs', and even those developed to their most elaborated
level of intensity ('articulated' [*differenzierte*] and 'dynamized' [*dynamis-*

ierte], that do the 'desiring' for him – this receptivity of the 'creative subject' is not simply the irrational opposite number of a rationality that would more consciously 'know' where it was in history. It is not some form of creative 'intuition' which is being opposed here to a different, more intellectual, form of self-consciousness. Rather, the immanent technical operations of the 'creative spirit' are themselves what Hegel would have called 'objective spirit', but what it is better in the present context to identify as the collective productivity of a society at a given moment of its development.

> By virtue of the infinitely minute and differential nature of his artistic choices and decisions, the individual artist in fact assumes the role of the executor of the collective objectivity of spirit itself [*Geist*], his own personal role vanishing into that in the process; something implicitly recalled in the traditional conception of the genius as passive-receptive. (AT 402–3/381)

This is perhaps the moment to register the fresh new light Adorno's productivism casts on his similarities and dissimilarities with the positions of Benjamin. The latter may be seen as equally 'productionist' from two relatively distinct standpoints: an emphasis on technology, and on the well-nigh allegorical value of the modifications of urban machinery for the transformations of the psyche (as in his essays on Baudelaire): alongside a rather different (and more Brechtian) stress on the role of 'productivity' in the work of the advanced artist – a position essentially laid out in 'The Author as Producer'. But what this essay seeks to affirm is quite different from Adorno's identification of the most advanced forms of social production *within* the work of art. For Benjamin is looking for a link and a form of class solidarity that might connect modernist vanguard artists with an industrial proletariat. He discovers it by affirming not the identity of the two productions, but rather the identity of the advanced character of each one, taken separately. Thus the artist's class solidarity with the values and attitudes of the factory worker passes through the high productivity embodied by each; whence the sympathy each may have with the other. The comparison thus yields more or less the results one might have anticipated: from Adorno's perspective, Benjamin's dialectic is either too external (the allegorical machinery) or too mediated; from Benjamin's, Adorno's dialectic is too idealistic in its immediate identification of industrial production and inner form.

But the model of productive forces alone (in Marxism a 'vulgar' or reductive conception of production) is at length completed by its orthodox complement, the notion of the *relations* of production (from class relations down to the articulated component positions of these, either in the labor process or in those expanding and contracting spaces for agency opened in business which were touched on in the analogies between the artist and the vanishing entrepreneur). The concept of productivity in Marx mediates between these 'levels' in such a way that it can only tactically be assigned to one or the other on any specific occasion: 'advanced' may here designate state-of-the-art machinery, or on the contrary what bourgeois thought generally considers to be expert scientific and technological knowledge and the experience of skilled workers (the true epistemological capital which alone explains the miraculous resurgence of this or that 'advanced' industrial power after the thoroughgoing wartime destruction of its material equipment). The so-called creative subject also incorporates this fund or level of collective competence, below which it falls only to its aesthetic peril. But to analogize artistic productions in these terms – as a socially average advanced productivity read in terms of labor rather than in terms of machinery – at once introduces hitherto unmentioned complications and contradictions which are no less central for Adorno's aesthetics.

Six

For when one passes from the concept of productive forces to that of productive relations, all the negative and diagnostic themes traditionally associated with Marxism reappear: first and foremost the division of labor itself, as deeply inscribed in the individual work of art as were the state of productive forces. It is at this point that what has been loosely referred to as 'creative subjectivity' proves to subsume two very different things: the mental operations of the composer, and that very different part of contemporary mutilated subjectivity which is the maimed and shrunken 'self', which tries to 'express' its subjective suffering through the work, in a situation where that suffering and the very 'subject' itself (with all its feelings of consciousness and precarious personal identity) turn out in reality to be part of the work's raw material and its content. This is the other sense in which 'the subjective component of the work is in reality a piece of objectivity' (AT 68/61) and in which the 'subjective' in art is never truly grasped until we reach a standpoint from which it is revealed as part of social and historical objectivity, a 'method' Adorno rather inadequately characterized as 'second reflection', as we shall see. (It will be more appropriate to deal with the implications of this view of subjectivity all together in a later chapter).

For the moment, only the contradictions involved – their various formulations are familiar in Marxian social science, but less so in the aesthetic forms Adorno gives them here – need be briefly enumerated. The division of labor, for instance, determines a process which is best not thought of in its traditional bourgeois form as an opposition between the individual and the collective, but rather as a tendential collectivization in which previous forms of individuation are recast, problematized, fragmented

197

and often threatened in their very being (*Dialectic of Enlightenment* recurs to this situation throughout in its systemic form, while *Minima Moralia* stages it from the standpoint of the subject). Yet it is an objective and dialectical process, which should neither be surrendered to the rhetoric of conservative pathos – for the loss of individuality is not something necessarily always to be deplored in and of itself – nor too frequently saluted with the triumphalist accents of socialist realism, as though collectivization *always* meant the rebirth of true cooperation in Marx's sense. The process is primarily a matter of the increasing, and increasingly complex, collective nature of social labor (as though the primal 'division of labor' were a kind of infernal machine that redivides and rearticulates itself *à la* Luhmann in a well-nigh infinite momentum); and only then a social matter of what Weber called bureaucratization, which in our society essentially designates the collective organization of the business firm and the multinational industry; it is also a political fact of life for oppositional groups in a situation, prevalent since the 1970s, where the very cultural image of either the isolated romantic rebel or the solitary anomic victim have virtually disappeared, and virtually all so-called 'marginal' or opositional groups have collectively, in one way or another, mobilized and acquired an institutional framework.

But this tension or contradiction in modern society is reinscribed in the individual work of art in the form of the distinction already referred to between the collective character of advanced artistic technique and the remnants of individual isolation and subjectivity that become the former's content and raw material at the very moment they seem to demand the work as their last remaining possibility of subjective expression. Indeed, postmodernism – if there is such a thing – may then be theorized as the moment in which that older subjectivity – now fully collectivized – disappears altogether; so that the tension that constituted Beckett's minimalism fully as much as Schoenberg's expressionistic moment – the silent cry of pain – evaporates, leaving advanced collective productivity and technology free to 'express' nothing but itself: a process whose end-product is at once no longer works of art but commodities.

But the distinction between productive forces and productive relations can also be rehearsed as a dialectic and as a contradiction in its own right, in a reversal of priorities whereby it is precisely the primacy of the productive forces which secures a momentary aesthetic triumph over everything that is repressive in productive relations or in other words in class society:

> Every intelligible unit of collective forces transported within the work of
> art – units that look subjective [in so far as they embody the know-how

PRODUCTIVITIES OF THE MONAD

of the individual creator] – marks the potential presence within it according
to the degree of socially average productivity: monads include all that in
windowless fashion. This can be most strikingly observed in the artist's reactions to criticism and in the corrections he makes in response to it. Through
such improvements, to which he feels compelled, often enough in conflict
with what he considered the work's initial impulse or inspiration, he functions
as an agent of society, whether consciously or not. He embodies the social
forces of production, without thereby feeling in any way bound by the censure
dictated by the relations of production, which he himself also feels able to
criticize on the basis of his own professional expertise [métier]. ... This is
why every true artist is obsessed with questions of technique and method;
here the fetishism of the means has genuine legitimacy. (AT 71–2/65)

Despite the pathos of maimed subjectivity, therefore – and because that
suffering is itself of a piece, dialectically, with the injustice of the social
or class system in general, that is, with the *relations* of production –
the artist who puts his blind trust in technique and in the *forces* of production – often, for example, altering the original content of a work for
what seem to be superior technical reasons – is the more authentic.

Yet the forces of production are also finally the place of rationalization,
in the Weberian sense or in the sense of what the Frankfurt School
rebaptized as 'instrumental reason'. We have already to a certain degree
recapitulated this dialectic as it turns on reification and the commodity
form:

In the rationalization of the means there lies in art, as everywhere else, the
telos of their fetishization. To the degree to which control over means becomes
absolute, to that degree they tend objectively to become ends in themselves.
(AT 439/412)

Adorno's valorization of productive forces thereby becomes a poisoned
gift, or a Trojan horse, in a situation where these carry instrumental
reason or the baleful 'dialectic of Enlightenment' at their very heart.
Yet this doctrine is, as I have tried to show, a beneficial one which can
liberate contemporary criticism from its subjectivizing tendencies and
make possible a new kind of analysis in which the formal and the social
or historical, far from being incompatible or antithetical, are at one.
Perhaps one should say, then, that it is when the doctrine of productivity
becomes wholly positive and undialectical that it begins at once to reso-
nate that other dialectical mirage which is the sense of the impending
'end of art'.

It is appropriate therefore to end this particular discussion negatively
and to reformulate its essential lesson in a paradoxical reversal. For what

the doctrine of productive forces really has to teach contemporary criticism is not how to identify aesthetic success, but rather how to diagnose aesthetic failure: 'There are many indications that in works of art metaphysical untruth can be identified by mistakes or ineptitude in technique' (AT 195/187). This observation – which opens a bridge between traditional ideological analysis and technical or formal interpretation – will not be fully measured, however, unless we remember that Adorno is never, in *Aesthetic Theory*, concerned with 'bad' art as such: the technical flaws he has in mind here are rather those to be detected in ambitious and advanced aesthetic production (the example that most frequently recurs is the music of Richard Strauss [AT 319/306]). The proposition is further strengthened, and perhaps paradoxically transformed or dialectized beyond recognition, by a different kind of reminder: that

> what is ideological and 'affirmative' about the idea of fully achieved works of art must be corrected and rebuked by the fact that in that sense there are no achieved or 'successful' works of art. If those were really capable of existing, it would mean that reconciliation [*Versöhnung*] was really possible in the midst of the universal absence of reconciliation that endows art with its vocation in the first place.' (AT 283/271)

The 'achieved' work of art draws its deepest truth from contradiction as such, and from its unreserved commitment to it – something which virtually by definition guarantees that it cannot be achieved or complete or successful in the sentimental sense of a traditional normative aesthetics. But this unexpected conception of the necessary failure of all authentic works was in reality always implicit in the doctrine of productivity, and even in the conception of the 'New' that is implicit in it. 'Every masterpiece', Gertrude Stein once remarked, 'came into the world with a measure of ugliness in it. ... It's our business as critics to stand in front of it and recover its ugliness.'[12] Here is Adorno's version of the same conception of the New as ugliness and as scar:

> Every meaningful work leaves a mark or a trace on its material and its technique; what constitutes the modern as a kind of logical necessity is the obligation to track down that mark or trace, and not the flair for the latest fashion. This obligation, concretely realized, can be called the critical moment within modern art. Those marks on the material and the artistic procedures – to which every qualitatively new work then commits itself – are in reality scars, they are the places in which the preceding works failed. As the new work goes to work on them, it ends up turning against those who left such traces behind themselves. (AT 60/52)

This is the sense in which one is tempted in general to characterize Adorno's aesthetics as an aesthetic of scars: in his implacable insistence on suffering fully as much as in his implacable identification of authenticity – in philosophical thought as well as in art – with contradiction as such, in its most acute and unresolvable form. None the less, there remains an open question – which *Aesthetic Theory* seems to raise more naggingly than the earlier, more local monographs and critical analyses – as to whether these two things – individual suffering and systemic contradiction – are finally, in Adorno, always one and the same. A further examination of the various polemics against subjectivism in *Aesthetic Theory* will not necessarily answer that question, but will be justified if it ends up confirming it as a deeper problem in Adorno's thinking.

Seven

Productive power, we have observed Adorno to say, 'is, deeply embedded within the technological processes, the true subject, which has coagulated into technology' (AT 69/62). Meanwhile, his approving citation of Adolf Loos's remark 'that ornaments cannot be *invented*' (AT 46/39) implies the far more sweeping corollary that aesthetic innovation is not to be seen as invention – let alone 'creation' – but rather very precisely as discovery, as an activity which, analogous to the natural sciences, seems to locate and to register ever new and hitherto unsuspected features in the thing itself – that is to say, in the artistic raw material (something which, as we shall see shortly, has very interesting implications for the notion of artistic *intention*).

These positions are now familiar; but they also imply the possibility, and indeed the obligation, to reread or rewrite the text, and demand a kind of estrangement effect or *ostranenia* by which what looks subjective in the work can somehow, by a dramatic enlargement of perspective, be revealed as objective in its deeper essence. In spite of Adorno's insistence on commitment to the objective logic of the work, therefore, there remains an open space in his aesthetics for the critical gesture and the act of the critical transformation of the text: something he only fragmentarily, and seemingly with great reluctance, theorized as 'second reflection'.

There will therefore be a certain ambiguity in the positions on subjectivity we are about to outline: they often present themselves as historical and philosophical analyses of what subjectivity is, or thinks itself to be – that is, its objective illusions (or even its ideologies); at the same time, however, they can also be read as methodological clues and indications of how one is to objectify these seemingly subjective components (or 'moments', to use the Hegelian term) in our reading of the works themselves.

Adorno's first published book, on Kierkegaard, to be sure, provocatively denounced the concept and the experience of bourgeois 'inwardness' in a famous passage that assimilated the bourgeois soul to the *interior* of a Biedermeier household.[13] This can also clearly be taken as an aesthetic judgement and a sentence passed on certain kinds of 'spiritualizing' art, which, however, were they works of great quality, could presumably in another sense be reobjectified and their more objective 'truth content' historically and philosophically disclosed. Once again the ideal of a kind of liquidation of the ego is variably situated: sometimes in the works themselves as their objective tendency, and sometimes in our relationship to them, as when the objectivizing spirit of Hegel's aesthetic is celebrated for the way in which, anticipating Constructivism long *avant la lettre*, 'it sought the subjective success of the art-work precisely in those moments where the subject vanishes from it' (AT 92/85).

But as we have shown, Adorno's philosophical procedure does not involve the destruction of older, sometimes even false categories (and the projection of some new hitherto non-existent utopian philosophical terminology or language), but rather a playing through them which mobilizes even their untruth to project its opposite. The category of 'expression' is, for example, both a philosophical and a historical problem (the social position of subjectivity) and an aesthetic value which stands in precarious and antagonistic tension with cognate but incompatible categories such as mimesis on the one hand and construction on the other, but above all with *Schein* or aesthetic appearance – something that will more immediately be appreciated when we remember that for Adorno expression is above all the expression of pain (which takes the aesthetic form of dissonance or a new and sharper kind of ugliness, themselves tendentially in conflict with the value of aesthetic appearance and a fundamental feature of that crisis in *Schein* which as we have seen is at one with the modern itself):

> The antithesis of expression and *Schein* is a primary one. In so far as expression can scarcely be conceived except as the expression of suffering – joy resists expression stubbornly, while bliss, one would think, remains inexpressible – expression constitutes then immanently that moment in which art wards off that utter and complete immanence towards which its formal law tends, by means of one of its own constitutive elements. (AT 169/161-2)

The immediacy of expression, therefore, the impatience of its passion, prevent the work from sealing over into a purely aesthetic object (and thereby ceasing to become art altogether but, rather, a commodity): art remains art only by holding to the anti-aesthetic claims of reality and truth. Yet this truth, secured by the commitment to subjective expression, also threatens tendentially to undermine aesthetic appearance altogether (as we have already seen technically in the shrinkage of expressionistic music into the briefest of instants).

This is not to say, however, that subjective expression in the work of art persists as some foreign body within it, or some alien impulse: it is also transformed and objectified in a peculiar manner, which Adorno characterizes after a fashion that can be said to be *his* version of Benjamin's concept of *aura* (with which *Aesthetic Theory* pursues an endless subterranean dialogue of pro and con): 'Expression is the gaze of the work of art' (AT 172/165). Yet what is most beautiful about this formulation is what it does not yet say, but what we might have deduced from the related figure of the windowless monad – namely, that this gaze is *blind* (AT 174/167), blind both because we see it as an object and because it cannot look back at us, or indeed out at any empirical reality.

But expression is also bound to the dialectic of time, and not merely because its contents – these particular passions, these strong but dated feelings – are always historical. In so far as beyond all specific contents (already, indeed, somehow reduced and de-differentiated by their assimilation to sheer suffering in general – that is to say, paradoxically, to what can never really be 'expressed' in the first place), expression characterizes the historical status of the psychic subject itself, its tendential compression and its ever more onerous historical constraints and unfreedom – to that degree, every moment of expression bears within itself synchronic history:

> The language of expression is in contradistinction to that of meaning something older, yet unresolved: as though the work of art, by assimilating itself to the subject in its structure, repeats the process of that very subject's emergence in the world and its liberation from it. Works of art possess expressivity, not when they communicate subjectivity, but rather when they tremble with its *Ur*-history, and the *Ur*-history of endowment with soul and life: the *tremolo* of willed expressions of subjectivity is an unbearable substitute for this primal historicity. This situation is what circumscribes the affinity of works of art with subjectivity: that affinity persists because that primal history lives on within the subject itself, beginning again and again throughout all history. Only the subject can constitute the vehicle for expression, no matter how mediated it is even where it imagines itself to be the most immediate. Even where what is expressed resembles the psychic subject, and where its impulses are 'subjective' in the conventional sense, these remain impersonal, passing

through the integrated ego rather than emerging from it. Expression in works of art is the non-subjective dimension of the subject itself, less its expression than its impression: there is nothing quite so expressive as the eyes of apes, that seem objectively to mourn the fact that they are not human beings. (AT 172/165)

This peculiar dialectic of a subjectivity that passes back and forth between the two poles of expression and of the psychic subject itself, in which each is alternately subjective and objective in opposition to the other's variability, finds its most dramatic formal rehearsal in an excursus on the lyric, and on its pronouns (themselves variably objective or subjective [AT 249–52/239–41]), which completes Adorno's earlier (and fundamental) programmatic essay on this topic, 'Lecture on Lyric and Society'.[14]

Indeed, the originality of Adorno's observations on language and on style as such lies in his emphasis on the objectivity that speaks through this most subjective of all phenomena (and it is an objectivity to be distinguished from Bakhtin's collective speech as well as from the non- or inhuman dimensions of language foregrounded by poststructuralism). Here that dimension of language alienated to the concept and the social totality is in effect used against itself and redirected:

If in fact lyric content is to be grasped as something objective that operates by way of individual subjectivity – and otherwise what most obviously defines it as a genre, its effects on others besides the monologic poet, can scarcely be explained – this can be so only if the withdrawal of the lyrical work, its interiorization and distanciation from the social surface, is itself socially motivated behind the back of the author himself. The medium for this is, however, very precisely language. ... The greatest lyric constructs are those in which, in the virtual elimination of mere content, the subject sounds through language in such a way that language itself becomes audible. The self-forgetfulness of the subject as it surrenders itself to language as to something objective, and the immediacy and involuntary nature of its expression, are one and the same: and this is how speech mediates lyric and society within itself. (NL 56)

This deeply Benjaminian idea will then be explored in two directions: the first most obviously and dramatically affords a dialectical and utopian 'method', particularly in Adorno's readings here of the way in which Mörike's and George's subjective expression stand as virtual photographic negatives of their experience of the social, which can be read back from them in reverse. The other path, however, tends towards forms of the objective in subjective language that finally lead out of the modern period itself:

In so far as language cuts through the threads that connect it to the subject, it speaks for the subject that can no longer speak for itself – Hölderlin was probably the first whose art sensed this. (NL 478)

But Hölderlin's neoclassicism leads back to epic and parataxis, and to the forms of social and linguistic experience already registered in the moment of their disappearance in *Dialectic of Enlightenment*:

> This murmur [of the hexameter in the *Odyssey*] is the very voice and intrinsic sound of epic speech, in which identity, the fixed and the univocal, mingles with the polysemous and the transitory, in order to separate itself from them once again triumphantly. The undifferentiated flow of myth is the ever-identical; the *telos* of narrative, however, is multiplicity and difference, so that implacably rigid commitment to identity in which the epic object is fixed serves precisely to ratify its non-identity from the badly identical and the unarticulated indifferentiation of sameness. (NL 34)

But this is the very point at which Adorno's intermittent literary analyses meet the fundamental work in which so much of the dialectical aesthetics of that period were crystallized – Lukács's *Theory of the Novel*, where the account of the historical fate of literary form itself prefigures the other dialectical trajectories – the concept, repression, the subject, technology, the senses – that the Frankfurt School was to explore so luminously. Here, then, the possibility of realism is itself tendentially excluded 'from the narrator's standpoint by sheer subjectivism that no longer tolerates a content that has not been transformed by subjectivity and thus undermines the epic commandment of objectivity itself' (NL 41).

At this point, however, a retroactive rewriting of history, and in particular the history of the relationship between lyric and society, language and the subject, imposes itself. In an astonishing passage that goes far towards establishing and clarifying Adorno's essential modernism, he will thus assert that lyric and its language could only be a modern phenomenon (the argument Lukács made for the novel in his fundamental work) and that

> its concept, as that is immediate for us and virtually 'second nature', is essentially modern. In a similar way landscape painting and the idea of 'nature' it proposes also first knew autonomous development in the modern period. I know I am exaggerating in this, and that you will find many counter-examples to oppose. The most powerful one would be Sappho. Of Chinese, Japanese, Arabic lyrics I will not speak, as I cannot read them in the original and must suspect that translation deploys mechanisms of adaptation that preclude adequate understanding. But the properly lyric statements that have come down to us from older times are only intermittent and fragmentary, like

those occasional backgrounds in older painting that anticipate something of what will become landscape painting. Such lyric instants do not constitute form. Those great poets of a more distant past that are classified under lyric in literary histories - Pindar, for example, and Alcaeus, but also the overwhelming bulk of the work of Walther von der Vogelweide - are very distant from lyric in its contemporary primary sense. They lack that character of the immediate and the desubstantialized that we have rightly or wrongly become accustomed to seeing as the very criterion of lyric, and that only intense training allows us to transcend. (NL 52-3)

Such essentially historicist positions - never developed elsewhere in Adorno, save for certain reflections on earlier music - suggest the retroactive effects Marx posited for his theory of the modes of production - namely that it was only in the more advanced social formations (above all capitalism) that the implicit 'truth' of the earlier ones came to light. But of course that truth of the earlier formations (here the intermittent presence of lyric) comes to light by fulfilling and abolishing the earlier forms in which it was only implicit.

These varied reflections on the objectivity of language then reach a kind of theoretical climax and codification, thereby returning very much to their Benjaminian inspiration, in the peculiar notion of the 'speech-like character' [Sprachähnlichkeit] of the work of art, developed in Aesthetic Theory: a notion which, paradoxically, is introduced in opposition to linguistic theories which see the individual linguistic work as a mere example of language as such, as well as to communicational ones which ignore the fact that 'more modern forms of art work to transform communicative speech into something mimetic' [AT 171/164]. The opposition of speech (as what is imitated on this view) and the specific text that imitates it - reminiscent of the great opposition between 'capital in general' and 'the many capitals' in Marx - thus not unexpectedly offers a different way of conceiving the relationship of general to particular:

Language is hostile to the particular yet seeks the latter's salvation. It mediates the particular through generality and within the constellation of the general, doing justice to its own universals, however, only when these are not static and endowed with the appearance of essential being, but rather concentrated to the extreme upon what is specifically to be expressed [that is to say, the particular]. The universals of language thereby draw their truth from a process antithetical to their own inner logic. (AT 304/292)

Meanwhile, the implications of Adorno's aesthetic positions for practical criticism generally are more wide-ranging than this important local probe into literary method. It has already been made clear that those critical

methods somehow defined and limited in advance by an a priori conception of subjectivity are here systematically excluded: reception was brack-
eted by way of the primacy of construction; psychological studies of
various kinds are peremptorily assigned to the manipulative techniques
of the objects of the Culture Industry; even Aristotelian catharsis is repudiated (although Freud's treatment at Adorno's hands is sometimes more
nuanced,[15] along with what may still seem 'psychological' in Kant).

What is more interesting here is the fate of the various critical
approaches to meaning, something all the more strategic in so far as
Adorno also – along with his historical critique of philosophical aesthetics
– wishes to restage the latter's claims in some new way, and to reinvent
a new kind of primacy of philosophy over artistic experience. In general,
however, more limited literary-critical doctrines of meaning are here dialectically undermined by an operation which transfers them into the
interior of the work of art, as the latter's content. The pretensions of
the symbol are thereby historically dispatched:

Art absorbs symbols by depriving them of what they 'symbolized'; advanced
artists have themselves concretely completed the philosophical critique of
the symbol. The indices and characteristics of the modern have thereby
become absolute in their own right, they are signs whose meaning is forgotten
even for them. Their penetration into the aesthetic medium and their resistance
to all forms of intention are two manifestations of the same process. (AT
147/140–41)

The crucial word here is 'intention', which marks the first stage of the
polemic against meaning. But Adorno's position is to be sharply distinguished from the way in which recent critical debates on this subject
have been conducted, and in particular from the twin questions of whether
'intention' could ever be determined on the basis of a text (to which
its putative formulation merely supplies an additional text to be deciphered, and not some deeper truth); and whether, even if intention could
be established, it would constitute the ultimate bedrock or foundation
for understanding. Adorno's is not in that sense a doctrine of understanding (or *Verstehen*), but he is also more historically variable about the
detectability of intentions in a given work. What changes everything
in his discussion of this matter is that even where intentions can be
determined, they are not to be grasped as something outside or behind
the text – which gives us hints as to its proper use – but rather as part
and parcel of the text itself, fully as much a component of its raw material
as the creative biographical subject, who is equally drawn into the work

as part of its aesthetic 'ruse of reason'. In fact, the appearance of intention in a given work is generally useful as a negative symptom:

> The distinction between truth and intention in the work of art becomes available for critical consciousness above all where intention stands in the service of the untrue, mostly of those eternal truths which are in reality little more than the repetition of the mythic. (AT 195/187)

What is meant here is surely the Heideggerian thematics (also reaffirmed by Gadamer) about the confrontation of great art with the eternal mysteries of death and being: but such eternal verities are also perpetuated on a garden-variety level by a humanistic criticism mesmerized by the 'human condition'. Here intention passes over into conventional versions of meaning itself, about which Adorno tirelessly insists that whatever it is, it is not the same as what he will call 'truth content': 'understanding, meaning and content are not equivalents' (AT 516/476). Meaning and intention, even in the traditional sense of the idea of the work, 'such as the inherent guilt of subjective moralizing in Ibsen's *Wild Duck*' (AT 515/475), is not 'truth content', since it merely identifies this particular component of the work without disposing of any further means of judging it – whether the judgement be couched in formal language (is the intention realized?), in philosophical language (is it 'true' or 'false'), or in historical and social language (that of the situation itself). The categories of meaning or message are inadequate, not merely because they do not allow for the possibility that, as in Beckett, it is the very absence of meaning that could be the work's meaning, constituting something like a 'judgement on the very nature of meaning itself which includes and develops the latter's very history' (AT 230/220).

They are also, in the conventional use, formally inadequate, yet by the same token indispensable as symptoms:

> No matter how irreducible the content of a work is to its intention – if only for the simple reason that no matter how carefully thought through, no intention is ever destined to be fully realizable in a representation – only a rigid dogmatism would disqualify the category of intention as a moment in the work of art. Intentions have their proper place within the dialectic between the mimetic pose of the work of art and its participation (*methexis*) in the historical dynamic of 'enlightenment' [or instrumental reason]: not merely as subjectively mobile organizing forces that are exhausted in the work itself but also in the form of an objectivity proper to them. ... If the materiality of the work of art constitutes its resistance to empty identity, then their fundamental process essentially involves a dialectic between materiality and intention. Without this last – which is the immanent form of the

identity principle – form could as little come into being as it could in the absence of the mimetic impulse. The surplus of intentions then proclaims the irreducibility of the work to mimesis alone. And the objective bearer of such aesthetic intentions, which synthesizes them with each other, is what is called meaning. (AT 226–7/217)

The category of intention, like that of 'meaning', is thus retained as one of a variety of traditional aesthetic categories without whose interplay and mutually canceling critique the discussion of the work of art would remain empty: there is at work here in Adorno something like what Freud called overdetermination, by which he not only characterized the simultaneous and multiple determination of the dream's final form, but also marked the discovery, in the course of analytic interpretation, that any one of those 'paths' could equally well lead back to the central nucleus of the dream itself. What functions as such a nucleus in Adorno is of course 'truth content' (which has not yet been examined in its own right); clearly the metaphoric spatiality of the Freudian hermeneutic is inappropriate here, where the work's truth content does not lie behind the work somewhere or deep within it as that 'substantificque moelle' archetypal in the imagery of hermeneutics.

The 'analytic method', however, by which one transcends the play of partial categories towards that truth-content, does make a fitful appearance in Aesthetic Theory, where it is called 'second reflection', a term by which Adorno seemed to want to convey something a little more than a second reading or a higher form of reflexivity. For the 'reflection' of a first order within the work surely designates its technological and productive energies, which mark the investment of collective knowledge and labor: this is the level of technique and of social productivity, as that becomes historically differentiated into the dynamic of the work's materials and the intentionalities of its producer (not excluding, as we have seen, the historical status of the subject itself).

'Second reflection', then, presumably means a drawing back from this in such a way that it becomes visible to the naked eye, not merely as features or energies within the work of art but as the work of art itself. The few tantalizing remarks Adorno consecrates to this 'method' – which in another sense is simply the dialectic itself in the realm of aesthetic thinking – suggest that it has the dual capacity to transform what looks subjective in the work into something objective, and to return the appearance of objectivity to its original productive dynamism:

> The truth of the new, or in other words of spaces and positions that have never yet been occupied, is situated in the non-intentional. This is what puts it in contradiction with reflection, the very motor force of the new, and

potentiates it to the second power. Second reflection is thus quite the opposite of its conventional philosophical embodiment, such as Schiller's doctrine of the '*sentimentalisch*', which ends up heaping further and further intentions on the work of art. Second reflection aims to grasp the procedures and the language of the work of art in as articulated and intensely conscious a fashion as possible, but essentially steers towards blindness. (AT 47–8/39–40)

This 'method', then, has as its rule the effort to avoid conceptual formulations which one might substitute for the work of art; yet it aims at a higher type of philosophical thinking (Adorno will explicitly evoke the Hegelian concept of the *Begriff*) which somehow remains concrete without losing itself in some ecstatic identification with the work itself. It maintains a distance from the work, which it intuits from a broader perspective (my language) and thereby certainly involves the positing of certain new kinds of meaning, whose formulation, however, is a matter of great tact and delicacy. We conclude this chapter with one of those provisional attempts:

What is mediated in the work of art, what makes it something other than its mere presence as an object in the world, must be mediated a second time through reflection, by way of the 'concept' [the Hegelian *Begriff*]. That can be successful, however, only if the concept addresses itself specifically to the details of the work rather than moving away from them into generalities. When, shortly before the end of the first movement of Beethoven's sonata *Les Adieux*, a fleeting association of three bars seems to quote the clatter of horses' hooves, this evanescent passage, which seems almost ashamed of any intellectual recognition, a sonorous expression of disappearance scarcely even identifiable within the context of the movement, bespeaks more of the hope of ultimate return than any general reflection on the nature of this sound itself, a mixture of transience and persistence, could make explicit. Only an aesthetic philosophy capable of securing such micro-logical details in their innermost spirit, within the construction of the aesthetic whole, could be said to live up to its promise. Such a philosophy would, however, also have to be a self-sufficient articulated and mediated form of thinking in its own right. (AT 531/490)

Eight

At length, at the term of this elaborate historical and often technical reflection on artistic form and the thoughts it is possible to think about it, aesthetics - to whose contradictions and historical impossibility *Aesthetic Theory* had so often seemed to testify - reasserts itself, in the abandoned draft preface published at the end of the posthumous volume, and philosophy once again lays claim to primacy over the whole field of aesthetic inquiry. We must therefore in conclusion speculate as to the concrete content of such philosophizing, whose lone and enigmatic watchword - 'truth-content', or *Wahrheitsgehalt* - inevitably raises the suspicion that it may be no more than a euphemism for that doctrine of authenticity whose emptiness and ideological character Adorno so tirelessly denounced in his great adversary Heidegger.

Even more disturbing - and yet another unexpected convergence with the philosophical opponent - is the seeming reappearance of ontology at the heart of Adorno's most probing philosophical attempt to character-ize the nature of the work of art, as a contact with non-identity or with nature for which the stigmatized term 'being' often scarcely seems a jarring substitute. It is not, to be sure, a question of accusing Adorno of the kind of reversion to Schopenhauer and to mysticism, if not to religion itself, which Max Horkheimer seems to have experienced towards the end of his life ('the appeal to an entirely other than this world ... led finally to a more positive evaluation of certain metaphysical trends').[16] Nonetheless, the ontological account of the work of art would seem to coexist uneasily, in *Aesthetic Theory* taken as a whole, with its relation-ship to social and historical contradiction - on which Adorno so strongly insists elsewhere throughout the text, as we have seen.

Paradoxically, it is the very will to wrest artistic experience from the aestheticizing language of sheer contemplation, as well as the reemphasized vocation of the dialectic to disqualify the aesthetic monisms of materialism and positivism alike, that leads Adorno to his ontology, in which the peculiar nature of the art-work as something both aesthetically autonomous and anti-aesthetic or profoundly social and historical is to be philosophically characterized:

The spiritual mediation of the work, by which it is able to stand in contrast to the empirical, cannot be realized without its integration of some properly discursive dimension. Were the work of art purely contemplative [*Anschauung* – 'intuition' – has the overtone of a quasi-visual contemplation], it would remain imprisoned in the contingency of the sensuously immediately given, against which, however, the work in reality opposes its own specific logic. Its quality is determined by the degree to which its concreteness and its articulated development and inner differentiation precisely shed that contingency. The purist, and in that sense profoundly rationalistic, opposition between the visually contemplative and the ideational in reality reinforces that dichotomy between rationality and material sensuousness perpetuated by society itself for its own ideological ends. Art must, on the contrary, struggle in effigy against that opposition with the objective critique it in effect embodies; if art is banished to the sensuous pole alone, the opposition is thereby merely reconfirmed. That untruth which is the deeper critical object of all art is not rationality itself, but rather the latter's static opposition to the particular; if art extracts the moment of the particular as an object of mere contemplation, it ratifies precisely that reified rigidity and valorizes precisely the waste products that social rationality abandons and excludes in order to draw attention away from itself. To the degree therefore that, according to traditional aesthetic precept, the work becomes ever more seamlessly an object of contemplation, to that very degree is its spirituality reified, outside sheer appearance and well beyond the more truly aesthetic event of apparition. (AT 151/144)

It is therefore as a relationship to otherness, nature, or being itself that the work of art can be rescued from the trivializing aestheticism of the doctrine of aesthetic contemplation, with the unexpected additional advantage that art need no longer find itself in opposition to technical rationality but can be seen as incorporating that form of collective social knowledge as well in the process.

In fact these twin results, which seem paradoxically to conjugate the two incompatible temptations of this aesthetic – the metaphysical relationship to non-identity on the one hand, the affirmation of art as advanced social productivity on the other – circumscribe the mystery of the work of art and the philosophical problem it poses:

The metaphysical questions raised by art today turn on the problem of how
something 'spiritual', a thing that is made and in the language of philosophy
merely 'posited', can also be true. What is at stake in this problem is not
immediately the individual work of art at hand, but rather its content [Gehalt].
The question about the possible truth of an object that is made is, however,
nothing less than that other question about aesthetic appearance and about
its possible redemption as the appearance of truth itself. Truth-content, however, cannot be made or constructed. All making in art is one long struggle
to say what that made object itself can never be and what art itself can never
know: that is what Geist or spirit means in aesthetics. And this is where
the idea of art as the restoration of a repressed nature submerged in the
dynamics of history comes in. Nature, whose imago art aspires to be, does
not yet exist; what is true in art is a non-existent. It comes to coincide with
art within that Other, which a reason fixated on identities and bent on reducing
it to sheer materiality calls Nature. That other is, however, neither a unity
nor a single concept, but rather the multiple. The truth-content of art therefore
takes the form of the multiple, rather than some ultimate abstraction under
which the individual works of art might be subsumed. There is therefore
an inseparable relationship between the way in which the truth-content of
art is realized only in individual works and the multiplicity of all those realities
reason seeks to reduce to so many identifications. The most profound of
all the paradoxes of art is probably this: that it can encounter the non-made
or truth only by means of the construction and the composition of particular
and specifically organized individual works, and never through any more
immediate access. Yet the individual works stand in the most extreme tension
with their truth-content. To the degree to which such truth appears only
within constructed objects without any conceptual form, to that very degree
it negates their construction. Every work of art disappears qua representation
in its own truth-content; the latter causes the work of art itself to sink into
sheerest irrelevance, something it is given only to the very greatest works
of art to experience. (AT 198-9/191)

The undertones of Dialectic of Enlightenment in this passage remind us
that the relationship between history and nature – what we have here
seemed to detect as an incompatibility between metaphysics (or ontology)
and Marxism – was there coordinated with no little philosophical
ingenuity as an alternation of history with nature: the process designated
by the title was described as the response to some initially hostile and
threatening nature which took the form of the latter's tendential domination, and the gradual emergence throughout history of the instrument
of that domination – 'enlightenment', or reason, instrumental reason,
'bad' rationality or Verstand (in distinction to Vernunft), which the authors traced back to the earliest forms of magic spells, rituals, sacrifice,

mimetic attempts to control and dominate nature which they saw as
earlier forms of 'enlightenment' and of a piece with it (save that the
dialectical twist in the transformation of this last into science marks
the turning of mimesis against itself, in the moment of the anti-mimetic
taboo on graven images). Even the theme of the tendentially repressed,
damaged, victimized subject was given in advance by the premiss that
Reason or 'Enlightenment' also requires the domination of an inner
human nature (in short, a repression of instinct) in order to secure its
primacy.

This means, in the context of Aesthetic Theory, as the above-cited passage
makes clear, that 'the idea of art as the restoration of a repressed nature'
will be capable of identifying the presence of nature or being somewhere
at the heart of all historical contradictions and conjunctural constellations
of social meaning, since the domination of nature is deeply inscribed
within them as their ultimate dynamic. Meanwhile, in this sense later
and more complex social forms of human drives and motivations – productivity fully as much as commodification (or that 'reason fixated on
identities' which is at work in the establishment of exchange value as
such) – will all carry within them the primal drive (or original sin) of
this first moment of the relationship to nature, which is not merely
fear but also the 'instinct' of self-preservation. Yet in the sense in which
this properly infinite 'dialectic of enlightenment' which is human history
can have no real beginning – that baleful fearful thing henceforth called
Nature having been conjured up by human terror of it in the first place
– one can also say, as Adorno does here, that 'nature does not yet exist':
an uncharacteristically Blochian note in Adorno, and particularly in Aesthetic Theory, where the utopian character of art and its commitment
to Hope and to the not-yet-existent has decisively receded and is sounded
only in a few sober local references.

What we have been calling the ontological motif in Adorno's aesthetics
now tactfully recapitulates many of these themes, particularly in his polemics against the aesthetic subject and against subjectivity and subjectivism, which now take on a somewhat different meaning and appearance.
For the true place of the subject in aesthetic experience is not to be
characterized by its purification (Aristotelian catharsis), nor in its 'reconciliation' with the object, still less in its creative mastery over this last
and objective contingency (as for example in Sartre), but rather in a
violent eclipse of the subject itself which is, however, sharply to be distinguished from annihilation, submission, the surrender of the subject
to what transcends it (as in Heidegger and on some readings of Kant's
concept of the sublime), let alone the virtual swoon or momentary
obliteration of the human:

Erschütterung [the shock of the aesthetic experience], which is in any case
the polar opposite of traditional notions of aesthetic experience, is unrelated
to any particular gratification of the ego, let alone its pleasure. Rather it
is to be seen as a memento of the liquidation of the ego, which by way
of such aesthetic shock becomes aware of its own constraints and finitude.
The experience is also sharply to be distinguished from that sapping and
weakening of the ego perpetuated by the Culture Industry. For this last such
a conception as that of aesthetic shock would be an idle vanity, an attitude
that justifies its deeper motivation in *ressentiment* to destroy art altogether
[*Entkunstung*]. But in order for the ego to reclaim even the most minimal
possibility of peering out over the prison that it is in its very nature, it requires
not distraction but the most extreme form of tense effort: this is what preserves
aesthetic shock – in any case an involuntary conduct – from regression. Kant
very correctly posited the strength of the subject as the necessary precondition
for his aesthetic of the sublime. (AT 364/347-8)

Yet this simultaneous strength or affirmation of the subject in its moment
of involuntary annihilation – a strength which allows it to confront
the experience without lapsing into the various regressive conducts
exhaustively enumerated by the Frankfurt School, from fascism and the
mythic to their various aesthetic equivalents – is also, momentarily, a
surrender of all the scars left on the ego by the dialectic of enlightenment,
most notably the drive to 'self-preservation':

> As Schopenhauer well knew, aesthetic experience is able to break through
> the spell of rigid self-preservation and to project the image of a state of con-
> sciousness in which the ego no longer finds its gratification in its own private
> interests, including that of its personal survival. (AT 515/475)

We should here note in passing how this new utopian account of the
relationship of aesthetic experience to the psychic subject decisively re-
absorbs Kant's two great motifs: that of the suspension of interests, and
also the doctrine of the sublime, which is here and throughout reread
or rewritten by Adorno as precisely this encounter with the not-I or
the Other that is ontologically central to his aesthetics. His account moves
dialectically through the various traditional descriptions, drawing its
power from their critique (and in particular the notion that aesthetic
experience is in any sense to be assimilated to pleasure or the satisfaction
of needs) but also sometimes modifying them in a positive way:

> The traditional mode of relating to art, whatever its relevance, was [not one
> of pleasure or enjoyment, but rather] one of admiration: admiration that
> works of art are what they are in themselves, and not merely for the viewer.
> What was felt to dawn in such works and what overpowered the viewer

was their truth, something that for example outweighs all the other components of a work such as that of Kafka. Works of art were not considered
instruments of enjoyment of some higher type. The relationship was not
seen as any sort of culinary incorporation, quite the opposite: the viewer
vanished into the thing itself: something fully realized only in those modern
representations that erupt out at you as onrushing locomotives used to do
from the movie screen. (AT 27/19)

This otherness of the work of art, which it may perhaps be more accurate
in the light of such passages to formulate as the otherness of its truth-
content, is now finally – in the obligatory yet peculiarly central pages
Adorno feels it necessary to devote to the traditional topic of 'natural
beauty' – identified as the *Ansich*, the in-itself of being or of nature:
'Natural beauty is the trace on things of the non-identical in a world
dominated by universal identity' (AT 114/108).

Several impulses need to be disentangled here: first of all, even the
most evanescent experience of nature registers the mystery, not merely
of the not-I, nor even of what resists identity (either in the ego-logical
or the rationalizing-commodifying sense), but above all of what has not
been *made* by the subject (a paradox already registered above for the
'truth-content' – unmade – of works of art which are 'made' or 'constructed' by definition):

> The experience of nature can only be that of appearance [or better still: *Erschei-
> nung*, of the act of appearance, the event of apparition], and not of some
> raw material for work and the reproduction of life, let alone of the substratum
> of scientific knowledge. (AT 103/97)

This essential distance of nature from the human or from praxis then
accounts for Adorno's unsatisfactory attempt to characterize nature itself
philosophically: 'For natural beauty, as an apparition, is already itself
image [*Bild*]' (AT 105/99), a description whose slippage into precisely
those accounts of our contemplative relationship to nature and to art
that he seeks to discredit it would seem difficult to prevent. We are
here, perhaps, at the closest point in Adorno to the various existential
philosophies: the suggestion that natural appearing or apparition is a
kind of event recalls the Heideggerian doctrine of Being itself as something
that happens; even though the simultaneous effort to endow this event
with the force of negativity and the shock of what is radically not the
subject seems more Sartrean in spirit, and should also be strongly empha-
sized.

But Adorno will then immediately remind us that even in this metaphysical or ontological sense all experiences of nature are mediated histori-

cally and socially: his discussion of natural landscape, for example, modulates almost at once as though by its own inner force of gravity towards
that rather different thing he calls 'cultural landscape' (AT 101-2/94-6),
in which natural perceptions have somehow become indissociable from
cultural and historical ones: 'without historical recollection or commem-
oration [*Eingedenken*], beauty would not exist' (AT 102/96). To be sure,
there is here a reversal from the ontological account of nature to the
history of the concept and the experience of the natural, which then
at once makes available more familiar dialectical solutions to this tension
(where, for example, we intuit nature itself by way of its destruction
by capitalism).

Still, as this motif of a contemplative glimpse of nature as image (or
better still as the sheer conceptual possibility of such a glimpse) is the
crucial pretext for all recent attempts to argue a philosophical *rapproche-
ment* between Adorno and his archenemy Heidegger, it is worth recalling
what is incompatible, in Adorno's conception of natural history, with
the *Seinsfrage* of Heideggerian existentialism. Even leaving aside the dizzying horror of the organic and Darwinian perspective disclosed by
Adorno's notion of 'natural history' (something which might, in a pinch,
find its more lofty, 'metaphysical' equivalent in the Heideggerian Being-
unto-death), the materialism of the body contained within Adorno's
insistence on the idea of happiness and his fleeting evocation of Utopia
is very different in spirit either from the mood of heroic fascism in early
Heidegger, or the latter's ritual solemnity, as in the wondrous pages
on the inauguration of the *polis* in 'The Origins of the Work of Art'.
This last is in fact a good deal more political (in all senses) than anything
in Adorno, whose physicality here demands at least the courtesy of a
comparison with the great Brechtian materialism of the soup and the
cigar.

We can also problematize this issue – essentially the tension between
history and nature – one last time in a somewhat different way before
we engage the crucial matter of the relationship of this aesthetic to 'truth-
content'. The dilemma can be dramatically staged by quoting what is
surely Adorno's most forthright statement on the historical semantics
of aesthetic experience and the social and historical character of the 'truth-
content' of great art:

> That a Beethoven symphony is as little accessible to someone who cannot
> grasp what are often called its purely musical or technical occurrences as
> it is to someone unable to perceive the echo in it of the French Revolution;
> and how both those moments mediate each other – is to be reckoned among
> the tough yet unavoidable problems confronting any philosophical aesthetics.
> (AT 519/479)

The example will seem less facile if it is augmented by even those scattered observations about Beethoven which have been quoted above; everything that is most admirable about Adorno as an aesthetic thinker and the embodiment of one possible form of the cultural and political intellectual is richly in evidence here. Our concern, however, is with the consistency between this account of Beethoven's historical 'truth-content' and the metaphysical or ontological aesthetic of non-identity which has just been outlined. In what way, in other words, can this aesthetic intuition of the great historical *Novum* of the French Revolution be reformulated in terms of the otherness of the experience of the natural? Thereby a supplementary problem, a third term, is added to the philosophical task Adorno describes above of mediating between formal and historical approaches. Meanwhile a certain mediatory thread is already given by Adorno's historical account of the history of aesthetics, which shifts for social and historical reasons from attention to beauty (still finally Kant's framework) to an emphasis on the constitutive relationship between art and freedom (Schiller, Hegel); perhaps the ontological motif in Beethoven is to be grasped here in some deeper relationship between the experience of political liberation and the dawning sense of freedom in nature itself. But whatever the elements of a solution, it should be clear that Adorno's multiple parameters demand an analysis of extraordinary complexity and range, which he himself failed to articulate theoretically with absolute coherence, all the while projecting the ideal of such analysis with a power that rebukes the ambitions of most contemporary criticism.

Nine

As for truth-content, however, it seems at least minimally possible that it cannot be philosophically described, since it is inscribed in a situation of well-nigh nominalistic multiplicity in which only individual works of art, but not Art itself, have their various truth-contents, which are therefore incomparable, incommensurable and not susceptible to abstract philosophical generalization. To say that it involves the correspondence of the work to its own specific concept [*Begriff*] is not apparently to say very much (except to Hegelians). To insist on the completion of aesthetic judgement and description with a properly philosophical form of judgement is perhaps to suggest a little more:

> The truth-content of a work is not what it means, but what decides whether it is in itself true or false, and it is this conception of the truth of the work in itself which is alone consistent with properly philosophical interpretation and which coincides with philosophical truth (at least in the Idea). (AT 197/190)

The difference between these kinds of truth judgements and Heideggerian 'authenticity' can at least be read off their respective critical practice, by comparing the emptiness of the content of this last (death and Being) with the historical specificity of Adorno's readings. But it should be clear that the notion of 'truth-content' is what enables Adorno to transcend the limits of a whole range of conventional interpretations and hermeneutic schemes and to step outside aesthetic meanings in such a way that they can be historically grasped. This larger capacity of 'second reflection' to foreground meaning in a historical way specifically includes ideological analysis and secures a philosophical innovative and original place for 'false consciousness' within the work's larger historical 'truth-content'. If Beethoven is a privileged example of one kind of truth about formal history, and Schoenberg and Beckett are examples of a more extreme kind of formal solution, here it is the figure of Richard Wagner which becomes Adorno's archetypal crux:

> That works of art transcend themselves in the process whereby they are concretely realized does not in itself guarantee their truth. Many works of very great quality are true as the expression of what is in itself false consciousness. This is something that can be grasped only from the standpoint of a transcendent critique, such as that of Nietzsche on Wagner. The limitations of Nietzsche's critique lie not merely in the fact that he judges the work from above rather than engaging its claims on their own merits. He has in fact a too limited conception of the very nature of truth-content itself: a kind of culture-philosophical conception, which takes no account of the historical moment which is immanent in aesthetic truth. The distinction between what is true in itself and something that is merely an adequate expression of false consciousness is untenable, if only because there has not yet to the present day ever existed anything like true consciousness, from which such a distinction might be observed somehow from above. The full representation of false consciousness properly names something which can also be named truth-content. The understanding of works of art, therefore, besides their exegesis through interpretation and critique, must also be pursued from the standpoint of redemption, which very precisely searches out the truth of false consciousness in aesthetic appearance. Great works cannot in that sense lie. Even where their content is mere appearance [Schein], in so far as it was historically necessary it includes a truth to which they testify; only the unsuccessful works are untrue. (AT 196/188)

Rightly or wrongly, Adorno felt that his Wagner book had made the most fundamental analytical contribution to this problem, which necessarily confronts anyone obliged to come to terms – whether intellectually, culturally or pedagogically – with classics of a conservative, if not indeed sometimes outright reactionary, stamp. His solution – the most difficult of all, since it requires one simultaneously to insist on what is false and ideological and also on what is utopian in the work – seems to me preferable to the alternatives, in which one either transforms a reactionary writer into a progressive one by fiat, or else smashes the canon altogether.

It has already become clear that the philosophical 'truth-content' of the work somehow – at least in 'great bourgeois' music and art – participates in its technical innovations. But these are themselves 'contradictions' in some very fundamental sense: thus the remarkable chromatic coloration of Wagner's music is deeply at one with the disintegration in it of the classical musical material (and even with his own technical ineptness). Yet the very splendor of that technical breakdown, whose tendentially atomistic logic releases all kinds of new 'productive forces', is itself a figure for the relationship between his 'moment of truth' and the regressive position of the subject in a bourgeois society that has already begun to anticipate its own limits. It should, however, be noted that this particular dialectic of ideology and truth excludes cheating and liberal whitewashing and wishful thinking: Wagner's character ('a sentimental Marat') has of course always offered a rich minefield of defects and imperfections, from egotism and cowardice all the way to the shame of the turncoat and the unreliability of the social toady. But nowhere have the crystallizations of these unlovely traits within the form and detail of the music drama been so implacably pursued as here by Adorno. This harshness, the remorselessness of the ideological judgement, is, however, the price that must be paid for the dialectical acknowledgement of the truth it also contains:

> Tristan's 'How could that vision leave me?', which refers to the presentiment of nothingness as something, seizes hold of the moment in which a complete negativity perfects the chimera of Utopia. It is the moment of awakening. The passage in Act III of *Tristan*, where the horn in the orchestra soars above the boundary separating nothingness from something to catch the echo of the shepherd's melancholy song as Tristan stirs – that passage will survive as long as the fundamental experiences of the bourgeois era can still be felt by human beings. Together with that other passage, the scene of Brünnhilde's awakening, it is evidence of that glimmering awareness without which the concept of nothingness, or so Wagner's music would have us believe, could not be conceived of. If compassion is reserved for animals, then it is logical for them to accompany such a moment: Brünnhilde's horse indeed seems to survive archaic times over into this now of consciousness (archaic time being, according to Schopenhauer, that of nothingness itself). (W 192/151)

(It does not seem superfluous to add that the motto of Adorno's book reads 'Horses are the survivors of an age of heroes'). The 'case' of Wagner, however, finally suggests that even formally, the doctrine of 'truth-content' cannot be generalized or transformed into an interpretive method: everything in Adorno's view of Wagner indeed returns us to the unique moment of this work, in which something of a German bourgeoisie that has not come to 'maturity' already lives its own decline, and where its very untimeliness generates a regressiveness that is at one and the same time formally innovative and productive. But it would be sheer critical mannerism to transfer this characteristic analysis to other figures of the modern, as though it alone embodied Adorno's 'method'. The method, however at least in principle, implies that every historical situation will be distinct, even though all are also frozen under the magic spell of the total system.

Adorno's aesthetics is therefore inseparable from ideological analysis, the necessity of whose historical 'moment' it repeatedly stresses: something which then brings us back in conclusion to what has already been characterized as the anti-political character of this same aesthetic. Adorno is very clear about the specific historical situation from which this position springs:

> The relationship between social praxis and art, always variable in any case, seems to have changed profoundly in the last forty or fifty years. During the First World War, and before Stalin, the artistic and political vanguards were always linked in spirit; whoever came of age in that time was inclined to feel that art was a priori what it had in fact rarely been historically, namely politically left by definition. (AT 373-7/359-60)

This is a useful reminder, since in the Anglo-American cultural field the constitutive affinity between modernism in art and revolutionary politics has rarely been stressed – indeed, most often reversed and denied for ideological purposes. Meanwhile, to stress the historical situation from which such opinions spring and to which they react is also to imply their historical variability and the possibility of the emergence of a different situation in which such antagonisms no longer hold or in which their very polar terms are perhaps transformed beyond recognition.

What must be principally stressed here, however, is that while Adorno seems to exclude the possibility of political works of art, often with some vehemence, what he in reality opposes may better be identified as a political aesthetic, one which stresses and valorizes the function of works of art within situations of immediacy, and in the realm of the day-to-day struggle and the Event, rather than their deeper expression of social struggle or historical contradiction (something, on the contrary, always implicit in *Aesthetic Theory*, as we have shown). What this means is that the individual works may wander out of one category into another: everything changes when something normally called 'political art' turns out to have been that seemingly different and incompatible thing called 'great art', as witness Adorno's subtle appreciation of his great adversary, Brecht:

> Brecht's efforts to smash subjective nuances and quarter tones with a tough objectivity which included conceptual toughness are very precisely aesthetic means, and in his finest works a principle of stylization rather than preaching; hard to tell exactly what the author 'meant' in *Galileo* or *The Good Person of Sezuan*, except to stress the distance and non-coincidence between the objec-

tivity of the representation and its subjective intention. Brecht's allergy to
expressive values, his preference for a quality that may have led him to misun-
derstand what the positivistic conception of a 'protocol sentence' was all
about – all of this is itself the figure for a certain kind of expression that
can come to language only through the latter's determinate negation. (AT
55/47)

(And later on, the song of the cranes from *Mahagonny* will be instanced
as a supreme realization of this peculiar and unique Brechtian aesthetic.)

It would seem, indeed, that what is for Adorno intolerable about any
specifically political aesthetic has less to do with its politics than with
its stress on art as such, rather than the individual works of art – the
monads – which Adorno wishes radically to distinguish from art as a
process or an institution. A peculiarly Hobbesian expression indeed recurs
in *Aesthetic Theory* from time to time to characterize the relationship
of the various individual works to each other: a *bellum omnium contra
omnes* (AT 47/60). And see elsewhere: 'they refuse to be compared. They
want to annihilate one another' (MM No. 47, 92/75). Sometimes the
Hegelian version is also offered (a permutation so significant, in a different
order of things, for French existentialism): 'each work of art seeks the
death of the other' (AT 60/52; 313–14/301). Yet such language, which
seeks to characterize the nominalism of 'truth-content' and the irreducibility of the unique historical conjunctures in which the great works
are embedded, does not always seem appropriate to describe this enormous historical sky in which the aesthetic monads hang gleaming like
so many planetary bodies; it might be better to say that they somehow
repel each other instinctively. Each one demands to exist as an absolute
in terms of which the existence of others can scarcely be acknowledged.
So Beethoven is not at war with Wagner, exactly, or with Greek tragedy;
but each can reveal its absolute truth only by means of the eclipse of
all the others. In much the same way the historical situation of each
one is an absolute present – a present of struggle, praxis, suffering –
whose claims on reality are sapped by any chronological historicism or
relativism of the archive. A political aesthetic also wishes to affirm this
primacy of the present and the event; but it is clear that for Adorno
it also means lining the monads up on sides and in teams, and substituting
general demands of style and discussions about art in general for engagement with the works themselves. The hostility to 'political art' this seems
to suggest might just as adequately be characterized as a hostility to avant-
gardes and to programmatic slogans.

It is self-defeating, however, to conclude an exploration of Adorno's
work within the aesthetic itself, a zone from which many readers will

wish to be heliported out and which will confirm their impressions of
the ultimately useless character of this philosophy, still evidently seeking
to stage a *Zweckhaftigkeit ohne Zweck*. (Significantly, in Germany today,
as we shall see in conclusion, the relegation of Adorno to mere aesthetics
is now the canonical method for dealing with this particular survival
of the dialectic.) And it is certain that aesthetic experience as such leads
nowhere, virtually by definition, save in the sense in which it stands
as a figure for a utopian existence that would not be dominated by instrumental motives and would above all be free of the ultimate 'end', which
is that of self-preservation. On the other hand, every reader of Adorno
will also remember that aesthetic experience is necessarily particular or
concrete, and not merely 'by definition': indeed, we have seen Adorno
argue that the guilt of art in general – the unjustifiable privilege and
luxury of 'aesthetic experience' in general – is unresolvable as such, and
qualifiable only in the individual work itself. But this then means that
aesthetic experience also always leads us back to history – to the history
of capitalism from which the work emerged, and to the constellation
of classes and instrumental rationality which is its semantic content and
makes its utopian dimension possible. It would then be equally justifiable
to say that aesthetics always leads back to history itself, and that for
art the 'non-identical' is society.

Meanwhile, the vital relationship of Adorno to political thinking lies
in the form rather than the content of his thoughts, which, conceptualizing aesthetic form or philosophical content rather than politics as such,
is capable of detecting within them – with a starker, more luminous
articulation than can normally be achieved within political analysis or
social history – the complex mobilities of the historical dialectic.

CONCLUSIONS

Adorno in the

Postmodern

One

One sometimes has the feeling that objections to Adorno's work and positions fall into two groups that ought under normal circumstances to cancel each other out. For one group, Adorno's work remains too Marxist; for the other (a much smaller group, it must be admitted) he is not Marxist enough, and maybe not even Marxist at all. The plot thickens if you introduce rumors of latent (or overt) Hegelianism, a reproach that could conceivably be anathema to both parties: for the anti-Marxists confirming the ineradicable Hegelian roots of Marxism itself, for the Marxists on the other hand signifying an idealism inconsistent in any number of ways with materialism, politics, Marxist aesthetics, or whatever.

Nor are these battle lines clarified by a second set of objections that seems obscurely related to the first, but across all their borderlines in a seemingly random manner: this view taxes Adorno with a 'modernism' whose sense, after the postmodern, now largely transcends any merely aesthetic commitment to modern art and has come to characterize a whole range of old-fashioned philosophical habits and procedures (by contrast with the way in which 'postmodern' philosophy, sociology, political science, history, aesthetic theory, is done today). It does not seem to me terribly promising to try to combine in advance the thematics of these two kinds of critique, the one turning on Marxism, the other turning on modernism: an effort that would probably take the form of wondering whether Marxism is a modernism, not necessarily a rewarding experiment. I will, however, try to introduce a certain symmetry into them by arguing, if not for a 'postmodern' Adorno, then at least for one consistent with and appropriate for the current postmodern age.

As far as the first set of objections is concerned I would, of course
be only too willing to agree with the denunciation of Adorno as a Marxist,
since that has been one of the arguments of this book; but even here,
the fact that the indictment arises from two such distinct philosophical
and ideological positions as those of Jean-François Lyotard[1] and of Jürgen
Habermas[2] must give us pause. Let me therefore first (in answer to the
'not-Marxist-enough' position) summarize my own findings, and the reasons for which I feel able to reassert the essential Marxism of this thinker.

The basic exhibits here are clearly enough the fundamental Marxian
law of value and also the omnipresent conceptual instrument called 'totality'. Both of these have already been addressed; I will therefore here
restate them with some concision. The law of value – or at least some
general Marxian sense of the dynamic of capitalism and of the tendential
laws of its development and history – is always presupposed by Adorno's
interpretations; I have also tried to show that the historical paradigm
of *Dialectic of Enlightenment*, in which the law of value seems to be
'only one principle among many principles of social integration by means
of instrumental reason',[3] is in fact an alternate rewriting of social history
in terms of natural history which leaves the Marxian paradigm intact.

I have observed in passing, indeed, that Adorno's philosophical presuppositions are not merely Marxist, they sometimes reflect a rather old-
fashioned Marxism: this is so particularly in the areas of culture and
of ideology. The title of the 'Culture Industry' chapter itself should have
alerted us to the discovery that Adorno has no conception of culture
as such, in the way in which more recent theorists like the late Raymond
Williams have developed the idea; in the notorious chapter in question,
Adorno's concern is with the entertainment business and not with a
theory of the cultural sphere he would never have accepted in the first
place. (Art or the aesthetic constitutes such a sphere, but its evaluation
is in Adorno irredeemably negative, as we have seen; the position of
the aesthete as such is absolutely refused; individual works of art, however,
negotiate another kind of vulnerable and provisional status on an *ad
hoc* basis.)

By the same token, the peculiar footwork that juxtaposes a slashing
and very often class-conscious ideological analysis of a text with some
evocation of its 'truth-content' strikes me as finding its explanation in
the relatively conventional and old-fashioned conception of ideology as
mere 'false consciousness' which Adorno shared with most of his generation (excepting Lukács, who was older, and Sartre, who reflected other
preoccupations; Adorno seems not to have known much about Gramsci).
This distinction, which of course once again makes a place for philosophy
as such, may no longer be necessary after the Althusserian rewriting

of 'ideology' in terms of subject-positions. But the problem to which it corresponds – how reactionary works can have value and even (Heidegger!) how reactionary ideas can have their 'truth-content' – is still very much with us. We lose it if we abandon the concept of ideology as such (to do so is, however, a fundamental proposition of the postmodern).

Meanwhile, it is also clear that if you reproach Marxism with its temporal dimension, which allows it to consign solutions to philosophical problems to a future order of things (Laclau–Mouffe[4]), then Adorno is, if anything, more Marxist than conventional Marxists, since his entire philosophy turns on just such a vision of postponement and lag, deferral and future reconciliation. But it may be admitted that this future-oriented philosophy – which prophesies catastrophe and proclaims salvation – is scarcely consistent with that perpetual present which is daily life under postmodernism and late capitalism.

I have reserved the matter of 'totality' for the final topic in this set of objections. When it is finally understood that this term signifies something like society or economic system, it slowly becomes clear that the only way to evade its use is resolutely to stigmatize the very concept of 'society', as Laclau and Mouffe have done, and to try to limit one's remarks and analyses to something more modest called 'the social' (they do not always succeed in doing this). I have already referred, on the matter of whether this is a transindividual or indeed transcendent concept in Adorno, to his short Encyclopaedia entry on 'Society', in which the quintessence of his sociological thought is made succinctly available.[5]

On totality, however, the reader is also directed to his extraordinary 'Introduction' to the so-called 'Positivist Dispute in German Sociology', where the bull's horns are seized a little more directly than in Negative Dialectics:

> It is almost tautological to say that one cannot point to the concept of totality in the same manner as one can point to the facts, from which totality distances itself as a concept.[6]

The misconception seems to be based on the idea that if you talk about something repeatedly, you must like it; to point something out insistently turns into the advocacy of the thing, very much on the principle of messengers who bring bad news (and suffer the consequences). But totality is not celebrated in Adorno, even though the critical use of its concept is: the much-quoted dictum that, as against Hegel, 'the whole is the untrue' does not imply that we ought to stop talking about it – quite the contrary:

Totality is not an affirmative but rather a critical category. Dialectical critique seeks to salvage or help to establish what does not obey totality, what opposes it or what first forms itself as the potential of a not yet existent individuation. The interpretation of facts is directed towards totality, without the interpretation itself being a fact. There is nothing socially factual which would not have its place in that totality. It is pre-established for all individual subjects since they obey its 'contrainte' even in themselves and even in their monadological constitution and here, in particular, conceptualize totality. To this extent, totality is what is most real. Since it is the sum of individuals' social relations which screen themselves off from individuals, it is also illusion – ideology. A liberated mankind would by no means be a totality. Their being-in-themselves is just as much their subjugation as it deceives them about itself as the true societal substratum. This certainly does not fulfill the desideratum of a logical analysis of the concept of totality, as the analysis of something free from contradiction, which Albert uses against Habermas, for the analysis terminates in the objective contradiction of totality.[7]

Ultimately, indeed, as I hope to have shown in the course of the preceding work, the critical instrument of contradiction is inseparable from a conception of totality; my impression is also, however, that these conceptual instruments survive today only in Marxism as such, so that on the whole, in my opinion, the refutation of Adorno's non-Marxism is sustained. I will have more to say about the imputation of Hegelianism below.

Two

The accusation of Marxism, however, is more complicated; it seems to me to include several distinct kinds of anxieties that can, I think, best be disentangled by examining the position on Adorno held by progressive (or Habermasian) currents in the Federal Republic today, here expertly summarized by Herbert Schnädelbach:

> What henceforth makes immediate commerce with Adorno's texts impossible for us today are in my opinion three developments in the history of theory. First of all, there has been a fundamental scene change on the philosophical stage in the last twenty years, and other fronts have come into being, quite different from those on which Critical Theory once sought to make its stand. Our problem is no longer logical positivism along with various kinds of idealistic system-building; but rather the undifferentiated celebration of the multiple, along with irrationalism [various kinds of French poststructuralism are evidently meant here], which however also still yokes its chariot to the [Frankfurt-School-type] 'critique of instrumental reason'.
>
> Then too, we must respect the new kinds of precise discrimination that the reception of analytic philosophy in [West] Germany has taught us, sometimes against our own will; this philosophy has not solved many problems, perhaps, but it has certainly allowed us to formulate them better.
>
> Thirdly, the problems of mentalism as a form of language impelled the reflections of Wittgenstein, Ryle and many others; and have also forced German academic 'consciousness philosophy' to rethink its traditional paradigms.[8]

As if all that were not enough, Schnädelbach later on adds that, in any case, 'negative dialectics as the well-known "ontology of the false condition" [*Ontologie des falschen Zustandes*, ND 22/11] is a concept that cannot be recuperated'.

There is, to be sure, no little irony in this West German expression
of satisfaction at having adopted the more advanced Anglo-American
philosophical fashions and at having liquidated, as a token of one's own
achievement of a higher stage, the final traces of the national heritage
in philosophy. It leads one to conjecture that Schnädelbach's first point
was not altogether accurate after all, and that some of the old enemies
– most notably positivism, in its broader sense – are still very much
alive! So that this particular 'analysis' strikes one as being little more
than the declaration that you have changed sides. The irony is of course
compounded by the general exhaustion of analytic philosophy in the
Anglo-American realm itself in recent years, and the search for a renewal
by way of the very continental philosophies here renounced (in the true
spirit of the dialectic of enlightenment) as archaic and old-fashioned.

A second paradox of Schnädelbach's interesting assessment lies in the
wilful separation between his first and third points, as though he were
somehow not aware that it was primarily by way of the very poststructuralism initially indicted for irrationality and obscurantism that
the critique of philosophies of the subject and of consciousness (centering
on, but certainly not limited to, phenomenology) was primarily staged.
What is under the first heading denounced as a renunciation of Reason
turns out, under the third heading, to be celebrated as a welcome critique
of philosophies of consciousness.

Leaving the polemic thrust of the passage aside, however, and without
wishing to undertake the reevaluation of poststructuralism which would
evidently be required (and would demand at least a full-length book in
its own right),[9] a few observations about the relationship of Adorno to
these trends may be offered. With respect to the relationship between
thinking and language, it is certain that Adorno is a traditional, that is
to say a prestructuralist, philosopher – or, if you prefer a different kind
of terminology, that he remains a philosopher rather than undergoing
the sea-change into that new and postmodern thing, a *theorist*. Poststructuralism's triumph and its linguistic obscurity, along with its idiosyncratic
forms of cultural politics, derived fundamentally from the conviction that
there could be no thinking separate from language, and that everything
identified or designated as 'thought' was rather already in some more
profound way a proto-linguistic event. What this 'discovery' does is to
dispel the illusion that the philosophical 'system' could be anything more
than a book or a *Darstellung* (and not a form of Truth, however you
used that word); it also makes for great discomfort with the category
of consciousness, most particularly with the notion of self-consciousness
as such, but also, in a secondary way, with the older notions of sensation
and perception (and thereby with the body in any immediate fashion).

Whatever Adorno says about philosophy's modern relationship to language itself, to rhetoric and to problems of material and linguistic *Darstellung* (these are primarily to be found at the end of the 'Introduction'
to *Negative Dialectics*), it can be asserted with some confidence that he
never 'goes as far' as the poststructuralists, and that some notion of thinking is preserved beyond a material embodiment in language which would
probably have seemed positivistic to him in the way in which it also,
effectively enough, squeezes out the last vestiges of transcendence, consciousness, and truth. However tortured the Archimedean problems of
the negative dialectic as such, they are only analogous to and not at
all identical with the even more elaborate Archimedean dilemmas of
deconstruction; both need something outside the system in order to criticize it, but in Adorno's case this something would remain an idea, while
in Derrida's it ought ideally to be a linguistic possibility: the similarity
comes from the fact that in neither case can this urgent need be met,
except by an elaborate formal subterfuge.

On the other hand, what needs to be added here is that the 'concept'
functions in Adorno as a constricting and reifying system almost as iron-
clad as language itself for poststructuralism. The concept – with its inner
properties of system and identity – is something we can scarcely think
our way out of or around; it stands between us and some utopian reinvention of thought just as impenetrably as does the 'language of Western
metaphysics' for the French critiques of philosophy – both then sharing
the premiss that a new kind of thinking (or a new kind of language)
will not be possible until the social system, to which the older one was
integral, has been transformed beyond recognition.

As for Reason,[10] I cannot feel that it offers the most vital standard
today under which to do battle, even though Habermas's notion of communication has rehabilitated it in ingenious ways. But those ways still
involve a leap and a metaphorical reidentification of the findings of contemporary language philosophy with philosophical ideals of the bourgeois
past that smack uncomfortably of the history manuals or the revolutionary museums. The staging of such an identification is a political and
cultural decision, and I have not seen any public discussion of the strategic
decision in question. One would be willing to accept Habermas's judgement on the utopian content of those great bourgeois revolutionary ideals,
but only provided that the reason he used to give is still attached –
namely, that their ongoing vitality results from their never having been
realized in the first place (an idea distantly reminiscent of Adorno himself).
Still, at a time when those ideals of parliamentary democracy and market
freedom are everywhere being celebrated as more advanced values than
the conceptions of economic equality that were in fact their historical

sequel – in such a period, which we now call postmodern, the revival
of the Enlightenment conception of Reason seems open to ambiguity,
nor is it clear that it can be recuperated from the enemy so easily.

The principal tactical weakness of the defense of reason lies, however,
in the very success of the critique of instrumental reason itself, which
in a time of universal cynicism can no longer be rolled back. But we
must also mention the remarkable achievements of some of the currents
of thought associated with poststructuralism which, following Freud,
set out to show in a variety of ways that what we used to call the 'irrational'
was by no means so unreasonable as all that, and amounted to a practice
of intentionality by other means. These demonstrations then went a
long way towards fulfilling Freud's own profoundly Enlightenment program: 'wo Es war, soll Ich werden' – 'the id shall be transformed into
consciousness'; what used to be unconscious shall be reclaimed from
the sea. So everything from the emotions to fascism, and from advertising
to religion and mysticism, looks far more transparent to us than it did
to the earliest respectable burghers (who needed a stronger concept of
the irrational to domesticate their own unconscious drives); and this
increasing sense of the deeper intentionality of everything we used to
think of as irrational – this widening of the terrain of a more supple
conception of meaning, if not reason – also accounts, incidentally, for
the transformations in the classical Marxian notion of ideology as false
consciousness which were mentioned above. From that perspective also,
Reason does not seem a great deal more contemporary than the older
Marxian notion of 'science' (which used to accompany 'ideology' as its
good sibling).

It is with any newer concept of reason as with Saussure's communicational loop: it makes a difference whether we are talking about the sender
or the receiver. In this case, reason does not mean the sender's point
of view, that is to say, always doing what is reasonable or rational; it
means the receiver's point of view – always *understanding* what the actor's
reasons were, why the thing was done in the first place (or why this
or that position or value is defended). But after Freud (indeed, after Marx),
after Nietzsche, after Foucault on madness, after a whole enormous enlargement in our *sympathy* with what people do (this word, however,
meant in Rousseau's sense as *Verstehen*, and not in any way approval
or endorsement) – our very notion of reason may be expected to have
expanded well beyond its former boundaries and to include much that
for strait-laced respectable burghers used to count as 'irrational'. (As for
exposing the 'reasons' in language, for the purpose of Kantian universality
tests, I fear that in the era of 'cynical reason' even the most 'irrational'
will be willing to tell you in great detail why they feel like doing what

they propose to do.)

Indeed, it seems possible to accommodate these newer modes of interpretation by way of the conceptuality of a somewhat different tradition
than the one in which the only opposite number to Reason is the Irrational
itself in all its demonic forms. Indeed, this other tradition was also that
of the Frankfurt School, which is surely why Habermas's reproach –
the apparently devastating demonstration that the critique incorporated
in *Dialectic of Enlightenment* provides no place of truth from which it
can be launched or sustained in the first place – falls oddly flat. For
in Hegel's restoration of the dialectic as a superior mode of truth (rather
than as the sophistical instrument of superstition for which Kant reserved
the term) the Kantian faculties become reordered; *Vernunft*, or dialectical
reason, now emerging above and subsuming the understanding or *Verstand*, the term for which the expression analytical reason (or, as the
Frankfurt School rebaptized it, instrumental reason) should be reserved.
Dialectical reason, which corresponds to a social organization that does
not yet exist, has not yet come into being in any hegemonic form. The
poststructuralists, individually as well as collectively, have themselves
been as hostile to the ideal of the dialectic as Habermas himself. On
the other hand, their various hermeneutics of the cultural and the 'irrational' must surely be thought of as contributions to some future enlargement of the power of dialectical thinking.

The problem with the concept of Reason is therefore not reason itself
but its opposite number, the private term of the irrational, or irrationalism, which is now enlarged to become the dumping ground for anything
one wishes to exclude. This leads us to the second objection to Adorno
current in the Federal Republic today, and at least implicit in Schnädelbach's remarks, but certainly explicit in Habermas himself – namely,
the conclusion that the critique of instrumental reason is dangerous,
since among other things it makes any concept of Reason – that is, of
philosophy itself – impossible. Adorno's 'philosophy' comes thus finally
be seen as a matter of aesthetics.[11] But it does not take a philosophically
very alert eye – indeed, any non-philosophical humanist will have
instantly grasped the further implication – to understand that in that
case 'what is living' is really the same as 'what is dead' in Adorno's
philosophy. For it is clear that the aesthetic – the third realm in Habermas's conception of modernity: he follows Kant fairly closely on this
point – is a kind of sandbox to which one consigns all those vague things
we have enumerated above under the heading of the irrational: but this
is the proper place for them, because here they can be monitored and,
in case of need, controlled (the aesthetic is in any case conceived as a
kind of safety-valve for irrational impulses). But if the reproach is not

a trivial one – something that would be the case if one argued for the aestheticality of Adorno's thought simply by denying validity to everything else he ever touched on – then it draws its force from a separation between abstract thinking and 'mere' aesthetic representation which must be argued as such (and is, for example, superseded in poststructuralism). The evocation of Schelling in this regard is suggestive, but hardly conclusive; indeed, it might slowly come to prove the opposite when one reviews Adorno's hostility to the Romantics and his commitment to Hegel as well as to Kant.

Habermas has opened a more interesting line of argument with his suggestion[12] that *mimesis* is the source of this tendential aestheticalization of Adorno's philosophy, in so far as it is both an indispensable and an indefinable concept. Mimesis is 'the placeholder for this primordial reason that was diverted from the intention of truth', but in order for the concept to occupy this now central position, 'Horkheimer and Adorno would have to put forward a *theory* of mimesis, which, according to their own ideas, is impossible'. But as we have tried to show above, they see mimesis as an impulse at work in thought and philosophy fully as much as in art, which is to say that it entertains no particularly privileged relationship to art itself.

To put all this the other way round (since in my opinion the misunderstanding develops fully as much in that direction): the presence, within Adorno's aesthetics, of a conception of the truth-content of the work of art is surely not at all the same thing as the assertion that the work of art affords the only means to truth and thereby replaces philosophy or, as Bubner outrageously puts it, 'reverses the relationship in which art and philosophy stand with respect to each other in Hegel'[13] – a characterization that might better apply to Lukács, for whom 'philosophy' as such has already been realized, but not to Adorno, for whom it notoriously 'lived on'. (Bubner goes on to deplore the philosophical demands with which Adorno overloaded denatured art proper, but this is another matter altogether and has more to do with his modernism than with the alleged 'aesthetic' character of his philosophy). A non-philosopher and 'culture-worker' may be forgiven the suspicion that these worries reflect the perplexities of social scientists and philosophers who have never taken culture or daily life seriously (let alone aesthetics) when confronted with a philosopher in whose texts the rate of aesthetic reference seems abnormally and incomprehensibly high.

But in fact Adorno, unlike Kant and unlike Lukács, has very little to say about the 'specificity' of aesthetic experience, which he takes for granted but is not concerned to ground or defend. The problems raised by Adorno's aesthetics – the problems his aesthetics wishes to raise

raise, those most urgent and interesting for it – are on the contrary always historical ones: the nature of the modern, the crisis of nominalism, the destiny of form. If everything in Adorno leads into the aesthetic, everything in Adorno's aesthetics leads out again in the direction of history. I have argued that his contribution to philosophy lay in the demonstration that all abstract philosophical questions are fundamentally historical ones, questions that 'participate' (in the sense of Platonic *methexis*) in the social and the economic. It is very precisely this same lesson that we confront repeatedly in all his aesthetic writings as well; these, as we have seen, are a veritable organon of the rewriting or transcoding of formal questions into substantive socioeconomic ones. In that case, it may by no means be so reassuring in the long run to have successfully demonstrated that Adorno's philosophy is 'merely' aesthetic.

The third objection current even in progressive thought in the Federal Republic today is in many ways the most interesting, but it is precisely because it points ahead to new kinds of explorations that it cannot be fully dealt with here. This is what stirs behind the seemingly perfunctory repudiation of the famous slogan *'Ontologie des falschen Zustandes'* [ND 22/11] and in some larger sense it stakes out Adorno's claim to 'have' a philosophy in any more basic (non-aesthetic) fashion. What is implicit in the slogan is in fact what later became known by the term Capital-logic – that is to say, the attempt of younger philosophers, very much inspired by Adorno himself, to develop a critique of traditional logic by way of the derivation of logical categories from commerce and from capital. One powerful 'chapter' of Capital-logic is already developed (and reviewed above) in the identification posited by Adorno between the 'identity' of the concept and the structure of exchange; but any fully fledged development of this new philosophical approach would involve a great deal more than that, and would clearly have to stipulate the two distinct stages in Marx already referred to: the logic of the commodity, first of all, and the rather different and far more complex and dialectical logic of capital or of value that develops on top of it.

Indeed, if the derivation from the moment of exchange is generally called 'identity', and summons in its train the group of themes and analyses we have already developed, that based on the more complex emergence of capital as such must be distinguished from it. Exchange (of a local variety) is presumably age-old, and notions of identity and logical comparison have been with us since the first hominids. Capital, however, is a later original historical construction on that, which brings with it its own original logical derivations, most of which center around the paradoxical movement of capital as a single general force which is also at one and the same time a multiplicity of individual forces. This movement, which constitutes the very architecture of the three volumes of Marx's *Capital*, has been identified and elaborated on by Rosdolsky in his commentary to the *Grundrisse*.[14] It may, then, be expected to generate logical forms rather distinct from those of simple identity; and in fact we will identify them in terms of Adorno's other great thematic motif, the tension between the universal and the particular. For this complex of themes there is, however, not quite the ready slogan that lay to hand for 'identity' (along with the ubiquitous 'non-identity'); but it will be convenient to see its operations clustering around the more historical crisis term, 'nominalism'. The working out of a more systematic capital-logic must then carefully disentangle these two motifs of identity and nominalism, which are themselves derivations of exchange and capital, respectively.

But Habermas's relatively perfunctory dismissal of this line of inquiry in fact conflates these two distinct moments:

> Marx analyzes the double form of the commodity as a use value and an exchange value, as well as the transformation of its natural form into the value form; for this purpose he draws upon Hegel's concept of abstraction and treats the relation between use value and exchange value like that between essence and appearance. Today this presents us with difficulties; we cannot employ unreconstructed basic concepts from Hegel's logic just like that. The extended discussion on the relation of Marx's *Capital* to Hegel's *Logic* has illuminated these difficulties rather than resolved them. I shall therefore not go any deeper into the analysis of the commodity form. Lukács doesn't either. He is interested only in the reification effects that come about to the degree that the labor power of producers becomes a commodity ...[15]

This statement is an important parting of the ways, this time from so-called reification theory, and it is if anything more significant than Haber-mas's critique of production in Marx (which, since Marx is not nearly so productionist as he argues, left Marx and Marxism relatively intact). The observations on Lukács himself are pertinent but irrelevant, since Capital-logic springs rather from Adorno, and necessarily goes well beyond the problem of the logical category that corresponds to the simple commodity form (Adorno's own impatience with simple 'reification theory' testifies to his sense of the complexity of the logical problems involved).

In the postmodern period it is generally not effective to seek to argue on the basis of acquired momentum; for example, to assert that this or that having been effectively disproven once and for all, we can now go on to something else. Kant was wiser; he understood that his own 'disproof' of the ontological proof of God (definitive if anything ever

was) would have 'no practical consequences' whatsoever. But where –
in various post-Marxisms, for example – it is asserted by a Habermas,
or a Derrida, or even a more banal Hindess and Hirst, that this or that
mode of looking at things is now definitively outmoded, we may confi-
dently expect the putatively extinct specimens to reappear in the lists
in the near future. (And much the same can be said of the way in which
analytic philosophy has been supposed to liberate us from various 'pseudo-
problems' or 'metaphysical survivals'.) The point is, however, that since
the postmodern eschews tradition and a canon, nothing of this kind
can in it *ever* be taken for granted; no one will admit that anything
has been proven or disproven once and for all; and as the movement
of theory has to be recreated at every moment, it cannot in this traditional
way 'acquire momentum'.

At any rate, I also happen to think that Habermas's prognosis of the
Zeitgeist (or the 'spiritual situation of our time') is simply incorrect: any
number of straws in the wind point to an impending Hegel revival,
of a new kind, likely to draw a revival of Capital-logic along with it,
and not only in those fields (essentially political theory of the so-called
state-derivation type[16]) where it still flourishes. But the Hegel who emerges
from this rereading will be an unfamiliar materialist-mathematical Hegel,
one who comes *after* the *Grundrisse*; quite unlike the idealist-conservative
Hegel who *preceded* the writing of Marx's first great work, the unpublished commentary on the *Philosophy of Right*. Meanwhile, an exploration
of the influence of the abstract or logical forms of capital in the whole
newly developing field of the study of everyday life and of 'culture'
(in a wider sense than Adorno was willing to use the term) may be
expected to correct some of the implications of the notorious, but seminal,
'Culture Industry' chapter.

Three

Another constellation of objections can now be formulated, as has already been suggested, in terms of some putative essential 'modernism' in Adorno's thinking – a theme which will lead us on to a few final reflections on his relevance for our own, 'postmodern' period. But this is now a somewhat different issue from Adorno's relationship to aesthetic modernism as such and turns on his own modernity as a writer – that is to say, essentially as a philosopher; one can indeed, without much difficulty, imagine 'modern' philosophical projects utterly unsullied by any cultural or aesthetic sympathies whatsoever.

It does not seem particularly effective to begin such an exploration with a check list, although we have already seen a number of traits in Adorno's work that would be candidates for such a list of the most characteristic signs and symptoms of the 'modern' – I have already mentioned the breath of auto-referentiality that hovers over his work, particularly when it assigns itself a unique function to preserve values and a language elsewhere in the process of dissolution and disappearance. The question of the standpoint then powerfully emerges – not yet the more desperate Archimedean point of the 1960s speculation (students or underclasses as the 'subject of history'?): and it is most often forthrightly answered in terms of class privilege, as in the opening paragraph of *Minima Moralia*, thrown down like a gauntlet, or the scarcely more evasive discussion in *Negative Dialectics* (51/41): 'Only those not completely molded [by the administered world] can resist it.' This goes further in the dialectic of intellectuals of a certain independent means than Horkheimer was ever willing to, but clearly makes for problems in the 1960s when the species has virtually become extinct. It is not clear that the charismatic artists of the modern period – who enthusiastically outfitted themselves with the trappings of seers and prophets – had any more clear-sighted grasp of the nature of the limbs they themselves sat on; but a comparable auto-referentiality is to be found in them whenever the question of the poet (which replaces this one of the philosopher) rears its head.

The immediate historicity of the theme in Adorno's hands then suggests an obvious next step, and everyone's principal candidate for the fundamental modernist characteristic *par excellence* – namely, time and temporality, and a certain kind of philosophical history, or perhaps we should rather more closely specify this motif as an attention to temporality as a mode of grasping history, the use of existential time protensions and retensions as an instrument for grasping the dynamics of an external collective history otherwise available only in the 'facts' and the *faits divers*. Neither perspective by itself would then be 'modern' – the historicist passion as such, or the 'inner sense' dear to diarists and autobiographers; on the other hand, the enormous technical – one wants to say, technological – expansion in subjectivity in the modern, which includes a remarkable new and enlarged laboratory for temporal registrations and inscriptions, does seem to develop hand in hand with a distracted alertness to those distant sounds from the street that betoken unimaginable historical convulsions in the making, and the ends and beginnings of whole worlds.

If this second, historical and social dimension of the modern has been lost on North Americans, whose modernist pantheon is mainly collected under the rubrics of 'time' and 'the self', this is – as Adorno is there to instruct us – because subjects of the American constitution prefer to think of crisis and catastrophe, revolution, *Weltuntergang* – even the passing of the old aristocracy and any number of 'ends of eras' as such – as profoundly European in some bad and reprehensible sense ('history' would then be what the Europeans have to be ashamed of, as opposed to the forthright monetary indecency Adorno attributes to North Americans in 'Olet' [MM 259–61/195–6]).

What qualifies for this specifically modern function of temporality in Adorno we have already begun to identify: most notably in the coordination between a personal and idiosyncratic sense of missed occasions and unseasonable survivals and a now more than merely non-synchronous historical paradigm, in which the 'stages' of social and productive development pile up, fall out, keep us waiting, or turn out to have happened already and already been forgotten.

But in my opinion no isolated theme of this kind, even one so fundamental as temporality itself, is sufficient to account for the modernist cast of a certain kind of thought (or formal expression); the reason has already

been given in advance in Benjamin's and Adorno's (profoundly modernist) fascination with the 'constellation' as such – a mobile and shifting
set of elements in which it is sheer relationship rather than substantive
content that marks their structure as a whole. This means that in a constellation there can be no 'fundamental' features, no centers, no 'ultimately
determining instances' or bottom lines, except for the relationship of
all these contents to each other. The notion is virtually Althusserian
avant la lettre; it also still retains something like a nostalgia for centered-
ness and for unified (if not necessarily organic) form, as Derrida has
shown in an influential essay on Lévi-Strauss's not unrelated concept
of structure.[17] In this essay, which has sometimes been taken as the opening
move in what we now call poststructuralism, it seems appropriate to
suggest that Derrida's unmasking of the secret *modernism* of Lévi-Strauss
constitutes a first step in the inauguration of a *post*modernism based on
play and randomness (in short, on the 'aesthetic' itself, when you stop
to think about it).

The representation of individual items is at best a matter of aesthetic
appreciation or belletristic interest; nor does representation really emerge
as an issue and a dilemma in its own right when the possibility of some
realistic access to the social totality is taken for granted and given in
advance. It is only with the second or monopoly stage of capitalism,
and the emergence of a classical imperialist system beyond the confines
of the various national experiences, that a radical aesthetic and epistemological doubt about the possibility of grasping society as a whole begins
to be felt: and it is precisely this radical doubt that inaugurates modernism
as such and constitutes the representational drama specific to it. On the
other hand, when, in the postmodern and the multinational era, 'totality'
no longer seems to be a relevant issue, becoming either something you

are resigned to missing or do not wish to achieve for moral and political reasons, then the most urgent representational problems (of a philosophical as well as of a formal nature) fall away.

The central tension in Adorno's work was, however, precisely that of a relationship between universal and particular which is at one with the objective tension between the social totality and its subjects. This specifically modernist tension is then inscribed in the individual sentences just as it determines the *ad hoc* architectonic solutions of the negative dialectic itself as a mode of philosophical *Darstellung*; it must also, as I have argued, be recaptured in the apologetics of the 'essay' as form, whose values are more easily mistaken for the now more familiar postmodern ones. Finally, Adorno's rehearsal of the modernist problematic of representation is belated enough to include a matter of crucial interest for us today, which we must ourselves generally bring from the outside of our own present to the modern classics, and this is a reflection on and a thematization of the passing of the modern itself, the reasons for its obliteration, and some dawning apprehension of an intellectual landscape in which the negative, or 'critical theory', will have definitively become a thing of the past.

Four

It is now time to assess the value of Adorno for us in full postmodernism as this last develops in uneven transnational zones, within which the national inequalities are also preserved. (Perhaps this should be qualified: for us, as intellectuals in the advanced capitalist countries; perhaps even only for 'us', as North American intellectuals.)

We must begin by acknowledging the possibility of a case for Adorno's postmodernism as well, or at least for a certain postmodern Adorno. But this case would have to be based on other musical writings than the canonical ones, the bleak retrospective monuments to the high moderns, such as the dolmens *Philosophy of Modern Music* erects to Schoenberg and Stravinsky. But less familiar texts – above all the essay 'Vers une musique informelle'[18] – abundantly document his sympathy with and support for the new postwar musical production organized around the Cologne radio station and the experimental music concerts in Kranichstein and Darmstadt associated with now famous names like Boulez and Stockhausen. Such sympathy, along with the books on Mahler and Berg, make it clear that we were wrong to confuse Adorno's historical assessment of the central significance of Schoenberg with any particular personal taste or inclination for the Viennese composer and theoretician, whose dead end he repeatedly characterized as such.

Meanwhile, we were also wrong to take the rhetoric of the analysis literally, and to assume that a powerful articulation of what looked like terminal contradictions in the musical system – but similar judgements were issued on the other arts, whose analogous contradictions betokened a blockage in the very nature of historical time – in any way implied that you should stop composing; nor did he do so himself. The concept of a *'musique informelle'* is thus already exceedingly postmodern, in the way it includes a revolt against the irreversible necessities of modernist aesthetic time, change, and progress, along with its more predictable reaction against systems of Schoenberg's type in the form of the occasional or the aleatory; rules made up to be used only once, along with the effort to drop out of (musical) history. (There is even a kind word for John Cage, and the whole thing makes one think a little of Italian *pensiero debole* translated into the musical realm.) This relaxation of the logic of history is of course very different from the new aesthetics Benjamin tried to invent and to project, in a similarly contradictory situation.

But it is very consistent with one particular strand in Adorno's thinking, which he sometimes staged as the very program of his own work: namely the stress, particularly in the essay on 'The Essay as Form',[19] on the repudiation of system and the commitment to the fragmentary and the occasional, to a freedom in the instant that eschewed the traditional Germanic longing for the *Hauptwerk* and the architectonic truth. This particular rhetoric, which has reminded some of Jena Romanticism,[20] does not strike me as particularly convincing in Adorno – or in Lukács, who started it,[21] and who may also, like Adorno, be seen to be arguing inconclusively against his own powerful *esprit de système*, rather than (like Nietzsche) expressing some blithe and irresponsible temperamental freedom from the temptation altogether.

It is true that Adorno wrote a great many short pieces, dabbled in the 'fragment' (above all in *Minima Moralia*), and produced aphorisms of a particularly deadly and unerring variety. But the crux of the matter lies in his conception of philosophizing itself, after the end of the great systems: do the 'models' of *Negative Dialectics* imply a practice of *philosophie informelle* of the type proposed by Richard Rorty and sometimes also described as 'postmodern'? This would imply philosophizing of a an occasional kind, an *ad hoc* problem-solving and a kind of 'open thinking', as he put it himself, 'unprotected against the risk of decline into randomness; nothing assures it of any ultimate saturation with the topic at hand that would rule out such a risk' (ND 45/35). The rhetoric of the open and the closed, which ought by now instantly to awaken the gravest suspicions and set the alarm bells ringing, is ominous enough; I have not, however, read the models of *Negative Dialectics* in this random or aleatory fashion, and it should be clear that I do not find characterizations of Adorno as postmodern any more convincing than those that see him as a 'late Romantic'. That he included a place for the possible emergence of postmodernism is, however, beyond any doubt.

But the relevance of Adorno for postmodernism, in its strong sense as a cultural dominant, is to be sought elsewhere, in the philosophical

and sociological polemics. In fact, what Adorno called positivism is very
precisely what we now call postmodernism, only at a more primitive
stage. The shift in terminology is to be sure momentous: a stuffy petty-
bourgeois republican nineteenth-century philosophy of science emerging
from the cocoon of its time capsule as the iridescent sheen of consumerist
daily life in the Indian summer of the superstate and multinational capitalism. From truth to state-of-the-art merchandise, from bourgeois respecta-
bility and 'distinction' to the superhighways and the beaches, from the
old-fashioned authoritarian families and bearded professors to permissive-
ness and loss of respect for authority (which, however, still governs).
The question about poetry after Auschwitz has been replaced with that
of whether you could bear to read Adorno and Horkheimer next to
the pool.

This, then, is indeed some first service they might do for us: to restore
the sense of something grim and impending within the polluted sunshine
of the shopping mall – some older classical European-style sense of doom
and crisis, which even the Common Market countries have cast off in
their own chrysalid transmogrification, but which the USA can now
use better than they can, being an older and a now ramshackle society
by contrast (a little like finally being older than your own father, as
Sartre once put it). It is, however, a representational problem – pictures
of decaying rails and abandoned factories we already had in the thirties;
critiques of consumer society and its images (bright teeth and smiles)
we had in the fifties. These are now old stuff, even in their unexpected
structural combination with each other; the real problem perhaps being,
as has been said above, the very matter of representation itself, of the
representation of this totality, about which all of postmodernism concurs
that even if it exists it would be unrepresentable and unknowable. The
dialectic – even that frustrating and infuriating thing, the *negative* dialectic
– is perhaps a way of squaring this circle that we haven't yet tried: starting
at least from way back inside the head and its stereotypes without believing for one minute that any of them are personal or subjective. If such
thought could finally manage to climb up, and look out of one of the
sockets (like the character in *Endgame*), it might glimpse something real
for a moment before the ladder collapsed.

Positivism becomes postmodernism when it has, like philosophy on
the older paradigm, fulfilled and thereby abolished itself. Adorno insists
on one side of its mission, thereby giving us one useful description: it
wants to abolish the subjective, as that takes the form of thoughts, interpretations and opinions (perhaps it also wants to abolish the language
that corresponds to those things: poetic, emotive, rhetorical). This is
to say that it is a nominalism, and as such wants to reduce us to the

empirical present (or to use the empirical present as the sole pattern for imagining other situations and other temporal moments). It wishes to abolish value as such, and any thinking that raises the issue of ends (the formulation of the so-called 'critique of instrumental reason'), not excluding the dialectic itself, but very much including all the other visionary ideologies of which it equally also promises the 'end'.

The postmodern is in that sense the fulfillment and abolition of liberalism as well, which, no longer tenable as an ideology and a value any more than traditional conservatism, can function more effectively after its own death as an ideology, realizing itself in its most traditional form as a commitment to the market system that has become sheer common sense and no longer a political program. All the critiques of such positivism are true and useless at the same time, because they can mobilize only antiquated representations and dated ideologies. At that point even talking about the not-being of thinking ceases to be effective, which was what was desired in the first place. What no longer is is as absent as what never was, or what is not yet or is not to be; only being is left, only we don't call it that any more since the word itself is meaningless without its opposite, nothingness, which has been withdrawn from circulation.

Adorno was a doubtful ally when there were still powerful and oppositional political currents from which his temperamental and cantankerous quietism could distract the uncommitted reader. Now that for the moment those currents are themselves quiescent, his bile is a joyous counter-poison and a corrosive solvent to apply to the surface of 'what is'. Even his archaic economics now seems apt and timely; very much in the spirit of his own construction of time, the utterly outmoded doctrine of monopoly capital may be just the image we need, in the absence of our own images, since it incited him to track the system into its most minute recesses and crannies, without paranoia, and with an effectiveness that can still set an example to those demoralized by the decentralization of the current one, which offers rows of identical products (or their modular transformations) instead of the grim and windowless headquarters we thought we were looking for.

In an earlier situation of uneven development, Adorno's dialectic (and so-called Western Marxism generally) could be grasped as a specific and restricted First World Marxism, the property of intellectuals, a specialized intellectual instrument very different from the ones demanded by underdevelopment or socialist construction (but no less valid, in its proper use and situation, than they were). Equally unevenly, an abrupt new expansion of the world system has annulled those inequalities and replaced them by others we as yet understand less well. Liberation movements across a neocolonial Third World have dried up overnight; while the institutions of actually existing socialism have seemed to melt away like the snow on a sunny day. The socialist transformation of human beings and social relations envisaged by Marx, however, had its condition of possibility in a regime of high productivity and advanced technology, which wishful thinking cannot conjure into being. Stalinism is disappearing not because it failed, but because it succeeded, and fulfilled its historical mission to force the rapid industrialization of an underdeveloped country (whence its adaptation as a model for many of the countries of the Third World). As Gorz has observed, in that sense communism is the 'first stage' towards socialism! (It is sufficient to remember how in Poland industrialization under a single global management – the state – was the precondition for the emergence of a national labor movement.) The problem, as yet nowhere resolved, is how to ensure the arrival of a *second* step.

In effect, what follows the abdication by the Party of its ideological responsibilities to reinvent and project a vision of the socialist model is a vacuum in the state which is at once, but only provisionally, filled by the spectacle of intellectuals, or the intelligentsia itself, in power: some future Marx may outdo the analogous pages of *The Eighteenth Brumaire* in satirizing the euphoria with which this caste celebrates and seals the acquisition of its own professional guild-values ('freedom' of speech and 'free' elections) and then aimlessly confronts its production crisis and begins to bicker, reuniting only to hold out a hand for money to the great ally and defender of 'freedom', a United States which, having benevolently neutralized the Soviet Union, goes on to reconquer Panama and to gear up for more such local 'defensive' operations around the world.

Into the void of this interregnum only big business can flow, buying up nationalized industries on the cheap and reaping the benefits of the cheap labor thrown open to the multinationals by the utter collapse of autonomous national states. The rapid deterioration of the former Second World into a Third World status *tout court* is then the *telos* of this current history, and the functional goal towards which it moves; the shedding of the old snake skin of a worn-out stage, and the emergence of a new and more genuinely global capitalism, determine the ruthless unmasking of the structural weakness of socialism in the East (as well as spelling the end and sounding the knell of autonomous development in the Third World), where an idealistic and revolutionary posture seems displaced into the popular opponents of the state for as long as it takes until the latter are fully transformed into consumers or 'immiserated' laborers for foreign capital.

None of which 'disproves' Marxism, which remains on the contrary the only current mode of thought intent on directing our attention to the economic consequences of the new 'Great Transformation', at the risk of throwing cold water on its superstructural illusions. Capital and labor (and their opposition) will not go away under the new dispensation; nor can there possibly exist in the future, any more than in the past, any viable 'third way' between capitalism and socialism, however tainted the rhetoric and conceptuality of this last may have become for people to whom bureaucrats fed it by rote. No future is conceivable, however, from which the deeper ideological commitment to politics – that is to say, left politics – is absent. Obviously, the sources of such commitment are unconscious and overdetermined by family and childhood, as well as by class, experience; and even a fully postmodernized First World society will not lack young people whose temperament and values are genuinely left ones and embrace visions of radical social change repressed by the norms of a business society. The dynamics of such commitment are derived not from the reading of the 'Marxist classics', but rather from the objective experience of social reality and the way in which one isolated cause or issue, one specific form of injustice, cannot be fulfilled or corrected without eventually drawing the entire web of interrelated social levels together into a totality, which then demands the invention of a politics of social transformation. The privilege of the Marxian texts – and the reason why his name, perhaps abusively, remains related to such a politics in contradistinction to other social thinkers – is that Marx made this totalizing experience at the very beginning of his career, as the trajectory of the very first published and unpublished articles demonstrates. Whether the word Marxism disappears or not, therefore, in the erasure of the tapes in some new Dark Ages, the thing itself will inevitably reappear.

As for the current situation, however, Korsch long ago showed us, within the Marxian corpus itself, how the very mood and methodology of the analyses varied across the great internal polarity of voluntarism and fatalism (or determinism) according to the changes in the objective social situation, and its great cyclical rhythms that alternate from situations of promise and change (so-called 'pre-revolutionary' ones) to those of a locked social geology so massive that no visions of modification seem possible (at least to those ephemeral biological subjects that we are). Ours seems for the moment closer to this last than to the former, and the thoughts we find useful must vary accordingly.

This is the spirit in which I have proposed Adorno as a dialectical model for the 1990s. His introspective or reflexive dialectic befits a situation in which – on account of the dimensions and unevenness of the new global world order – the relationship between the individual and the system seems ill-defined, if not fluid, or even dissolved. The over-emphasis in Adorno on what he calls theory – defined as the detection of the absent presence of totality within the aporias of consciousness or of its products – is not a bad lesson for intellectuals today, when the older notion of critical theory as permanent negativity and implacable social critique seems better to characterize the practice of a Sartre than the ideals of postmodern thinkers. The 'current situation' to be sure has any number of urgent demands besides dialectical theory; still, 'not only theory, but also its absence, becomes a material force when it seizes the masses'.

Notes

NOTES ON TRANSLATION

1. Quoted by Walter Benjamin in 'The Task of the Translator', in *Illuminations*, transl. Harry Zohn, New York, 1969, p. 81.
2. In *Telos*, no. 65, Fall 1985, pp. 147-52.

INTRODUCTION

1. As on a book jacket: Born 11 September 1903 in Frankurt-am-Main, died 6 August 1969 in Switzerland. Dissertation in Philosophy (on Husserl), 1924, University of Frankfurt; 1925, studied musical composition in Vienna with Alban Berg; 1927 on, frequent visits in Berlin to Benjamin, Brecht, Bloch, Weill, and others; inaugural lecture as Assistant Professor of Philosophy at Frankfurt, 1931, not yet in close association with Horkheimer's Institute for Social Research; definitive emigration to the United States in 1938, after failure to establish himself at Oxford; participation in the Princeton Radio Research Project; closer collaboration with Horkheimer and a move to Southern California; definitive return to West Germany in 1953 as Professor of Philosophy and Sociology at the University of Frankfurt; succeeds Horkheimer as Director of the Institute in 1964. See, for more bibliographical and historical detail, Rolf Wiggershaus, *Die Frankfurter Schule*, Munich 1987. This book, which draws richly on unpublished material and letters and has obviously had the benefit of Habermas's participation, offers the most substantial historical picture of the Frankfurt School from its beginnings to its most recent mutations. Unlike Martin Jay's pioneering work (*The Dialectical Imagination*, Boston, MA 1973), which told the story (only up to the return to Germany) from Horkheimer's point of view, Wiggershaus presents a decidedly critical perspective on the Institute's central figure.
2. Susan Buck-Morss has in particular insisted on the way in which virtually the whole program of *Negative Dialectics* is already present in the so-called inaugural lecture of 1931, entitled 'The Actuality of Philosophy' and reprinted in *Gesammelte Schriften*, vol. 1, Frankfurt 1983, pp. 325-44; transl. in *Telos*, no. 31, Spring 1977, pp. 120-33. See her *Origins of Negative Dialectics*, New York 1977, pp. 24-5, 63-5.
3. Wiggershaus, pp. 688-9.

4. Wiggershaus, pp. 503-8; the volume also includes detailed accounts of the various 'empirical' projects, before and after (and during) the Emigration.

5. See Axel Honneth, 'Communication and Reconciliation: Habermas's Critique of Adorno', in *Telos*, no. 39, Spring 1979, pp. 45-61; and see of course Habermas himself, especially *Theorie des kommunikativen Handelns*, vol. 1, (Frankfurt 1981, ch. 4, esp. pp. 489-534; and *The Philosophical Discourse of Modernity*, transl. Frederick Lawrence, Cambridge, MA 1987, ch. 5, pp. 106-30.

6. See, for example, the assessment of Kant: 'His timid bourgeois detestation of anarchy matches his proud bourgeois antipathy for tutelage' (ND 248/250). The analysis of Wagner's 'social character' is also rich in such judgements, e.g.: 'It is the fawning stance of the momma's boy who talks himself and others into believing that his kind parents can deny him nothing, for the very purpose of making sure they don't' (W 15/16).

7. See, for example, H. Mörchen, *Macht und Herrschaft im Denken von Heidegger und Adorno*, Stuttgart 1980; or R. Bubner, 'Kann Theorie aesthetisch werden?' in *Materialien zur Aesthetischen Theorie*, ed. Lindner and Ludke, Frankfurt 1979, esp. p. 111.

8. *Gesammelte Schriften*, vol. 6, Frankfurt 1976, pp. 637/8.

9. See his interview with Gérard Raulet entitled 'Structuralism and Poststructuralism', *Telos*, no. 55, Spring 1983, pp. 195-211 (in Wiggershaus, p. 12).

10. See 'Immanence and Nominalism in Postmodern Theory', in *Postmodernism, Or The Cultural Logic of Late Capitalism*, Durham, NC 1990. The most stimulating and judicious comparison of French poststructuralism with the various Germanic traditions is to be found in Peter Dews, *Logics of Disintegration*, London 1987; on Derrida and Adorno, see also Rainer Nägele, 'The Scene of the Other', in *Literature*, vol. 11, nos 1-2, Fall-Winter 1982-3, pp. 59-79. Perry Anderson draws a very interesting parallel between Adorno and Althusser in *Considerations on Western Marxism*, London 1976, pp. 72-3.

PART I

1. Sabine Wilke astutely points out the fundamental structural ambiguity at work in parataxis as such, in 'Kritische und Ideologische Momente der Parataxis: Eine Lekture von Adorno, Heidegger und Hölderlin', *Modern Language Notes* 102 (3), April 1982, pp. 627-47, esp. p. 646. And note Empson's cognate discussion of classical parataxis – 'the Homeric *but* where one expects "and"' – in *Some Versions of Pastoral*, New York 1960, p. 136.

2. *Marxism and Form*, Princeton, NJ 1971, p. 307.

3. Lévi-Strauss, *Structural Anthropology*, vol. 1, New York 1963, pp. 341-78.

4. We have all problably overstressed the 'Freudo-Marxism' of the Frankfurt School, which is finally realized only in Marcuse. The attacks on Freud in *Minima Moralia* are ferocious (see, for example, No. 136), although it is true that he is there seen as a profoundly *American* thinker whose 'therapy' goes along with obligatory good health, clean teeth and a permanent smile on your face. This assessment of Freud should be juxtaposed with the remarkable appreciation in 'Sociology and Psychology', Part II, *New Left Review*, no. 47, 1968 (or *Gesammelte Werke*, vol. 8, Part I, Frankfurt 1972, pp. 42-85).

5. It should be noted that his valorization of the essay as form has very different consequences in the social sciences, where it undermines the belief in the exhaustiveness of empirical detail (their version of a belief in representation) and substitutes for that the provisional model or the local hypothesis. The essay here opens a wedge between full history and abstract sociology, and as it were allows each of these tendencies to correct or defamiliarize the other. But see notes 19 and 20 to Conclusions, below.

6. Le Président de Brosses, *Du Culte des dieux fétiches*, Paris 1760. But see also Part II, note 12.

7. Thus Hegel's 'logic deals only with particularity, which is already conceptual' (ND 322/328).

8. Pollock's work is often discussed – by Martin Jay (*The Dialectical Imagination*, ch. 5), Helmut Dubiel (*Theory and Politics*, transl. B. Gregg, Cambridge, MA 1985) and others; to my knowledge only Giacomo Marramao discusses the relationship to Grossman, in 'Political Economy and Critical Theory', *Telos*, no. 24, Summer 1974. I make a few suggestions of my own below, but in my opinion the definitive study of the Frankfurt School's economic dimension remains to be written. It should be added that what Pollock calls 'late capitalism' has nothing to do with the current or postmodern stage of the world system, for which some of us also use this term.

9. See Gilles Deleuze, *Cinéma I: L'Image-mouvement*, Paris 1983, chs 2 and 3.

10. Quoted in Karl-Heinz Bohrer, *Plötzlichkeit*, Frankfurt 1981, p. 14.

11. Dolf Oehler, 'Charisma des Nicht-identischen', in T.W. Adorno, special issue, ed. H.L. Arnold, text + kritik (1977), p. 155. Indeed, if one likes to put it that way, he scarcely says anything else in his great essay on Beckett either, but I defy any intelligent reader to come away with a similar impression! (NL, 281–321; or 'Trying to Understand *Endgame*', *New German Critique*, no. 26 [Spring-Summer 1982]).

12. A next step which will be called 'Capital-logic' (see Conclusions).

13. 'Gesellschaft', in *Gesammelte Schriften*, vol. 8, Frankfurt 1972 or 'Society', *Salmagundi*, nos 10–11, Fall 1969/Winter 1970, pp. 144–53. This volume of the *Collected Works* contains the most extensive collection of Adorno's sociological interventions (but for an English translation of some of these, see note 23 below). And see also, in English, the useful collaborative volume *Aspects of Sociology*, Boston, MA 1972.

14. 'Society', p. 145.

15. 'Society', p. 146.

16. 'Sociology and Psychology', *New Left Review*, no. 46, November–December 1967, pp. 67–80; no. 47, January–February 1968, pp. 79–97; no. 46, p. 69.

17. Ibid., p. 69.

18. Ibid., p. 70.

19. Ibid., p. 73.

20. Ibid., p. 74.

21. Ibid., pp. 77–8.

22. Ibid., p. 78.

23. *The Positivist Debate in German Sociology*, ed. G. Adey and D. Frisby, New York 1976, p. 84.

24. See the volume referred to in the preceding note for the protocols of its most dramatic confrontation.

25. 'Society', p. 148.

26. 'History does not merely touch on language, but takes place in it' (MM 293/219); yet 'Lyric and Society' also reminds us that it can there 'take place' negatively (see below).

27. T.W. Adorno, *Prismen*, Frankfurt 1955; transl. S. and S. Weber: *Prisms* London 1967, p. 50/49.

28. Manfredo Tafuri, *Architecture and Utopia*, Cambridge, MA., 1979.

29. Pierre Bourdieu renews this position in our own time, with the powerful anti-cultural and anti-intellectual demystifications of books like *Distinction* (London 1985).

30. *Prisms*, p. 82/75.

31. Ibid., 18/26.

32. *Origin of German Tragic Drama*, Walter Benjamin, *Ursprung des deutschen Trauerspiels*,

Gesammelte Schriften, Frankfurt 1980, vol. 1, Part I; transl. J. Osborne, London, 1977): 'Epistemo-Critical Prologue', p. 207/27. All further refs in text as OGT.

33. See below, Conclusions, note 20.

34. See Introduction, note 2 and, on the *Passagenwerk*, Susan Buck-Morss, *Dialectics of Seeing: Walter Benjamin and the Arcades Project*, Cambridge, MA 1990.

35. *In These Great Times: A Karl Kraus Reader*, ed. Harry Zohn, Montreal 1976, p. 70.

36. Benjamin, *Gesammelte Schriften*, vol. 4, p. 142.

37. 'Aura' seems to have been derived from the 'irrationalist' philosopher Ludwig Kages (see Wiggershaus, pp. 224 ff). The source of mimesis is more obscure, particularly since Adorno's use of the concept has very little in common with Benjamin's. See, however, Michael Cahn, 'Subversive Mimesis; T.W. Adorno and the Modern Impasse of Critique', in *Mimesis in Contemporary Theory*, vol. 1, ed. M. Spariosu, Philadelphia 1984. Habermas interprets the centrality of the concept as a compensation for the lack of any positive conception of Reason:

As the placeholder for this primordial reason that was diverted from the intention of truth, Horkheimer and Adorno nominate a capacity, *mimesis*, about which they can only speak as they would about a piece of uncomprehended nature. They characterized the mimetic capacity, in which an instrumentalized nature makes its speechless accusation, as an 'impulse'. The paradox in which the critique of instrumental reason is entangled, and which stubbornly resists even the most supple dialectic, consists then in this: Horkheimer and Adorno would have to put forward a *theory* of mimesis, which, according to their own ideas, is impossible. (*The Theory of Communicative Action*, vol. 1, transl. Thomas McCarthy, Boston, MA 1984, p. 382).

Dialectic of Enlightenment will be discussed below; in my opinion, however, mimesis is rather the substitute for the traditional subject–object relationship.

38. In his *Figuren des Scheins*, Bonn 1984, Rainer Hoffman makes a beginning on the stylistic-syntactic analysis of Adorno. Friedemann Grenz's valuable *Adornos Philosophie in Grundbergriffen*, Frankfurt 1974, posits the practice of two fundamental types of sentences in Adorno (both of them *'geschichtsphilosophisch'* – p. 12): these are 'physiognomic negations' on the one hand, and the more familiar Hegelian 'determinate' negation on the other (pp. 180, 202, 203). Gillian Rose, meanwhile, suggests that in Adorno arguments

taken from traditional philosophy ... are transformed into principles of social criticism by use of the figure of chiasmus: arguments which expose illegitimate abstraction in philosophy reveal principles of abstraction in society; arguments which expose the illegitimate dominance of the subject in philosophy reveal modes of social domination. (*The Melancholy Science*, New York 1978).

This is all the more pertinent, since chiasmus is in general the fundamental deep figure of the Marxian or materialist dialectic (I believe that it occurs seldom in Hegel).

39. See David Bordwell, Janet Staiger and Kristin Thompson, *The Classical Hollywood Cinema*, New York 1985, ch. 31, 'Alternative modes of film practice'.

40. That of F. Pollock; see above, note 8.

41. R. Bubner, 'Adornos Negative Dialektik', in *Adorno-Konferenz 1983*, ed. Friedeburg and Habermas, Frankfurt 1983, p. 36.

42. I. Kant, *Critique of Pure Reason*, transl. J.M.D. Meiklejohn, Chicago 1952, p. 43.

43. J.P. Sartre, *Search for a Method*, transl. H. Barnes, New York 1963, pp. 8 ff.

44. Georg Lukács, *History and Class Consciousness*, transl. R. Livingstone, Cambridge, MA. 1971, esp. 'Reification and the Consciousness of the Proletariat'.

45. See, for example, *The Differentiation of Society*, New York 1982.

46. See, for a near-contemporary period piece, Richard M. Weaver's *Ideas Have Consequences*, Chicago 1948, which uses the diagnosis of nominalism for a classic Cold

War jeremiad on the decadence of the modern age. I am grateful to Richard Rorty and Gayatri Spivak for this reference. In general, superstructural (or 'spiritual') diagnoses of the breakdown of the social order will be right-wing (see also, and above all, Heidegger himself); while infrastructural ones will be left-wing.

47. See above, Introduction, note 2.

48. 'The words that are not means appear senseless; the others seem to be fiction, untrue' (DA 132/147).

49. Significantly, this is the only passage lifted without modification into the later text (see *Gesammelte Schriften*, vol. 1, pp. 354-5).

50. The following reflection, from 'Sociology and Psychology', seems to me enormously revealing:

Fear constitutes a more crucial subjective motive of objective rationality. It is mediated. Today anyone who fails to comply with the economic rules will seldom go under straight away. But the fate of the *déclassé* looms on the horizon. Ahead lies the road to an asocial, criminal existence: the refusal to play the game arouses suspicions and exposes offenders to the vengeance of society even though they may not yet be reduced to going hungry and sleeping under bridges. But the fear of being cast out, the social sanctions behind economic behaviour, have long been internalized along with other taboos, and have left their mark on the individual. In the course of history this fear has become second nature; it is not for nothing that the word 'existence' in usage uncontaminated by philosophy means equally the fact of being alive and the possibility of self-preservation in the economic process. (*New Left Review*, no. 46, 1967, p. 71.)

51. Marshall Sahlins, 'The First Affluent Society', in *Stone Age Economics*, Chicago 1972, ch. 1.

52. 'No differently will the world one day appear, almost unchanged, in its constant feast-day light, when it stands no longer under the law of labor, and when for homecomers duty has the lightness of holiday play' (MM 144/112).

53. See, on Weber, my 'Vanishing Mediator', in *The Ideologies of Theory*, vol. 1, Minnesota 1988.

54. See, on Greek concepts of labor, J.P. Vernant, 'Travail et nature dans la Grèce ancienne', in *Mythe et pensée chez les Grecs*, Paris 1965; also the Cahn reference in note 24 above.

55. This is the way in which a focus on the media reinflects and displaces Pollock's theory of state capitalism, a kind of left version of the James Burnham managerial-society thesis current during this period. The convergence features of the two theories save them from lapsing into the simpler idea of 'totalitarianism' that came to dominate Cold War apologetics shortly thereafter; but the stress here on emergent technology, shared across the advanced countries, and in particular between Roosevelt's USA and Hitler's Germany, anticipates contemporary trends in media theory (see my forthcoming *Signatures of the Visible*).

56. Thus I cannot agree with Martin Jay's notion of a gradual disillusionment of the Frankfurt School with Marxism (but see his valuable *The Dialectical Imagination* and *Marxism and Totality*): one must distinguish between personal opinion (or cowardice) and the deeper principles that inform an intellectual work. As for Helmut Dubiel, he takes the following line (in *Theory and Politics*):

The fact that so many readers of the Circle's writings of the 1940s do not recognize the conscious abandonment of the Marxist theoretical tradition can be explained by the fact that their basic positions are not developed as criticisms of Marx. Their philological distance from his writings, maintained throughout the various development periods of the Circle's theory, of course do not aid the reader in recognizing the break with Marxist theory once it had been made. A critique of Marx from the perspective of *Eclipse of Reason* was developed for the first time by pupils of Horkheimer and Adorno. But the break remained unrecognizable in subsequent years because Horkheimer and, especially, Adorno maintained a Marxian form of argumentation ... (p. 93). When is a break not a break? A clever defense attorney would tear this equivocal analysis to shreds; not least because the 'pupils' mentioned turn out to be Habermas and Wellmer, who may have developed 'a critique' of Marx, but certainly developed an even more devastating one of Horkheimer and Adorno themselves!

57. *Minima Moralia* is even more explicit; speaking of buildings, space and dwelling (in 18); it says: 'The possibility of residence is annihilated by that of socialist society, which, once missed, saps the foundations of bourgeois life' (41/39).

58. But the not always disinterested defense of contemplation and disengagement is certainly everywhere in Adorno (see, for instance, MM No. 82, 'Keeping one's distance', where the figure and the strategy of 'distance' are strongly and internally related to the 'bad immediacy' of the various positivisms).

59. But see also MM 143/III, 157/121, 224/170.

PART II

1. See below, Part III, chapter 7.

2. See, most famously, Adorno on the *intérieur*: *Kierkegaard, Gesammelte Schriften*, vol. 2 (1979) , pp. 38–69; and MM No. 106.

3. T.S. Eliot, 'Tradition and the Individual Talent', *Selected Essays*, New York 1950, pp. 10–11.

4. 'Just as, in the nature and finite areas of its life, art has its *before*, so also does it have an *after*, that is to say, a circle that passes beyond art's mode of apprehending and representing the Absolute ...' G.W.F. Hegel, *Aesthetik*, vol. I, 1955, p. 110.

5. See also AT 465/433.

6. See Joseph Horowitz, *Understanding Toscanini*, Minnesota 1987; also Adorno's own essay on Toscanini, called 'Die Meisterschaft des Maestro', in *Gesammelte Schriften*, vol. 16, Frankfurt 1978, pp. 52–67.

7. Raymond Williams, *Marxism and Literature*, Oxford 1977, p. 110.

8. See my 'On Negt and Kluge', *October* 46, Fall 1988, pp. 151–77.

9. Terry Eagleton's complaint in *Against the Grain*, London 1986; see also MM 280/210: 'He who has laughter on his side has no need of proof.'

10. The Culture Industry 'builds the need for happiness in and exploits it. It thus has its moment of truth in the way in which it satisfies a substantial need developing out of the tendentially increasing renunciation demanded by society; but becomes the absolutely untrue in the way in which it offers that satisfaction.' (AT 461/430)

11. Actually, we owe this brilliant formula to the translator!

12. See above, Introduction, note 5.

13. Andreas Huyssens has pointed out (in *After the Great Divide*, Bloomington, IN 1986) the intimate relationship between the Wagner book and Adorno's theory of the Culture Industry. Indeed, the emergence of this last now proves to be endogamous, something that art does to itself in its disintegration during the imperialist period (Adorno suggests, in the light of the *Gesamtkunstwerk*, that Nietzsche should have called *his* Wagner book 'The Birth of Film out of the Spirit of Music'). In Benjamin's thought the stage of the 'reproducible work of art' follows that of the emergence of high modernism in

the language and form of Baudelaire; in Adorno, both are simultaneous with Wagner. In addition, a rich discussion of 'phantasmagoria' (ch. 6) lays claim to prolong and continue Marx's notion of commodity fetishism in the aesthetic realm.

PART III

1. Adorno did allow himself to say things like this: 'Music down to this very day has existed only as a product of the bourgeois class, a product which, both in the success and failure of its attempts at formulation, embodies this society and gives aesthetic documentation of it. ... Within the existing order it must be doubted whether any music other than bourgeois music exists' (*Philosophy of Modern Music*, Frankfurt 1958; New York 1973).

2. As in *War and Peace*, Book VIII, chapter 9:
In the second act there was scenery representing tombstones, and there was a round hole in the canvas to represent the moon, shades were raised over the footlights, and from horns and contrabass came deep notes while many people appeared from right and left wearing black cloaks and holding things like daggers in their hands. They began waving their arms. Then some other people ran in and began dragging away the maiden who had been in white and was now in light blue. They did not drag her away at once, but sang with her for a long time and then at last dragged her off, and behind the scenes something metallic was struck three times and everyone knelt down and sang a prayer. All these things were repeatedly interrupted by the enthusiastic shouts of the audience. (transl. Louise and Aylmer Maude, New York 1942, p. 622)

3. 'Great architecture finds its transfunctional voice there where it is able to express its own instrumental purposes mimetically from the inside as its content. Scharoun's Philharmonic [in Berlin] is beautiful because – in order to establish spatially ideal conditions for orchestral music – it becomes *like* orchestral music, without borrowing allusions programmatically from it' (AT 72/66).

4. *Mahler*, Frankfurt 1960, p. 127.

5. In his *Theory of the Avant-garde*, Minnesota 1984.

6. See also the beautiful meditation on the meaning and origin of the 'disinterested' in art, in MM No. 144.

7. See on this above, pp. 21–2; and also 182–3.

8. In *What is Literature?* and vol. 3 of *L'Idiot de la famille*.

9. See, however, the very balanced and reasonable discussion of hearing in ch. 1 of the *Introduction to the Sociology of Music*, where, after passing in review a typology of musical listeners – the expert, the good listener, the cultural consumer, the emotional listener, the listener out of *ressentiment*, the jazz expert and the jazz fan, and the consumer of music as entertainment, concluding with anti-listeners such as the indifferent, the unmusical and the anti-musical – Adorno wisely suggests that the problem of musical education must pass through the mediation of the social totality:
The antagonistic condition of the whole is expressed in the fact that even musically correct forms of behavior can realize aspects of the whole that are relatively negative by way of their structural position within it. ... The expert listener requires a specialization of a type hitherto inconceivable, the proportional regression of the type of the merely good listener – is probably a function of that specialization. ... The failure in the face of culture, however, ought to lead to some further conclusions as to the failure of culture before human beings, and as to what the world has made of them in the first place. (*Einleitung in die Musiksoziologie*, in *Gesammelte Schriften*, vol. 14, Frankfurt 1973, pp. 197–8.)

10. 'Vers une musique informelle', *Gesammelte Schriften*, vol. 16, p. 523.

11. See my 'Marxism and Historicism', in *The Ideologies of Theory*, vol. 2.

12. Gertrude Stein, *Four in America*, intro. Thornton Wilder, New Haven, CT 1947, p.vii.

13. See Part II, note 2.

14. Translated in *Telos*, no. 20 (Summer 1974), pp. 56–66.

15. But see Part I, note 4.

16. Introduction to M. Jay, *The Dialectical Imagination*, Boston, MA 1973, p. xii.

CONCLUSIONS

1. Jean-François Lyotard, 'Adorno como diavolo', in *Des dispositifs pulsionnels*, Paris 1973, pp. 115–33.

2. See above, Introduction, note 5.

3. Dubiel, *Theory and Politics*, p. 93.

4. Ernesto Laclau and Chantal Mouffe, *Hegemony and Socialist Strategy*, London 1985.

5. See above, Part I, note 13.

6. *The Positivist Dispute in German Sociology*, p. 10.

7. Ibid., p. 12.

8. 'Dialektik als Vernunftdkritik', in *Adorno-Konferenz 1983*, ed. Friedeburg and Habermas, Frankfurt 1983, pl.69.

9. But see Peter Dews, *Logics of Disintegration*.

10. See the Habermas references in Introduction, note 5, above.

11. See above all Bubner, 'Kann Theorie aesthetisch werden?' in *Materialien zur Aesthetischen Theorie*, ed. Lindner and Ludke, Frankfurt 1976. Adorno repudiates a 'literary' or 'aesthetic' conception of philosophy in *Negative Dialectics* (26–7/24–5).

12. *Theory of Communicative Action*, vol. 1, Boston, MA 1984), transl. T. McCarthy, pp. 382–3.

13. *Materialien*, p. 132.

14. Roman Rosdolsky, *The Making of Marx's Capital*, London 1977. See also the pathbreaking commentaries on the *Grundrisse* and the manuscripts of the 1860s by Enrique Dussel: *la Producción teórica de Marx*, Mexico City 1985; and *Hacia un Marx desconcido*, Mexico City 1988.

15. Habermas, *Theory of Communicative Action*, vol. 1, p. 357.

16. See, for an expert and thorough summary of this tradition, Bob Jessop, *The Capitalist State*, New York 1982, ch. 3. See also *Value, Social Form and the State*, ed. Michael Williams, New York 1988, whose editor begins:
The chapters which follow have all been sparked by opposition to the widespread reversion of contemporary Marxism to the methodological preoccupations of orthodox social science: positivism, analysis, individualism and naturalism. This reversion, manifested most recently in self-styled 'analytical Marxism' . . ., is based upon the tacit (and sometimes explicit) rejection of the crucial place of the Hegelian dialectic in Marxist theory, the role of forms of consciousness in regulating bourgeois society and of the insights of Marx's early writings on the state, civil society and critique of right. (p. 1)

17. J. Derrida, 'La Structure, le signe et le jeu dans le discours des sciences humaines', *L'Ecriture et la différence*, Paris 1967, pp. 409–28.

18. *Gesammelte Schriften*, vol. 16, Frankfurt 1978, pp. 493–540.

19. *Noten zur Literatur*, pp. 9–33. He also considered the 'Introduction' to his Husserl

book something of a manifesto in this same respect (see *Against Epistemology*, transl. Willis Domingo, Cambridge, MA 1983, pp. 3–40). What one misses in the 'Essay as Form' is any consideration of the generic and institutional infrastructure of the 'essay' in cultural journalism, the feuilleton, etc., determinants which considerably reduce and demystify the putative 'freedom' of the genre.

20. Any reading of the 'Fragment' chapter in the now canonical account by P. Lacoue-Labarthe and J.L. Nancy of the Jena Romantics, called *The Literary Absolute*, will bring considerable differences to mind; even if one does not consider the Jena Romantics to be charlatans, their self-defeating insistence on the necessarily incomplete nature of all expression is very distant in spirit from Adorno's way of confronting what for him also was a *necessary* dilemma of the representation of 'totality'.

21. See 'On the Nature and Form of the Essay', in *Soul and Form*, transl. Anna Bostock, London 1974.

INDEX

Che Guevara *see* Guevara
Christianity 95
class 8, 9, 66, 130
  society 166, 198, 199
  solidarity 195
  struggle 95, 129, 184
Collingwood, R. G. 192
commodity
  exchange 69
  fetishism 138, 148, 180
  form 43, 140, 142, 149, 161, 162, 167,
    168, 181, 198, 199, 204, 239, 240
  production 21, 24
  world 47
Communism 250
Comte, Auguste 112, 161
concept [*Begriff*] 15, 17, 18, 19, 20, 21, 22,
  24, 26, 28, 30, 32, 36, 46, 48, 49,
  51, 53, 56, 57, 59, 63, 69, 203, 206,
  211, 235, 239
La Condition humaine (Malraux) 119
constellation 50, 51, 54–60 *passim*, 63,
  68, 96, 207, 244
constructivism 175, 203
consumption 23, 44, 142, 182
Croce, Benedetto 9, 26, 157
cubism 193
culture 43, 46, 75, 77, 87, 124
  critique of 33, 44, 45, 47–8, 109
  industry 69, 103, 106, 107, 108, 125, 128,
    136, 137, 139–45 *passim*, 147, 148, 151,
    152, 154, 158, 162, 166, 167, 168, 173,
    186, 206, 216, 230, 241, 258 n11
  see also mass culture

Dante Alighieri 131
Darstellung, concept of 49, 50, 51, 52,
  54, 55, 59, 60, 62, 78, 80, 182, 234,
  235, 245
Darwin, Charles 35, 94, 95, 97, 98
  Origin of the Species 94
de Man, Paul 10, 183
deconstruction 9
Deleuze, Gilles 16, 22, 31
democracy 140, 235

Derrida, Jacques 5, 9, 10, 58, 182, 235,
  241, 244
Dews, Peter 254 n10
dialectic, concept of 4, 5, 7, 8, 11, 16,
  17, 22, 24, 25, 27, 28, 29, 30, 31, 35,
  36, 43, 50, 71, 72, 73, 105, 116, 120,
  145, 147, 180, 213, 225, 237, 249, 252
  of enlightenment 10, 65, 74, 99, 100,
    102, 108, 110, 129, 148, 179, 199, 215,
    216
  negative 47, 62, 112, 235, 248
Dialectic of the Enlightenment (Adorno
  and Horkheimer) 3, 9, 15–16, 37,
  39, 50, 64, 65, 96, 99, 103, 104, 108,
  109, 114, 118, 119, 137, 139, 141, 154,
  161, 163, 180, 198, 206, 214, 237,
  256 n37
  'Culture Industry' chapter 106–7,
    143, 153, 230, 241
  'Odyssey' chapter 18, 19, 129, 136, 149,
    150, 151, 152
difference, concept of 16, 17, 23
division of labour 41, 42, 43, 69, 102,
  109, 197, 198
Döblin, Alfred, *Berlin-Alexanderplatz*
  137
domination 22, 24, 30, 37, 67, 68, 90,
  96, 101, 103, 105, 110, 179, 214, 215
Dubiel, Helmut 257–8 n56
Durkheim, Émile 38, 39, 91

Eagleton, Terry 6
ecological politics 110
economic, category of 19, 23, 24, 162,
  189
  see also base, Marxist concept of
Eisenstein, Sergei 31, 173
Elias, Norbert 101
Eliot, T. S. 129
empiricism 7, 41, 73, 131
Engels, Friedrich 45, 46
enlightenment 20, 28, 43, 67, 81, 82, 83,
  101, 103, 105, 107, 149, 150, 162, 166,
  209, 214, 236
  dialectic of 10, 65, 74, 99, 100, 102,
  108, 110, 129, 148, 179, 199, 215, 216

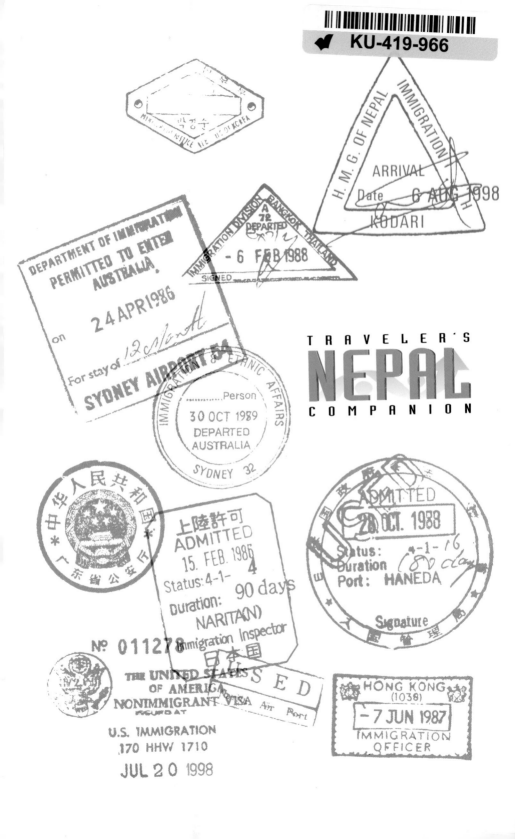

The 2000–2001 Traveler's Companions
ARGENTINA • AUSTRALIA • BALI • CALIFORNIA • CANADA • CHILI • CHINA • COSTA RICA • CUBA •
EASTERN CANADA • ECUADOR • FLORIDA • HAWAII • HONG KONG • INDIA • INDONESIA • JAPAN • KENYA •
MALAYSIA & SINGAPORE • MEDITERRANEAN FRANCE • MEXICO • NEPAL • NEW ENGLAND • NEW ZEALAND •
PERU • PHILIPPINES • PORTUGAL • RUSSIA • SOUTHERN ENGLAND • SOUTH AFRICA • SPAIN • THAILAND •
TURKEY • VENEZUELA • VIETNAM, LAOS AND CAMBODIA • WESTERN CANADA

Traveler's NEPAL Companion
First Published 2000 in the United Kingdom by
Kümmerly+Frey AG,
Alpenstrasse 58, CH 3052 Zollikofen, Switzerland
in association with
World Leisure Marketing Ltd
Unit 11, Newmarket Court, Newmarket Drive,
Derby, DE24 8NW, England
Web Site: http://www.map-world.co.uk

ISBN: 1-84006-066-2

© 2000 Kümmerly+Frey AG, Switzerland

Created, edited and produced by
Allan Amsel Publishing
53, rue Beaudouin, 27700 Les Andelys, France.
E-mail: Allan.Amsel@wanadoo.fr
Editor in Chief: Allan Amsel
Editor: Fiona Nichols
Original design concept: Hon Bing-wah
Picture editor and designer: David Henry

Printed by Samhwa Printing Co. Ltd., Seoul, South Korea

TRAVELER'S NEPAL COMPANION

By Chris Taylor
Photographed by Mohamed Amin and
Duncan Willetts

Kümmerly+Frey

Contents

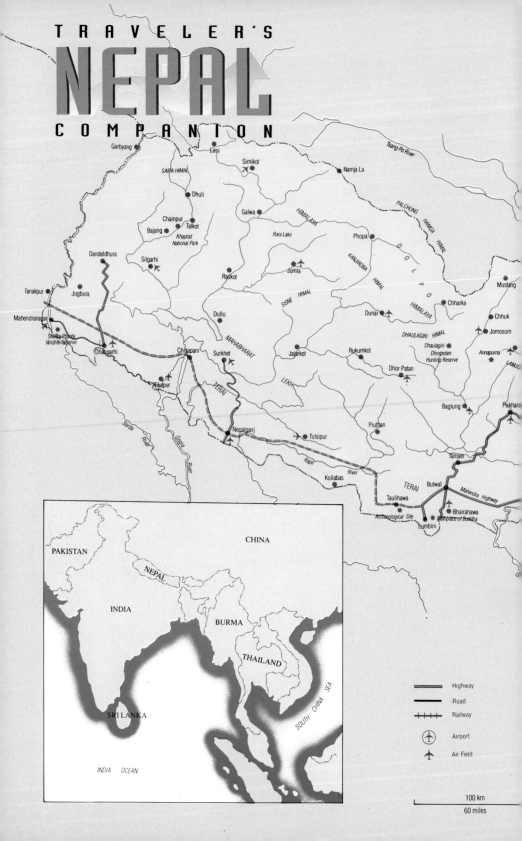

TRAVELER'S NEPAL COMPANION

Garbyang
Limi
Simikot
Namja La
SAIPA HIMAL
Tsang Po River
Dhuli
PALCHUNG HAMGA HIMAL
Chainpur
Galwa
HIMALAYA
Talkot
Phopa
Bajang
Rara Lake
KANJIROBA HIMAL
Khaptad National Park
DOLPO
Dandeldhura
Silgarhi
Mustang
Raskot
Jumla
SISNE HIMAL
HIMALAYA
Chharka
Tanakpur
Jogbura
Chhuk
Dunai
Jomosom
Mahendranagar
Dullu
DHAULAGIRI HIMAL
Shukla-Phanta Wildlife Reserve
MAHABHARAT
Dhaulagiri
Annapurna
Dhangarhi
Chisapani
Surkhet
Jajarkot
Rukumkot
Dhorpotan Hunting Reserve
LAMJU
Tikapur
Jumla
Dhor Patan
TERAI
LEKH
Baglung
Pakhara
Sarda River
Gogra River
Nepalganj
Tulsipur
Piuthan
Tansen
Rapti River
Koilabas
Butwal
TERAI
Taulihawa
Mahendra Highway
Bhairahawa
Archaeological Site
Birthplace of Buddha
Lumbini

Inset map

CHINA
PAKISTAN
NEPAL
INDIA
BURMA
THAILAND
SOUTH CHINA SEA
SRI LANKA
INDIA OCEAN

Legend

═══	Highway
───	Road
┼┼┼┼	Railway
✈ (circled)	Airport
✈	Air Field

100 km
60 miles

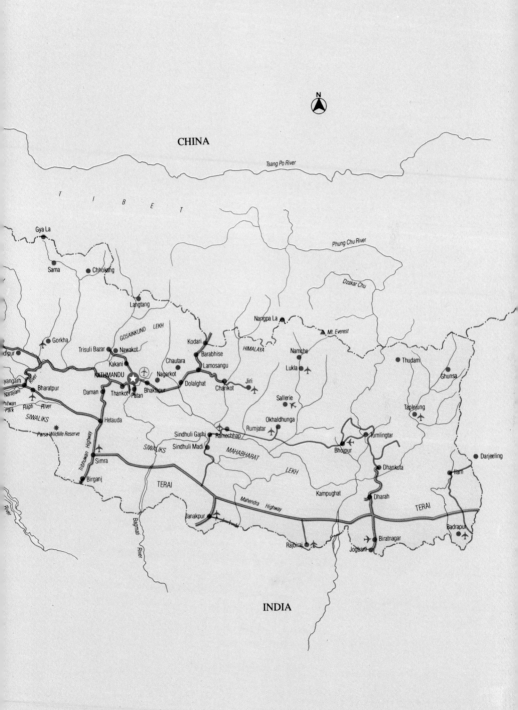

CHINA

Tsang Po River

T I B E T

Phung Chu River

Gya La

Sama   Chhokang   *Dzakar Chu*

            Langtang

                    GOSAINKUND LEKH   Nangpa La ●   ▲ Mt. Everest

    ● Gorkha   Kodari   ● Thudam
            Trisuli Bazar ● Nawakot   Barabhise   *HIMALAYA* Namche
dipur   Kakani   Chautara   Lukla   Ghunsa ●
yangarh   *River*   KATHMANDU Nagarkot Lamosangu   ✈
Narayani   ● Bharatpur Daman Thankot ✈ Bhaktapur Dolalghat Jiri   Taplejung
hitwan   Patan   Charikot   ✈
Park   Rapti *River*   Sallerie ✈
    SIWALIKS   Hetauda   Okhaldhunga
        ● Parsa Wildlife Reserve   Rumjatar   ● Darjeeling
                                Sindhuli Garhi Ramechhap   Tumlingtar
                      SIWALIKS Sindhuli Madi   Bhojpur ✈
            Simra   *MAHABHARAT*   Dhankuta   Ilam ●
        Birganj   *LEKH*   Dharah
                    TERAI   ✈   TERAI
                            Mahendra Highway Kampughat
        River   Janakpur ✈   Badrapur
                                        Rajbiraj ✈   ✈
                                            Jogbani Biratnagar ✈

                    INDIA

TOP SPOTS

Cruise the Himalayan Skyline

THE LURE OF EVEREST MIGHT BE IRRESISTIBLE IF IT WERE NOT FOR THE SMALL FACT of 15 days of walking at altitudes that reach over 5,000 m (16,400 ft) — a fabulous trek for those with the endurance, energy and the time, but one that many visitors decide to decline. Fortunately there's an easy option: every morning from September to May Royal Nepal Airlines and other domestic carriers offer a mountain-hugging cruise past Everest and two dozen more great peaks.

The **Mountain Flight** heads east of Kathmandu for 160 km (99 miles), in what is an unparalleled spectacle: ice-encrusted peaks on one side; a verdant patchwork of cultivated fields on the other. In the course of the flight, you pass just 25 km (16 miles) from the world's highest mountains. And at a flight altitude of 7,500 to 8,500 m (24,600 to 27,900 ft), you see them at eye-level. If weather conditions obscure the peaks, you get your money back.

If the Mountain Flight sounds a little too jet-age, the soft option is **Balloon Sunrise Nepal (** (01) 418214 FAX (01) 424157, P.O. Box 1273, Hattisar, Kathmandu, an Australian company that offers hot-air balloon flights over Kathmandu valley.

Starting shortly after sunrise, when the light is at its best and the air is clearest, the balloon ascends from Kirtipur to a height of around 3,000 m (10,000 ft), where you find yourself in a large wicker basket with a small group of strangers gazing out on the world's most impressive skyline and trying not to think about how far you are from the ground. If nothing else, it's exhilarating.

Gaze on the Eyes of Buddha

THERE IS NO IMAGE MORE EVOCATIVE OF NEPAL THAN THE HEAVY-LIDDED, SUMMER-SKY-BLUE EYES OF THE BUDDHA at **Swayambhunath temple**, near Kathmandu. The question-mark nose that sits beneath them is in fact the

OPPOSITE: The heavy-lidded eyes and question-mark nose of the Buddha at Swayambhunath temple is, along with the Annapurna skyline, the most evocative image of Nepal. ABOVE: Machhapuchhare, the holy fishtail peak of the Annapurna range, wreathed in clouds, is an unforgettable sight for those who've trekked in its shadow.

Nepal numeral "one", symbolic both of unity and the one path to salvation as preached by the Buddha. If you look carefully, you'll see a delicate whorl rising from the gilt background above the eyes — the third eye, all-seeing, symbolic of Buddha's omniscience.

There can be few more pleasant ways to while away a late afternoon in Kathmandu than to walk out to Swayambhunath. Start the walk from Durbar square. Behind the Kasthamandap, in the south-west corner of the square is **Pie Alley** or Maru Tole, although the pie shops for which it was once famed are now all gone. Follow it down to the river and cross via a footbridge that rocks and sways with the continuous passage of local pedestrian commuters. A path leads up to a road lined with houses and shops, where you turn left towards the green at the foot of Swayambhunath hill.

The climb to the temple involves puffing up more than 300 steps — some sources claim 365, a number that is disputed but you can check yourself if you wish. Along the way sellers of Tibetan jewelry, their wares spread out on rugs, will call to you. Look in particular for the carvers of miniature *mani* stones. Mani stones are inscribed with prayers and are usually seen at the tops of passes, where they are laid in thanks for a successful journey. Watch out too for the monkeys, which scamper about mischievously, and are best kept at a distance. Manjushri, the Tibetan Buddha of Discriminative Awareness, is said to have once had his hair cut here: the shorn hairs became trees; the lice became monkeys.

After you've recaptured your breath at the summit, choose a quiet spot to survey the scene. At your feet is spread a fabulous view of Kathmandu, while circling the stupa in a clockwise direction, one outstretched hand slapping the prayer wheels into a devotional spin, lips muttering a mantra, is a Tibetan monk or two. All around, prayer flags flutter in the breeze, scattering their prayers

heavenward for the salvation of all beings.

The famous eyes gaze out in the four cardinal directions. Over them is a staggered cone of 13 gilded rings, representing the 13 steps to enlightenment. At the summit the "umbrella" with its saffron skirt, represents enlightenment itself.

It's almost chastening, the air of antique devotion that hangs about this place, particularly late in the afternoon as the warm light deepens into the searing reds and lambent shadows of sunset. But then, before you know it, worldly concerns sweep such thoughts aside: it's getting dark and time to turn back to Kathmandu for dinner.

Little Tibet

NEPAL IS A PATCHWORK OF ETHNIC GROUPS, EACH WITH THEIR OWN RELIGION, LANGUAGE AND DRESS. But if most of these ethnic groups are obscure to the nonspecialist, the one that everyone has heard of is the Tibetans.

In October 1950 the Chinese People's Liberation Army rolled into Tibet, sweeping aside the poorly equipped Tibetan forces. For the Chinese, Tibet was in this way "liberated"; for most Tibetans, their country had been invaded. And with their religious and other individual rights suppressed in their own country, many have made their way to the more tolerant soil of Nepal.

There are probably around 100,000 Tibetans in Nepal, and many of them have settled around **Bodhnath,** a stupa that long has had a Tibetan connection. Walking around Bodhnath you momentarily leave Nepal and find yourself in Tibet. The many new temples here are known as *gompa* and were built with help of donations from overseas.

The gompa are active places of worship; although you may enter, it is always polite to ask permission of one of the many maroon-cloaked monks. Don't

The weaving of colorful Tibetan carpets, a tradition near extinction in Tibet, has found a new lease of life in Nepal.

forget to remove your shoes and hat
before entering the main chapel.
If you wish to take photographs, a
small donation or a gift — the white
kata scarf is the customary Tibetan
gift for monks — is appreciated.

Entering a gompa when a service is
in progress is a unique, mysteriously
atmospheric experience that you will
never forget. The interior is dark, shifting
with flickering pools of luminescence
thrown off by innumerable candles.
In Tibet these candles are made of yak
butter, making the air heavy with a
slightly rancid, slightly sweet smell,
but in Nepal vegetable ghee is usually
substituted. Add to this the rolling
drone of meditating monks kneeling
on cushions and muttering a tape-loop
mantra, and you have a heady concoction.

If you're lucky, your visit to Bodhnath
may coincide with a ceremony that
requires a musical accompaniment.
Such performances are not melodious;
but the crashing of cymbals, pounding
of drums and the booming of the three-
meter (10-ft) *radung* — something like
a cross between a Swiss horn and a
didgeridoo — combine to create a
haunting cacophony of sound.

Trekking with the Royals

PRINCE CHARLES HAS DONE IT;
MICK JAGGER HAS IT DONE IT; there's
no reason why you can't.

A long, arduous trek is not for
everyone; in fact only around 10
percent of Nepal visitors go trekking.
But trekking doesn't necessarily entail
weeks in the wilderness, and Nepal is
also blessed with numerous short and
less taxing walks in the hills. The most
famous is the so-called **Royal trek** from
Pokhara. Combining rugged scenes of
the world's highest mountains with all
the effort of a strenuous amble in the
countryside, the only drawback of
the Royal trek is that it doesn't offer
tea house accommodation en route.

The reward of an arduous uphill climb.

afternoon camp in the vicinity allows you to feast your eyes on the mountains in the glow of sunset while you enjoy a meal cooked over a campfire.

The second day involves a gradual climb, passing through villages where it is possible to buy an average *dahl bhat* (rice and lentils) lunch — of interest if you haven't tried one before. The Gurung village of **Shakhlung**, at 1,750 m (5,740 ft), is the usual place to overnight.

By the third day, the ground you've covered even in this short time means that the skyline is changing. As the trail descends steeply, Annapurna II and Himalchuli come into view. After pausing at a checkpoint, which also has a couple of tea shops, the trail ascends once again, making for **Chisophani**, a village with a small temple and a campsite that commands beautiful mountain views.

With the exception of a final ridge, just before entering the Pokhara valley again, you spend most of the final day of the trek descending, first along a ridge and then sharply down a series of steps. The walk ends, as it began, through rice fields. At the village of **Begnas** you can catch a taxi 12 km (7 miles) back to Pokhara.

But then again this drawback is precisely what keeps the crowds at bay.

The three- to five-day trek never goes above 2,000 m (6,600 ft), and the climbs are of the gentle variety, making it a perfect trek for children or anyone who is not as fit as they might be.

It begins with a short taxi ride from Pokhara to **Biyajapur** (an army camp), from where a trail ascends through rice fields, past a small village to a resting place under a pipal tree. Such trees were planted long ago with the purpose of providing shade for travelers, and often — like this one — have a stone bench, or *chautara*, beneath them.

The trail follows a ridge, providing stunning views (weather permitting) of Machhapuchhare and Annapurna. A late

Safari on Elephant-Back

THE INDIAN RHINOCEROS IS A MASSIVE LUMBERING CREATURE that stands at around 1.7 m (5.6 ft) and weighs around two tons. Combine this with notoriously poor eyesight and a tendency to charge anything that moves, and you have a dangerous beast indeed. If you find yourself in the path of a charging rhino, you are advised to make a dash for it (in a curve), dropping an item of clothing as you go. Better still, do your rhino-seeing on the back of an elephant.

ABOVE: The safest way to see Nepal's animal life is on elephant-back. LEFT: An elephant is about the only thing a 300-kg (650-lb) rhino will leave alone. OPPOSITE: Fording the *tals* of the Terai (top), a favored rhino haunt, is not something you'd want to do on foot. Rare gurials bask in the sunny waters of Chitwan National Park (bottom).

Rhinos leave elephants alone, as do tigers, making elephants the safest mode of transport for a safari in the **Royal Chitwan National Park**. The elephants themselves are curious enough, munching their way through up to 300 kg (660 lb) of food and quaffing 200 liters (52 gallons) of water per day, not to mention resignedly obeying the commands of their diminutive human masters — the mahout or, in Nepali, *pahit*; but the real attraction of Chitwan — and other national parks of Nepal's lowland Terai — is its wild animals.

From your railed *howdah* — the platform "saddle" used on elephants — you have a sweeping view of the marshy grasslands, the preferred habitat of the Indian one-horned rhino. More often than not, you'll find them wallowing muddily in the *tals* — lakes formed by the monsoonal shifts in river courses — of the Terai.

Almost everyone is on the lookout for a Bengal tiger. You will have to keep your eyes peeled. With just 120 (or so) of them spread out over an area of nearly 2,000 sq km (760 sq miles), this shy creature bestows the gift of a sighting on only the luckiest of visitors.

But if tigers are scarce, other animals are not. The chital is the most numerous of the park's four species of deer; others include the barking deer. Golden jackals scavenge on the plains. The gaur is the world's largest species of wild ox, growing to a maximum height of 2.2 m (7.2 ft). Sloth bears, langur monkeys and wild pigs may also be seen, along with a host of smaller mammals such as squirrels, leopard cats and porcupines. And if you weren't worried enough about the rhinos, the rivers harbor two species of crocodile; while lurking in the tall grass is the world's most venomous snake, the king cobra.

At Chitwan, it's a world of discovery aboard an elephant. For many first-timers, however, an unwelcome discovery is that, while riding an elephant may be the safest way to search out horned rhinoceroses and rare Bengal

tigers, it is by no means painless: a couple of hours on the back of an elephant will leave you feeling the following day as if you had done an unaccustomed workout in the gym.

Bazaar Experiences

DON'T SPEND YOUR TIME IN KATHMANDU BEING FERRIED AROUND IN RICKSHAWS AND TAXIS: get out and walk.

One of Kathmandu's best strolls is from Indra Chowk to Asan Tole, taking you through the heart of the **Old Bazaar**, once the start of the long trade route to Tibet.

Chowk means "intersection", and **Indra Chowk** is an intersection *par excellence*, a swirling juncture of six bustling streets and alleys. Presiding over the shops and shoppers is the upstairs shrine of **Akash Bhairav** — *akash* means "sky", which is where this bhairav (a ferocious manifestation of Shiva)

On Kathmandu's Durbar square, amongst the temples and statuary, a young woman OPPOSITE sells fruit. While ABOVE, a Newari woman vends fresh fruit on a curbside.

is supposed to have miraculously fallen
from. Opposite the shrine, in a narrow
alley is the **bead bazaar,** where stalls
glitter with the glass beads much coveted
by Nepali women for use in necklaces.
Also on Indra Chowk is a **Shiva temple**,
its platform cluttered with woolen rugs
and shawls for sale.

The walk from Indra Chowk is short
but brimming with interest. Try and keep
to a slow amble, and pause when you
reach **Kel Tole**, where you will find the
Seto Machhendranath temple, dedicated
to the patron saint of Kathmandu's
Buddhists. Wander into the temple
courtyard and linger in a quiet corner
for a few moments to take in the scene:
women make *puja* (ritual offerings) of
flowers and incense; a few children dash
in and out of the shadows; a sacred cow
lumbers sleepily out into the street;
shopkeepers preside hopefully over
small piles of grain and domestic items.
At night, from around 9 PM, musicians
often perform here.

From here continue your walk up to
Asan Tole. If you have not been long in
Nepal, chances are you will be suffering
from a kind of sensory overload by now.
This bazaar area in the heart of old
Kathmandu is so chock-a-block with the
unfamiliar that before long it becomes
difficult to process it all. A sacred goat
bleats from inside the pushing crowd;
you pause over a pile of brown
vegetative bricks wondering what they

are (Tibetan tea) and are nearly knocked
aside by two hurrying porters, vast,
overstuffed sacks hanging from their
crowns; in the square are sacks
of mysterious spices and
baskets of vegetables.

In amidst all this buying and
selling, pushing and shoving, stands
the delightful **Annapurna temple**, and
beside it smaller temples to **Ganesh**
and **Vishnu**. The Annapurna temple
is home to a manifestation of Lakshmi,
the Goddess of Wealth. Watch the
never-ending flow of worshippers calling
upon her favor in this most secular of
places, a bazaar that wakes before the
sun and continues long after it has set.

Toothache Gods and
Child-Devouring Demons

*A MYRIAD OF DISCOVERIES AWAIT YOU
IN KATHMANDU.* Myths, legend and
superstition have nested in the most
unlikely corners of the city, and for
those who know how to seek them

out there are countless tiny shrines and temples that mark their presence.

In **Asan Tole**, that busy square where vegetable and spice sellers hawk their goods, is a paving stone with an impression of a fish that fell from the sky one day. The story goes that an astrologer was once awaiting the tolling of a bell that would announce the birth of his son. When at last the bell rang, he immediately cast the boy's horoscope and discovered that he was not after all the father. In horror and anger he quit town.

Years later he returned to study under a gifted young astrologer, who asked him to make a prediction. He duly predicted a fish would fall from the sky, stating the time and even the precise spot where it would fall. "Surely," suggested the younger astrologer, "you've failed to account for the wind." Sure enough, he repeated his sums and discovered that his calculations were slightly off. And in the same moment he remembered another time he had failed to account for the wind. He cast that horoscope of

so many years ago again, and discovered the boy whose birth he had been awaiting was his after all; indeed he was no other than the gifted young astrologer who now sat before him.

If fish falling from the sky and leaving dents in the paving stones isn't curious enough for you, take the road that leads west out of Asan Tole. About halfway along before you reach the next crossroads, on the left, is the **Ugratara temple**, where locals come to pray when their eyes are troubling them. Stroll up to the crossroads, turn left and look to your left for a piece of wood that has had thousands of nails hammered into it. If you look carefully amongst all the coins, you will find an image of the **toothache god** — sooner a prayer and a coin for him than a visit to the dentist.

OPPOSITE: Shiva in his most terrifying aspect as an incarnation of Bhairav, on a mask carved in the eighteenth century. ABOVE: The accomplishment of Newar woodcarving in the Royal Palace of Kathmandu is breathtaking — there are sections where you might stand transfixed for an hour and still discover new details.

It is this mixture of the surreal and fanciful that makes Kathmandu so bewitching. In the area around the toothache god, in amongst the shops and houses, you can find shrines to Ganesh and Vishnu, stone lions, a miniature replica of Swayambhunath — those unable to mount the 300-odd stairs of the real thing may instead circumambulate this one — and dozens of small pagodas and temples. Best of all is the **Kichandra Bahal**, an erstwhile Buddhist monastery west of Kel Tole. Its unassuming courtyard, complete with a small stupa and pagoda sanctuary is noted for four brass plaques, one of which shows the demon Gurumapa devouring a small child whole. This demon's hunger for children is insatiable and must be appeased with an annual festival in which a buffalo is slaughtered for fear that the demon will start on the local infants.

Funny Business

IF YOU'RE THE PRUDISH SORT, IT WON'T DO TO LOOK TOO CLOSELY AT THE CARVINGS THAT ADORN SOME TEMPLES OF THE KATHMANDU VALLEY — if there's bliss here, it's certainly not the spiritual kind.

Erotic carvings can be seen on the slanting wooden struts that support the curved roofs of pagodas. Usually the

images carved onto the struts are of manifestations of the deity to which the pagoda is dedicated, ferocious protective griffins at the far corners. But from time to time you will find a concourse of sexual athletics, in which everybody — from the servants to the pets — gets a turn. It's dizzying stuff, particularly when you consider you're looking at a place of worship.

The explanations are legion; yet no theory seems more compelling than another. Scholars point to the influence of Tantric practices, in which sexuality is used as a stepping stone to higher states of consciousness; some look to connections with fertility rites; while many local guides will tell you the lewd images deter the Goddess of Lightning, a chaste, virginal creature who wouldn't dare strike such an obscene structure with her bolts from the heavens.

In Kathmandu some of the finest erotic carvings can be seen on the struts of **Basantapur tower** of the Hanuman Dhoka palace in Durbar square. Close by the entrance to the palace is **Jagannath temple**, where you will find more erotic carvings. And in the center of Durbar square, the **Shiva temple** is also adorned with some interesting erotica.

Kathmandu's neighboring city of Patan does not have a great deal of erotic carving, though the struts on **Charanarayan temple** in Durbar square will reveal some imaginative group contortions for those who take the time to look.

But overall it's hard to beat Bhaktapur's **Café Nyatapola**, a restaurant that started out as a place of worship. Nowadays you can sit and watch the crowds in the square, sip a drink, and occasionally, if you are that way inclined, look to the ceiling and enjoy your erotica at leisure.

Erotic carving ABOVE on an ancient Kathmandu valley temple. OPPOSITE: Crowds ambling through Patan's Durbar square in the late afternoon.

TOP SPOTS

Cycle into the Hills

YOU DON'T NEED TO BE TOUR DE FRANCE FIT TO CYCLE INTO THE HIMALAYAS, but a little exercise in the weeks leading up to your Nepal trip won't go astray. **Himalayan Mountain Bikes** ((01) 416596 FAX (01) 411055, P.O. Box 2247, Kathmandu, on the other hand, gamely claim that they "cater for all levels of fitness."

Nagarkot has the best views of the Himalayas in all Kathmandu valley, and an overnight stay that takes in both sunset and sunrise is an obligatory Nepal experience. Of course, you can take a bus or a taxi up there, but why not cycle up on a top-of-the-range mountain bike, guided by an expert? You're sure to feel you've earned the views when you get to the top.

The first day entails a 38-km (24-mile) ascent to Nagarkot. Now this may sound like a long way, but remember you have all day to do it. Besides, the tour stops half way, in **Bhaktapur**, where you have several hours to look at some of the valley's best preserved historic buildings and temples, cool off and have lunch. The climb to Nagarkot is rewarded with lodgings at a rustic guesthouse complete with a breathtaking panorama of the Himalayas.

The second-day descent to Kathmandu keeps the Himalayas in view, following a track past villages and rice fields to **Changu Narayan**, a sixth-century temple complex dedicated to Vishnu. The descent continues to Bhaktapur, where you have lunch and then cycle on to Kathmandu with a stopover in Thimi, a town known for its pottery.

It's a ride that is guaranteed to produce some aches and pains if you're not a regular cyclist, but the memories linger long after the aches are gone, and the second day is downhill anyway… mostly.

Celebrate with a Living Goddess

NEPAL IS SUCH A FESTIVE COUNTRY THAT IT'S ALMOST IMPOSSIBLE FOR YOUR VISIT NOT TO COINCIDE WITH SOME KIND OF ANNUAL EVENT. Some of these are small, local affairs, but the best of them are vast colorful pageants that involve the whole country.

Indra Jatra, a September festival, is one of the big ones. Indeed, it has been called the quintessential Nepali festival: all-encompassing and inclusive, a celebration of the gods, of history and of the end of the monsoon, it involves eight days of music, dance and drama, as well as the towing of chariots around Kathmandu.

According to local legend, Indra, the God of Rain, was arrested for stealing flowers for his mother in Kathmandu valley. She came down to rescue him, and Indra's jailers, realizing they had a god on their hands, released him and carried Indra and his mother through the streets in celebration. The celebrations continue to this day.

Not that this is all there is to celebrate: also remembered is the 1768 conquest of Kathmandu valley by Prithvi Narayan. Bhairav, that ferocious manifestation of Shiva, also gets a look in — his horrific visage, concealed from view the rest of the year, is displayed on Kathmandu's Durbar square and at Indra Chowk in the old city of Kathmandu.

On the third day of the celebrations, **Kumari Jatra** — the inner core of the bigger festival — begins. Golden temple chariots are assembled outside the home of the Kumari, Kathmandu's living diminutive goddess. Hidden from public view for most of the year, she is carried out accompanied by attendants: two boys in the roles of Bhairav and Ganesh, who will accompany the Kumari in chariots of their own. The Kumari's chariot is greeted from Hanuman Dhoka by the king, and

TOP SPOTS

then the procession makes its way towards the image of Bhairav, from whose mouth beer pours. Men compete for the honor of getting a gulp of the beer, and for the good luck it brings.

The living goddess's chariot continues its course around Kathmandu for the next few days, accompanied wherever it stops by performances of music and dance and costumed drama. The festival culminates with the Kumari anointing the king's forehead with a holy *tika* — that third-eye splash of red — thus confirming his right to rule for another year.

Only in Nepal, you find yourself thinking, does beer flow from the mouth of a demon and a living goddess confirm the right of a king to rule.

Festive crowds are watched over by the all-seeing eyes of the Buddha.

YOUR CHOICE

The Great Outdoors

NEPAL IS TOPOGRAPHICALLY THE MOST DRAMATIC COUNTRY IN THE WORLD. STARTING IN THE LOWLAND TERAI, a mere 60 m (200 ft) above sea level, Nepal climbs all the way to the highest point on earth: the top of Everest (8,848 m or 29,028 ft). With trails crisscrossing the foothills and mountain passes, Nepal is a walker's paradise.

Not that anyone talks about "walking", or even "hiking" in Nepal. Trekking — from Afrikaans — is what outdoors enthusiasts come to Nepal for. A trek may be as short as one day (there are several one-day treks around Kathmandu and Pokhara), but is more likely to last from three or four days to as long as a month.

Before setting out on a trek, there are a couple of local organizations that are worth referring to for up-to-date information. The Himalayan Rescue Association (HRA) has a Trekkers' Information Center in the Hotel Tilicho ((01) 418755, Kathmandu. The Kathmandu Environment Education Project (KEEP) ((01) 410303, is in the Potala Tourist Home, Kathmandu.

The chief drawing card of a trek in Nepal is the incomparable mountain scenery. Where else can you wake in the first light of dawn with the snow-capped peaks of the Himalayas towering overhead? But the wonder of trekking in Nepal is not just the peaks: as you head towards the mountains, you pass through lowland villages, wayside temples, past checkerboard rice paddies. At higher altitudes there are alpine meadows, awash with flowers in the spring, and evergreen forests. Add to this a constant stream of Nepali villagers who share the trails with trekkers, the Sherpa plodding along unflinchingly under heavy loads, the trader urging along a pack of loaded yaks, and you have an irresistible brew.

There are different treks for different folks, each offering its own delights: long and arduous does not necessarily

OPPOSITE: Trekking in Nepal is not just mountain ridges, but also lowland paddy fields, meadows and even eerie moss-covered forests such as this one in the Everest region. ABOVE: Wild flowers bloom in the spring, usually March, in a beautiful profusion of pinks, reds and whites.

mean better. If you've never trekked in the mountains before and are not sure whether you are up to it, try one of the shorter treks, such as the four-day **Royal trek** — so named because Prince Charles and a small party of 90 once walked it — out of Pokhara. An even shorter warm-up exercise is **Baglung** to **Tatopani**, which takes just two days. Slightly more ambitious is the Jhomsum trek, a nine-day walk that reaches a maximum elevation of 3,800 m (12,500 ft) and has good hotels and food all the way.

Of course there's also no shortage of hardship for those who fancy pitting themselves against the elements and testing their mettle. The 18-day trek around **Annapurna** reaches an elevation of 5,400 m (17,700 ft) and involves some hard climbs, but at least offers the compensation of mostly decent places to stay. The 20-day slog to Makalu base camp, on the other hand, has no accommodation en route and has a steep climb up to 5000 m (16,400 ft).

Almost at the other extreme to trekking in the Himalayas is a safari in Nepal's lowland Terai. The most popular safari destination is **Royal Chitwan National Park**, one of the few places in the world where you can see a Bengal tiger in the wild. In all honesty your chances of seeing a tiger are remote, but you will undoubtedly feast your eyes on some of the park's one-horned Indian rhinoceroses, deer, wild boars, sloth bears, monkeys and over 450 species of birds.

Getting around the Royal Chitwan National Park is half the fun. The official mode of transport is by elephant, which is reckoned to be the safest way to view a herd of rhinos. If, after a few hours on the back of an elephant — an exercise that will leave you aching the next day — you've had enough, rest assured that you can also get around the park in a vehicle, in canoes or even on foot.

The Royal Bardia National Park is a more remote and less touristed alternative to Chitwan. And, more importantly, nowhere else in Nepal do you have a better chance of laying your eyes on the elusive Bengal tiger.

Rhinoceroses are present in much smaller number than at Chitwan, but there are a host of other mammals — including the barking deer, blue cow and leopard — present in the park. Like Chitwan, local transport is on the back of an elephant.

Sporting Spree

NEPAL'S SPORTING OPPORTUNITIES ARE ASSOCIATED WITH ITS GREAT OUTDOORS, with its mountains, its crashing rivers and its mountain trails.

MOUNTAIN BIKING
Mountain biking is still in its infancy in Nepal, but it's catching on rapidly. The

Kathmandu valley in particular is crisscrossed by trails and minor roads, many of which wind up to spectacular viewpoints where bikers can rest before enjoying the adrenaline rush of a near free-fall descent.

Unless you're an experienced biker and can manage your own repairs (and have your own spares), it's a good idea to book a mountain-bike tour. **Himalayan Mountain Bikes** ((01) 416596 FAX (01) 411055 E-MAIL info@hmb.wlink.com.np, P.O. Box 2247, Kathmandu, are the experts. They have the bikes, the mechanics, the spares, have researched dozens of routes, and can even provide vehicular backup for the more demanding tours.

Serious mountain bikers can even throw themselves at the Himalayas in a competitive spirit. Himalayan Mountain Bikes and the newly formed Nepal Mountain Bikes Association sponsor the annual Himalayan Mountain-Bike Championships, which is held in March. The 27-km (17-mile) course follows the razor-sharp ridges that ring the Kathmandu valley, a grueling but spectacular and exhilarating run.

For the less experienced, Himalayan Mountain Bikes offers some fabulous introductory rides. A good taster is the

Few places are able to offer such exhilarating white-water rafting as Nepal, where the water runs down from the highest places in the world.

two-day ride from Kathmandu to Nagarkot and Sanku, which takes you past farms and villages, the Narayan forest and provides views of the Himalayas at Nagarkot. The uphill section follows the asphalt road to Nagarkot via Bhaktapur and Thimi. The switchback ascent to Nagarkot at 2,000 m (6,600 ft) is a serious workout. The downhill section plunges 900 m (3000 ft) into the Sali Nadi valley and the village of Sanku on a rutted jeep track. From Sanku a metaled road returns to Kathmandu.

Other popular rides include the four-day 125-km (78-mile) ride from Kathmandu to Dhulikhel and Namobuddha, a tour that takes you into the stunning ravines of the Sun Khosi and its tributaries; and the five-day "Goat Tracks" tour, which as the name suggests is mostly off-road.

WHITE WATER

Nepal is considered by many experts to rate among the best places in the world for kayaking and white-water rafting. And with some highly professional rafting and kayaking agencies operating out of Kathmandu, it's worth taking the plunge and shooting the rapids for a few days.

Among the white-water specialists in Kathmandu, the following are highly recommended: **Ultimate Descents (** (01) 419295 FAX (01) 411933 E-MAIL rivers @ultimate.wlink. com.np, P.O. Box 6720, Northfield Café, Thamel. Other agencies include **Equator Expeditions (** (01) 416596 FAX (01) 411933, P.O. Box 8404, Thamel; **Himalayan Encounters (** (01) 417426 FAX (01) 417133, P.O. Box 2769, Thamel; and **Himalayan River Expeditions (** (01) 420322 FAX (01) 414075, P.O. Box 242, Durbar Marg.

Although it's possible to try rafting or kayaking somewhere in Nepal at any time of the year, the best times are from March to early June and from September to early December. From December to

early March, many of Nepal's rivers are icy cold, requiring wetsuits; from June through September, the monsoon runoff turns the rivers into dangerous, raging torrents.

The most frequently rafted river in Nepal is the **Trisuli river**. Its easy access from the Kathmandu-Pokhara highway, means that many budget operators take tours down the river. If you are short of time or just want to dip your toes into the white-water rafting experience, this is probably where you will end up. The remoter rivers of Nepal offer a very different experience, however.

The **Sun Kosi river**, for example, is not just a collection of rapids but a river journey. Starting up near the Tibetan border, you travel 270 km (167 miles) over a nine- to 10-day period, ending up at Chatara on the Gangetic plain. The rapids on the early days of the trip are light, allowing inexperienced rafters to learn as they go along. The combination of foaming rapids, gorgeous mountain and rural scenery, followed by a quiet evening camped by a river, provides an unforgettable experience.

The **Karnali river** is Nepal's longest. It is also one of the most remote: access involves a flight to Nepalganj, a five-hour bus journey to Surkhet and then a two-day trek to Sauli. From here you experience seven exhilarating days on the river, traveling 180 km (112 miles) through some of the remotest parts of Nepal before finishing at Chisophani, close to the Royal Bardia National Park.

AT THE SAME TIME...

Fitness freaks and thrill seekers who are not content to settle on either rafting or mountain biking have the option of taking a tour that incorporates both. Himalayan Mountain Bikes and Ultimate Descents (see above for contact details) have joined together to make a tour that involves two days of rafting on the Bhoti Khosi river and two days of mostly off-road mountain biking out of Dhulikhel. It's a combination that is guaranteed to cure you of the office blues and get the cricks out of your neck.

Breakfast on the rooftop of one of Pokhara's many inexpensive lodges.

The Open Road

UNLESS YOU BRING YOUR OWN VEHICLE, ONE THING YOU WON'T BE DOING IN NEPAL IS DRIVING. While car-hire is available, self-drive rental is not. This is not as great a loss as you might imagine. Nepal's road network is in a poor state of repair and local driving habits range from aggressive to suicidal — overtaking on blind corners and the crests of hills are both accepted road behavior. The highways are littered with the wrecks of vehicles.

Nepal's road infrastructure is expanding at least. Many of the popular trekking routes now have road access to the trailheads, saving days of walking. Bear in mind, however, that in Nepal "road access" is an elastic concept — a rutted trail on which speeds of 20 kph (12 mph) are a bone-jarring nightmare are not uncommon.

It's an unfortunate fact of life that, despite the incomparable views, the open road in Nepal is usually an uncomfortable, aggravatingly slow and dangerous experience. Some old-hands and tour operators recommend flying, even on such popular road routes as Kathmandu to Pokhara.

Backpacking

NEPAL HAS LONG BEEN A MECCA FOR BACKPACKERS. Back in the heady "flower power" era, the very word Kathmandu was the stuff of dreams, and the city's **"Freak Street"** was a magnet to the lost in space generation. Times change. Freak Street's glory days are long gone and today's "freaks" likely as not have a credit card in their money pouch. But for all that, Nepal remains the perfect destination for a backpacking holiday.

ABOVE: Some of Kathmandu's tourist products may incline towards kitsch, but no one can accuse them of being unimaginative. OPPOSITE: A typical Thamel street scene, where the street signs scream food! exports! trekking! and the touts sidle up hopefully and mutter, "Something?"

After all, Nepal is a great bargain. Keeping costs down doesn't mean scrimping and saving, sleeping in a tent and eating out of cans. There's no need for dormitory-style hostel accommodation either. Hotels and guesthouses, even in Kathmandu, cost as little as US$5 a night for a room with an attached bathroom. And, unless you take one of the less-trodden treks, beds are available in tea houses strategically situated three to four hours walk from each other on most of the popular trekking routes. Many young budget travelers take to the high mountain paths to enjoy some of the most spectacular scenery in the world on less than US$10 per day.

If accommodation charges make backpacking a breeze, so too do meals. The restaurants of Kathmandu and Pokhara have a near legendary status among backpackers on the Asian trail. Pokhara's **Lakeside district** and Kathmandu's **Thamel district** are wall-to-wall with restaurants whose menus read like introductory samplers to the cuisines of the world. Hungry diners frequently find themselves forced to choose between dishes as diverse as chicken korma, Mexican burrito, vegetarian lasagna, sizzling steak, moussaka, Tibetan momos and Chinese stir-fry.

Perhaps the ambitious inclusiveness of these assaults on international cuisine leads to a certain lack of authenticity, but there are few who'll deny that the results are tasty. And cheap... . In most such restaurants it's possible to sit down to an enormous sizzling steak and a bottle of beer and, when you've finished, be presented with a bill for no more than US$4.

This remarkable good value extends into the restaurants that offer genuine quality dining, so that it's perfectly possible to splurge on, say, some of the best Indian cuisine the world can offer and spend only US$15 to US$20. It's near impossible to spend more than US$25 per head on a meal anywhere in Nepal.

Nepal's great asset as a backpacking destination is that it is one of the few places in the world where economizing doesn't mean missing out. With the exception of the Mountain Flight and ballooning, there are almost no activities or sights in Nepal that do not have a budget option. Even the jungle safaris of **Royal Chitwan National Park**, where the well-heeled may spend upwards of US$200 per day on the full safari experience, can be done on a budget of US$20 per day if you stay in the village of Sauraha and organize your own safari — on elephant back, by jeep, by canoe or even on foot.

As for the mountains, independent trekking has long been a popular activity in Nepal. Essentially, you organize your permit and set off into the hills. If you're reasonably fit, the **Annapurna** and **Everest** treks can be done without guides and porters at a cost of US$10 per day for accommodation and food, plus US$5 per week for the permit. The easiest and most popular treks to do independently at these rates are the Everest trek, the Langtang trek, the Helambu trek, the Jhomsum trek, and the Annapurna circuit trek.

One more thing you won't have to resort to in Nepal is hitchhiking. Most budget travelers get around on Nepal's long-haul buses. The driving is erratic, there's never enough legroom and speeds rarely get above a tortured trot, but you do eventually get to your destination. The bus journey from Kathmandu to Pokhara, for example, takes around eight hours and costs US$4. And for the hardy budget traveler the US$60 saved in that eight hours of not flying is equal to six days trekking in the Himalayas.

Living It Up

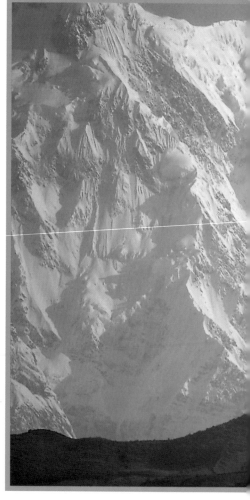

THE KINGDOM OF NEPAL MAY NOT BE MONTE CARLO, BUT IT STILL OFFERS FIVE-STAR HOTELS, WORLD-CLASS DINING, as well as trekking and adventure tour operators who are in a league of their own when it comes to providing for the needs of their guests.

EXCEPTIONAL HOTELS
Nepal's best hotels are all in Kathmandu. They cannot compare in opulence with the top hotels in Bangkok or Delhi, but they put on a good show given their limited resources. See WHERE TO STAY in the section on Kathmandu for information on hotels such as the Hotel Yak and Yeti, the Everest Hotel and the Hotel Shangri-la.

Elsewhere in Nepal, the best hotels are usually mid-range in standard. The new Shangri-la Village in Pokhara is an exception. Pokhara's Fish Tail Lodge is also an excellent hotel by local standards, but its popularity is due more to its splendidly isolated position overlooking the Phewa Lake than anything else.

The Tiger Tops Jungle Lodge may not offer five-star comforts, but there are few places in the world where you can rough it in such style. Built in the style of a traditional Tharu longhouse with traditional wall paintings and locally woven rugs and bedspreads, the lodge is the perfect base from which to set out into the Terai on the back of an elephant.

EXCEPTIONAL RESTAURANTS
When it comes to dining out, the high life in Nepal is something just about any traveler can splurge on — it's very difficult to spend more than US$20 per head on a meal even in Kathmandu's finest restaurants. Indian cuisine is what Nepal does best, and restaurants such as Ghar-e-Kabab in Kathmandu can be compared with the best anywhere. See the Kathmandu part in the WHERE TO EAT section for recommendations of top-notch restaurants in the capital.

NIGHTLIFE

By 10 PM, Kathmandu is mostly tucked in to bed and nodding off to sleep. Elsewhere around the kingdom the day might have ended even earlier.

If it's drinking and carousing you are looking for, your options will be decidedly low key. There are several bars in the Thamel area, the best of them being the New Orleans and the Blue Note — small, intimate places with good jazz offerings. Both of them close at 10 PM.

The only discos are in the international hotels such as the Soaltee Oberoi, Yak and Yeti, and Everest Sheraton hotels.

Kathmandu has four casinos: the Casino Nepal ((01) 270244, Soaltee Oberoi Hotel; Casino Anna ((01) 223479, Hotel de l'Annapurna; Casino Everest ((01) 220567, Everest Hotel; and the Casino Royale ((01) 228481, Yak and Yeti Hotel. The patrons are mostly Indian visitors, who stake small fortunes on the turn of a card at baccarat, chemin de fer, and the turn of the roulette wheel. The chips are valued in Indian rupees or other foreign currencies. The casinos are off-limits to Nepali citizens.

Soaring high over the valleys of Nepal, the Himalaya are never far from view.

Family Fun

THERE'S NO POINT PRETENDING THAT
NEPAL IS THE PERFECT HOLIDAY DESTINATION
FOR THE KIDS. For a start, there's little in
the way of children's amusements in
Nepal; but even more importantly, there
are some health matters to consider.
Be sure that your children have had all
their vaccinations and any additional
immunizations that your doctor
recommends for Nepal. Many diseases
that have been eradicated or are very
rare in developed countries are still
present and a threat to the health of
children in Nepal.

The narrow, crowded streets of the
cities are also a concern. If you have very
small children, a stroller is next to useless
in such conditions. Bring a baby carrier
that straps onto your back or chest. The
risk for bigger children is of getting lost.
Keep a close eye on them, and as an
extra precaution ensure that they carry
a photocopy of their passport with
them at all times.

Now for the good news: Many people
who have traveled with their children in
Nepal come back with glowing reports.
For a start the Nepalis, like all Asians, are
wonderfully tolerant of children, and in
the budget and mid-range hotels they'll
find playing companions in the adult
staff. Most hotels and guesthouses, like
many of the restaurants, have garden
areas, which are perfect for kids to
play in.

There are no theme parks or fun
parks and no beaches to keep children
amused in Nepal, and it's a rare child
who can find as much interest in the
architectural and artistic delights of
the Kathmandu valley as his or her
parents can. What Nepal does have
in abundance, however, is mountains.
Taking one of the easier treks with
good views of the mountainous
skyline can be great fun for kids —
they'll sleep like logs at night.

Trekking companies can provide
advice and make arrangements that will
make a trek with children easier. As a bare
minimum, it is a good idea to hire porters
to carry your luggage and, in the case of
small children, the kids themselves in
case they become tired or sick.

Cultural Kicks

MENTION NEPAL AND MOST PEOPLE THINK
MOUNTAINS. But while it's impossible to
visit Nepal without at least catching a
glimpse of the towering Himalayas,
many visitors are content to admire
these peaks from afar and restrict
their sightseeing to the cultural
attractions of Kathmandu valley.

Early European visitors to
Kathmandu valley came away with
tales of a land in which every second
building was a temple. This is an
exaggeration, of course; but to refer
to the valley as a "treasure trove" —
of art and architecture is to do no
more than state the obvious.

THE ARCHITECTURAL LEGACY
For most of the last millennium the
compact valley of Kathmandu has been
home to three kingdoms: Kathmandu,

Bhaktapur and Patan or, as they were known in the Malla era, Kantipur, Bhadgaon and Lalitpur. The rivalry between the three, no more than a day's march from each other, has bestowed the valley with a remarkable architectural legacy.

To fully appreciate the dizzying scale and painstaking details of the Durbar squares of Kathmandu, Bhaktapur and Patan, you will have to spend at least a day in each. The design of the Newar palaces is based on the same principles as Newar home design, the thick mud walls enclosing a central courtyard. But in the case of the palaces, the architectural design pales in comparison with the carvings that decorate them.

Scattered through the streets and squares of the Newar cities are a multitude of Hindu pagoda temples, and it is arguably here that local artistic expression is at its most eloquent. The pagoda, like the mandala, is a three-dimensional representation of the universe and, like the crowded mandala thangkas you see for sale in around the squares, the surfaces of the pagoda are a mass of carved detail of deities and demons, sometimes erotica. See the **Nyatapola pagoda** in Bhaktapur, one of the valley's few five-storied pagodas (most are three-storied), for the happy convergence of all that is best in Newar architectural design.

MUSEUMS

It is frequently remarked that Kathmandu valley is one big museum. There's no denying this. You might easily spend months scouring the streets of Kathmandu alone and still come up with fascinating daily discoveries: a roadside shrine, a particularly beautifully carved window frame.

Items that have been collected into museums tend to be moveable art pieces that might otherwise be sold or stolen. The National Museum ((01) 271504, Chhauni, for example, has a fascinating collection of religious art, including sculptures, wood carvings and best of all an impressive display of metalwork —

most of it Buddhist in inspiration and created by Patan artisans in the fourteenth century. Look for the life-sized Lokeshvara mandala.

The National Art Gallery ((01) 610004, Durbar square, Bhaktapur, is another essential stop for anyone interested in Nepal's cultural legacy. Displayed inside is a collection of Buddhist thangkas, sculptures and murals from Bhaktapur's Palace of 55 Windows. Bhaktapur also has the National Woodcarving Museum and the Bronze and Brass Museum.

PERFORMANCES

The best cultural performances are held in Kathmandu, where all the major hotels provide cultural entertainment of one kind or another in the evenings. It is also worth checking the noticeboards in Thamel for announcements of performances. Some of the better restaurants in Thamel have live traditional music.

OPPOSITE: Garuda perches on high, hands in prayer. ABOVE: A holy man pores over religious texts in a quiet corner. OVERLEAF: King Yoganendra Malla presides serenely over Patan's Durbar square.

The Everest Cultural Society performs folk dances daily from 7 PM at the Hotel de l'Annapurna. The New Himalchuli Cultural Group stages classical and folk dances together with songs and music at the Hotel Shankar's Cultural Hall daily from 6:30 to 7:30 PM (November to February), and 7 to 8 PM (March to October).

Less touristy performances are held at the Hotel Vajra ((01) 272719, P.O. Box 1084, Bijeswori, Kathmandu. You will need to check for times. Performances vary from folk dances to modern productions, but a trip out to this hotel near Swayambhunath temple is always worth the effort.

Try the Ghar-e-Kabab restaurant, Annapurna Hotel, Durbar Marg, for the best in Indian classical music.

Shop Till You Drop

NEPAL IS NOT HONG KONG OR SINGAPORE — BUSTLING, MODERN PARADIGMS OF THE ASIAN SUCCESS STORY — where tourists depart reeling under the weight of the latest consumer electronics. Rather, the Nepal traveler leaves with bags straining from unexpected purchases of Nepali, Indian and Tibetan arts and crafts.

It's difficult to imagine anywhere in the world in which so many fascinating artistic traditions converge in such

tempting profusion. In Kathmandu and Pokhara, entire days can be frittered away browsing through mandalas, textiles, Tibetan carpets, handmade paper, terracotta pottery and ritual artifacts from Tibet and the high mountain valleys of the Himalayas.

There is such a dazzling array of fascinating bric-a-brac, fabrics and clothes that it is easy to rush into purchases. The sensible shopper spends some time exploring Kathmandu, checking prices and comparing quality. Beware: antiques may be no more than a few days old; and anything older than 100 years cannot be taken out of the country.

BARGAINING

For many visitors prices seem so reasonable in Nepal that it seems difficult to believe that prices might be cheaper still with a little bargaining — in some cases the "real" price may be as little as half the asking price.

It takes time to learn successful bargaining, but for starters if you're interested in something (never ask the price or begin to bargain for something you don't want to buy) try a smile and a counter-offer somewhere between a third and a half of the price quoted. If you remain relaxed and lighthearted about the negotiation, you'll probably find that a couple more offers and counter-offers will result in a price that is significantly cheaper than you might have paid.

TIBETAN CARPETS

The Tibetan refugee carpet industry sprang into existence in 1961, when a Swiss foreign aid program started carpet production at the Tibetan refugee camp of Jawalkhel in Patan. Today, Tibetan carpets are Nepal's biggest industry, accounting for around half of the country's foreign exchange. Jawalkhel is still a good place to buy carpets. And not only can you buy the carpets here, you can also watch them being made.

Tibetan carpets are designed to be sat upon, slept upon, but never walked upon: if they seem small, this is the reason. The weave is far less fine than Persian carpets, usually around 40 to 60 knots per square inch (a good Persian carpet may have many times more). The experienced buyer notes the weave, but even more important is the intensity and harmony of the colors. The dyes used are mostly chemical, and have been ever since chemical dyes were first introduced into Tibet in the nineteenth century.

If you want to take a look at some genuinely valuable Tibetan carpets before heading out to see new ones being produced in Jawalkhel, a visit to the **Karma Lama Ritual Gallery** ((01) 226409, Durbar Marg, is recommended.

ART

Almost all Nepali and Tibetan art is religious. *Thangka* is a Tibetan word signifying an illuminated Buddhist scroll

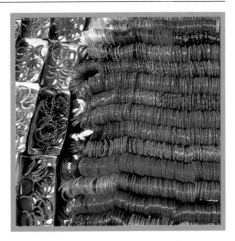

mounted on silk. Every multitudinous detail in such paintings is symbolic — a Bodhisattva might be pictured seated in the center of a geometric *mandala*, concentration on which is used as a meditation aid. When judging prices, take a close look at the quality of execution of the detail and at the quantity of gold leaf, which is used as a highlight in good quality thangka. You will see them for sale in shops all over Kathmandu, and in areas with large numbers of Tibetans.

At one time the metalwork of Nepalese artisans was among the best in the world. Figurines and statues depicting Hindu and Buddhist deities were — and still are — created by the lost-wax method, whereby an image is modeled in wax, coated in clay and then baked to melt away the wax leaving a clay mold into which molten metal may be poured. You can see this process and shop for metalwork at the **Patan Industrial Estate** in Patan.

MODERN ART

Nepal is so steeped in history, that many visitors do not realize that a new breed of

No place in Asia sports a more tempting profusion of traditional souvenirs than Nepal. OPPOSITE: Metalwork masks glitter on the sidewalk (left) while a shop just off Kathmandu's Durbar square (right) displays its colorful wares. LEFT: Tibetan carpets are hung out to tempt passersby on a Kathmandu sidestreet. Bangles ABOVE much beloved by Nepali women, sparkle and dazzle.

young artists are at work, looking for ways to express the modern Nepali experience. The **Indigo Gallery** ((01) 424303, Naxal, is in the same building as Mike's Breakfast, providing a good opportunity to enjoy a splendid meal in soothing surroundings while taking a look at the latest exhibition. The **October Gallery** ((01) 271545, Swayambhu, is another space that exhibits the work of contemporary Nepali artists.

CLOTHES

It's difficult to resist Nepal's silk-embroidered T-shirts. Designs range from unique and fetching to plain off-the-wall, but there is something for nearly everyone. You can have your clothes custom embroidered if you like — at bargain prices.

Elsewhere, clothes in Nepal are a mixed bag. Much of the clothing on sale in Thamel is poor quality and likely to be considered eccentric outside Nepal: conservative dressers are unlikely to find much they like. Items such as the inexpensive cotton drawstring trousers and skirts are fine for in and around Kathmandu, but you are unlikely to wear them out when you get home. The sweaters widely on sale around Thamel look great, but they rarely make it through a winter without starting to fall apart. The claims by shopkeepers that the sweaters are made of yak wool are simply a sales pitch.

Local clothing can make good souvenirs. Saris and lungi are widely available. Look, too, for *topi*, the jaunty caps that are as essential an adjunct to Nepalese formal wear as the tie is to ours.

For local clothing that is a cut above the average, look for **Durga Design** ((01) 610048, Thamel, across from the Potala Guesthouse.

JEWELRY

Traditionally the women of Nepal and Tibet display their wealth in their jewelry. Family savings in many poor villages may go into women's jewelry, which becomes an heirloom passed down through the generations. Such

jewelry — differing in design from village to village — is almost impossible to buy; but the importance of such traditions has bestowed Nepal with fine gold and silver smiths who produce some superb ready-made jewelry and who can also produce high-quality work according to your own design.

For Tibetan jewelry, Bodhnath is the best area to look, though you will see the characteristic silver and turquoise colors of Tibetan jewelry all through the Kathmandu and Pokhara valleys. Patan is commonly agreed to have the best gold and silver smiths.

MISCELLANEOUS CRAFTS

Nepali woodcarving belongs to a long and noble tradition. A few moments gazing at the wood carvings on the struts of temple roofs, the frames of windows in the Durbar squares of Kathmandu, Patan or Bhaktapur is enough to make you realize that the Newar artisans who produced them were in a league of their own.

Nowadays you can buy miniatures of such work — no match for the originals they are modeled on perhaps, but still a popular souvenir. The best place to shop for wood carvings in Bhaktapur, particularly in Dattatreya Square, where you will also find the **National Woodcarving Museum.**

In Kathmandu's Durbar square and in tourist areas such as Thamel, itinerant peddlers carrying "flute trees" are a common sight. For those who seek a greater musical challenge, the *saranghi* is a bowed fiddle-like instrument.

Puppets and masks make good gifts for adults and children alike. Thimi is a particularly good place to look for papier maché masks. The masks are usually depictions of Ganesh, Kumari or Bhairav, and are used in festive masked dances. When buying puppets, check that the heads are made of papier maché rather than clay — the latter are liable to break in transit. Bhaktapur is a good hunting ground for puppets, particularly the woodcarving shops of Durbar square. Bhaktapur is also the place to seek out block-printed handmade paper — perfect for wrapping an unusual gift.

BOOKS

Few travelers go to Nepal expecting to buy books; few leave without an armful of them. If you have interest is in Oriental religions, in the Indian Sub-Continent, in Tibet, or if you simply wish to find some literature with a local setting, the bookshops of Kathmandu are among the best-stocked in the world. Thamel shops are the place for second-hand books — some of them fabulously well stocked with titles in English (mostly), French, German, Dutch, Swedish and Japanese.

For some of the best browsing in town, go to Pilgrim's ((01) 231040, Thamel, next door to the Kathmandu Guesthouse. It's a warren of heaving bookshelves — the kind of shop you pop into for five minutes and emerge two hours later with half-a-dozen books you simply had to buy.

Short Breaks

Most of Nepal's best attractions are within easy striking distance of Kathmandu. With little time needed to get around, you can pack a lot into a short stay in Nepal.

Kathmandu makes a perfect base. You might spend two or three days exploring the city's attractions, wandering the maze-like alleys of the old city, marveling at the temples and palaces of Durbar square and striking out to the nearby Buddhist stupas of Swayambhunath and Bodhnath. Just as simple is to spend the mornings in Kathmandu and the afternoons in the ancient Buddhist city of **Patan**, half an hour distant by taxi, or in the predominantly Hindu city of **Bhaktapur**, about one hour away, where city and international efforts have

OPPOSITE: A typical rickety suspension bridge on an Everest region trek. Watch out for yaks coming the other way! ABOVE: Gokyo Peak in the Everest region, with views of the lake and glacier of the same name.

achieved a time-warping preservation job on the local architecture.

An excursion out of Kathmandu you will never forget involves an overnight stay at either **Nagarkot** or **Dhulikhel**. Both towns are on ridges that offer panoramic views of the Himalayas. Nagarkot has the best views, but Dhulikhel has better access and is quicker to get to (around two hours by bus). You can arrive in the late afternoon, check into one of the many hotels or guesthouses — there's something to suit all budgets and tastes — and then settle down somewhere comfortable — perhaps the verandah of your hotel room or the rooftop of your guesthouse — to watch shifting colors play over the Himalayas as the sun goes down. The next morning you should be up early to watch a repeat performance (though no two are ever the same) in the light of the rising sun.

A short holiday in Nepal would seem to make a trek out of the question. But this is not entirely true. There are some magical day-walks you can do that serve as the perfect trekking sampler, leaving you fulfilled but hankering for the day you can come back and do something longer.

One of the best day-walks in Kathmandu is the **Namobuddha trek** out of Dhulikhel (see above). The beauty of this six-hour circuit hike is not only that it provides stunning views of the Himalayas, but that it takes you through villages with tea houses, through pine forests, to a stupa, and past water mills just as the longer treks do.

If wildlife is your main interest, even a safari on elephant back at **Royal Chitwan National Park** need not be out of the question on a short trip. Chitwan is just five hours away from Kathmandu by taxi or bus; providing you arrive in Kathmandu by mid-afternoon, you can be in Chitwan Park by the evening, ready to mount your elephant the next morning. And if time is of the essence, don't worry: two days on the back of an elephant is more than enough for most people.

YOUR CHOICE

Festive Flings

HARDLY A WEEK PASSES IN NEPAL WITHOUT A FESTIVAL. They fall into three categories: Hindu or Buddhist festivals; historical festivals commemorating the royal family or an epic event from the past (perhaps the mythological past); and seasonal festivals, where offerings are made for good harvests.

Most festivals are local affairs, but there are some large national ones too. All dates are based on Nepal's lunar calendar, and are approximate only.

SPRING
One of the earliest spring festivals is **Ghode Jatra,** which is held in Tundikhel, Kathmandu in March. Held to appease Demon Gurumapa, the King of Nepal is the chief guest. The principal attractions are horse races, acrobatic shows, and a procession of chariots of the goddesses.

Ramavami (March to April) commemorates the epic victory of Rama, hero of the Ramayana, over his arch-rival Ravana. Elephants, ox-carts and horses

OPPOSITE: A Vishnu statue in Bhaktapur glistens with oil and pollen anointed by passing worshippers. ABOVE: All Kathmandu valley turns out to join the eight-day Indra Jatra Festival, the annual celebration of the monsoon rains and the conquest of the area by the ruling dynasty in the eighteenth century. OVERLEAF: Flour fills the air as Buddhist monks at Kathmandu valley's famed Bodhnath stupa celebrate yet another religious festival.

lead thousands of devotees through Janakpur in a milling throng. Other Ramavami celebrations are held in Kathmandu and elsewhere for those unable to travel to Janakpur.

Chaitra Dasain (March) is one of Kathmandu's most colorful festivals. It is often referred to as "little Dasain," a reference to Dasain in October, the greatest celebration of the year. The towering chariot of White Matsyendranath is pulled through the city for three days, and sacrifices are offered to Durga, Shiva's consort, in one of her most terrifying aspects.

Nepali New Year falls in March or April and is celebrated most enthusiastically in Bhaktapur, where it's known as **Bisket Jatra.**

The highlight of the festival is the parade of chariots: one houses Bhairav; the other the goddess Bhadrakali. The chariots lumber through the streets, pause for a tug of war between the east and west parts of town, before descending to a field beside the river, where a 25-m (82-ft) wooden lingam is erected and then sent crashing down. The New Year officially begins with the fall of the lingam. The pennants that flutter

from the top of the lingam represent two snakes that were vanquished from a princess of Bhaktapur by a visiting prince who was a manifestation of Bhairav.

The next day, in nearby Thimi, is **Bal Kumari Jatra**, a festival where teams of men from all over Thimi and surrounding districts carry palanquins — known as *khat* — with neighborhood deities on board. Proceedings reach fever pitch with the arrival of a khat bearing Ganesh.

The **Rato Matsyendranath Jatra** festival is held in the first month of the

New Year (April to May), but the actual date is decided on the basis of propitious signs by Hindu priests. Matsyendranath is patron of the rains, and with the monsoon imminent he is drawn through every neighborhood of Patan, on a meandering route that may take a month or more to complete.

Buddha Jayanti celebrates the birth of Buddha with an all night vigil of butter lamps and electric lights in late April or early May at the Swayambhunath stupa in Kathmandu valley.

Overshadowing hundreds of smaller images, a massive gilded figure of Buddha is carried in a colorful procession down the many steps to a cloister where religious rites continue throughout the day before the Buddha is returned to its hilltop shrine.

At the Bodhnath stupa, on the other side of the valley, an image of Buddha is mounted on the back of an elephant and paraded around the dome. Ribbons of colorful flags stretch from the gilt-copper pyramid that surmounts the stupa, as the monks below blow their long copper horns. In the crescendo of the climax everyone hurls fistfuls of ground wheat into the air.

The centerpiece of the festivities is the large portrait of the Dalai Lama held head high and shielded under a large canopy.

SUMMER
Gunla (July to August) is a month-long celebration marked by massive pilgrimages to the Buddhist shrine at Swayambhunath.

Snakes and snake gods — *naga* — are associated with the monsoon rains. At **Nagpanchami,** which usually falls in July, Hindus paste pictures of naga on their front doors and make offerings of milk and boiled rice.

Ghantakama, held in Kathmandu in July, is one of the most riotous Newar celebrations. It celebrates the slaying of Ghantakama, a demon whose name means "bell ears," a reference to the bells he wore on his ears to drown out the name of Vishnu. On the last day

OPPOSITE: Folk dance (top) of a remote Tamang community in Langtang valley's remote Gharku village. A flower seller (bottom) parades his blooms through the streets of ancient Patan during the annual Matsyendranath Jatra festival. ABOVE: Carved stone image of Ganesh (left), the elephant-head god, Kathmandu. Stone carving (right) of Shiva in his incarnation as Bhairav.

before the new moon, worshippers place tripods of fresh reed stalks at crossroads and indulge in cheerful obscenities. At twilight, amid much good humored banter and jostling, an effigy of the demon, is symbolically drowned and evil is banished.

Janai Purnima is the full moon Hindu celebration of the renewal of the sacred thread — *janai* — worn looped over the shoulders of high-caste Brahmins.

as they walk around the city. In Bhaktapur, celebrations are rowdier, with singing, stamping, joking, shouting and much drinking.

Krishna Jantra, in August, celebrates the birth of Krishna, a manifestation of Vishnu in the aspect of Love. Processions bear pictures detailing Krishna's exploits and at night women gather at the Krishna temple in Patan to sing praise.

Celebrations center around the Khumbheshwar temple in Patan. Pilgrims mark the occasion by making a pilgrimage to Gosainkund, the sacred lake at the head of Trisuli valley, 4,300 m (14,100 ft) above sea level, and which is said to have a subterranean connection with the lake at Khumbheshwar temple.

Gai Jatra, which falls in July, is Kathmandu valley's "cow festival." Cows, it is believed by Hindus, lead the way into the other world after death. This festival is held in memory of those who have died in the past year. Cows, cow effigies and children dressed as cows are paraded through the streets. It is also a day for merry-making and fancy dress — in Patan the crowds impersonate cows, holy men, *sadhus*, or madmen

AUTUMN

A favorite with photographers, **Teej Brata**, which falls in August or September, is the colorful Festival of Women. Hundreds of thousands of Nepali women, all dressed in striking dresses of various hues of red, gather on the banks of the Bagmati at Pashupatinah.

Married women wear their scarlet and gold wedding saris, and the unmarried sing and dance in their brightest clothes to pray to Shiva and his consort Parvati for a long and happy marriage. They bathe in the Bagmati in honor of their husbands or husbands-to-be. Throughout Kathmandu valley, there is feasting on the first day and fasting on the second and third.

September in Kathmandu is the time for one of the year's most important festivals: **Indra Jatra** is eight days of noise and color, celebrating the release of Indra, the King of Gods, who, disguised as an ordinary mortal, was arrested for stealing flowers in Kathmandu. When his mother came down to earth to find him, the people, overcome with remorse, fell down before them and then carried them in triumph through the streets in a week-long festival.

Before the event starts, King Birendra consults the Bal Kumari for assurance that all augurs well. The Kumari anoints the King on the forehead with the Hindu's sacred red mark, the *tika*, and he presses his forehead on her feet. Then, watched by foreign and Nepali dignitaries, the Kumari is carried from her temple to a large chariot, for her feet must not touch the ground.

King Birendra and his queen watch from the balcony of their Durbar square palace as the Kumari's chariot, accompanied by images of Ganesh and Bhairav, is drawn through the square and the streets of Kathmandu. Sheep or goats are laid in the path of the juggernaut's wheels, sacrifices to save those who may stumble or fall before the giant vehicle.

Ashwin, which falls in September or October, is the Ganesh Festival, held in honor of the pot-bellied elephant god without whose blessings no journey or religious ceremony, be it private or public, is ever begun. Nepalis believe that even Surya, the Sun God, offers puja to Ganesh before he journeys across the heavens.

October is the month of the biggest of Nepal's national festivals: **Dasain**. Starting at the new moon and lasting for 10 days, this is a time for family and home, a time for gifts and feasts. The "nine nights" — *navaratri* — of Dasain are marked by masked dances, and on the eighth night, the "black night," sacrifices are performed by all who can afford one — preferably on a black goat. Another Dasain activity is the erection of swings and primitive ferris wheels at entrances to villages around the country.

November sees the arrival of India's biggest Hindu festival, **Tihar Dipawali**, known in English as the Festival of Lights. In Nepal Tihar is second only to Dasain. The five days of rituals held in honor of Yama, the God of Death, are probably the most splendid of Nepal's national festivals. On the third day — **Lakshmi Puja** — Kathmandu valley fills with spluttering oil lamps, which are lit to welcome Lakshmi, the Goddess of

Wealth. The fifth and final day is Bhai Tika, when sisters offer gifts to their brothers along with the blessing: "I plant a thorn at the door of death; may my brother be immortal."

WINTER
Bibaha Panchami, which falls in November or December, is a week-long festival held in Janakpur commemorating Rama and Sita's wedding. On the first day, everybody joins the great procession from Rama's

Clad in rich scarlets, reds and golds, women OPPOSITE purify themselves in the waters of a sacred river at Kathmandu's Pashupatinah temple during the Teej festival in a ritual of bathing and ABOVE feasting as they pray for the continuing love and devotion of their husbands.

temple. Rama's idol, dressed as a bridegroom, is placed in a gaily-decorated sedan chair that rides on the back of an elephant — just as elegantly bedecked in brocades and silks — and led to Sita's temple, Naulakha Mandir. Next day, Sita's idol is carried with great fanfare to the side of Rama in a symbolic re-enactment of their marriage.

Maghesnan is a Hindu purification ceremony in which thousands swarm along the banks of the Bagmati river in Kathmandu and elsewhere at the full moon of the 10th month of the Nepali year (January to February).

The new moon in February is Tibetan New Year, or **Losar**. Like Dasain for the Nepalis, Losar for the Tibetans is a family celebration. Go to Bodhnath temple just outside Kathmandu to see lamas parading around the stupa bearing portraits of the Dalai Lama.

The beginning of spring in January or February is marked by **Sri Panchami**, also known as Basant Panchami. Celebrations begin on the fifth day of the new moon during the 10th month of the Nepali year, honoring Saraswati, Brahma's consort and the Goddess of Learning, and Manjushri, legendary Buddhist patriarch of Kathmandu valley, regarded as the God of Learning. It is a festival with special significance for students and scholars. At Kathmandu's Hanuman Dhoka palace, the King is anointed with a tika and slices of coconut while a 31-gun salute is fired and poems and songs are performed in honor of spring.

Temples are decorated with flowers, and schoolchildren parade in the streets, carrying their text and exercise books for blessing by Saraswati. The next day new primary students start their lessons. Older students go to Swayambhunath or Chabahil to ask Saraswati for success in their examinations.

One of the year's most bizarre festivals is **Maha Shivatri**, held in February or March and honoring the birth of Shiva. Hindu devotees make their way from all over Nepal to Pashupatinah temple, but the main attraction (for foreign witnesses) is the huge numbers of Indian sadhus

who have covered vast distances on foot to reach the temple.

Also known as the Festival of Colors, **Holi–Phagu**, which falls in March, heralds the coming of the monsoon with a nationwide water festival. The colors are powdered dyes added to buckets of water everybody hurls at each other. If you're out and about this day, be sure to wear the sort of clothes you don't mind getting stained with a kaleidoscope of colors.

Galloping Gourmets

OUTSIDE KATHMANDU AND POKHARA, THERE IS LITTLE SUSTENANCE FOR GOURMETS. The basic fare is dhal bhat, and on some of the tea house treks this is the only food available. *Dhal bhat* is as humble a dish as you can imagine — lentils and rice. How good it tastes depends on what it is flavored with — some spicy fried vegetables if you are lucky. If you are on an overnight or day trip from Kathmandu, you can at least bring the makings of a picnic.

The Nepali diet is largely vegetarian, though for most Nepalis this is by economic necessity rather than choice. As cows are sacred, beef is not eaten; water buffalo is the popular alternative. Nowadays, in the international restaurants of Kathmandu, frozen steaks are flown in from India and farther afield.

Tibetan cuisine has had an influence on Nepal, and in some trekking regions the diet is distinctly Tibetan. As anyone who has traveled extensively in Tibet will tell you, this is not the most fortunate of influences. The Tibetan diet is bland: *thukpa*, is a vegetable noodle soup; while *momos* are small meat-filled dumplings, fried or steamed. Together they encompass the extremes of a modest cuisine. Tibetan yak-butter tea is only for the brave or foolhardy.

Momos are not, perhaps, a great contribution to international cuisine, but on a cold night a steaming bowl of them are a treat.

Without a doubt the best that Nepal has to offer it owes to its vast southern neighbor: India. The top Indian restaurants in Kathmandu rate with the best anywhere in the world. If you are not familiar with Indian cuisine or have only eaten take-outs, you should treat yourself to a modest splurge in one of the Indian restaurants while you are in Kathmandu.

DRINKS
Soft drinks and mineral water are widely available. Always drink bottled or boiled water. Tea, *chiyaa*, is served sweet and milky, and is safe to drink. You should try Indian yogurt, *lassi*, either salted or sweet.

Nepal doesn't produce its own wines. *Chhang* is the Tibetan equivalent of beer, and is made from fermented barley, maize, rye, or millet. *Arak* (potato alcohol), and *rakshi* (wheat or rice alcohol), also have their adherents. The local brewers also produce strong spirits — whisky, rum, and gin.

Nepal's Star and Golden Eagle lager beers are excellent. Imported beers, spirits, and wines are available in most major tourist centers — at a price.

HEALTH
Few travelers make it through a Nepal trip without getting some kind of gastrointestinal upset. For most people this is simply a minor inconvenience, slowing them down for a day or two. But it still pays to be careful.

The number one health rule is never to drink water that has not been boiled and filtered. This is especially true during the wet season, when water supplies frequently become contaminated. Uncooked food such as sandwiches and especially salads are also risky. In Kathmandu, many restaurants claim their salads are washed in water treated with iodine solution; if true, such salads are probably safe. Salads washed in untreated water are most definitely not safe.

The meringue pies and cheesecakes of Thamel should be avoided. Chocolate cakes are safe.

Special Interests

BIRDWATCHING
KATHMANDU IS JUST FIVE HOURS BY BUS OR TAXI FROM ROYAL CHITWAN NATIONAL PARK, which is a birdwatcher's paradise: with over 450 species of birds, there are few destinations in the world that compare. In the more remote Royal Bardia National Park, some 250 species of birds have been counted.

It's unlikely that you will be able to find guides with a particular expertise in birdwatching, but you can at least try to track down a copy of the indispensable *Birds of Nepal* by R.L. Fleming *et al* (Kathmandu: Avalok 1979). A good alternative is the *Collins Handguide to the Birds of the Indian Sub-Continent* by Martin Woodcock (Collins 1990).

TREKKING PEAKS

Most people, when they think of mountaineering, think of huge, lavishly funded caravans snaking their way through the foothills of the Himalayas to a base camp, from where a meticulously planned assault of the mountain is undertaken. While expeditions of this type are still common, not all climbing in Nepal is done on such a massive scale.

In 1978 the Nepal Mountaineering Association (NMA) opened 18 peaks, ranging from 5,500 m (18,040 ft) to 6,584 m (21,596 ft), to trekkers. These so-called "trekking peaks" provide an opportunity to avid climbers — who lack the resources to undertake a major expedition — to tackle a Himalayan mountain.

Application procedures are straightforward and involve a fee of US$200 for peaks under 6,100 m (20,000 ft), US$300 for those over. You are required, however, to have a liaison in Kathmandu, and for most trekkers this means a trekking company. See TRAVELERS' TIPS , TRAVEL AGENCIES for some reliable trekking companies in Kathmandu. Look, too, for the highly recommended *Trekking Peaks of Nepal* by Bill O'Connor (England: Crowood Press 1989).

SPIRITUAL MATTERS

Yoga and Buddhist (the Tibetan variety) meditation are alternatives to trekking and white-water rafting for some Nepal travelers. In addition to the recommendations here, the noticeboards of Thamel in Kathmandu are rarely short of inspirational advertisements aimed at the spiritually inclined.

For meditation, the main center catering to Westerners is **Kopan monastery** ((01) 226717, P.O. Box 817,

---

OPPOSITE: Drifting in search of wildlife in the Royal Chitwan National Park. ABOVE: Annapurna rears its head above the clouds.

Bodha, near Bodhnath temple. Short courses are available year-round, but month-long courses are available on a periodic basis, and attract students from around the world. Prices for the month course, with full board in the monastery, are very reasonable.

Affiliated with Kopan monastery is the **Himalayan Yogic Institute and Buddhist Meditation Center** ((01) 413094 FAX (01) 410992, which also has short courses on Buddhism and meditation.

Yoga Studio ((01) 417900, P.O. Box 5098, Kathmandu, is a popular school for would-be yogis.

LANGUAGE COURSES

Nepali may not be one of the most widely spoken languages in the world, but those who take the time to learn some — and in comparison to other Asian languages it is not particularly difficult — find that trekking and touring rural Nepal become an altogether more enjoyable experience. It's surprising how quickly a repertoire of useful phrases can be learned.

Two schools in Kathmandu that provide classes and individual lessons are the **School of International Languages** ((01) 211713, and **Insight Nepal** ((01) 418963.

Taking a Tour

NEPAL TOURS USUALLY MEAN TREKKING AND/OR SAFARI TOURS. If you are planning to be in Nepal for a short period and want to restrict your sightseeing to the cultural attractions of Kathmandu valley, you will probably find it easier to book accommodation from home and then sign up for tours of the valley when you arrive.

Tours of the Kathmandu valley are reasonably priced, and you have the option of either joining a group of other tourists in a minibus or of hiring your own driver and guide. Naturally, it is cheaper to join a group tour — around US$5 per half day — than have a personal tour — between US$20 to US$30 per half day.

For group tours, Gray Line ((01) 412899, is the best bet. Their tours take in a large number of destinations around the valley, including Bhaktapur, Patan, Swayambhunath, Bodhnath and Pashupatinah, among others. For personalized tours with a driver and guide of your own, Natraj Tours and Travel ((01) 220001, Durbar Marg, and Adventure Travel Nepal ((01) 223328, Durbar Marg, are the two best options.

Adventure tours that involve trekking, mountain biking and white-water rafting can be booked either in Nepal or at home. If your time is limited, it is best to organize the tour at home. For information on white-water rafting and mountain biking, see the SPORTING SPREE, page 28. For information on local trekking companies, see the TRAVELERS' TIPS, TRAVEL AGENCIES.

Australian travelers can book adventure tours of Nepal from the following agencies: Peregrine Adventures ((03) 9663 8611 FAX (03) 9663 8618, 258 Lonsdale Street, Melbourne, Victoria 3000; and World Expeditions ((02) 9264 3366, 3rd Floor, 441 Kent Street, Sydney, New South Wales 2000.

UK travelers can book adventure tours of Nepal at: Encounter Overland Expeditions ((0171) 370 6845 FAX (0171) 244 9737, 267 Old Brompton Road, London SW5 9JA ; and Exodus Expeditions ((0181) 673 0859, 9 Weir Road, London, SW12 OLT.

Travelers from the USA can book adventure tours of Nepal at: Adventure Center TOLL-FREE (800) 227 8747 FAX (510) 654 4200, 1311 63rd Street, Suite 200, Emeryville, CA 94608; and Himalayan Travel TOLL-FREE (800) 225 2380 FAX (203) 622 0084, 112 Prospect Street, Stamford, CT 06901.

A lowland scene in the Annapurna region, where wooded hills give way to snow-dusted peaks.

Vertical
Perspec-
tives

IMAGINE a land where the only sound is the wind flowing through the mountain passes far above, a river crashing through a canyon far below, a rice mill clicking rhythmically on a verdant hillside, goats or roosters calling from the next valley. Imagine a panorama of green steep hills rising to rolling crests of glissading stone, soaring peaks of sheer white ice towering overhead: These peaks are the Himalayas, the Roof of the World; the land at their feet is Nepal.

From the medieval push and shove of Kathmandu to the precipitous trails that link far-flung villages, from the lowland forests of the Terai to the wind-swept vistas of the high Himalayas, from the Hindi-speaking people of the plains to the proud and kindly Sherpas and Tibetans of the mountain passes, Nepal is fascinating, complex, compelling and un-forgettable. Not many people visit Nepal just once: to go to Nepal is to promise to return.

How could it be otherwise? Nepal casts a spell on those who journey there. The peaks seem to leap skywards. Flowers bloom in dazzling profusion, littering the terracotta earth in a kaleidoscope of color. Elsewhere are dappled forest greenery and verdant paddies, granite gray cliffs and glacial ice. Meanwhile the carved façades, gilded temples and sparring roof-tops of Kathmandu conjure up visions of centuries past.

Indeed, there are times when the entire Nepal experience seems to belong to a forgotten time — hardly surprising when you consider that until the 1950s the country was the "hermit kingdom." Today, amenities we take for granted elsewhere — roads, vehicles, telephones, television — are in short supply in Nepal. But then some might say that the most magnificent mountain scenery in the world is best appreciated in the absence of such things.

It is the mountains that draw most travelers to Nepal. Eight of the world's ten highest peaks, all of them above 8,000 m (26,250 ft), can be found in Nepal. Not that the country is particularly big — somewhat larger than the state of Florida, or England and Wales combined. But

wedged between the world's two most populous countries, India and China, this small area of 141,414 sq km (53,737 sq miles) packs in more cultural and topographical contrasts than countries many times its size.

Nepal's sub-tropical location and stag-gering altitude range — from 60 to 8,848 m (200 to 29,028 ft) above sea level — provide conditions under which most types of vegetation can grow, producing a wondrous variety of mammals, birds, rep-tiles, insects and plants. And although

population growth and increasing compe-tition for scarce natural resources has ex-terminated many species and reduced others, for those who are prepared to take to the hills on foot, Nepal can still call to mind the Shangri-La of *Lost Horizons*, a place so exotic, so serene and so far away that its very existence comes as a surprise.

PREVIOUS PAGES: Prayer flags (left) flutter in the breeze in the Everest region. Holy man (right) on a high mountain pass. OPPOSITE: The divine fishtail peaks of Nepal's most sacred mountain, Machhapuchhare, which rises 6,993 m (22,940 ft) northwest of Pokhara. ABOVE: An ice-melt stream in the Langtang region.

The
Country
and its
People

THE HIMALAYAS, which curve like a scimitar more than 3,000 km (1,860 miles) across the subcontinent from northern Pakistan in the west to Burma in the east, form the backbone of Nepal. The average elevation of northern Nepal is well above 6,000 m (19,686 ft), yet all this was once a sea. The peak of Everest, Sagarmatha (goddess of the universe), at 8,848 m (29,028 ft), is composed of marine rock from the Cretaceous age. Eighty to 60 million years ago, it formed the bed of the Tethys Sea, separating Asia and India. Then, at the end of the Mesozoic era, the Asian continent collided with the island of India. The tremendous pressure forced up the bed of the Tethys Sea, forming the Tibetan Marginal range on the Nepal-Tibet border.

Later, in the Miocene era, some 10 to 15 million years ago, the movement of the earth's tectonic plates again forced the Indian subcontinent against Asia, folding the Himalayas into existence. These peaks formed buttresses against moist sea winds approaching from oceans to the south, causing increased precipitation on their steep southern slopes. Torrential rivers came into being, cutting through the mountains almost as quickly as they were raised.

It was not until the Pleistocene period, 600,000 years ago, that a final continental collision brought the Himalayas to their current heights. The Mahabharat range and Siwalik hills in southern Nepal also formed at this time, damming rivers and creating a large prehistoric lake in the Kathmandu valley. The lake dried up approximately 200,000 years ago.

The Himalayas run along Nepal's entire 885-km (549-mile) northern border with Tibet. The youngest mountain range in the world, they are still engaged in their slow assault on the heavens. From the air, they present a panorama that stretches farther than the human eye can see; it seems impossible that anyone, or anything, can live within their frozen embrace. Yet locked in

PREVIOUS PAGES: Festive bathing (left) in the waters of the lowland Terai. A minority girl (right) smiles a greeting. RIGHT: Distant view of the highest point on earth, 8,848 m (29,028 ft) Everest, surrounded by its cohorts, Nuptse and Lhotse.

thousands of secret valleys are Nepal's mountain towns and villages, accessible only by narrow footpaths carved or worn into the rock.

All length and little breadth, Nepal measures only 240 km (149 miles) at its widest point, and 150 km (93 miles) at its narrowest. From the narrow strip of flat, fertile, checkerboard plain that lies 67 m (220 ft) above sea level along the Indian border, it climbs to more than 8,848 m (29,028 ft).

Within a span of 12 hours you can fly with the rising sun along the daunting barrier of the Himalayas, from Annapurna to Kanchenjunga and back to Kathmandu then drive along a road cut into the side of a deep Himalayan river gorge and down the precipitous flanks of the Mahabharat range to the emerald plains of the Terai, and there ride an elephant among a herd of rhino as the sun sets. Similarly, the south-north land journey by car from the sea-level border to the mountains is a swift and stunning transformation of environment. You can leave the Indian border in early morning, reach the Tibetan border by late afternoon and be back in Kathmandu by nightfall. The east-west traverse, however, takes many weeks and is only possible on foot. It is one of the world's toughest, most difficult treks.

No more than 160 km (99 miles) separates Mount Everest from the tropical plains where its melting snows swell the floodwaters of some of the major tributaries of the sacred Ganges. Nepal's rivers begin as a trickle of ice melt and become raging waters as they are joined and swollen by countless tributaries. Over millennia these waterways have cut some of the deepest gorges in the world, plunging from 5,180 m (17,000 ft) to just above sea level. At full flood, these waters take just 12 hours to complete a journey from Arctic ice to tropical jungle.

Among Nepal's plains, mountains and rivers is a tapestry of vivid cultural contrasts; there are 35 ethnic groups including those of the Gurkha and the Sherpa. But with an average per capita income of less than $160 a year, Nepal's people live,

many of them, on the edge of or in the midst of poverty. The majority of farmers scratch a frugal living from their rice paddies and grain fields in the hills, mountains or the overcrowded Terai plains of the south. In the towns and cities there is also much poverty, particularly among the Tibetan refugees chased out of their own mountain kingdom by the conquering, ravaging Chinese armies in recent years.

Yet whatever faith the people of Nepal follow, be it Hinduism, Buddhism, animism or cheery paganism, they tend to celebrate each other's feasts notwithstanding, and within a poverty of means commemorate life and faith year round with festivals saluting incarnate and reincarnate deities alike.

Kathmandu, the capital and seat of the royal family, lies at the center of the country, 1,331 m (4,368 ft) above sea level, on roughly the same latitude as Florida. Neither too hot in summer months nor too cold in the winter season, Kathmandu, like most of midland Nepal, is favored with one of the world's more agreeable climates. Summer temperatures reach around 30° C (86° F) and the mean winter temperature is 10° C (50° F). The Nepalis attribute the pleasant climate to the generosity of the gods, and justifiably celebrate their divine fortune by reaping at least three harvests a year.

THE MISTY PAST

Some archaeologists believe that even before the Himalaya mountain range reached its present grandeur, *Orepithecus*, one of our early ancestors, inhabited the region's valleys and plains. Primitive humans had formed hill tribes and were making and using primitive tools as long as one million years ago. Little is known about these early inhabitants; however, both Hindu and Buddhist legends confirm that humans resided here during the time a lake filled the Kathmandu valley, and that there were relatively developed societies with oral traditions and an animistic religion.

THE KIRANTI INVADERS AND THE BIRTH OF BUDDHA

Somewhere around 700 BC Kiranti invaders arrived from India. Their military exploits are described in ancient Indian texts such as the Mahabharata and Ramayana, but their influence probably only extended over a portion of the Terai and the midlands, where they established Patan as their stronghold. They assimilated the pre-existing cultures, and, for at least seven centuries, controlled north-south trade and travel.

It was during this epoch that Buddha was born — in 540 BC at Lumbini. Buddha himself preached in the Kathmandu valley as well as northern India, and his teachings spread throughout Asia. In 250 BC the Indian Emperor Ashoka, recently converted to Buddhism, journeyed to Nepal, where he erected a memorial to Buddha in Lumbini and founded a disputed number of *stupas* in Patan. Nepal then, as now, enjoyed a happy coexistence of both Buddhism and Hinduism.

Over the next two centuries, until perhaps 50 BC, Kiranti influence waned in the valley. Other groups migrated here and mingled with existing populations to become the people commonly referred to as Newaris. In the hills and mountains tribal societies and kingdoms also expanded and diversified.

After the Kiranti, the valley was ruled by the Somavashis, who also originally came from India. Under the Somavashis, the Hindu religion flourished and a four-caste system was introduced. They renovated the holy shrine, Pashupatinah, and in the first century AD constructed a temple on the site. It was also during their

rule that the roofs of the temples in Patan were gilded.

THE GOLDEN AGE

Eventually the Somavashis were conquered by the Licchavi, who ruled the valley from the fifth through seventh centuries. These Hindu rulers also came from India and are credited with bringing an age of enlightenment with them. They fostered the study of Sanskrit and the production of carvings, many with elaborate inscriptions and dedications.

Buddha's 540 BC birthplace at Lumbini on the Terai plains which border India.

One notable Licchavi ruler, Manadeva, built the Changu Narayan temple in 388 Saka Sambat (AD 467), so its inscriptions tell us. A stele there praises Manadeva's victories over the Malla tribes and the subjugation of the Thakuris.

Two centuries later the last Licchavi ruler, Shevadeva, gave his daughter in marriage to one of his strongest Thakuri vassals, Amsuvarman, who was well-educated and had written a Sanskrit grammar. As Shevadeva preferred the monastic life to his royal duties, Amsuvarman assumed many of his father-in-law's duties during the latter's lifetime.

On the death of Shevadeva in AD 605, Amsuvarman appointed himself king. He expanded his influence beyond the valley by marrying his daughter Bhrikuti to the Tibetan King Sron Tsan Gampo. Bhrikuti is credited with converting the Tibetan king and his other wife, a Chinese princess, to Buddhism, thus beginning the eventual transmission of the religion to Tibet and China. The two brides have been canonized in the Buddhist tradition and are worshipped as the goddesses of compassion, Green Tara (Bhrikuti) and White Tara (Wen-cheng, the Chinese princess).

In AD 643 and 647 the Chinese sent their first diplomatic missions to the Kathmandu valley. The records of Wang Huen Tse, the leader of the second mission, show that he had mixed feeling about Ni-Po-Lo and its inhabitants: "The kingdom of Ni-Po-Lo... is situated in the middle of snowy mountains and indeed presents an uninterrupted series of hills and valleys. Its soil is suited to the cultivation of grain and abounds in flora and fruits.... Coins of red copper are used for exchange. The climate is very cold. The national character is stamped with falseness and perfidy; the inhabitants are all of a hard and savage nature: to them neither good faith nor justice nor literature appear, but they are gifted with considerable skill in the art. Their bodies are ugly and their faces are mean. Among them are both true believers [Buddhists] and heretics [Hindus]. Buddhist's convents and the temples of the Hindu gods touch each other. It is reckoned that there are about two thousand religious who study both the Greater and Lesser Vehicle. The number of Brahmans and the nonconformists has never been ascertained exactly."

Other members of the missions were more impressed with the Nepali culture and art. Years later, Nepali architects were invited to China to build the first pagodas there.

This golden age of Nepal was followed by a dark age during which tribes were at constant war with one and other. Gone was art, learning and religious tolerance; few records or relics remain from this period. Some historians believe that during this era in the reign of a Thakuri king, Guakanadeva, around 950, the city of Kathmandu, then known as Kantipur, became the regional capital, and the towns of Bhadgaon and Kirtipur were established. Commerce with India and Tibet increased and Tantric rites and ideals were introduced and integrated into the religions.

THE MALLA DYNASTY

In the eleventh century Muslims took power in India. Under Muhammed Ghauri, they extended their empire into the northern kingdoms, causing both Hindus and Buddhists to flee north to Nepal and Tibet. The Malla dynasty arose from these refugees, and it dominated the valley until the eighteenth century.

According to popular legend, the name of the dynasty came about when a son was presented to Arideva, one of the earliest Malla rulers, about the year 1200. Arideva was wrestling at the time, and he gave the child the title Malla, meaning "wrestler" in Sanskrit.

There were peaceful periods under the Mallas, but these were interrupted by Muslim invasions from India. During a fourteenth century attack, the Muslims sacked many temples and shrines in the valley. Nonetheless arts, architecture and learning advanced; there were three universities in the valley; religious tolerance was so complete that Buddhists and Hindus worshipped in the same temples and celebrated each other's religious festivals.

During the Malla rule, Christian monks came to the valley and were allowed to preach their religion. For many years there was a Catholic church near Kathmandu. But in their religious fervor, these Christian missionaries supposedly burned more than 3,000 pagan books and manuscripts as works of the devil. For this they were expelled, taking only a handful of native converts with them.

Under the reign of Jaya Sthiti Malla, which began in 1382, a caste system was reintroduced after a Brahman priest convinced the king that the gods look with disfavor upon casteless societies. The Brahman priests placed themselves at the top of the caste, with 64 professional groups below and shoemakers, butchers, blacksmiths and sweepers at the bottom, the untouchables. The second caste was the warriors, to which the royal families belonged. This caste was again subdivided into sub-castes, which led to suspicion and dissent among rulers and contributed substantially to the civil strife of the time.

The most aggressive of the Malla rulers, Jaksha Malla, extended the boundaries of his kingdom to include much of what is now modern Nepal. His territory extended north to Tibet and south to the Ganges river. He oversaw the construction of canals and water supply systems.

Unfortunately, shortly before his death he divided the valley amongst his children: Bhadgaon (also known as Bhaktapur), Banepa and Kathmandu went to his three sons, Patan to his daughter. The heirs, not content with their inheritances, were soon warring with each other. Banepa became part of Bhadgaon and Patan eventually lost its independence to Kathmandu.

The valley remained divided during the next 200 years, but there were several rulers of note in Kathmandu, Patan and Bhadgaon. Pratap Malla, king of Kathmandu from 1640 to 1674, was a man of letters, and demonstrated his knowledge of fifteen languages on a plaque in the Royal palace. He also erected the statue of Hanuman, the monkey god, at the entry to the palace, which since then has been known as Hanuman Dhoka. He was also responsible for the construction of the steps and gold thunderbolt at Swayambhunath.

Under King Siddhi Narasimba Malla (1618–1661), Patan grew considerably. Siddhi Narasimba oversaw a major construction effort that included 2,400 individual houses. He was a religious man, and one day left on a pilgrimage from which he never returned.

The life of King Bhupatendra Malla of Bhadgaon reads much like a fairy tale. The wicked witch was his father's second wife, who wanted her own son to inherit the throne. Bhupatendra was the son of the first wife and therefore first in line. The second

wife decided to have the young prince killed. Her conspirators took the boy from the palace into the forest to murder him. However, they did not have the courage to carry out the stepmother's wish, and abandoned the child instead. The prince was found by a carpenter who raised him as his own son.

Years later, the carpenter took his son with him to work in the Royal palace. The king, the boy's real father, recognized him and welcomed him back as the rightful heir.

Sculptures of Buddhist and Hindu deities encircle an ornamental pool where Patan's eighteenth-century royal families bathed. The pool is surrounded by a protective symbol, a large stone snake known as Nagbandh. OVERLEAF: Elegant medieval architecture in Kathmandu.

Bhupatendra became king in 1696 when his father died, and his reign was marked by incessant construction. The best remaining structures from this period are the Palace of 55 Windows and the temple of Nayatapola. This was one of the most prosperous eras in the city.

THE UNIFICATION OF NEPAL

In spite of, or perhaps because of, the relative prosperity of the many divided kingdoms in the valley, they were at constant

war with each other. Outside the valley, meanwhile, other principalities were flourishing. Little is documented about life in these outlying kingdoms, but from one, Gorkha, came the leader of modern Nepal, Prithvi Narayan Shah.

The following story is told of him as a young boy in the land of the Gurkhas and fortified towns: One day when he was six years old, Prithvi Narayan went to the temple where he met an unhappy old man. "I am hungry. Can you give me some curd?" begged the old man. Prithvi Narayan fetched some curd. The old man ate his fill but kept a little in his mouth.

"Hold out your hand!" ordered the old man. The boy obeyed and the old man spit

what was left in his mouth into it. "Eat!" he commanded. Prithvi Narayan was not inclined to follow this order and dropped the curdled milk to the ground.

"If you had eaten my spittle from your hand, the old man said, you would have been able to conquer all the countries of your dreams. Since you have thrown it away, you will only be able to conquer those kingdoms into which you can walk." And the ancient one suddenly disappeared.

After becoming king of Gorkha in 1742, Prithvi Narayan spent 25 years expanding his territory and unifying a large part of Nepal. He was a great conqueror, but, as prophesied, he never did realize all his dreams.

Prithvi Narayan began his assault on the valley with careful planning and sound tactics. He first took over the fortifications of Nawakot in the Trisuli valley, through which passed much of the commerce with Tibet. The Malla kings united to send troops against Nawakot but were unsuccessful in breaking Prithvi Narayan's commercial blockage. Prithvi Narayan moved on to isolate the valley by cutting off the remaining trade routes and sent Brahman priests into the valley to stir up unrest.

The intrigues in the valley kingdoms helped advance Prithvi Narayan's plans. In Kathmandu, King Jaya Prakash had been exiled by his wife, whom he eventually killed. Jaya's brother, the King of Patan, was deposed by the Pradhans, a rival family, who spared his life but blinded him. Jaya came to his brother's aid, suppressed the Pradhan coup, forced them to beg in the streets and paraded their wives as witches.

Prithvi Narayan's economic blockage was not as successful as he had anticipated. Apparently only Patan offered allegiance in return for the right of passage. Prithvi Narayan sent his brother to rule Patan, but he was deposed and killed after a short time. Changing his tactics, Prithvi Narayan decided to lay siege to the valley, and chose Kirtipur as the first point of attack. He offered amnesty in return for surrender and was flatly refused. He swore to raze the city to the ground and mark every inhabitant for life.

After a two-year siege, the starving city surrendered. Prithvi Narayan forced the men to tear down their own temples and palaces, after which they were led one by one to the executioner who cut off their noses and lips. Only those who played wind instruments were exempt. One account of the episode claims Prithvi Narayan weighed this flesh bounty at 86 pounds in all. For generations the Kirtipur was hence known as Naskatipur, The City of the Noseless Ones.

Neither Patan nor Kathmandu offered much resistance to Prithvi Narayan and his

because he died four years later, leaving his two-year-old son, Rana Bahadur Shah, on the throne. Administration of the kingdom fell to a regent who also followed in the footsteps of Prithvi Narayan. He sent armies to Kashmir, Sikkim and Tibet. The Gurkha invasion of Tibet in 1790 and sacking of the Grand Lama's palace at Tashi-Lhumpo brought China into the conflict. Afraid of being overrun, Nepal requested military aid from the British East India Company. British troops, however, did not arrive until after a treaty had been signed

Gurkha armies. He easily took Kathmandu on September 1768 during the festival of Indra Jatra, when most of the population was celebrating. Jaya Prakash took refuge in Bhadgaon, but within a year the Gurkhas had taken it also. With control of the valley, Prithvi Narayan now held everything from Lamjung to Everest. He made Kathmandu his capital and maintained a policy of exclusion of Europeans, particularly missionaries. "First the Bible, then trading stations, then the cannon," he said. He planned a campaign to conquer Tibet, but died in 1774 without realizing his goal.

Prithvi Narayan was succeeded by his son, Pratap Singh Shah, who made little progress on his father's grand empire

in 1792 at Nawakot. Under the Nawakot treaty, Nepal agreed to honor the Tibetan boundaries and to pay an annual tribute to the Chinese emperor. A British representative remained in Nepal in a semiofficial capacity.

In 1795, at the age of 19, Rana Bahadur Shah assumed leadership of his country and had his regent imprisoned and killed. Bahadur Shah was an erratic if not insane ruler; his wife Tripura Sundavi and chief counselor Bhim Sen Thapa held the reigns of the kingdom. After Bahadur Shah was

OPPOSITE: Young sentinel of the famed Gurkha force of soldiers. ABOVE: Gurkha unit of the Nepali Army on parade in Kathmandu.

stabbed to death by his brother, Bhim Sen assumed the title of Prime Minister while serving as regent for the infant heir, Rajendra Bikram Shah. Bhim Sen directed Nepal for the next 30 years. He oversaw the army during a two-year border conflict (1814–1816) with the British East Indian Company. Against the well-equipped British and Indian armies, he led 12,000 men, some of whom were armed with bows and arrows. For heavier weapons they had only a few leather Tibetan cannons, made from yak hides tightly rolled together.

THE RANA RULE

Rajendra Bikram Shah's wife was a scheming, ambitious and unfaithful queen. When one of her lovers was murdered, she decided to revenge herself, and enlisted the help of one Jang Bahadur Rana, an equally ambitious officer in the Royal Guard. Convinced that a member of the Royal Council was responsible, she asked Jang Bahadur to call a meeting of the Council at the Kot, in the center of Durbar square. Closing the

The Treaty of Segauly, signed in 1816, was a compromise, not a victory for either side. The Prime Minister ceded some territories along his southern border, agreed to the stationing of a permanent British Resident in Kathmandu, and permitted the enrollment of three Gurkha regiments into the British Army.

When Rajendra Bikram Shah came of age, he progressively reduced Bhim Sen's power and eventually removed him as Prime Minister. Later Bhim Sen was imprisoned and in 1839 committed suicide. Another short period of relative chaos and royal intrigue followed out of which came the Rana prime ministers who ruled Nepal until after World War II.

gates to the courtyard, she demanded of the more than 500 noblemen that the person responsible for her lover's death be identified and punished accordingly. One pointed to Jang Bahadur as the murderer; in the ensuing mayhem, all the leading nobles were massacred by three regiments under Jang Bahadur's command. The identity of the assassin is not certain. Some accounts of the Kot massacre claim that Rajendra Bikram Shah himself was responsible for his wife's lover's death.

Nonetheless Jang Bahadur Rana installed himself as "His Highness the Maharaja" and Prime Minister. He then forced Rajendra Bikram Shah to abdicate in favor of his son, and exiled the king and queen to India. He gave the crown to the young prince, Sirendra Bikram Shah, and his eventual heirs, as it was believed that the spirit of Vishnu lived in the royal Shah line. However, Sirendra and his successors were in essence little but royal captives of Jang Bahadur and the other Ranas. Thereafter, only once a year did the Ranas permit the king to show himself before the general public which believed, as some Nepalis still do today, that they would receive forgiveness for all their sins merely by looking at him.

Thus the Prime Minister came to hold supreme command in Nepal; Jang Bahadur Rana decreed the position hereditary, passing from brother to younger brother, or brother to cousin. This first Rana Prime Minister was an adept statesman and politician. He sought the friendship of Europe but kept his country isolated from foreign influences. In 1850 he accepted an invitation from Queen Victoria and Napoleon III to visit Europe. He was royally received in London and Paris, as though he were the king.

His year long journey firmed international friendships but angered the local Brahmans who believed that anyone crossing the "black waters" of the ocean would return an untouchable. On his return, Jang Bahadur Rana purified himself in the Ganges and visited most of the major Hindu shrines in India and Nepal to prove he had not been contaminated by his trip.

The following Rana reign was notable for oppressive policies and favoritism based on its own set of castes within the family. There were A-, B- and C-Ranas, a breakdown that greatly contributed to the demise of the dynasty. The top government position went to A-Ranas, who were the pure Ranas in the direct line descending from Jang Bahadur. The A-Ranas had the right to live in palaces of more than 100 rooms. B-Ranas, descendants of Rana men who had married below them, received important civilian and military posts but could not have more than 70 rooms in their palaces. C-Ranas, offspring of harem girls, had large villas and high army posts, but could never rise to the rank of general.

Autocratic though they were, the Ranas

did bring about some positive advances in the country. Slavery and *sati* (suttee), the practice of the wife throwing herself on the burning body of her dead husband, were abolished; a university was founded, and a railroad, short though it was, constructed. Still, unrest and dissatisfaction with the Ranas was growing.

Nepal had sent 50,000 Gurkha soldiers to the First World War and continued to fill its three regiments in the British Army thereafter. In addition many served as mercenaries in the India Army. These returning

soldiers were Nepal's major contact with the outside world, and came to form a core of resistance to the Rana rule.

In 1940 the Prime Minister arrested 100 men and executed four of their leaders for the crime of communicating with the king. Many of the royal supporters remained in prison for extended periods of time; others took refuge in India. Martyrs' Memorial in Kathmandu commemorates these independence fighters. Although there was not a revolution in the sense of widespread open

OPPOSITE: Members of Nepal's royal family, including King and Queen, acknowledge the salute of the crowds from the balcony of a Kathmandu palace. ABOVE: Sherpa porter climbs a high pass in the Everest region.

warfare, during the last years of Rana domination persecution of the educated non-Rana Nepalis was commonplace, with little or no interference from the British. As Danish journalist Karl Eskerlund wrote, but for the alliance between the British and the Ranas, the country would not have stagnated so long. The British left Nepal alone because they wanted a buffer between India and Tibet. It was in their interest to keep Nepal as primitive as possible.

After World War II, the liberal Prime Minister Padma Shamsher realized that the days of autocracy were numbered. He moved to create a city council for which there were open elections and a new constitution. As far as the other A-Ranas were concerned, however, the Prime Minister took his reforms too far when he proposed an independent judiciary system. In 1948 Padma Shamsher was forced to resign in favor of Mohan Shamsher, a conservative.

Meanwhile, a liberation army of political exiles had formed in India, as well as several underground opposition movements in Kathmandu. On November 6, 1950 King Tribhuvan Shah and his family succeeded in escaping from Rana custody by detouring into the Indian embassy on the way to a picnic. They then flew to New Delhi and joined their supporters in exile. To insure survival of the royal line in the event that the escape failed, Tribhuvan left his four-year-old grandson, whom Mohan Shamsher immediately placed on the throne.

For the next three months, Mohan Shamsher sought international recognition for the new child-king, while from his exile in India King Tribhuvan organized support for himself within Nepal. In February, 1951, liberation forces entered the Terai; there were demonstrations in Kathmandu demanding a new constitution; and a group of C-Rana army officers announced they would no longer support a government which excluded them from the right of succession. The power of the Ranas was broken.

TOWARDS DEMOCRACY

On February 15, 1951, King Tribhuvan returned to Nepal and brought the Shah family back to power after 104 years. Mohan

Shamsher remained as Prime Minister; half the cabinet positions went to revolutionary leaders. Mohan resigned soon after, and went into exile in India. Nepal had finally emerged from isolation to take its place among the nations of the world.

King Tribhuvan ruled for four more years with several different cabinets, and died March 1955 while undergoing medical treatment in Zurich. His son, Mahendra Bir Shah, ascended to the throne and saw the new nation through the establishment of a constitution and its admission to the United Nations.

King Mahendra's coronation marked the first time in history that Nepal opened its borders to foreign heads of state and the international press. It was a gala affair organized and catered by a flamboyant retired Russian ballet star, Boris Lissanevitch, and his Scandinavian wife, who had started the only western-style hotel in Nepal at the request of Mahendra's father.

The King instituted a constitution that established a parliament and allowed political parties. Elections were held from February to April, 1959. The two-month time for voting was essential in this young nation where no internal communications existed except footpaths. The elections were publicized and carried out by *gaines*, wandering chanters. B.P. Koirala, leader of the liberation movement and supporter of the King's father, became Prime Minister.

The first parliament, however, was not long-lived. Locked in continual conflicts with his Prime Minister, the King dissolved Parliament, outlawed political parties, and imprisoned Koirala and several other ministers on December 15, 1960. Mahendra ruled the country until 1962, when he inaugurated a new constitution based on a system of *panchayats,* a pyramidal system that started in village communities and culminated in the king.

In 1963 King Mahendra passed a new social code guaranteeing equality to all citizens, freedom of speech and religion and the right of assembly. Castes were abolished, polygamy forbidden and the mar-

Tethering yaks (top) at Nar Valley. Phortse village clings to a barren mountainside (bottom) near Solu Khumbu.

The Country and Its People

riage of minors prohibited. Mahendra opened Nepal's doors to foreign visitors, aid and investment, and fostered nationalism in this country where previously many citizens did not even understand the concept of a nation or the meaning of Nepal.

When Mahendra died on January 31, 1972, he was succeeded by his son, Birendra Bir Bikran Shah. By 1990 pro-democracy protests had put pressure on King Birendra to agree to multiparty democratic elections. Nepal's first democratic elections in 32 years were duly held in May 1991, and the country became a constitutional monarchy.

GEOGRAPHY FROM BOTTOM TO TOP

Nepal is divided into five geographical regions: the Terai, Siwalik, Mahabharat, midlands or Pahar, and Himalaya. The government separates the country into 14 administrative zones subdivided into 75 development districts of varying importance.

The Terai, part of the great Ganges Plain, accounts for just over 20 percent of Nepal's land area, extending north from the southern border with India to the first foothills. Never wider than 35 km (22 miles), it is hot and humid most of the year. Until recently it was covered by dense forests filled with wildlife, from rare butterflies to Bengal tigers, but in the last two or three decades these forests have been widely encroached on, the forests cut and the wildlife exterminated. A large influx of settlers means that the Terai is where the majority of the Nepalis live nowadays.

This human settlement has ravaged the Terai. Where British hunter and explorer Jim Corbett in the 1930s stalked man-eating tigers and fished for huge fighting bream in the shade of ancient forests, there are now only eroded river valleys up to a mile wide and a patchwork of forest and cultivated areas. For much of the year river beds are dry; during the summer they are flooded from bank to bank with silted torrents changing course from year to year. Many houses stand on stilts. Like so many places on the planet, the Terai has become proof of the instantaneous and irreversible damage of population growth.

The Siwalik zone, with the Churia range, rises from the Terai to 1,200 m (4,000 ft). Its steep slopes and dry climate have left it relatively uninhabited. To the north are wide valleys, such as Rapti Dun, which in places separate the Siwalik from the Mahabharat.

The Mahabharat forms a barrier between the plains and the fertile midlands. It too is sparsely populated, but covered with terraced slopes. Most of Nepal's water passes through this region, which until very recently had lush deciduous forests that have nearly all been cut for fuelwood. Somewhat off the beaten track, it has mountain passes as low as 210 m (700 ft) and peaks over 2,700 m (9,000 ft).

More than 40 percent of the population occupies the temperate valleys of Kathmandu and Pokhara that dominate the Pahar zone or midlands. Here the soil is largely alluvial and fertile; crops of nearly every kind can be grown at altitudes between 600 and 2,100 m (2,000 and 7,000 ft).

Higher in the Himalayas, human habitation is isolated in remote valleys or sheltered where possible on the elevated plateaus. Here people live much as they did a thousand years ago, some still rooted in the Stone Age. Most of the high country is above treeline, for much of the year its rocky slopes covered by snow.

Nepal has one of the world's highest birthrates, with its population growing so fast the country may soon find itself hardpressed for food. Over-cultivation of the precipitous valley slopes above the river gorges has already turned the landscape into a textbook case of deforestation and soil erosion. With its steep farmlands unprotected by the deep root systems and sheltering foliage of perennial vegetation, the fierce monsoon rains wash away the fragile topsoil and can bring thousands of tons of mountainside landsliding down the slopes. Yet the beauty of Nepal's landscape remains virtually indestructible. The sheer scale and form, even of the eroded walls of the valleys, are still magnificent enough to take the breath away.

It is these same mountain walls that have kept Nepal remote from the world until this century.

MONSOON CLIMATE

Nepal's climate is dominated by the monsoons of southern Asia. The rains usually come in late April or early May and continue with steady persistence until October. Drought conditions prevail generally for the remainder of the year, with only occasional thunderstorms or snows in the mountains.

October and November are probably the best months to visit Nepal, as the countryside is still lush from the monsoon rains and

Although the monsoon cycle is relatively predictable, remember that the weather, like the hiking trails, can offer surprises. The following note appears on many trekking maps and should be kept in mind:

"In Nepal all paths and bridges are liable to disappear or change at no notice due to monsoons, acts of gods, etc."

FAITH AND SUPERSTITION

In Nepal two of the world's great religions — Buddhism and Hinduism — coexist

neither too hot in the lowlands nor too cold in the mountains. December can be too cold to enjoy trekking in the mountains, and from January to March heavy snowdrifts close the mountain passes. In March and April the countryside is generally very dry, but the rhododendrons are in bloom on the hillsides, and multicolored butterflies and summer birds are omnipresent. May is a fickle month — some years it is dry and pleasant, other wet and gray.

In contrast to the hot-cold extremes of the Terai and the Himalaya, Kathmandu's temperate climate is near perfect. The Kathmandu valley does, however, become dusty in March and April, and can often be shrouded in haze.

The Country and Its People

peacefully, and it seems that everywhere you look there is a shrine or temple commemorating a god or deity. Indeed, *himalaya* is a Sanskrit word meaning "abode of the gods": The north summit of sacred Gaurisankar, 7,144 m (23,438 ft), represents Shiva; the south Parvati, his consort. Scores of other gods and goddesses make their home among the Himalayas: Sagarmatha atop Everest, and Annapurna, "Goddess of Plenty," atop the 8,091-m (26,545-ft)-high peak of Annapurna I; while Ganesh, the elephant-headed god, resides on top of 7,406-m

Giant statue of reclining Vishnu at Buddhanilkantha in the Kathmandu valley, which measures 4.6 m (15 ft), undergoes daily cleaning by a priest or temple acolyte.

(24,298-ft)-high Ganesh Himal I. All are
living deities to most Nepalis.

BUDDHA'S BIRTHPLACE

Lumbini, in the Terai of southern Nepal, is
the birthplace of Siddhartha Gautama
Buddha. It is as sacred to the world's 300
million Buddhists as Mecca to the Muslims
and Jerusalem to the Judeo-Christian faiths.
The Buddha was born in 540 BC in a garden
under a grove of leafy trees. His mother,
Maya Devi, had been on her way to her
mother's home in Devadaha when she went
into labor and sought sanctuary in the
garden. It was hot and humid and the grove
of trees provided welcome shade.

Son of King Suddhodhan, the Buddha
wanted for nothing as he grew up at his
palace home at Tilaurokot, about 27 km
(17 miles) from Lumbini. When he played
in the garden within the palace walls his
eyes often turned northward to the distant
Himalayan peaks, then already an inspiration for the founder of what would become
one of the world's major religious forces.

At the time of his birth, there was great
poverty and hardship among the people,
but Siddhartha Gautama, sheltered by royal
privilege, knew nothing of this.

He was 29 before he set foot outside the
palace, persuading his charioteer to drive
him around the nearby countryside. So
overwrought was the prince by what he saw
that he quit the palace and his family and
became an ascetic, wandering the countryside, exploring the religions of the day.
Finally, he abandoned his search and
became a recluse. He spent his days meditating on life until, under a pipal tree at Gaya
near Benares, India, he evolved the philosophy that would sustain millions through the
next 2,500 years. Out of this came his name,
Enlightened One — the Buddha.

He reasoned that the way to enjoy life to
the full was to reject extremes of pleasure
or pain and follow an "Eightfold Path"
based on "Four Noble Truths." Mankind
suffered, pronounced the Buddha, because
of its attachment to people and possessions
in a world where nothing is permanent.
Desire and suffering could be banished by
an attachment to rightfulness.

The individual, he theorized, was simply
an illusion created by the chain of cause and
effect, karma, and trapped in the cycle of
incarnation and reincarnation. Nirvana, the
highest point of pure thought, could only
be attained by the extinction of self — and
the abolition of karma.

In the centuries that have followed the
Buddha's death sectarian differences have
caused schisms in Buddhism so that,
broadly, in India there is the Mayahana
school of Buddhism and in Southeast Asia
and Sri Lanka the Hinayana school. The
latter more closely follows the Buddha's
original teachings.

The Buddhism of Nepal belongs to the
Mayahana school. This school emphasizes
less the individual pursuit of nirvana than
compassion and self-sacrifice on behalf of
all sentient creatures treading the wheel of
life. An enlightened being who postpones
personal salvation in order to help others
on the path to enlightenment is known as
a *bodhisattva*. Tibetan Buddhism, the predominant local influence, features a vast
pantheon of bodhisattvas — these can be
seen featured in the intricate mandalas of
the Kathmandu markets.

At his coronation, on February 24, 1975,
King Birendra declared Nepal an international zone of peace in keeping with the first
tenet of the Buddhist religion — and 10 years
later this zone had been endorsed by 75 of
the world's nations.

Both the motif and the heart of this international zone is Lumbini garden, which
was visited in 1967 by U Thant, the Secre-
tary General of the United Nations. Many
Buddhist nations have constructed their
own commemorative shrines to the Enlightened One in Lumbini.

A GARRISON OF GODS

To the outsider Hinduism is a bewildering
religion, a remarkable convergence of
miraculous gods, moral codes and minutely
graded social castes. The codes of Hinduism are set forth in ancient texts such as the

One of Nepal's treasured five-storied temples—
Nyatapola in the ancient city of Bhaktapur. When it
was dedicated more than two centuries ago its
doors were locked, never to be opened again.

Vedas, Ramayana, Upanishads and Bhaga-vad Gita. But the religion finds popular expression mostly in the worship of seemingly countless gods.

The three gods you cannot help hearing about as you explore the countless temples and shrines of Nepal are Brahma the Creator, Vishnu the Preserver and Shiva the Transformer and Destroyer. Each of these gods has many manifestations or avatars, depending on the attribute they represent: Bhairav the Destroyer of Evil, for example, is an avatar of Shiva and comes in 64 forms. Add to this

but by no means exclusively so. The Hindu pantheon jostles with deities who must be propitiated and entertained with a daily round of offerings and oblations *(puja)*.

Sacred to all Hindus is the domestic cow, also Nepal's national animal. It plays a significant role in the country's religious rites. It is used to exorcise evil spirits and to turn an unlucky horoscope into one of good augury. Devout Hindus often touch a cow's tail in the belief that it will help them across the river Vaitarani on their way to paradise.

the fact that the gods all have their consort and deified "vehicle" on which they travel (Garuda, for example, is Vishnu's mount) and already you have a small host of gods. Other supernumerary deities, such as Ganesh the Elephant-headed, bring the number in the full constellation into the thousands — one source claims 33,000.

Hinduism divides into sects. Most Nepalis are Shaivites (followers of Shiva), Vaishnites (followers of Vishnu), Shaktas (followers of Shakti) or Ganpatyas (followers of Ganesh) — there are many others —

As in India, these bovids are left to wander freely in both town and country. The Hindu religious epic, the Mahabharata, avers that those who kill, eat or allow any cow to be slaughtered are condemned to hell.

When someone dies, families give a cow to one of the Brahmans in the belief that the cow will reach their dead kin in heaven. These days the animal has been replaced by a token gift of one or two rupees to the presiding priest at the funeral.

SHAMANISM

ABOVE: Buddhist prayer stones, *mani* (left), on the trail to Everest, at Solu Khumbu. Buddhist stupa (right) at the village of Chaunrikharka on the approach to Everest.

More ancient than either Hinduism or Buddhism, is a belief in a spirit world that is mediated by the *jhankri*, or shaman. In the

isolated communities of the Nepal Himalayas all illnesses are believed to hail from
the spirit world and must be banished by
means of exorcisms, sacrifices and herbal
medicines.

Thus spirits with names like "Warrior
King of the Black Crag" and "Great Lord of
the Soil God" and "Fierce Red Spirit" are
invoked from the shadows of eternity.
These take hold of the shaman and then
exorcise evil and sickness from the patient.

Convulsive shaking during a ceremony
known as *puja* is the key sign of possession.

date on which King Vikramaditya of India
defeated Saka in 57 BC. That was when the
Nepali calendar, Vikram Samvat, began.

Under the Vikram Samvat, the country
is now more than half a century ahead of
the rest of the world. Thus, Nepal and its
citizens celebrated the dawn of the twenty-
first century in splendid isolation. This
auspicious event took place in April 1943
at a time when the country's borders were
still sealed, and the rest of the world — including some brave Gurkhas — was at
war.

If the shaman cannot find the lost soul of the
patient then the victim will die.

Minor illnesses, however, are less trau-
matic, for both patient and witchdoctor. The
jhankri invokes a magic formula called
phukne, and caresses away the pain of the
affliction with a broom while reciting sacred
prayers, *mantras*.

THE NEPALI CALENDAR — AHEAD OF THE TIMES

Just like the rest of the world, except Ethio-
pia, Nepal has 365 days and 12 months in
each year. But the length of the months dif-
fers — from 29 to 32 days. Nepal's first century began at the start of the Vikram era, the

There are four other New Year days —
one based on the solar calendar, two on the
lunar calendar and one on the Christian
Gregorian calendar.

The Vikram Samvat, the official calendar
used for administration and followed by all
Nepalis, is based on a lunar-solar system of
reckoning.

The second most popular of Nepal's
calendars — no doubt because it is widely
used by many professional astrologers —
is the Shakya Samvat, which also follows a

ABOVE: Buddhist *mani* stones (left), adorned with
prayer flags, in the high country of the Himalaya. A
Buddhist stupa (right) at Thangboche monastery,
Khumbu, which stands at 4,267 m (14,000 ft) on the
slopes of Mount Everest.

lunar-solar system of calculation. But, it can be confusing. This calendar dates back to the accession of an ancient king, Salivahan. Under this scheme, Nepal has only just begun the second decade of the twentieth century.

What might be called Kathmandu's calendar, the Newar Samvat introduced by the Malla dynasty, is roughly 900 to 1,000 years behind the other two.

Perhaps the most confusing of all is the Tibetan calendar. Based on the cycle of Jupiter, which works in spans of 12 and 60

day), *Budhabar*; Jupiter Day (Thursday) or Day of the Lord, *Brihaspatibar*; Venus Day (Friday), *Sukrabar*; and Saturn Day (Saturday), *Shanisharbar*.

BUDDHIST AND HINDU ART FORMS

Nepal is perhaps the world's greatest treasury of Buddhist and Hindu art — most art in Nepal is of a religious nature. More than 2,500 years of the Hindu and Buddhist faith have given Nepal an unrivaled collection of

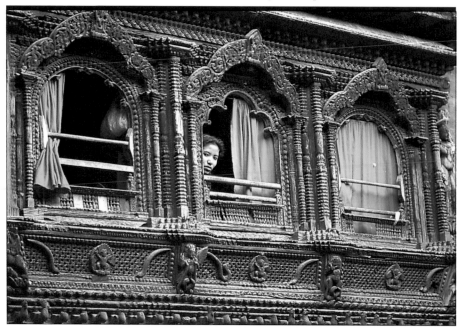

years, it was established in Western Nepal about 1,400 years ago. It does not begin with any given year nor is there any certainty about its dates. But it's easily the most colorful, each year bearing the name of one of 12 animals: rat, bull, tiger, hare, dragon, serpent, horse, sheep, monkey, rooster, jackal and pig.

Most Nepalis therefore have a choice of three or four New Year days to celebrate but the universal choice, based on the official calendar, falls somewhere in the middle of April.

The seven days of the Nepal week are named after the planets — Sun Day, *Aityabar*; Moon Day, *Somabar*; Mars Day (Tuesday), *Mangalbar*; Mercury Day (Wednes-

religious architecture and art, from the simple Buddhist stupas to the ornate Hindu pagoda temples.

The Indian Emperor Ashoka was one of the earliest known contributors to Nepal's artistic heritage. Not only did he construct stupas in Patan and Lumbini, and numerous monasteries or gompas elsewhere, but he also established trade, cultural and religious ties between the two areas. Ashoka's priests probably originally brought their own Indian artists (wood and stone cutters, carvers, architects and painters); eventually a professional artist class developed in Nepal with its own style.

The development of a wholly Nepali form of artistic expression seems to have begun between the fourth and seventh centuries AD. Five centuries later, Tibetan influences began to appear in the native art forms: Tantric and Lamaistic themes filled with sinister and demoniac images such as Bhairav, the Destroyer of Evil.

In the thirteenth century Chinese influences became apparent, but the admiration for each other's art proved to be mutual. The Nepali architect Araniko was so venerated for his style that the mandarins of China invited him to Beijing to work for them.

The richest periods of Nepali expression were during the early Licchavi dynasty, between the fourth and ninth centuries, and in the Malla epoch, from the thirteenth to eighteenth centuries. These royal houses were great patrons of the arts, as is the ruling house of Nepal today. Many of the art treasures from these periods were destroyed, not only in the recurrent earthquakes, but also by the Muslim marauder Shamsu-din-Ilyas of Bengal, who swept with his armies through the valley in the fourteenth century, and desecrated virtually every temple and piece of religious art he could find in Patan, Kathmandu and Bhaktapur. But those that have survived are considered so priceless that in 1970 West

Germany undertook to finance their renovation and preservation, and also to make an inventory of the major works, especially the temples.

It is said there are more temples in Kathmandu than houses, but the same seems to hold true outside the valley. And although much of this heritage from the Malla dynasty and that of other eras was destroyed in the great earthquakes of 1833, 1934 and 1988, an incomprehensible amount remains. Students of religion, art or architecture need many months to absorb the wonders of Nepal.

THE PAGODA

Of the many architectural styles in Nepal, one of the most striking is the pagoda. The pagoda temple originated here and is said to have derived from the practice of animal sacrifice. One theory on the evolution of the pagoda argues that worshipers found it necessary to have an altar that was sheltered to keep the rain from extinguishing the fire. It was also necessary, however, to cut a hole in the roof in order to let out the smoke. To keep the rain from entering the hole a second roof was added atop the first.

Most pagodas stand on a square base, or plinth, of brick or wood and have two to five roofs, each smaller than the one below. The uppermost roof is usually made of metal and gilded, as are frequently the lower ones. The buildings are richly adorned with carved pillars, struts, doors and other woodwork. Most decorative carvings are of various deities of all sizes and shapes, such as gods with many arms or deified, humanized animals, often in erotic poses.

The deity to whom the temple is dedicated is normally housed on the ground floor; the upper levels are more decorative than functional. Some art historians believe that the receding upper tiers are intended to represent the umbrellas that protect the deity from the elements. Above the main

OPPOSITE: Ornately carved windows testify to the skills of the famed Newari craftsmen of Kathmandu valley. ABOVE: Intricately made door to Buddhist temple in Patan.

entrance is a semi-circular tympanum or to-rana usually with the enshrined deity as the central figure.

The Nyatapola temple in Bhaktapur is considered the most impressive pagoda in the country.

THE *SHIKARA*

Although the *shikara* is of northern Indian rather than Nepali origin, many of Nepal's temples follow its architectural form: a simple square tower of bricks or stones and mortar, with a small room at the base that houses the god or goddess. Variations on the shikara have pillars, balconies and surrounding interconnected towers, which may also house deities.

The Krishna Mandir in Patan is an excellent example of a stone shikara, but the most interesting shikara in Nepal is the Mahabuddha, temple of One Thousand Buddhas, also in Patan. This shikara is built with bricks, each containing an image of Buddha.

THE *GOMPA* AND THE HINDU MONASTERY

Another form of architecture indigenous to Nepal and neighboring Tibet is the *gompa*, the Buddhist monastery of the high-mountain regions. Although they follow a fairly simple floor plan, all gompas are finely adorned and embellished and many date back to the time of Ashoka. The most striking example of this architecture in Nepal is the Thangboche monastery at Khumbu, near Mount Everest. There are about 400 Buddhist monasteries in Kathmandu valley; those near the stupa at Bodhnath are open to visitors.

Of a more intricate style are the Hindu monasteries, thirty of which are located in the Kathmandu valley. These serve as centers of Hindu study and learning. The most beautiful is probably the Pujahari Math in Bhadgaon.

THE STUPA

The Buddhist stupa is the oldest and simplest of the Nepali art forms. On its base, most often a stepped pyramidal platform, is a solid hemispherical mound in white adorned by a spire. The mound represents the universe and the pairs of eyes on the four sides of the spire symbolize the four elements of earth, fire, air and water. The 13 steps between the dome and the spire represent the 13 degrees of knowledge needed to attain nirvana; the canopy that surmounts the top of the spire represents nirvana. Each stupa is usually ringed by prayer wheels, each of which is given a twirl by devotees as they circle the shrine clockwise.

The oldest known stupas in Nepal are those erected by Ashoka in Patan, but the most famous are those of Swayambhunath and Bodhnath.

DELICATE WORKMANSHIP

Most Nepali art is worked in stone, metal, wood or terracotta. Compared to other art forms, there is very little painting in the history of the country's art, but the fine, filigree detail of Nepali sculptures, in these four materials, is as delicate as any brushstroke.

The earliest expression is Buddhist, dating from about the third century BC. Its surviving examples are four stupas in Patan, Kathmandu and the Ashoka pillar at Lumbini.

Nepali art reached a zenith in the Licchavi dynasty. Working in stone, local artists learned all that they could from India's Gupta, Deccan and Pala schools of art. These they refined and presented in indigenous creations with distinctive Nepali features.

They also began to work in a variety of metals, producing incredibly wrought bronzes of mythical and religious figures. Some of their 1,500-year-old works, exquisite in their detail and imagery, still survive in Kathmandu valley.

The metallic sculptures of Tara, Vajrapani, Maitreya, Umamaheshwara and the Buddha are among the most illustrious, both for their style and their antiquity.

Cairn of *mani* mark the entrance to the Thangboche monastery which guards the approach to Mount Everest, Sagarmatha, revered as "The Mother of the Universe."

More recent examples of Nepali metal work exist in the hollow cast statues of kings and queens, in the gilded sculpted doors and in other artifacts of the ancient art cities of Patan, Bhaktapur and Kathmandu.

Tibetan bronzes are notable for the holes set in them for paper prayers, mantras, votive offerings of grain and precious stones, or for religious icons.

Dating some of these masterpieces defies the art historian. Inscribed with the images of a pantheon of gods, both Bud-

dhist and Hindu, most are believed to be from the Pala or an earlier era.

Even more detailed and expressive than stone and metal are the wood and ivory carvings which grace the buildings of Nepal, on struts, pillars, beams, doors, windows, cornices, brackets and lintels inside and outside temples and private homes. The ivory windows of the Royal palace in Kathmandu's Durbar square are a well-known example of this art form, but countless others can be found in varying stages of repair and disrepair on the once-elegant Rana palaces and villas in Kathmandu. On a walk through the back streets of Kathmandu's Old Town, you can find windows peeking through the tail of a peacock, others grotesquely circled by skulls and a variety of suggestive and erotic motifs.

Developed from the twelfth century as an integral part of Nepali traditional architecture, wood art has always been the specialty of the Newaris.

The Newaris established a large vocabulary including every component part and

exact detail of traditional carving. These medieval texts have been passed down through the generations and still serve as the instructional handbooks for today's wood carvers.

The skill of the Newar craftsman is seen in the absence of either nails or glue in his works. And the erotica that adorn the temples throughout the country leave no doubt about the vividness of their artistic imaginations. Given the Hindu philosophy that worships Shiva's lingam, the religious of old considered the sexual nature of such art and temple decoration profoundly significant.

Nepal's history of terracotta craft stretches back to the third century BC, but in Kathmandu it reached its glory during the sixteenth and eighteenth centuries. Outstanding examples of friezes and moldings decorate the buildings from this era in the Kathmandu valley and can also be found in the region's museums. Of particular note are the long bands of male and female figures, *nagbhands*, that stretch around some temples, depicting Hindu narratives and epics. The main gateway of the Taleju temple in Hanuman Dhoka, Bhaktapur and Patan's Mahabuddha and Maya Devi temples are outstanding examples of this art form.

Pottery-making has been practiced for over one thousand years in Nepal and some fine examples survive. The pottery center of Kathmandu valley is Thimi, where potters turn out outstanding figurines, smoking pipes, lamp stands and flower pots.

RELIGIOUS PAINTINGS

Most Nepali painting is of a religious nature and has existed since the ascendancy of the Lichhavi dynasty in the fourth century. The earliest surviving specimens, however, in the form of illustrated manuscripts, date back only to the eleventh century. These manuscripts were produced in Buddhist monasteries and,

ABOVE: Children gaze from the window of an old Newar house on the sidestreets of Bhaktapur. OPPOSITE: Colorfully attired and bedecked in beads, this wizened old man seems to personify the spirit of Nepal's tribespeople.

together with *thangkas* — a form of painting that features favorite gods and lesser deities and are inevitably subdued in form and color — represent the major form of painting in Nepal.

In recent years the government has asked donor nations and UNESCO to help in the restoration and preservation of Nepal's art works.

It has been estimated that at least half of Kathmandu's most priceless works from the last 2,000 years have been lost in the 40 years since Nepal opened its borders to the

rest of the world, much of it spirited away in a vacuum of control by ruthless middlemen and art dealers acting on behalf of wealthy art collectors and museums in the West, thus robbing Nepal of its artistic treasures.

Out of the country's 200 most valuable paintings — all more than one thousand years old — only three still remain in Nepal.

ETIQUETTE

The idea that foreigners are wealthy is deeply ingrained in Nepali minds. Palms extended, children in the streets chant — "Rupee! Paisa!" Ignore them and they usually smile and run away. And if they persist,

adults normally send them away, for the idea of begging is abhorrent to the Nepali people.

The people are immensely friendly and travelers, even lone women, can move almost everywhere with complete confidence. But bear in mind that the Nepalis have different values and standards from our own. For reasons that may be obscure to you, they may ask you not to enter a certain precinct or photograph a certain shrine. The fact is that they regard any foreigner as ritually polluted.

Superstition and religion are indivisible and are deep-rooted, in Nepali society. Never step over someone's feet or body when you can walk around them and never offer "polluted" food — food that you have tasted or bitten into.

In Nepali custom, the left hand is tainted and it is impolite to pass things or offer something with the left hand. It is just as impolite to receive anything with the left hand. Always use the right hand — or both hands together. This will signify that you honor the offering and the recipient or donor. Most Nepalis take off their shoes before they enter a house or a room, so avoid entering any house unless you wish to spend some time in there — for instance, to eat or to drink tea. The cooking and eating areas must be especially respected. Never enter these when wearing shoes — and remember that the fireplace in any home is regarded as sacred. Most Nepalis squat cross-legged on the ground to eat, so take care not to stand in front of them because your feet will point directly at their food.

RACIAL GROUPS

The two main racial groups are Indo-Aryan and Mongoloid. The southern communities, Brahmins and Chhetris, are of Aryan stock. The Sherpas and Tamangs of the north are pure Mongoloid. In between come such groups as the Newars of Kathmandu, the Kirantis of the midlands, the Gurungs and the Magars, who are a mixture of both.

The main ethnic groups of the midlands are the Kirantis (Rais and Limbus), Tamangs, Gurungs, Thakalis and the Newar. Those of the Himalayan mountains are the Sherpas, Lopas and the Dolpos of remote northwest Nepal who number just a few hundred people. On the lowlands, the main groups are the Tharus, Satars, Dhangars, Rajbansis, Danwars, Majhis and Darais. Among the minorities is a Muslim population that numbers around two percent of the population and about 6,000 Tibetan refugees who have settled in Nepal and obtained citizenship.

Nepal's many diverse cultures have been shaped over thousands of years by the weather and the environment and there is a direct living link between groups still in the Stone Age and the metropolitan elite of Kathmandu who have entered the Jet Age. The country's Stone Age groups, where people still make fire with flint and iron and use stone axes, are found in Bajhang and the high, hidden valleys of the west.

THE GURKHAS

Perhaps the best known of all these communities are the Gurkhas and the Sherpas. In fact, the Gurkhas are not an ethnic but a warrior grouping, with more than 300 years of tradition in the armies of Nepal and as mercenaries in the pay of the Indian and British armies. After tourism, military service in foreign armies is the country's second-largest single source of foreign exchange. Salaries, pensions and related services bring between US$15 and $20 million a year.

The bravery of the Gurkha soldier who forms the elite force of the Royal Nepali Army, is legendary. Short and stocky hillsmen, they have fought and distinguished themselves in some of the greatest battles in military history. During the last two centuries, their daring feats have earned them endless awards, notably 13 Victoria Crosses, considered to be Britain's highest award for valor. Most recently, in the 1982 Falklands War between Argentina and Britain, their bravery was acknowledged yet again.

The name Gurkha denotes their status as the bravest of the brave. It originated from the Gorkhali community of central Nepal, which raised the first two Gurkha battalions in 1763 to serve the founder of the present royal dynasty. Calling themselves the Sri Nath and the Purano Gorakh, these battalions first saw action against the British in 1768. They also took part in separate campaigns against Tibet.

By 1814 this force, made up mainly of Thakuri, Magar and Gurung tribesmen, had slashed their way through the central Himalayas with the *kukhuri* — the fearsome, long, curved blade that by the end of

the nineteenth century had become the most celebrated weapon in the arsenal of hand-to-hand combat.

Their derring-do during the two-year Anglo-Nepal War (1814–1816) impressed Western observers and the British East India Company began recruiting Gurkhas on an informal basis. These informal arrangements continued for another 70 years. When the Gurkhas were formally acknowledged as a fighting force, eight units were already in continuous service in India. Most units were made up of Magar and Gurung tribesmen, but officers had already begun

Women of the Tamang community OPPOSITE and ABOVE, one of the major ethnic groups of the Nepal midlands region.

to draw other recruits from the Rais, Limbu and Sunwar tribes of the east and from the Khasas in the west. During the 1857 Indian Mutiny, they demonstrated not only tenacity and bravery but also loyalty that would become equally as legendary. As Bishop Stortford, in a 1930 introduction to Ralph Lilley Turner's Nepali Dictionary, remembered:

...my thoughts return to you... my comrades... Once more I hear the laughter with which you greeted hardship... I see you in your bivouacs... on forced marches

or in the trenches, now shivering with wet and cold, now scorched by a pitiless and burning sun. Uncomplaining you endure hunger and thirst and wounds; and at last your unwavering lines disappear into the smoke and wrath of battle. Bravest of the brave, most generous of the generous, never had country more faithful friends than you.

In the last half of the nineteenth century, these warriors fought all across south Asia, from Malaya to Afghanistan — even in Africa, in Somaliland — displaying remarkable endurance as well as courage.

Several Gurkhas have also distinguished themselves as mountain climbers. In 1894, Amar Singh Thapa and Karbir

Burathoki climbed 21 major peaks and walked over 39 passes in the European Alps in an epic 86-day trek during which they covered more than 1,600 km (990 miles). Thirteen years later, Karbir Burathoki, with Englishman Tom Longstaff, completed the first major ascent of any Himalayan peak, 7,119-m (23,357-ft)-high Trisul. (Between 1921 and 1937, Gurkha porters helped to mount five attempts on the then unclimbed Everest.)

By the end of World War I, more than 300,000 Gurkhas had seen service across Europe, Africa and in the Indian Army. In a battle in Flanders in 1915, Kulbir Thapa won the first of the 13 Victoria Crosses; Karna Bahadur Rana won the second in Palestine in 1918. Certainly, without these doughty stalwarts, Britain would have been even more hard pressed to defend itself and its colonies in World War II. Expanded to 45 battalions, Gurkha troops distinguished themselves in action across the Middle East, the Mediterranean and in Burma, Malaya and Indonesia. Two battalions were formed into crack paratroops. By war's end, the Gurkhas had accumulated another 10 Victoria Crosses.

In 1947, Britain began to dismantle its empire and the Gurkha regiments were divided. Six became the Indian Gurkha Rifles and four the British Brigade of Gurkhas. Subsequently, the Gurkha regiments of the Indian Army fought against China in 1962 and in successive conflicts with Pakistan in 1965 and 1971. The British sector served with distinction in Malaya, Indonesia, Brunei and Cyprus and, in 1965, in action in Sarawak, Lance Corporal Rambahadur Limbu won the Gurkhas their 13th Victoria Cross, for "heroism in the face of overwhelming odds".

Today, the descendants of these brave men sign up for service in faraway British outposts — Hong Kong, Singapore, Brunei and Belize in Central America. It was from there that the Gurkhas were rushed into action when war broke out in 1982 between Argentina and Britain. Described by the Argentinean press as a cross between

ABOVE: Grizzled face of a veteran Sherpa mountain porter. OPPOSITE: Young Sherpa boy at Lukla, the community's high country capital.

The Country and Its People

dwarfs and mountain goats, they presented such a ferocious mien as they advanced on the Argentinean positions that the Latin Americans dropped their weapons and fled — not wishing to discover the Gurkhas' legendary skill at disemboweling the enemy with their wicked-looking *kukhuri* blades.

The Kiranti hillsmen from eastern Nepal are now among the principal recruits to the Gurkha regiments. Of Mongoloid and Tibetan stock, they are said to have won the myth-shrouded battle of

THE SHERPAS

The Sherpas are a Nepali ethnic group that have earned fame as the world's most skillful high-altitude mountain porters and climbers. Of Mongoloid stock and numbering between 25,000 and 30,000 they migrated centuries ago over the Himalayas from Minyak in eastern Tibet. It was Sherpa Norgay Tenzing who, with Sir Edmund Hillary, conquered Everest; and it is the Sherpas who accompany every

Mahabharat. Their religion is a blend of Animism, Buddhism and Hindu Shivaism.

Numbering more than half a million, they speak a language that derives from Tibet.

Most Kirantis, military mercenaries or farmers, carry the Gurkha kukhuri tucked beneath the folds of their robes. Tradition says that once this is drawn it cannot be put back in its scabbard until it has drawn blood.

Until recently, Kiranti honor could only be satisfied by the slaughter of a chicken or duck. Now they settle for yet another compromise. It is cheaper by far simply to nick a finger and spill their own blood to satisfy this centuries-old tradition.

major mountain-climbing expedition. For endurance few are known to equal them. They are Buddhists and they earn their living by trading, farming and herding yaks.

It was A.M. Kellas who first brought Sherpas on a mountain ascent in 1907 in the Indian state of Sikkim. But renown came with the opening of the Nepal Himalayas in the 1950s; so courageous and skillful were they on the perilous slopes that the Alpine Club gave them the title, Tigers of the Snow.

Sherpa Tenzing earned immortality from his ascent with Hillary, but he died penniless in exile in Delhi, India, in 1986. Others of his kin have since followed him to the top of the world. One, Pertemba Sherpa, has been there twice.

The high altitude of the Sherpas' environment has prepared them physically and mentally for the challenges of climbing 8,800 m (29,000 ft) into the sky.

Since the Mongol invasions 700 or 800 years ago, they have maintained much of their nomadic lifestyle; in summer they move up to the sparse pastures above 5,800 m (19,000 ft). In the past, they migrated to Tibet in summer, returning in winter to the Khumbu region. Slowly, they

Yaks provide butter for the lamps that burn in the monasteries and private homes and for the rancid Tibetan tea served in these parts. Arts and handicrafts are limited but images, scrolls, murals and rock carving provide lucrative rewards for those Sherpa priests, or lamas, who have become skilled artisans. The Sherpas belong to the oldest Buddhist sect in Tibet, still largely unreformed.

The priests borrow freely from the arts of sorcery and witchcraft to sustain their authority and sacrifice is a ritual tool to

settled in more permanent communities, tilling the fields and growing vegetables and root crops.

Made up of 18 clans, each speaking its own dialect, Sherpas follow tribal laws that prohibit intermarriage not only among members of the same clan but also between members of specific clans. Gifts of the Sherpa home-brewed beer, *chhang*, are exchanged between heads of families when their offspring become engaged. Weddings are elaborate and lavish affairs with great feasting and drinking.

Traders and money-lenders are prominent in Sherpa society. Usury is widespread, loans at 30 percent interest not uncommon.

deal with the mythological demons and gods who inhabit every peak and recess of the high-mountain region and whose presence is confirmed in the Buddhist scriptures.

THARUS

The Tharus are the indigenous inhabitants of the most fertile part of Nepal, the southern corn and rice belt of the Terai. They number close to a million. Over the cen-

Nepal is a diverse mix of ethnic groups. OPPOSITE: Tamang man (left) at Namche Bazaar on the slopes of Mount Everest. Newari man (right) and two Newari girls ABOVE from the Kathmandu valley, represent the country's oldest community.

turies they have been joined by many migrants from the midland valleys and the mountain highlands. The Terai is also host to the majority of Nepal's 300,000 Muslims — lured to the plains by the climate and fertile soil.

The Tharus, especially those of high-caste birth, are much more conservative and rigid in their values than the rest of their countrymen. In the south they live, together with non-caste communities such as the Danuwar, Majhi and Darai, along the Terai's northern edge, and in the west with the Rajbansi, Satar, Dhimal and Bodo people; they can also be found in the east and Morang.

The Tharus have lived there longest, building up a resistance to malaria and living in cool, spacious, airy houses with lattice-work brick walls to allow in any breeze. Besides farming, they hunt, breed livestock and fish.

Their bejeweled women are noted for their stern demeanor. They marry early, but if the groom cannot afford the dowry he must work for the bride's family — up to five years — to be eligible.

They worship tigers, crocodiles and scorpions, in a form of Hinduism tinged with animism.

NEWARS

In Kathmandu valley, the oldest community is that of the Newars. Descended from the Mongols, they practice a form of the Hindu caste system, ranking hereditary occupations such as carpentry, sculpture, stonework, goldsmith and others according to ritual purity. Their crafts adorn almost every corner of the Kathmandu valley and its cities.

To the Newars, every day is a celebration of life and death. Together with their extended families, they observe a constant round of rituals, worshipping and placating the many deities whose blessings rule their daily lives.

Once a year they honor one of the family cows, usually a calf, which personifies Lakshmi, the goddess of wealth, treating it to grain and fruit. Windows are lit throughout the night to please the divinity who circles the earth at midnight and to bring her blessings on cash boxes and grain stores.

Each stage of a Newar's life is marked by colorful ceremonies. In a land where few people live more than 50 years, the old are venerated. When a man reaches the golden age of 77 years, seven months and seven days, there's a re-enactment of the rice-feeding ceremony, *pasni,* which marks the seventh month of every male child. The elder is hoisted on a caparisoned palanquin and paraded through the town, his wife following behind on a second palanquin. He's given a symbolic gold earring that marks him out as a wise one for the rest of his life.

Death is marked by cremation at any one of the many burning places near the holy Hindu bathing sites, or *ghats,* which in Kathmandu, in particular, line the banks of the Bagmati river.

Mourners walk around the body three times before setting the funeral pyre alight, while relatives shave their heads and ritually purify themselves with the slimy algae-laden waters of the river. After this, the ashes are scattered in the Bagmati and the wind-borne smoke carries the soul to the abode of Yama, the god of death, where it will merge with the divine.

Young Newar girls are symbolically wedded to Vishnu. Thus, married for life, they escape any stigma if widowed or divorced from their earthly husband.

These little sisters also pay homage to their brothers — often their only source of support in old age — during the Tihar Bhaitika festival. The boys, seated behind decorative symbols of the universe, *mandalas,* receive the mark of the *tika* and the blessing, "I plant a thorn at the door of death; may my brother be immortal".

OTHER COMMUNITIES

In the Dhaulagiri region, slashes of brilliant orange or white mark the farms of the Brahmins, Chhetris, Gurungs and Magars. Their gardens are filled with the colors of poinsettias, marigolds and other flowers,

In a small village in the Everest region an infant in a topi peers around a corner.

and shady banyan trees. Barley, wheat, millet, rice and maize are grown in the valleys that lie between the mountains.

The people of the Manang valley, however, are famous for their trading. Tibetan in culture, they travel to many parts of the Orient — Singapore, Hong Kong and Bangkok — to do business.

Another trading community is that of the Thakali people, whose colorful trade caravans of mules, loaded with sugar, kerosene and rice, travel through the low-lying Kali Gandaki gorge, the deepest in the world and, for centuries, one of the most important trade routes linking Tibet with Nepal and India. Like the Manang community, their settlements are distinguished by the flat roofs of their houses.

Of Nepal's diverse communities perhaps the smallest is that of the Dolpos, a few hundred people who herd their yaks and goats in the sterile stony moors of Nepal's western Himalayas. They also grow wheat, barley and potatoes. Lamaist Buddhists speaking a Tibetan dialect, they are mainly traders who use pack beasts to move their goods in caravans from Tibet to the more populous areas of Nepal. They ride tough highland ponies and are adept horsemen.

NATIONAL EMBLEMS

Nepal's national bird is a rare, brilliantly colored pheasant, of the species *Galliformes*, found between the 2,400- and 4,500-meter (7,800- and 15,000-ft) contours of the Himalayas. It belongs to the same family as the peacock.

The ubiquitous rhododendron — of which there are about 32 species, most with red and pink flowers, rarely white — is the national flower. Crimson-red, *simrik*, is Nepal's national color. Regarded as both sacred and auspicious it is considered a symbol of progress, prosperity and action and is visible at all national and sacred occasions. Shiva is supposed to draw power from this dark red hue.

During Nepal's many Hindu festivals, red flowers are presented as votive offerings to the different gods and goddesses. Crimson is also the color that symbolizes married bliss and virtually every Nepali

woman wears crimson during festivals and other sacred occasions.

Red is usually the color of the country's national dress, *labeda suruwal*, which is made of homespun cotton. On some occasions the color of this dress is gray or light brown. It consists of a seamed, double-breasted tunic that extends almost to the knees, fastened by two ribbons; and trousers that are baggy around the thighs but tight at the ankles, similar to the *shalwa qamiz* of India.

For some occasions sophisticated Nepali women wear the Indian sari.

Nepal's national flag comprises two adjoining red triangles — symbolizing morality, virtue and unity — bordered by blue. The top triangle contains a crescent moon emitting eight rays, the lower one, a sun emitting 12 rays. These are symbols of the many legendary solar and lunar dynasties to which the royal family belongs.

The family's coat of arms is decorated with leaf-shaped pieces symbolizing the title of Sri Panch five times glorified. For the crest, the heraldic device uses the plume of a bird of paradise which is believed to have been introduced to Nepal by a former premier, Mathbar Singh Thapa. Below this are the footprints of Paduka, the guardian god of Gorkha, ancestral home of the ruling dynasty. Crossed kukhuris represent the national weapon, the traditional, curved sword of the famed Gurkha battalions. On either side are the sun and the moon, symbol of enlightenment and eternity.

The shield depicts Nepal, from the Himalaya to the Terai and at the center, hands clasped, sits Pashupatinah, creator as well as destroyer of the Universe.

The Sanskrit motto avers that love of mother and motherland is superior even to love of heaven. The soldier recruit and veteran are also represented by a prayer exhorting them to defend their country, so long as the universe shall exist.

Nepal's national anthem wishes for the continued prosperity of the "excellent, illustrious, five times glorified King" and a fivefold increase in the number of his subjects.

Tamang woman at Lukla. Highland people like the Sherpas and the close-knit Tamang are descended from Tibeto-Mongoloid stock. They number about one million and are mainly Buddhist.

The Cities of Kath- mandu Valley

KATHMANDU VALLEY

The Kathmandu valley, seat of the Malla kings and repository of Nepali art and culture, is the heart of Nepal. A fertile oasis in the foothills of the Himalayas, Kathmandu valley measures just 25 km (15 miles) east to west and 20 km (12 miles) north to south. But within the compass of that small area, the valley packs in the attractions of three ancient cities and a treasure trove of endowments from antiquity.

Not that Kathmandu valley's attractions are all cultural: Set 1,350 m (4,425 ft) above sea level, the valley is ringed by gentle, evergreen hills touching about 2,370 m (7,800 ft), slate-blue in the misty haze of spring and summer. The eternal backdrop is the Himalayas. From the top of 2,200-m (7,175-ft)-high Nagarkot, you can see the Annapurna massif, Dhaulagiri in the west and Everest in the east.

BACKGROUND

Eons ago the Kathmandu valley was a lake; it was probably drained by one of the cataclysmic earthquakes that occasionally shake the region. Legend has it that the sage Manjushri used his sword to slash a gorge — now spanned by a Scottish-built suspension bridge — at Chobar about eight kilometers (five miles) southwest of the modern capital where the Bagmati, one of Kathmandu valley's major rivers, begins its plunge to the Ganges. There's a temple, of course, right by the gorge — Jal Binayak — that pays homage to the myth. Whatever the cause, the waters left behind a loam so rich that Kathmandu farmers can count themselves blessed. Abundant rains and sunshine combine with the loam to ensure that no land goes fallow.

The ox-plow keeps dominion still over the grain and paddy fields and, outside the metropolitan area, most of Kathmandu's 300,000 people seem to have a small patch of ground to till. Indeed, from a distance, this richly fertile basin must look much the same as it did when it was first farmed. Before then, the only communities lived near the shrines and pilgrimage sites that lay on the slopes of the encircling hills. The earliest settlements in the valley go back well beyond 2,500 years, their beginnings shrouded in ancient myths and legends.

Those that remain, such as the Buddhist stupas, evoke eras long before Kathmandu itself came into existence. The Kathmandu valley is peppered with such stupas — the two most visible are Swayambhunath and Bodhnath

KATHMANDU

Kathmandu is one of the world's most intriguing cities. First impressions can be disappointing — the boulevards and thoroughfares are often choked with traffic and air pollution is a major problem nowadays. But step into the back streets and you enter another world — a medieval maze of narrow alleys lined with old world shops, ornately carved windows overhead. Crowds throng these alleys, a sturdy porter trots past under what looks to be a cargo-hold of goods tucked into a vast sack, a woman stoops to leave an offering of flowers and uncooked rice at a centuries old shrine, the plangent strains of unfamiliar music sing out, curious smells assail the nostrils.

Naturally, Kathmandu, like every other city in the region, is on a collision course with the twenty-first century. As everyone knows — Pico Iyer made it the title of a book — in the tourist district the restaurants show videos; fax and e-mail services are abundant; rush-hour traffic jams are a regular occurrence. But for all this Kathmandu manages to retain its charm.

GENERAL INFORMATION

For a country that generates so much income from tourism, the Department of Tourism is surprisingly listless about the task of supplying information to visitors. Kathmandu has three offices: ((01) 470537, at the international terminal of the airport; ((01) 220818, at Basantapur on Ganga

PREVIOUS PAGES: Gilded conical canopy of the Swayambhunath stupa west of Kathmandu (left), known as the monkey temple and (right) an eighth or ninth-century mask depicting Shiva as an incarnation of Bhairav. OPPOSITE: Beautiful Kathmandu valley.

KATHMANDU

GALKOPAKHA

NAYABAJAR

LAINCAUR

LAJIMPAT

Bisnumati

Lekhnath Marg

PAKNAJOL

KALDHARA

THAMEL

NARAY

Narainhiti Royal Palace

Nag Pokhri

Siwa Ma

Narayan Hiti

DHOBICAUR

NAKSAL

Kamal Pokhri

KWABAHAL

CHETRAPATI

JYATHA

THAHITI

Kanti Path

KAMALACHI

NAGHAL

KAMALADI

TENGAL

Srigha Chaitya • Bahal

TYAURA

Nara Devi •

BANGEMURHA

Ugratara

Rani Pokhri

NARDEWI

KILAGAL

ASAN TOLE

BHOTAHITI

Narsingha Temple •

Annapurna Temple

• Clock Tower

YATKHA

KHEL TOLE

BAGBAJAR

PYAPHAL

INDRA CHOWK

MAHABAUDDHA

DILLIBAJAR

MAKHANTOL

Ratna Park

• Taleju

GUCCATOL

Durbar Square •

Hanuman

Darbar Marg

Kumari Bahal • Dhoka

YENGAL

MARU

BASANTPUR

Ganga Path

KALIKA

BHIMSENTHAN

JHOCHE

New Road

Dharma Path

Hari Shankar •

CIKAMUGAL

TEBAHAL

Bhrikutimandap Marg

OMBAHAL

KHICAPOKHRI

JAISIDEWAL

Tundikhel

Vegetable Market

GANABAHAL

Prithwi

Path

Kanti Path

Machhendranath •

Martyr's Memorial

Prithwi Path

KALIMATI

BRAMHATOL

LAGANTOL

HYUMATA

Ram San Path

Tripureswar Marg

N

TEKU

TRIPURESWAR

Bagmati

KALMOCAN

THAPATHALI

500 meters

1500 feet

Path; and ((01) 233581, at Babar Mahal. Free fold-out maps of Kathmandu should be available.

The following contacts may be of assistance:

Tribhuvan International Airport ((01) 470537.

Bus bookings can be made by any of the hundreds of travel agents operating in Kathmandu with a minimum of fuss.

Car Rental: Avis is represented by American Express Yeti Tours ((01) 221234.

Health emergencies: Patan Hospital ((01) 521333, is staffed by Western doctors and is the best of Nepal's hospitals. CIWEC Clinic ((01) 410983, is also recommended.

WHAT TO SEE

Kathmandu divides into the Old City in the west and the New City in the east. The dividing line is Kanti Path, or King's Way, which runs from north to south, skirting the Royal palace and cutting across the diplomatic precinct of Lazimpat and north to the reclining Vishnu of Buddhanilkanth.

Kathmandu's main attractions are in the Old City, with most of the highlights clustered in and around Durbar square and on the far-flung edges of town, notably Swayambhunath, Bodhnath and Pashupatinah. Good views of the city can be had from Swayambhunath and Bodhnath. Unfortunately Kathmandu's most visible landmark, **Bhimsen tower**, Dharahara, a 70-m (200-ft)-high edifice, was damaged in the 1934 earthquake that shook the valley, and is now closed to the public — thus denying what was once a popular and spectacular 360-degree view of the city.

Durbar Square

You might consider pausing and taking a deep breath before entering **Durbar square**. You are about to enter a living museum, a miraculous clutter of pagodas, temples, carved windows and timbered gables, statues of man and beast and gods and goddesses, in a happy collision of styles. The result is an organic devotional growth that is quite unlike anything else in the world. Perhaps its only equals are those a few kilometers away in Patan and Bhaktapur.

It's worth bearing in mind as you explore the square that there is much dispute among scholars about the historical details of the structures and statues you're looking at; but such quibbles are best left to professionals.

Entering from **Basantapur square**, immediately ahead and slightly to the right is a **Narayan temple** with a raised seventeenth-century gray stone statue of Vishnu's personal mount, Garuda, in a kneeling position outside. What's inside nobody's quite sure since the inner sanctum has long been closed.

Facing it is the **Gaddi Baithak**, an ornate annex of the old **Royal palace** built early in the twentieth century by a Rana premier, Chandra Shamsher, during the reign of King Tribhuvan Bir Bikram Shah Dev. It's here that Nepal's top brass gather with the royal family to celebrate Indra Jatra and other festivals and state occasions. There's a throne for King Birendra in the main room, which is lined with portraits of his ancestors.

On the other side of the square, behind the Narayan temple, is a temple dedicated to **Kamdeva**, god of love and lust, built by King Bhupatendra's queen, Riddhi Laxmi and adorned with an immaculate sculpture of Vishnu and Lakshmi. Close by, on a flank of **Vishnumati Bridge**, is the fourteenth-century wooden **Kasthamandap** built from the wood of a single tree, from which it derives its Sanskrit name: *kastha*, wood and *mandap*, pavilion. Renovated in the seventeenth century, it's from this structure also that Kathmandu derives its name. Built in

Beckoning customers, tinsel glitters in the afternoon sun in a Kathmandu bazaar.

the pagoda style, with balconies and raised platforms, it was for many years a place for Tantric worship but is now a shrine with an image of Gorakhnath, a deified yoga disciple of Shiva, as its centerpiece.

On the corner of **Chikan Mugal**, opposite this inspiring fountainhead of the capital, is the lion house, **Singha Satal** — built from the surplus timber left over from the Kasthamandap — with a second-story balcony and several small shops on the ground floor. Standing in the shadows of the Laxmi Narayan is a nineteenth-century temple,

built by King Surendra Bir Bikram Shah Dev and dedicated to **Ganesh**, the elephant-headed god, where the kings of Nepal worship before their coronation. Near the temple to the god of love and lust is an eighteenth-century temple, dedicated to **Shiva** and **Parvati**, **Nava Yogini**, guarded by lion statues. Opposite this is another dedicated to the goddess Bhagvati.

Move along past the Big Bell and a stone temple dedicated to Vishnu and you'll come to a **Krishna temple**. Diagonally opposite is the entrance of Durbar square's inner treasury, the **Hanuman Dhoka** palace, which derives its name from a large statue of Hanuman the monkey-god and the Nepali word for gate, *dhoka*.

All this is something of a royal mall. For three centuries or more, the kings of Nepal have been enthroned here. The most noticeable feature is the house on the corner overlooking Durbar square, which has three distinctive carved windows on one side where the Malla kings used to watch processions and festivals. Two of them are carved from ivory, a discovery made in 1975 during preparations for King Birendra's coronation.

Next door you'll find another large, latticed window with a gargoyle face — a grinning mask in white of Bhairav. Carved in the eighteenth century by Rana Bahadur Shah to ward off evil, it's still there offering benedictions. Each Indra Jatra festival thousands clamor to siphon off sanctified rice beer, *jand*, as it pours from Bhairav's mouth. They'll be particularly blessed, it's believed, if cursed with a hangover next day.

The old **Royal palace** — parts of it have survived six centuries — stands next door and is difficult to miss not only for its scale and form but also because of its massive golden door guarded by stone lions. Elaborately decorated with intricate motifs and emblems, it's a fitting entrance for kings-to-be. In the courtyard inside, on February 24, 1975, Birendra Bir Bikran Shah was crowned King of Nepal. At each corner of the palace stands a colored tower representing one of Kathmandu's four cities — the fourth is Kirtipur.

The Hanuman statue stands at the gate and just by its right-hand side a low fence guards an inscribed seventeenth-century dedication to the goddess Kalika on a plaque set into the wall. The inscription in at least 15 different languages — among them English, French, Persian, Arabic, Hindi, Kashmiri and, of course, Nepali — was written by King Pratap Malla, a gifted linguist and poet. Facing the Hanuman Dhoka there's the sixteenth-century **Jagannath temple**, outstanding for the erotic carvings on its struts.

ABOVE: On Kathmandu's Durbar square colorful foreigners are as much a part of the spectacle as locals and their historical heritage. OPPOSITE: The *chowks* — intersections — of Kathmandu bustle with bazaars. A vegetable vendor (top) weighs his products the old-fashioned way. Two women (bottom) pause to chat at a fabric store.

None of these, however, compare to the **Taleju temple** that rises from a mound to the right of the palace, considered the most beautiful in Kathmandu. Dedicated to Taleju Bhavani, the tutelary goddess of the Malla dynasty who was a consort of Shiva, the three-storied temple reaches about 36 m (120 ft) high and each of the three pagoda roofs is gilded with copper and embellished with hanging bells. The temple is only open to the public once a year, and nobody but members of the royal family are allowed to enter the main sanctum.

that support the second story. Nearby is the small **Hari Shankar temple**, dedicated to Shiva. Walk on to a crossroads where the struts of the three-storied, seventeenth-century Shiva temple, **Jaisi Dewal**, on top of a seven-stepped pyramid, has very finely carved erotica. Set in a yoni behind it is a massive, free-shaped lingam. It's thought the lingam may date back to the Lichhavi era.

Not far away is more classic erotica, on the struts of the **Ram Chandra Mandir** — delicate, but explicitly detailed carvings. Next you come to a stupa ruined in the four-

Durbar Square Environs

One of Kathmandu's most famous attractions is "**Freak Street**", just off Basantapur square. Its apple pies and hashish were once celebrated the length of the overland trail, from London to… well, Kathmandu. Nowadays, it's a down at heel version of Thamel and the only reminder of the heady days of the sixties and early seventies are a few T-shirts shops and a couple of poorly patronized restaurants.

Some distance south of Durbar square, faced in ceramic, is the three-storied **Adko Narayan temple**, one of the four main Vishnu temples of Kathmandu, guarded by an image of Garuda and lions and liberally adorned with erotic carvings on the struts

teenth century — the **Takan Bahal**, a round stucco mound mounted by a brick building.

From here you can wander around the narrow streets and alleys of the southern end of the Old City, discovering ancient houses and more ancient religious shrines. One, **Machhendra temple** plays a significant role during the Seto Machhendranath festival, when the deity's chariot must be driven three times around the temple as part of the final ceremony, after which the chariot is dismantled and the image returned in a colorful palanquin to its principal temple near Asan Tole.

Southwest of Durbar square, near the Vishnumati bridge, is a revered shrine dedicated to Bhimsen, the god of traders and artisans, whose shops occupy its ground floor. Another manifestation of Shiva, Bhimsen has been worshipped in the valley since the seventeenth century. In the days when Nepal's main commercial trade was with Tibet, every 12 years this shrine was carried to Lhasa on the Silk Road. There are some Buddhist stupas next to the temple.

In the opposite direction, to the north of Durbar Square, is a popular three-storied temple, the **Nara Devi**, guarded by red and white lions, dedicated to one of the Ashta Matrikas. Inside women prostrate them-

bar square, is approached through the six-meter (20-ft)-wide Makhan Tole, flanked by a many-hued façade with wooden balconies and columns. Six streets radiate out from the Indra Chowk. Various peddlers wander among the cloth and flower sellers, past a dried-fish market into the bead bazaar where the colors of the tawdry bangles and necklaces dazzle the eye. The Chowk is noted for its three temples, of which the most important is a three-storied house to the south, with white, purple and green ceramic tiles, yellow windows and two

selves surrounded by dazzling ceramic tiles and paintings. Nearby is the three-tiered **Narsingha temple** with its image of Vishnu with a lion's head. Along the same road is an open courtyard with a Swayambhunath-like stupa, **Yaksha Bahal**, with four sensual fourteenth-century carvings of the female form. It faces a painted metal door with two figures, one with four eyes, while above, an attractive woman's face appears out of a carved window frame, entrance to the house of the deity, Kanga Ajima.

Indra Chowk

The Indra Chowk, an area praised for its silk bazaar with many fine blankets and textiles, including woolen shawls, northeast of Dur-

balconies, from one of which hang four gilded griffins. The temple holds a highly revered shrine to Akash Bhairav. During the Indra Jatra festival a large image of Bhairav is displayed in the square when a huge lingam pole is raised in the center. Other important shrines and buildings in the Chowk include a highly venerated shrine to **Ganesh** and the Shiva Mandir, a simpler version of Patan's Krishna temple. This solid stone building is set above a four-stepped plinth where carpet sellers lay out their wares.

OPPOSITE: Old men while away an afternoon in the sunshine on Patan's Durbar square. ABOVE: Religious icon in front of Kathmandu's Jagannath temple.

Beyond Indra Chowk is the open space of **Kel Tole** — a fast and furious Nepali bazaar area, a never-ending hubbub of shoppers, peddlers, sightseers, beeping scooter rickshaws and even automobiles, forging through the narrow street watched by families from the balconies of their houses.

Seto Machhendranath

At the other end of the Chowk, to the east, past a small shrine smeared with blood, is one of Nepal's most revered temples: Seto

Machhendranath is at the center of a monastic courtyard, with its entrance guarded by two splendid brass lions. Each evening, beneath the porch that leads to the courtyard, groups of musicians gather and chant sacred verses, gazing at the temple as it rises behind a foreground of steles, *chaityas* (smaller stupas) and carved pillars, with its gilt-copper roof glowing in the evening sun.

The shrine guards the image of Kathmandu valley's most compassionate deity, Padmapani Avalokiteshwara, also known as Jammadyo or Machhendra. Once a year, around March and April, the image is taken from the temple for chariot processions through the city during the Seto Mach-

hendra festival. Built at an unknown date, the temple was restored in the early seventeenth century. Around the inside courtyard are many shops selling a variety of goods — wool, paper prints, cloth, string, ribbons, beads, curios, Nepali caps and pottery. Near the temple, on a street corner, is a small, Tantric temple, the three-storied **Lunchun Lunbun Ajima**, which carries, between portraits of the king and queen, erotic carvings.

Asan Tole

Northeast from here is Asan Tole, the capital's rice bazaar, where mountain porters gather seeking employment. It's a large open space with three temples, including the three-storied **Annapurna temple**, notable for the upturned corners of its gilded roofs. Many come to worship at its shrine, which contains nothing more than a pot. There's a mini-Narayan shrine near the center of the square and a smaller Ganesh temple.

Kanti Path

Leaving Asan Tole to wander through the fascinating narrow alleys and byways of the ancient Old Town you eventually come to **Kanti Path**, one of the city's main thoroughfares, with a notable ghat on one side of it, the **Rani Pokhari**. In the sixteenth century the wife of the Malla King Pratap built a temple in the center to honor her young son after his death, but it later collapsed. Since then a new shrine has been built. Beside the lake stands **Trichandra College**, built by the Ranas, with its clock tower and the wide expanse of the Tundikhel and the landmark column of the **Bhimsen tower**.

If you head northwest from Asan Tole through the city's vegetable and fruit market, the street becomes narrower and narrower until you reach a door that opens into the **Haku Bahal courtyard**. This has a notable carved window balcony, supported by small carved struts and an exquisitely carved door frame, all dating from the seventeenth century. Nearby is

ABOVE: Every byway in the Kathmandu valley turns up religious icons like this one. OPPOSITE: Bhaktapur's Jamuna goddess, mounted on a turtle.

the three-storied **Ugratara temple**, dedicated to the relief of eye infections and ail-
ments. The temple wall is adorned with
reading spectacles that have been donated
to whatever Hindu deity presides over the
gift of sight.

Continue on now until you see the two-
storied **Ikha Narayan temple**, with its magnificent four-armed Sridhara Vishnu, dating
from the tenth to eleventh century, flanked
by Lakshmi and Garuda. There's another
monument to a healing deity, Viasha Dev,
the toothache god, opposite this shrine. The
idea is that you hammer a nail into this large
piece of wood and thus nail down the evil
spirits causing the pain. If this fails, there's
a street of friendly, neighborhood dentists,
complete with off-the-peg molars of all
shapes and sizes, in the nearby lane.

If you walk futher north, past a sixteenth-century Narayan temple, you'll find
one of the capital's oldest and most remarkable antiquities — a carved black stone
fifth-century image of Buddha; and beyond that a bas-relief **Shiva-Parvati** as Uma
Maheshwar set in a brick case. Continue on
now to a passage guarded by lions that
leads into a monastery courtyard containing the shrine of Srigha Chaitya, a miniature likeness of the Swayambhunath stupa.
It's believed that those too old or sick to
climb the hill to Swayambhunath can earn
the same merit by making a pilgrimage
here.

Swayambhunath

The stupa of Swayambhunath looks down
from the top of a 100-m (350-ft)-high hill in
the west of the city, the rays of the rising sun
setting fire to its burnished copper spire as
it floats above the sea of early morning mist
that fills the valley. Buddha's all-seeing
eyes, in vivid hues, adorn all four sides of
the base of the spire, keeping constant vigil
over Kathmandu. Many believe this sacred
ground protects the divine light of Swayambhunath, the Self Existent One who,
when the waters drained from the valley,
emerged as a flame from a lotus blossom
atop this hill.

In the Kathmandu valley, temples and dwellings
merge into one another in what must be one of the
world's most bewitching urban landscapes.

The site of Swayambhunath was holy ground long before the advent of Buddhism, perhaps at a projecting stone that now forms the central core of the stupa. Here, it is said, Manjushri discovered the Kathmandu lotus that floated in its ancient lake.

The stupa's earliest known work was carried out in the fifth century by King Manadeva — confirmed by an inscription dated AD 460, some 600 years after emperor Ashoka is reputed to have paid homage at the site. Destroyed by Bengali troops in the

mid-fourteenth century, it was rebuilt by the seventeenth-century Malla monarch, King Pratap, who added a long stairway leading to it, two adjoining temples and a symbolic thunderbolt at the top.

The stupa is shaped like a lotus flower and in the last two thousand years saints, monks, kings and others have built monasteries, idols, temples and statues there; they now encircle the original stupa and the entire hilltop. Today pilgrims and the curious climb laboriously up King Pratap's 365 flagstone steps. Even if you have no sense of religion or history, you'll find the antics of the monkeys, which inhabit the temples and the shops, fascinating — they use the handrails of the steps as a slide — and the

views over Kathmandu as breathtaking as the stiff climb. Nepali legend says the monkeys are descended from the lice in Manjushri's hair which, as they dropped to the ground as he had his hair cut, sprang up as monkeys. It is also said that each strand of his hair which fell also sprang up again — as a tree.

On the stupa, the Buddha's all-seeing eyes gaze out in the four cardinal directions. Beneath the eyes, where you would expect a nose, is the symbol for the Nepali numeral "one", a representation of the one path to enlightenment. Above the eyes is the third eye, which represents the omniscience and wisdom of Buddha.

Mounted on a brass pedestal before the stupa is the thunderbolt, or *vajra* — all powerful — representing the divine strength of Lord Indra, King of the Heavens, in contrast to Buddha's all-pervading knowledge. Beneath the pedestal stand the 12 animals of the Tibetan zodiac: rat, bull, tiger, hare, dragon, serpent, horse, sheep, monkey, rooster, jackal and pig.

There's a daily service in the monastery, or *gompa*, facing the stupa — a rowdy and, to western ears, discordant clanking of instruments, blaring horns and a mêlée of saffron-robed worshippers. The eternal flame, Goddesses Ganga and Jamuna, is enshrined in a cage behind the stupa where a priest makes regular offerings.

Opposite, on a neighboring hill, the serene image of Saraswati, goddess of learning, gazes on the often frantic throng around Swayambhunath in benign astonishment.

Bodhnath

For all its size, Swayambhunath takes second place to a stupa northeast of the capital. Dedicated to Bodhnath, the god of wisdom, it's the largest stupa in Nepal — an immense mound surrounded by a self-contained Tibetan township and ringed by the inevitable prayer wheels, each given a twirl as devotees circle the shrine clockwise.

Basic fare in Kathmandu is flavored with seasonings such as chilies ABOVE laid out to dry in a Kathmandu street. OPPOSITE: Kathmandu skyline (top). A jumble of handcrafts and souvenirs (bottom) beckons in a Kathmandu bazaar.

The Cities of Kathmandu Valley

Most worshippers here are from Tibet. The Bodhnath lama is said to be a reincarnation of the original Dalai Lama, for the stupa's obscure origins are tenuously linked to Lhasa, ancestral home of the now exiled spiritual leader.

Legend says the stupa was constructed by the daughter of a swineherd, a woman named Kangma. She asked the king of Nepal for as much land as the hide of a buffalo would cover on which to build the stupa. When the king agreed, Kangma sliced the hide into thin ribbons, which

ambiance. There are a number of new monasteries in the Bodhnath region, and one, in the form of a castle, on the forestd slopes beside Gorakhnath cave. This monastery guards the footprints of a fourteenth-century sage who lived in the cave as a hermit.

Not far from this cave, the Tibetans have built another monastery — commemorating the memory of Guru Padma Rimpoche Sambhava, a saint who rode down to Kathmandu from Tibet to conquer a horde of demons.

were joined into one and laid out to form the square in which the stupa stands. Legend says that a relic of the Buddha lies within the solid dome, which symbolizes water and is reached by 13 steps, again symbolizing the 13 stages of enlightenment from which the monument derives its name, *bodh* meaning enlightenment and *nath*, meaning god.

Saffron and magenta-robed Tibetan monks celebrate their colorful rituals with worshippers chanting prayer verse, mantras and clapping their hands as travelers, especially those heading for the high Himalayas, seek blessings for their journey.

With about 5,000 exiles living in the valley, Kathmandu has a distinctly Tibetan

Godavari Royal Botanical Gardens
Nepal's flora enchanted early European visitors, who exported it lock, stock and root to their own climes. In the words of Nobel laureate Rudyard Kipling:
Still the world is wondrous large —
seven seas from marge to marge —
And it holds a vast of various kinds of man;
And the wildest dreams of Kew
are the facts of Kathmandu
Perhaps the easiest place to see many examples of Nepal's unique flora is Godavari Royal Botanical Gardens, located at the foot of the valley's highest point, 2,750-m (9,000-ft)-high Pulchoki hill, where the sacred waters of the Godavari spring from a natural cave.

Godavari has some 66 different species of fern, 115 orchids, 77 cacti and succulents and about 200 trees and shrubs as well as many ornamentals — though this represents only a small proportion of the country's 6,500 botanical species. It also features orchid and cacti houses, as well as fern, Japanese, and water gardens. Throughout, by lily ponds and on grassy slopes, the visitor finds rest and shade in thatched shelters.

Every 12 years, thousands of pilgrims journey from all over Nepal and India to bathe in the divine and healing waters of the Godavari spring.

Changu Narayan temple

On another hilltop stands Kathmandu's most ancient temple, Changu Narayan, glorious in its almost derelict splendor; its struts and surroundings are decorated with hundreds of delicately-carved erotic depictions. Founded around the fourth century AD, it represents the very best in Nepali art and architecture. It's difficult indeed to imagine a more stunning example of what Kathmandu valley is all about. Woodwork, metalwork and stonework come together in dazzling harmony nowhere to greater effect than in the sculptures of Bhupatendra, the seventeenth-century Malla king and his queen. There's also a human-sized figure of Garuda, with a coiled snake around his neck, close to the country's oldest stone inscription which records the military feats of King Mana Deva who ruled from AD 464 to 491. Although fire and earthquake have often damaged Changu Narayan and its environs over the centuries, this link with the ancient past is still evident in the image of a lion-faced Vishnu ripping the entrails out of his enemy.

Life's daily rhythms here in the cobblestone square are unchanged, too, with its pilgrim's platforms and lodges, *dharmsalas*, surrounding the square and the central temple. Cows, chickens, pye-dogs and runny-nosed urchins wander around while women hang their saris out to dry in the warm evening sunlight, which like some pastoral idyll of old, bathes the red brick in glowing orange.

The Cities of Kathmandu Valley

Pashupatinah

Pashupatinah is the holiest and most famous of all Nepal's Hindu shrines. Perched on the banks of the Bagmati, at **Deopatan**, Pashupatinah is reserved exclusively for Hindu worshippers. A series of terraces on the opposite bank — thickly populated with hundreds of rhesus monkeys, regarded by Hindu believers as kin of the gods, sun and stars — provides the best view of the pagoda's gilded copper roof, sadly surrounded by tatty, corroded tin roofs and higgledy-piggledy power lines.

There was a temple here as early as the first century AD; a settlement here in the third century BC may well have been the valley's first.

In the age of mythology Lord Shiva and his consort lived here by this tributary of the holy Ganges, making it, by the reckoning of some, a more sacred place of pilgrimage even than Varanasi on the Ganges. The Hindu holy men, *sadhus*, dressed in loin cloths and marked with cinder ash, looking immensely wise — but still wanting cash for picture sessions — sit cross-legged everywhere meditating, surrounded by the

Novice monks OPPOSITE at a Kathmandu monastery and ABOVE Buddhist monks at Bodhnath stupa in Kathmandu valley.

temple's delicate gold and silver filigree work.

For the visitor, the most astonishing thing about almost any Hindu shrine is its shabbiness. It's best to bear in mind that after centuries of use these are not historic monuments or museums but living places of worship, in many cases sadly in need of immediate renovation to preserve their glories. Pashupatinah is no exception. Much of the exterior is close to collapse, stained with the patina of centuries and with litter lying everywhere. Pashupatinah's most precious

treasure is its carved Shivalings or Shiva's phallus, stepped in a representation of the female sex organ, or yoni, of Parvati, Shiva's consort.

Gokarna Safari Park

Pashupatinah is not far from the forested slopes of Gokarna, close to the open glades and myriad birds of a Royal Game Sanctuary that's now open to the public as a safari park. For those who hanker after a touch of Maharajah-style travel, elephant rides are available between 9:30 AM and 4:30 PM across a nine-hole golf course among herds of grazing chital, rare black buck and other deer, rabbits, monkeys and pheasants.

New City

New road (Juddha Sadak) connects the Old City and the New City. Built over the devastation caused by the 1934 earthquake, it runs east from Basantapur and Durbar square to Tundikhel, the vast swathe of land that serves as Kathmandu's parade ground. The royal pavilion is used by the king to review parades on state occasions. It is decorated with statues of the six Gurkha heroes of the two world wars and around the park are equestrian statues. The park, according to local lore, was the home of a mythical giant, Gurumapa and each year, during the Ghode Jatra festival, a buffalo and mounds of rice are laid out in supplication to Gurumapa, to keep the peace.

As for New road itself, it is a commercial hub, harboring everything from the latest electronic appliances, cosmetics, expensive imported food and drugs, to jewels and priceless antiques. Halfway along the road is a small square shaded by a pipal tree, where intellectuals meet to philosophize and debate. Facing the Crystal Hotel at the end of New road is a supermarket close to a small, isolated shrine. There's also a statue of Juddha Shamsher Rana, prime minister from 1932 to 1945, who masterminded the building of New road.

Running off New road are a network of paved alleys, each with squares and corner patis, central chaityas and occasional temples, between traditional terraced houses. The medieval ambiance creates an authentic time warp, save for the gossiping crowds and the persistent whine of transistor radios. Westward is Basantapur, a large open space where the royal elephants were once kept — it takes its name from a large tower looming over the massive Hanuman Dhoka palace.

When New road was completed, the square turned into a marketplace, to be replaced by a brick platform built for King Birendra's coronation celebrations in 1975. Touts sell an assortment of cheap bric-a-brac — local trinkets, bracelets, bangles, religious images, swords and knives — throughout the square.

The two architectural triumphs of the

New City are the imposing **Narainhiti Royal palace**, built during the reign of King Rana Bahadur Shah and extended in 1970 to commemorate the wedding of Crown Prince Birendra, who is now the king; and Kathmandu's most impressive architectural work, the **Singh Durbar**. With the restoration of royalty in 1951, the Singh Durbar's 1,000 rooms, in the middle of a 31-hectare (77-acre) compound, were put to use as government offices. Unfortunately, much of it burned down in 1973. Its most impressive feature, the mirrored Durbar hall furnished

Auto-Rickshaw

Kathmandu's auto-rickshaws or "public scooters" follow fixed routes. Sensibly, very few foreigners use them. Black-and-yellow metered scooters are more popular. Although metered, fares are negotiated and should cost about half that of the taxis.

Rickshaw

Kathmandu's gaudy, honking rickshaws form part of the capital's vibrant street canvas. These large tricycles accommodate

with a throne, statues, portraits of dead rulers and a line of stuffed tigers, still survives. Today the Nepali Parliament, the Rastriya Panchayat, meets in the Singh Durbar, which also serves as the headquarters of the national broadcasting system (the first television transmissions didn't begin until May 1986).

GETTING AROUND

Trolley Bus

A fleet of quiet, pollution-free trolley buses, provided by China, ply the 18 km (11 miles) between the traffic circle beside the National Stadium and Bhaktapur; they cost next to nothing.

two passengers under cover in the back. Be sure that you agree on the fare before you set off and that the driver knows your destination. They should not cost more than taxis.

Taxi

Taxis, with white on black registration plates, travel throughout the Kathmandu valley. Fares are negotiated before setting off — the meter is purely decorative. Special half- and full-day rates may be negotiated.

OPPOSITE: A woman prostrates herself in prayer at the ancient Buddhist Swayambhunath temple, Kathmandu. ABOVE: Giant Buddha statue at Swayambhunath .

Bicycle

Cycling is one of the most popular means of exploring the capital and the valley. These days, mountain bikes can be hired from many shops in the Old City and near the main hotels, though standards vary enormously — check that the bell, brakes and lights work. If there are no lights carry a flashlight as it is required by law — and enforced. For a few rupees children will take care of the bicycle when you visit a popular tourist spot. Elsewhere, it is safe to leave it unattended (but locked) while you go sightseeing.

Motorbike

Motorbike hire is popular among young travelers. An international license is essential. Rates are economical for Indian-made 100 cc Hondas motorbikes, but more substantial motorcycles are also available for hire.

Bus

Kathmandu's severely overcrowded local buses are not recommended. For long-distance buses, the main bus station is on the Ring road, northwest of town, though most foreign travelers make their bus journeys on tourist buses which leave from the Thamel end of Kanti Path.

WHERE TO STAY

Kathmandu provides travelers with a wide range of accommodation options — from the lap of luxury to basic guesthouse bed and washroom standards — and everything in-between. There is truly something for everyone.

LUXURY

The best all-around choice if you're looking for five-star standards combined with some local color is the **Hotel Yak and Yeti** ((01) 248999 or (01) 240520 FAX (01) 227782, P.O. Box 1016, Durbar Marg, Kathmandu. Located in the city center and built around the wing of an old Rana palace, with 270 rooms, 19 suites, swimming pool, tennis courts, gymnasium, jogging trail, casino, shopping plaza and all the other services you might expect, the Yak and Yeti also

maintains a much cherished historical association with Boris Lissanevitch's Royal Hotel: the copper chimneyed fire place from Boris's legendary Yak and Yeti bar (once the only expatriate haunt in all Kathmandu) can now be found in the Yak and Yeti's Chimney Room Restaurant (see WHERE TO EAT, below). The rooms with garden views are particularly sought after.

One of the great attractions of the **Hotel Shangri-la** ((01) 412999 FAX (01) 414184, P.O. Box 655, Lazimpat, Kathmandu, is its back garden, much favored as a sunny

retreat to while away an afternoon with a book — the unusual swimming pool is constructed along the lines of a traditional bathing ghat. The Shangri-la has the full complement of services and restaurants, the latter including Tien Shan, probably the best Chinese dining in all Nepal. As is the case at the Hotel Yak and Yeti, request a room with a garden view.

Less conveniently located but also boasting impeccable standards is the **Everest Hotel** ((01) 220567 FAX (01) 224421, P.O. Box 569, New Banesworth, Kath-

OPPOSITE: A treasury of ornate medieval architecture (top and bottom) adorns the cities of Kathmandu valley. ABOVE: The delicate filigree on Bhaktapur's Golden Gate.

mandu. First impressions in the lobby, which brims with fascinating displays and bric-a-brac, are unlikely to be dashed elsewhere in the hotel — the room furniture is tasteful, if slightly worn in some rooms. The hotel has a swimming pool, tennis court, shopping arcade, restaurants, a rooftop bar and restaurant (at eight floors, the Everest is Kathmandu's tallest hotel) a casino and one of the few discos in Kathmandu.

MID-RANGE

Without a doubt the most unique hotel in Kathmandu is **Dwarika's Kathmandu Village Hotel (** (01) 470770 FAX (01) 471379, P.O. Box 459, Battisputali, Kathmandu. A winner of the Heritage Award from the Pacific Asia Tourist Association (PATA), Dwarika's is a hotel that comes close to being a museum. Many of the fittings in the hotel have been rescued from buildings slated for demolition or on the verge of collapse and faithfully restored by a team of craftspeople employed by the hotel. The rooms combine modern comforts with tasteful antique fittings and there's a wonderful sense, if you stay here, of having made a small contribution to the maintenance of Nepal's rich but threatened artistic heritage.

Coming in at the expensive end of the mid-range is the **Hotel Shanker (** (01) 410151 FAX (01) 412691, P.O. Box 350, Lazimpat, Kathmandu. This is one instance, however, where that little extra makes all the difference. The majestic old building — in the style of a European palace — makes staying here is a grand experience. The one catch is that room standards and sizes vary considerably, and some of the rooms are disappointing.

There's a lot to be said for the convenience of a Thamel location — great shopping and almost unlimited opportunities for dining out. One place that provides this along with standards above the average Thamel guesthouse is the **Hotel Manang (** (01) 410933 FAX (01) 415821, P.O. Box 5608, Thamel, Kathmandu. Rooms are air-conditioned, sport mini-bars and satellite television and on the upper floors offer good views.

INEXPENSIVE

Most of Kathmandu's best deals are in the tourist enclave of Thamel, an area in which sizzling steak restaurants rub shoulders with handicraft stalls, providers of e-mail services and trekking agencies. Of near legendary status is the **Kathmandu Guest House (** (01) 413632 or 418733 FAX (01) 417133, P.O. Box 2769, Thamel, Kathmandu. The rooms are simple, ranging from back-to-basics to lower mid-range comfort, but praise is reserved mostly for the garden area, which in Kathmandu's perennially sunny weather is usually littered with basking travelers recuperating from the rigors of the last trek or reading up on the next one. Services are basic — laundry, travel bookings and so on — but the building is a delightful warren and it's in the heart of Thamel.

A relative newcomer to the crowded Thamel accommodation scene is the Tibetan-managed **Utse Hotel (** (01) 226946 FAX (01) 226945, Jyatha, Thamel, Kathmandu. The spotless, carpeted rooms with television and private bath are a good value, but it is the rooftop garden that wins most guests' hearts. Downstairs, off the lobby, is a popular Tibetan restaurant.

For inexpensive lodgings outside the busy Thamel area, the embassy district of Lazimpat has the appropriately named **Hotel Ambassador (** (01) 410432 FAX (01) 413641, P.O. Box 2769, Lazimpat, Kathmandu. Given that you're still only a 10-minute walk from Thamel, the Ambassador provides the best of both worlds — peace from the touts and bustle and easy access to the restaurants and attractions of Kathmandu. The hotel has a good range of well-maintained rooms; downstairs are a sunny coffee shop and Indian restaurant.

WHERE TO EAT

For weary world travelers, Kathmandu has a reputation as the gourmet capital of the sub-continent. Whether you feel this sobriquet is deserved will probably depend on where you have arrived from. It has to be said that most of the restaurants in Thamel,

A Thamel souvenir stand displaying gleaming metalwork.

which offer a vast range of continental, Mexican, Tibetan, Chinese and even Thai cuisine, are doing a good job under the pressure of limited resources; but few Thamel restaurants bear up to repeat visits.

Most of Kathmandu's best restaurants are outside Thamel, on Durbar Marg, or in the major hotels around town. Prices here are very reasonable: even scaling Kathmandu's culinary heights, you'll be hard pressed to spend more than US$20 per person. Naturally it is Nepali and Indian food that locals do best, but there are also one or

Al'Fresco Restaurant, Soaltee Oberoi ((01) 272550/6, may be indoors but it does at least offer pleasant views of the hotel gardens, not to mention the best Italian dining in Kathmandu. It's popular with the "expat" community — who like to forget they are in Kathmandu from time to time. Open daily. Reservations are recommended.

The **Chimney Room**, Hotel Yak and Yeti ((01) 413999, owes its reputation at least in part to a nostalgic connection with Boris Lissanevitch, the Russian ballet dancer,

two good Chinese, Japanese and Italian restaurants for those seeking a break from the spices.

EXPENSIVE

Universally lauded as Kathmandu's premiere Indian restaurant, **Ghar-e-Kabab**, Hotel de l'Annapurna ((01) 221711, is the perfect spot for a memorable evening out. The tandoori here is as good as you'll find anywhere. You can watch the chefs at work, and in the evenings listen to the exotic sounds of live classical Indian music. Open daily. Reservations are recommended.

A rickshaw operator ABOVE waits for customers while a sidewalk vendor OPPOSITE sells garlic and shallots in a Kathmandu street.

world traveler and chef who is remembered as having established Kathmandu's first hotel. The name is taken from the copper fireplace that came from Boris's Royal Hotel. The Russian–continental menu features some of Boris's specialties, such as his celebrated borscht and chicken Kiev. Open daily. Reservations recommended.

Providing you are prepared to forego sushi and sashimi, you can have a surprisingly good Japanese meal at **Fuji Restaurant** ((01) 225272, Kanti Path. The setting — French windows giving out onto a pond and summer alfresco dining — is as much a treat as the food. Regular diners wax enthusiastically about the *obento*, set meals — for both lunch and dinner.

Closed Mondays. Reservations recommended.

Probably the best Chinese food in town is the Sichuan and Cantonese fare at **Tien Shan** ((01) 412999, Shangri-la Hotel. Try the Sichuan dishes — the chef, from Chengdu, knows what he is doing.

INEXPENSIVE

Thamel is teeming with inexpensive restaurants, but if you want to take a look at where the locals eat and drink, wander down to **Nanglo** ((01) 222636, Durbar

to the original Mike's, which of course does it better. Open daily.

The **Old Vienna Inn** ((01) 419183, Thamel, is one of the few Thamel restaurants that deserve a special mention. It's another long-runner, with a small army of aficionados. The menu features Austrian and German favorites. The chocolate cake is legendary. Open daily.

Another excellent Thamel restaurant is the **Third Eye** ((01) 227478, Thamel. It has two major selling points: the best tandoori in Thamel; and an intimate, sit-on-the-floor

Marg. There's a rough and ready bar and Chinese restaurant downstairs, but out the back and on the roof is a beer garden with tasty barbecue dishes and some average generic Western cuisine. In the winter months, local "expats" gather downstairs, knock back the beers and munch on Tibetan momos. Open daily.

Mike's Breakfast, Naxal, is an institution. As the name suggests, breakfasts are the specialty, but lunch and dinner are excellent too. Meals are served in a delightful garden. There's an art gallery upstairs featuring local artists and occasional exhibitions by foreign photographers and painters. The **Northfield Café** in Thamel is run by the same management, but this is no excuse to skip a trip out

room at the back. This is one of the few Thamel restaurants where a reservation is a good idea. Open daily.

It's impossible to leave Thamel without mentioning two more restaurants: **Le Bistro** ((01) 411170, Thamel, and **KC's** ((01) 416911, Thamel. It is the upstairs views over one of Thamel's busiest intersections, the faint strains of blues and jazz coming from the Blue Note café next door, that make Le Bistro an essential stop on the Thamel restaurant circuit — the food is average. KC's, on the other hand, is remembered as one of the Thamel pioneers: many of the Thamel standards — such as sizzling steak — had their start here. The sizzling steaks and vegetarian lasagna are still good.

NIGHTLIFE

Kathmandu is not a place for late night carousing. Everything closes at 10 PM. For a quiet drink before an early night, try **Blue Note**, an upstairs Thamel bar with candlelit tables and a wide selection of jazz and blues.

Kathmandu's casinos are an exception to the early-to-bed rule. There are four of them these days, catering largely to an Indian clientele — Nepalis are denied entry. Kathmandu's casinos are: **Casino Anna**

((01) 223479, Hotel de l'Annapurna; **Casino Everest** ((01) 220567, Everest Hotel; **Casino Royale** ((01) 228481, Hotel Yak and Yeti; and **Casino Nepal** ((01) 270244, Hotel Soaltee Oberoi.

HOW TO GET THERE

For details of air and bus services to Kathmandu see GETTING AROUND and GETTING THERE sections of TRAVELERS' TIPS.

The easiest way into town from the airport is by taxi. There is an official taxi stand just outside the exit to the Departure Lounge at Tribhuvan International Airport. Avoid touts offering free taxi rides into town. The major hotels all offer airport connections.

PATAN

Patan, around five kilometers (three miles) south of Kathmandu, over the Bagmati River, is less a distinct city than a district of Kathmandu these days. But in medieval times, until the Gurkha conquest of the valley in 1768, it was the largest of the three Kathmandu valley kingdoms. As Kathmandu rose to prominence, Patan became a quiet backwater.

It is this that makes Patan such a charming retreat from Kathmandu. The city is resolutely Newari; there's an old-world ambiance to the tangled skein of alleys, where domestic animals wander freely and locals still have time to pass the time of day with each other. When you need a break from Kathmandu but you're still not ready for the hills, Patan is the perfect getaway.

WHAT TO SEE

Durbar square

At the entrance to Patan's Durbar square, another royal mall, is an octagonal **Krishna temple**. Nearby is an immense copper bell cast in the eighteenth century by Vishnu Malla and his queen, Chandra Lakshmi. Traditionally, its deep sonorous clanging summoned worshippers, but it was also used as an early warning system in the event of emergencies: fires, earthquakes and raiding armies. How the people of Patan distinguished between the call to divine duty and the warning to take cover remains unexplained.

Set next to the Krishna temple is a three-storied **Vishnu temple** notable for its tympanums, the ornate triangular recesses set between the cornices of its low gables.

One of Patan's oldest temples, **Charanarayan,** is believed to have been built around 1566 by King Purendra, although now architectural historians suspect it belongs to the seventeenth century. The struts of this two-storied pagoda building, embellished with lively erotica — either inspiring or inspired by the *Kama Sutra* — will impress gymnastics enthusiasts.

The centrally placed **Krishna temple** is unmistakable. One of the most beautiful

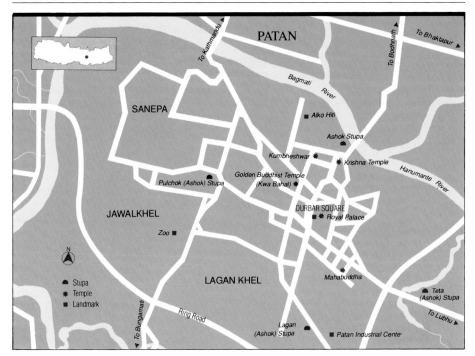

temples in the country, generally regarded as a masterpiece of Nepali architecture, it's built entirely of limestone, a legacy of King Siddhi Narsimha Malla, who reigned for 41 years in the seventeenth century. The annual focus of thousands of devotees celebrating Krishna's birthday around August to September is the narrative carving on the frieze, depicting the stories of the epic Mahabharata and Ramayana. It was the king's son, Shri Nivasa Malla, who in 1682 restored the undated Bhimsen temple after it was damaged by fire. Since then, following the 1934 earthquake, it's been restored once more. The gods make Patan tremble frequently.

Not only the gods wreak havoc in Patan. When King Prithvi Narayan Shah swept into the valley in 1768 to oust the Mallas, Patan's fourteenth-century Royal palace was badly damaged, but its ornate gates, delicately-carved struts, statues, open courtyards and many rooms — conference halls, sleeping chambers, kitchens and so forth — remain to recall the glory of Malla architectural splendor. One of these many splendors is the eighteenth-century **Taleju temple,** built as an additional story to the palace itself and tragically destroyed in

1934. Now rebuilt, it's open only 10 days each year, during the September to October Chaitra Dasain festival. This temple, **Taleju Bhavani,** though smaller and less impressive than the original, is held more sacred.

Of all of its statuary, Patan's most imposing monument is the sculpture of **King Yoganarendra Malla** seated on a lotus atop a six-meter (20-ft)-high pillar in front of the **Degatule Taleju temple.** He ruled at the beginning of the seventeenth century and is the subject of a still popular belief among Patan folk that one day he will return to take up his rule again. For this reason, one door and one window in the palace always remain open to welcome him.

Patan's treasures are not confined to the immediate precincts of its Durbar square. Five minutes walk away there's a **Golden Buddhist temple** and another Buddha shrine, Mahabuddha, two kilometers (1.2 miles) distant. There's also **Kumbheshwar,** one of two five-storied temples in Kathmandu valley where Shiva is believed to winter for six months before leaving to spend his summer with Parvati on the crest of Gaurisankar.

A Kathmandu vegetable market.

SHOPPING

Be sure to shop around before committing yourself to any purchases: prices — and quality — vary considerably.

The best **Tibetan carpets,** old and new, are found at Jawalkhel, near Patan, in the **Tibetan Refugee Center** and many shops.

The **Cheez Beez Bhandar, (Nepali Handicraft Center)** near Jawalkhel, sells **handicrafts** from all parts of Nepal.

Excellent quality **antiques and rare art objects** are on display at the **Tibet Ritual Art Gallery,** Durbar Marg, above the Sun Kosi restaurant; it's run by two experts in the subject.

Woodcarvings, metalwork and thang-kas can be seen at **Patan Industrial Estate**. Bear in mind that it is forbidden to export thangkas and bronzes if they are more than 100 years old.

WHERE TO STAY

Patan has few hotels. Most travelers stay in Kathmandu, which is just twenty minutes away by taxi.

LUXURY

The top hotel in Patan is the **Hotel Hima-laya** ((01) 523900 FAX (01) 523909, P.O. Box 2141, Sahid Sukra Marg, Lalitpur, Kath-mandu. Although it does not match the standards of the best hotels in Kathmandu, the Himalaya can justly boast of its views of the mountains for which it is named. Ask for a room with a view.

MID-RANGE

The **Hotel Narayani** ((01) 525015 FAX (01) 525017, Pulchowk, Patan, was once Patan's best. These days, competition from the newer Himalaya has forced it to bring its prices down. The expansive garden and large swimming pool are winning features of this hotel, but otherwise it is undistin-guished.

For many repeat visitors, the **Summit Hotel** ((01) 521894 FAX (01) 523737, Kupon-dole Height, Patan, is in a class of its own. It may be slightly inaccessible, but this con-tributes to the hideaway character of the hotel. There's a pleasant garden and swim-ming pool; but best of all are the views of Kathmandu and the Himalayas from the rooms.

Patan's Durbar square holds matchless treasures of medieval architecture and art.

INEXPENSIVE

The **Aloha Inn (** (01) 522796 FAX (01) 524571, Jawalkhel, Patan, is a good escape if you're fed up with big impersonal hotels. It has a family guesthouse atmosphere, with a small well-tended garden, while maintaining higher standards than the average guesthouse.

Lastly, for a room with a view, the **Third World Guesthouse (** (01) 522187, overlooks Patan's Durbar square. Wake up here in the first glimmerings of dawn and it's easy to feel that you've been spirited into an ancient Oriental citadel.

WHERE TO EAT

Nobody goes to Patan for the dining. The most popular restaurants are more notable for their views of Durbar square than for the dishes they turn out. **Café de Pagode** is typical. It overlooks the square and serves an eclectic range of local and international dishes. If you stop here for lunch, stick to what they do best: the Indian and Nepali dishes. Other, similar, restaurants around the square include the **Café de Patan** and the **Café de Temple**. None of these has a phone or will take a reservation — they are simple, informal places that are perfect for watching life go by.

The **Chalet Restaurant (** (01) 523900, Hotel Himalaya, does good quality Indian, continental and even Japanese food. The ambiance can't compare with the cafés on the square, however.

HOW TO GET THERE

Getting to Patan from Kathmandu is easy — you could walk if the traffic wasn't so disagreeable. Taxis make the 15-minute run from Thamel for less than US$2. The public buses are best avoided.

AROUND PATAN

At the southwestern edge of Patan is **Jawalkhel,** site of the valley's largest Tibetan refugee camp. This area is a center for **Tibetan handicrafts.** In two large buildings, 200 men and women are always busy carding wool and weaving carpets. In the

first building, five rows of women in traditional costume sit on the floor, one to three on a carpet, weaving traditional patterns, chatting and singing. In the next building, old men and women comb the wool and spin it into threads. Shops display these handicrafts for sale. Portraits of the King and Queen of Nepal and the Dalai Lama look down from the walls on a maze of carpets, blankets, woven bags and small coats.

Jawalkhel Zoo, near the craft shops in the industrial area, has a selection of exotic

south-Asian animals, especially Himalayan species. Open daily.

South of Patan, various vehicle and walking tracks line settlements and sacred sites of the one-time capital. West of the Bagmati river are **Kirtipur** and its satellite hamlets, **Panga** and **Nagaon.** The twin settlements of **Bungamati** and **Khokana** lie on either side of the sacred Karma Binayak site. There is a road leading to the **Lele valley** and a trail to **Godavari** and **Phulchoki**, passing through **Harisiddhi, Thaibo** and **Bandegaon.** An eastern lane takes travelers to **Sanagaon** and **Lubhu.** All these villages have close links to Patan.

BHAKTAPUR

About 16 km (10 miles) from Kathmandu is Bhaktapur, eastern gateway of the valley. In its present form the city dates back to the

OPPOSITE: Carved stone sentinels guard the secrets locked inside the temple of Nyatapola in Bhaktapur. ABOVE: Bhaktapur after rain shower.

ninth century — King Anand Malla made it his seat in AD 889.

Central Bhaktapur, particularly its Durbar square is something of a showcase. Of the three historic cities in Kathmandu valley, Bhaktapur best retains the medieval flavor of the Malla era. This is no accident. Since the 1970s the German-funded Bhaktapur Development Project has set out to ensure that Bhaktapur's development takes place along lines that best suit the heritage and character of the old city.

good hour can be spent sipping the piquant local tea and studying the erotica on the tea room struts.

Nyatapola is one of two five-storied temples in the valley. (Kumbheshwar is the other; see page 127). From as far back as you can stand it looks like a fretted pyramid climbing up to the clouds, reaching a height of more than 30 m (100 ft). Its inspiration is said to have been appeasement to the terrifying menace of Bhairav, who stands in another temple. There seems to be more than just fancy to this tale. Now more than

Bhaktapur is not just the historically best preserved of the three valley cities, it is also the most thoroughly Hindu and Newar. Even though Kathmandu is just a day's walk away, the Newar people of Bhaktapur speak a different dialect.

WHAT TO SEE

Nyatapola Pagoda
Durbar square is dominated by Nyatapola Pagoda. Tourists stand before it overwhelmed not only by the dimensions of the temple but also by the nonstop hurly-burly of hawkers, pedestrians and children who overrun the place. You can find sanctuary in the Café Nyatapola, opposite, where a

200 years old, its doors were sealed and bolted when the builders finished their job, and have never been opened since. What's inside is anyone's guess. Certainly, no menace terrifies the hordes who swarm over its plinth and up its steps. After all, they are guarded at the bottom by legendary sentinels, Jaya Mal and Patta, two wrestlers said to have the strength of 10 men; next, two huge elephants, each 10 times stronger than the wrestlers; then, two lions, each as strong as 10 elephants; now, two griffins each as strong as 10 lions; and finally, on the uppermost plinth, two demi-goddesses — Baghini in the form of a tigress and Singhini, as a lioness — each 10 times stronger than a griffin. It's a pattern of sentinels

found nowhere else in Nepali temple architecture and considered significant evidence of the measure of appeasement required to placate Bhairav.

Durbar Square

You'll need time to digest all this ambiance, both exotic and enthralling, before walking on to Durbar Square to feast on its treasures which begin at its very gate, built of lime-plastered brick in the eighteenth century by Bhupatendra. Its arch is a depiction of the face of glory, Kirtimukha,

gate, alas, is only bronze, but when it catches the sun's rays it glitters and sparkles like the precious metal itself. Ranjit Malla commissioned it in 1754 to adorn the outer entrance to the Taleju temple within the Royal palace, a one-storied shrine with many struts. During the Vijaya Dashami festival the goddess is believed to take up residence in the south wing of the building. It's a superlative example of the artwork of Kathmandu valley, regarded by many as its finest. One of the carved windows is believed to be the personal handicraft of Bhupatendra, whose

guarded on either side by two wooden carvings: one of Bhairav, the other of Hanuman. The gate looks out on three remarkable temples of different styles, whose divine proportions are concealed by all being huddled together: one, the single-storied Jagannath, housing an image of Harishankara; the second, a two-storied Krishna temple standing in front of it and housing images of Krishna, Radha and Rukmani; and the third, the Shiva Mandir, built in the shikara style with four porticoes each with a niche above them for plated images of gods.

Both evening and morning, the sun falls on the north-facing **Golden Gate,** the entrance to the **Palace of 55 Windows.** The

bronze statue — sitting, hands folded reverently before Taleju — faces the Golden Gate. Each of the corners has images of Hindu goddesses Devashri and Lakshmi and in the temple area there's a large bell cast out of copper and iron. The temple opens its doors only once a year — between September and October — during the Dasain festival celebrations, when Taleju's golden statue is placed on the back of the horse that is stabled in the courtyard and led around town in a procession.

After a day craning their necks at the beautiful roofs of Newar temples OPPOSITE, travelers can relax and while away the evening in one of the Thamel district's countless rooftop restaurants such as the Brezel Bakery ABOVE.

The Cities of Kathmandu Valley

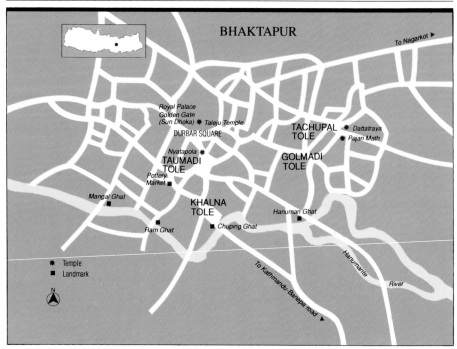

The adjacent palace is renowned mainly for its 55-windowed Hall of Audience, an elaborately carved balcony and its collection of priceless wood carvings, some damaged in the 1934 earthquake but still considered invaluable. Originally built in the fifteenth century, the palace was remodeled by Bhupatendra. Again, this Durbar square also boasts a large bell that was used both to summon worshippers and to give alarms, particularly if there was a night curfew, when it was rung to send citizens scurrying home. There are many more temples in Bhaktapur's Durbar square: to **Kumari, Vatsala, Durga, Narayan, Shiva,** and **Pashupatinah.** The last is the oldest in the city, built around the end of the fifteenth century by the widow and sons of King Yaksha Malla to honor his memory, though some argue it was built much later in 1682 by Jita Malla, father of Bhupatendra.

Bhaktapur legend avers that Lord Pashupatinah appeared before him in a dream and ordered him to build the temple. Another legend has it that the king wanted to visit the temple at Deopatan but was unable to cross the Bagmati since it was in full flood and so ordered another temple to Pashupatinah to be built in Bhaktapur.

The western end of the palace, previously known as Malati Chowk, has been converted into the **National Art Gallery** ℂ (01) 610004. Highlights include wall murals from the Palace of 55 Windows, a large collection of thangkas and some superb sculpture — both Buddhist and Hindu. It's open from 10:30 AM to 4 PM. Closed Tuesdays and national holidays.

Tachupal Tole

It's just a 10-minute walk along the fascinating Main Bazaar from Nyatapola Pagoda to Tachupal Tole, the original center of the old city. Some architectural historians maintain this part of the city may date back to the eighth century. The heart of this district is Dattatreya square, named after **Dattatreya temple.** The temple is very old indeed; it was built in 1427, though alterations were made half a century later. Look for Jaya Mal and Patta flanking the entrance — the same two wrestlers you saw at Nyatapola Pagoda.

Behind Dattatreya temple is the **Bronze and Brass Museum** ℂ (01) 610488, which has a collection of metalwork from around the valley — both ritual and domestic in function. Most visitors find the **National Woodcarving Museum** ((01) 610005, opposite, more interesting. The collection of both architectural carvings and free-standing sculptures is not extensive but quite captivating. Both museums are open from 10 AM to 5 PM (3 PM on Fridays). Closed Tuesdays.

WHERE TO STAY

Bhaktapur is a day-tripper's city. Your ac-

commodation choices are more limited than even Patan. Most of the accommodation is of the extreme budget variety.

INEXPENSIVE

The Golden Gate Guesthouse ((01) 610534, Durbar square, Bhaktapur, may be somewhat spartan, but it's just a hop away from the gate from which it takes its name. The roof offers great views.

If you're looking for a little more comfort, try the **Bhadgaon Guesthouse** ((01) 610488 FAX (01) 610481, Durbar square, Bhaktapur. The rooms are simple but comfortable with basic bathrooms. Again, the rooftop views are picture postcard material.

The Cities of Kathmandu Valley

WHERE TO EAT

Though not a true restaurant city, Bhaktapur, at least provides you with the rare opportunity to dine in a converted pagoda. The **Café Nyatapola**, opposite Nyatapola temple, started life in the eighteenth century as a place of worship; nowadays it does palatable pizzas and tasty samosa, along with all the other international fare you've come to expect of Nepali tourist restaurants.

The **Café Peacock** is on Dattatreya square and possesses what many find to be one of the most charming prospects in the whole Kathmandu valley. The international menu is both cheaper and better than that of the Café Nyatapola.

THIMI

Just three kilometers (1.9 miles) west of Bhaktapur is Thimi — Kathmandu valley's fourth-largest settlement. Founded by the Malla dynasty, Thimi takes its name from the Nepali word *chhemi*, which means "ca-

Potters shape their vessels in traditional fashion at the village of Thimi, near Bhaktapur in the Kathmandu valley.

pable". It's an honor bestowed upon Thimi's residents by the Bhaktapur monarchs for their skill in fighting the forces of the rival kingdoms in the valley.

Thimi is a town of potters where families, taught skills handed down from generation to generation, turn out handsome stoneware fashioned from the red clay of the valley — vessels for domestic use and art works such as peacock flower vases and elephant representations. The colorful sixteenth-century **Balkumari temple** is the town's main shrine and nearby in a much smaller dome-shaped shrine is a brass likeness Bhairav.

Thimi is most renowned as the location, along with two other adjacent villages — **Nade** and **Bode** — of the most riotous of Nepal's New Year (Bisket Jatra) celebrations. Nade is noted for its multicolored, three-storied Ganesh temple, while on the other side of the many dikes that meander through the rice paddies, Bode boasts a famous two-storied seventeenth-century **Mahalakshmi temple**. It stands on the site of an early temple built, according to local lore, in 1512, after Mahalakshmi appeared in a dream to the king of Bhaktapur.

Every year on New Year's Day, the square around the Balkumari temple in Thimi witnesses a spectacular gathering of 32 deities carried in elaborate multi-roofed palanquins under the shade of ceremonial umbrellas after which the Nade idol of Ganesh arrives. Later the crowds move across the field to Bode to witness another extraordinary New Year's ritual (see also YOUR CHOICE, FESTIVE FLINGS, pages 45–53).

LAND OF THE NEWARS

KIRTIPUR

About five kilometers (three miles) southwest of Kathmandu, perched on a twin hillock, twelfth-century Kirtipur was to become an independent kingdom and ultimately the last stronghold of the Mallas when Prithvi Narayan Shah rode into Kathmandu to conquer the valley in 1769–70.

Bhaktapur woman preparing traditional Nepali bread, *roti*.

The city withstood a prolonged siege, during which the Malla army taunted Pritthvi's Gorkha forces as they hurled them back down the fortress-like hill.

It was a mistake. When Kirtipur finally fell, the vengeful Gorkha ruler ordered his men to amputate the nose and lips of all Kirtipur's male inhabitants — the only exception being those musicians who played wind instruments.

Now only the ruined walls remain to remind Kirtipur's 8,000 residents of this epic battle. These days Kirtipur is a place of

trade and cloistered learning. Part of nearby Tribhuvan University's campus now sprawls across the former farmlands.

The traditional occupations, apart from farming, are spinning and weaving. At Kirtipur's **Cottage Industry Center**, 900 handlooms spin fine cloth for sale in Kathmandu.

Though it has withstood the savage earthquakes that have caused so much damage elsewhere in the valley, Kirtipur has been unable to withstand the ravages of time: there's a decayed and neglected air to the city. Still, a walk beneath the exquisitely-carved windows of its multistoried houses — laid out on terraces linked by ramps and sloping paths — is a worth-

while excursion and there are some fine temples to command your interest.

Kirtipur lies on the saddle between two hills, beside a small lake. The main approach is via a long flight of stairs. Atop the hill to the south there's a huge stupa, the **Chilanchu Vihar,** encircled by eight shrines decorated at their cardinal points by stone images. There are many Buddhist monasteries around the stupa also. On the hill to the north, which is higher, Hindus have settled around a restored temple dedicated to **Uma Maheshwar.**

The three-storied **Bagh Bhairav temple** stands at the high point of the saddle between the two hills, a place of worship for both Hindus and Buddhists. It's decorated with swords and shields taken from its Newar troops after Prithvi Narayan Shah's eighteenth-century victory. It contains an image of Bhairav, manifested as a tiger and the *torana* above the main sanctum shows Vishnu riding Garuda and Bhairav attended on either side by Ganesh and Kumar. From the temple there are striking views of the valley and the brightly colored patchwork of farm fields below, with the villages of **Panga** and **Nagaon** in the southeast.

You can take a path through the rice fields from Kirtipur to Panga, which was established by the Mallas as a fortress town to stall invaders from the north. None of its six or so temples dates prior to the nineteenth century. The path continues from Panga to Nagaon, a name that means "new village".

The sixteenth-century Malla who ruled Kathmandu from Patan, concerned that his subjects might move too far from the city to serve its defense, established the twin settlements of **Bungamati** and **Khokana,** near the Karma Binayak Shrine, amid fertile fields. During a major drought, the king sought the blessings of the rain god, Machhendra, at a temple in India, inviting the deity to come and settle in the valley. He built a shrine at Bungamati where, in the last decade of the sixteenth century, it became the custom to keep the image of the Rato Machhendra during winter, moving it back to Patan by palanquin in summer.

Guardian elephant outside a temple at Kirtipur village in Kathmandu valley.

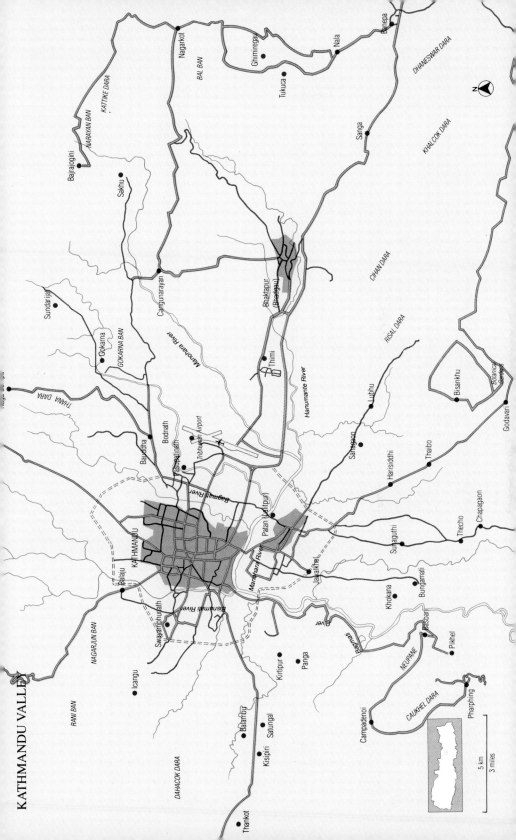

KATHMANDU VALLEY

Bajrajogini

Sakhu

Nagarkot

BAL BAN

Ghimiregau

Nala

Banepa

DHANESWAR DARA

N

KATTIKE DARA

NARAYAN BAN

Tukuca

Sanga

KHALCOK DARA

Sundarijal

Cangunarayan

Bhaktapur
(Bhadgau)

CIHAN DARA

Gokarna

GOKARNA BAN

Manohara River

Thimi

RISAL DARA

Botanical
Gardens

THANA DARA

Bodnath

Pasupatinath

Tribhuvan Airport

Hanumante River

Lubhu

Bisankhu

Godavari

Balaju

Bagmati River

Patan (Lalitpur)

Sanagaon

Thaibo

KATHMANDU

Manohara River

Jawalkhel

Harisiddhi

Sulaguthi

Thecho

Chapagaon

Swayambhunath

Bisnumati River

River

Khokana

Bungamati

Icangu

RANI BAN

NAGARJUN BAN

Kintipur

Panga

Bagmati River

Basbari

NEUPANE

Pikhel

Balambu

Satungal

Campadenoi

CAUKHEL DARA

Pharphing

Kisipiri

DAHACOK DARA

Thankot

5 km

3 miles

Many small votive chaityas line the processional way from Patan to Bungamati, which nestles against a hillside, surrounded by terraced rice paddies and small copses of trees. The village is noted for its strongly-stated, shikhari-style **Rato Machhendranath temple**. The adjacent Lokeshwar shrine contains an image of Bhairav's massive head in full, demoniac fury.

There's another shrine, **Karma Binayak**, on a tree-clad hill and beyond that, a 10-minute walk away, is a brick-paved village famous for the manufacture of mustard oil, **Khokana**. It has a temple dedicated to the nature goddess Shukla Mai, or Rudrayani. Rebuilt after the 1934 quake, its main street is noticeably wider than in similar villages.

THROUGH KATHMANDU VALLEY

TO THE WEST

Many interesting rural communities, with fascinating temples and shrines, are close to Kathmandu. In the west, on the old "Silk Road" to Tibet, stand the villages of **Satungal, Balambu, Kisipidi** and **Thankot**. The first three cluster together within walking distance, no more than six kilometers (3.7 miles) from the capital city.

Satungal, Balambu, Kisipidi

The first, **Satungal**, was built in the sixteenth century as a fortress to thwart invaders from the north. Many of its 1,000 residents work in Kathmandu. Its **main square** is notable for the two-meter (6.5-ft) stone image of a seated Buddha on a free-standing platform. Nearby, to the north of the square, steps lead through an embellished gate to a **Vishnu Devi temple.**

Several inscriptions testify to the antiquity of the second village, **Balambu,** built more than a thousand years ago when the Lichhavi dynasty ruled Kathmandu valley, but fortified later. Its main feature is the two-storied **Mahalakshmi temple,** in the central square along with some smaller temples. Among the three-storied houses that line the square is one dedicated as the god house of Ajima Devi.

The third village, **Kisipidi,** with its lush green trees and small, stone-walled gardens, is renowned for the two-storied **Kalika Mai temple** in its center.

Thankot

Travel on along the main highway, the Raj Path and after two kilometers (1.2 miles) you come to the fourth village, **Thankot,** built by the Mallas and later made a fortress by Prithvi Narayan Shah — its name, in fact, means "military base". On a hill above the village stands an impressive two-storied

Mahalakshmi temple, much admired for its patterned tympanum and columns, erotic carvings, open shrine and images of kneeling devotees.

Four kilometers (2.5 miles) to the southwest of Thankot stands the 2,423-m (7,950-ft) peak of **Chandragadhi**, "The Mountain of the Moon", reached by a trail through a dense forest of bamboo, pine and sal trees. At the crest there's a small Buddhist chaitya and splendid views of Kathmandu valley.

Back on the Raj Path look for the **monument to King Tribhuvan,** built to com-

OPPOSITE : Typical village sights in Kathmandu valley: Serene bathing ghat (top) in Bhaktapur. A market stall (bottom) in Nala village. ABOVE: Ancient, yet elegant house in Patan.

memorate the re-establishment of royalty after the Rana regime. It has a raised hand. There's another monument along the road that honors the men who built it between 1953 and 1956 — Indian engineers and Nepali laborers. Before then, goods were moved laboriously from India to the Nepal border by railway, then transferred from the Terai to Daman via overhead cables, and finally carried by porters to Kathmandu.

The Lele Valley Road

Two of the valley's most ancient villages, **Chapagaon** and **Lele,** date back to Lichhavi times. The road to them cuts through a green and yellow quilt of mustard fields and rice paddies stretched out beneath the hazy gray-blue foothills of the mighty Himalayas.

Sixteenth-century **Sunaguthi,** standing on a high plateau at the edge of another valley, has a **shrine to Bringareshwar Manadeva**, which houses one of the most sacred lingams in the Kathmandu valley. Next to the shrine is a two-storied **Jagannath temple.** Now the path climbs gently upward through the emerald, terraced fields to **Thecho** with its brightly decorated **Balkumari temple.** There's another one, to **Brahmayani,** in the north of the village guarded by the deity's vehicle — a duck, of all things — atop a column, with the usual lion on the steps of this two-storied temple.

About two kilometers (1.2 miles) beyond Thecho, guarded by a metal Ganesh shrine and a statue of Brahma beside a huge yoni, the road enters **Chapagaon** where, says a famous valley legend, one of the Malla kings sent his son into exile for founding a caste of his own. The central square contains two temples, both two-storied, dedicated to **Narayan** and **Krishna.** The struts carry incredibly-detailed erotic carvings. Close by, in a single-storied building, is an image of **Bhairav,** the village's major deity. South of Chapagaon are the two small hamlets of **Bulu** and **Pyangaon.**

TO THE EAST

King Anand Malla, founder of the Bhaktapur dynasty, is said to have built seven new villages in the east of Kathmandu valley, but of these, three predated him: Banepa, Nala and Dhulikhel. The four that he did build are Panauti, Khadpu, Chaukot and Sanga, though not all lie within the valley. Nonetheless, King Anand Malla's vision gave Banepa and Dhulikhel, situated, as they were, on the main Silk Road from Kathmandu to Tibet, status and a greater strategic value.

SANGA AND THE ARANIKO HIGHWAY

The road climbs out of the valley over a pass, five kilometers (three miles) east of Bhaktapur, where it cuts through **Sanga.** There's a small lane to the north, off the Araniko highway, that takes you into

Sanga, where a vantage point offers an incredible panorama of the entire valley. Despite its antiquity, the only object of historical merit is a small **Bhimsen shrine** to commemorate a Kathmandu legend that, when the valley was a lake, Bhimsen crossed it by boat, rowing from Tankhot in the west to Sanga.

From Sanga, the Araniko highway zigzags steeply down into the lush **Banepa valley** and the village from which it takes its name. Standing at the foot of a forested hill, much of the village was razed by fire in the early 1960s, but it remains the main center of commerce for the surrounding hill areas. Banepa's **Chandeshwari shrine** overlooks the valley from the top of a hill to the northeast of the town. Northwest, there's a

rough trail to **Nala**, seat of a Buddhist meditation site and **Lokeshwar,** about 100 m (330 yards) west of Nala, by the old Bhaktapur road. Pilgrim shelters surround the temple, which has a water tank in front of it. A steep alley in the village center takes you to the four-storied **Bhagvati temple** in the center of a square — the locale for many colorful processions during the village's annual festivals.

DHULIKHEL

Back on the highway at Banepa, you can drive on to Dhulikhel, which is popular as

Annapurna's majestic beauty dominates the landscape of Nepal's midlands and provides an awe-inspiring backdrop for its many small villages.

a place to stop and contemplate the Himalayas. Not that the views are the only reason to linger. Dhulikhel's main square contains a **Narayan shrine** and a **Harisiddhi temple**. The village houses are renowned for their beautiful, carved woodwork. On a northern hill above the village stands the magnificent three-storied **Bhagvati temple**, which is famous for its ceramictiled façade.

Dhulikhel remains one of the trade gateways between Kathmandu valley, eastern Nepal and Tibet.

mountain-facing rooms are a good value — there can be few more exhilarating feelings than to open your eyes in the morning to a view of the world's highest peaks. The hotel has a good restaurant.

INEXPENSIVE

The **Dhulikhel Lodge** ((011) 61152, P.O. Box 6020, Kathmandu, has long been a favorite with budget travelers. Though it's a convivial place, expect only the bare minimum of creature comforts. The lodge's guestbooks make for fascinating reading.

WHERE TO STAY

MID-RANGE

The **Dhulikhel Mountain Resort** ((011) 61466 FAX (01) 226827, P.O. Box 3202, Kathmandu, is something of a luxury trekking lodge. The resort's 43 rooms are thatchroofed chalets in a garden with Himalayan views. The Mountain Resort has a good restaurant and even a bar. If you want a few days away from it all contemplating the mountains, there are few places in which you can do it in such comfort.

The **Himalayan Horizon Sun-N-Snow Hotel** ((011) 61296 FAX (011) 61476, P.O. Box 1583, Kathmandu, is a step down in comfort and price from the Mountain Resort, but its

PANAUTI

One of the most fascinating Newar towns in this area, Panauti stands at the confluence of two rivers south of Banepa in a small valley surrounded by mountains. There used to be a king's palace in the square and the town is noted for two fine examples of Malla temple architecture. Both the three-storied sixteenth-century **Indreshwar Mahadev temple** and a **Narayan Shrine** have been restored.

Architecturally and historically, the Indreshwar Mahadev temple is one of the most important Newar shrines in Kathmandu valley and is thought to have replaced an earlier one built in the eleventh to twelfth centuries. The carving on its struts conveys the profound serenity of Shiva, in his many incarnations. Two shrines guard the courtyard; one is to Bhairav, another to a primeval nature goddess, represented by a simple stone. There's another **Krishna temple** on a peninsula at the confluence of the two rivers, with several Shiva lingams nearby and a sacred cremation ghat. On the other side of the Bungamati river is a famous seventeenth-century temple, also restored, where a chariot festival is held each year. It's dedicated to **Brahmayani,** chief goddess of Panauti after Indreshwar Mahadev.

the same management as the Kathmandu Guesthouse in Thamel. The rooms all have balconies with views of the Himalayas and the resort also has an indoor swimming pool — it gets cold up here in the winter months.

The Fort ((012) 90896 FAX (012) 228066, Nagarkot , strives hard for ambiance, decking out its rooms with Tibetan rugs and thangkas. The effect is quite traditional, with an unobtrusive overlay of modern comforts and amenities. The rooms all have good views.

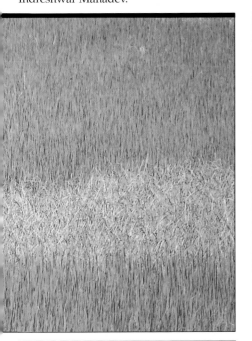

THE ROAD TO NAGARKOT

The village of Nagarkot is, like Dhulikhel, a popular Himalayan viewpoint on the eastern rim of the Kathmandu valley. It's north of Dhulikhel and is approached by a rough road via Bhaktapur and Thimi. Unlike Dhulikhel there is little in the way of village life in Nagarkot; but the views are indisputably better.

INEXPENSIVE
The **View Point Hotel (** (01) 417424, Nagarkot, is an agreeable compromise between the rock-bottom budget hotels and the more expensive and mid-range places. It's a cozy affair, with views, rooms with attached bathrooms and even some cottages for a more private retreat. The restaurant at the View Point is also good; while you eat, a glowing fireplace keeps the cold at bay.

WHERE TO STAY

MID-RANGE
The most desirable of Nagarkot's hotels is the **Club Himalaya Resort (** (012) 90883 FAX (012) 417133, Nagarkot, which is run by

OPPOSITE: Verdant rice paddies of the Suikhet valley near Pokhara. Women harvest grain ABOVE at Pokhara. OVERLEAF: Above the rice fields north of Pokhara rise (left) Machhapuchhare and (right) 7,525-m (24,688-ft) Annapurna IV and 7,937-m (26,041-ft) Annapurna II.

The Cities of Kathmandu Valley

THE ROAD TO TIBET

KODARI

Kodari's setting is remarkable enough — no more than 50 km (31 miles) from the crest of 8,013-m (26,291-ft)-high Shisha Pangma, or Gosainthan in the west and much the same distance from 8,848-m (29,028-ft)-high Everest, in the east. Just 100 km (62 miles) from Kathmandu, Kodari also marks the official border crossing with Tibet.

Chinese. Although fairly new, it is already badly damaged by the frequent landslides and washouts that send whole sections of road — and sometimes the vehicles on them — plunging to the swollen torrents below.

Though it winds through the foothills of the greatest mountain range in the world, these hills themselves are so high and sheer that views of the snow-capped peaks are rare. **Dhulikhel,** which offers a stunning vista of the Himalayas, including Everest, is an exception.

Kodari itself is of little interest — a cluster of wooden shacks straggling along the roadway that links Nepal and China. But the journey to Kodari presents a picturesque panorama of raging rivers, valley towns and green, forested slopes. Visas for China are difficult to obtain for non-group tourists in Kathmandu. If you organize your visa before you get to Nepal, however, you are free to walk across the border at Kodari and travel all the way to Lhasa and beyond.

ARANIKO HIGHWAY (RAJMARG)

Like most roads in midland Nepal, the Araniko highway was constructed by the

A few kilometers after Dhulikhel, at **Dolalghat,** a long low bridge crosses the wide bed of the Sun Kosi, just below its confluence with the Indrawati river. Almost half a kilometer (1500 ft) long, the bridge was built in 1966. Not long after Dolalghat, on the Sun Kosi, is one of the country's first hydroelectric schemes, built in 1972 with Chinese aid.

The power station lies less than 900 m (3,000 ft) above sea level between Lamosangu and Barabise. Continuing north from bustling Barabise the road begins to climb upwards. All along the road the sparse winter and spring waters are tapped for irrigation and domestic use through ancient but well-maintained aqueducts, models of traditional engineering. Dug out above the sides of the stream and lined with stone, the aqueducts move the fast-flowing water off the main body which soon descends below.

Many visitors stop at **Tatopani,** where hot springs from the raging cauldron beneath the Himalayas have been tapped, pouring forth day and night an everlasting supply of hot water.

At occasional intervals there's the inevitable temple — and at **Khokun,** only seven kilometers (four miles) from the Tibetan

Business here is still slow; but a trickle of Tibet-bound tourists arrive daily and the occasional day-trippers descend from their coach to be photographed with the Tibetan town of **Khasa,** 600 m (2,000 ft) higher up the gorge and the brilliant snows of 6,000-m (19,550-ft)-high Choba-Bahamare in the background. To the east, directly in line with Kodari, mighty Gaurisankar, only 35 km (22 miles) distant, remains invisible beyond the rise of the gorge wall.

A yellow line across the middle of the bridge marks the border between China's

border, a temple occupies a rock in the middle of the gorge — with no indication of how worshippers climb up its sheer rock faces. A magnificent waterfall leaps and jumps like scintillating diamonds hundreds of meters down the sheer lush green wall of the mountain.

The perpendicular rock walls of the gorge press inexorably closer and closer. They seem to lean over the narrow ribbon of road that clings so precariously to the hillside. The road cuts beneath a cliff and you can almost reach out and touch either side of the gorge. Round one more bend and there's the immigration post and beyond the police post. Finally you reach the border spanned by the **Friendship Bridge.**

Tibet and Nepal. Nepalis can cross unhindered. Foreigners must have a visa. (See FORMALITIES, page 231.) The best hotel in the Tibetan border town of Khasa is the grim Zhangmu Hotel, run by a depressed crew of Han Chinese who can rarely summon the energy to turn on the hot water in the rooms.

Where the border actually crosses — which side of the hill is Tibet or Nepal — is anyone's guess. On the other side the road winds back into what, hypothetically anyway, must be Nepal. The waters of the Bhote Kosi rage down the intervening gorge with a thunderous roar even though it's

OPPOSITE: Every afternoon clouds roll into the vertiginous valleys surrounding Gokyo peak.
ABOVE: Evening settles on Phewa lake, Pokara.

the dry season. It's an awesome thought, the Bhote in flood during the monsoons and thaw. Thick, strong walls that buttress the bridge foundations suggest the power they are designed to withstand.

THE ROAD TO POKHARA AND THE WEST

PRITHVI–TRIBHUVAN HIGHWAY

Southwest of Kathmandu, the Trisuli gorge meets that of the Mahesh Khola

river. From the capital to the confluence of the two rivers you take another of Nepal's major roads, the **Prithvi–Tribhuvan high-way,** as scenic as it is dramatic. A memorial to those who died building both highways stands at the top of the pass close to a Hindu shrine.

PRITHVI HIGHWAY

The pass out of the valley leads down the almost sheer escarpment in a series of tortuous and terrifying hairpin bends to the Prithvi highway, which starts at the town of **Naubise,** leaving the older Tribhuvan highway and heading southward to He-tauda. The building of the Prithvi highway — in 1973 with Chinese aid — is marked at Naubise by a stone tablet set in the side of the rock wall.

Hamlets and villages — the main highway being their one street — abound along the road. On the level sections on either side are emerald-green rice paddies. Cultivating rice is a family affair — the men bullying the

oxen teams with the plows, the women and children planting young green shoots with astonishing speed and dexterity. Paddies cling to the mountain hundreds of meters above, protected from sliding away only by a fragile buttress of precious topsoil. Fields end abruptly at the edge of a gully or cliff. Many disappear in the monsoons, leaving only a void where once stood half an acre of sustenance.

Charoudi, the most popular "put-in" place for shooting the Trisuli's rapids, is a small one-street hamlet after which the road drops quickly to **Mugling,** veering westward over the elegant suspension bridge. Not long after Mugling there's a northward turn off the highway that leads to **Gorkha,** ancestral seat of the Shah dynasty, rulers of Nepal since the eighteenth century. King Prithvi Narayan Shah's old palace still stands on a mountain ridge overlooking this ancient capital from which the Gurkha soldiers derive their name. There are some famous and distinctive temples in the town, including the pagoda-style **Manakamana** dedicated to a Hindu deity with the power to make dreams come true.

Between October and March there are stunning views from Gorkha of Annapurna and its sister mountains, but nothing beats the panorama that awaits you in the trekking and climbing capital of Pokhara, where the mirror reflection of sacred Machhapuchhare shimmers in the still, crystal waters of **Phewa lake.** Just 50 km (31 miles) from the village street at 900 m (3,000 ft) above sea level, Annapurna and its surrounding peaks rise up another 7,176 m (23,545 ft).

POKHARA VALLEY

Like the valley of Kathmandu, Pokhara valley is blessed with fertile soil. Add to this an average of more than 420 mm (155 inches) of rain a year and it is no surprise that the land burgeons with lush vegetation: cacti, bananas, rice, citrus trees, mustard fields, hedges of thorny spurge spiked with red blossoms, walls studded with ficus. The patchwork terraces are cut through by gorges channeled by the Seti river and scattered with lakes that glitter like diamonds in the spring sunshine. The ochre mud-and-thatch homes of the Hindu migrants from the Terai contrast with the white-walled, slate-roofed homes of the native Lamaistic tribes from the flanks of the mountain.

POKHARA AND PHEWA LAKE

Thirty years ago, Pokhara was an insignificant, little-known town. The first motor vehicle, a Jeep, arrived in 1958 — by airplane. Progress since then has been swift, encouraged by tourists and climbers, the advent of hydroelectric power in 1967 and the completion of the Prithvi highway in 1973. Within a decade Pokhara's population doubled to 50,000. There's even a movie house.

Local legend says Phewa lake covers an ancient city engulfed during a cataclysmic earthquake millennia ago. Today local fishermen ply their *donga* (long dug-out canoes, fashioned from tree trunks) on the placid waters, ferrying pilgrims to the **shrine of Vahari,** a golden temple nestled on an island. There's also a **Royal Winter Palace** for winters on the lake shore.

WHAT TO SEE

Unlike the Kathmandu valley, which is teeming with cultural attractions, Pokhara's sights are mostly natural. Try and find the time to hike out of town and gaze at the mountains; alternatively, hire a bicycle, pony or a donga.

Bicycle rental rates are next to nothing (always check the brakes and tires before setting out). Pony hire is more expensive — around US$30 per day with a guide. **Pokhara Pony Trek (** (061) 20339 is a long-established operator. Those who want to cruise the lake can hire dongas for around Rs 50 per hour — a bit more if one of the boat-boys does the paddling. Modern boats are also available.

Swimming in **Phewa lake** is probably not advisable given that it's used as a dumping ground by many villagers. You can take a boat out to the small pagoda-style temple situated on the lake's tiny island, however. This temple is dedicated to goddess Barahi and is one of the most famous places of pilgrimage in the region.

There are three natural sites of interest in the area. **Devlin's falls** is located southwest from the airport along the Siddhartha highway. This dramatic but seasonal waterfall, known locally as Patle Chhango, is created when a small stream flows out of the lake and suddenly collapses and surges down the rocks into a steep gorge. **Seti gorge** is equally fascinating. To get there, drive to the middle of the first bridge along the Kathmandu highway. Look down below and you will see the four-and-a-half-meter (15-ft)-wide gorge carved more than

14-m (36-ft)-deep by the flow of the Seti River. The third interesting natural site is at **Mahendra cave,** north of Shining Hospital and the university campus near **Batulechaur** village. It is one of the few stalagmite and stalactite caves in Nepal, known locally as a holy place. Carry a flashlight.

SHOPPING FOR CRAFTS

Near the Himalayan Tibet Hotel and the airport is **Pokhara Craft,** a shop specializing in local handicrafts and featuring nettle fabric (made from the stinging hill nettle)

OPPOSITE: Decorated house in central Nepal.
ABOVE: Village craftsman weaving rush baskets.

and woodcrafts. You can see local craftsmen at work there during the day.

The entire Lakeside area of Pokhara is one big art and crafts fair. Shops here sell everything from second-hand books and hiking gear to Tibetan thangkas.

WHERE TO STAY

Pokhara has three main accommodation areas: Lakeside, Damside and the airport. The airport area has a couple of Pokhara's better hotels but it has little going for it as

hara, south of the airport. This luxury development has 61 rooms and is run by the Shangri-la group — bookings can be made at the Shangri-la Hotel ((01) 412999 in Kathmandu.

Despite the emergence of competition, for many Pokhara visitors the **Fish Tail Lodge** ((061) 20071 FAX (061) 20072, Lakeside, Pokhara, is still the only place to stay. Accessible only by a pontoon raft, it stands on a rocky promontory at the eastern end of the Phewa lake. The views are spectacular and the glass-walled restaurant over-

a base. Lakeside is the busy part of town — a colorful, bustling enclave of shops, restaurants and guesthouses. Few of the hotels or guesthouses have views of the lake, however. Damside, in the south of Pokhara, is a quieter version of Lakeside.

Accommodations in Pokhara are not as sophisticated as in Kathmandu. Generally you'll find that the luxury and inexpensive categories of accommodation provide the best value for money. Most of the true mid-range hotels are disappointing.

LUXURY

The latest arrival on the Pokhara accommodation scene is the **Pokhara Shangri-la Village** ((061) 22122 FAX (061) 21995, Pok-

looking the lake and the Annapurna massif is one of the best places to dine in all Pokhara. In Kathmandu reservations can be made at the Hotel de l'Annapurna ((01) 221711.

MID-RANGE

The **New Hotel Crystal,** Nadhunga ((061) 20035 FAX (061) 20234, Pokhara, has the look of a hotel that was constructed with the tour group market in mind. Although many mid-range travelers put up here, it's worth bearing in mind that there are rooms at half the price in Lakeside that come close to the same standards provided here.

The **Hotel Tragopan** ((061) 21708 FAX (061) 20474, Damside, has just one drawback: its location on a busy intersection. Otherwise, it's a good mid-range hotel, with a restaurant, pub, garden and shops.

The **Base Camp Resort** ((061) 21226 FAX (061) 20990, Lakeside, is a good alternative to the mainstream mid-range accommodations. It's an informal affair, with two-storied bungalows grouped around a pleasant leafy garden, and offers all the amenities you would expect of a good hotel — air conditioning, international phone service and satellite television — at affordable prices.

FAX (061) 21670, Lakeside, you'll find another new hotel with a charming ambiance. All rooms have attached bathroom with 24-hour hot water, satellite television and international direct-dial telephones. Located in the same lane are two excellent lodge-style accommodations with rates starting around US$10. The **Tranquility Lodge** ((061) 21030, Lakeside, as its name suggests, is a restful spot set in an expansive garden. Close by is the **Butterfly Lodge** ((061) 22892, Lakeside, a similar operation.

INEXPENSIVE

The best advice for finding inexpensive accommodation is to hire a taxi to Lakeside or Damside and take a look around at the hotels. There's no shortage of very comfortable rooms, with attached bathrooms and balconies from US$10 to US$20 per night.

The **Hotel Meera** ((061) 21031 FAX (061) 20335, Lakeside, is one of the new breed of budget hotels. It's right in the heart of Lakeside and the comfortable rooms are fitted with large windows to make the most of the lake views. The downstairs restaurant serves good Nepali and Indian cuisine.

At the **Hotel Khukuri** ((061) 21540

WHERE TO EAT

Lakeside is the area for dining, but frankly, there's little to distinguish the dozens of restaurants in this area from one another. Some have better views, some better service, but mostly they all serve up the same eclectic mix of dishes from around world and play the same music over their sound systems.

The **Fish Tail Restaurant** (Fish Tail Lodge) ((061) 20071, is an exception and

OPPOSITE: A team of yaks plods through the barren high-altitude landscape on the road to Muktinath. ABOVE: Wooden aqueducts (left) irrigate fields in the Annapurna region. A tumble-down stone wall (right) snakes across the barren earth.

highly recommended. If you go for an evening meal, try to be there in time to see the sun set — whether in the garden or in the restaurant itself, the Fish Tail is a wonderful spot to see out the day. The menu is the usual mix of European, Nepali and Indian dishes, but done to higher standards than at most other places around Pokhara. There's live Nepali music and dance every evening.

For Lakeside dining, the **Fewa Park Restaurant** is a tranquil spot. It's better for breakfast or an afternoon snack than for dinner or

lunch. Next door is **Beam Beam**, another Lakeside restaurant with views. The food is better here, but the alfresco dining area is cluttered and the live music performed in the bar area can sometimes be too loud.

Over in Pokhara's Damside area, **KC's** ((061) 21560, is a branch of the successful Kathmandu chain and is generally packed with diners. Vegetable lasagna and sizzling steaks are popular orders. As is the case elsewhere in Pokhara, the European dishes rarely approach authenticity but they are often tasty just the same.

AROUND POKHARA

Ram Bazaar
East of Pokhara, Ram Bazaar is a small but picturesque village with shops, a school and artisans.

Tibetan Villages
The most interesting of the Tibetan settlements, situated just to the north of Pokhara in Lower Hyangja, is **Tashi Phalkhel**. South-

west of the airport, and beyond Devlin's falls, is another settlement, **Tashiling**.

Batulechaur
A few miles north of town, Batulechaur is famous for its *gaine* singers who tell of the rich history of Nepal in their rhapsodic songs. They accompany their voices with a small four-stringed, violin-like instrument, *saranghi*, played with a horse-hair bow.

Sarangkot
At the peak of the 1,600-m (5,250-ft) Sarangkot, are the remains of a fortress used by King Prithvi Narayan Shah the Great during the eighteenth century. Going west of Pokhara, past Kaskidanda ridge to Gyarajati village, you climb to the summit.

Muktinah
One of many places of pilgrimage in these hills that line the Kali Gandaki basin, is **Muktinah**. Set at 3,800 m (12,460 ft), its eternal flame draws Hindu and Buddhist worshippers alike. Black ammonite fossils, thought of as the embodiment of the god Vishnu, are found in profusion and pilgrims travel long distances over rugged trails to collect these.

Kali Gandaki Gorge
The deepest gorge in the world, Kali Gandaki, is flanked on one side by the daunting massif of Annapurna and on the other side, only 35 km (22 miles) away, by 8,167-m (26,795-ft)-high Dhaulagiri I. In between, almost eight kilometers (five miles) below, at only 1,188 m (3,900 ft), sits the village of **Tatopani**. (See also page 149).

With Dhaulagiri and Annapurna you are at the frontier of the highest land in the world. The peaks of Annapurna and its cohorts form the world's greatest natural amphitheater. Its only equal — in scale, form and drama — is directly opposite, across the Kali Gandaki valley, where Dhaulagiri's six peaks and those around them, form another breathtaking panorama.

MAJESTIC MOUNTAINS

On Nepal's western border, the Himalayas curve southward enfolding the country and dividing it physically from the northern-most reaches of India. The highest of these western peaks is **Api**. Though small by comparison with its sister peaks in central and eastern Nepal, few mountains in the world outside Asia rise as high as Api's 7,131 m (23,396 ft), forming a formidable massif in the far west. Peak to peak, directly in line with Api, only 60 km (37 miles) away is its easterly neighbor, **Saipal**, just 97 m (318 ft) lower. The actual Nepal–India border is marked by the Kali river, which flows at the foot of lonely Api.

through tough country — winds between these two massifs, cresting a saddle more than 5,500 m (18,000 ft) high between Nampa and Firnkopf West, before entering Tibet over the Urai pass.

Eastward of the remote western regions the Himalayas climb steadily higher. In the little-known **Kanjiroba Himal**, a cluster of mountains that takes its name from the highest peak, 11 crests rise above 6,000 m (20,000 ft), including 7,409-m (22,583-ft)-high Kanjiroba Himal. The mountains encircle the ancient **kingdom of Dolpo** and

Api dominates a range of magnificent but rarely seen and little-known peaks including **Jetibohurani**, 6,848 m (22,468 ft); **Bobaye**, 6,807 m (22,333 ft); **Nampa**, 6,755 m (22,163 ft); and **Rokapi**, 6,466 m (21,214 ft). Not far from Saipal stands the jagged peak of **Firnkopf West** at 6,683 m (21,926 ft); to the north is the lonely **Takpu Himal** gazing down on the lovely Humla valley and its remote capital of **Simikotat** from 6,634 m (21,766 ft).

Minnows compared to the peaks of central and eastern Nepal, these mountains remain relatively untouched by climbers. Japanese teams conquered Api in 1960, Saipal in 1963 and Nampa in 1972. A major trade route from the plains — a long trek

the sacred **Crystal Mountain** (see DOLPO, page 179–180), forming the natural boundaries of the 3,540-sq-km (1,345-sq-mile) **Shey-Phoksondo National Park.** Dolpo came into the kingdom in the eighteenth century as a result of King Bahadur Shah's conquests.

Eastward, across the fortress of Langtang Himal's peaks, lies the **Rolwaling Himal,** that little-known and overshadowed annex of the great Everest massif. Accessible only from the west, it is considered as beautiful as Langtang.

Main street of Chapagoan village OPPOSITE in Kathmandu valley where legend says a famous Malla king exiled his son for founding a caste of his own. ABOVE: Traditional scene in Chame village en route to Annapurna.

The Cities of Kathmandu Valley

At the far end of the Bhote Kosi gorge, 7,180-m (23,557-ft)-high **Menlungtse** and the slightly lower 7,144-m (23,438-ft)-high mass of **Gaurisankar** stand sentinel, as do Lhotse and Nuptse, for Sagarmatha — Everest — hiding her massive pyramid from prying and curious eyes.

The twin citadels of Gaurisankar and Menlungtse are the westernmost bastions of the Everest massif. Peak to peak, a distance of about 70 km (43 miles) separates Shiva's abode from that of Sagarmatha, Goddess of the Universe. In between, around and about, are literally dozens of lesser ramparts extending to the central pinnacle, most rising above 6,100 m (20,000 ft). Thirty kilometers (18 miles) from Everest, 8,153-m (26,750-ft)-high **Cho Oyu** guards the northwest approach while, less than eight kilometers (five miles) from the pinnacle of the world, 8,511-m (27,923-ft)-high **Lhotse** guards the eastern flank and 7,879-m (25,850-ft)-high **Nuptse** the southwestern flank. Sixteen kilometers (10 miles) beyond Lhotse, 8,481-m (27,825-ft)-high **Makalu** and its four other peaks barricade the approach from the southeast. Well-guarded, from the ground or the air, Everest hides herself, demurely, behind her cluster of courtier peaks.

The first major attempt to scale Everest took place in 1924 when George Mallory and Andrew Irvine disappeared on the mountain close to the summit. Their bodies still lie somewhere beneath Sagarmatha's eternal snows. They took a route along the northeast ridge from Tibet. It was only when Nepal opened its borders that the south face, the line taken by Hillary and Tenzing, was approachable.

Leaving behind the shadows of the brave and foolish who still lie on Sagarmatha's slopes, (including an English religious zealot without any mountain experience who fell to his death in the 1930s, leaving in his diary this epitaph: "Off again. Gorgeous day.") It's 125 km (78 miles) eastward from Everest as the crow flies to the top of 8,598-m (28,208-ft)-high **Kanchenjunga** astride Nepal's border with India's Sikkim state. Here too is a massif of giant peaks — 15 of them are above 7,000 m (23,000 ft).

A remote chorten in the Everest region.

The Terai

WILDLIFE AND RICE PADDIES

Along Nepal's southern border with India lies a narrow band of fertile plains, the Terai. Flat and never wider than 35 km (22 miles), it covers 24,000 sq km (9,120 sq miles). In addition to providing a dramatic contrast to the rest of the terrain of the world's most mountainous nation, the Terai has a charm all its own.

During monsoon season, tributaries of the Ganges flood the Terai's fields and pad-

countryside is a lush hub of activity. The recently completed Mahendra or East-West highway links the major towns of the region; footpaths connect everywhere else. Buses travel the main route and can get you to the birthplaces of Buddha and Sita and the jungle wildlife parks and reserves, but your feet or a bicycle are the only ways to get off the beaten track.

BIRATNAGAR

On the eastern reaches of the Terai lies

dies, depositing soil eroded from the Himalayas. Often rivers and streams change course, uprooting stilted huts and villages, washing out roads and destroying communication links. In the following months, crops are planted — rice, wheat, cane, jute, tobacco, beans and lentils — and harvested before the scorching desert winds arrive, preceding the next year's monsoons. Home for more than half Nepal's population and most of the kingdom's industries, this one fifth of Nepal's land area produces more than 50 percent of the gross domestic product and provides habitat for the country's remaining Bengal tigers and horned rhinoceros. In October and November, the ideal months for visiting this part of Nepal, the

Biratnagar, Nepal's second largest city with over 100,000 people. A major industrial center with sugar, textile and jute mills, small- and medium-scale factories for timber products and rice mills, in itself it is a town to pass by rather than through, but nearby attractions make it a worthwhile stopover.

WHERE TO STAY

Reservations for hotels in Biratnagar can be made in Kathmandu travel agencies before setting out. One of the better places to stay in town is the **Hotel Himalaya Kingdom** ((021) 27172 FAX (021) 24141, Mahendra Chowk, Biratnagar. Rooms are inexpensive and come with attached bathroom.

AROUND BIRATNAGAR

To the west of Biratnagar lie the principal natural resources of the area: green rice paddies, jute fields, floodplains and marshes. On the Indian border, the massive Kosi dam impounds the Sun Kosi river, which is fed by the Tamar river from the slopes of Mount Kanchenjunga and the Arun river from the snows of Makalu. Built by India, the Kosi dam is one of Nepal's major hydroelectric projects. Besides con-

to have been the ancient capital of Maithili and birthplace of Sita, consort of Rama (one of Vishnu's incarnations and hero of the epic Ramayana). It is a major pilgrimage center for Hindus from all over the subcontinent.

An eight-kilometer (five-mile) brick-paved road encircles the city and its many sacred Hindu shrines and ponds, of which **Gangasagar** and **Dhanushsagar** are the most outstanding. Pilgrims to its two famous festivals, commemorating Rama and Sita's wedding and Rama's epic vic-

trolling unpredictable floods and generating much of the country's energy, the dam has created new wetlands that now form the **Kosi Tappu Wildlife Reserve**. Here you can see one of the few remaining herds of wild buffaloes and thousands of migratory birds. The only accommodation in the reserve is at the **Tappu Wildlife Camp** ((01) 226130 FAX (01) 224237, P.O. Box 536, Kamaladi, Kathmandu.

JANAKPUR

Of more historical interest is Janakpur, 120 km (74 miles) west of Biratnagar, on the Indian border. With 40,000 Maithili-speaking inhabitants, Janakpur is reputed

tory over evil, immerse themselves in these sacred waters and flock to **Janaki temple** to pay homage to Rama and Sita. Built by a queen of Tikamgarh (in Madhya Pradesh, northern India) in 1900, its delicately-carved marble traceries were inspired by seventeenth-century Mughal architecture. The delicate exquisitely-shaped filigrees are seen at their best on the elaborate cupolas, ceilings and tiles. Nearby is the **Vivah Mandap** where legend holds that Rama and Sita were wed.

PREVIOUS PAGES: Stone-walled rice paddies of the Midlands region (left) and Tharu youngster (right) of the Terai plains. Farm workers tend the fertile fields of the Terai using the ubiquitous oxen for ploughing OPPOSITE and ABOVE transportation.

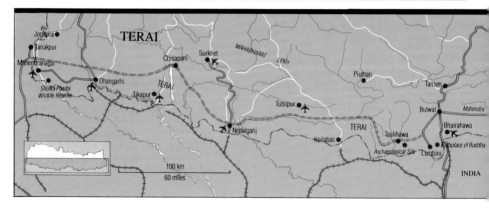

The town is also famous as the main stop on one of the worlds shortest railways — the 52 km (32 mile) narrow-gauge **Nepal Railway** that links Nepal with Jayanagar, India. The line is a colorful anachronism that delights inveterate travelers, a time-serving echo of the old British Raj.

WHERE TO STAY

Most hotel accommodation in Janakpur is primitive. The **Hotel Rama (** (041) 20059, is the only place in town that comes close to deserving a recommendation. The air-conditioned rooms are best and cost about US$15.

BIRGANJ

Eighty kilometers (50 miles) west of Janakpur, the Mahendra highway links up with the Tribhuvan Rajpath, for many years the country's main trans-Asia link. To the south is the border town of Birganj; to the north, through Amlekhganj and across the Mahabharat Lekh hills, is Kathmandu valley. Along the route is a dramatic view at Daman.

Birganj has seen better days. In the sixties and seventies, western hippies and mystics queued for clearance into Nepal on the Indian side at Raxaul and spent the night in one of Birganj's many cheap lodging houses before taking the high road to Kathmandu.

It is, however, still a bustling industrial area with timber yards, a sugar mill, match factory and a raucous bus depot where itinerants jostle each other in their eagerness to catch the next, often over-crowded,

coach to Kathmandu. It is also a jump-off point for visitors to Royal Chitwan National Park and Parsa Wildlife Reserve.

ROYAL CHITWAN NATIONAL PARK AND PARSA WILDLIFE RESERVE

The highlight for most visitors to the Terai is a visit to Royal Chitwan National Park and Parsa Wildlife Reserve, wilderness retreats recreated out of the once fertile rice and wheat fields that swiftly covered the Rapti valley after the fall of the Rana dynasty in the 1950s.

Royal Chitwan, spread over 932 sq km (354 sq miles), was the first of Nepal's extensive network of wildlife sanctuaries that now protect over seven percent of the nation's territory. The valley in which the park lies forms the flood plains of the Narayani river, joined here by the waters of the Rapti and other streams and feeders to become the second largest tributary of the sacred Ganges that flows approximately 200 km (124 miles) to the south.

Before the park's creation in 1973, Nepal's population explosion had pushed migrants down from the hills, forcing the indigenous Tharu tribes into this area formerly reserved as royal hunting grounds. Using slash-and-burn techniques, they opened up the forests and planted rice and grain.

Concerned with the destruction of its traditional hunting grounds, the Nepali royal family planned new strategies for the protection of its wildlife and in 1973 King Mahendra established Chitwan. The grasslands were rehabilitated, along with the sal (*Shorea robusta*) forests and slowly

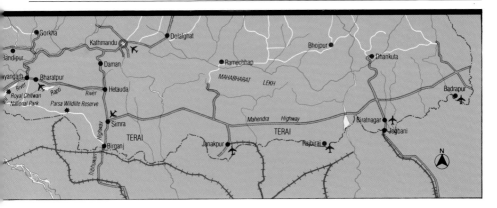

the game began to creep back from the uncertain havens it had found outside. An exemplary model of wildlife management, Royal Chitwan and its denizens have continued to prosper. Subsequent extensions, Parsa Wildlife Reserve, have given it a much larger area, embracing smaller forests of khani (*Acacia catechu*), sisso (*Dalbergia sisso*) and simal (*Bombax malabaricum*) — all valuable indigenous woods.

Monsoon fluctuations in the course of the rivers have created new ponds and lakes in a park–reserve that now covers an area of 1,200 sq km (456 sq miles) of sub-tropical lowland, bounded by the Rapti river in the north, the Reu river and the Churia or Siwalik range in the south and the Narayani river in the west.

Several animal observation blinds have been constructed next to water holes where patient visitors might see leopards and tigers and most will sight rhinoceros, wild boar, deer, monkeys and a multitude of birds. Throughout the park, small fenced enclosures contain varieties of grasses from which agronomists and conservationists hope to determine the ideal pastures for Chitwan's wild animals.

On clear winter days this jungle has one of the most dramatic backdrops in the world: the stunning ice slopes of Ganesh Himal, Annapurna and Himal Chuli stand out on the horizon in magnificent detail. Travel in the park is difficult during the monsoon season (May to September) and the best animal-viewing is from February to April. Any stay shorter than two days is probably not worth the effort as the key to enjoying the wild animal park is patience. Accommo-

dations should be arranged before leaving Kathmandu or from Birganj, if you are entering Nepal from India.

Riding an elephant is the best form of transport in the park. The Royal Nepali Army, which polices the park and enforces conservation laws, makes its patrols by elephant and park workers move about in similar fashion. It is not uncommon to see a small work crew resting in the shade of a clump of bombax trees around midday, the elephants' trunks relentlessly foraging; their *pahits*, handlers, perhaps sleeping on their backs with umbrellas raised as protection against the sun.

Elephants can usually be rented at the park offices or at one of the lodges listed below. Each beast has its own handler and individual gait. For most, these game rides are the memories that will last longest. The pahit, astride the elephant's neck, brushes the lianas and giant ferns aside with his steel goad and the seemingly ungainly three-ton steed steps nimbly over fallen logs.

In the dark shadows of a thicket, a sudden flash of fawn reveals the flight of a startled sambar deer. Giant butterflies flit from leaf to leaf and beyond the wall of leaves shadows move — perhaps a tiger or a leopard. However briefly, you can be the last of the maharajahs. Out on the plains the great Asiatic one-horned rhinos are moving with steadfast purpose, cropping the grass as a herd of *chital* — timid, fawn-like deer, edge nervously away from the young elephant. Back in the forest, a jungle fowl suddenly struts across the trail and from a low-lying branch a wild peacock takes off in a brilliant cascade of feathers.

It is also possible to travel part of the way down the Rapti river and its streams by canoe, to view crocodiles basking in the sun, as well as a variety of riparian flora and fauna. Arrangements for a canoe trip are best made at the Sauhara park office, four miles south of Tadi Bazaar (on the Mahendra highway between Marayangarh and Hetauda).

Hiking is allowed in the Chitwan jungle, but an experienced guide is necessary as trails are not marked and the wildlife can be dangerous. Rather than being an encumbrance, a guide is an asset who can find and identify animals and many can reel off with computer-like accuracy the names of the sanctuary's prolific yet rare bird species.

WHERE TO STAY

Most visitors to Chitwan arrive on a package tour from Kathmandu that includes guides, accommodation and meals. Advance bookings are essential. Accommodation standards vary surprisingly little. Budget travelers organizing their own Chitwan trip stay in the nearby village of Sauhara.

A more remote wildlife jungle can be experienced in far west Nepal, five hours drive from Nepalgunj, in the Royal Bardia National Park (see page 169).

LUXURY

Luxury here reflects prices rather than five-star comfort. If it's pampered treatment you want, then you should probably avoid Chitwan. Even the resorts run by Tiger Tops, where you might shell out upwards of US$1,000 for a two-night, three-day package, comprise accommodation made from local materials and lacking amenities such as electricity.

Tiger Tops ((01) 420322 FAX (01) 414075, P.O. Box 242, Durbar Marg, Kathmandu, is the original and still the most prestigious of the resorts in Chitwan. There are three Tiger Tops resorts in total: the **Jungle Lodge**, the **Tented Camp** and the **Tharu Village Safari Resort**. In all three you can expect high standards of guide services, solar heated water and a beautiful rustic environment. The Jungle Lodge is home to the famous

tree-house accommodation; as the name suggests, in the Tented Camp you stay in safari-style tents fitted with twin beds and stools; the Tharu Village Safari Resort is the most luxurious of the three, even having a swimming pool and holding Tharu dances in the evenings.

The **Chitwan Jungle Lodge** ((01) 228918 FAX (01) 228349, P.O. Box 1281, Durbar Marg, Kathmandu, is an operation in which rooms are provided in traditional mud-wall Tharu huts — all with private bathrooms and hot water. The lodge is deep in the

jungle and when traditional dances are held in the rustic restaurant in the evenings it's easy to imagine yourself on safari in another era.

The **Island Jungle Resort** ((01) 225615 FAX (01) 223814, P.O. Box 2154, Durbar Marg, Kathmandu, has a beautiful location on an island in the middle of the Narayani river — crocodiles are frequently seen in the river and if you are lucky you might even see Gangetic dolphin. Accommodation is available in both cottages and safari tents.

BHARATPUR AND NARAYANGHAT

The twin towns of Bharatpur and Narayanghat are the nearest urban centers to Chitwan.

OPPOSITE: Sunrise travelers take an early morning wildlife safari abroad an elephant in Royal Chitwan National Park (top) where park workers (bottom) rest in shade during the midday heat. Wild monkey ABOVE at Chitwan.

Bharatpur's role in the lowland infrastructure is as an airfield for what the domestic air carrier rashly promises are daily flights to Kathmandu. Renowned for the reliability of its international schedules, Royal Nepal Airlines has an equal reputation for the erratic time-keeping of its internal flights: understandable in mountain regions where weather suddenly closes in but perplexing to passengers waiting in the balmy and reliable climes of the Terai.

Narayanghat —lying on the banks of one of Nepal's three largest rivers, the

Narayani, and known as the "Gateway to Chitwan" — is in fact the major junction on the Mahendra highway with a spur climbing up through the hills along the east bank of the Narayani to the town of **Mugling**, the main junction between Kathmandu and Pokhara on the Prithvi highway. It is also a vital administrative and commercial center of the Terai region and indeed the economic capital of the indigenous people of this region, the Tharus.

Bustling Narayanghat, with sizable industries and flourishing markets, is also something of a pilgrimage spot. Each year, in January, a major fair attracts tens of thousands to the nearby village of **Deoghat**, where they immerse in the waters at the

confluence of the Kali Gandaki and Trisuli-Marsyangdi rivers.

Travelers continue their westward journey from Narayanghat over the modern bridge that spans the river, veering southwest along the Narayani's flood plains and over the shallow crest of a spur of the Siwalik hills to join the **Siddhartha highway** — a direct India–Pokhara link — at **Butwal,** on the banks of the river Tinau. This market town, with 25,000 to 30,000 inhabitants, is famous for its produce gardens and fruit orchards.

TANSEN

Northward of Butwal, a small eastward spur of the Siddhartha highway doubles back on itself as it climbs, in just a few miles, to **Tansen** — a town of 15,000 souls, famed for the erotic carvings decorating its **Narayan temple.** Tansen is also justly renowned as a landscape artist's *El Dorado*. Craft industries and the traditional Newar houses also make the town a worthwhile stopover. Its **Bhairavnath temple,** legend says, was carried — lock, stock and timber beams — all the way from the Kathmandu valley by King Mani Kumarananda Senior: one of history's biggest removal jobs. For anglers, Tansen's leaping streams provide fine sport.

BHAIRAWA

Hugging the Indian border, 40 km (25 miles) south of Tansen, Bhairawa is the Terai's second largest industrial center and a major producer of liquor. There's another British military base, five kilometers (three miles) outside the town, which signs up more of the stout Gurkha military stock.

WHERE TO STAY

The only reason to stay in Bhairawa if you're not leaving for or arriving from India is to visit Lumbini. Bear in mind that there is also some accommodation in Lumbini itself, notably the Japanese-managed Hokke Hotel.

ABOVE: Stone carving of Buddha in Patan.
OPPOSITE: Terraces are cut into the hillsides to enable the cultivation of grains here in the Everest region and elsewhere in Nepal.

The Terai

MID-RANGE

Bhairawa's best accommodation is the **Hotel Yeti ℂ** (071) 20551 FAX (071) 20719. It has clean, air-conditioned rooms with attached bathrooms and a reasonable restaurant.

The **Hotel Himalayan Inn ℂ** (071) 20347, offers basic mid-range to budget accommodation in an uninspiring setting.

LUMBINI

Nineteen kilometers (12 miles) southwest of Bhairawa is Lumbini, the birthplace of Sid-

one was born here," had been split in two, probably by lighting.

Later excavation has revealed a brick temple, Maya Devi — said to mark the exact spot where the Buddha was born.

WHERE TO STAY

If your finances stretch to a worthwhile splurge, the **Lumbini Hokke Hotel ℂ** (071) 20236, is that most surprising of things: a Japanese-managed hotel in the Terai. Its raison d'être is the large number of Japanese

dhartha Gautama Buddha in 540 BC. Since 1958 Lumbini has been in the hands of an international committee established by the Fourth World Buddhist Conference and initially funded by a substantial contribution from King Mahendra.

At the turn of the century, German archaeologist, Dr. Feuhrer, began excavating the ruins of the area, including the Lumbini palace and gardens, several shrines and a monastery. He discovered a sandstone sculpture depicting Buddha's nativity (now in the National Museum) and a soaring obelisk erected to honor Buddha by Mauryan emperor Ashoka when he visited the Lumbini gardens in 249 BC. The pillar, inscribed in Brahmin, "Buddha Sakyamuni, the blessed

pilgrims who come to Lumbini in homage to Buddha. The Japanese-style rooms complete with *tatami*, *shoji* and deep baths will be a nostalgic treat for anyone who has ever traveled in Japan.

TILAUROKOT

When Buddha was born, his father King Suddhodhan had as his capital Tilaurokot, 27 km (17 miles) west of Lumbini. Although the stupas, monasteries and palaces that Chinese travelers wrote about over two centuries ago no longer exist, the Nepalis have preserved it as a heritage site. Unfortunately very little distinguishes this site from the rest of the present-day Terai.

NEPALGUNJ

The western-most city in Nepal and capital of its region, Nepalgunj is an industrial center on the Indian border. It has a population of 40,000 and little to recommend it to tourists.

ROYAL BARDIA AND SHUKLA PHANTA RESERVES

The Royal Bardia National Park and the Shukla Phanta Wildlife Reserve have been

growing in popularity since the construction of the Mahendra highway linking the east and west of Nepal.

The Royal Bardia National Park is the Terai's largest wilderness area and offers the best opportunities in all Nepal to see a tiger in the wild. The park is home to over 30 species of mammal and hundreds of species of birds. **Karnali,** part of Royal Bardia, located on the eastern bank of the Karnali river, is a sanctuary for the endangered swamp deer. Accommodation in the park is still developing.

Shukla Phanta, in Kanchanpur district in the westernmost reaches of Nepal, is one of the few places in the country where the endangered black buck are found.

The Terai

Like Bardia, you have a good chance here of seeing tigers and rhinos. Tourist facilities are virtually non-existent, however.

WHERE TO STAY

As at Chitwan, **Tiger Tops** resorts ((01) 420322 FAX (01) 414075, P.O. Box 242, Durbar Marg, Kathmandu, provide superb accommodation. There are two resorts: **Tiger Tops Karnali Lodge** and **Karnali Tented Camp**. The lodge is at the park boundary, the camp — as comfortable a

camp as you'll ever come across — is inside the park. Rates are around US$165 per night all inclusive. Some budget accommodation is also starting to spring up: a good option is the **Forest Hideaway Cottages,** where you can make reservations by calling ((01) 41768, in Kathmandu.

There is no accommodation at Shukla Phanta, but **Silent Safari** ((099) 21230 FAX (099) 22220, P.O. Box 1, Mahendranagar, runs tours into the reserve.

OPPOSITE: A forest skyline overlooks the Rapti river in the Royal Chitwan National Park. ABOVE: Threatened survivor of the greatest of the world's cats, the royal Bengal tiger (left), pads through Chitwan's lush grasslands. One of Nepal's two species of crocodiles, the gurial (right) basks in the muddy shallows of a river.

The
Eastern
Midlands

ILAM AND THE ILAM VALLEY

In the narrow neck of land that connects northeast India with the rest of that vast country — and also divides Nepal from Bhutan, another tiny Himalayan kingdom — are West Bengal and Sikkim. From **Siliguri** the road crosses the **Mechi river,** a tributary of the Ganges, to **Kakar Bhitta** in Nepal. You can also take an alternative hill road from **Darjeeling** through the **Mane pass** and down to the rolling tea fields of Ilam.

Set at around 1,300 m (4,000 ft), the tea fields are particularly lovely, rolling away from either side of the road in every direction, a carpet of vivid green laid out at the feet of Nepal's northeastern mountains with dramatic views of mighty Kanchenjunga, the world's third-highest mountain, astride the Sikkim–Nepal border.

With its weathered brick houses, **Ilam** is a gracious town, by Nepali standards, of about 12,000 people. Its principal industry is tea and you can visit the factory where the leaf is cured before it is shipped to Kathmandu and to the rest of Nepal. Villagers also run cottage industries turning out a wide and attractive range of handmade cloth, blankets, sweaters and carpets.

Access is by bus from **Biratnagar** or **Dhahran** to **Birtamodh** and another bus from **Birtamodh** to **Ilam.** Ilam is also one hour by bus from **Bhadrapur (Chandragadhi).**

DHANKUTA REGION

DHARAN BAZAAR

Focal point of this region, lying at the base of the ever-green Vijaypur hills, is Dharan Bazaar. An unusual feature of town life is the Union Jack that flies over one of the squat single-storied buildings. This is one of the British Army Gurkha recruiting centers. Wiry teenagers from the hills continue a long and noble tradition, enlisting — usually for life — while older generations, now retired, make the long trek each month from the same hills to pick up their pensions.

The orchards of the Vijaypur hills are rich and productive and surplus fruit is preserved in a recently established canning factory. Access is by bus from Biratnagar.

DHANKUTA

Dhankuta stands on a ridge in the hills above Dhahran, pleasantly cool at an elevation of 1,200 m (4,000 ft) and famous for its ancient orange groves and its leafy scenery punctuated by many mountain streams, their crystal clear waters dancing between grassy banks flanked by pine and oak forests. Its streets are lined with myriad tea houses, the market town itself serving as a commercial, banking and government center. One modern wonder for townsfolk has been the arrival of electric power. Its gabled black-and-white houses and dreamy ways are strikingly reminiscent of an Alpine village. A modern motor road winds its way from Dhahran to Dhankuta. By foot

PREVIOUS PAGES: In spring and summer, ice-melt streams (left) pour in torrents from the mountains down into the lush valleys and lowlands. A fisherman (right) poses with his triangular net. ABOVE: An old Tibetan woman sells turquoise jewelry and metalwork in Namche Bazaar. OPPOSITE: Worn brick façades (top) provide a pleasant backdrop to village life. A weaver (bottom) works a handloom.

it takes about five hours to climb the 32 km (20 miles), via Bijaipur to this ancient Newar town.

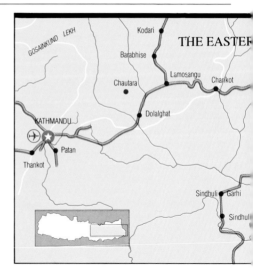

TUMLINGTAR AND THE ARUN VALLEY

Close to Dhankuta lies one of Nepal's most remote and beautiful regions. Nowhere are the country's stunning scenic contrasts more sharply defined than in the **Arun valley,** lying in the shadows of the Khumbu Harkna Himal, below Makalu's daunting 8,481-m (27,825-ft)-high peak with the wide and lazy Arun river meandering along the valley floor.

The river bestows a mantle of verdant green and nourishes the cool leafy trees, which provide shade all along this enchanted valley and its many companion valleys, equally as lovely. Its villages have remained unchanged for centuries.

Flights touch down in the meadow at **Tumlingtar**, the Arun valley's main settlement, on scheduled runs from Kathmandu or the Terai. There is access by road from Biratnagar.

Though only a short distance northward above the tree-clad hills rise the world's mightiest mountains, at its lowest levels the valley could be part of Africa.

The red bare earth is dotted with stunted sparse semi-arid savanna grassland. Groves of succulents and stands of banana trees repeat the African image. The heat of the sun's rays, funneled into the valley by the rising hills, is merciless. Brickmakers use the heat to bake their product for the thatched Tudor-like cottages of the hamlets that dot the valley and perch on the hillsides.

In the north, the valley is bounded by the snow-covered 4,100-m (13,500-ft)-high Shipton pass — beyond which lie the mountain ranges surrounding the three great peaks of Everest, Makalu and Lhotse.

Anglers delight in the **Ishwa valley,** its slopes thick with rhododendrons and magnolias and its mountain streams alive with fish.

Barun, another valley, its walls a tangled jungle of undergrowth, with rushing streams and plunging waterfalls, forms an amphitheater with distant Makalu center-stage.

It was in one of the rivers in this area — at a height of almost 5,000 m (17,000 ft) — that a wildlife expert discovered what may well be the only high-altitude salamander in the world.

RUMJATAR

A stiff two- to three-day trek over the western ridge takes the fit and the active out of the Arun valley and down into **Rumjatar,** at 1,300 m (4,500 ft) in the valley of the **Dudh Kosi river.**

OKHALDUNGA REGION

Some kilometers away, **Okhaldunga,** a pleasant unspoiled village with an old fortress, has given its name to this lyrical essay of hill and valley, river and lake.

Many of the birds, which give Nepal one of the most richly varied collections of avifauna in the world, are found on the forest-clad 3,000-m (10,000-ft)-high crests of the **Neche Dahuda hills,** overlooking the valley floors. Flocks of them, some vividly colored, flit from tree to tree — their dawn chorus in springtime a hosanna to life reborn.

Okhaldunga lies directly at the foot of Everest but few attempt the exhausting trek through these foothills to the roof of the world.

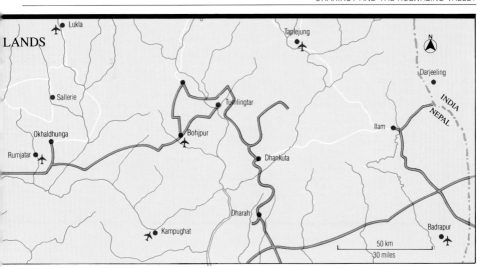

CHARIKOT AND THE ROLWALING VALLEY

West by northwest from Okhaldunga as the Himalayan crow flies, **Rolwaling valley** (*rolwaling* is a Sherpa word that means "the furrow") lies in the shadows between the Everest region of Khumbu Himal and Langtang Himal.

Long has this valley — shaped by the floodwaters that burst out of a nine-meter (30-ft)-wide opening in a sheer rock wall on the east bank of the Bhote Kosi river — fascinated those who visit it. Many pilgrims believe that this is the spot where Shiva thrust his trident into the mountainside to let the waters cascade down to the holy Ganges. It's in the upper reaches of the Rolwaling valley that members of the Sherpa and Tamang communities talk about the *yeti* — that elusive Abominable Snowman that has been seen so often by the Sherpa guides who live in the valley.

Perched at around 2,000 m (6,500 ft), just a few hours drive from Kathmandu, the small pleasant village of **Charikot,** with hotels and shops, is gateway to this region. But progress through Rolwaling valley from thereon is solely by foot (see SOME CLASSIC TREKS, ROLWALING HIMAL, page 199).

Three dining chairs stand outside the tea house in the tiny 10-house hamlet of **Piguti,** its quietness broken only by the scurry of pye-dogs chasing a lone trekker through its one street.

Here too trekkers are few, leaving Rolwaling's many splendors — including the magnificent amphitheater of Gaurisankar — to delight only the rare visitor.

Higher up, one-, two- and three-storied houses cling to the edge of the precipitous rice paddies, now brown, awaiting the monsoons, as cotton wool clouds dab the little knolls and grassy shoulders with a cool balm to ease the sting of the sun.

The paths that climb up the mountain slopes veer left and right, across perilous-looking rope or steel-hawsered suspension bridges. Many require a toll.

Slowly the trail winds through the forests to the highest settlement — a small close-knit Sherpa community. The 200 families of **Beding** live in small but striking stone houses with elegantly painted and carved exteriors.

There's also a monastery. Among the many holy places of the Himalayas, Beding is remembered as the refuge of Guru Padma Sambhava, the mystic Tantric recluse who chose the small cave in the cliff, about 150 m (500 ft) above the monastery, as his place of meditation 1,200 years ago.

Soon after this the trail passes beyond the tree line to the land of the yeti...

Off the Beaten Track

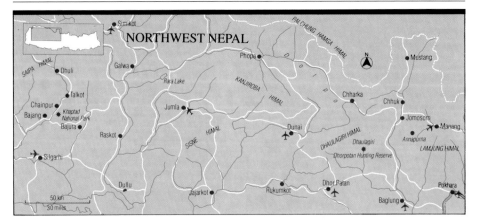

JUMLA AND LAKE RARA

Southwest of Pokhara lies **Baglung** — approachable only on foot or by dubious road from the Terai — gateway to the **Royal Dhorpotan Hunting Reserve.** Handmade paper, used for packing and bamboo crafts, is its most famous product. It's the home of the Thakalis, a small group of no more than 20,000 people of Tibetan–Mongoloid stock, speaking a Tibetan–Burmese vernacular, whose faith is a mixture of Buddhism, Hinduism and Bonpo.

Baglung also earns praise, from the impotent and those on the wane, for the power of the local aphrodisiac, *silajit*. Locals travel far north to exploit deposits of this tar-like substance that oozes from rocks and fetches high prices in India. Tastefully produced crafts include woolen vests, blankets, rugs and other sewn or woven handicrafts.

After Baglung you're deep into Nepal's mystical west: closed, barred and still little known. Yet it once nurtured a great kingdom of the Mallas that reached its height in the fourteenth century. The capital of this ancient kingdom, **Jumla**, set almost 2,400 m (8,000 ft) above sea level, and only reachable by plane — unless you're an untiring trekker prepared to walk for weeks. There are few visitors to this region.

Ringed by magnificent peaks, Jumla is truly a natural paradise, a quaint rural town with a bazaar, lined by the flat-roofed houses of the region and boasting no more than 50 shops, a bank, police station and the inevitable tea houses.

The Mallas kept a winter capital at Dullu, in the south of the Mahabharat Lekh range of hills and maintained a territory that stretched from the humid Terai to the Taklahar in western Tibet — connected by trails that even today few tackle. Yet the Mallas left a magnificent legacy in Jumla: sculptured temples, stone pillars and the still-living folk songs of the region. This beauty is well-guarded; few disturb its tranquillity and population is sparse. The **Karnali** — one of 14 Nepali zones — has a total population of around 300,000: no more than 12 people to every square kilometer.

There's an old highway along the Tila Nadi valley where you measure your pace by the distance between the ancient milestones placed here as long ago as the fifteenth century. Two days hard slog bring reward — a refreshing dip in the hot springs at **Seraduska.** Walk east for three days and you'll reach **Gothichaur,** an alpine valley set more than 2,900 m (9,500 ft) above sea level. In the valley's pine forests a stone shrine and a water spout are a reminder of the Malla dynasty. The area offers marvelous views of two little-known peaks, Chyakure Lekh and Patrasi Himal. Jumla is also the stepping off point for a long, hard trek to the Shangri-la valley of **Humla.**

Best of all, make a four-day trek over high passes like **Padmara, Bumra,** and the 3,456-m (11,341-ft)-high **Ghurchi pass** and finally **Pina,** to **Lake Rara,** Nepal's most en-

PREVIOUS PAGES: Porters (left) toil over high mountain passes. A young Sherpa woman (right) pauses to rest from her labors. OPPOSITE: A yak on the banks of Gokyo Lake.

chanting national park. The lake is the kingdom's largest body of water, covering 10 sq km (four square miles) almost 3,000 m (10,000 ft) above sea level. Snow lingers here as late as May and June but its crystal-blue waters are haven to a treasury of hardy avian visitors, particularly mallards, pochards, grebes, teals and other species from the north. The park itself covers 104 sq km (40 sq miles). Alpine meadows line the lake shores and fields of millet and wheat are flanked by pine forests.

There are apple orchards and the lake waters are rich with fish. Several villages stand on Rara's shores, their houses, terraced like the land, backed on to steep hillsides. Wildlife includes hordes of impertinent monkeys who raid farms and grain stores with seeming impunity. Set like a sapphire in its Himalayan brooch, Lake Rara is both a botanical and zoological treasure.

Another national park, **Khaptad** — several days distant, southwest of Rara — stands at much the same elevation, covering 187 sq km (71 sq miles): a floral repository of high-altitude conifers, oak and rhododendron groves, its open meadows reserved for royalty.

To the west lie more little-known valleys reachable only on foot. Southwards the trade caravans — even goats and sheep are used as pack animals — must travel daunting distances over forbidding terrain before reaching the temperate and fertile lands of the Mahabharat and the tropical fields of the Terai.

HOW TO GET THERE

Permits are needed for travel to these areas. If you obtain one, you next face the obstacle of getting on a flight. Guides can be difficult to find in this part of Nepal, as can be food.

DOLPO

Northeast of Jumla, so remote from the nearest road it takes three weeks of tough walking to reach, Dolpo and its monasteries straggle up a pitch of long, tortuous ridges, above an expanse of rumpled, brown and barren mountains. The creed of the shaman — spirit-possessed holy man — still rules here, as it has done for 15 centuries. In the rarefied air of these 3,000- to 5,000-m (10,000-to 16,000 ft-)-heights, perceptions and sensations are acute. Sitting atop a mountain ridge in the dark night in a yak-hair tent, wind howling, rain lashing down, watching the Shaman as he is taken hold of by "Fierce Red Spirit with the gift of the life force of seven black wolves" is enough to convince even the most cynical witness from western civilization of the power of the supernatural.

The population of a few hundred in Dolpo has been swollen by Tibetan refugees. All make votive offerings, some of tablets made from a compound of clay and funeral ash and delicately carved with a pantheon of Buddhist deities. At a height of more than 4,000 m (13,000 ft), Dolpo's grain fields are among the highest cultivated land in the world. The paths and trails that lead through this tiny principality of old are often no more than fragile, crumbling shale strata sticking out of sheer cliff faces. With a precipitous drop a step away on one side, as you stoop low beneath an overhang, you'll agree it's a climb only for the agile.

This is a land of holy peaks of which the most revered is the valley's sacred Crystal Mountain. According to local legend, a thousand years ago a Tibetan ascetic, Drutob Senge Yeshe, flew to the top of the harsh slab of rock, a massif that rises out of the shale around it, aboard a magic snow lion and challenged the god who lived there. When he defeated the deity, the rock turned to crystal. Now Dolpo people circle the

16 km (10 mile) circumference of the mountain's base in an annual pilgrimage, or *kora*. Its many strata — layers of rock — also draw pilgrims of a different faith: geologists hunting fossils.

HOW TO GET THERE

The only way to get into the Dolpo area is to trek. A special permit is required, as are experienced guides. It takes at least 14 days from Pokhara to hike into the region.

MUSTANG

Dolpo's neighboring kingdom, Mustang, is reached by a long trek through the Kali Gandaki gorge and over the one, desperately high, southeast facing pass into Dolpo. The native name for this lunar land of canyons and ridges is Lo. In the capital, **Mantang,** dominated by fortress walls, the central feature is the massive white-walled **Royal palace** in which lives the world's least-known monarch. Schools are bringing change. But while the youngsters come home filled with stories of space flights, which they've heard on the classroom wireless, their grandparents still believe the world is flat and shaped like a half moon.

Lo Mantang, in fact, is the full name of the 2,000-sq-km (760-sq-mile) kingdom of His Highness King Jigme Parwal Bista, founded in the fourteenth century by the Tibetan warlord Ama Pal. It lies on a barren valley floor at around 4,800 m (15,000 ft), snug against the Tibetan border on three sides and guarded by formidable 7,300-m (24,000-ft)-high mountains, pierced only by narrow passes. On the Nepal side, massive Dhaulagiri I, at 8,167 m (26,795 ft) the world's seventh-highest mountain, provides the defense that has sealed Lo from the outside world through the centuries.

Fabled Mustang, as it's now known on the maps, is only an "honorary" kingdom these days but each night King Jigme, the 25th monarch since the 1480s, orders the only gate of the mud-walled capital shut and barred to keep out invaders. Twelve dukes, 60 monks, 152 families and eight witches occupy the capital. King Jigme still owns serfs who plow his stony fields for

grain crops. But Lo's treasures are many and priceless: a wealth of Tibetan art, monasteries and forts set in its 23 villages and two other towns. Many of Mustang's monasteries — the name derives from the Tibetan phrase meaning "plain of prayer", *mon thang* — are carved into cliff faces. You climb a ladder to reach them. Other wealth lies in the rocky hills: turquoise and rich deposits of alluvial gold on the beds of the rivers that course through the land. But Lo's citizens consider the task of panning for this metal beneath their dignity.

The King's subjects — Lopas, who are Lamaist Buddhists — number around 8,000 and speak a dialect of the Tibetan language. The women practice polyandry — often marrying two or three brothers. The king

keeps his authority as a ruler by virtue of a 160-year-old treaty with King Birendra Shah's dynasty and annual payment to Nepal of 886 rupees and one horse. In return King Jigme holds the rank of colonel in the Nepali Army.

So archaic is the kingdom, matches were unknown until a few years ago and superstitious fears are rampant. The whole land goes to bed in terror of Lo's 416 demons of land, sky, fire and water and life is dedicated to warding off the evil spirits that cause Lo's 1,080 known diseases as well as five forms of violent death. Thus, for three days each year, King Jigme's subjects celebrate New Year by "chasing the demons": with the noise of cymbals, drums and notes made by playing on human skulls, filling the air.

Not a single tree grows in this arid and withered land. To supplement their monotonous diet of yak milk and sour cheese, the Lopas nurture fragile gardens. For trade, they deal in salt from Tibet. The trail they follow winds for 240 km (149 miles) along the Kali Gandaki gorge between Dhaulagiri and Annapurna.

How to Get There

Closed for many years, Mustang can now be reached on foot from Pokhara with guides and porters. Permits for the region cost US$700 for 10 days.

Valley in the shadows of Tibet's Cho Oyu, one of the world's highest mountains.

High Altitude Trekking and Treks

THE HIGH MOUNTAIN VALLEYS AND PASSES

For many visitors, the reason for coming to Nepal is the prospect of a high-altitude trek. The best time to trek is late September and early October when the mountain views are superb (and can continue to be so throughout crisp winter). The first quarter of the year provides perfect trekking conditions, with the one drawback that views of the peaks are often obscured by hazy conditions. Summer

from Pokhara with dozens of high-altitude walks to choose from, including the Royal trek that follows in the footsteps of the Prince of Wales and gives you three to five days in Gurung and Gurkha country, east of the Pokhara valley. Highlights of the six- to 10-day Ghandrung to Ghorapani trek are outstanding panoramas of Machhapuchhare, Annapurna and Dhaulagiri. The 17- to 19-day Kali Gandaki to Muktinah route is in excellent condition in the winter, although you might encounter some snow at Ghorapani.

is usually condemned as sticky and the trails are infested with leaches; but those who have trekked in the summer say that the leaches are found only in fairly low altitudes and summer treks are gloriously free of crowds.

There are literally hundreds of treks to choose from in the eight major trekking regions of Nepal. Your choice will depend upon the time you have and the season.

The major trekking regions are: **Annapurna Himal, Dhaulagiri Himal, Manaslu, Langtang Himal-Jugal-Himal Ganesh Himal, Khumbu Himal, Kanchenjunga, Makalu,** and **Rolwaling Himal.**

The most popular trekking areas are **Annapurna Himal** and **Dhaulagiri Himal**

Treks in **Dhaulagiri** take you through a veritable wonderland of meadows, forest and villages and among some of the happiest and most generous people in the world, allowing you to savor the simple lifestyles — and delightful scenery — to the full. The contrast between the stark, ice-white peaks set against the conifer and rhododendron forests, the azure sky above, verdant spring and summer fields below, can steal your breath as much as climbing these heights.

Villages straggle down the hillsides in a series of terraces, just like the paddies and grain fields and there's always time and reason enough to rest in one of the many tea houses, simple little cafés where the refreshments help beat the debilitating dehydration brought about by high altitudes and exercise.

In contrast to the dozens of trekking options around Dhaulagiri and Annapurna, there are few around **Manaslu.** This is all the more delightful because these tracks take you to the feet of such giants as 8,158-m (26,766-ft)-high Manaslu and its sister peaks, including sacred 7,406-m (24,298-ft)-high Ganesh Himal I with its seven lesser peaks and forbidding 7,893-m (25,895-ft)-high Himal Chuli.

lakes up to a height of more than 4,500 m (15,000 ft).

Close to the border is **Somdu,** Nepal's most remote permanent settlement, a village of 200 souls — about 40 families — whose fields and paddies are covered with snow until late in the year. Nearby, there are also the twin villages of **Li** and **Lo.** All along the way the trails are lined with the inevitable prayer stones, *mani,* of the staunch Buddhists who inhabit the region.

Retracing your footsteps to **Trisuli Bazaar,** turn northeast and climb the trail that

Take the Trisuli valley through Trisuli Bazaar around the north face of Himal Chuli and Manaslu and you'll walk through hills clad with evergreen forests, thundering waterfalls and alpine flora: oaks, alders, firs and rhododendrons. Village houses are sturdy gabled, two-storied brick and thatch affairs. Among the many large and striking monasteries are some which are surprisingly small — one, with a pagoda-style roof and a circular top, is like a cross between a lighthouse and a Suffolk grain store.

A 14-day trek leaves **Ganesh Himal** in the east and takes you around the north face of **Himal Chuli** and **Manaslu** — almost into China's backyard, through bleak and windswept passes, skirting glaciers and frozen

winds along the east bank of the Trisuli river to enter one of Nepal's most enchanted regions and another classic trekking region — fabled **Langtang Himal** with its monasteries, stupas, prayer walls and places made sacred by the Hindu scriptures.

When Nepal opened its doors to foreigners in 1950, the first to venture into its hidden mountain sanctuaries were British climbers Eric Shipton and H.W. Tilman who "discovered" Langtang Himal's many

PREVIOUS PAGES: Trekking along a precipitous trail in the high country of the Himalayas (left). A mountain woman (right) enjoys the fine weather. OPPOSITE: The Sherpa village of Namche Bazaar, main gateway to Everest, glows at night. ABOVE: Namche Bazaar, by day, nestles in neat rows beneath icecapped Khumde.

High-Altitude Trekking and Treks

marvels — just 75 km (47 miles) north of Kathmandu — unknown then to many Nepalis. No city in the world can claim a more incredible backdrop. Tilman's comment that it is "one of the most beautiful valleys in the world" is still considered an understatement by some.

Outside the rustic tea houses that refresh the traveler, ancient bo trees, their gnarled limbs like rheumy fingers, spread a thick canopy of shade over Langtang's version of the patio, old stone terraces with seats stepped into the stonework.

Dominating the valley at its north end is Nepal's 7,245-m (23,769-ft)-high Langtang Lirung, a few kilometers beyond which, on the Tibetan border, rises its sister peak, 7,238-m (23,748-ft)-high Langtang Ri; both overshadowed by Shisha Pangma — sacred 8,013-m (26,291-ft)-high Gosainthan of Hindu mythology — one of the legendary abodes of Shiva. You get sudden and unexpected views of some of these peaks as you take the trail hacked out of the gorge above Trisuli Bazaar. On the more level areas, it cuts through stands of juniper and rhododendron, blue pine and cushion plants.

Shops and boarding rooms ABOVE in Namche Bazaar, at Solu Khumbu. OPPOSITE: Sherpa porters on market day at Namche Bazaar.

For centuries this trail has been a trade route between Kathmandu and Rasuwa Garhi across the border in Tibet. During July and August this rocky track becomes a mass of humanity as devout Hindu pilgrims, worshippers of Shiva, head for Langtang's **Gosainkund** lakeland. These half-a-dozen small lakes sparkle like jewels in the midday sunshine and are said to have been formed when Shiva thrust his trident into the mountainside. From Gosainkund it's possible to continue over the pass into the remote but eternally beautiful reaches of upper **Helambu,** best in springtime when the rhododendrons bloom. Here, too, the headwaters of Nepal's major river, the **Sun Kosi,** mingle together from scores of tumbling waterfalls, roaring rivers and laughing streams.

Swiss explorer, geologist, adventurer Tony Hagen shared Tilman's passion for Langtang Himal and ignited the same feelings in another Swiss — a UN farm advisor — who built a Swiss cheese factory close to Kyangjin monastery at around 3,840 m (12,500 ft) and which, whatever the quality of the cheese, provides some of the most spectacular mountain views found anywhere.

Langtang's principal purpose is as a wildlife and botanical sanctuary — **Langtang National Park,** a haven for the endangered snow leopard, leopard, Himalayan black bear, red panda and wild dog. Outside the 20 or so alpine villages roam 30 different species of wildlife, while more than 150 different kinds of birds have nested among the region's 1,000 botanical species. It is the most popular of all Nepal's wilderness areas — a wonderland of hardy mountain people, animals, birds, forests and mountains — much of it preserved within the nation's second largest national park spread across 1,243 sq km (472 sq miles).

Khumbu Himal is for the serious, hardy trekker — a 25- to 30-day walk interspersed with Sherpa villages. Though the scenery is sensational, it's extremely cold. If you are flying in and out, expect some delays. **Lukla** flights are inextricably tied to the weather — and if you miss your flight the staff drop you back to the bottom of the list which, on one occasion, meant an extended

stay of some three weeks for one unlucky person.

By plane it is only forty minutes from Kathmandu to Lukla, more than 2,700 m (9,000 ft) above sea level. Its landing strip is on an uphill gradient, one side of which drops precipitously thousands of meters to the floor of the Dudh Kosi valley.

Namche Bazaar is well above Lukla. There is also a 4,000-m (13,000-ft)-high airfield nearby — at **Syangboche** where guests of the Everest View Hotel alight. Each bedroom in this hotel is equipped with oxygen.

Almost everybody who visits Nepal dreams of standing at the foot of the world's greatest mountain, but it's a realistic goal only for the fittest. Most of the trail takes you above 4,000 m (13,000 ft) in thin, freezing, raw air — chest pounding, lungs gasping — to the 6,000-m (20,000-ft)-high Everest base camp, higher than any point in Africa or Europe.

Yet it's not just the mountain and its huddle of neighboring peaks, three of the world's seven highest, which is the sole attraction, for this is also a land of fable and monastery, remote meadows, wildlife and the home of the hardy Sherpas and their colorful culture.

The trail from Lukla climbs up the Dudh Kosi canyon zigzagging from side to side through stone-walled fields, rustic villages and hardy forests. The Buddhist prayer — *Om mani padme hum,* Hail to the jewel in the lotus — is carved everywhere, on the huge boulders that look like enormous tables standing by the side of the trail and on top of long stone walls.

These carvings are built to pacify local demons, deities or the spirit of some dead person and should be circled clockwise, because the earth and the universe revolve in that direction. If you are walking straight on, keep them on the left as a mark of respect. These are prayers and supplications artistically inscribed with great devotion. Don't take them as souvenirs — it's sacrilege, much as defiling a Christian church or Muslim mosque would be.

Elsewhere, scraps of colored cloth flutter in the breeze, or a bamboo framework is covered with colored threads woven into an

intricate design; sometimes you may find dyed wheat-flour dumplings lying on the ground — offerings to malignant demons or deities and not to be touched or disturbed by strangers. These prayer flags may look old and ragged but to the Nepalis, especially the Sherpas, they never fade — their prayers of supplication and gratitude are always carried on the breeze to Buddha, the Compassionate One.

Before Namche Bazaar, at the village of Josare, lies the headquarters of **Sagarmatha National Park** where rangers and wardens, used to high-altitude living, relax at 4,000 m (13,000 ft) with volleyball games. More than 5,000 trekkers a year climb this trail to enter the national park's 1,243 sq km (472 sq miles) of mountain wilderness; the rumpled

brown-green buttresses of Everest ascending ever higher as you climb.

The town, capital of the Sherpa community, is set on a small plateau at the foot of sacred 5,760-m (18,901-ft)-high Khumbila which stanches the long run of the Ngojumba glacier as it slides down from the base of Cho Oyu. It is the focal point of everything that occurs in the Everest region. Every Saturday morning there's a colorful market when hundreds trek in from the surrounding villages and towns to haggle and argue, buying and selling. Namche's streets step up the barren, rocky slopes of Khumbila lined with pleasant white-washed two-story homes with shingle and tin roofs.

Sherpa monasteries, reflecting their Tibetan heritage, are the most striking in

Nepal. You'll find them in the towns of **Khumjung** and **Kunde**, which stand above Namche Bazaar on the slopes of Khumbila. They are well worth visiting if you can make the climb. West of Namche, at the foot of the Bhote Kosi valley, which is fed by the Jasamba glacier, there's a particularly impressive monastery in the village of **Thami.**

You can use Namche to approach **Cho Oyu,** either west up the Bhote Kosi valley or north of Khumbila up the Dudh Kosi valley. The westward route takes you up the Renjo pass, coming down to **Dudh Pokhari,** a beautiful glacial lake in the Ngojumba glacier. There's a passable chance en route

Buddhist prayer stones, *mani,* mark the trails to many sacred mountains in the high Himalayas.

of seeing some of Sagarmatha National Park's wildlife: wolf, bear, musk deer, feral goat species, even the brilliantly colored crimson-horned or Impeyan pheasants of this region.

A hard four-hour slog, or a full day's strenuous effort from Namche on the trail to Everest, you'll come to Khumbu and the most famous of its monasteries, **Thangboche,** known the world over for its stupendous views of Everest, Lhotse, with the unmistakable 6,855-m (22,491-ft)-high obelisk of Ama Dablam, in the background.

After his successful ascent of Everest, on May 29, 1953, Sir Edmund Hillary became New Zealand's Ambassador to India and Nepal and devoted much of his diplomatic career and personal life to improving the lot of the Sherpa community that he has come to love. He is a frequent visitor to the monastery and its presiding lama. It was his initiative that led to the establishment of Sagarmatha National Park in 1975. The park was run by New Zealand experts until 1981 when Nepal took over its management. Hillary has been back frequently, helping to build schools and community centers.

Civilizing forces, not all for the better, have come apace to the once-isolated Sherpas whose festivals add color and fantasy to life in this otherwise barren but beautiful region. There's also a much more relaxed trek — for those who don't wish to scale great heights — by foot or pony along the old trade route between Kathmandu and Pokhara. Including a visit to Gorkha, this takes between eight and 10 days.

In the far west, trekking from **Jumla** always poses problems — simply because it's so difficult to reach this remote region. But the spectacular scenery makes the effort worthwhile. The trekking "high season" — between October and December — is the best time for high-altitude climbing when the more popular routes — Khumbu, Pokhara, Ghandrung, Ghorapani and Annapurna — are congested.

SOME CLASSIC TREKS STEP BY STEP

KANCHENJUNGA

Astride the Sikkim border with eastern Nepal, **Kanchenjunga** is the world's third-highest mountain and this 13-day outward journey depends on absolute fitness and acclimatization, as it takes the trekker from the subtropical lowlands to a height of more than 5,000 m (16,000 ft) above sea level — around the base of some magnificent satellite peaks — to Yalung glacier. You need Sherpa guides and first-class equipment including rugged tents, together with adequate rations as food supplies are not easy to obtain in this region.

It should go without saying that a trek of this sort will need to be organized with a reliable trekking agency. Permits are only issued to groups. See the TREKKING AGENCIES section of the TRAVELERS' TIPS chapter for some recommended agencies.

Most agencies will organize a flight to Biratnagar. From here a rented vehicle should be able to get you to the trailhead, Basantpur, on the same day. The alternative is an 11- to 13-hour bus journey from Kathmandu to Dhahran, where you stay overnight before traveling on to Basantpur.

First Day

From Basantpur the path goes to **Dobhan**; it splits into two — one continuing along the ridgeback, the other winding up and down the hillside to the right. Stick to the ridge: it's shorter and the mountain views are spectacular.

An irrigation duct takes water to the nearby fields as the trail climbs a gentle slope through the twin villages of Tsute. Beyond them, through the forest, the path turns right, leaving the ridge to climb through stands of rhododendrons before emerging in a delightful alpine meadow — ideal for camping but without water.

Re-enter the forest, however and climb gently upwards for about another fifteen minutes to the two houses of **Door Pani,** at a height of 2,780 m (9,000 ft), where there's a beautiful meadow in which to camp with plentiful water.

Second Day
From the meadow you now climb through the forest to another ridge where the trail now begins to switchback — up and down — in true Himalayan fashion. Follow this for approximately half an hour before descending steeply to the left for about 200 m (650 ft) to the village of Tinjure Phedi with its tea house.

From here the trail follows a ridgeback through copses of rhododendrons beneath sprawling alpine meadows and is relatively smooth and even, until the hamlet of **Chauki,** with its 11 houses and a tea shop.

There's no cultivation around these parts and the meadows are used for summer pastures. As you walk from Chauki, the magnificent peak of Makalu dominates the horizon, but not long after this you get your first glimpse — and what a glimpse — of Kanchenjunga. Soon after this, the trail arrives at the foot of the Mongol Bharari pass.

Lined with mani stones, it winds gently up to the saddle, through rhododendron forest, cresting the ridge at the hamlet of Ram Pokhari — two lakes and five small houses.

Now the trail winds along the top of a grassy, undulating ridge before descending to **Gupha Pokhari** and its enchanting lake, at a height of 2,985 m (9,790 ft).

Third Day
Take the pass to the right, skirting the ridge directly in front of you, when you leave Gupha Pokhari. You'll get your last glimpse of Makalu and Chamlang before turning northeast into the Kanchenjunga massif.

You enter this range on your right, along a winding switchback trail; after an hour's

walk you come to the crests of a 3,025-m (10,000-ft)-high pass that descends to **Dobhan.** Along the downward trail are many bunkhouses for trekkers and porters where it's possible to spend the night.

After passing the bunkhouses, the trail climbs the second of two small hills before beginning the real descent, through thick forest, to the bottom of the pass and the rice paddies and grain fields of the hamlet of **Gurja Gaon.** From this trail, there are magnificent views of Jannu and Kanchenjunga.

The path continues its descent from Gurja Gaon, rejoining, on the right, the alternate route from Basantpur, to a campsite near **Nesum,** at 1,650 m (5,400 ft).

Fourth Day
Trekking in the Himalayas is not for those who seek to climb ever upward. Trails plunge up and down 3,000 m (10,000 ft) or more and from Nesum the trail continues its descent through a maze of rice paddies to Dobhan and the valley of the **Tamar river.**

Trekkers OPPOSITE rest outside a tea house on the trail to Mount Everest and Sherpa women take to the trail ABOVE near Lukla.

There are many hamlets, villages and tea houses along the way. After about a 90-minute walk you reach **Dobhan**, a picturesque Newar settlement, with a village store and many houses.

It's here that the trail crosses the **Meiwa Khola,** a tributary of the Tamar, on to a level plain with a small hamlet, after which it reaches the **Tamar.** Cross here to the left bank, via the suspension footbridge, where the road divides — one a narrow path to Ghunsa, the other a long, climbing ridgeback trail to **Taplejung.**

From here, the track starts climbing steeply as it zigzags its way to **Deoringe school** before easing back into a more moderate climb through terraced fields and scattered forests, passing by the hamlet of **Taribun.** There are many more houses along this well-traveled route.

Finally, just above a public bathhouse, you reach **Taplejung** at 1,798 m (5,800 ft), the administrative headquarters of this district with a post and telegraph office, hospital, government offices and a military post. Taplejung is a good place to replenish food and other supplies, but fresh meat and vegetables are only available on Saturdays, when the city's markets are open.

Fifth Day

You leave Taplejung and its cobblestone streets, pass the water reservoir, and follow the path to the airfield — a very steep climb.

There's a hotel at the edge of the airfield on a level plateau and there's now a gentle climb through the flower-filled meadowlands to the forest, with the mountains to your right, before descending to **Lali Kharka.**

Across the valley stands **Bhanjyang,** which you reach the next day but for now your descent culminates in the fertile fields around **Tambawa,** at 2,000 m (6,500 ft), where you can camp in the fields or near the school.

Sixth Day

From Tambawa to **Pa Khola** takes around 90 minutes, first to get to a ridgeback trail and then circuitously down the mountain to Pa Khola.

At Pa Khola, the trail cuts through terraced rice paddies, then across a suspension footbridge to **Kunjar.** Before you reach this lovely alpine village, surrounded by thick rain forest, it passes through a few hamlets.

The path carries on gently upward out of Kunjar until you are high above **Tambawa.** Soon it reaches **Bhanjyang** with many tea houses and striking views of Kanchenjunga, framed by South peak, Main peak and Yalung Kang.

The path descends again, to the left, on a pleasantly easy slope to the terraced fields of **Khesewa,** at 2,100 m (6,800 ft), where you can camp in the surrounding fields.

Seventh Day

From Khesewa, the trail descends through forest to the **Nandeva Khola** on the left and, crossing the river, continues down along its banks before entering the forest to the left to begin the climb up the next range of hills to **Loppoding.**

Now the path switchbacks up and down to the rest area, at the delightfully-named hamlet of **Fun Fun.** After this, follow the ridgeback into the hills on the right bank of the **Kabeli Khola,** before a gradual descent through rice paddies and grain fields to the village of **Anpan.**

From Anpan, the trail follows a ridge-back up an easy slope to **Ponpe Dhara,** which sits on its crest. You can pause here to take in the splendid view of distant Jannu before continuing the winding descent through hamlets and farm fields to the Kasshawa Khola, which you cross by suspension bridge. On the other side you make the slow climb to the village of **Mamankhe.**

Eighth Day

This hike starts with an easy climb, skirting a formidable ridge, to the village of Dekadin. After this, the trail follows the right bank of the Kabeli Khola, about 200 to 300 m (600 to 900 ft) above its raging waters, winding around various ridges, cliffs and streams.

On the whole, this three-and-a-half hour walk is an easy up and down trek with constant views of the river below and the little farmsteads and their fields on the hills opposite.

Finally, you descend some stone steps to the river itself and then on to another that takes you on a gradual climb away from the river through villages and fields.

Eventually, after about two hours hard climbing, the trail reaches the remote village of **Yamphudin,** at 2,150 m (7,000 ft). Report to the checkpost.

Camp here in fields or in house compounds. You may prefer to engage new porters for the hazards of cold, snow and altitude ahead, as those from Dhahran are not well-suited to the rugged challenge of the Kanchenjunga range.

Ninth Day

Yamphudin is where the real climbing begins. There are two options for the route to Lamite Bhanjyang. The favorite choice is to cross the river and trek through Dhupi Bhanjyang.

For those who prefer a tougher challenge, the second route requires a climb up a mountain path from **Yamphudin,** on the right bank of **Omje Khola,** that crosses a stream early in its course.

It then plunges down two hours through the fields back to the **Omje Khola,** which you must cross again to reach an extremely steep mountain ridge that, at first, demands

care with every step. But the trail soon enters the forest where there is little or no sense of height. Gradually the severity of the gradient eases into a relaxed climb, still through thick forest, until it emerges on a level open saddle.

Eventually the trail reaches the climbing hut at **Chitre** where you can spend the night. However, in the dry season there's no water and you will have to walk on another 90 minutes to a little tarn beneath **Lamite Bhanjyang.** You can ask at **Yamphudin** before you set off if water is available.

Tenth Day

The ridgeback from Chitre is lined with magnolias and bamboo but when the trail climbs beyond the bamboo belt it reaches **Lamite** and its single shelter — a simple structure consisting of a roof with supporting posts.

The trail then ascends through thick stands of rhododendron, along a ridge to **Lamite Bhanjyang,** at 3,430 m (11,250 ft), with Jannu rising up before you above the ridge in all its magnificence and behind you panoramic views of the foothills around Dhahran.

Climb about 150 m (550 ft) from here on the right before descending, through thick forests of rhododendron, to the **Simbua Khola,** with Kanchenjunga's majestic snowclad peak floating above the trees.

The gentle descent takes the trail almost to the river and then climbs along the left

Sherpa woman and children OPPOSITE outside a high country tea shop on one of Nepal's many popular trekking trails. Sherpa father and son ABOVE at Lukla.

bank for a short distance before crossing over a wooden bridge to the right bank and the campsite at **Torontan**, at 3,080 m (10,100 ft), where you can sleep in one of the caves.

Eleventh Day
Follow the path, past the caves, along the right bank of the **Simbua Khola**. The forested walls of the valley are thick with pine and rhododendron.

Eventually, after about two hours walking, the trail reaches **Whata** with its single hut, where it crosses to the right bank of the stream in front of the hut and continues through the thick forest to the snowline.

You'll see a Sherpa shrine with a huge boulder, shaped like a snake. It's designed to ward off the demons, for the Sherpas believe that if anyone dies beyond this point, evil spirits will fall upon the mountains.

The path leads down to the river bank and up a difficult trail to **Tseram** where you can see your ultimate destination — the terminal moraine of **Yalung glacier.** Behind it are the 7,353-m (24,120-ft)-high Kabru and 7,349 m (24,112 ft) Talung peak. Camp in one of the caves.

Twelfth Day
A steep slope, descending from the left, bars the way out of Tseram and you have to retrace your trail to the bank of the **Simbua Khola,** then around its base, before climbing up through stony, terraced field to **Yalung Bara** where a single stone hut marks the end of the tree line. From here you have to carry enough fuelwood for the rest of the trek.

Just above, past several small stone huts, the path comes to the right bank of the entrance to the **Yalung glacier** and **Lapsang,** with Lapsang La valley at the left.

Now the trail comes to a tiny pond and skirts a protruding cliff face — when you suddenly see before you a stunning panorama: the peaks of 7,317-m (24,005-ft)-high Kabru S., 6,678-m (21,910-ft)-high Rathong and 6,147-m (20,168-ft)-high Kokthan. Follow the flat trail to the **Ramze** at 4,560 m (15,000 ft) where there is a hut in which you can sleep.

Chortens and temples appear unexpectedly in the high places of Nepal.

Thirteenth Day

The magnificent Yalung glacier veers left at Ramze and just around the corner next morning you will get your first close up views of mighty Kanchenjunga.

Now the trail climbs the lateral moraine to a **Buddhist stupa** from which it descends steeply to the glacier floor and a path marked by cairns. Lungs gasp in the rarefied air but eventually, after about four hours of really intense effort, you reach the campsite atop the glacier, at 4,890 m (16,000 ft), with magnificent views of 7,710-m (25,294-ft)-high Jannu.

The vista of the mountains surrounding Yalung glacier opens before you — and at the final camp, **Corner Camp,** at 5,140 m (16,900 ft), on the left bank of the glacier, there is a stupendous mountain panorama — a fitting reward for the effort it takes to reach this point.

Fourteenth to Twenty-Second Day

Depending on how your agency has staged your trek, you will either trek nine days back to Basantpur or six days to Suketar, which has flights to Biratnagar and sometimes direct connections to Kathmandu.

MAKALU

One of Nepal's most splendid — and demanding — treks, takes you from **Tumlingtar** north through the subtropical **Arun valley** and over the 4,000-m (13,000-ft)-high **Shipton pass,** to the slopes of the three great peaks of Makalu, Everest and Lhotse. You must carry all your supplies and Sherpa guides are absolutely essential. Altitude sickness is an ever present threat and, until the monsoons, Shipton pass is buried in snow.

First Day

From **Tumlingtar** airfield, climb the hill and walk through level rice paddies and scattered houses and then across a series of terraced hills. To the right you see the waters of the **Shawa Khola.** In the distance stands

Chamlang. Soon the path becomes a ridge-back with many travelers, tea houses and shaded rest areas.

After passing a bubbling spring the path moves to the right flank of the ridge and, after a short climb, you will see more houses and finally arrive at the checkpost at the entrance to **Khandbari,** with its shop-lined main street and large open bazaar.

Khandbari is the administrative capital of the district with a bank, hospital and school. It's a good place to stock up on food and other essentials. A meadow out-

side the village makes an excellent campsite.

The ridge trail continues to **Mane Bhanjyang,** where it divides — one branch going left to the ridge route; the other straight through the rice paddies. Follow this latter route on the gentle climb to the village of **Panguma.**

There's not too much to see here and the walk is somewhat monotonous as you climb to **Bhote Bash,** set at about 1,720 m (5,600 ft), where you can camp in one of the fields.

Second Day

When you leave Bhote Bash, you also leave the farmlands and turn right onto

A precarious log and stone bridge leads across the swollen floodwaters that interrupt a rough mountain trail.

the left side of the ridge as it climbs to the pass above. The level path passes through scrub and fields to **Gogune** and on into forest.

After a walk of about two hours, the switchback trail exits at the Gurung village of **Chichira,** set on top of a ridge, then continues to Kuwapani. At this point you get impressive but far distant views of Makalu.

From the three-house settlement of **Kuwapani,** the path veers to the right of the ridge, arriving at **Samurati's** lone house,

with the fields of **Sedua** visible on the hillside opposite and, beyond, the walls of the Shipton pass.

Not long after this, the trail cuts down the ridge where it veers left, at a single house, to **Runbaun.** Now the trail becomes extremely steep and rough.

Great care must be exercised — and not only on the trail. The suspension bridge over the Arun river, which takes about three-and-a-half hours to reach, is narrow and precarious with missing footboards. One careless step could be fatal.

where there are painted mani stones and a cave in which you can sleep.

Leaving the village, the path divides into two. Take the left fork into the forest through **Fururu** to the rest area in **Daujia Dhara Deorali,** where the path levels out. Down in the forest on the left, across a small stream and over another ridge, there's an unusual combination of painted mani stones.

Eventually, the trail reaches **Mure,** a village at the right of the path, where you can camp in the fields or in one of the house compounds.

Third Day
Leave the village down a slope facing it

After the bridge, the trail climbs steeply along a precarious and crumbling incline on the right bank up to the grain fields and hamlet of **Rumruma.**

The trail leaves the hamlet through terraced fields to **Sedua,** at 1,480 m (4,855 ft), where you can camp at the school near a spring.

Fourth Day
From **Sedua,** the trail leaves the Arun river and enters the watershed of the **Kashuwa Khola.** Climb a mountainside dotted with terraced fields and forests. After about two hours walk a *chorten,* or Buddhist stupa, marks the Sherpa village of **Naba Gaon** with its monastery.

Climb a ridge, lined with mani stones on the right and follow the trail along the right bank of the **Kashuwa Khola** through **Kharshing Kharka,** which has two huts. The path cuts through thick hill forest where fallen trees can make walking difficult. Eventually, it crosses a small stream and leads into the remote village of **Tashi Gaon,** at 2,050 m (6,700 ft), with its attractive timber houses covered with bamboo roofing. You can camp in the fields near the village.

Fifth Day
Leave **Tashi Gaon** through forest up a gentle slope, across a rocky area and stream, to the meadows of **Uteshe.** From the top of the next ridge there are striking mountain panoramas where the path veers right.

The path continues gradually upwards, across a stream into thick bamboo. When it leaves the bamboo, the trail enters a rhododendron forest and becomes markedly steeper; passing Dhara Kharka on the crest of the ridge and then to **Unshisa** on the Ishwa Khola side of the ridge, finally reaching the campsite at **Kauma,** at the top of the ridge, after about five hours walking. Just below the ridge, about 20 m (60 ft) down on the Kashuwa Khola side, there are some caves where you can sleep.

Sixth Day
From Kauma, the trail climbs to the top of a ridge that offers the best mountain landscape of the whole trail — a truly dramatic panorama at the far end of the valley of 7,317-m (24,005-ft)-high Chamlang, 6,739-m (22,110-ft)-high Peak Six, 6,105 m (20,030 ft) Peak Seven and the long-awaited 8,481-m (27,825-ft)-high Makalu, with the outline of the Kanchenjunga range to the east.

The trail now begins to climb **Shipton pass.** In fact, there are two passes — **Keke La** and **Tutu La.** Rugged cliffs bar the way and the trail traverses left to a small pond, then climbs up to **Keke La,** at 4,127 m (13,500 ft), then down into an s-shaped valley, past a small tarn and up to **Tutu La.**

Here the trail descends to a level stretch before veering left, past a waterfall and across a stream and on through forest to **Mumbuk,** set at 3,500 m (11,500 ft) amid pines and rhododendron.

Seventh Day
The trail leaves the campsite, following the course of a winding stream for about 200 m (650 ft) before turning left and down along the side of another stream, turning left yet again, past a cave, to the **Barun Khola.**

The path takes the right bank with views of Peak Six. Beware of the frequent rockfalls. Soon Makalu comes into view and the trail exits onto a terraced hill and the meadows of **Tematan Kharka.**

The trail continues along flat hills to **Yangre Kharka** where there are some caves, and on into rhododendron forest.

Here it leaves the **Barun Khola,** climbing gently up the side of a wide valley and turns right, across a stream, to the single hut of **Nehe Kharka** 2,670 m (8,760 ft).

Eighth Day
Leave the campsite, past a cave and cross to the left bank of the **Barun Khola** over a bridge set on a large boulder in midstream, into rhododendron forest. The path becomes steep as it zigzags up to the meadowlands on the slopes of **Ripock Kharka.**

Here the path leads away from the Barun Khola, on a modest gradient, through **Jark Kharka** to **Ramara** — offering views along the way, one after the other, of 6,830-m (22,409-ft)-high Pyramid Peak, 6,720-m (22,048-ft)-high Peak Four, 6,477-m (21,251-ft)-high Peak Three, 6,404-m (21,101-ft)-high Peak Five, Peak Six and Chamlang.

At Ramara, approaching the Barun Khola, the trail reaches the snout of **Lower Barun glacier** and continues along the glacier's left bank to the headwaters of the **Barun Khola** and **Mere** where there is a cave for camping. There are no more forests and you must carry fuelwood with you from this point.

The trail continues on the right across some rocky, glacial terrain to **Shershon,** at 4,615 m (15,000 ft).

Ninth Day
The majestic crest of Makalu dominates the horizon at Shershon as the trail skirts the base of its southeast ridge in an easy climb onto lateral moraine. Here, glowering down from its massive height, the mountain seems to fill the sky.

Take the trail down to the riverbed, across the stream and up a terraced hill to **Makalu base camp,** set in a pastoral meadow at 4,800 m (15,750 ft), where there's a stone hut without a roof.

Makalu base camp is an ideal place from which to explore the area around the foot of this great mountain, including the Barun glacier.

Tenth to Sixteenth Day
The return trek to **Tumlingtar** takes about seven days.

Turn right in the village square to a steep ridge route that descends to the right bank of the Tamba Kosi and the bridge, which crosses to a trail just above the rushing water.

Eventually, the trail arrives at **Piguti** where it crosses the **Gumbu Khola** to a pleasant meadow where you can camp.

Second Day
Leave camp, past the suspension bridge over the main stream and follow the path along the right bank with views of Gauri-sankar rising up at the far end of the valley.

ROLWALING HIMAL

Few tourists or trekkers visit Rolwaling Himal — getting permits for the region is not easy — yet it offers some of the finest mountain trekking anywhere. You need full equipment, including durable tents and Sherpa guides. To reach the trailhead take a bus from Kathmandu to Lamosangu and then a van to **Charikot.**

First Day
From Charikot, Rolwaling Himal is clearly visible in the distance. The trail out of town leads down a wide, gentle gradient through many hamlets to the village of **Dolakha,** with its striking three-storied houses.

Soon the trail reaches **Shigati,** where there is a checkpost and a large tributary of the Bhote Kosi that enters the river from the left.

Once across the suspension bridge over the Shigati Khola, the valley narrows and walls become precipitous cliff faces. The trail leads on to another suspension bridge that takes it back to the left bank and along an undulating path to the village of **Suri Dhoban.**

Leaving this settlement, the trail crosses the **Khare Khola** over another suspension bridge and on through the precipitous

ABOVE: Three generations of Sherpa women.
OVERLEAF: Winter sunset on Lhotse.

Bhote Kosi valley. The trail is reasonably good, but occasional landslides may mean making a detour down to the riverbed or up over the hills.

Eventually, the trail reaches the terraced hills and cultivated fields of **Manthale,** at around 1,070 m (3,200 ft), where you can camp.

Third Day

Leave the village by taking the winding path through the fields and over a bridge to the right bank and a moderately sloping,

undulating, walled path to Congar, at which point the trail crosses a stream.

After some distance, the valley narrows and becomes precipitous and the trail traverses an area of tumbled rock and boulders to a waterfall on the opposite bank.

Here there is a crossroads, where you leave the old Silk Road to Tibet and take the path on the right, down to the bridge and the river below, which then climbs steeply in zigzag fashion through breaks in the valley walls.

At the top the path exits onto terraced fields, where it is lined with many stones and chortens, to **Simgaon,** set at 1,950 m (6,300 ft). No longer visible, but still audible far below, the Bhote Kosi cuts deep through

the valley gorge, its waters diverted to the fields spread over the hills on either side.

Fourth Day

Follow the path from the campsite, through terraced fields, to the summit of the next ridge — with splendid views of 7,146-m (23,438-ft)-high Gaurisankar — and into a dense rhododendron forest that zigzags up the mountain to the crest of another ridge.

The trail follows the crest of the ridge through more rhododendron to emerge in the fields and meadows around **Shakpa** and then up the mountains on the Rolwaling side of the valley into more thick forest.

Leaving this, the path climbs steeply down some dangerous and tricky sections to cross a stream. It then skirts a ridge to reach **Cyalche,** at 1,760 m (5,570 ft), where you can camp on the grass.

Fifth Day

From the campsite, the path descends steeply and diagonally to the **Rolwaling Chhu**. It then follows the riverbed, before veering to the left bank and through a narrow valley and over a covered wooden bridge to the right bank.

The path continues across a stream by the bridge and climbing gently, follows an undulating course to **Nyimare,** then **Ramding** and **Gyabrug,** where the roofs of the rock-walled houses are weighted down with stones.

Follow the path across another stream before climbing, briefly, to the last permanent village in this region, **Beding,** set at 3,690 m (12,100 ft), which boasts 32 houses and a monastery. You can camp near the river with panoramas of 7,180-m (23,557-ft)-high Menlungtse, Rolwaling Himal's major peak.

From this base you can make a three-day diversion to **Manlung La** by taking the trail, along the mountain flank on the right bank, just after the village.

The first day, the trail climbs to a 4,900-m (16,000-ft)-high campsite, via Taten Kharka. The second day takes you to Manlung La, set at 5,510 m (18,000 ft) and back. The trail is crevassed and you will need ropes, picks and ice axes.

Sixth Day

Leave the village, past the **Manlung La** diversion on your left, follow the right bank of the Rolwaling Chhu on a gradual climb through the valley to **Na Gaon**, a village with terraced and walled potato fields.

Leaving the village, the trail crosses a wooden bridge and mountains come into view — 6,698-m (21,976-ft)-high Chobutse and 6,269-m (20,569-ft)-high Chugimago — before the snout of the Ripimo Shar and Tram Bau glaciers push in to block the valley.

Seventh to Eleventh Day

It takes five days to return to Charikot from Rolpa Chobu.

MANASLU

An inspiring 14-day outward trek, from **Trisuli Bazaar** to the **Burhi Gandaki,** winding through huge and steep valleys, over snowclad passes and foaming rivers, to the three peaks of Manaslu, known as "the Japanese peaks". Long a restricted area, this trek was only opened to tourists in 1991.

The trail crosses a wooden bridge, shortly thereafter leaving the main path and turning left to **Omai Tsho** up a ridge that offers a spectacular vista of 6,735-m (22,097-ft)-high Kang Nachungo and the mountains surrounding Ripimo glacier.

The path to **Tsho Rolpa** skirts the base of the Ripimo glacier and passes between **Ripimo** and **Tram Bau glaciers** on to the right bank of Tram Bau glacier. It becomes narrower and narrower as the valley becomes shallower.

At the far end of the valley are 6,730-m (22,081-ft)-high Pigphera-Go Shar and 6,666-m (21,871-ft)-high Pigphera-Go Nup.

Soon you arrive at the last camp, **Rolpa Chobu**, at 4,540 m (15,000 ft).

Trekkers must be part of an organized group and be accompanied by a liaison officer. There is an annual quota on the number of people that may take this trek. Excellent equipment and guides are essential and because of its duration, so are adequate food supplies and physical fitness. Build in extra rest days to help you recover during the trek.

Board a bus at **Sorkhuti** on the northern side of Kathmandu for **Trisuli Bazaar.** Reserve your seat in advance. The journey takes four hours.

Dry stone wall OPPOSITE marks the trail into the Himalayan village of Phakdingma. Harvesting potatoes ABOVE in a high country village on the approach to Mount Everest.

High-Altitude Trekking and Treks

First Day
Camp in the meadow in front of the military post, a short climb up from Trisuli Bazaar town. Take the path along the riverbed and up the right-hand plateau to Raxun Bazaar.

It's a wide, smooth pathway that cuts through the rice paddies to **Gote Thati.** The path crosses a suspension bridge over the Somrie Khola, runs along the river's right bank and continues on through the villages of **Ghorakki, Shiraune Bash** and **Kaple Bash.**

Before long, signs of cultivation vanish and the river is dry. Now the path climbs a ridge to **Somrie Bhanjyang,** at 1,290 m (4,200 ft), continuing over a tea house-lined pass to the valley floor and the hamlet of **Kinu Chautara** with its many tea houses.

The path continues through farmland and then crosses to the right bank of the **Thofal Khola,** down a gradual incline to the hamlet of **Jor Chautara.** Soon after this, it reaches **Baran Gurun** where you can camp in the compound of people's homes or in the fields.

Second Day
Leaving camp, the trail crosses a small stream and then up some steep stone steps to **Baran,** through a small hamlet and along a winding mountain path, to the Tamang village of **Tharpu.**

Shortly afterwards, it reaches **Tharpu Bhanjyang,** with its one general store, then climbs down a pass to Boktani. Not long after reaching here it begins to climb a ridge to **Col Bhanjyang,** where it joins the mountain trail along the side of the Thofal Khola.

It's gentle, pastoral countryside — small foothills rolling away to distant horizons, sheltering gentle valleys — and eventually the trail takes you through **Katunche,** which boasts a bank and post office, onto the trail to **Charanki Pauwa** and **Charanki Phedi,** where you can camp in the fields outside the village.

Third Day
Leaving the village, the narrow path crosses a small stream, over Achani Bhanjyang pass and down to the left bank of the Ankhu

Khola where it crosses a suspension bridge to **Kale Sundhara Bazaar.**

At this point, the landscape is sweltering and subtropical all the way to **Gaili Chautara** where, just beyond the village, you leave the main path and take the trail to the left, much of it along the side of the river, through **Hansi Bazaar,** with its tea houses and shops and between rice paddies in the riverbed.

Where the Ankhu Khola bends to the left, the path veers to the right on its way to **Arughat Bazaar,** through a small, narrow valley and over a sprawling terraced hill that stands between the Ankhu Khola and Burhi Gandaki.

Reaching the village of **Soliental** and the **Burhi Gandaki,** you can see Arughat Bazaar below. Take the path along the left bank of the Burhi Gandaki for **Arughat Bazaar,** a small, bustling town on either side of the river. Its central shopping area, with bank, is on the right side of the river across a suspension bridge.

You can camp in the grove near the school, just outside town.

Fourth Day
Out of Arughat Bazaar the trail follows the right bank of the Burhi Gandaki to its source, along a path through farm fields and **Mordar.**

When you reach **Simre** the dry season trail follows the riverbed to **Arket.** During the monsoon it climbs over the hills. You cross the Arket Khola at **Arket,** through a village and its tea houses and across more farmland to the **Asma Khola** which you cross to climb up to **Kyoropani.**

From this hamlet, the path is straight and level for a short distance and then descends to the river bank and on through another hamlet to its confluence with the Soti Khola where you can camp in the fields on the right bank.

Fifth Day
Follow the trail along the riverbed for about ten minutes and then take the winding path up the forested hill to **Almara, Riden** and **Riden Gaon.**

Tea house and restaurant (top) in Trisuli Bazaar's main street (bottom).

Soon the Burhi Gandaki valley becomes a precipitous gorge until it reaches another valley that cuts into the opposite bank and opens up. Now the trail crosses farmlands to **Lapbesi** and then down to the white riverbed of the **Burhi Gandaki.**

Another path follows the mountain contours, rejoining the trail from the riverbed near the hamlet of **Kani Gaon.**

Continue along an undulating path above the river to **Machha Khola,** with its tea house, where you can camp in the fields outside the village.

Sixth Day

Leave across the Machha Khola and follow the path along the river bank into a precipitous valley and across the abundant flow of the Tado Khola to **Kholabensi,** a hamlet of eight houses.

The trail now continues along the bank of the **Burhi Gandaki,** between two walls of sheer cliff, to the hot springs of **Tatopani.** Soon after, it crosses a suspension bridge to the left bank into forest and then along a gravel path by the river to **Dobhan** where there is a tea house.

Here the trail crosses the Dobhan Khola and some rocks, to the point where the Burhi Gandaki bends right into raging rapids. It climbs up the hill above the rapids

which suddenly broaden out into a sluggish, meandering stream between white beaches.

Now cross the **Yaru Khola,** climb into the forested hillside to **Lauri** and the suspension bridge to the right bank, where the trail climbs again — along a winding path that dips down once more to the riverbed and an easy walk through the fields to the checkpost at **Jagat,** set at 1,350 m (4,400 ft). This is the last village with a shop. You can camp in the fields outside the village.

Seventh Day

You leave Jagat down some stone steps to the river, crossing the tributary flowing in from the left and then walk along the right bank before climbing a terraced hill to **Saguleri** where you can suddenly see 7,177-m (23,540-ft)-high Sringi Himal rising up at the end of the valley.

Follow the undulating path along the right bank to **Sirdi Bash** and on to the next village, **Gata Khola,** where you cross the suspension bridge to the left bank. This is where the trekking trail to Ganesh diverges to the right. You continue along the river bank to **Seirishon Gaon.**

It is here that the hills surrounding the valley start closing in, trapping the Burhi Gandaki between sheer and precipitous cliffs. A bit further on, you reach the **Chhulung Khola** tributary, flowing in through the opposite bank and you cross the bridge to the right bank.

The trail climbs for about l00 m (328 ft) before turning right, following a winding path through a pine forest above the Shar Khola stream, that flows in from the opposite bank.

The trail follows the river through the center of the valley before crossing over to the left bank. Walk for about another thirty minutes and it returns once more to the right bank.

Soon you come to the junction of the **Nyak trail** that climbs up to the left, the main trail continuing along the river's right bank until you have to climb up to traverse its gorge.

Finally, you cross the **Deng Khola** into the tiny hamlet of **Deng,** with four houses. You can camp in the fields outside.

Eighth Day

Leave the village along the high, winding path that soon takes you down to the river bank where you cross a suspension bridge to the left bank and start the steep ascent to **Lana.** Then begins a more gentle, gradual climb through **Unbae,** with its stone gate and mani stones, before the trail dips down once more to the river, curving past a waterfall on the right.

Now the path climbs up again across a terraced hill, past the village of **Bih** and across the **Bihjam Khola,** on a twisting course lined with mani stones, to a tiny hamlet near the Burhi Gandaki.

The trail soon reaches farm fields and a stone gate — entrance to the Tibetan village of **Ghap,** at 2,095 m (6,800 ft) — where there is a suspension bridge across the Burhi Gandaki. You can camp in the meadow on the left bank, near the entrance to the village.

Ninth Day

Follow the path along the right bank, past a long mani-stone wall, into the forest and then through **Lumachik,** with its one lone house, and across the wooden bridge over the **Burhi Gandaki gorge**. Here the trail climbs upward through forest to a wooden bridge that takes it across to the right bank and on through the forest to the checkpost at **Namru.**

Leave Namru by crossing a stream to a grassy field with a waterfall and stone cliff to the left, over the pastures to **Bengsam** where the trail climbs out of the village through a stone gate and continues on to **Li.**

Here the trail crosses the **Hinan Khola,** streaming down from the Lidanda glacier, to climb up to **Sho,** guarded by its stone gate. Soon afterwards, it rounds a bend to and reveals enchanting views of Naike peak, 7,154-m (23,500-ft)-high Manaslu North and finally, 8,158-m (26,766-ft)-high Manaslu.

Climbing gradually, the path passes between houses, farm fields and a bubbling spring to **Lo,** at 3,150 m (10,300 ft) and its stone-walled fields. Behind you, at the head of the valley below, stands 7,406-m (24,298-ft)-high Ganesh Himal I. You can

camp by the spring at the entrance to the village.

Tenth Day

Cut through the village, lined by a long mani stone wall, down across the **Damonan Khola** and then climb along the river. Ahead, the horizon is dominated by the snowcap of 7,835-m (25,690-ft)-high Peak 29, while the Shara Khola flows in from the right.

After a few minutes the trail comes to a left fork — the main path ascends the ridge to **Sama** — that climbs to **Pungen glacier,**

via **Honsansho Gompa** and despite the effort is a worthwhile diversion simply for the views of Peak 29 and Manaslu.

The narrow path climbs through thick forest to **Honsansho Gompa** and over a gentle ridge and cuts diagonally across a rocky riverbed to another small ridge. Not long after this it reaches seven stone huts at **Kyubun,** then climbs over a small ridge formed by the moraine of Pungen glacier, from which you get a stunning view of the battlements of Peak 29 and graceful Manaslu.

Trekkers OPPOSITE cross the foaming waters of the Dudh Kosi in the Everest region. Porters ABOVE trek high into the great mountain fastness of Nepal.

This moraine leads onto **Ramanan Kharka** but to reach Sama climb down the glacier and, from the small ridge, cut across its snout to the rock-strewn riverbed and a chorten.

From this point it is just a short climb back down to the main path and the potato fields and houses of Sama village, set at 3,500 m (11,500 ft). Just twenty minutes of hiking will bring you to the meadow at **Sama Gompa** where you can spend the night before a panoramic view of Manaslu peak.

climbs above the trickle of the Burhi Gandaki before climbing down to the riverbed.

Cross the river, up a terraced hill on the opposite bank and through a stone gate to the remote village of **Somdu,** where around 40 families share life's alpine travail. There's no more fuelwood after this so take what you will need with you.

The path goes down the mountain from the village, through a stone gate and across the **Gyala Khola,** before climbing gradually upwards. Below you, to the left, you may see the ruins of Larkya Bazaar.

Eleventh Day

Leave the meadows, skirting a ridge of lateral moraine, to the banks of the **Burhi Gandaki** after crossing a stream born in the ice-melt of Manaslu glacier. If you turn left you can make a 60- to 70-minute excursion to a glacial lake.

Meanwhile, the main trail leaves the grasslands, traveling down to the riverbed and onto **Kermo Kharka** with stupendous views of Manaslu. From here it passes a long mani-stone wall, at **Kermo Manan,** where the valley begins to close in and the trail

Larkya glacier soon appears on the opposite side of the valley after the trail crosses two streams and skirts around **Sarka Khola.** Then it climbs to a strong shelter, at 4,450 m (14,600 ft) where you can spend the night.

Twelfth Day

From the shelter, a short climb takes the trekker up to a glacial valley with fine views of Cho Dhanda along the way. As the gradual ascent continues, the unmistakable image of Larkya peak comes into sight opposite a small glacier on the other side of the valley.

Soon the trail leads into a level glacier and gradually upwards until a final short,

Four thousand eight hundred meters (16,000 ft) up in the Himalaya, rough, scattered moraine ABOVE and a smooth, glassy lake OPPOSITE are contrasting elements of a glacial landscape.

steep climb brings you to **Larkya La,** set at 5,135 m (16,850 ft) — and a breathtaking view to the west of 7,126-m (23,380-ft)-high Himlung Himal, Cheo Himal, Gyaji Kang, 7,010-m (23,000-ft)-high Kang Gulu and 7,937-m (26,041-ft)-high Annapurna II.

Climbing down the steep, snow-covered west face of the pass, unlike the east face, is a tricky business, so be careful.

Continue down to **Larcia,** opposite a hill on the other side, called Pangal, that also offers superb mountain views. From Larcia, the trail climbs down some glacial moraine

Now follow the riverbed, cross over the wooden bridge above the headwaters of the Dudh Khola and up a lateral moraine, before descending through a magnificent rhododendron forest to **Hampuk.**

Finally, before reentering the forest, draw breath for your last look at the west face of Manaslu, then continue through the forest along the right bank of the **Dudh Khola** to **Sangure Kharka** and its one hut.

Manaslu North peak and Larkya peak are now behind you as the trail continues

to the roofless stone hut of **Tanbuche,** at around 3,900 m (12,800 ft).

Thirteenth Day

Leaving Tanbuche, as you head for **Bimtang,** you can study the west face of Manaslu and 6,398-m (20,100-ft)-high Phungi. From the ghost town of **Bimtang,** with its mani stones and deserted houses, the trail climbs a lateral moraine and then continues down to a riverbed where it enters the Burdin Khola to **Manaslu base camp.**

If you climb the 4,160-m (13,600-ft)-high ridge hereabouts you'll be rewarded by fine views of the west face of 7,154-m (23,500-ft)-high Manaslu North, Annapurna II and 6,893-m (22,609-ft)-high Lamjung Himal.

down the right bank of the narrow valley, crossing the **Surki Khola** where it enters from the right, to the farm fields of **Karche,** set at 2,785 m (9,130 ft), on the opposite bank.

Fourteenth Day

The trail leads up to the paddy fields on top of the terraced hill and over **Karche La pass,** then down through the fields to **Goa** and along the right bank of the Dudh Khola to **Tilije.**

Here the trail crosses a wooden bridge to continue down along the left bank to the Marsyangdi Khola where it returns, across a wooden bridge, to the right bank and the checkpost at **Thonje.**

From here you will leave the village of Karte and follow the trail on the left bank of the **Marsyangdi Khola,** returning to the right bank across a covered wooden bridge. Now there's a short climb and the trail joins the trekking trail that leads around Annapurna.

Fifteenth to Eighteenth Day
Now the path leads gradually down to the checkpost at **Darapani** and, on to **Bhotehura** and **Dumre,** where you can take a bus to Kathmandu.

An 11-day outward trek along the **Marsyangdi Khola,** into the **Manang basin,** over **Thorung pass** and down into the **Kali Gandaki gorge** — the world's deepest — gives the trekker a roundabout tour of the Annapurna massif. It is also one of the most varied and comfortable. There are many hotels and tea houses en route so you do not have to carry camping equipment.

If you are traveling by bus from Kathmandu to Pokhara, you can bypass Pokhara altogether and start this trek from Dumre. Road improvements mean that it is now possible to take a bus from Dumre to Besi Sahar. If you fly in to Pokhara, you will have to take a Kathmandu-bound bus to Dumre.

First Day
The trek begins with a long walk through the bazaar of **Besi Sahar,** before ascending steeply over marble rocks.

Now Manaslu and Peak 29 rear their heads above the far end of the valley as the

trail reaches **Khudi,** at the base of a suspension bridge across the Khudi Khola.

Walk through the village, past a school on the lower right, to the path on the right bank. Just after the school it crosses a stream and then travels through two hamlets, across a suspension bridge to the left bank, to **Bhul Bhule,** which has hotels and tea houses.

The path begins to climb but in the dry season you can follow the riverbed and then up a gradual incline to the Manang village of **Ngatti,** lined with hotels and tea houses.

The trail out of the village crosses a stream to the left bank of Ngatti Khola, a tributary that has its source in the snows of 7,893-m (25,895-ft)-high Himal Chuli and across a long suspension bridge to the right bank.

The trail soon leaves the bank and climbs up to the crest of the ridge that divides the Marsyangdi and Ngatti. By the tea house at the summit is a well-shaded rest area.

From the rest area the path follows the left bank of the **Marsyangdi river,** climbing gradually all the way, through the village of **Ranpata,** to the **Bahundhara pass** set at 1,270 m (4,100 ft) where there is a checkpost. There's a village on the hill overlooking the pass. Here you'll find tea houses, shops and hotels. You can stay overnight in one of the hotels or camp somewhere in the fields around the **Bahundhara** pass.

Approximate walking time: six hours.

Second Day
Follow a small ridge, branching out from the pass, down to flat and fertile farm fields, then through a forest, across a stream and up again to a tea house, on to a stone path that takes about ten minutes to traverse before it crosses the rice paddies and grain fields into Kani Gaon.

Ahead, the Marsyangdi valley narrows into a steep and precipitous gorge, along a winding mountain path. On the opposite bank of the river a waterfall heralds the approach to **Sange,** passes over a suspension bridge to the right bank, past hotels, tea shops and houses and down to the riverbed where the trail almost at once begins to climb upwards, past a single house, to a flat plateau.

Not long after this, the rocky trail dips down some 200 to 300 m (650 to 1,000 ft), past a spring, to the riverbed and then into **Jagat,** at 1,290 m (4,200 ft), where there are hotels and tea houses. You can also camp in the fields near the village.

Approximate walking time: three and a half hours.

Third Day

From Jagat, the path leads down almost to the riverbed and then climbs an extremely precipitous trail opposite a sheer cliff. When

closed by precipitous walls of rock. But the path is level, extremely soothing after the perilous journey that preceded it. It goes down to the river bank and into **Tal,** which has hotels and tea houses.

Soon after this village, the valley narrows and the riverbed becomes much narrower, while the trail cuts through rock walls high above, before descending to **Karte.**

(For a day-and-a-half diversion, take the steps behind Karte, past **Naje,** and climb up to **Kurumche Kharka** with a view of the southwest face of Manaslu.)

the climb ends, the trail levels out all the way to **Chyamche,** which is notable for the splendid waterfall on the opposite bank.

Soon after it dips down to cross a suspension bridge to a hair-raising trail on the left bank — precarious and narrow along the edge of the gorge's sheer wall. One slip could be fatal. It's not for the dizzy.

Now the path undulates until it reaches a tributary that flows in from the other bank. The main river is littered with massive boulders, some as big as office blocks and in the dry season it's hard to see the river water at all.

Not long after this, the trail leaves the river bank and takes a zigzag course to the top of a hill overlooking the Tal river, en-

From Karte, the path continues down to the river bank and across a suspension bridge to the right bank, close to **Darapani** and its checkpost, at 1,860 m (6,000 ft).

You can sleep in one of many hotels or camp in the fields behind the checkpost.

Approximate walking time: five hours, possibly longer if you exercise extreme caution on the dangerous sections.

Fourth Day

Follow the trail through a narrow field when you leave the village and come to the confluence with the **Dudh Khola,** spawned

OPPOSITE: On the trekking trail around the mighty Annapurna massif. ABOVE: Rain sheds its blessings over the terraced paddies of Chame Valley.

in the ice-melt of Manaslu's south face, on the opposite bank.

Below, to the right as you climb the path through, you will be able to make out the roofs and streets of the village of **Thonje.** Now the Marsyangdi bends left and when you see Annapurna II ahead, you are at the entrance to the Bhote village of **Bagarchap,** prayer flags fluttering in the breeze.

The path continues its climb, past the tea houses at **Dhanagyu,** across a stream and by a cascading waterfall on the left, to where the Marsyangdi Khola valley becomes a gorge traversed by steep stone steps.

Look back here for splendid views of Manaslu and Phungi, then continue the lung-sapping climb to a level path through a colorful rhododendron forest and two houses at **Ratamron,** then on up and across a stream to the lone house at **Tanzo Phedi.**

Here the trail cuts through pine forest, over an area of crumbling rocks, to the checkpost of **Kodo,** dominated by the mighty mass of Annapurna II and Peak 29 towering, it seems, almost directly over the hamlet.

The trail cuts through the village and up through more pine forest to **Chame,** at 2,670 m (8,750 ft), with government offices, shops and hotels. It's a good place to replenish your food rations. You can stay in one of the hotels or camp near the school — or by the hot springs across the bridge on the left bank.

Approximate walking time: six hours.

Fifth Day

Cross a wooden bridge as you leave the village to the left bank and, with wonderful views of the shimmering snows of 6,893-m (22,609-ft)-high Lamjung Himal, pass through **Chame.**

As the trail climbs up the valley, past **Kreku,** the mountain is hidden by the foothills and then the trail cuts deep into pine forest and up a winding rocky face. On the other side, the valley wall is a sheer cliff, evidence of the change of terrain.

A narrow footbridge spanning an alpine gorge makes a challenging passage for trekkers and porters on the trail.

This valley is extremely steep and the path leaps back and forth across the river, following the easiest route available until it crosses a wooden bridge to the former military fortress at Buradhan on the right bank. Now only ruins remain of the fortifications.

From here, the trail climbs a rocky path to first one wooden bridge and then up again to another timber bridge leading into thick forest on the right bank.

When you leave this forest the valley broadens out into more gentle terrain and the east peak of Annapurna II dominates the horizon as the track leads gradually down, past a mani stone, to a level field with a pond. The trail leads to another timber bridge over the river and through a terraced field with scattered clumps of trees. There are good views of the north face of Annapurna II.

Finally, the trail skirts the lower level of the village of **Upper Pisang** and crosses the Marsyangdi to **Lower Pisang,** set at 3,200 m (10,500 ft). You can stay in one of the village's many hotels or camp in the meadow next to the spring.

Approximate walking time: five hours.

Sixth Day

Take the timber bridge across the **Tseram Tsang Changu,** past a mani stone and some chortens, to the right bank and through a thick forest, climb up to the mountain pass marked by a chorten. From here you can see Manang airfield dead ahead.

The trail descends to a level section, past **Ongre** where the northeast face of Annapurna III is visible, to the airstrip at **Omdu** and then across flat broad plain and across the Sabje Khola. Here the massive peak of 7,525-m (24,688-ft)-high Annapurna IV appears on the horizon.

The trail then traverses another bridge, over the trickle of the newborn Marsyangdi Khola, over to the left bank and the village of **Mungji,** encircled by verdant farm fields. To the right, sheltered beneath a small mountain, stands **Braga** with its magnificent monastery.

Here there are many large chortens and mani stones and before long you arrive at **Manang,** set at 3,520 m (11,500 ft) beneath

a panoramic vista most certainly made in heaven — from a terraced hill above the town spread out before you are Annapurna II, Annapurna IV, Annapurna III, 7,555-m (24,787-ft)-high Gangapurna and, behind, 7,134-m (23,406-ft)-high Tilitso peak.

Manang's streets and houses are lined with many fluttering prayer flags and there are numerous hotels. You can stay the night in one of these or camp on their rooftops.

Total walking time to Manang is about four hours.

Tinke. All along this route you will see Annapurna Himani on the horizon with Peak 29 and Himalchuli in the distance behind it.

Tinke is the last permanent settlement in the Marsyangdi Khola valley but the path continues along up through the summer village of **Kutsuan** and, soon after a deserted village, the trail flattens out and crosses a bridge over the Gundon Khola. Carved out of the mountains ahead you can see the walls of the Thorung pass — your destination.

Seventh Day

Most experienced trekkers recommend having a rest day in Manang to acclimatize to the high altitudes. Manang is a good place to stock up on anything you may have forgotten to bring — medical supplies, warm socks and gloves and so on — and the hotels here are a cut above the average, providing luxuries such as hot showers. Throughout the trekking season, the Himalayan Rescue Association operates an aid post in the village, giving lectures on altitude sickness and providing a doctor's services.

Eighth Day

Now begins the toughest part of the trek, through Manang and up to the village of

The trail now becomes a gentle switch-back before crossing a delta with many yak meadows and then across the Kenzan Khola to **Churi Latter** (also spelled Letdar or Lathar), where there are three hotels. You should consider staying here for the night. Some trekkers push on to Thorung Phedi, but in the interests of acclimatizing to the high altitudes, it is far better that you take this leg of the trip at a more leisurely pace. Besides the lower altitudes (4,250 m or 14,000 ft), accommodation and food are better here than at Thorung Phedi, and **Churi Latter i**s less likely to be crowded with other trekkers.

Approximate walking time: three to four hours.

Ninth Day

From here the trail climbs a gradual incline to the snout of a ridge. Then it dips down to cross the bridge over the Marsyangdi Khola and ascending the mountain path on the right bank, then down a rocky section to the riverbed which it follows for 10- to 15-minute walk.

Finally, the path climbs a rocky track to the plateau and **Thorung Phedi,** at 4,500 m (14,750 ft), which has one combined hotel-tea house, serving very basic Tibetan fare. You can bed down on its earth floor or camp

rear, passes out of sight. Now the angle eases as you begin the ascent to Thorung pass at 5,416 m (17,770 ft), its crest marked only by cairns and no shelter from the cruel wind.

This is one of the entrances to the eight-kilometer (five-mile)-deep **Kali Gandaki gorge** and ahead — as you enter an old lateral moraine for the precipitous descent — Dhaulagiri II, III and Tashi Kang, rise up over the valley. The final leg is down an extremely steep cliff. Finally, you arrive at **Chabarbu** and its one hotel.

nearby. When there's snow on the pass, this cramped and not particularly friendly place can be host to up to 100 trekkers.

Approximate walking time: three hours.

Tenth Day

Leave early, prepared for extreme cold and severe gale-force winds as you climb the most testing section of this trek — **Thorung pass.** Climb the zigzag trail up the steep hill in front of the hotel, through a rocky area to the top of the ridge. Here it crosses a frozen stream, then some lateral moraine and continues over a frozen lake to the glacier.

The trail then traverses to the left, between small hill-like ridges above 5,000 m (16,500 ft) and soon Annapurna II, in the

From here on out, the path flattens out through the valley and across the **Khatung Kang** which flows in from the left, to the lunar landscape of the Jhong Khola valley which you descend with magnificent views of 8,167-m (26,795-ft)-high Dhaulagiri I and 6,920-m (22,704-ft)-high Tukuche peak.

Once through the valley, you are approaching the checkpost at **Muktinah,** set at 3,798 m (12,500 ft). There are no hotels, and no camping is allowed in Muktinah itself, but after an easy 10-minute walk down to **Ranipauwa** you'll find a rash of

OPPOSITE: A baby goat in a remote highland village. Two youngsters at Dhampus ABOVE in the shadows of mighty Annapurna.

houses, hotels, tea houses and camping
sites — apple pies await the foot-weary
trekker here.

Approximate walking time: seven to
nine hours.

Eleventh Day
With Dhaulagiri I, Tukuche peak and Dhaulagiri II and III still in view, the trail leads
down from Muktinah to **Jharkot**, where
there are the ruins of an ancient fortress and
several hotels.

Now the path passes through two stone
walls to a gradual descent down the mountains and leading along a wide level trail to
Khingar, after which it dips gradually to a
crossroads. The right turning leads to Kag-
beni, famous for the ruins of its medieval
castle.

The path on the left leads you down the
mountain flank to the left bank of the Kali
Gandaki river and **Akkara Bhatti** and then
on to **Jhomsumba** (also spelled Jomsom) in
the afternoon.

Jhomsumba has an airfield which offers
daily flights to Pokhara — they tend to be
heavily booked. It also has a large selection
of accommodation, including **Om's Home**,
a cut above the average, where rooms have
heaters and attached bathrooms.

Twelfth to Nineteenth Day
The trek from Jhomsumba to Pokhara, is the
return leg of the Jhomsum trek, sometimes
referred to as the "classic tea house trek".
There are decent hotels all along the route
and it's unlikely that you will ever be short
of company: it's probably the most popular trek in Nepal and it's also used heavily
by locals. The altitude on the Jhomsum trek
never exceeds 3,000 m (9,800 ft) — easy
streets after the heights from which you've
just come.

DHAULAGIRI

Beginning in **Pokhara,** this trek leads you
through some of the most beautiful mountain and pastoral landscapes in Nepal —
providing the savor of simple lifestyles in
and around the **Myagdi Khola basin.** You
need full camping equipment, rations and
Sherpa guides.

First Day
Although it is possible to hike directly out
of Pokhara in around three days, improvements in road conditions mean that most
trekkers take the bus to Maldhunga (three
hours), which is directly below the trailhead
at **Baglung.**

From Baglung the trail goes to **Pharse,**
where there are tea houses and hotels and
houses.

Still on the left bank, the path crosses
a stream into **Diranbhora,** then up a gentle
incline to **Beni,** on the opposite bank of the
Myagdi Khola, where there is a checkpost.

It's a bustling town and administrative
center and you can camp in fields outside
the village.

Second Day

The trail from Beni cuts through **Beni Mangalghat**'s single street of shops and into desolate mountain country, past the lone tea house at **Jyanmara** and on a wide, level path to **Singa,** with many shops and tea houses.

Beyond the village of Singa, the trail follows the left bank of the **Myagdi Khola** above the riverbed, past a hot spring to the left below and through the farm fields that herald the approach to **Tatopani** and its **hot springs.**

Soon after leaving this village, the trail crosses a suspension bridge to the right bank, through the hamlet of **Bholamza,** and more fields, before swinging back to the left bank via another suspension bridge, to

Simarchor. Some distance beyond this village there's a bridge across the Newale Khola which flows in from the right.

The trail continues along the left bank of the **Myagdi Khola,** past the villages of **Shiman** and **Talkot** and then climbs up to the shops and tea houses of **Babichor.** You can camp on the grass next to the village granary.

Third Day

From Babichor, the high, winding trail crosses the mountainside into a broad and fertile valley, across grain fields and through the cobblestone street of **Shahasharadhara,** where you cross the Duk Khola. Continue

The peaks of regal Annapurna, crowned with snow.

through the rice paddies to the hamlet of **Ratorunga** where the valley ends.

Now the undulating trail follows the river bank on the left, past **Bodeni** to **Chachare**. The valley narrows at the town of **Darbang,** its main street lined with shops. Here the trail crosses to the right bank, via a suspension bridge, past the Ritum Khola tributary at left and through the hamlet of **Darbang.**

The trail then skirts a gaunt cliff face to **Phedi,** set at 1,100 m (3,500 ft), where there are some tea houses. It's not a pretty place but it's the only camping site for several miles around.

Fourth Day

When you leave Phedi you face a lengthy climb to **Phalai Gaon** and should make an early start. Not long after leaving the village the trail crosses the **Dang Khola,** where it flows in from the left and climbs a ridge on the opposite bank in a series of hairpins, above the Myagdi Khola.

Soon the gradual climb brings you to **Dharapani** and steeply out again, before descending to the farm fields beyond **Takum.**

After **Sibang,** it cuts through forest, past **Mattim,** to the crest of a ridge which provides a magnificent view of Dhaulagiri Himal, dipping down to the Gatti Khola, to skirt the base of the ridge and enter **Phalai Gaon,** at 1,810 m (6,000 ft). You can camp in the school grounds outside the village.

Fifth Day

Follow the stonewalled path from Phalai Gaon over the terraced fields to the right and cross the suspension bridge over the Dhara Khola river. During the dry season the trail goes down the valley next to the school, across to the opposite bank and up a steep hill.

But the main path from the suspension bridge climbs up the mountain, above the village of Dhara and through a hamlet to an undulating walk that joins up with the shortcut. After skirting a ridge it emerges once more on the right bank of the Myagdi Khola.

Now the path climbs again, in a series of hairpins and then skirts another ridge, to reveal astounding views of Dhaulagiri I and

7,193-m (23,600-ft)-high Gurja Himal. Soon it reaches the Magar village of **Muri** which you leave by walking down a gentle slope, across a rocky stream.

Continue down to the farm fields along the Dhara Khola, cross the river and then climb up the mountain on the right to **Ghorban Dhara pass** with its superb views — including your first glimpse of 6,465-m (21,211-ft)-high Ghustung South.

From the pass, the trail leads down to the right bank of the **Myagdi Khola** and a lone house where you can camp in the surround-

ing fields — beneath the village of **Jugapani,** perched on the mountainside above.

Sixth Day

Leave along the right bank, past **Naura** and climb the mountain for a short while to a path that traverses a steep, grass-covered hill. Where the traverse ends, the Myagdi Khola valley becomes a precipitous gorge. Even though the path along the steep, grassy edge of the gorge is well-constructed with many stone steps, take care.

At the top of the climb, the trail traverses right — take great care to avoid falling into the gorge. Eventually, the trail dips down through forest, across a ridge and some terraced fields to **Boghara,** at 2,080 m (6,800 ft).

You can camp in the compounds of the houses or the terraced fields.

Seventh Day

Leaving Boghara, the trail descends through the fields, crossing a small ridge to the left and on through thin forest to **Jyardan,** the region's most remote village.

From the village the trail is high and winding, then it cuts across a boulder-strewn landscape to a grass-covered traverse, before dropping down some steep stone steps to the river bank.

Here the trail continues through thick forest with occasional glimpses, through breaks between the trees, of the west face of majestic Dhaulagiri I. Some distance beyond, the trail dips down and the Myag-di Khola comes into view. You cross to the left bank by a wooden bridge with a hand-rail.

Once again the path cuts through forest as it climbs the course of the **Pakite Khola,** never too far from the river. The crest of 6,062-m (19,889-ft)-high Jirbang dominates the end of the valley and then you cross a

The path goes upstream some distance, then starts climbing again, crossing a stream beneath a beautiful high waterfall, where it eases into a gradual incline to **Lipshe.**

Now the trail continues its undulating course through the forest-lined walls of the steep **Myagdi Khola gorge** before emerging at a little glade, **Lapche Kharka,** where you camp overnight.

Eighth Day

When you leave camp, the trail continues to climb through forest to a level area at **Dobang.** Soon after this, it crosses a timber bridge over the Konabon Khola, flowing down from the Konabon glacier.

High-Altitude Trekking and Treks

stream, to the plateau at **Chartare,** set at 2,820 m (9,250 ft).

There's a crystal clear stream flowing through the middle of the meadow, making it excellent for camping.

Ninth Day

From Chartare, return to and follow the forest trail until it passes two small caves. Here it leaves the forest, cutting across a rocky mountainside, then crossing a small stream, to the **Choriban Khola** which it

OPPOSITE: The contents of a wooden aqueduct freeze in the frosty winter weather of the high mountains. Woman ABOVE carries firewood up a precipitous stone walkway overlooking lush, terraced hillsides.

skirts for some distance, before finally crossing it to climb the bank on the other side.

Look behind at this point and you will
get a splendid view of the ice-white silhou-
ette of 6,380-m (20,932-ft)-high Manapati.
Soon after climbing the steep hill, the path
narrows into a gentle gradient, through the
forest, to a small grassy clearing at **Puchhar.**

The trail now crosses a small glacier
down to another glacier born on the west
face of Dhaulagiri and then climbs the
opposite wall to another grassy area, **Pakabon,** set at 3,585 m (11,750 ft), where you
can camp.

Ahead stand the massive western ramparts of Dhaulagiri I. To the right is Manapati — and behind, the granite walls of
Tsaurabong peak shadow the sky as if
about to fall over the camp.

Tenth Day
From Pakabon, you will follow a lateral moraine to a rocky ridge which you descend
to the right and into a valley deep in snow
and glacial detritus. Approaching the headwaters of the Myagdi Khola, you are closed
in by daunting and forbidding rock walls.

The precipitous path runs high above
the right bank before descending to the
valley floor and on, by an intermittent foot-
path through the gorge, to the terminal
moraine of **Chhonbarban glacier.** It enters
the glacier area from the right bank, crossing the undulating glacial surface where the
valley bends right through a large gorge.

At this point, 6,837-m (22,432-ft)-high
Tukuche peak West stands brooding over
the far end of the glacier.

Soon the trail levels out into easy walking up the gradual gradient of this section,
then the glacier veers left and the trail
moves onto the right bank.

The trail terminates at **Dhaulagiri base
camp,** at 4,750 m (15,500 ft), with stunning
perspectives of Dhaulagiri I to the north
and, to the west: 7,751-m (25,429-ft)-high
Dhaulagiri II; 7,703-m (25,271-ft)-high
Dhaulagiri III; and 7,660-m (25,133-ft)-high
Dhaulagiri IV — a sheer ice fall streaming
from the northeast col.

*Early morning sun lights up a frosty trekkers' camp
at 5,500 m (18,000 ft).*

Eleventh Day

By this point, you have a sound risk of getting altitude sickness as the trail climbs out from the camp, up the right bank of the glacier and then ascends another mountainside to where it cuts across the flank and crosses the moraine on the side of 6,611-m (21,690-ft)-high Sita Chuchura, to an easy snow-covered incline on the right that brings you to **French pass,** at 5,360 m (17,600 ft).

From here you can see Sita Chuchura, the mountains of Mukut Himal and the 6,386-m (21,000-ft)-high Tashi Kang. To the

right is Tukuche peak West and to the rear stands Dhaulagiri I.

Twelfth to Twenty-First Day

It takes nine to 10 days to retrace this route to Pokhara.

LANGTANG

Regarded as the most perfect alpine landscape in the world, the **Langtang massif** — visible from Kathmandu — is right on the city's back door and this five- to six-day outward trek allows you to enjoy it in full. With many hotels and eating places it's also one for the casual and not-so-hardy trekker. However, to extend the trek from **Langshisa Kharka** to **Langtang glacier** you must be well-equipped and in excellent physical condition.

ABOVE: A wall, where wood, stone and mortar meet in a delightful combination. OPPOSITE: A distant view of Manang airport, a place so remote that staff often have to chase away grazing yaks for incoming flights.

First Day

From Kathmandu take a bus to **Trisuli Bazaar,** a journey that can take up to six hours. Change there for a bus to **Dunche,** set at 2,040 m (6,700 ft), focal point of the district with hotels, shops and government offices.

Second Day

The road leaves Dunche across some fields, down the forested banks of the **Trisuli Khola,** across a suspension bridge and up a steep hill along a small stream.

After some twenty minutes of walking, the trail leaves the stream and travels up the hillside on the left to a tea house atop a ridge. There's a fork in the trail here — straight on to **Gosainkund**, the sacred Shiva lake and left to Syabru, a rather narrow path past the tea house.

The trail skirts the ridge, with Dunche in view on the opposite bank and carries along the mountainside on the left bank of the Trisuli river to some fields where the path to **Syabrubensi** branches left, near **Bharkhu.**

Leaving Bharkhu, cross the fields and climb the steep mountain pass, an exercise rewarded — to your rear where the path flattens out and leads left through forest — by a view of Ganesh Himal. Then it passes another village, to the left below and through more forest to a rest area at the crest of a ridge.

From here the path dips down gradually to **Syabru,** at 2,230 m (7,300 ft), where you can camp in the monastery grounds or hotel garden.

Approximate walking time: five and a half to six hours.

Third Day

Walk down the ridge, between the houses, turn right past some fields, then through forest, across a stream and a flat mountain trail on the left that leads to a ridge crest.

The other side leads down a steep slope through thick forest to the **Langtang Khola,** then follows the left bank. Soon it crosses a stream and continues to climb the valley to a wooden bridge across the Langtang Khola which takes it to the right bank.

Here the path climbs high, leaving the river far below and then down around the

flank of the mountain, to join the path from Syarpa Gaon.

Not far from this junction the trail veers back to the river bank and later, climbs up to the **Lama Hotel,** surrounded by other tea houses and hotels. When the trail cuts into forest, through breaks in the tree cover you will see majestic Langtang Lirung off in the distance.

The path climbs steadily past **Gumna-chok** and its lone hotel, to a short steep hill where it leaves the river bank and the valley broadens. Not long after this it reaches the checkpost at **Ghora Tabela,** set at 3,010 m (9,900 ft).

Approximate walking time: six hours.

Fourth Day

The trail leaves Ghora Tabela through the farm fields that stud the valley floor and after a short distance crosses over a steep hill. Here the forest ends and the path becomes gentle, running through colorful shrubs and meadows.

Now Langtang appears, against the backdrop of 6,387-m (21,000-ft)-high Gan-chempo. The trail climbs gradually up a grassy knoll, above a monastery, to **Lang-tang,** where gardens are enclosed by stone walls. Some little distance from the village there is a chorten followed by one of the longest mani walls in Nepal.

The trail leads along the top of green and lovely hillsides, past two villages, after which the valley broadens out and the path enters a flat, dry riverbed. Where it crosses the flow from **Lirung glacier,** 6,745-m (21,250-ft)-high Kimshun and 6,543-m (21,467-ft)-high Yansa Tsenji can be seen to the left.

Now the trail crosses a moraine covered with loose stones to **Kyangjin Gompa,** at 3,840 m (12,500 ft) where there's a cheese factory.

To the north of the village, on a 4,000-m (13,000-ft)-high crest there are magnificent views of Langtang Lirung's north face and the surrounding mountains.

You can stay in the town hotel or camp in one of the stonewalled fields. Beyond this point you will need tents and supplies and should be watchful for symptoms of altitude sickness.

Approximate walking time: five to six hours.

Fifth Day

The trail from Kyangjin Gompa crosses a wide alluvial delta, across a stream, to an airstrip with stupendous vistas of Langtang Lirung's full profile.

From the airstrip, the trail follows the river and 6,300-m (20,600-ft)-high Lang-shisa Ri comes into view at the far end of the narrow valley, with Ganchempo visible on the opposite side.

Up from the river, the trail goes through the rocky hills, to the seven stone huts of **Jatang.** Just beyond, the path descends once more to the dry riverbed, then up some more hills with views of Shalbachum glacier pushing its snout into the valley. Near the glacier is the hamlet of **Nuba-matang,** with five stone huts.

Now the trail cuts across the grassy fields and climbs the glacial moraine with perspectives of the far end of the valley, dominated by 6,830-m (22,400-ft)-high Pemthang Karpo Ri, Triangle and 6,842-m (22,490-ft)-high Pemthang Ri; to the right is Langshisa Ri.

Now the trail descends to **Langshisa Kharka,** at 4,125 m (13,500 ft) for views of 6,078-m (20,000-ft)-high Kanshurum and

6,151-m (20,200-ft)-high Urkinmang at the far end of the Langshisa glacier.

You can camp in the stone huts at **Langshisa Kharka** or in the grassy fields.

Approximate walking time: four hours.

Sixth to Ninth Day

The return to Dunche from this point takes three or four days.

Extension I

To trek from Langshisa Kharka to **Langtang glacier** you have to be exceptionally fit and well equipped.

Extension II

It is possible to visit Langshisa glacier, following the trail upstream from **Langshisa Kharka** for a short distance to a log bridge. (It sometimes gets hurled away by landslides so check before you start if it is there).

Then the trail climbs through scrub before descending to one of the streams running off the glacier which you enter at the snout. It gradually climbs until 6,966-m (22,855-ft)-high Dorje Lakpa comes into view — magnificent from Kathmandu, fabulous when so close.

The trail from Langshisa follows the top of a level hill and down a winding path to the riverbed. Here it begins to climb, past a small stone hut and through thorny scrub, to a second hut. The trail now becomes vague and difficult as the trek is not often used.

Some distance after this a valley leads to the **Morimoto peak base camp** on a wide plain with views of 6,874-m (22,550-ft)-high Gur Karpo Ri and 6,750-m (22,150-ft)-high Morimoto peak.

The trail crosses the plain and enters the valley again. Around the corner, where the valley ends, it begins to climb to the glacier. This is the terminus for most trekkers, with an excellent camp and outstanding views.

The glacier veers right and when you round the corner you get a breathtaking view of 7,083-m (23,240-ft)-high Lenpo Gang, the highest of the Jugal Himal's peaks.

You can camp at a site set at 4,800 m (15,750 ft) often used as a base camp by climbing expeditions.

High-mountain denizens frolic on a wall.

Travelers' Tips

GETTING TO NEPAL

By Air

Most international visitors — more than 90 percent — fly into Nepal's **Tribhuvan International Airport**, eight kilometers (five miles) from Kathmandu.

If the skies are clear there is no more exciting flight in the world. Passengers in left-hand seats on eastbound flights to Kathmandu will see in succession Gurja Himal, 7,193 m (23,600 ft); Dhaulagiri I, 8,167 m (26,795 ft); the deep gorge of the Kali Gandaki river leading north to Mustang; the six peaks of the Annapurna range; Manaslu, 8,158 m (26,766 ft); and finish their flight with the three humps of Ganesh Himal at 7,406 m (24,298 ft) dominating Kathmandu valley.

Passengers in right-hand seats on westbound flights will see, in succession, Kanchenjunga, 8,598 m (28,208 ft) on the border with Sikkim; Makalu, 8,481 m (27,825 ft); Everest, 8,848 m (29,028 ft); Cho Oyu, 8,153 m (26,750 ft); Gaurisankar, 7,144 m (23,438 ft); Dorje Lhakpa, 6,966 m (22,855 ft); and finish their promenade with Langtang Lirung, 7,245 m (23,769 ft) above Kathmandu valley.

There are few direct flights to Kathmandu from outside Asia. Most travelers will have to change — usually in Bangkok if they're coming from the USA; from Delhi if they're coming from Europe. Royal Nepal Airlines has the greatest number of direct flights, including London, Paris, Frankfurt, Delhi, Calcutta and Bangkok. Lufthansa also operates direct flights through London and a number of flights to the USA via Frankfurt.

All those departing Nepal on international flights pay Rs 700 airport tax as they check-in.

The major international airlines with offices in Kathmandu are (all in the 01 area code):
Aeroflot Soviet Airlines (227399, Kamaladi.
Air India (419649, Hattisar.
Bangladesh Biman (416852, Durbar Marg.
British Airways (222266, Durbar Marg.
Cathay Pacific (411725, Kamaladi.

China Southwest Airlines (411302, Kamaladi.
Dragonair (223162, Durbar Marg.
Druk Air Royal Bhutan Airlines (225166, Durbar Marg.
Indian Airlines (410906, Hattisar.
Lufthansa (223052, Durbar Marg.
Myanmar Airways Corporation (224839, Durbar Marg.
Northwest Airlines (215855, Kanti Path.
Pakistan International (223102, Durbar Marg.
Royal Nepal Airlines (220757, Kanti Path.
Singapore Airlines (220759, Durbar Marg.
Thai International (224917, Durbar Marg.

By Land

Land travelers have a vast choice of routes and means of transport by which to enter Nepal. In addition to Tribhuvan Airport, there are 11 other official entry points:
Kakar Bhitta (Mechi zone), with connections to Darjeeling and Siliguri, India;
Rani Sikijha (Kosi zone), just south of Biratnagar;
Jaleshwar (Janakpur zone); Birganj (Narayani zone), near Raxaul, India, the most common entry point for overland travelers;
Kodari (Bagmati zone), on the Chinese–Tibetan border; and
Sunauli (Lumbini zone), near Bhairawa on the road to Pokhara.

The other entry points, which can only be reached on foot, are at **Kakarhawa** (Lumbini zone); **Nepalgunj** (Bheri zone); **Koilabas** (Rapti zone); **Dhangadi** (Seti zone); and **Mahendranagar** (Mahakali zone). These entry points are all unsuitable for motor vehicles.

By Rail
India provides frequent railroad service throughout the country including trains to the Nepal border. But there are only two lines in Nepal. The 47-km (29-mile) line between Raxaul, India and Amlekhganj, built in 1925, is no longer used. The only line still

Royal Nepal Airlines Twin Otter takes off PREVIOUS PAGES from Lukla's clifftop runway (left) at 2,760 m (9,200 ft) as trekkers (right) make their way on foot to Everest base camp. OPPOSITE: Moonrise over the distinctive peak of Ama Dablam on the trail to Everest base camp.

working in Nepal, for freight only, built in 1940, runs a brief 27 km (17 miles) through Janakpur.

By Road and Rail

The combined rail–road route to Nepal from Delhi offers two viable options. The quickest route is via **Gorakhpur,** while the other allows an interesting stopover in **Varanasi.** From either city, buses go to Kathmandu or Pokhara via **Sunauli.** Taking this route allows one to visit **Lumbini,** Buddha's birthplace, close to Sunauli.

Seasoned travelers might consider making their way by train from **Darjeeling** to **Siliguri,** followed by a 60-minute taxi drive to **Kakar Bhitta.** Here you can catch a bus to **Kathmandu.** The advantages to be gained from taking this route are the ride on the miniature Darjeeling railway followed by traveling through almost 400 km (248 miles) of the Terai, including panoramic views of the Siwalik hills.

You will need a special permit to enter Darjeeling (required for all, including British Commonwealth passport holders). And

If traveling on to **Kathmandu,** you can also stop over at **Narayanghat** and visit **Royal Chitwan National Park,** just two hours away by local transport.

Similarly, taking the combined rail–road route to Nepal from **Calcutta, India** offers two interesting alternatives — traveling through **Muzaffapur** or **Patna** — with bus connections to Kathmandu by way of **Birganj.** The land journey takes about 36 hours altogether. Taking a ferry from Muzaffapur, across the Ganges river to Patna, takes approximately 90 minutes. Most other routes to the Nepali border from inside India require a great deal of effort, patience and aggravation and are of little interest to the traveler.

on your return from Nepal remember that you'll need an Indian visa to enter India through a border post. If you intend on traveling more than once between Nepal and India, a multiple-entry Indian visa is useful.

Driving into Nepal

Those who drive to Nepal by private car should allow at least two hours to clear the Indian border and make sure that they carry a *carnet de passage en douanes* (for cars and motorcycles) which gives a three-month exemption from customs duty.

Motor vehicles in Nepal are driven on the left side of the road. Drivers must hold a valid international driver's license.

FORMALITIES

All visitors require a visa and must carry a valid passport. Three kinds of visa are available: 15 days (US$15); 30 days (US$25) and 60 days multiple re-entry (US$60). Visas are available on arrival at Tribhuvan International Airport or at Nepal embassies and consulates. Be warned, the lines for visas at the airport are glacially slow and payment is required in US dollars (bring some with you). You will also need one passport photo.

Visas issued for travel in Nepal are valid only for the Kathmandu and Pokhara valleys, Chitwan National Park and for major roads between these destinations. To leave these areas you will need additional permits.

TREKKING PERMITS

Trekking Permits are available at the Central Immigration Office ((01) 412337, in Maiti Devi, Kathmandu. The office is open 10 AM to 1 PM (closing at noon on Fridays)

Visas can also be extended for up to 150 days, at a rate of US$1 per day. Tourists are not allowed to spend any more than 180 days in Nepal in any calendar year.

Visa extensions (and trekking permits) are issued at the Central Immigration Office ((01) 412337, in Maiti Devi, Kathmandu. Office hours are 10 AM to 1 PM (closes at noon on Fridays) for applications; 3 to 5 PM for picking up passports; closed Saturdays. Bring your passport and two passport-sized photos.

Visitors wishing to cross the border at the Friendship Bridge to the Tibetan town of Khasa need a Chinese visa. It's best to organize one before you arrive in Kathmandu. The Chinese Embassy in Nepal only gives visas to group tourists.

for applications; 3 to 5 PM for picking up passports; closed Saturdays. Bring your passport and two passport-sized photos. If you are part of an organized group, the permit will be arranged for you, saving a great deal of time and effort.

Costs for permits vary according to where you plan to trek. Most areas, such as Annapurna, Everest and Langtang (among others), cost US$5 for the first week and

Young women of Pokhara OPPOSITE reap an additional harvest of small fish from the muddy waters of their rice paddies. ABOVE: Other youngsters (left) use a fish trap in the rushing waters of the Trisuli river to catch their supper while a conical net (right) hauls in a writhing catch for another group fishing the same waters.

US$10 for every additional week. Kanchenjunga and Lower Dolpo cost US$10 for the first week, US$20 for every additional week. Manaslu is US$75 per week in the low season, US$90 in the high season. Permits for Mustang and Upper Dolpo cost US$700 for 10 days, and you must be accompanied by a government liaison officer.

CUSTOMS

Duty Free Travelers are allowed to carry 200 cigarettes, 50 cigars, one bottle of spir-

its and two bottles or 12 cans of beer free of duty. Personal effects exempt from duty include one pair of binoculars, one camera, 15 rolls of film, one video camera, one tape recorder, one transistor radio and one fishing rod and accessories.
Forbidden imports Firearms and ammunition (unless you hold an import license obtained in advance), radio transmitters, walkie-talkies and drugs.
Movie cameras require special permits.
Souvenirs On departure, souvenirs can be exported freely but antiques and art objects need special clearance.
Antiques and art objects need special clearance from the Department of Archaeology, National Archives Building, Ram Shah Path,

Kathmandu, which takes at least two days. Nepal is concerned to preserve its priceless art treasures and forbids the export of any object more than 100 years old. If in doubt, consult the Department of Archaeology.
Forbidden exports Precious stones, gold, silver, weapons, drugs, animal hides, trophies, wild animals.
Pets such as Tibetan dogs, may be exported.

NEPAL EMBASSIES AND CONSULATES ABROAD

AUSTRALIA **Sydney** ((02) 9233 6161, Level 1, 17 Castlereagh Street, NSW 2000, or **Melbourne** ((03) 9379 0666, 72 Lincoln Road, Essendon, Victoria 3040, or **Brisbane** ((07) 3232 0336, Level 21, AMP Place, 10 Eagle Street, Queensland 4066, or **Perth** ((08) 9386 2102, Suite 2, 16 Robinson Street, Nedlands, Western Australia 6009.
BANGLADESH **Dhaka** (601890, United Nations Road, Road 2, Baridhara Diplomatic Enclave, Baridhara.
BELGIUM **Genese** ((02) 358 5808, 21 Avenue Champel, B-1640 Rhode Street.
CANADA **Toronto** ((416) 226 8722, Royal Bank Plaza, South Tower, Ontario.
CHINA **Beijing** Embassy (010) 532 1795, № 1 Sanlitun Xilujie or **Lhasa** Consulate ((0891) 36890, Norbulingka Road 13, Tibet.
DENMARK **Copenhagen** ((01) 3312 4166, 2 Teglgaardstraede, 1452.
FRANCE **Paris** ((01) 46 22 48 67, 45 bis rue des Acacias, 75017, or **Toulouse** ((061) 329 1222, 7 bis allée des Soupirs, 31000.
GERMANY **Bonn** ((0228) 343097, Im-Hag 15, D-5300, Bad Godesberg 2, or **Frankfurt am Main** 60 Z 069-40871, Flinschstrasse 63, D-6000; **Munich** 21 (089-5704406, Landsbergerstrasse 191, D-8000, or **Berlin** 15 ((030) 881 4049, Uhlandstrasse 171/2, 1000.
INDIA **New Delhi** Embassy ((011) 332 9969, Barakhamba Road, 110001, or **Calcutta** ((033) 711224, 19 Woodlands, Sterndale Road, Alipore, 700027.
ITALY **Rome** Consulate ((06) 348176, Piazza Medaglie d'Oro 20, 00136.
JAPAN **Tokyo** ((03) 3705 5558, Tokoroki 7-chome, Setagaya-ku 158.
MYANMAR (BURMA) **Rangoon** (550633, 16 Natmauk Yeiktha (Park Avenue), P.O. Box 84, Tamwe.

PAKISTAN **Karachi**-2 (200979, 4th floor Qamar House, 419 MA Jinnah Road.
RUSSIA, FEDERAL REPUBLIC **Moscow** (2447356, or (2419311, 2nd Neopolimovsky Pere Look 14/7.
SPAIN **Barcelona** ((03) 323 1323, Mallorca 194 Pral 2A, 08036.
SWITZERLAND **Zurich** ((01) 475993, Asrylstrasse 81, 8030.
THAILAND **Bangkok** Embassy (391 7240, 189, Soi 71, Sukhumvit Road, 10110.
UK **London** ((0171) 229-6231, 12A Kensington Palace Gardens, W8 4QU.

India ((01) 410900, Lainchaur.
Israel ((01) 411811, Lazimpat.
Italy ((01) 412743, Baluwatar.
Japan ((01) 231101, Durbar Marg.
Myanmar (Burma) ((01) 521788, Chakupat, Patan City Gate, Patan.
Pakistan ((01) 411421, Pani Pokhari.
Russia, Federal Republic ((01) 412155, Baluwatar.
South Korea ((01) 211172, Tahachal.
Thailand ((01) 213910, Thapathali.
UK ((01) 410583, Lainchaur.
USA ((01) 411179, Pani Pokhari.

USA **Washington, District of Columbia** ((202) 667 4550, 2131 Leroy Place N.W., 20008, or **San Francisco** ((415) 434-1111, Suite 400, 909 Montgomery Street, CA 94133, or **Dallas** ((214) 931-1212; 16250 Dallas Parkway, Suite 110, TX 75248, or **Atlanta** ((404) 892-8152, 15th Street N.E., GA 30309.

EMBASSIES

Australia ((01) 411578, Bhat Bhateni.
Bangladesh ((01) 414943, Naxal.
Canada ((01) 415193, Lazimpat.
China ((01) 411740, Baluwatar.
France ((01) 412332, Lazimpat.
Germany ((01) 412786, Gyaneshwor.

CULTURAL CENTERS

British Council ((01) 223000, Kanti Path.
French Cultural Center ((01) 224326, Bag Bazaar.
Indian Cultural Center and Library ((01) 211497, RNAC Building.
Goethe Institute ((01) 220528, Sundhara.

TOURIST INFORMATION

Nepal's tourist information offices are of limited use to the traveler, though they may have a map or two on hand. The offices are:

Trekkers rest OPPOSITE on the Everest trail while umbrellas guard rickshaw drivers against sun and rain ABOVE in Kathmandu valley's benign climate.

Main office (English-language) ((01) 220818, Ganga Path, Basantapur, (in front of Hanuman Dhoka palace; open 10 AM to 4 PM, Sunday to Friday).
Tribhuvan Airport Exchange ((01) 470537 (other offices in airports at **Pokhara, Bhairawa, Birganj** and **Kaka Bhitta**).
Department of Tourism ((01) 214519.

RELIGION

Minority faiths practice freely in the Hindu kingdom of Nepal. The major places of worship are:

Roman Catholic
Jesuit St. Xavier College ((01) 521050, Jawalkhel.
Annapurna Hotel (Sunday Mass) ((01) 211711.

Protestant
Church of Christ, Nepal, Ram Shah Path.
Blue Room, USIS, ((01) 213966, Rabi Bhawan.

Muslim
Main Mosque, Durbar Marg.

Jewish
Israeli Embassy ((01) 211251.

TRAVEL AND TREKKING AGENCIES

There are hundreds of travel and trekking agencies in Nepal — far more than it would be practical to list here. The agencies below are some of the best-known, longest-running and most reliable.
Adventure Nepal Trekking ((01) 412508 FAX (01) 222026, Tridevi Marg .
Annapurna Mountaineering and Trekking ((01) 222999 FAX (01) 226153, Durbar Marg.
Asian Trekking ((01) 413732 FAX (01) 411878, Tridevi Marg.
Equator Expeditions ((01) 425800 FAX (01) 425801 E-MAIL equator@expeds.wlink.com .np, Thamel.
Himalayan Adventures ((01) 411866 FAX (01) 418561, Maharajganj.
Himalayan Encounters ((01) 417426 FAX (01) 417133, Thamel.
Himalayan Expeditions ((01) 226622 FAX (01) 526575, Thamel Chowk.

Lama Excursions ((01) 220186 FAX (01) 227292, Durbar Marg.
Malla Treks ((01) 410089 FAX (01) 423143 E-MAIL trekinfo@mallatrk.mos.com.np, Lainchaur.
Tiger Mountain ((01) 414508 FAX (01) 414075 E-MAIL tiger@mtn.mos.com.np, Lazimpat.
Wayfarers ((01) 212810, Thamel.

CURRENCY AND EXCHANGE

There are 100 *paisa* to one Nepali *rupee*. Banknotes are in denominations of 1,000, 500, 100, 50, 20, 10, five, two and one rupee. Coins are in denominations of one rupee; and 50, 25, 10 and five paisa. The *mohar* is a half rupee (50 paisa); the *sukaa*, 25 paisa.

The official exchange rate is set by the Nepal Rastra Bank and published daily in *The Rising Nepal* newspaper. It is also broadcast by Radio Nepal in the Nepali language. At press date the exchange rate was approximately 56 rupees to the US dollar.

Excess Nepali rupees can be converted back into dollars as long as they do not exceed 15 percent of the total amount changed. Keep your exchange receipts as you will need to show them in order to be able to change rupees back into US dollars.

There is an exchange counter at Tribhuvan Airport open nonstop, daily. The New road gate exchange counter of Rastriya Banijya Bank is open daily from 8 AM to 8 PM. The Nepal Bank on New road is open from 10 AM to 3 PM, Sunday to Thursday, from 10 AM to noon on Fridays.

Official exchange rates fluctuate against all currencies. Dollars are in high demand, but exchanging money unofficially is illegal.

TRAVELING IN NEPAL

INTERNAL FLIGHTS

Flying is the quickest way of getting around Nepal; just bear in mind that flights are subject to cancellations and delays due to weather conditions. Low visibility flying is simply too dangerous to be risked in a mountainous country like Nepal.

A Newar priest dressed in sacred crimson, Kathmandu.

The domestic monopoly enjoyed and operated by national flag carrier, **Royal Nepal Airlines** ((01) 220757 is a thing of the past, though it still has the most extensive network with a fleet of 44-seat Avro 748s, 19-seat Twin Otters and five-seat Pilatus Porters.

Other domestic operators are: Necon Air ((01) 473860; Nepal Airways ((01) 412388; Everest Air ((01) 480431; Asian Airlines ((01) 410086; Manakamana Airways ((01) 416434; and Gorkha Airlines ((01) 423137. The last three operate helicopters.

From **Kathmandu** there are scheduled services to **Dang, Dhangadi, Jumla, Mahendranagar, Nepalgunj, Rukumkot, Safi Bazaar, Siliguri Doti, Surkhet,** in the west; to **Baglung** and **Bhairawa** in the midlands; and to **Bhadrapur, Biratnagar, Janakpur, Lukla, Lamidanda, Rajbiraj, Rumjatar Taplejung, Tumlingtar** in the east.

Book well ahead, especially to destinations only served by the smaller aircraft. If you cancel 24 hours in advance, you pay a 10-percent cancellation fee; 33-percent if less than 24 hours in advance and 100-percent if you fail to show up. If the flight is canceled the fare is refunded.

Charter flights are available.

If you are flying to a restricted area you will need to produce your trekking permit before you depart from Tribhuvan Airport.

AIRPORT TRANSFERS

Royal Nepal and Indian Airlines provide a bus service from Tribhuvan Airport to Kathmandu. Travelers on the other airlines must use a taxi, which accommodates three passengers. Rates are set at Rs 200. The driver often has an "interpreter". Travelers from Kathmandu to the airport can board the bus that leaves the RNAC building, New road.

HIRE CARS

Hire cars are available from most travel agencies, though it is not possible to drive yourself in Nepal. The hire fee is high, but the cars are comfortable and likely to be in good repair. A car holds three or four people; metered taxis usually no more than two.

Yeti Travels, near the Annapurna Hotel, runs the **Avis** agency ((01) 227635, and Gorkha Travels, also on Durbar Marg, runs the **Hertz** franchise ((01) 224896.

ROADS IN NEPAL

Until the fifties Nepal was virtually roadless. The only links between different communities were village trails and mountain paths. Trading was a laborious affair, conducted over weeks and months. Since then, there has been a major highway con-

struction program supported mainly by Nepal's neighbors, India and China.

There are six main roads: the **Tribhuvan Raj Path**, linking Kathmandu with Raxaul at the Indian border, 200 km (124 miles) away, opened in 1956 and was built with Indian aid.

The **"Chinese road"** or **Araniko highway,** 110-km (68-mile)-long, to the Tibetan border at Kodari, was built by China and opened in the mid-Sixties.

Chinese engineers also helped build the 200-km (124-mile)-long **Prithvi Raj Marg** between Kathmandu and Pokhara, opened in 1973. There have been two extensions: Dumre to Gorkha and Mugling to Narayanghat and in 1970, Indian engineers completed the 188 km (117 mile) extension from Pokhara to Sunauli on the Indian Border, the **Siddhartha Raj Marg**.

Nepal's most ambitious road building project came about as a cooperative effort between the Soviet Union, United States, Britain and India. The 1,000 km (620 mile) east-west **Mahendra Raj Marg** through the southern lowlands is part of the planned Pan-Asian highway, linking the Bosphorus with the Far East.

The new 110-km (68-mile)-long highway, from **Lamosangu** to **Jiri** east of Kathmandu,

routes. Bookings are best made a day ahead with a travel agency.

ON FOOT

Nepal is a land best explored on foot. The most beautiful and the most interesting places can only be reached by walking. True Nepalis don't count distance by kilometers or miles, but by time traveled. And a leisurely promenade through the green terraced rice paddies and mustard fields, through villages and hamlets, up, down

built with Swiss help was opened in September 1985.

During the rainy season, whole portions of existing roads are damaged and must be repaired. It is essential to inquire locally before setting off on a long-distance road trip.

BUS SERVICES

Nepal's bus services remain primitive, no matter what travel agents may say about "tourist buses", "luxury coaches" and "express services". On the road, the buses are invariably slow, cramped and erratically driven. **Minibuses**, less crowded, faster, but more dangerous, operate along the same

and around trails — is certainly the best way to soak up Kathmandu valley and the other regions of the country, the people and their culture.

TREKKING

Every trekker — or traveler for that matter — needs a permit to visit areas outside those included in your Nepali visa. These special permits are issued for one destination at a time on a set route. The charges

Fields under snow OPPOSITE and weathered roofs ABOVE at Nar village. OVERLEAF: Warden's house nestles beneath the high peaks of Sagarmatha National Park.

are based on weekly rates and the permits can be obtained in Kathmandu and Pokhara.

Any reasonably fit person can trek, but the fitter you are, the more you will enjoy it. Do as much walking and exercise as possible to prepare yourself for Nepal's mountain trails.

Health and Precautions on the Trail

Trekkers should have inoculations against tetanus, polio, cholera, typhoid and paratyphoid. A gamma globulin injection pro-

vides some protection against hepatitis, an endemic infection in Nepal.

A risk the trekker shares with climbers is altitude sickness: a combination of nausea, insomnia, headaches and potentially lethal edemas, both cerebral and pulmonary. Sudden ascents to heights of 3,650 m (12,000 ft) and more, without acclimatization, can lead to accumulations of water, either in the lungs or brain. Swift descent for medical treatment is the only answer (see ALTITUDE SICKNESS, following page).

Trekking Gear

Trekking along Nepal's rough, rocky trails demands that you wear strong, comfortable boots with good soles. At low altitude, tennis shoes or running shoes provide adequate cushioning for the feet. But good boots are essential at higher elevations and in the snow; they should be large enough to allow one or two layers of heavy woolen or cotton — never nylon — socks. Wearing light casual shoes or sneakers after the day's hike will help rest your feet.

For women, wrap-around skirts are preferable to slacks or shorts, which offend many mountain communities. Men should wear loose fitting trousers or hiking shorts. For clothing, two light layers are better than a single thick one. If you get too hot, you can peel the top layer off. At extremely high altitudes wear thermal underwear. It's best to carry too many clothes than not enough. Drip-dry fabrics are best.

Your pack should be as small as possible, light and easy to open. The following gear is recommended:

Two pairs of woolen or corduroy trousers or skirts; two warm sweaters; three drip-dry shirts or T-shirts; ski or thermal underwear (especially from November to February); at least half-a-dozen pairs of woolen socks; one pair of walking shoes; an extra pair of sandals; light casual shoes or sneakers; a woolen hat; gloves or mittens; a strong, warm sleeping bag with hood; a thin sheet of foam rubber for a mattress; a padded anorak or parka; a plastic raincoat; sunglasses; toilet gear; some towels; medical kit; water bottle; and a light day pack.

Your medical kit should include pain killers (for high-altitude headaches); mild sleeping pills (for high-altitude sleeplessness); streptomagna (for diarrhea); septram (for bacillary dysentery); tinidozole (for amoebic dysentery); throat lozenges and cough drops; ophthalmic ointment or drops; one broad spectrum antibiotic; alcohol (for massaging feet to prevent blisters); blister pads; bandages; antiseptic solution and cotton; a good sun block; and a transparent lip salve.

In addition to these, you should carry a flashlight, candles, lighter, pocket knife, scissors, spare shoelaces, string, safety pins, toilet paper and plastic bags to protect your food, wrap up wet or dirty clothes, carry your litter, and protect your food, tents and photographic equipment. Much of this can be bought in Kathmandu.

Cooking and eating utensils are normally provided by the trekking agency and carried by the porters.

Always carry your trekking permit in a plastic bag where you can get to it easily. Lock your bag against theft or accidental loss. Make sure you have plenty of small currency for minor expenses along the way.

Carry a good supply of high-energy food like chocolate, dried fruits, nuts and whisky or brandy for a warming nightcap.

Water is contaminated so do not drink from streams no matter how clear or sparkling they look. Chlorine is not effective against amoebic cysts. All water should be well boiled or treated with iodine: four drops per liter (¼ gallon) and left for twenty minutes before drinking.

But note that at high altitude water boils at temperatures below 100°C (212°F) — not hot enough to kill bacteria. A pressure cooker solves the problem and also cooks food quicker.

Normally the day starts with early morning tea at around six o'clock. Trekkers break camp and pack, then breakfast on hot porridge and biscuits. Everyone is ready to begin the day's march by around seven o'clock.

Lunch is taken around noon, the cook having gone ahead to select the site and prepare the meal. By late afternoon, the day's trek comes to an end. Trekkers pitch camp and then sit down to dinner. At these high altitudes, after a long hard day's walking, there's little dallying over the campfire. Though sleep is often fitful and shallow, most are ready to hit the sack by 8 PM.

Speed is not of the essence. Pause frequently to enjoy the beauty of a particular spot, talk to the passing locals, take pictures or sip tea in one of the rustic wayside tea shops.

Walk at your own pace. Drink as much liquid as possible to combat high altitude and heat dehydration. Never wait for blisters to develop but pamper tender feet with an alcohol massage.

ALTITUDE SICKNESS

There are three main types of altitude sickness. Early altitude sickness is the first and acts as a warning. It can develop into pulmonary edema (waterlogged lungs) or cerebral edema (waterlogged brain). The symptoms are headache, nausea, loss of appetite, sleeplessness, fluid retention and swelling of the body.

Altitude sickness develops slowly, manifesting itself two or three days after reaching high altitude. The only cure is to climb no higher until the symptoms have disappeared.

Pulmonary edema is characterized, even when resting, by breathlessness and a persistent cough, accompanied by congestion of the chest. If these symptoms appear, descend at once.

Cerebral edema is less common. The symptoms are extreme tiredness, vomiting, severe headache, staggering when walking,

abnormal speech and behavior, drowsiness, even coma. Victims must return at once to a lower altitude and abandon all thoughts of their trek.

If left untreated altitude sickness can lead to death. It's endemic in the high Himalayas where even experienced mountaineers sometimes forget that the mountains begin where other mountain ranges end. Everest base camp, for instance, is some 1,000 m (more than 3,000 ft) higher than the summit of the Matterhorn. Above 3,000 m (10,000 ft) the air becomes noticeably thinner.

Kathmandu's Freak Street LEFT where the beats and hippies of the 1950s and 1960s found their pot if not their gold. Traditional Nepali dance ABOVE honors Bhairav, Shiva's demoniac incarnation.

Youth, strength and fitness make no difference. Those who climb too high, too quickly, expose themselves to the risk of **acute altitude sickness**. At elevations of 4,300 m (14,108 ft), for example, the body requires three to four liters (three quarts to one gallon) of liquid a day. At lower altitudes try to drink at least one liter (one quart) a day.

You should schedule frequent rest days between the 3,700- and 4,300-m (12,000- and 14,000-ft) contours, sleeping at the same altitude for at least two nights. Climb

higher during the day but always descend to the same level to sleep.

Never pitch camp more than 450 m (1,500 ft) higher in any one day, even if you feel fit enough for a climb twice that height.

If you begin to suffer early altitude sickness, go no higher until the symptoms have disappeared. If more serious symptoms appear, descend immediately to a lower elevation. Mild symptoms should clear within one to two days.

If the victim is unable to walk he should be carried down on a porter's back or by yak. No matter what the reason, never delay, even at night.

Some victims are incapable of making correct decisions and you may have to force them to go down against their will. The victim must be accompanied.

Treatment is no substitute for descent. If a doctor is available, he can treat the victim but the patient must descend.

Because of a lack of radio communications and helicopters, emergency evacuations are difficult to organize. Rescue operations take time and cost a great deal of money.

Some agencies may be able to arrange helicopter rescues for its client trekkers but individual trekkers stand no chance of such aid.

COMMUNICATIONS

Few travelers bother with the government-run post offices and communications centers. In Kathmandu and Pokhara numerous private operators offer postage, international phone calls and faxes and even e-mail.

The Central Post Office in Kathmandu has three sections, each located close to one another at the junction of Kanti Path and Kicha-Pokhara road. The **Foreign Post Office** ℓ (01) 211760, handles parcels sent or received from abroad, but the best strategy is to avoid the need of sending or receiving anything during your stay as it will just cause headaches. If you do want to send a parcel, take advantage of the packaging and parcel service offered by many shopkeepers.

Letters can be received poste restante at the **General Post Office** ℓ (01) 211073, 10 AM to 5 PM, daily except Saturdays and holidays; the closing time is 4 PM between November and February. When mailing letters, check that stamps are franked in front of your eyes. Major hotels and bookshops such as Pilgrim's in Thamel, Kathmandu, will also handle your mail, which is much easier.

The **Telecommunication Office** at Tripureshwar handles telephone calls, cables and telexes. The telex at the Central Telegraph Office works only during government hours. The country code for Nepal is 277. Dialing from abroad, drop the "0". There are no city codes in Nepal.

TIPPING

As a rule, for good and exceptional service, a gratuity of about five percent will be appreciated. For exceptional service by taxis, a tip of 10 percent of the fare is in order. This is also now customary in restaurants that cater to tourists and travelers.

CLIMATE

Nepal enjoys an extreme variety of climates. Altitude and exposure to sun and rain are the most influential factors.

Kathmandu valley has three seasons. The winter — from October to March — is the best time to visit Nepal. Night time temperatures drop close to freezing point, but by day these climb from 10°C to 25°C (50°F to 77°F) and the skies are generally clear.

Mornings and evenings are invigorating. There is often an early-morning mist. October and February are particularly pleasant.

Pokhara valley is much warmer — temperatures rise to 30°C (86°F) at midday in the lower altitudes.

From April to early June the weather becomes hot and stuffy, with occasional evening thunderstorms. The land is frequently shrouded in heat mist.

Temperatures in Kathmandu can range between 11°C and 28°C (52°F and 83°F) in April to between 19°C and 30°C (66°F and 86°F) in June, with maximum temperatures of 36°C (97°F).

Pre-monsoon rains usually start in May and the monsoon, normally at the end of June, lasts three months. For most of this time the Himalayas remain hidden. The torrential downpours cause much flooding but it is still possible to tour Kathmandu valley.

With the rains come the leeches (jugas), however — trekking stops and the lowlands are cut off by swollen rivers and landslides.

When the monsoon ends, around mid-September, the skies clear, the nights become cooler and the landscape is a symphony of fall colors, brown and gold.

CLOTHING

Comfortable, casual clothing is recommended unless meetings with businessmen and government officials are planned.

During winter days in the Kathmandu valley you'll be warm enough with light clothing but carry a warm sweater, padded anorak or jacket for the evenings.

Forget fashion. Jeans, cord trousers or long skirts, are fine and casual shoes essential, even if you don't intend to walk much.

During the rainy season you can buy umbrellas locally for protection from both rain and sun.

Trekking gear, in standard sizes, can be bought or rented in Kathmandu and Pokhara together with sweaters, ponchos, caps and other woolen or down clothing.

During the hot season, between April and September, all you will need is light summer clothing, preferably cotton. This is true for most of the year in the Terai except in December and January when you need a sweater or jacket for evening wear.

HEALTH

Travelers are advised to have inoculations and immunization against typhoid, hepatitis, cholera and tetanus.

Never drink unboiled and unfiltered water. Avoid ice cubes and raw vegetables. Always peel fruit and clean your hands often. Never walk barefoot.

Stomach upsets are known locally as the "Kathmandu Quickstep". If trouble persists, it can develop into more serious amoebic or bacillary dysentery or giardiasis, so get a stool test and seek medical help.

OPPOSITE: Happy Sherpa youngsters reflect the spirit of their mountain homeland. ABOVE: Colorful market stall.

Malaria is on the rise, but most of Kathmandu is too high to support the malaria-carrying species of mosquitoes. For visits to the south, however, take a recognized prophylactic two weeks before you arrive in the Terai and continue to take this for six weeks after you leave. Carry mosquito repellent during the warm months.

Pharmacies in Kathmandu, mainly along New road, offer a wide range of Western drugs at low prices and some traditional Indian ayurvedic remedies.

Most international hotels have a doctor

sometimes fluctuates. Outside Kathmandu blackouts are frequent. At least three varieties of power sockets are used: three round pins (small); three round pins (large); and two round pins (large). Plug adapters are available in electronics stores on Kanti Path.

PHOTOGRAPHY

Film stock is only available in Kathmandu and Pokhara. Prices are only slightly higher than you would pay, for example, in Bangkok, though about twice the price of Hong

on call and there are several treatment centers in Kathmandu that have Western doctors and nurses on their staff. In the event of an emergency or a serious illness, however, you will have to either go home or to Bangkok, which has excellent facilities.

The following hospitals and clinics in Kathmandu and Patan are recommended: **Patan Hospital** ((01) 521034 or (01) 522266, Lagankhel, Patan; **CIWEC** ((01) 228531, Durbar Marg, Kathmandu; **Nepal International Clinic** ((01) 412842, Naxal.

POWER

Major towns in Nepal are on the 220-volt alternating current system, though power

Kong or Singapore. Color print film can be processed quickly in Kathmandu and Pokhara, but you should leave slide film to be processed somewhere else no matter what local shop owners tell you.

TIME

Nepal is fifteen minutes ahead of Indian Standard Time and five hours forty-five minutes ahead of Greenwich Mean Time.

Government office hours are from Sunday to Friday between 10 AM and 5 PM. They close one hour earlier during the three winter months. Only embassies and international organizations enjoy a two-day weekend. Shops, some of which remain open on

Travelers' Tips

Saturdays and holidays, seldom open before 10 AM but do not usually close until 7 or 8 PM.

Remember that in this deeply religious country there are many holidays devoted to various deities, mythological events, astrological signs, traditional festivals, in addition to several secular holidays marking phases of Nepal's modern history.

ACCOMMODATION

Travelers to Kathmandu have a wide range of choices — from five-star international hotels to basic board and lodging with shared toilets and bathrooms.

Apart from the five-star game lodges in Royal Chitwan National Park the choice outside Kathmandu valley is more homey and less expensive.

During the high seasons — spring and fall — Kathmandu's international hotels have near 100-percent occupancy, so it's advisable to book well in advance. At the lower end of the price scale there are plenty of comfortable hotels. Most offer a choice of bed and breakfast; half board (breakfast and one other meal); or full board.

There are also a number of basic lodges with minimal amenities. Rates vary depending on facilities. Toilets and showers are generally communal, heating extra. Most are in old Kathmandu, around Durbar square or in Thamel district.

Tariffs are subject to a 12 to 15 percent government tax.

MOUNTAIN LODGES

In the mountains there are many basic lodges, usually near airstrips, as well as the many traditional Nepali tea houses found in every village on the trekking routes. The most comfortable accommodation available in the high Himalayas are at **Lukla** (see page 186) and **Jumla** (see page 178).

NATIONAL PARKS AND WILDLIFE DIRECTORY

CHITWAN NATIONAL PARK: 932 sq km (354 sq miles). Elephants, tigers, leopards, rhinoceros, wild boar, deer, monkeys and a multitude of birds (see pages 16–19 and 162).

GODAVARI ROYAL BOTANICAL GARDENS: 66 different species of fern, 115 orchids, 77 cacti and succulents and about 200 trees and shrubs (see page 116).

KHAPTAD NATIONAL PARK: A floral repository of high-altitude conifers, oak and rhododendron forests (see page 179).

KOSI TAPPU WILDLIFE RESERVE: Wild buffaloes and thousands of migratory birds (see page 161).

LAKE RARA NATIONAL PARK: 187 sq km (71 sq miles). Repository of high-altitude conifers, oak and rhododendron forests (see page 178).

LANTANG NATIONAL PARK: 1,243 sq km (472 sq miles). Haven for the endangered snow leopard, leopard, Himalayan black bear, red panda and wild dog (see page 186).

PARSA WILDLIFE RESERVE: 1,200 sq km (456 sq miles). Elephants, tigers, leopards, rhinoceros, wild boar, deer, monkeys and a multitude of birds (see page 162).

ROYAL BARDIA RESERVE: A sanctuary for the endangered swamp deer (see page 169).

SAGARMATHA NATIONAL PARK. 1,243 sq km (472 sq miles). Wolf, bear, musk deer, feral goat species, and the brilliantly colored crimson-horned or Impeyan pheasants (see page 188).

SHEY-PHOKSONDO NATIONAL PARK: (see page 155).

SHUKLA PHANTA WILDLIFE RESERVE: Endangered black buck (see page 169).

OPPOSITE: The 7,131-m (23,771-ft) Langtang Lirung near the Tibetan border at the head of Trisuli valley. Protected against glaring snow and high-altitude ultraviolet rays, a climber ABOVE reaches 4,500 m (15,000 ft) during an attempt on one of the major peaks of the Himalayas.

JAWALKHEL ZOO, Patan: A selection of exotic south Asian animals, especially Himalayan species (see page 131).

MEDIA

English language news bulletins are broadcast twice daily by Radio Nepal at 8 AM and 8:30 PM, with a special 45-minute "tourist program" at 8 PM. Local television is unlikely to be of much interest to the average visitor, but satellite TV is now available at the international hotels and at many of the mid-range hotels in Kathmandu.

Several English language newspapers are published in Kathmandu, as well as many in Nepali.

The Rising Nepal and *Kathmandu Post* both cover local and international events in a style that puts most foreign readers to sleep. Both devote much of their front page to the activities of the royal family.

The *International Herald Tribune,* one day old, is on sale at newsstands and in hotels, as are *Time, Newsweek, The Far Eastern Economic Review, Asiaweek, The Economist* and *India Today.* Newspapers from Germany, France, Australia and Britain are often available, several days old, in Kathmandu bookshops.

LANGUAGE

Nepali is an atonal and phonetic language. No matter how long the word, the accent is always placed on the first or second syllable. Words are pronounced exactly as they are spelled.

Apart from a few peculiarities, consonants are pronounced as in English:
ch is pronounced *tch* as in bench
chh is pronounced *tch-h* as in **pitch here**
th is pronounced *t-h* as in **hot head**
kh is pronounced *k-h* as in **dark hole**
ph is pronounced *p-h* as in **top hat**
j is pronounced *d-j* as in **Jesus**
dh is pronounced *d-h* as in **adhere**

The *t, d, th and dh,* with a dot beneath them are pronounced by rolling the tongue back and putting it in the center of the roof of the mouth, so that the sound produced is like *"rt"* in "cart" or *"rd"* in **card.**

Pronounce vowels either long or short:
e is always *e (ay)* as in **café**
u is pronounced *oo* as in **moon** (never *yu* as in *mute*)
y is pronounced *yi* as in **yield** (never *ai as in my*)
i is pronounced *oh* as in **toe.**

Further Reading

AMIN, WILLETTS, TETLEY. *Journey through Nepal*. London: The Bodley Head.

ANDERSON, MARY. *The Festivals of Nepal*. London: George Allen and Unwin, 1971.

ARMINGTON, STAN. *Trekking in the Nepal Himalaya*. Melbourne: Lonely Planet, 1994.

BERZRUSCHKA, STEPHEN. *A Guide to Trekking in Nepal*. Seattle: The Mountaineers, 1981.

FLEMING, R.L., et al. *Birds of Nepal*. Kathmandu: Avalok, 1979.

GREENWALD, JEFF. *Shopping for Buddhas*. Melbourne: Lonely Planet, Journeys, 1996.

HAGEN, TONI. *Nepal: The Kingdom in the Himalaya*. Berne: Kümmerly and Frey, 1961. (Second edition, 1971).

INDRA. *Joys of Nepali Cooking*. New Delhi: 1982.

IYER, PICO. *Video Night in Kathmandu*. Vintage: 1989.

MATTHIESSEN, PETER. *The Snow Leopard*. London: Chatto and Windus, 1979.

MACDONALD, A.W. AND ANNE VERGATI STAHL. *Newar Art*. New Delhi: Vikas, 1979.

PEISSEL, MICHEL. *Tiger for Breakfast*. London: Hodder, 1966.

O'CONNOR, BILL. *Trekking Peaks of Nepal*. England: Crowood Press, 1989.

PYE-SMITH, CHARLIE. *Travels in Nepal*. Penguin.

SCHALLER, GEORGE B. *Stones of Silence*. London: Andre Deutsch, 1980.

SCOTT, BARBARA J. *The Violet Shyness of Their Eyes: Notes from Nepal*. Calyx, 1993.

SNELLGROVE, DAVID L. *Himalayan Pilgrimage*. Shambala, 1981

SUYIN, HAN. *The Mountain Is Young*. London: Jonathan Cape, 1958.

TILMAN, W. *Nepal Himalaya*. Cambridge: Cambridge University Press, 1952.

UNSWORTH, WALT. *Everest*. London: Allen Lane, 1981.

WOODCOCK, MARTIN. *Collins Handguide to the Birds of the Indian Sub-Continent*. Collins, 1990.

Photo Credits

Photographs by Mohamed Amin and Duncan Willetts except:

Peter Danford: pages 26, 27, 31, 40 *(top left)*, 42, 43, 57, 61, 97, 123, 148, 152, 153 *(left and right)*, 167, 172, 179, 214, 218, 222, 223, 224–225.

Robert Holmes: cover and pages 3, 4, 5 *(right)*, 6 *(right)*, 10, 12–13, 14–15, 16 *(top and bottom)*, 17 *(top and bottom)*, 25, 28–29, 34–35, 41 *(top and bottom)*, 54 *(bottom left)*, 54–55 *(top)*, 58, 59, 77 *(bottom)*, 81, 84, 85, 105, 107 *(bottom)*, 109, 118, 119, 120 *(top and bottom)*, 126, 130, 131, 140 *(top)*, 142–143, 149, 165, 168, 169 *(left and right)*, 171, 173 *(top and bottom)*, 184, 187, 200–201, 210, 213, 228, 243.

Chris Taylor: pages 18, 20–21 *(top)*, 23, 32, 33, 36, 38–39, 40 *(bottom right)*, 44, 88, 107 *(top)*, 108, 110, 111, 121, 132, 133.

Nik Wheeler: pages 37, 52, 77 *(top)*, 94 *(right)*, 106, 150, 156–157, 158, 159, 194–195, 236, 237.

Publisher's Note: *Traveler's Companion* is the series title under which the international series of Kümmerly+Frey *Insider's Guides* are published in North America. The content both editions is the same.

Quick Reference A–Z Guide
to Places and Topics of Interest with Listed Accomodations, Restaurants and Useful Telephone Numbers